Praise for *Head First JavaScript Programming*

"Warning: Do not read *Head First JavaScript Programming* unless you want to learn the fundamentals of programming with JavaScript in an entertaining and meaningful fashion. There may be an additional side effect that you may actually recall more about JavaScript than after reading typical technical books."

— **Jesse Palmer, Senior Software Developer, Gannett Digital**

"If every elementary and middle school student studied Elisabeth and Eric's *Head First HTML and CSS*, and if *Head First JavaScript Programming* and *Head First HTML5 Programming* were part of the high school math and science curriculum, then our country would never lose its competitive edge."

— **Michael Murphy, senior systems consultant, The History Tree**

"The *Head First* series utilizes elements of modern learning theory, including constructivism, to bring readers up to speed quickly. The authors have proven with this book that expert-level content can be taught quickly and efficiently. Make no mistake here, this is a serious JavaScript book, and yet, fun reading!"

— **Frank Moore, Web designer and developer**

"Looking for a book that will keep you interested (and laughing) but teach you some serious programming skills? *Head First JavaScript Programming* is it!"

— **Tim Williams, software entrepreneur**

"Add this book to your library regardless of your programming skill level!"

— **Chris Fuselier, engineering consultant**

"Robson and Freeman have done it again! Using the same fun and information-packed style as their previous books in the *Head First* series, *Head First JavaScript Programming* leads you through entertaining and useful projects that, chapter-by-chapter, allow programmers—even nonspecialists like myself—to develop a solid foundation in modern JavaScript programming that we can use to solve real problems."

— **Russell Alleen-Willems, digital archeologist, DiachronicDesign.com**

"Freeman and Robson continue to use innovative teaching methods for communicating complex concepts to basic principles."

— **Mark Arana, Strategy & Innovation, The Walt Disney Studios**

Praise for other books by Eric T. Freeman and Elisabeth Robson

"Just the right tone for the geeked-out, casual-cool guru coder in all of us. The right reference for practical development strategies—gets my brain going without having to slog through a bunch of tired, stale professor-speak."

— **Travis Kalanick, CEO Uber**

"This book's admirable clarity, humor and substantial doses of clever make it the sort of book that helps even non-programmers think well about problem-solving."

— **Cory Doctorow, co-editor of Boing Boing, Science Fiction author**

"I feel like a thousand pounds of books have just been lifted off of my head."

— **Ward Cunningham, inventor of the Wiki**

"One of the very few software books I've ever read that strikes me as indispensable. (I'd put maybe 10 books in this category, at the outside.)"

— **David Gelernter, Professor of Computer Science, Yale University**

"I laughed, I cried, it moved me."

— **Daniel Steinberg, Editor-in-Chief, java.net**

"I can think of no better tour guides than Eric and Elisabeth."

— **Miko Matsumura, VP of Marketing and Developer Relations at Hazelcast Former Chief Java Evangelist, Sun Microsystems**

"I literally love this book. In fact, I kissed this book in front of my wife."

— **Satish Kumar**

"The highly graphic and incremental approach precisely mimics the best way to learn this stuff..."

— **Danny Goodman, author of *Dynamic HTML: The Definitive Guide***

"Eric and Elisabeth clearly know their stuff. As the Internet becomes more complex, inspired construction of web pages becomes increasingly critical. Elegant design is at the core of every chapter here, each concept conveyed with equal doses of pragmatism and wit."

— **Ken Goldstein, former CEO of Shop.com and author of *This is Rage: A Novel of Silicon Valley and Other Madness***

Other O'Reilly books by Eric T. Freeman and Elisabeth Robson

Head First Design Patterns

Head First HTML and CSS

Head First HTML5 Programming

Other related books from O'Reilly

Head First HTML5 Programming

JavaScript: The Definitive Guide

JavaScript Enlightenment

Other books in O'Reilly's *Head First* series

Head First HTML and CSS

Head First HTML5 Programming

Head First Design Patterns

Head First Servlets and JSP

Head First SQL

Head First Software Development

Head First C#

Head First Java

Head First Object-Oriented Analysis and Design (OOA&D)

Head First Ajax

Head First Rails

Head First PHP & MySQL

Head First Web Design

Head First Networking

Head First iPhone and iPad Development

Head First jQuery

Head First
JavaScript
Programming

Wouldn't it be dreamy if there was a JavaScript book that was more fun than going to the dentist and more revealing than an IRS form? It's probably just a fantasy...

Eric T. Freeman
Elisabeth Robson

Beijing • Cambridge • Köln • Sebastopol • Tokyo

Head First JavaScript Programming

by Eric T. Freeman and Elisabeth Robson

Printed in the United States of America.

Published by O'Reilly Media, Inc., 1005 Gravenstein Highway North, Sebastopol, CA 95472.

O'Reilly Media books may be purchased for educational, business, or sales promotional use. Online editions are also available for most titles (*http://my.safaribooksonline.com*). For more information, contact our corporate/institutional sales department: (800) 998-9938 or *corporate@oreilly.com*.

Editors:	Meghan Blanchette, Courtney Nash
Cover Designer:	Randy Comer
Code Monkeys:	Eric T. Freeman, Elisabeth Robson
Production Editor:	Melanie Yarbrough
Indexer:	Potomac Indexing
Proofreader:	Rachel Monaghan
Page Viewer:	Oliver

Printing History:

March 2014: First Edition.

Nutshell Handbook, the Nutshell Handbook logo, and the O'Reilly logo are registered trademarks of O'Reilly Media, Inc. The *Head First* series designations, *Head First JavaScript Programming*, and related trade dress are trademarks of O'Reilly Media, Inc.

Many of the designations used by manufacturers and sellers to distinguish their products are claimed as trademarks. Where those designations appear in this book, and O'Reilly Media, Inc., was aware of a trademark claim, the designations have been printed in caps or initial caps.

While every precaution has been taken in the preparation of this book, the publisher and the authors assume no responsibility for errors or omissions, or for damages resulting from the use of the information contained herein.

In other words, if you use anything in *Head First JavaScript Programming* to, say, run a nuclear power plant, you're on your own. We do, however, encourage you to visit Webville.

No variables were harmed in the making of this book.

ISBN: 978-1-449-34013-1

[M]

To JavaScript—you weren't born with a silver spoon in your mouth, but you've outclassed every language that's challenged you in the browser.

Authors of Head First JavaScript Programming

Eric Freeman

Elisabeth Robson

Eric is described by Head First series co-creator Kathy Sierra as "one of those rare individuals fluent in the language, practice, and culture of multiple domains from hipster hacker, corporate VP, engineer, think tank."

Professionally, Eric recently ended nearly a decade as a media company executive—having held the position of CTO of Disney Online & Disney.com at The Walt Disney Company. Eric is now devoting his time to WickedlySmart, a startup he co-created with Elisabeth.

By training, Eric is a computer scientist, having studied with industry luminary David Gelernter during his Ph.D. work at Yale University. His dissertation is credited as the seminal work in alternatives to the desktop metaphor, and also as the first implementation of activity streams, a concept he and Dr. Gelernter developed.

In his spare time, Eric is deeply involved with music; you'll find Eric's latest project, a collaboration with ambient music pioneer Steve Roach, available on the iPhone app store under the name Immersion Station.

Eric lives with his wife and young daughter on Bainbridge Island. His daughter is a frequent vistor to Eric's studio, where she loves to turn the knobs of his synths and audio effects.

Write to Eric at `eric@wickedlysmart.com` or visit his site at `http://ericfreeman.com`.

Elisabeth is a software engineer, writer, and trainer. She has been passionate about technology since her days as a student at Yale University, where she earned a Masters of Science in Computer Science and designed a concurrent, visual programming language and software architecture.

Elisabeth's been involved with the Internet since the early days; she co-created the award-winning Web site, The Ada Project, one of the first Web sites designed to help women in computer science find career and mentorship information online.

She's currently co-founder of WickedlySmart, an online education experience centered on web technologies, where she creates books, articles, videos and more. Previously, as Director of Special Projects at O'Reilly Media, Elisabeth produced in-person workshops and online courses on a variety of technical topics and developed her passion for creating learning experiences to help people understand technology. Prior to her work with O'Reilly, Elisabeth spent time spreading fairy dust at The Walt Disney Company, where she led research and development efforts in digital media.

When not in front of her computer, you'll find Elisabeth hiking, cycling or kayaking in the great outdoors, with her camera nearby, or cooking vegetarian meals.

You can send her email at `beth@wickedlysmart.com` or visit her blog at `http://elisabethrobson.com`.

Table of Contents (summary)

Table of Contents (the real thing)

Intro

Your brain on JavaScript.
Here *you* are trying to *learn* something, while here your *brain* is doing you a favor by making sure the learning doesn't *stick*. Your brain's thinking, "Better leave room for more important things, like which wild animals to avoid and whether naked snowboarding is a bad idea." So how *do* you trick your brain into thinking that your life depends on knowing JavaScript programming?

a quick dip into javascript

1 Getting your feet wet

JavaScript gives you superpowers. The **true programming language** of the web, JavaScript lets you **add behavior** to your web pages. No more dry, boring, static pages that just sit there looking at you—with JavaScript you're going to be able to reach out and touch your users, react to interesting events, grab data from the web to use in your pages, draw graphics right in your web pages and a lot more. And once you know JavaScript you'll also be in a position to create **totally new** behaviors for your users.

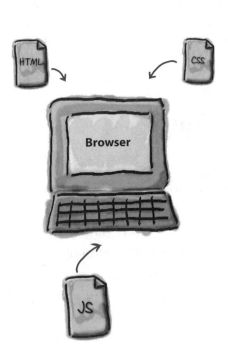

writing real code

Going further

You already know about variables, types, expressions... we could go on.

The point is, you already know a few things about JavaScript. In fact, you know enough to write some **real code**. Some code that does something interesting, some code that someone would want to use. What you're lacking is the **real experience** of writing code, and we're going to remedy that right here and now. How? By jumping in head first and coding up a casual game, all written in JavaScript. Our goal is ambitious but we're going to take it one step at a time. Come on, let's get this started, and if you want to launch the next casual startup, we won't stand in your way; the code is yours.

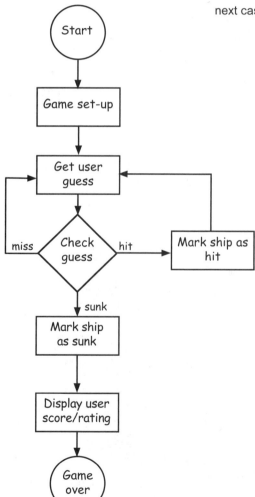

introducing functions

Getting functional

3

Get ready for your first superpower. You've got some programming under

your belt; now it's time to really move things along with **functions**. Functions give you the power to write code that can be applied to all sorts of different circumstances, code that can be **reused** over and over, code that is much more **manageable,** code that can be **abstracted** away and given a simple name so you can forget all the complexity and get on with the important stuff. You're going to find not only that functions are your gateway from scripter to programmer, they're the key to the JavaScript programming style. In this chapter we're going to start with the basics: the mechanics, the ins and outs of how functions really work, and then you'll keep honing your function skills throughout the rest of the book. So, let's get a good foundation started, *now*.

putting some order in your data

4 Arrays

There's more to JavaScript than numbers, strings and booleans.
So far you've been writing JavaScript code with **primitives**—simple strings, numbers and booleans, like "Fido", 23, and true. And you can do a lot with primitive types, but at some point you've got to deal with **more data**. Say, all the items in a shopping cart, or all the songs in a playlist, or a set of stars and their apparent magnitude, or an entire product catalog. For that we need a little more *ummph*. The type of choice for this kind of ordered data is a JavaScript **array**, and in this chapter we're going to walk through how to put your data into an array, how to pass it around and how to operate on it. We'll be looking at a few other ways to **structure your data** in later chapters but let's get started with arrays.

understanding objects

A trip to Objectville

So far you've been using primitives and arrays in your code. And, you've approached coding in quite a **procedural manner** using simple statements, conditionals and for/while loops with functions—that's not exactly **object-oriented**. In fact, it's not object-oriented *at all!* We did use a few objects here and there without really knowing it, but you haven't written any of your own objects yet. Well, the time has come to leave this boring procedural town behind to create some **objects** of your own. In this chapter, you're going to find out why using objects is going to make your life so much better—well, better in a **programming sense** (we can't really help you with your fashion sense *and* your JavaScript skills all in one book). Just a warning: once you've discovered objects you'll never want to come back. Send us a postcard when you get there.

interacting with your web page

6

Getting to know the DOM

You've come a long way with JavaScript. In fact you've evolved from a newbie to

a scripter to, well, a **programmer**. But, there's something missing. To really begin leveraging your JavaScript skills you need to know how to interact with the web page your code lives in. Only by doing that are you going to be able to write pages that are **dynamic**, pages that react, that respond, that update themselves after they've been loaded. So how do you interact with the page? By using the **DOM**, otherwise known as the **document object model**. In this chapter we're going to break down the DOM and see just how we can use it, along with JavaScript, to teach your page a few new tricks.

Browser here, I'm reading the page and creating a DOM of it.

types, equality, conversion, and all that jazz

Serious types

It's time to get serious about our types. One of the great things about JavaScript is you can get a long way without knowing a lot of details of the language. But to truly **master the language**, get that promotion and get on to the things you really want to do in life, you have to rock at **types**. Remember what we said way back about JavaScript? That it didn't have the luxury of a silver-spoon, academic, peer-reviewed language definition? Well that's true, but the academic life didn't stop Steve Jobs and Bill Gates, and it didn't stop JavaScript either. It does mean that JavaScript doesn't have the... well, the most thought-out type system, and we'll find a few **idiosyncrasies** along the way. But, don't worry, in this chapter we're going to nail all that down, and soon you'll be able to avoid all those embarrassing moments with types.

bringing it all together

8 Building an app

Put on your toolbelt. That is, the toolbelt with all your new coding skills, your knowledge of the DOM, and even some HTML & CSS. We're going to bring everything together in this chapter to create our first true **web application**. No more **silly toy games** with one battleship and a single row of hiding places. In this chapter we're building the **entire experience**: a nice big game board, multiple ships and user input right in the web page. We're going to create the page structure for the game with HTML, visually style the game with CSS, and write JavaScript to code the game's behavior. Get ready: this is an all out, pedal to the metal development chapter where we're going to lay down some serious code.

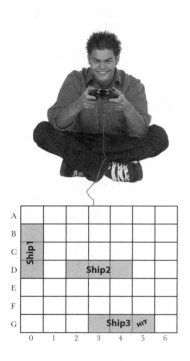

asynchronous coding

9

Handling events

After this chapter you're going to realize you aren't in Kansas anymore.
Up until now, you've been writing code that typically executes from top to bottom—sure, your code might be a little more complex than that, and make use of a few functions, objects and methods, but at some point the code just runs its course. Now, we're awfully sorry to break this to you this late in the book, but that's **not how you typically write JavaScript code**. Rather, most JavaScript is written to **react to events**. What kind of events? Well, how about a user clicking on your page, data arriving from the network, timers expiring in the browser, changes happening in the DOM and that's just a few examples. In fact, all kinds of events are happening **all the time**, behind the scenes, in your browser. In this chapter we're going rethink our approach to JavaScript coding, and learn how and why we should write code that reacts to events.

first class functions

Liberated functions

Know functions, then rock. Every art, craft, and discipline has a key principle that separates the intermediate players from the rock star virtuosos—when it comes to JavaScript, it's truly understanding **functions** that makes the difference. Functions are fundamental to JavaScript, and many of the techniques we use to **design and organize** code depend on advanced knowledge and use of functions. The path to learning functions at this level is an interesting and often mind-bending one, so get ready... This chapter is going to be a bit like Willy Wonka giving a tour of the chocolate factory—you're going to encounter some wild, wacky and wonderful things as you learn more about JavaScript functions.

anonymous functions, scopes, and closures

Serious functions

You've put functions through their paces, but there's more to learn.

11

In this chapter we take it further; we get hard-core. We're going to show you how to **really handle** functions. This won't be a super long chapter, but it will be intense, and at the end you're going to be more expressive with your JavaScript than you thought possible. You're also going to be ready to take on a coworker's code, or jump into an open source JavaScript library, because we're going to cover some common coding idioms and conventions around functions. And if you've never heard of an **anonymous function** or a **closure**, boy are you in the right place.

Darn it! Judy was right again.

Wait a sec... what is this closure thing? It looks related to what we're doing. Maybe we can get a leg up on her yet.

advanced object construction

12

Creating objects

So far we've been crafting objects by hand. For each object, we've used an **object literal** to specify each and every property. That's okay on a small scale, but for serious code we need something better. That's where **object constructors** come in. With constructors we can create objects much more easily, and we can create objects that all adhere to the same **design blueprint**—meaning we can use constructors to ensure each object has the same properties and includes the same methods. And with constructors we can write object code that is much more **concise** and a lot less error prone when we're creating lots of objects. So, let's get started and after this chapter you'll be talking constructors just like you grew up in Objectville.

using prototypes

Extra strength objects

13

Learning how to create objects was just the beginning. It's

time to put some muscle on our objects. We need more ways to create **relationships**
between objects and to **share code** among them. And, we need ways to extend
and enhance existing objects. In other words, we need more tools. In this chapter,
you're going to see that JavaScript has a very powerful **object model**, but one that
is a bit different than the status quo object-oriented language. Rather than the typical
class-based object-oriented system, JavaScript instead opts for a more powerful
prototype model, where objects can inherit and extend the behavior of other objects.
What is that good for? You'll see soon enough. Let's get started...

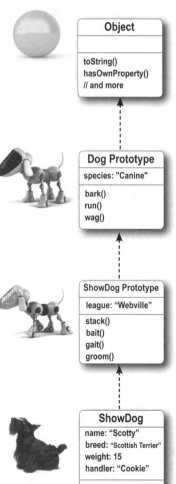

Object

toString()
hasOwnProperty()
// and more

Dog Prototype

species: "Canine"

bark()
run()
wag()

ShowDog Prototype

league: "Webville"

stack()
bait()
gait()
groom()

ShowDog

name: "Scotty"
breed: "Scottish Terrier"
weight: 15
handler: "Cookie"

14

Appendix: Leftovers

The top ten topics (we didn't cover)

We've covered a lot of ground, and you're almost finished with this book.

We'll miss you, but before we let you go, we wouldn't feel right about sending you out into the world without a little more preparation. We can't possibly fit everything you'll need to know into this relatively small chapter. Actually, we *did* originally include everything you need to know about JavaScript Programming (not already covered by the other chapters), by reducing the type point size to .00004. It all fit, but nobody could read it. So we threw most of it away, and kept the best bits for this Top Ten appendix. This really *is* the end of the book. Except for the index, of course (a must-read!).

 **Index**

how to use this book

Intro

In this section, we answer the burning question: "So, why DID they put that in a JavaScript book?"

Who is this book for?

If you can answer "yes" to all of these:

(1) Do you have access to a computer with a **modern web browser** and a **text editor**?

(2) Do you want to **learn, understand** and **remember** how to **program with JavaScript** using the best techniques and the most recent standards?

(3) Do you prefer **stimulating dinner party conversation** to **dry, dull, academic lectures?**

this book is for you.

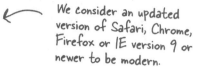

We consider an updated version of Safari, Chrome, Firefox or IE version 9 or newer to be modern.

[Note from marketing: this book is for anyone with a credit card.]

Who should probably back away from this book?

If you can answer "yes" to any one of these:

(1) **Are you <u>completely</u> new to web development?**

Are HTML and CSS foreign concepts to you? If so, you'll probably want to start with *Head First HTML and CSS* to understand how to put web pages together before tackling JavaScript.

(2) Are you a kick-butt web developer looking for a *reference* book?

(3) Are you **afraid to try something different**? Would you rather have a root canal than mix stripes with plaid? Do you believe that a technical book can't be serious if JavaScript objects are anthropomorphized?

this book is not for you.

We know what you're thinking.

"How can this be a serious book?"

"What's with all the graphics?"

"Can I actually learn it this way?"

And we know what your brain is thinking.

Your brain craves novelty. It's always searching, scanning, *waiting* for something unusual. It was built that way, and it helps you stay alive.

Today, you're less likely to be a tiger snack. But your brain's still looking. You just never know.

So what does your brain do with all the routine, ordinary, normal things you encounter? Everything it *can* to stop them from interfering with the brain's *real* job—recording things that *matter*. It doesn't bother saving the boring things; they never make it past the "this is obviously not important" filter.

How does your brain *know* what's important? Suppose you're out for a day hike and a tiger jumps in front of you. What happens inside your head and body?

Neurons fire. Emotions crank up. *Chemicals surge.*

And that's how your brain knows…

This must be important! Don't forget it!

But imagine you're at home, or in a library. It's a safe, warm, tiger-free zone. You're studying. Getting ready for an exam. Or trying to learn some tough technical topic your boss thinks will take a week, ten days at the most.

Just one problem. Your brain's trying to do you a big favor. It's trying to make sure that this *obviously* non-important content doesn't clutter up scarce resources. Resources that are better spent storing the really *big* things. Like tigers. Like the danger of fire. Like how you should never again snowboard in shorts.

And there's no simple way to tell your brain, "Hey brain, thank you very much, but no matter how dull this book is, and how little I'm registering on the emotional Richter scale right now, I really *do* want you to keep this stuff around."

Your brain thinks THIS is important.

Great. Only 661 more dull, dry, boring pages.

Your brain thinks THIS isn't worth saving.

We think of a "Head First" reader as a <u>learner</u>.

So what does it take to *learn* something? First, you have to *get* it, then make sure you don't *forget* it. It's not about pushing facts into your head. Based on the latest research in cognitive science, neurobiology and educational psychology, *learning* takes a lot more than text on a page. We know what turns your brain on.

Some of the Head First learning principles:

Make it visual. Images are far more memorable than words alone, and make learning much more effective (up to 89% improvement in recall and transfer studies). It also makes things more understandable. **Put the words within or near the graphics** they relate to, rather than on the bottom or on another page, and learners will be up to twice as likely to solve problems related to the content.

Unlike other languages, JavaScript is delivered, as code, directly to your browser. That's different!

Web Server   "Found the code, here ya go"

Use a conversational and personalized style. In recent studies, students performed up to 40% better on post-learning tests if the content spoke directly to the reader, using a first-person, conversational style rather than taking a formal tone. Tell stories instead of lecturing. Use casual language. Don't take yourself too seriously. Which would you pay more attention to: a stimulating dinner party companion, or a lecture?

I really think JavaScript should go in the <head> element.

Not so fast! There are performance and page loading implications!

Now that I have your attention, you should be more careful using global variables.

Get the learner to think more deeply. In other words, unless you actively flex your neurons, nothing much happens in your head. A reader has to be motivated, engaged, curious and inspired to solve problems, draw conclusions and generate new knowledge. And for that, you need challenges, exercises and thought-provoking questions, and activities that involve both sides of the brain and multiple senses.

Get—and keep—the reader's attention. We've all had the "I really want to learn this but I can't stay awake past page one" experience. Your brain pays attention to things that are out of the ordinary, interesting, strange, eye-catching, unexpected. Learning a new, tough, technical topic doesn't have to be boring. Your brain will learn much more quickly if it's not.

Touch their emotions. We now know that your ability to remember something is largely dependent on its emotional content. You remember what you care about. You remember when you *feel* something. No, we're not talking heart-wrenching stories about a boy and his dog. We're talking emotions like surprise, curiosity, fun, "what the...?" , and the feeling of "I Rule!" that comes when you solve a puzzle, learn something everybody else thinks is hard, or realize you know something that "I'm more technical than thou" Bob from engineering *doesn't*.

Metacognition: thinking about thinking

If you really want to learn, and you want to learn more quickly and more deeply, pay attention to how you pay attention. Think about how you think. Learn how you learn.

Most of us did not take courses on metacognition or learning theory when we were growing up. We were *expected* to learn, but rarely *taught* how to learn.

I wonder how I can trick my brain into remembering this stuff...

But we assume that if you're holding this book, you really want to learn how to create JavaScript programs. And you probably don't want to spend a lot of time. And you want to *remember* what you read, and be able to apply it. And for that, you've got to *understand* it. To get the most from this book, or *any* book or learning experience, take responsibility for your brain. Your brain on *this* content.

The trick is to get your brain to see the new material you're learning as Really Important. Crucial to your well-being. As important as a tiger. Otherwise, you're in for a constant battle, with your brain doing its best to keep the new content from sticking.

So how *DO* you get your brain to think JavaScript is as important as a tiger?

There's the slow, tedious way, or the faster, more effective way. The slow way is about sheer repetition. You obviously know that you *are* able to learn and remember even the dullest of topics, if you keep pounding on the same thing. With enough repetition, your brain says, "This doesn't *feel* important to him, but he keeps looking at the same thing *over* and *over* and *over*, so I suppose it must be."

The faster way is to do **anything that increases brain activity,** especially different *types* of brain activity. The things on the previous page are a big part of the solution, and they're all things that have been proven to help your brain work in your favor. For example, studies show that putting words *within* the pictures they describe (as opposed to somewhere else in the page, like a caption or in the body text) causes your brain to try to make sense of how the words and picture relate, and this causes more neurons to fire. More neurons firing = more chances for your brain to *get* that this is something worth paying attention to, and possibly recording.

A conversational style helps because people tend to pay more attention when they perceive that they're in a conversation, since they're expected to follow along and hold up their end. The amazing thing is, your brain doesn't necessarily *care* that the "conversation" is between you and a book! On the other hand, if the writing style is formal and dry, your brain perceives it the same way you experience being lectured to while sitting in a roomful of passive attendees. No need to stay awake.

But pictures and conversational style are just the beginning.

Here's what WE did:

We used *pictures*, because your brain is tuned for visuals, not text. As far as your brain's concerned, a picture really *is* worth 1024 words. And when text and pictures work together, we embedded the text *in* the pictures because your brain works more effectively when the text is *within* the thing the text refers to, as opposed to in a caption or buried in the text somewhere.

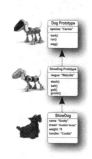

We used *redundancy*, saying the same thing in *different* ways and with different media types, and *multiple senses*, to increase the chance that the content gets coded into more than one area of your brain.

We used concepts and pictures in *unexpected* ways because your brain is tuned for novelty, and we used pictures and ideas with at least *some* *emotional* content, because your brain is tuned to pay attention to the biochemistry of emotions. That which causes you to *feel* something is more likely to be remembered, even if that feeling is nothing more than a little *humor*, *surprise* or *interest.*

We used a personalized, *conversational style*, because your brain is tuned to pay more attention when it believes you're in a conversation than if it thinks you're passively listening to a presentation. Your brain does this even when you're *reading*.

Be the Browser

We included more than 100 *activities*, because your brain is tuned to learn and remember more when you *do* things than when you *read* about things. And we made the exercises challenging-yet-do-able, because that's what most *people* prefer.

We used *multiple learning styles*, because *you* might prefer step-by-step procedures, while someone else wants to understand the big picture first, while someone else just wants to see a code example. But regardless of your own learning preference, *everyone* benefits from seeing the same content represented in multiple ways.

BULLET POINTS

We include content for *both sides of your brain*, because the more of your brain you engage, the more likely you are to learn and remember, and the longer you can stay focused. Since working one side of the brain often means giving the other side a chance to rest, you can be more productive at learning for a longer period of time.

Puzzles

And we included *stories* and exercises that present *more than one point of view,* because your brain is tuned to learn more deeply when it's forced to make evaluations and judgements.

We included *challenges*, with exercises, and by asking *questions* that don't always have a straight answer, because your brain is tuned to learn and remember when it has to *work* at something. Think about it—you can't get your *body* in shape just by *watching* people at the gym. But we did our best to make sure that when you're working hard, it's on the *right* things. That *you're not spending one extra dendrite* processing a hard-to-understand example, or parsing difficult, jargon-laden or overly terse text.

We used *people*. In stories, examples, pictures, etc., because, well, *you're* a person. And your brain pays more attention to *people* than it does to *things*.

We used an *80/20* approach. We assume that if you're going to be a kick-butt JavaScript developer, this won't be your only book. So we don't talk about *everything*. Just the stuff you'll actually *need*.

Here's what YOU can do to bend your brain into submission

So, we did our part. The rest is up to you. These tips are a starting point; listen to your brain and figure out what works for you and what doesn't. Try new things.

Cut this out and stick it on your refrigerator.

---

① Slow down. The more you understand, the less you have to memorize.

Don't just *read*. Stop and think. When the book asks you a question, don't just skip to the answer. Imagine that someone really *is* asking the question. The more deeply you force your brain to think, the better chance you have of learning and remembering.

② Do the exercises. Write your own notes.

We put them in, but if we did them for you, that would be like having someone else do your workouts for you. And don't just *look* at the exercises. **Use a pencil.** There's plenty of evidence that physical activity *while* learning can increase the learning.

③ Read the "There are No Dumb Questions"

That means all of them. They're not optional sidebars—*they're part of the core content!* Don't skip them.

④ Make this the last thing you read before bed. Or at least the last *challenging* thing.

Part of the learning (especially the transfer to long-term memory) happens *after* you put the book down. Your brain needs time on its own, to do more processing. If you put in something new during that processing-time, some of what you just learned will be lost.

⑤ Drink water. Lots of it.

Your brain works best in a nice bath of fluid. Dehydration (which can happen before you ever feel thirsty) decreases cognitive function.

⑥ Talk about it. Out loud.

Speaking activates a different part of the brain. If you're trying to understand something, or increase your chance of remembering it later, say it out loud. Better still, try to explain it out loud to someone else. You'll learn more quickly, and you might uncover ideas you hadn't known were there when you were reading about it.

⑦ Listen to your brain.

Pay attention to whether your brain is getting overloaded. If you find yourself starting to skim the surface or forget what you just read, it's time for a break. Once you go past a certain point, you won't learn faster by trying to shove more in, and you might even hurt the process.

⑧ *Feel* something!

Your brain needs to know that this *matters*. Get involved with the stories. Make up your own captions for the photos. Groaning over a bad joke is *still* better than feeling nothing at all.

⑨ *Create* something!

Apply this to something new you're designing, or rework an older project. Just do *something* to get some experience beyond the exercises and activities in this book. All you need is a pencil and a problem to solve... a problem that might benefit from using JavaScript.

⑩ *Get Sleep.*

You've got to create a lot of new brain connections to learn to program. Sleep often; it helps.

Read Me

This is a learning experience, not a reference book. We deliberately stripped out everything that might get in the way of learning whatever it is we're working on at that point in the book. And the first time through, you need to begin at the beginning, because the book makes assumptions about what you've already seen and learned.

We teach the GOOD parts of JavaScript, and warn you about the BAD parts.

JavaScript is a programming language that didn't come up through the ivy leagues with plenty of time for academic peer review. JavaScript was thrown out into the world out of necessity and grew up in the early browser neighborhood. So, be warned: JavaScript has some great parts and some not so great parts. But, overall, JavaScript is brilliant, if you use it intelligently.

In this book, we teach you to use the great parts to best advantage, and we'll point out the bad parts, and advise you to drive around them.

We don't exhaustively cover every single aspect of the language.

There's a lot you can learn about JavaScript. This book is not a reference book; it's a learning book, so it doesn't cover everything there is to know about JavaScript. Our goal is to teach you the fundamentals of using JavaScript so that you can pick up any old reference book and do whatever you want with JavaScript.

This book does teach you JavaScript in the browser.

The browser is not only the most common environment that JavaScript runs in, it's also the most convenient (everyone has a computer with a text editor and a browser, and that's all you need to get started with JavaScript). Running JavaScript in the browser also means you get instant gratification: you can write code and all you have to do is reload your web page to see what it does.

This book advocates well-structured and readable code based on best practices.

You want to write code that you and other people can read and understand, code that will still work in next year's browsers. You want to write code in the most straight-forward way so you can get the job done and get on to better things. In this book we're going to teach you to write clear, well-organized code that anticipates change from the get-go. Code you can be proud of, code you'll want to frame and put on the wall (just take it down before you bring your date over).

We encourage you to use more than one browser with this book.

We teach you to write JavaScript that is based on standards, but you're still likely to encounter minor differences in the way web browsers interpret JavaScript. While we'll do our best to ensure all the code in the book works in all modern browsers, and even show you a couple of tricks to make sure your code is supported by those browsers, we encourage you to pick at least two browsers and test your JavaScript using them. This will give you experience in seeing the differences among browsers and in creating JavaScript code that works well in a variety of browsers with consistent results.

Programming is serious business. You're going to have to work, sometimes hard.

If you've already had some programming experience, then you know what we're talking about. If you're coming straight from *Head First HTML and CSS*, then you're going to find writing code is a little, well, different. Programming requires a different way of thinking. Programming is logical, at times very abstract, and requires you to think in an algorithmic way. But no worries; we're going to do all that in a brain-friendly way. Just take it a bit at a time, make sure you're well nourished and get plenty of sleep. That way, these new programming concepts will really sink in.

The activities are NOT optional.

The exercises and activities in this book are *not* add-ons; they're part of the core content of the book. Some of them are to help with memory, some are for understanding, and some will help you apply what you've learned. Don't skip the exercises. The crossword puzzles are the only things you don't have to do, but they're good for giving your brain a chance to think about the words in a different context.

The redundancy is intentional and important.

One distinct difference in a Head First book is that we want you to really get it. And we want you to finish the book remembering what you've learned. Most reference books don't have retention and recall as a goal, but this book is about learning, so you'll see some of the same concepts come up more than once.

The examples are as lean as possible.

Our readers tell us that it's frustrating to wade through 200 lines of an example looking for the two lines they need to understand. Most examples in this book are shown within the smallest possible context, so that the part you're trying to learn is clear and simple. Don't expect all of the examples to be robust, or even complete—they are written specifically for learning, and aren't always fully-functional.

We've placed all the example files on the Web so you can download them. You'll find them at http://wickedlysmart.com/hfjs.

The 'Brain Power' exercises don't usually have answers.

For some of them, there is no right answer, and for others, part of the learning experience of the Brain Power activities is for you to decide if and when your answers are right. In some of the Brain Power exercises you will find hints to point you in the right direction.

We often give you only the code, not the markup.

After we get past the first chapter or two, we often give you just the JavaScript code and assume you'll wrap it in a nice HTML wrapper. Here's a simple HTML page you can use with most of the code in this book, and if we want you to use other HTML, we'll tell you:

```
<!DOCTYPE html>

<html lang="en">

    <head>

        <meta charset="utf-8">

        <title>Your HTML Page</title>

        <script>


                        ⟵——— Your JavaScript code will typically go here.


        </script>

    </head>

    <body>

                ⟵——— Any web page content will go here.


    </body>

</html>
```

⟰

But don't worry; at the beginning of the
book we'll take you through everything.

Get the code examples, help and discussion

You'll find everything you need for this book online at `http://wickedlysmart.com/hfjs`, including code sample files and additional support material including videos.

Tech Reviewers

These guys really rocked it; they were there for us throughout the review process and provided invaluable, detailed feedback on everything!

Ismaël Martin "Bing" Demiddel

Jeff Straw

Frank D. Moore

Alfred J. Speller

Bruce Forkush

Javier Ruedas

Thank you to our amazing review team

This book has been more carefully reviewed than any of our previous books. In fact, over 270 people joined our WickedlySmart Insiders program and participated in reading and critiquing this book in real time as we wrote it. This worked better than we ever imagined and was instrumental in shaping every aspect of *Head First JavaScript Programming*. Our heartfelt thanks to everyone who participated; the book is so much better because of you.

The amazing technical reviewers pictured above provided feedback above and beyond, and each made significant contributions to this book. The following reviewers also made contributions across different aspects of the book: **Galina N. Orlova, J. Patrick Kelley, Claus-Peter Kahl, Rob Cleary, Rebeca Dunn-Krahn**, Olaf Schoenrich, Jim Cupec, Matthew M. Hanrahan, Russell Alleen-Willems, Christine J. Wilson, Louis-Philippe Breton, Timo Glaser, Charmaine Gray, Lee Beckham, Michael Murphy, Dave Young, Don Smallidge, Alan Rusyak, Eric R. Liscinsky, Brent Fazekas, Sue Starr, Eric (Orange Pants) Johnson, Jesse Palmer, Manabu Kawakami, Alan McIvor, Alex Kelley, Yvonne Bichsel Truhon, Austin Throop, Tim Williams, J. Albert Bowden II, Rod Shelton, Nancy DeHaven Hall, Sue McGee, Francisco Debs, Miriam Berkland, Christine H Grecco, Elhadji Barry, Athanasios Valsamakis, Peter Casey, Dustin Wollam and Robb Kerley.

Acknowledgments*

We're also extremely grateful to our esteemed technical reviewer **David Powers**. The truth is we don't write books without David anymore, he's just saved our butts too many times. It's getting a little like Elton and Bernie; we're starting to ask ourselves if we actually could write a book without him. David ~~helps us~~ forces us to make the book more sound and technically accurate, and his second career as a standup comic really comes in handy when we're tuning the more humorous parts of the book. Thank you once again David—you're the ultimate professional and we sleep better at night knowing we've passed your technical muster.

Esteemed Reviewer, David Powers

At O'Reilly:

A huge, massive thanks to our editor, **Meghan Blanchette**, who cleared the path for this book, removed every obstacle to its completion, waited patiently and sacrificed family time to get it done. She's also the person who keeps us sane in our relationship with O'Reilly (and keeps O'Reilly sane in their relationship with us). We love you and can't wait to collaborate with you again!

Don't let the smile fool you, this guy is hard core (technically of course).

Meghan Blanchette

And another big shoutout to our Chief Editor Emeritus, **Mike Hendrickson**, who spearheaded this book from the very beginning. Thanks again Mike; none of our books would have happened without you. You've been our champion for well over a decade and we love you for it!

*The large number of acknowledgments is because we're testing the theory that everyone mentioned in a book acknowledgment will buy at least one copy, probably more, what with relatives and everything. If you'd like to be in the acknowledgment of our *next* book, and you have a large family, write to us.

Mike Hendrickson

Also At O'Reilly:

Our sincerest thanks as well to the whole O'Reilly team: **Melanie Yarbrough**, **Bob Pfahler** and **Dan Fauxsmith**, who wrangled the book into shape; to **Ed Stephenson**, **Huguette Barriere,** and **Leslie Crandell** who led the way on marketing and we appreciate their out-of-the-box approach. Thanks to **Ellie Volkhausen**, **Randy Comer** and **Karen Montgomery** for their inspired cover design that continues to serve us well. Thank you, as always, to **Rachel Monaghan** for her hardcore copyedit (and for keeping it all fun), and to **Bert Bates** for his valuable feedback.

1 a quick dip into javascript

Getting your feet wet

Come on in, the water's great! We're going to dive right in and check out JavaScript, write some code, run it and watch it interact with your browser! You're going to be writing code in no time.

JavaScript gives you superpowers. The **true programming language** of the web, JavaScript lets you **add behavior** to your web pages. No more dry, boring, static pages that just sit there looking at you—with JavaScript you're going to be able to reach out and touch your users, react to interesting events, grab data from the web to use in your pages, draw graphics right in your web pages and a lot more. And once you know JavaScript you'll also be in a position to create **totally new** behaviors for your users.

You'll be in good company too, JavaScript's not only one of the **most popular** programming languages, it's also **supported** in all modern (and most ancient) browsers; JavaScript's even branching out and being **embedded** in a lot of environments outside the browser. More on that later; for now, let's get started!

The way JavaScript works

If you're used to creating structure, content, layout and style in your web pages, isn't it time to add a little behavior as well? These days, there's no need for the page to just *sit there*. Great pages should be dynamic, interactive, and they should work with your users in new ways. That's where JavaScript comes in. Let's start by taking a look at how JavaScript fits into the *web page ecosystem*:

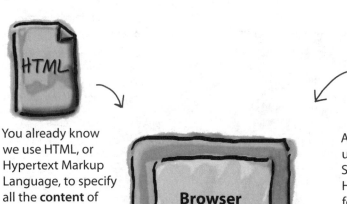

You already know we use HTML, or Hypertext Markup Language, to specify all the **content** of your pages along with their **structure**, like paragraphs, headings and sections.

And you already know that we use CSS, or Cascading Style Sheets, to specify how the HTML is presented...the colors, fonts, borders, margins, and the layout of your page. CSS gives you **style**, and it does it in a way that is separate from the structure of the page.

So let's introduce JavaScript, HTML & CSS's computational cousin. JavaScript lets you create **behavior** in your web pages. Need to react when a user clicks on your "On Sale for the next 30 seconds!" button? Double check your user's form input on the fly? Grab some tweets from Twitter and display them? Or how about play a game? Look to JavaScript. JavaScript gives you a way to add programming to your page so that you can compute, react, draw, communicate, alert, alter, update, change, and we could go on... anything dynamic, that's JavaScript in action.

How you're going to write JavaScript

JavaScript is fairly unique in the programming world. With your typical programming language you have to write it, compile it, link it and deploy it. JavaScript is much more fluid and flexible. With JavaScript all you need to do is write JavaScript right into your page, and then load it into a browser. From there, the browser will happily begin executing your code. Let's take a closer look at how this works:

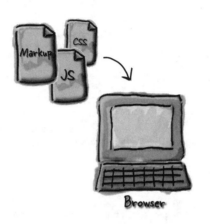

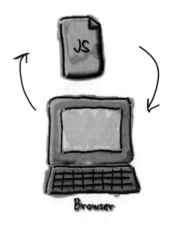

```
<html>
<head>
<title>Icecream</title>
<script>
 var x = 49;
</script>
<body>
<h1>Icecream Flavors</h1>
<h2><em>49 flavors</em></h2>
<p>All your favorite
flavors!</p>
</body>
</html>
```

Writing
1

You create your page just like you always do, with HTML content and CSS style. And you also include JavaScript in your page. As you'll see, just like HTML and CSS, you can put everything together in one file, or you can place JavaScript in its own file, to be included in your page.

We'll talk about the best way in a bit...

Loading
2

Point your browser to your page, just as you always do. When the browser sees code, it starts parsing it immediately, getting ready to execute it. Note that like HTML and CSS, if the browser sees errors in your code, it will do its best to keep moving and reading more JavaScript, HTML and CSS. The last thing it wants to do is not be able to give the user a page to see.

For future reference, the browser also builds an "object model" of your HTML page that JavaScript can make use of. Put that in the back of your brain, we'll come back to it later...

Executing
3

The browser starts executing your code as soon as it encounters it in your page, and continues executing it for the lifetime of your page. Unlike early versions of JavaScript, today's JavaScript is a powerhouse, using advanced compilation techniques to execute your code at nearly the same speed as many native programming languages.

How to get JavaScript into your page

First things first. You can't get very far with JavaScript if you don't know how to get it into a page. So, how do you do that? Using the `<script>` element of course!

Let's take a boring old, garden-variety web page and add some dynamic behavior using a `<script>` element. Now, at this point, don't worry too much about the details of what we're putting into the `<script>` element—your goal right now is to get some JavaScript working.

> Here's our standard HTML5 doctype, and `<html>` and `<head>` elements.

> And we've got a pretty generic `<body>` for this page as well.

> Ah, but we've added a script element to the `<head>` of the page.

```html
<!doctype html>
<html lang="en">
  <head>
    <meta charset="utf-8">
    <title>Just a Generic Page</title>
    <script>
      setTimeout(wakeUpUser, 5000);
      function wakeUpUser() {
        alert("Are you going to stare at this boring page forever?");
      }
    </script>
  </head>
  <body>
      <h1>Just a generic heading</h1>
      <p>Not a lot to read about here. I'm just an obligatory paragraph living in
an example in a JavaScript book. I'm looking for something to make my life more
exciting.</p>
  </body>
</html>
```

> And we've written some JavaScript code inside it.

> Again, don't worry too much about what this code does. Then again, we bet you'll want to take a look at the code and see if you can think through what each part might do.

A little test drive

Go ahead and type this page into a file named "behavior.html". Drag the file to your browser (or use File > Open) to load it. What does it do? Hint, you'll need to wait five seconds to find out.

Just relax. At this point we don't expect you to read JavaScript like you grew up with it. In fact, all we want you to do right now is get a feel for what JavaScript looks like.

That said, you're not totally off the hook because we need to get your brain revved up and working. Remember that code on the previous page? Let's just walk through it to get a feel for what it might do:

> *Perhaps a way to count five seconds of time? Hint: 1000 milliseconds = 1 second.*

```
setTimeout(wakeUpUser, 5000);
function wakeUpUser() {
    alert("Are you going to stare at this boring page forever?");
}
```

A way to create reusable code and call it "wakeUpUser"?

Clearly a way to alert the user with a message.

there are no Dumb Questions

Q: I've heard JavaScript is a bit of a wimpy language. Is it?

A: JavaScript certainly wasn't a power lifter in its early days, but its importance to the web has grown since then, and as a result, many resources (including brain power from some of the best minds in the business) have gone into supercharging the performance of JavaScript. But, you know what? Even before JavaScript was super fast, it was always a brilliant language. As you'll see, we're going to do some very powerful things with it.

Q: Is JavaScript related to Java?

A: Only by name. JavaScript was created during a time when Java was a red hot popular language, and the inventors of JavaScript capitalized on that popularity by making use of the Java name. Both languages borrow some syntax from programming languages like C, but other than that, they are quite different.

Q: Is JavaScript the best way to create dynamic web pages? What about solutions like Flash?

A: There was a time when Flash may have been the preferred choice for many to create interactive and more dynamic web pages, but the industry direction is moving strongly in favor of HTML5 with JavaScript. And, with HTML5, JavaScript is now the standard scripting language for the Web. Many resources are going into making JavaScript fast and efficient, and creating JavaScript APIs that extend the functionality of the browser.

Q: My friend is using JavaScript inside Photoshop, or at least he says he is. Is that possible?

A: Yes, JavaScript is breaking out of the browser as a general scripting language for many applications from graphics utilities to music applications and even to server-side programming. Your investment in learning JavaScript is likely to pay off in ways beyond web pages in the future.

Q: You say that many other languages are compiled. What exactly does that mean and why isn't JavaScript?

A: With conventional programming languages like C, C++ or Java, you compile the code before you execute it. Compiling takes your code and produces a machine efficient representation of it, usually optimized for runtime performance. Scripting languages are typically interpreted, which means that the browser runs each line of JavaScript code as it gets to it. Scripting languages place less importance on runtime performance, and are more geared towards tasks like prototyping, interactive coding and flexibility. This was the case with early JavaScript, and was why, for many years, the performance of JavaScript was not so great. There is a middle ground however; an interpreted language can be compiled on the fly, and that's the path browser manufacturers have taken with modern JavaScript. In fact, with JavaScript you now have the conveniences of a scripting language, while enjoying the performance of a compiled language. By the way, we'll use the words *interpret*, *evaluate* and *execute* in this book. They have slightly different meanings in various contexts, but for our purposes, they all basically mean the same thing.

JavaScript, you've come a long way baby...

JavaScript 1.0

Netscape might have been before your time, but it was the first *real* browser company. Back in the mid-1990s browser competition was fierce, particularly with Microsoft, and so adding new, exciting features to the browser was a priority.

And towards that goal, Netscape wanted to create a scripting language that would allow anyone to add scripts to their pages. Enter LiveScript, a language developed in short order to meet that need. Now if you've never heard of LiveScript, that's because this was all about the time that Sun Microsystems introduced Java, and, as a result, drove their own stock to stratospheric levels. So, why not capitalize on that success and rename LiveScript to JavaScript? After all, who cares if they don't actually have anything to do with each other? Right?

Did we mention Microsoft? They created their own scripting language soon after Netscape did, named, um, JScript, and it was, um, quite similar to JavaScript. And so began the browser wars.

JavaScript 1.3

Between 1996 and 2000, JavaScript grew up. In fact, Netscape submitted JavaScript for standardization and ECMAScript was born. Never heard of ECMAScript? That's okay, now you have; just know that ECMAScript serves as the standard language definition for all JavaScript implementations (in and out of the browser).

During this time developers continued struggling with JavaScript as casualties of the browser wars (because of all the differences in browsers), although the use of JavaScript became common-place in any case. And while subtle differences between JavaScript and JScript continued to give developers headaches, the two languages began to look more and more like each other over time.

JavaScript still hadn't outgrown its reputation as an amateurish language, but that was soon to change...

JavaScript 1.8.5

Finally, JavaScript comes of age and gains the respect of professional developers! While you might say it's all due to having a solid standard, like ECMAScript 5, which is now implemented in all modern browsers, it's really Google that pushed JavaScript usage into the professional limelight, when in 2005 they released Google Maps and showed the world what could really be done with JavaScript to create dynamic web pages.

With all the new attention, many of the best programming language minds focused on improving JavaScript's interpreters and made vast improvements to its runtime performance. Today, JavaScript stands with only a few changes from the early days, and despite its rushed birth into the world, is showing itself to be a powerful and expressive language.

1995   **2000**   **2012**

Sharpen your pencil

Look how easy it is to write JavaScript

You don't know JavaScript yet, but we bet you can make some good guesses about how JavaScript code works. Take a look at each line of code below and see if you can guess what it does. Write in your answers below. We've done one for you to get you started. If you get stuck, the answers are on the next page.

```javascript
var price = 28.99;

var discount = 10;

var total =
     price - (price * (discount / 100));
if (total > 25) {
   freeShipping();
}


var count = 10;
while (count > 0) {
   juggle();
   count = count - 1;
}


var dog = {name: "Rover", weight: 35};
if (dog.weight > 30) {
    alert("WOOF WOOF");
} else {
    alert("woof woof");
}


var circleRadius = 20;
var circleArea =
   Math.PI * (circleRadius * circleRadius);
```

Create a variable named price, and assign the value 28.99 to it.

create a variable named discount - assign value of 10

make a total
price (28.99) - (price 28.99 [X] (discount 10 / 100))

if the total is more than 25 then give free shipping

Create a variable named count value = 10

if the count is greater than 0

juggle

reduce the value of count by 1

var dog = dog - name if Rover w/ weight of 35

if its more than 30

alert - woof woof

if its not more than 30

lower case woof woof

var name circleRadius value of 20

calculate the

PI + ?

Look how easy it is to write JavaScript

You don't know JavaScript yet, but we bet you can make some good guesses about how JavaScript code works. Take a look at each line of code below and see if you can guess what it does. Write in your answers below. We've done one for you to get you started. Here are our answers.

```javascript
var price = 28.99;
```
Create a variable named price, and assign the value 28.99 to it.

```javascript
var discount = 10;
```
Create a variable named discount, and assign the value 10 to it.

```javascript
var total =
    price - (price * (discount / 100));
```
Compute a new price by applying a discount and then assign it to the variable total.

```javascript
if (total > 25) {
```
Compare the value in the variable total to 25. If it's greater...

```javascript
    freeShipping();
```
...then do something with freeShipping.

```javascript
}
```
End the if statement

```javascript
var count = 10;
```
Create a variable named count, and assign the value 10 to it.

```javascript
while (count > 0) {
```
As long as the variable count is greater than 0...

```javascript
    juggle();
```
...do some juggling, and...

```javascript
    count = count - 1;
```
...reduce the value of count by 1 each time.

```javascript
}
```
End the while loop

```javascript
var dog = {name: "Rover", weight: 35};
```
Create a dog with a name and weight.

```javascript
if (dog.weight > 30) {
```
If the dog's weight is greater than 30...

```javascript
    alert("WOOF WOOF");
```
...alert "WOOF WOOF" to the browser's web page

```javascript
} else {
```
Otherwise...

```javascript
    alert("woof woof");
```
...alert "woof woof" to the browser's web page

```javascript
}
```
End the if/else statement

```javascript
var circleRadius = 20;
```
Create a variable, circleRadius, and assign the value 20 to it.

```javascript
var circleArea =
```
Create a variable named circleArea...

```javascript
    Math.PI * (circleRadius * circleRadius);
```
...and assign the result of this expression to it (1256.6370614359173)

Look, if you want to go beyond creating *just* static web pages, you gotta have JavaScript chops.

It's True.

With HTML and CSS you can create some great looking pages. But once you know JavaScript, you can really expand on the kinds of pages you can create. So much so, in fact, you might actually start thinking of your pages as applications (or even experiences!) rather than mere pages.

And usually increase the size of your paycheck too!

Now, you might be saying, "Sure, I know that. Why do you think I'm reading this book?" Well, we actually wanted to use this opportunity to have a little chat about learning JavaScript. If you already have a programming language or scripting language under your belt, then you have some idea of what lies ahead. However, if you've mostly been using HTML & CSS to date, you should know that there is something fundamentally different about learning a programming language.

With HTML & CSS what you're doing is largely declarative—for instance, you're declaring, say, that some text is a paragraph or that all elements in the "sale" class should be colored red. With JavaScript you're adding *behavior* to the page, and to do that you need to describe computation. You need to be able to describe things like, "compute the user's score by summing up all the correct answers" or "do this action ten times" or "when the user clicks on that button play the you-have-won sound" or even "go off and get my latest tweet, and put it in this page."

To do those things you need a language that is quite different from HTML or CSS. Let's see how…

How to make a statement

When you create HTML you usually **mark up** text to give it structure; to do that you add elements, attributes and values to the text:

```html
<h1 class="drink">Mocha Caffe Latte</h1>

<p>Espresso, steamed milk and chocolate syrup,
just the way you like it.</p>
```

With HTML we mark up text to create structure. Like, "I need a large heading called Mocha Cafe Latte; it's a heading for a drink. And I need a paragraph after that."

CSS is a bit different. With CSS you're writing a set of **rules**, where each rule selects elements in the page, and then specifies a set of styles for those elements:

```css
h1.drink {
    color: brown;
}
p {
    font-family: sans-serif;
}
```

With CSS we write rules that use selectors, like h1.drink and p, to determine what parts of the HTML the style is applied to.

Let's make sure all drink headings are colored brown...

...and we want all the paragraphs to have a sans-serif type font.

With JavaScript you write **statements**. Each statement specifies a small part of a computation, and together, all the statements create the behavior of the page:

A set of statements.

Each statement does a little bit of work, like declaring some variables to contain values for us.

```javascript
var age = 25;
var name = "Owen";

if (age > 14) {
    alert("Sorry this page is for kids only!");
} else {
    alert("Welcome " + name + "!");
}
```

Here we create a variable to contain an age of 25, and we also need a variable to contain the value "Owen".

Or making decisions, such as: Is the age of the user greater than 14?

And if so alerting the user they are too old for this page.

Otherwise, we welcome the user by name, like this: "Welcome Owen!" (but since Owen is 25, we don't do that in this case.)

Variables and values

You might have noticed that JavaScript statements usually involve variables. Variables are used to store values. What kinds of values? Here are a few examples:

`var winners = 2;` ← This statement declares a variable named winners and assigns a numeric value of 2 to it.

`var name = "Duke";` ← This one assigns a string of characters to the variable name (we call those "strings," for short).

`var isEligible = false;` ← And this statement assigns the value false to the variable isEligible. We call true/false values "booleans." ← Pronounced "boo-lee-ans."

Notice we don't put quotes around boolean values.

There are other values that variables can hold beyond numbers, strings and booleans, and we'll get to those soon enough, but, no matter what a variable contains, we create all variables the same way. Let's take a little closer look at how to declare a variable:

We always start with the <u>var</u> keyword when declaring a variable.

NO EXCEPTIONS! Even if JavaScript doesn't complain when you leave off the var. We'll tell you why later...

Next we give the variable a name.

$$\text{var winners = 2;}$$

We always end an assignment statement with a semicolon.

And, optionally, we assign a value to the variable by adding an equals sign followed by the value.

We say optionally, because if you want, you can create a variable without an initial value, and then assign it a value later. To create a variable without an initial value, just leave off the assignment part, like this:

$$\text{var losers;}$$

By leaving off the equals sign and value you're just declaring the variable for later use.

No value?! What am I supposed to do now?! I'm so humiliated.

Back away from that keyboard!

You know variables have a name, and you know they have a value.

You also know some of the things a variable can hold are numbers, strings and boolean values.

But what can you call your variables? Is any name okay? Well no, but the rules around creating variable names are simple: just follow the two rules below to create valid variable names:

1 Start your variables with a letter, an underscore or a dollar sign.

2 After that, use as many letters, numeric digits, underscores or dollar signs as you like.

Oh, and one more thing; we really don't want to confuse JavaScript by using any of the built-in *keywords*, like **var** or **function** or **false**, so consider those off limits for your own variable names. We'll get to some of these keywords and what they mean throughout the rest of the book, but here's a list to take a quick look at:

break	delete	for	let	super	void
case	do	function	new	switch	while
catch	else	if	package	this	with
class	enum	implements	private	throw	yield
const	export	import	protected	true	
continue	extends	in	public	try	
debugger	false	instanceof	return	typeof	
default	finally	interface	static	var	

there are no Dumb Questions

Q: What's a keyword?

A: A keyword is a reserved word in JavaScript. JavaScript uses these reserved words for its own purposes, and it would be confusing to you and the browser if you started using them for your variables.

Q: What if I used a keyword as part of my variable name? For instance, can I have a variable named ifOnly (that is, a variable that contains the keyword if)?

A: You sure can, just don't match the keyword exactly. It's also good to write clear code, so in general you wouldn't want to use something like `elze`, which might be confused with `else`.

Q: Is JavaScript case sensitive? In other words, are myvariable and MyVariable the same thing?

A: If you're used to HTML markup you might be used to case insensitive languages; after all, <head> and <HEAD> are treated the same by the browser. With JavaScript however, case matters for variables, keywords, function names and pretty much everything else, too. So pay attention to your use of upper- and lowercase.

WEBVILLE TIMES

How to avoid those embarassing naming mistakes

You've got a lot of flexibility in choosing your variable names, so here are a few Webville tips to make your naming easier:

Choose names that mean something.

Variable names like _m, $, r and foo might mean something to you but they are generally frowned upon in Webville. Not only are you likely to forget them over time, your code will be much more readable with names like angle, currentPressure and passedExam.

Use "camel case" when creating multiword variable names.

At some point you're going to have to decide how you name a variable that represents, say, a two-headed dragon with fire. How? Just use camel case, in which you capitalize the first letter of each word (other than the first): twoHeadedDragonWithFire. Camel case is easy to form, widely spoken in Webville and gives you enough flexibility to create as specific a variable name as you need. There are other schemes too, but this is one of the more commonly used (even beyond JavaScript).

Use variables that begin with _ and $ only with very good reason.

Variables that begin with $ are usually reserved for JavaScript libraries and while some authors use variables beginning with _ for various conventions, we recommend you stay away from both unless you have very good reason (you'll know if you do).

Be safe.

Be safe in your variable naming; we'll cover a few more tips for staying safe later in the book, but for now be clear in your naming, avoid keywords, and always use var when declaring a variable.

Syntax Fun

- Each statement ends in a semicolon.
  ```
  x = x + 1;
  ```

- A single line comment begins with two forward slashes. Comments are just notes to you or other developers about the code. They aren't executed.
  ```
  // I'm a comment
  ```

- Whitespace doesn't matter (almost everywhere).
  ```
  x    =       2233;
  ```

- Surround strings of characters with double quotes (or single, both work, just be consistent).
  ```
  "You rule!"
  'And so do you!'
  ```

- Don't use quotes around the boolean values true and false.
  ```
  rockin = true;
  ```

- Variables don't have to be given a value when they are declared:
  ```
  var width;
  ```

- JavaScript, unlike HTML markup, is case sensitive, meaning upper- and lowercase matters. The variable `counter` is different from the variable `Counter`.

BE the Browser

Below, you'll find JavaScript code with some mistakes in it. Your job is to play like you're the browser and find the errors in the code. After you've done the exercise look at the end of the chapter to see if you found them all.

A

```
// Test for jokes
var joke = "JavaScript walked into a bar....';
var toldJoke = "false";
var $punchline =
   "Better watch out for those semi-colons."
var %entage = 20;
var result

if (toldJoke == true) {
    Alert($punchline);
} else
    alert(joke);
}
```

Don't worry too much about what this JavaScript does for now; just focus on looking for errors in variables and syntax.

B

```
\\ Movie Night
var zip code = 98104;
var joe'sFavoriteMovie = Forbidden Planet;
var movieTicket$    =    9;

if (movieTicket$ >= 9) {
    alert("Too much!");
} else {
    alert("We're going to see " + joe'sFavoriteMovie);
}
```

Express yourself

To truly express yourself in JavaScript you need *expressions*.
Expressions evaluate to values. You've already seen a few in passing in
our code examples. Take the expression in this statement for instance:

*Here's a JavaScript statement that assigns the result of
evaluating an expression to the variable total.*

*We use * for multiply
and / for divide.*

```
var total = price - (price * (discount / 100));
```

*Here's our
variable total.*

*And the
assignment.*

And this whole thing is an expression.

*This expression evaluates
to a price reduced by
a discount that is a
percent of the price. So
if your price is 10 and the
discount is 20, we get 8
as a result.*

If you've ever taken a math class, balanced your checkbook or done your
taxes, we're sure these kinds of numeric expressions are nothing new.

There are also string expressions; here are a few:

```
"Dear " + "Reader" + ","
```

*This adds together, or concatenates, these strings to
form a new string "Dear Reader,".*

```
"super" + "cali" + youKnowTheRest
```

*Same here, except we have a variable that
contains a string as part of the expression. This
evaluates to "supercalifragilisticexpialidocious". **

```
phoneNumber.substring(0,3)
```

*Just another example of an expression that results in a string.
We'll get to exactly how this works later, but this returns the
area code of a US phone number string.*

We also have expressions that evaluate to **true** or **false**, otherwise
known as boolean expressions. Work through each of these to see how
you get true or false from them:

```
age < 14
```

*If a person's age is less than 14 this is true, otherwise it is false.
We could use this to test if someone is a child or not.*

```
cost >= 3.99
```

*If the cost is 3.99 or greater, this is true. Otherwise it's
false. Get ready to buy on sale when it's false!*

```
animal == "bear"
```

This is true when animal contains the string "bear". If it does, beware!

And expressions can evaluate to a few other types; we'll get to these
later in the book. For now, the important thing is to realize all these
expressions evaluate to something: a value that is a number, a string or
a boolean. Let's keep moving and see what that gets you!

* *Of course, that is assuming the variable youKnowTheRest is "fragilisticexpialidocious".*

Sharpen your pencil

Get out your pencil and put some expressions through their paces. For each expression below, compute its value and write in your answer. Yes, WRITE IN... forget what your Mom told you about writing in books and scribble your answer right in this book! Be sure to check your answers at the end of the chapter.

Can you say "Celsius to Fahrenheit calculator"?

`(9 / 5) * temp + 32`

What is the result when temp is 10? __50__

This is a boolean expression. The == operator tests if two values are equal to each other.

`color == "orange"`

Is this expression true or false when color has the value "pink"? __FALSE__
Or has the value "orange"? __TRUE__

`name + ", " + "you've won!"`

What value does this compute to when name is "Martha"? __Martha, you've won!__

This tests if the first value is greater than the second. You can also use >= to test if the first value is greater than or equal to the second.

`yourLevel > 5`

When yourLevel is 2, what does this evaluate to? __FALSE__
When yourLevel is 5, what does this evaluate to? __FALSE__
When yourLevel is 7, what does this evaluate to? __TRUE__

`(level * points) + bonus`

Okay, level is 5, points is 30,000 and bonus is 3300. What does this evaluate to? __153,300__

`color != "orange"`

Is this expression true or false when color has the value "pink"? __TRUE__

The != operator tests if two values are NOT equal to each other.

Extra CREDIT!

`1000 + "108"`

Are there a few possible answers? Only one is correct. Which would you choose? __1000108__

Serious Coding

Did you notice that the = operator is used in assignments, while the == operator tests for equality? That is, we use one equal sign to assign values to variables. We use two equal signs to test if two values are equal to each other. Substituting one for the other is a common coding mistake.

```
while (juggling) {
    keepBallsInAir();
}
```

Doing things more than once

You do a lot of things more than once:

Lather, rinse, repeat…

Wax on, wax off…

Eat candies from the bowl until they're all gone.

Of course you'll often need to do things in code more than once, and JavaScript gives you a few ways to repeatedly execute code in a loop: **while**, **for**, **for in** and **forEach**. Eventually, we'll look at all these ways of looping, but let's focus on **while** for now.

We just talked about expressions that evaluate to boolean values, like `scoops > 0`, and these kinds of expressions are the key to the while statement. Here's how:

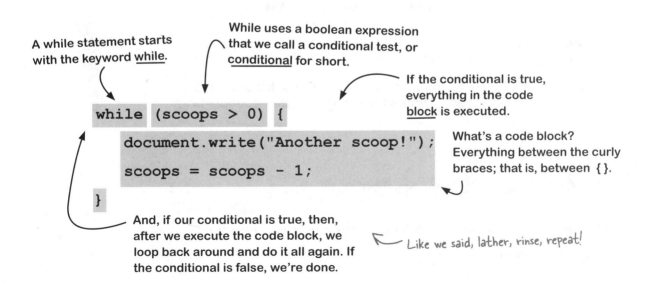

A while statement starts with the keyword <u>while</u>.

While uses a boolean expression that we call a conditional test, or <u>conditional</u> for short.

If the conditional is true, everything in the code <u>block</u> is executed.

```
while (scoops > 0) {
    document.write("Another scoop!");
    scoops = scoops - 1;
}
```

What's a code block? Everything between the curly braces; that is, between { }.

And, if our conditional is true, then, after we execute the code block, we loop back around and do it all again. If the conditional is false, we're done.

Like we said, lather, rinse, repeat!

How the while loop works

Seeing as this is your first while loop, let's trace through a round of its execution to see exactly how it works. Notice we've added a declaration for scoops to declare it, and initialize it to the value 5.

Now let's start executing this code. First we set scoops to five.

```javascript
var scoops = 5;
while (scoops > 0) {
    document.write("Another scoop!<br>");
    scoops = scoops - 1;
}
document.write("Life without ice cream isn't the same");
```

After that we hit the while statement. When we evaluate a while statement the first thing we do is evaluate the conditional to see if it's true or false.

```javascript
var scoops = 5;
while (scoops > 0) {
    document.write("Another scoop!<br>");
    scoops = scoops - 1;
}
document.write("Life without ice cream isn't the same");
```

Is scoops greater than zero? Looks like it to us!

Because the conditional is true, we start executing the block of code. The first statement in the body writes the string "Another scoop!
" to the browser.

```javascript
var scoops = 5;
while (scoops > 0) {
    document.write("Another scoop!<br>");
    scoops = scoops - 1;
}
document.write("Life without ice cream isn't the same");
```

The next statement subtracts one from the number of scoops and then sets scoops to that new value, four.

I scoop gone, 4 left!

```javascript
var scoops = 5;
while (scoops > 0) {
    document.write("Another scoop!<br>");
    scoops = scoops - 1;
}
document.write("Life without ice cream isn't the same");
```

That's the last statement in the block, so we loop back up to the conditional and start over again.

```javascript
var scoops = 5;
while (scoops > 0) {
    document.write("Another scoop!<br>");
    scoops = scoops - 1;
}
document.write("Life without ice cream isn't the same");
```

Evaluating our conditional again, this time scoops is four. But that's still more than zero.

Still plenty left!

```javascript
var scoops = 5;
while (scoops > 0) {
    document.write("Another scoop!<br>");
    scoops = scoops - 1;
}
document.write("Life without ice cream isn't the same");
```

Once again we write the string "Another scoop!
" to the browser.

```javascript
var scoops = 5;
while (scoops > 0) {
    document.write("Another scoop!<br>");
    scoops = scoops - 1;
}
document.write("Life without ice cream isn't the same");
```

The next statement subtracts one from the number of scoops and sets scoops to that new value, which is three.

2 scoops gone, 3 left!

```javascript
var scoops = 5;
while (scoops > 0) {
    document.write("Another scoop!<br>");
    scoops = scoops - 1;
}
document.write("Life without ice cream isn't the same");
```

That's the last statement in the block, so we loop back up to the conditional and start over again.

```javascript
var scoops = 5;
while (scoops > 0) {
    document.write("Another scoop!<br>");
    scoops = scoops - 1;
}
document.write("Life without ice cream isn't the same");
```

Evaluating our conditional again, this time scoops is three. But that's still more than zero.

Still plenty left!

```javascript
var scoops = 5;
while (scoops > 0) {
    document.write("Another scoop!<br>");
    scoops = scoops - 1;
}
document.write("Life without ice cream isn't the same");
```

Once again we write the string "Another scoop!
" to the browser.

```javascript
var scoops = 5;
while (scoops > 0) {
    document.write("Another scoop!<br>");
    scoops = scoops - 1;
}
document.write("Life without ice cream isn't the same");
```

And as you can see, this continues... each time we loop, we decrement (reduce scoops by 1), write another string to the browser, and keep going.

3 scoops gone, 2 left!

```javascript
var scoops = 5;
while (scoops > 0) {
    document.write("Another scoop!<br>");
    scoops = scoops - 1;
}
document.write("Life without ice cream isn't the same");
```

And continues...

4 scoops gone, 1 left!

```javascript
var scoops = 5;
while (scoops > 0) {
    document.write("Another scoop!<br>");
    scoops = scoops - 1;
}
document.write("Life without ice cream isn't the same");
```

Until the last time... this time something's different. Scoops is zero, and so our conditional returns false. That's it folks; we're not going to go through the loop anymore, we're not going to execute the block. This time, we bypass the block and execute the statement that follows it.

5 scoops gone, 0 left!

```javascript
var scoops = 5;
while (scoops > 0) {
    document.write("Another scoop!<br>");
    scoops = scoops - 1;
}
document.write("Life without ice cream isn't the same");
```

Now we execute the other document.write, and write the string "Life without ice cream isn't the same". We're done!

```javascript
var scoops = 5;
while (scoops > 0) {
    document.write("Another scoop!<br>");
    scoops = scoops - 1;
}
document.write("Life without ice cream isn't the same");
```

```
if (cashInWallet > 5) {
    order = "I'll take the works: cheeseburger, fries and a coke";
} else {
    order = "I'll just have a glass of water";
}
```

Making decisions with JavaScript

You've just seen how you use a conditional to decide whether to continue looping in a `while` statement. You can also use boolean expressions to make decisions in JavaScript with the `if` statement. The `if` statement executes its code block only if a conditional test is true. Here's an example:

Here's the if keyword, followed by a conditional and a block of code.

This conditional tests to see if we're down to fewer than three scoops.

```
if (scoops < 3) {
    alert("Ice cream is running low!");
}
```

And if we've got fewer than three left, then we execute the if statement's code block.

alert takes a string and displays it in a popup dialog in your browser. Give it a try!

http://localhost
Ice cream is running low!
OK

With an `if` statement we can also string together multiple tests by adding on one or more `else if`'s, like this:

We can have one test, and then another test with if/else if

```
if (scoops >= 5) {
    alert("Eat faster, the ice cream is going to melt!");
} else if (scoops < 3) {
    alert("Ice cream is running low!");
}
```

Add as many tests with "else if" as you need, each with its own associated code block that will be executed when the condition is true.

And, when you need to make LOTS of decisions

You can string together as many `if/else` statements as you need, and if you want one, even a final catch-all `else`, so that if all conditions fail, you can handle it. Like this:

In this code we check to see if there are five or more scoops left...

```
if (scoops >= 5) {
    alert("Eat faster, the ice cream is going to melt!");
} else if (scoops == 3) {
    alert("Ice cream is running low!");
} else if (scoops == 2) {
    alert("Going once!");
} else if (scoops == 1) {
    alert("Going twice!");
} else if (scoops == 0) {
    alert("Gone!");
} else {
    alert("Still lots of ice cream left, come and get it.");
}
```

...or if there are precisely three left...

...or if there are 2, 1 or 0, and then we provide the appropriate alert.

And if none of the conditions above are true, then this code is executed.

there are no Dumb Questions

Q: What exactly is a block of code?

A: Syntactically, a block of code (which we usually just call a block) is a set of statements, which could be one statement, or as many as you like, grouped together between curly braces. Once you've got a block of code, all the statements in that block are treated as a group to be executed together. For instance, all the statements within the block in a while statement are executed if the condition of the while is true. The same holds for a block in an if or else if.

Q: I've seen code where the conditional is just a variable that is sometimes a string, not a boolean. How does that work?

A: We'll be covering that a little later, but the short answer is JavaScript is quite flexible in what it thinks is a true or false value. For instance, any variable that holds a (non-empty) string is considered true, but a variable that hasn't been set to a value is considered false. We'll get into these details soon enough.

Q: You've said that expressions can result in things other than numbers, strings and booleans. Like what?

A: Right now we're concentrating on what are known as the *primitive types*, that is, numbers, strings and booleans. Later we'll take a look at more complex types, like arrays, which are collections of values, objects and functions.

Q: Where does the name boolean come from?

A: Booleans are named after George Boole, an English mathematician who invented Boolean logic. You'll often see boolean written "Boolean," to signify that these types of variables are named after George.

Code Magnets

A JavaScript program is all scrambled up on the fridge. Can you put the magnets back in the right places to make a working JavaScript program to produce the output shown below?. Check your answer at the end of the chapter before you go on.

Arrange these magnets to make a working JavaScript program.

```
document.write("Happy Birthday dear " + name + ",<br>");
```

```
document.write("Happy Birthday to you.<br>");
```

```
var i = 0;
```

```
var name = "Joe";
```

```
i = i + 1;
```

```
}
```

```
document.write("Happy Birthday to you.<br>");
```

```
while (i < 2) {
```

Your unscrambled program should produce this output.

localhost/~Beth/HFJS/chapter1/birthday.html

Happy Birthday to you.
Happy Birthday to you.
Happy Birthday dear Joe,
Happy Birthday to you.

```
var name = "Joe";
var i = 0;
i
       )
while (i < 2) {
document.write ("Happy Birthd to you.<br>");
     i = i+1;
   }
↑ document
```

Use this space for your re-arranged magnets.

Reach out and communicate with your user

We've been talking about making your pages more interactive, and to do that you need to be able to communicate with your user. As it turns out there are a few ways to do that, and you've already seen some of them. Let's get a quick overview and then we'll dive into these in more detail throughout the book:

Create an alert.

As you've seen, the browser gives you a quick way to alert your users through the `alert` function. Just call `alert` with a string containing your alert message, and the browser will give your user the message in a nice dialog box. A small confession though: we've been overusing this because it's easy; `alert` really should be used only when you truly want to stop everything and let the user know something.

Write directly into your document.

Think of your web page as a document (that's what the browser calls it). You can use a function `document.write` to write arbitrary HTML and content into your page at any point. In general, this is considered bad form, although you'll see it used here and there. We've used it a bit in this chapter too because it's an easy way to get started.

We're using these three methods in this chapter.

Use the console.

Every JavaScript environment also has a console that can log messages from your code. To write a message to the console's log you use the function `console.log` and hand it a string that you'd like printed to the log (more details on using console log in a second). You can view `console.log` as a great tool for troubleshooting your code, but typically your users will never see your console log, so it's not a very effective way to communicate with them.

The console is a really handy way to help find errors in your code! If you've made a typing mistake, like missing a quote, JavaScript will usually give you an error in the console to help you track it down.

Directly manipulate your document.

This is the big leagues; this is the way you want to be interacting with your page and users—using JavaScript you can access your actual web page, read & change its content, and even alter its structure and style! This all happens by making use of your browser's *document object model* (more on that later). As you'll see, this is the best way to communicate with your user. But, using the document object model requires knowledge of how your page is structured and of the programming interface that is used to read and write to the page. We'll be getting there soon enough. But first, we've got some more JavaScript to learn.

This is what we're working towards. When you get there you'll be able to read, alter and manipulate your page in any number of ways.

WHO DOES WHAT?

All our methods of communication have come to the party with masks on. Can you help us unmask each one? Match the descriptions on the right to the names on the left. We've done one for you.

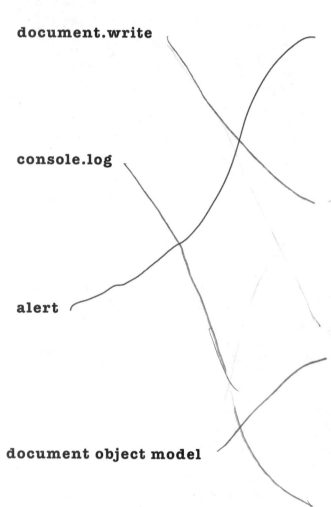

document.write

console.log

alert

document object model

I'll stop your user in his tracks and deliver a short message. The user has to click on "ok" to go further.

I can insert a little HTML and text into a document. I'm not the most elegant way to get a message to your users, but I work on every browser.

Using me you can totally control a web page: get values that a user typed in, alter the HTML or the style, or update the content of your page.

I'm just here for simple debugging purposes. Use me and I can write out information to a special developer's console.

A closer look at console.log

Let's take a closer look at how `console.log` works so we can use it in this chapter to see the output from our code, and throughout the book to inspect the output of our code and debug it. Remember though, the console is not a browser feature most casual users of the web will encounter, so you won't want to use it in the final version of your web page. Writing to the console log is typically done to troubleshoot as you develop your page. That said, it's a great way to see what your code is doing while you're learning the basics of JavaScript. Here's how it works:

Take any old string...

```
var message = "Howdy" + " " + "partner";
console.log(message);
```

...and give it to console.log, and it will be shown in the browser's console, like this.

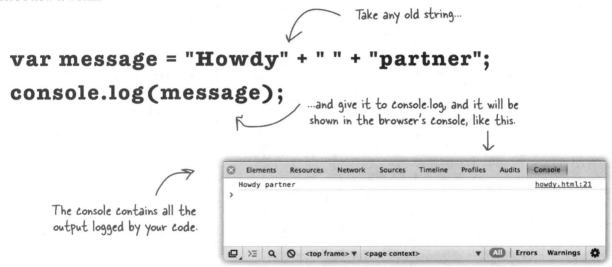

The console contains all the output logged by your code.

there are no
Dumb Questions

Q: I get that console.log can be used to output strings, but what exactly is it? I mean why are the "console" and the "log" seperated by a period?

A: Ah, good point. We're jumping ahead a bit, but think of the console as an object that does things, console-like things. One of those things is logging, and to tell the console to log for us, we use the syntax "console.log" and pass it our output in between parentheses. Keep that in the back of your mind; we're coming back to talk a lot more about objects a little later in the book. For now, you've got enough to use console.log.

Q: Can the console do anything other than just log?

A: Yes, but typically people just use it to log. There are a few more advanced ways to use log (and console), but they tend to be browser-specific. Note that console is something all modern browsers supply, but it isn't part of any formal specification.

Q: Uh, console looks great, but where do I find it? I'm using it in my code and I don't see any output!

A: In most browsers you have to explicitly open the console window. Check out the next page for details.

Opening the console

Every browser has a slightly different implementation of the console. And, to make things even more complicated, the way that browsers implement the console changes fairly frequently—not in a huge way, but enough so that by the time you read this, your browser's console might look a bit different from what we're showing here.

So, we're going to show you how to access the console in the Chrome browser (version 25) on the Mac, and we'll put instructions on how to access the console in all the major browsers online at http://wickedlysmart.com/hfjsconsole. Once you get the hang of the console in one browser, it's fairly easy to figure out how to use it in other browsers too, and we encourage you to try using the console in at least two browsers so you're familiar with them.

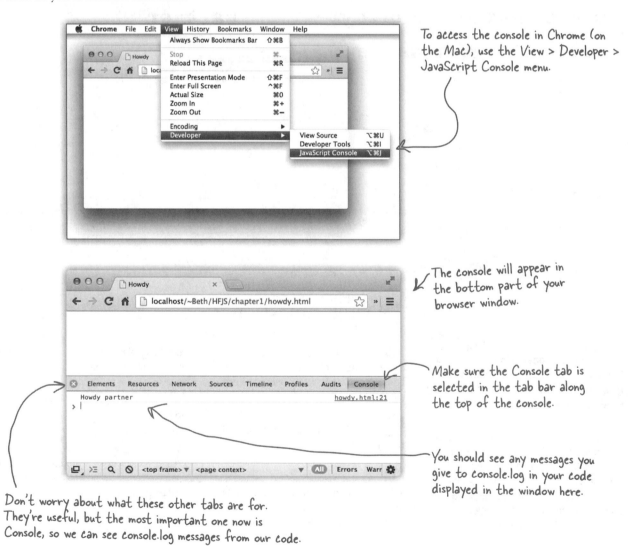

To access the console in Chrome (on the Mac), use the View > Developer > JavaScript Console menu.

The console will appear in the bottom part of your browser window.

Make sure the Console tab is selected in the tab bar along the top of the console.

You should see any messages you give to console.log in your code displayed in the window here.

Don't worry about what these other tabs are for. They're useful, but the most important one now is Console, so we can see console.log messages from our code.

Coding a Serious JavaScript Application

Let's put all these new JavaScript skills and `console.log` to good use with something practical. We need some variables, a `while` statement, some `if` statements with `else`s. Add a little more polish and we'll have a super-serious business application before you know it. But, before you look at the code, think to yourself how you'd code that classic favorite, "99 bottles of beer."

```javascript
var word = "bottles";

var count = 99;

while (count > 0) {

    console.log(count + " " + word + " of beer on the wall");

    console.log(count + " " + word + " of beer,");

    console.log("Take one down, pass it around,");

    count = count - 1;

    if (count > 0) {

        console.log(count + " " + word + " of beer on the wall.");

    } else {

        console.log("No more " + word + " of beer on the wall.");

    }

}
```

There's still a little flaw in our code. It runs correctly, but the output isn't 100% perfect. See if you can find the flaw, and fix it.

Shouldn't we be putting this code in actual web pages so we can see the output? Or are we just going to keep writing answers on paper?

Good point! Yes, it's time. Before we got there we wanted to make sure you had enough JavaScript under your belt to make it interesting. That said, you already saw in the beginning of this chapter that you add JavaScript to your HTML just like you add CSS; that is, you just add it inline with the appropriate `<script>` tags around it.

Now, like CSS, you can also place your JavaScript in files that are external to your HTML.

Let's first get this serious business application into a page, and then after we've thoroughly tested it, we'll move the JavaScript out to an external file.

A Test Drive

Okay, let's get some code in the browser... follow the instructions below and get your serious business app launched! You'll see our result below:

↖ To download all the code and sample files for this book, please visit http://wickedlysmart.com/hfjs.

① Check out the HTML below; that's where your JavaScript's going to go. Go ahead and type in the HTML and then place the JavaScript from two pages back in between the <script> tags. You can use an editor like Notepad (Windows) or TextEdit (Mac), making sure you are in plain text mode. Or, if you have a favorite HTML editor, like Dreamweaver, Coda or WebStorm, you can use that too.

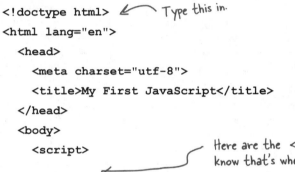

```
<!doctype html>   ⟵  Type this in.
<html lang="en">
  <head>
    <meta charset="utf-8">
    <title>My First JavaScript</title>
  </head>
  <body>
    <script>



    </script>
  </body>
</html>
```

Here are the <script> tags. At this point you know that's where you should put your code.

② Save the file as "index.html".

③ Load the file into your browser. You can either drag the file right on top of your browser window, or use the File > Open (or File > Open File) menu option in your favorite browser.

④ You won't see anything in the web page itself because we're logging all the output to the console, using console.log. So open up the browser's console, and congratulate yourself on your serious business application.

Here's our test run of this code. The code creates the entire lyrics for the 99 bottles of beer song and logs the text to the browser's console.

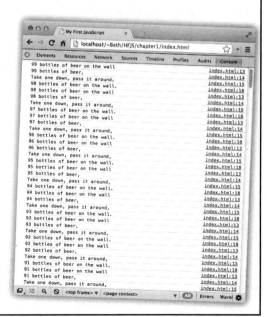

How do I add code to my page? (let me count the ways)

You already know you can add the `<script>` element with your JavaScript code to the `<head>` or `<body>` of your page, but there are a couple of other ways to add your code to a page. Let's check out all the places you can put JavaScript (and why you might want to put it one place over another):

You can place your code inline, in the `<head>` element. The most common way to add code to your pages is to put a `<script>` element in the `<head>`. Sure, it makes your code easy to find and seems to be a logical place for your code, but it's not always the best place. Why? Read on…

Or, you can add your code inline in the body of the document. To do this, enclose your JavaScript code in the `<script>` element and place it in the `<body>` of your page (typically at the end of the body).

This is a little better. Why? When your browser loads a page, it loads everything in your page's `<head>` before it loads the `<body>`. So, if your code is in the `<head>`, users might have to wait a while to see the page. If the code is loaded after the HTML in the `<body>`, users will get to see the page content while they wait for the code to load.

Still, is there a better way? Read on…

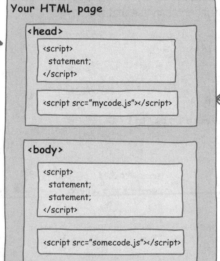

Your HTML page

```
<head>
  <script>
    statement;
  </script>

  <script src="mycode.js"></script>
</head>
```

```
<body>
  <script>
    statement;
    statement;
  </script>

  <script src="somecode.js"></script>
</body>
```

Or, put your code in its own file and link to it from the `<head>`. This is just like linking to a CSS file. The only difference is that you use the src attribute of the `<script>` tag to specify the URL to your JavaScript file.

When your code is in an external file, it's easier to maintain (separately from the HTML) and can be used across multiple pages. But this method still has the drawback that all the code needs to be loaded before the body of the page. Is there a better way? Read on…

Finally, you can link to an external file in the body of your page. Ahhh, the best of both worlds. We have a nice, maintainable JavaScript file that can be included in any page, and it's referenced from the bottom of the body of the page, so it's only loaded after the body of the page. Not bad.

> Despite evidence to the contrary, I still think the `<head>` is a great place for code.

We're going to have to separate you two

Going separate ways hurts, but we know we have to do it. It's time to take your JavaScript and move it into its own file. Here's how you do that...

1 Open index.html and select all the code; that is, everything between the `<script>` tags. Your selection should look like this:

```
<!doctype html>
<html lang="en">
  <head>
    <meta charset="utf-8">
    <title>My First JavaScript</title>
  </head>
  <body>
    <script>
      var word = "bottles";
      var count = 99;
      while (count > 0) {
         console.log(count + " " + word + " of beer on the wall");
         console.log(count + " " + word + " of beer,");
         console.log("Take one down, pass it around,");
         count = count - 1;
         if (count > 0) {
            console.log(count + " " + word + " of beer on the wall.");
         } else {
            console.log("No more " + word + " of beer on the wall.");
         }
      }
    </script>
  </body>
</html>
```

Select just the code, not the `<script>` tags; you won't need those where you're going...

2 Now create a new file named "code.js" in your editor, and place the code into it. Then save "code.js".

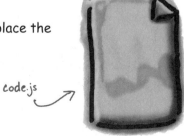

code.js

③ Now we need to place a reference to the "code.js" file in "index.html" so that it's retrieved and loaded when the page loads. To do that, delete the JavaScript code from "index.html", but leave the <script> tags. Then add a src attribute to your opening <script> tag to reference "code.js".

```
<!doctype html>
<html lang="en">
  <head>
    <meta charset="utf-8">
    <title>My First JavaScript</title>
  </head>
  <body>
    <script src="code.js">

    </script>
  </body>
</html>
```

Use the src attribute of the <script> element to link to your JavaScript file.

Where your code was.

Believe it or not we still need the ending <script> tag, even if there is no code between the two tags.

④ That's it, the surgery is complete. Now you need to test it. Reload your "index.html" page and you should see exactly the same result as before. Note that by using a src="code.js", we're assuming that the code file is in the same directory as the HTML file.

You should get the same result as before. But now your HTML and JavaScript are in separate files. Doesn't that just feel cleaner, more manageable, more stress-free already?

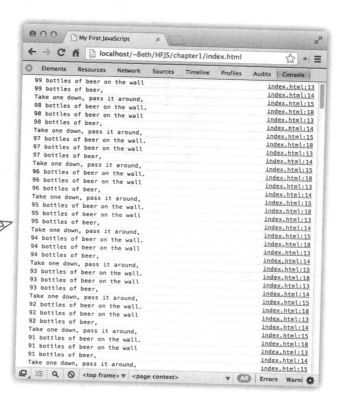

Anatomy of a Script Element

You know how to use the <script> element to add code to your page, but just to really nail down the topic, let's review the <script> element to make sure we have every detail covered:

The type attribute tells the browser you're writing JavaScript. The thing is, browsers assume you're using JavaScript if you leave it off. So, we recommend you leave it off, and so do the people who write the standards.

Don't forget the right bracket on the opening tag.

The <script> opening tag.

```
<script type="text/javascript" >
        alert("Hello world!");
</script>
```

Everything between the script tags must be valid JavaScript.

You must end the script with a closing </script> tag, always!

And when you are referencing a separate JavaScript file from your HTML, you'll use the <script> element like this:

Add a src attribute to specify the URL of the JavaScript file.

```
<script src="myJavaScript.js" >
</script>
```

Use ".js" as the extension on JavaScript files.

When referencing a separate JavaScript file, you don't put any JavaScript in the content of the <script> element.

Again, don't forget the closing </script> tag! You need it even when you're linking to an external file.

Watch it!

You can't use inline and external together.

If you try throwing some quick code in between those <script> tags when you're already using a src attribute, it won't work. You'll need two separate <script> elements.

```
<script src="goodies.js">
    var = "quick hack";
</script>
```

WRONG

JavaScript Exposed

This week's interview:
Getting to know JavaScript

Head First: Welcome JavaScript. We know you're super-busy out there, working on all those web pages, so we're glad you could take time out to talk to us.

JavaScript: No problem. And, I *am* busier than ever these days; people are using JavaScript on just about every page on the Web nowadays, for everything from simple menu effects to full blown games. It's nuts!

Head First: That's amazing given that just a few years ago, someone said that you were just a "half-baked, wimpy scripting language" and now you're everywhere.

JavaScript: Don't remind me. I've come a long way since then, and many great minds have been hard at work making me better.

Head First: Better how? Seems like your basic language features are about the same…

JavaScript: Well, I'm better in a couple of ways. First of all, I'm lightning fast these days. While I'm considered a scripting language, now my performance is close to that of native compiled languages.

Head First: And second?

JavaScript: My ability to do things in the browser has expanded dramatically. Using the JavaScript libraries available in all modern browsers you can find out your location, play video and audio, paint graphics on your web page and a lot more. But if you wanna do all that you have to know JavaScript.

Head First: But back to those criticisms of you, the language. I've heard some not so kind words… I believe the phrase was "hacked up language."

JavaScript: I'll stand on my record. I'm pretty much one of, if not *the* most widely used languages in the world. I've also fought off many competitors and won. Remember Java in the browser? Ha, what a joke. VBScript? Ha. JScript? Flash?! Silverlight? I could go on and on. So, tell me, how bad could I be?

Head First: You've been criticized as, well, "simplistic."

JavaScript: Honestly, it's my greatest strength. The fact that you can fire up a browser, type in a few lines of JavaScript and be off and running, that's powerful. And it's great for beginners too. I've heard some say there's no better beginning language than JavaScript.

Head First: But simplicity comes at a cost, no?

JavaScript: Well that's the great thing, I'm simple in the sense you can get a quick start. But I'm deep and full of all the latest modern programming constructs.

Head First: Oh, like what?

JavaScript: Well, for example, can you say dynamic types, first-class functions and closures?

Head First: I can say it but I don't know what they are.

JavaScript: Figures… that's okay, if you stay with the book you will get to know them.

Head First: Well, give us the gist.

JavaScript: Let me just say this, JavaScript was built to live in a dynamic web environment, an exciting environment where users interact with a page, where data is coming in on the fly, where many types of events happen, and the language reflects that style of programming. You'll get it a little more a bit later in the book when you understand JavaScript more.

Head First: Okay, to hear you tell it, you're the perfect language. Is that right?

JavaScript tears up…

JavaScript: You know, I didn't grow up within the ivy-covered walls of academia like most languages. I was born into the real world and had to sink or swim very fast in my life. Given that, I'm not perfect; I certainly have a few "bad parts."

Head First with a slight Barbara Walters smile: We've seen a new side of you today. I think this merits another interview in the future. Any parting thoughts?

JavaScript: Don't judge me by my bad parts, learn the good stuff and stick with that!

BULLET POINTS

- JavaScript is used to add **behavior** to web pages.

- Browser engines are much faster at executing JavaScript than they were just a few years ago.

- Browsers begin executing JavaScript code as soon as they encounter the code in the page.

- Add JavaScript to your page with the <script> element.

- You can put your JavaScript inline in the web page, or link to a separate file containing your JavaScript from your HTML.

- Use the **src** attribute in the <script> tag to link to a separate JavaScript file.

- HTML **declares** the structure and content of your page; JavaScript **computes** values and adds behavior to your page.

- JavaScript programs are made up of a series of **statements**.

- One of the most common JavaScript statements is a variable declaration, which uses the **var** keyword to declare a new variable and the assignment operator, **=,** to assign a value to it.

- There are just a few rules and guidelines for naming JavaScript variables, and it's important that you follow them.

- Remember to avoid JavaScript keywords when naming variables.

- JavaScript expressions compute values.

- Three common types of expressions are **numeric**, **string** and **boolean** expressions.

- **if/else** statements allow you to make decisions in your code.

- **while/for** statements allow you to execute code many times by looping.

- Use **console.log** instead of **alert** to display messages to the Console.

- Console messages should be used primarily for troubleshooting as users will most likely never see console messages.

- JavaScript is most commonly found adding behavior to web pages, but is also used to script applications like Adobe Photoshop, OpenOffice and Google Apps, and is even used as a server-side programming language.

JavaScript cross

Time to stretch your dendrites with a puzzle to help it all sink in.

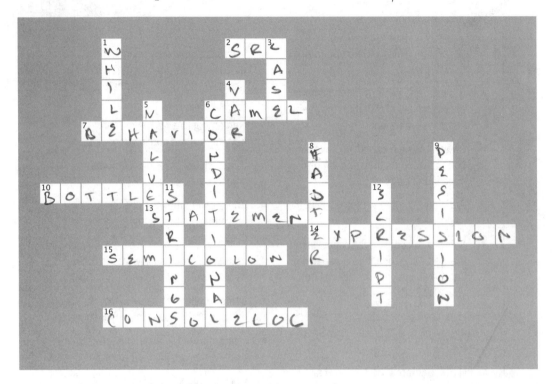

ACROSS

2. To link to an external JavaScript file from HTML, you need the _____ attribute for your <script> element.
6. To avoid embarrassing naming mistakes, use _____ case.
7. JavaScript adds _____ to your web pages.
10. There are 99 _____ of beer on the wall.
13. Each line of JavaScript code is called a _____.
14. 3 + 4 is an example of an _____.
15. All JavaScript statements end with a _____.
16. Use _____ to troubleshoot your code.

DOWN

1. Do things more than once in a JavaScript program with the _____ loop.
3. JavaScript variable names are _____ sensitive.
4. To declare a variable, use this keyword.
5. Variables are used to store these.
6. Each time through a loop, we evaluate a _____ expression.
8. Today's JavaScript runs a lot _____ than it used to.
9. The if/else statement is used to make a _____.
11. You can concatenate _____ together with the + operator.
12. You put your JavaScript inside a _____ element.

BE the Browser Solution

Below, you'll find JavaScript code with some mistakes in it. Your job is to play like you're the browser and find the errors in the code. After you've done the exercise look at the end of the chapter to see if you found them all. Here's our solution.

Delimit your strings with two double quotes (") or two single quotes ('). Don't mix!

A

```
// Test for jokes
var joke = "JavaScript walked into a bar....';
var toldJoke = "false";
var $punchline =
   "Better watch out for those semi-colons."
var %entage = 20;
var result
```

Don't put quotes around boolean values unless you really want a string.

It's okay, but not recommended, to begin a variable with a $.

Don't forget to end statements with a semi-colon!

Can't use % in variable names.

Another missing semi-colon.

```
if (toldJoke == true) {
    Alert($punchline);
} else
    alert(joke);
}
```

Should be alert, not Alert. JavaScript is case-sensitive.

We're missing an opening brace here.

B

```
\\ Movie Night
var zip code = 98104;
var joe'sFavoriteMovie = Forbidden Planet;
var movieTicket$    =    9;
```

Comments should begin with // not \\.

No spaces allowed in variable names.

No quotes allowed in variable names.

But we do need quotes around the string "Forbidden Planet".

```
if (movieTicket$ >= 9) {
    alert("Too much!");
} else {
    alert("We're going to see " + joe'sFavoriteMovie);
}
```

This if/else doesn't work because of the invalid variable name here.

Sharpen your pencil
Solution

Get out your pencil and let's put some expressions through their paces. For each expression below, compute its value and write in your answer. Yes, WRITE IN... forget what your Mom told you about writing in books and scribble your answer right in this book! Here's our solution.

⌐ Can you say "Celsius to Fahrenheit calculator"?

`(9 / 5) * temp + 32`

What is the result when temp is 10? __50__

⌐ This is a boolean expression. The == operator tests if two values are equal to each other.

`color == "orange"`

Is this expression true or false when color has the value "pink"? __false__
Or, has the value "orange"? __true__

`name + ", " + "you've won!"`

What value does this compute to when name is "Martha"?
__"Martha, you've won!"__

⌐ This tests if the first value is greater than the second. You can also use >= to test if the first value is greater than or equal to the second.

`yourLevel > 5`

When yourLevel is 2, what does this evaluate to? __false__
When yourLevel is 5, what does this evaluate to? __false__
When yourLevel is 7, what does this evaluate to? __true__

`(level * points) + bonus`

Okay, level is 5, points is 30,000 and bonus is 3300. What does this evaluate to? __153300__

`color != "orange"`

Is this expression true or false when color has the value "pink"? __true__

⌐ The != operator tests if two values are NOT equal to each other.

⌐ Extra CREDIT!

`1000 + "108"`   Are there a few possible answers? Only one is correct. Which would you choose? __"1000108"__

Serious Coding

Did you notice that the = operator is used in assignments, while the == operator tests for equality? That is, we use one equal sign to assign values to variables. We use two equal signs to test if two values are equal to each other. Substituting one for the other is a common coding mistake.

Code Magnets Solution

A JavaScript program is all scrambled up on the fridge. Can you put the magnets back in the right places to make a working JavaScript program to produce the output shown below?. Here's our solution.

Here are the unscrambled magnets!

```javascript
var name = "Joe";

var i = 0;

while (i < 2) {

    document.write("Happy Birthday to you.<br>");

    i = i + 1;

}

document.write("Happy Birthday dear " + name + ",<br>");

document.write("Happy Birthday to you.<br>");
```

Your unscrambled program should produce this output.

```
● ● ●    □ Happy Birthday        ×
← → C A   □ localhost/~Beth/HFJS/chapter1/birthday.html  ☆ » ≡
Happy Birthday to you.
Happy Birthday to you.
Happy Birthday dear Joe,
Happy Birthday to you.
```

JavaScript Cross Solution

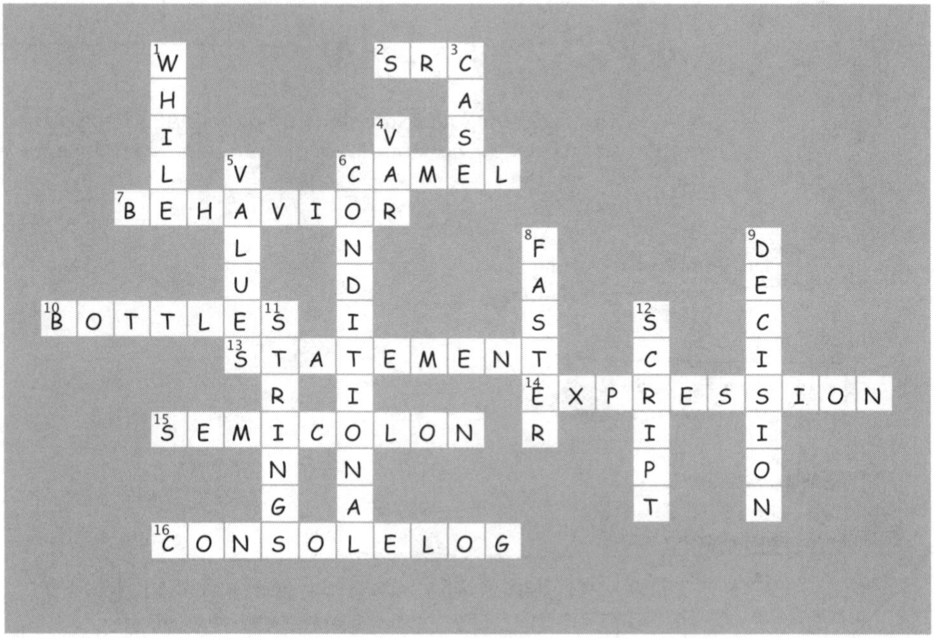
1 WHILE
2 SRC
3 CASE
4 V
5 VALUE
6 CONDITIONAL
6 CAMEL
7 BEHAVIOR
8 FASTER
9 DECISION
10 BOTTLES
11 STRING
12 SCRIPT
13 STATEMENT
14 EXPRESSION
15 SEMICOLON
16 CONSOLELOG

WHO DOES WHAT? SOLUTION

All our methods of communication have come to the party with masks on. Can you help us unmask each one? Match the descriptions on the right to the names on the left. Here's our solution:

document.write

console.log

alert

document object model

I'll stop your user in his tracks and deliver a short message. The user has to click "ok" to go further.

I can insert a little HTML and text into a document. I'm not the most elegant way to get a message to your users, but I work on every browser.

Using me you can totally control a web page: get values that a user typed in, alter the HTML or the style, or update the content of your page.

I'm just here for simple debugging purposes. Use me and I can write out information to a special developer's console.

2 writing real code

Going further

Yeah, I've done a little JavaScript coding.

Pffft... To get any further with me you're going to have to get some real experience writing code.

**You already know about variables, types, expressions...
we could go on.** The point is, you already know a few things about
JavaScript. In fact, you know enough to write some **real code**. Some code that
does something interesting, some code that someone would want to use. What
you're lacking is the **real experience** of writing code, and we're going to remedy
that right here and now. How? By jumping in head first and coding up a casual
game, all written in JavaScript. Our goal is ambitious but we're going to take it one
step at a time. Come on, let's get this started, and if you want to launch the next
casual startup, we won't stand in your way; the code is yours.

Let's build a Battleship game

It's you against the browser: the browser hides ships and your job is to seek them out and destroy them. Of course, unlike the real Battleship game, in this one you don't place any ships of your own. Instead, your job is to sink the computer's ships in the fewest number of guesses.

Goal: Sink the browser's ships in the fewest number of guesses. You're given a rating, based on how well you perform.

Setup: When the game program is launched, the computer places ships on a virtual grid. When that's done, the game asks for your first guess.

How you play: The browser will prompt you to enter a guess and you'll type in a grid location. In response to your guess, you'll see a result of "Hit", "Miss", or "You sank my battleship!" When you sink all the ships, the game ends by displaying your rating.

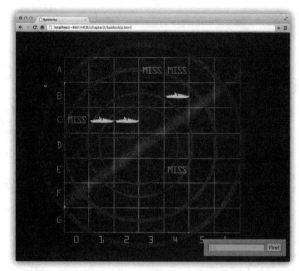

Here's what we're shooting for: a nice 7x7 grid with three ships to hunt down. Right now we're going to start a little simpler, but once you know a bit more JavaScript we'll complete the implementation so it looks just like this, complete with graphics and everything...we'll leave the sound to you as extra credit.

Our first attempt...
... a simplified Battleship

For our first attempt we're going to start simpler than the full-blown 7x7 graphical version with three ships. Instead we're going to start with a nice 1-D grid with seven locations and one ship to find. It will be crude, but our focus is on designing the basic code for the game, not the look and feel (at least for now).

Don't worry; by starting with a simplified version of the game, you get a big head start on building the full game later. This also gives us a nice chunk to bite off for your first real JavaScript program (not counting the Serious Business Application from Chapter 1, of course). So, we'll build the simple version of the game in this chapter, and get to the deluxe version later in the book after you've learned a bit more about JavaScript.

Instead of a 7x7 grid, like the one above, we're going to start with just a 1x7 grid. And, we'll worry about just one ship for now.

Notice that each ship takes up three grid locations (similar to the real board game).

First, a high-level design

We know we'll need variables, and some numbers and strings, and if statements, and conditional tests, and loops... but where and how many? And how do we put it all together? To answer these questions, we need more information about what the game should do.

First, we need to figure out the general flow of the game. Here's the basic idea:

1 **User starts the game**

    A Game places a battleship at a random location on the grid.

2 **Game play begins**
Repeat the following until the battleship is sunk:

    A Prompt user for a guess ("2", "0", etc.)

    B Check the user's guess against the battleship to look for a hit, miss or sink.

3 **Game finishes**
Give the user a rating based on the number of guesses.

Now we have a high-level idea of the kinds of things the program needs to do. Next we'll figure out a few more details for the steps.

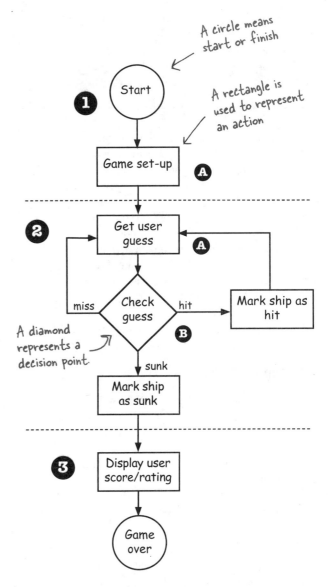

A circle means start or finish

A rectangle is used to represent an action

A diamond represents a decision point.

Whoa. A real flowchart.

A few more details...

We have a pretty good idea about how this game is going to work from the high-level design and professional looking flowchart, but let's nail down just a few more of the details before we begin writing the code.

Representing the ships

For one thing, we can start by figuring out how to represent a ship in our grid. Keep in mind that the virtual grid is... well, *virtual*. In other words, it doesn't exist anywhere in the program. As long as both the game and the user know that the battleship is hidden in three consecutive cells out of a possible seven (starting at zero), the row itself doesn't have to be represented in code. You might be tempted to build something that holds all seven locations and then to try to place the ship in those locations. But, we don't need to. We just need to know the cells where the ship is located, say, at cells 1, 2 and 3.

Getting user input

What about getting user input? We can do that with the `prompt` function. Whenever we need to get a new location from the user, we'll use `prompt` to display a message and get the input, which is just a number between 0 and 6, from the user.

Displaying the results

What about output? For now, we'll continue to use `alert` to show the output of the game. It's a bit clunky, but it'll work. (For the real game, later in the book, we'll be updating the web page instead, but we've got a way to go before we get there.)

1 **Game starts**, and creates one battleship and gives it a location on three cells in the single row of seven cells.

The locations are just integers; for example, 1,2,3 are the cell locations in this picture:

2 **Game play begins**. Prompt user for a guess:

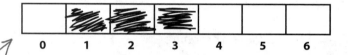

A

The page at localhost says:
Ready, aim, fire! (enter a number from 0–6):

Cancel   OK

B Check to see if user's input hit any of the ship's three cells. Keep track of how many hits there are in a variable.

3 **Game finishes** when all three cells have been hit and our number of hits variable value is 3. We tell the user how many guesses it took to sink the ship.

Sample game interaction

Working through the Pseudocode

We need an approach to planning and writing our code. We're going to start by writing *pseudocode*. Pseudocode is halfway between real JavaScript code and a plain English description of the program, and as you'll see, it will help us think through how the program is going to work without fully having to develop the *real code*.

In this pseudocode for Simple Battleship, we've included a section that describes the variables we'll need, and a section describing the logic of the program. The variables will tell us what we need to keep track of in our code, and the logic describes what the code has to faithfully implement to create the game.

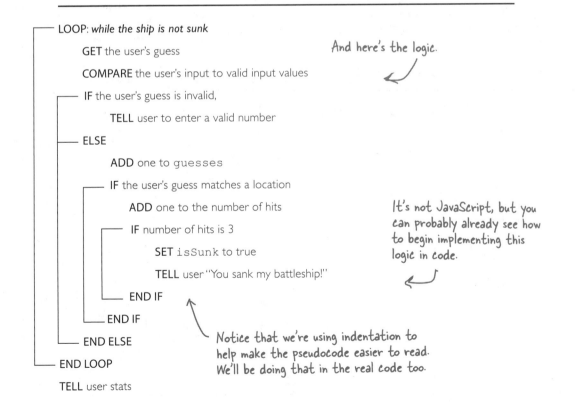

DECLARE three *variables* to hold the location of each cell of the ship. Let's call them `location1`, `location2` and `location3`.

DECLARE a *variable* to hold the user's current guess. Let's call it `guess`.

DECLARE a *variable* to hold the number of hits. We'll call it `hits` and *set* it to 0.

DECLARE a *variable* to hold the number of guesses. We'll call it `guesses` and *set* it to 0.

DECLARE a *variable* to keep track of whether the ship is sunk or not. Let's call it `isSunk` and *set* it to `false`.

The variables we need.

LOOP: *while the ship is not sunk*

    GET the user's guess

    COMPARE the user's input to valid input values

    IF the user's guess is invalid,

        TELL user to enter a valid number

    ELSE

        ADD one to `guesses`

        IF the user's guess matches a location

            ADD one to the number of hits

            IF number of hits is 3

                SET `isSunk` to true

                TELL user "You sank my battleship!"

            END IF

        END IF

    END ELSE

END LOOP

TELL user stats

And here's the logic.

It's not JavaScript, but you can probably already see how to begin implementing this logic in code.

Notice that we're using indentation to help make the pseudocode easier to read. We'll be doing that in the real code too.

Sharpen your pencil

Let's say our virtual grid looks like this:

And we've represented the ship locations using our location variables, like this:

```
location1 = 3;
location2 = 4;
location3 = 5;
```

Use the following sequence as your test user input:

```
1, 4, 2, 3, 5
```

Now, using the pseudocode on the previous page, walk through each step of code and see how this works given the user input. Put your notes below. We've begun the exercise for you below. If this is your first time walking through pseudocode, take your time and see how it all works.

← *If you need a hint, take a quick peek at our answer at the end of the chapter.*

location1	location2	location3	guess	guesses	hits	isSunk
3	4	5	—	0	0	false
3	4	5	1	1	0	false
3	4	5	4	2	1	False
3	4	5	2	3	0	False
3	4	5	3	4	2	False
3	4	5	5	5	3	True

The first row shows the initial values of the variables, before the user enters their first guess. We're not initializing the variable guess, so its value is undefined.

Oh, before we go any further, don't forget the HTML!

You're not going to get very far without some HTML to link to your code. Go ahead and type the markup below into a new file named "battleship.html". After you've done that we'll get back to writing code.

 The HTML for the Battleship game is super simple; we just need a page that links to the JavaScript code, and that's where all the action happens.

```html
<!doctype html>
<html lang="en">
  <head>
    <title>Battleship</title>
    <meta charset="utf-8">
  </head>
  <body>
    <h1>Play battleship!</h1>
    <script src="battleship.js"></script>
  </body>
</html>
```

We're linking to the JavaScript at the bottom of the <body> of the page, so the page is loaded by the time the browser starts executing the code in "battleship.js".

Here's what you'll see when you load the page. We need to write some code to get the game going!

⚛ BRAIN POWER

Flex those dendrites.

This is thinking ahead a bit, but what kind of code do you think it would take to generate a random location for the ship each time you load the page? What factors would you have to take into account in the code to correctly place a ship? Feel free to scribble some ideas here.

Writing the Simple Battleship code

We're going to use the pseudocode as a blueprint for our real JavaScript code. First, let's tackle all the variables we need. Take another look at our pseudocode to check out the variables we need:

We need three variables to hold the ship's location.

DECLARE three *variables* to hold the location of each cell of the ship. Let's call them `location1`, `location2` and `location3`.

DECLARE a *variable* to hold the user's current guess. Let's call it `guess`.

And three more (guess, hits and guesses) to deal with the user's guess.

DECLARE a *variable* to hold the number of hits. We'll call it `hits` and *set* it to 0.

DECLARE a *variable* to hold the number of guesses. We'll call it `guesses` and *set* it to 0.

DECLARE a *variable* to keep track of whether the ship is sunk or not. Let's call it `isSunk` and *set* it to `false`.

And another to track whether or not the ship is sunk.

Let's get these variables into a JavaScript file. Create a new file named "battleship.js" and type in your variable declarations like this:

```javascript
var location1 = 3;
var location2 = 4;
var location3 = 5;
```

Here are our three location variables. We'll go ahead and set up a ship at locations 3, 4 and 5, just for now.

We'll come back later and write some code to generate a random location for the ship to make it harder for the user.

```javascript
var guess;
var hits = 0;
var guesses = 0;
```

The variable guess won't have a value until the user makes a guess. Until then it will have the value undefined.

We'll assign initial values of 0 to both hits and guesses.

```javascript
var isSunk = false;
```

Finally, the isSunk variable gets a value of false. We'll set this to true when we've sunk the ship.

Serious Coding

If you don't provide an initial value for a variable, then JavaScript gives it a default value of `undefined`. Think of the value `undefined` as JavaScript's way of saying "this variable hasn't been given a value yet." We'll be talking more about undefined and some other strange values a little later.

Now let's write the game logic

We've got the variables out of the way, so let's dig into the actual pseudocode that implements the game. We'll break this into a few pieces. The first thing you're going to want to do is implement the loop: it needs to keep looping while the ship isn't sunk. From there we'll take care of getting the guess from the user and validating it—you know, making sure it really is a number between 0 and 6—and then we'll write the logic to check for a hit on a ship and to see if the ship is sunk. Last, we'll create a little report for the user with the number of guesses it took to sink the ship.

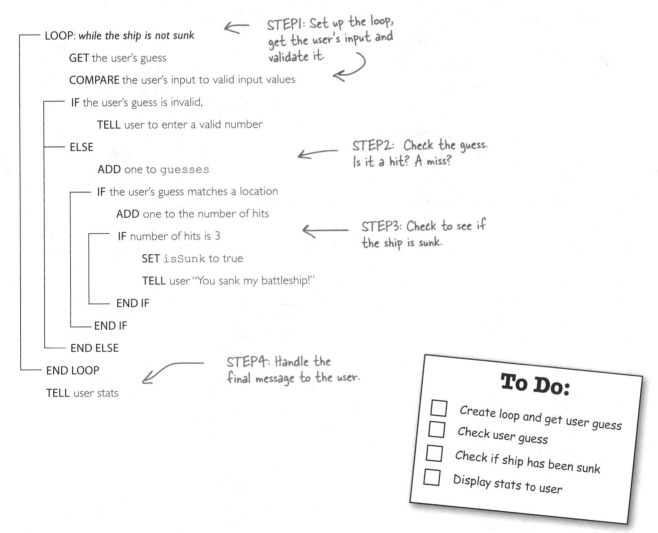

LOOP: *while the ship is not sunk*

    GET the user's guess

    COMPARE the user's input to valid input values

    IF the user's guess is invalid,

        TELL user to enter a valid number

    ELSE

        ADD one to guesses

        IF the user's guess matches a location

            ADD one to the number of hits

            IF number of hits is 3

                SET `isSunk` to true

                TELL user "You sank my battleship!"

            END IF

        END IF

    END ELSE

END LOOP

    TELL user stats

STEP1: Set up the loop, get the user's input and validate it.

STEP2: Check the guess. Is it a hit? A miss?

STEP3: Check to see if the ship is sunk.

STEP4: Handle the final message to the user.

To Do:

☐ Create loop and get user guess

☐ Check user guess

☐ Check if ship has been sunk

☐ Display stats to user

Step One: setting up the loop, getting some input

☐ Create loop and get user guess
☐ Check user guess
☐ Check if ship has been sunk
☐ Display stats to user

Now we're going to begin to translate the logic of our game into actual JavaScript code. There isn't a perfect mapping from pseudocode to JavaScript, so you'll see a few adjustments here and there. The pseudocode gives us a good idea of *what* the code needs to do, and now we have to write the JavaScript code that can do the *how*.

Let's start with all the code we have so far and then we'll zero in on just the parts we're adding (to save a few trees here and there, or electrons if you're reading the digital version):

DECLARE variables

We've already covered these, but we're including them here for completeness.

```javascript
var location1 = 3;

var location2 = 4;

var location3 = 5;

var guess;

var hits = 0;

var guesses = 0;

var isSunk = false;
```

LOOP: *while the ship is not sunk*

```javascript
while (isSunk == false) {
```

Here's the start of the loop. While the ship isn't sunk, we're still in the game, so keep looping.

Remember, while uses a conditional test to determine whether to keep looping. In this case we're testing to make sure that isSunk is still false. We'll set it to true as soon as the ship is sunk.

GET the user's guess

```javascript
    guess = prompt("Ready, aim, fire! (enter a number 0-6):");

}
```

Each time we go through the while loop we're going to ask the user for a guess. To do that we use the prompt built-in function. More on that on the next page...

How prompt works

The browser provides a built-in function you can use to get input from the user, named `prompt`. The `prompt` function is a lot like the `alert` function you've already used—`prompt` causes a dialog to be displayed with a string that you provide, just like `alert`—but it also provides the user with a place to type a response. That response, in the form of a string, is then returned as a result of calling the function. Now, if the user cancels the dialog or doesn't enter anything , then `null` is returned instead.

Here we're assigning the result
of the prompt function to
the guess variable.

```
guess = prompt("Ready, aim, fire! (enter a number 0-6):");
```

You provide prompt with a string,
which is used as instructions to
your user in the dialog box.

The prompt function's job is to get input
from the user. Depending on your device,
that usually happens in a dialog box.

The page at localhost says:

Ready, aim, fire! (enter a number from 0–6):

| 5 |

Cancel   OK

"5"

Once the prompt function obtains input from the user, it
returns that input to your code. In this case the input, in the
form of a string, is assigned to the variable guess.

Watch it!

You might be tempted to try this code now...

...but don't. If you do, your browser will start an *infinite loop* of asking you for a guess, and then asking you for a guess, and so on, without any means of stopping the loop (other than using your operating system to force the browser process to stop).

Checking the user's guess

If you look at the pseudocode, to check the user's guess we need to first make sure the user has entered a valid input. If so, then we also check to see if the guess was a hit or miss. We'll also want to make sure we appropriately update the `guesses` and `hits` variables. Let's get started by checking the validity of the user's input, and if the input is valid, we'll increment the `guesses` variable. After that we'll write the code to see if the user has a hit or miss.

```
// Variable declarations go here


while (isSunk == false) {
    guess = prompt("Ready, aim, fire! (enter a number from 0-6):");
    if (guess < 0 || guess > 6) {
        alert("Please enter a valid cell number!");
    } else {
        guesses = guesses + 1;
    }
}
```

We check validity by making sure the guess is between zero and six.

If the guess isn't valid, we'll tell the user with an alert.

And if the guess is valid, go ahead and add one to guesses so we can keep track of how many times the user has guessed.

Let's look a little more closely at the validity test. You know we're checking to see that the guess is between zero and six, but how exactly does this conditional test that? Let's break it down:

Try to read this like it's English: this conditional is true if the user's guess is less than zero OR the user's guess is greater than six. If either is true, then the input is invalid.

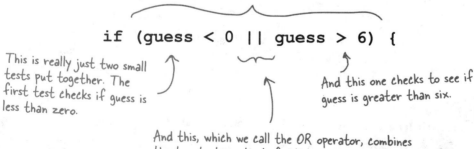

```
if (guess < 0 || guess > 6) {
```

This is really just two small tests put together. The first test checks if guess is less than zero.

And this one checks to see if guess is greater than six.

And this, which we call the OR operator, combines the two tests so that if either test is true, then the entire conditional is true. If both tests are false, then the statement is false, and the guess is between 0 and 6, which means it's valid.

writing real code
/

there are no Dumb Questions

Q: I noticed there is a cancel button on the prompt dialog box. What gets returned from the prompt function if the user hits cancel?

A: If you click cancel in the prompt dialog box then prompt returns the value null rather than a string. Remember that null means "no value", which is appropriate in this case because you've cancelled without entering a value. We can use the fact that the value returned from prompt is null to check to see if the user clicked cancel, and if they did, then we could, say, end the game. We're not doing that in our code, but keep this idea in the back of your mind as we might use it later in the book.

Q: You said that prompt always returns a string. So how can we compare a string value, like "0" or "6", to numbers, like 0 and 6?

A: In this situation, JavaScript tries to convert the string in guess to a number in order to do the comparisons, guess < 0 and guess > 6. As long as you enter only a number, like 4, JavaScript knows how to convert the string "4" to the number 4 when it needs to. We'll come back to the topic of type conversion in more detail later.

Q: What happens if the user enters something that isn't a number into the prompt? Like "six" or "quit"?

A: In that case, JavaScript won't be able to convert the string to a number for the comparison. So, you'd be comparing "six" to 6 or "quit" to 6, and that kind of comparison will return false, which will lead to a MISS. In a more robust version of battleship, we'll check the user input more carefully and make sure they've entered a number first.

Q: With the OR operator, is it true if only one or the other is true, or can both be true?

A: Yes, both can be true. The result of the OR operator (||) is true if either of the tests is true, or if both are true. If both are false, then the result is false.

Q: Is there an AND operator?

A: Yes! The AND operator (&&) works similarly to OR, except that the result of AND is true only if both tests are true.

Q: What's an infinite loop?

A: Great question. An infinite loop is one of the many problems that plague programmers. Remember that a loop requires a conditional test, and the loop will continue as long as that conditional test is true. If your code never does anything to change things so that the conditional test is false at some point, the loop will continue forever. And ever. Until you kill your browser or reboot.

Two-minute Guide to Boolean Operators

A boolean operator is used in a boolean expression, which results in a true or false value. There are two kinds of boolean operators: comparison operators and logical operators.

Comparison Operators

Comparison operators compare two values. Here are some common comparison operators:

< means "less than"

> means "greater than"

== means "equal to"

=== means "exactly equal to" (we'll come back to this one later!)

<= means "less than or equal to"

>= means "greater than or equal to"

!= means "not equal to"

Logical Operators

Logical operators combine two boolean expressions to create one boolean result (true or false). Here are two logical operators:

|| means OR. Results in true if *either* of the two expressions is true.

&& means AND. Results in true if *both* of the two expressions are true.

Another logical operator is NOT, which acts on one boolean expression (rather than two):

! means NOT. Results in true if the expression is false.

you are here ▶ **55**
/

So, do we have a hit?

This is where things get interesting—the user's taken a guess at the ship's location and we need to write the code to determine if that guess has hit the ship. More specifically, we need to see if the guess matches one of the locations of the ship. If it does, then we'll increment the `hits` variable.

Here's a first stab at writing the code for the hit detection; let's step through it:

```
if (guess == location1) {
    hits = hits + 1;
} else  if (guess == location2) {
    hits = hits + 1;
} else if (guess == location3) {
    hits = hits + 1;
}
```

If the guess is at location1, then we hit the ship, so increment the hits variable by one.

Otherwise, if the guess is location2, then do the same thing.

Finally, if the guess is location3, then we need to increment the hits variable.

And if none of these are true, then the hits variable is never incremented.

Notice we're using indentation for the code in each if/else block. This makes your code easier to read, especially when you've got lots of blocks nested inside blocks.

☑ Create loop and get user guess
☐ Check user guess
☐ Check if ship has been sunk
☐ Display stats to user

Sharpen your pencil

What do you think of this first attempt to write the code to detect when a ship is hit? Does it look more complex than it needs to be? Are we repeating code in a way that seems a bit, well, redundant? Could we simplify it? Using what you know of the || operator (that is, the boolean OR operator), can you simplify this code? *Make sure you check your answer at the end of the chapter before moving on.*

Adding the hit detection code

Let's put everything together from the previous couple of pages:

☑ Create loop and get user guess
☑ Check user guess
☐ Check if ship has been sunk
☐ Display stats to user

```
// Variable declarations go here
```

LOOP: *while the ship is not sunk*

GET the user's guess

ADD one to guesses

IF the user's guess matches a location

ADD one to the number of hits

```
while (isSunk == false) {
    guess = prompt("Ready, aim, fire! (enter a number from 0-6):");
    if (guess < 0 || guess > 6) {          ← Check the user's guess...
        alert("Please enter a valid cell number!");
    } else {                                    The user's guess looks valid, so let's
        guesses = guesses + 1;      ←          increase the number of guesses by one.

    if (guess == location1 || guess == location2 || guess == location3) {
        hits = hits + 1;
    }                                    ←     If the guess matches one of the ship's
                                               locations we increment the hits counter.
    }
}
```

We've combined the three conditionals into one if statement using || (OR). So read it like this: "If guess is equal to location1 OR guess is equal to location2 OR guess is equal to location3, increment hits."

Hey, you sank my battleship!

☑ Create loop and get user guess
☑ Check user guess
☑ Check if ship has been sunk
☐ Display stats to user

We're almost there; we've almost got this game logic nailed down. Looking at the pseudocode again, what we need to do now is test to see if we have three hits. If we do, then we've sunk a battleship. And, if we've sunk a battleship then we need to set `isSunk` to true and also tell the user they've destroyed a ship. Let's sketch out the code again before adding it in:

First check to see if there are three hits.

Take another look at the while loop above. What happens when isSunk is true?

```
if (hits == 3) {
    isSunk = true;          ←     And if so, set isSunk to true.  ←
    alert("You sank my battleship!");
}
```

And also let the user know!

Provide some post-game analysis

☑ Create loop and get user guess
☑ Check user guess
☑ Check if ship has been sunk
☐ Display stats to user

After `isSunk` is set to true, the while loop is going to stop looping. That's right, this program we've come to know so well is going to stop executing the body of the while loop, and before you know it the game's going to be over. But, we still owe the user some stats on how they did. Here's some code that does that:

```
var stats = "You took " + guesses + " guesses to sink the battleship, " +
            "which means your shooting accuracy was " + (3/guesses);

alert(stats);
```

↖ Here we're creating a string that contains a message to the user including the number of guesses they took, along with the accuracy of their shots. Notice that we're splitting up the string into pieces (to insert the variable guesses, and also to fit the string into multiple lines) using the concatenation operator, +. For now just type this as is, and we'll explain more about this later.

Now let's add this and the sunk ship detection into the rest of the code:

```
// Variable declarations go here
```

LOOP: *while the ship is not sunk*

GET the user's guess

```
while (isSunk == false) {
    guess = prompt("Ready, aim, fire! (enter a number from 0-6):");
    if (guess < 0 || guess > 6) {
        alert("Please enter a valid cell number!");
    } else {
```

ADD one to guesses

```
        guesses = guesses + 1;
```

IF the user's guess matches a location

ADD one to the number of hits

IF number of hits is 3

```
        if (guess == location1 || guess == location2 || guess == location3) {
            hits = hits + 1;

            if (hits == 3) {
```

SET isSunk to true

TELL user "You sank my battleship!"

```
                isSunk = true;

                alert("You sank my battleship!");
            }
        }
    }
}
```

TELL user stats

```
var stats = "You took " + guesses + " guesses to sink the battleship, " +
            "which means your shooting accuracy was " + (3/guesses);
alert(stats);
```

Remember we said pseudocode often isn't perfect? Well we actually left something out of our original pseudocode: we're not telling the user if her guess is a HIT or a MISS. Can you insert these pieces of code in the proper place to correct this?

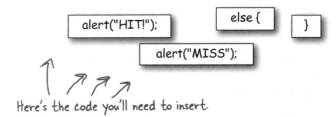

Here's the code you'll need to insert.

```
// Variable declarations go here

while (isSunk == false) {
    guess = prompt("Ready, aim, fire! (enter a number from 0-6):");
    if (guess < 0 || guess > 6) {
        alert("Please enter a valid cell number!");
    } else {
        guesses = guesses + 1;
        if (guess == location1 || guess == location2 || guess == location3) {
            hits = hits + 1;
            if (hits == 3) {
                isSunk = true;
                alert("You sank my battleship!");
            }
        }
    }
}
var stats = "You took " + guesses + " guesses to sink the battleship, " +
                "which means your shooting accuracy was " + (3/guesses);
alert(stats);
```

This is a lot of curly braces to match. If you're having trouble matching them, just draw lines right in the book, to match them up.

And that completes the logic!

Alright! We've now fully translated the pseudocode to actual JavaScript code. We even discovered something we left out of the pseudocode and we've got that accounted for too. Below you'll find the code in its entirety. Make sure you have this typed in and saved in "battleship.js":

☑ Create loop and get user guess
☑ Check user guess
☑ Check if ship has been sunk
☑ Display stats to user

```javascript
var location1 = 3;

var location2 = 4;

var location3 = 5;

var guess;

var hits = 0;

var guesses = 0;

var isSunk = false;


while (isSunk == false) {
    guess = prompt("Ready, aim, fire! (enter a number from 0-6):");
    if (guess < 0 || guess > 6) {
        alert("Please enter a valid cell number!");
    } else {
        guesses = guesses + 1;

        if (guess == location1 || guess == location2 || guess == location3) {
            alert("HIT!");
            hits = hits + 1;
            if (hits == 3) {
                isSunk = true;
                alert("You sank my battleship!");
            }
        } else {
            alert("MISS");
        }
    }
}
var stats = "You took " + guesses + " guesses to sink the battleship, " +
            "which means your shooting accuracy was " + (3/guesses);
alert(stats);
```

Doing a little Quality Assurance

QA, or quality assurance, is the process of testing software to find defects. So we're going to do a little QA on this code. When you're ready, load "battleship.html" in your browser and start playing. Try some different things. Is it working perfectly? Or did you find some issues? If so list them here. You can see our test run on this page too.

QA Notes

Jot down anything that doesn't work the way it should, or that could be improved.

Here's what our game interaction looked like.

First we entered an invalid number, 9.

Then we entered 0, to get a miss.

But then we get three hits in a row!

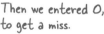

On the third and final hit, we sink the battleship.

And see that it took 4 guesses to sink the ship with an accuracy of 0.75.

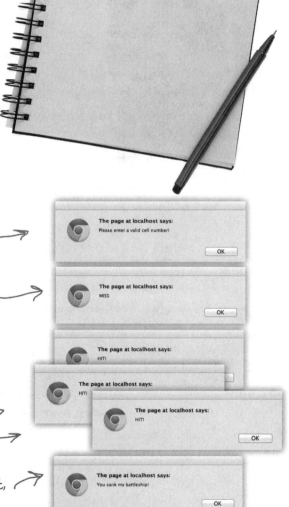

The game logic is pretty clear to me, except for the boolean operators. Is that just giving me a way to combine conditionals together?

Boolean operators allow you to write more complex statements of logic.

You've seen enough conditionals to know how to test, say, if the temperature is greater than 32 degrees. Or, that a variable that represents whether an item is inStock is true. But sometimes we need to test more. Sometimes we need to know not only if a value is greater than 32, but also if it's less than 100. Or, if an item is inStock, and also onSale. Or that an item is on sale only on Tuesdays when the user is a VIP member. So, you see, these conditions can get complex.

Let's step through a few to get a better idea of how they work.

Say we need to test that an item is inStock AND onSale. We could do that like this:

First, see if the item is in stock...

```
if (inStock == true) {
    if (onSale == true) {
        // sounds like a bargain!
        alert("buy buy buy!");
    }
}
```

And, if so, then see if it is on sale.

And if so, then take some action, like buy a few!

Notice this code is executed only if both conditionals are true!

We can simplify this code by combining these two conditionals together. Unlike in Simple Battleship, where we tested if guess < 0 OR guess > 6, here we want to know if inStock is true AND onSale is true. Let's see how to do that...

Here's our AND operator. With AND this combined conditional is true only if the first part AND the second part are true.

↓

```
if (inStock == true  &&  onSale == true) {
        // sounds like a bargain!
        alert("buy buy buy!");
}
```

↖ Not only is this code more concise, it's also more readable. Compare this code with the code on the previous page to see.

We don't have to stop there; we can combine boolean operators in multiple ways:

Now we're using both AND and OR in the same conditional expression. This one says: If an item is in stock AND it's either on sale, OR the price is less than 60, then buy.

↙

```
if (inStock == true  &&  (onSale == true || price < 60)) {
        // sounds like a bargain!
        alert("buy buy buy!");
}
```

↑

Notice we're using parentheses to group the conditions together so we get the result of the OR first, and then use that result to compute the result of the AND.

Sharpen your pencil

We've got a whole bunch of boolean expressions that need evaluating below. Fill in the blanks, and then check your answers at the end of the chapter before you go on.

```
var temp = 81;
var willRain = true;
var humid = (temp > 80 && willRain == true);
```

What's the value of **humid**? __TRUE__

```
var guess = 6;
var isValid = (guess >= 0 && guess <= 6);
```

What's the value of **isValid**? __TRUE__

```
var kB = 1287;
var tooBig = (kB > 1000);
var urgent = true;
var sendFile =
    (urgent == true || tooBig == false);
```

What's the value of **sendFile**? __FALSE__

```
var keyPressed = "N";
var points = 142;
var level;
if (keyPressed == "Y" ||
    (points > 100 && points < 200)) {
    level = 2;
} else {
    level = 1;
}
```

What's the value of **level**? __2__

Exercise

Bob and Bill, both from accounting, are working on a new price checker application for their company's web site. They've both written if/else statements using boolean expressions. Both are sure they've written the correct code. Which accountant is right? Should these accountants even be writing code? Check your answer at the end of the chapter before you go on.

Bob →

```
if (price < 200 || price > 600) {
    alert("Price is too low or too high! Don't buy the gadget.");
} else {
    alert("Price is right! Buy the gadget.");
}
```

```
if (price >= 200 || price <= 600) {
    alert("Price is right! Buy the gadget.");
} else {
    alert("Price is too low or too high! Don't buy the gadget.");
}
```

Bill →

Can we talk about your verbosity...

We don't know how to bring this up, but you've been a little verbose in specifying your conditionals. What do we mean? Take this condition for instance:

We often compare our boolean variables to true or false to form our conditional.

```
if  (inStock == true) {
    ...

}
```

And, inStock is a variable that holds a boolean value of true or false.

As it turns out, that's a bit of overkill. The whole point of a conditional is that it evaluates to either true or false, but our boolean variable `inStock` already *is* one of those values. So, we don't need to compare the variable to anything; it can just stand on its own. That is, we can just write this instead:

```
if  (inStock) {
    ...

}
```

If we just use the boolean variable by itself, then if that variable is true, the conditional test is true, and the block is executed.

And if inStock is false, then the conditional test fails and the code block is skipped.

Now, while some might claim our original, verbose version was clearer in its intent, it's more common to see the more succinct version in practice. And, you'll find the less verbose version easier to read as well.

Exercise

We've got two statements below that use the onSale and inStock variables in conditionals to figure out the value of the variable buyIt. Work through each possible value of inStock and onSale for both statements. Which version is the biggest spender?

```
var buyIt = (inStock || onSale);
```

onSale	inStock	buyIt	buyIt
true	true	TRUE	TRUE
true	false	TRUE	FALSE
false	true	TRUE	FALSE
false	false	FALSE	FALSE

```
var buyIt = (inStock && onSale);
```

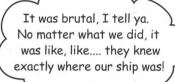

Finishing the Simple Battleship game

Yes, we still have one little matter to take care of because right now you've hard coded the location of the ship—no matter how many times you play the game, the ship is always at locations 3, 4 and 5. That actually works out well for testing, but we really need to randomly place the ship to make it a little more interesting to the user.

Let's step back and think about the right way to place a ship on the 1-D grid of seven cells. We need a starting location that allows us to place three consecutive positions on the grid. That means we need a starting location from zero to four.

We can start in locations 0, 1, 2, 3 or 4 and still have room to place the ship in the next three positions.

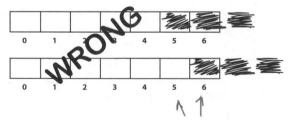

But, starting at position 5 or 6 won't work.

How to assign random locations

Now, once we have a starting location (between zero and four), we simply use it and the following two locations to hold the ship.

```
var location1 = randomLoc;
var location2 = location1 + 1;
var location3 = location2 + 1;
```

← Take the random location along with the next two consecutive locations.

Okay, but how do we generate a random number? That's where we turn to JavaScript and its built-in functions. More specifically, JavaScript comes with a bunch of built-in math-related functions, including a couple that can be used to generate random numbers. Now we're going to get deeper into built-in functions, and functions in general a little later in the book. For now, we're just going to make use of these functions to get our job done.

The world-famous recipe for generating a random number

We're going to start with the `Math.random` function. By calling this function we'll get back a random decimal number:

Our variable randomLoc. We want to assign a number from 0 to 4 to this variable.

Math.random is part of standard JavaScript and returns a random number.

```
var randomLoc = Math.random();
```

The only problem is it returns numbers like 0.128, 0.830, 0.9, 0.42. These numbers are between 0 and 1 (not including exactly 1). So we need a way to use this to generate random numbers 0–4.

What we need is an integer between 0 and 4—that is, 0, 1, 2, 3 or 4—not a decimal number, like 0.34. To start, we could multiply the number returned by `Math.random` by 5 to get a little closer; here's what we mean…

First, if we multiply the random number by 5, then we get a number between 0 and 5, but not including 5. Like 0.13983, 4.231, 2.3451, or say 4.999.

```
var randomLoc = Math.random() * 5;
```

Remember, * means multiplication.

That's closer! Now all we need to do is clip off the end of the number to give us an integer number. To do that we can use another built-in Math function, Math.floor:

We can use Math.floor to round down all these numbers to their nearest integer value.

```
var randomLoc = Math.floor(Math.random() * 5);
```

So, for instance, 0.13983 becomes 0, 2.34 becomes 2 and 4.999 becomes 4.

there are no Dumb Questions

Q: If we're trying to generate a number between 0 and 4, why does the code have a 5 in it, as in
`Math.floor(Math.random() * 5)`?

A: Good question. First, Math.random generates a number between 0 and 1, but not including 1. The maximum number you can get from Math.random is 0.999.... When you multiply that number by 5, the highest number you'll get is 4.999...
Math.floor always rounds a number down, so 1.2 becomes 1, but so does 1.9999. If we generate a number from 0 to 4.999... then everything will be rounded down to 0 to 4. This is not the only way to do it, and in other languages it's often done differently, but this is how you'll see it done in most JavaScript code.

Q: So if I wanted a random number between 0 and 100 (including 100), I'd write
`Math.floor(Math.random() * 101)`?

A: That's right! Multiplying by 101, and using Math.floor to round down, ensures that your result will be at most 100.

Q: What are the parentheses for in Math.random()?

A: We use parentheses whenever we "call" a function. Sometimes we need to hand a value to a function, like we do when we use alert to display a message, and sometimes we don't, like when we use Math.random. But whenever you're calling a function (whether it's built-in or not), you'll need to use parentheses. Don't worry about this right now; we'll get into all these details in the next chapter.

Q: I can't get my battleship game to work. I'm not seeing anything in my web page except the "Play battleship" heading. How can I figure out what I did wrong?

A: This is where using the console can come in handy. If you've made an error like forgetting a quote on a string, then JavaScript will typically complain about the syntax of your program not being right, and may even show you the line number where your error is. Sometimes errors are more subtle, however. For instance, if you mistakenly write isSunk = false instead of isSunk == false, you won't see a JavaScript error, but your code won't behave as you expect it to. For this kind of error, try using console.log to display the values of your variables at various points in your code to see if you can track down the error.

QA Notes

Back to do a little more QA

That's all we need. Let's put this code together (we've already done that below) and replace your existing location code with it. When you're finished, give it a few test runs to see how fast you can sink the enemy.

```javascript
var randomLoc = Math.floor(Math.random() * 5);
var location1 = randomLoc;
var location2 = location1 + 1;
var location3 = location2 + 1;
var guess;
var hits = 0;
var guesses = 0;
var isSunk = false;

while (isSunk == false) {
    guess = prompt("Ready, aim, fire! (enter a number from 0-6):");
    if (guess < 0 || guess > 6) {
        // the rest of your code goes here....
```

Go ahead and replace your location variable declarations with these new statements.

Here's one of our test sessions. The game's a little more interesting now that we've got random locations for the ship. But we still managed to get a pretty good score…

Play battleship!

We get a hit on our first guess.

On our second guess, we miss.

But then we get two hits in a row.

On the last hit, we sink the battleship!

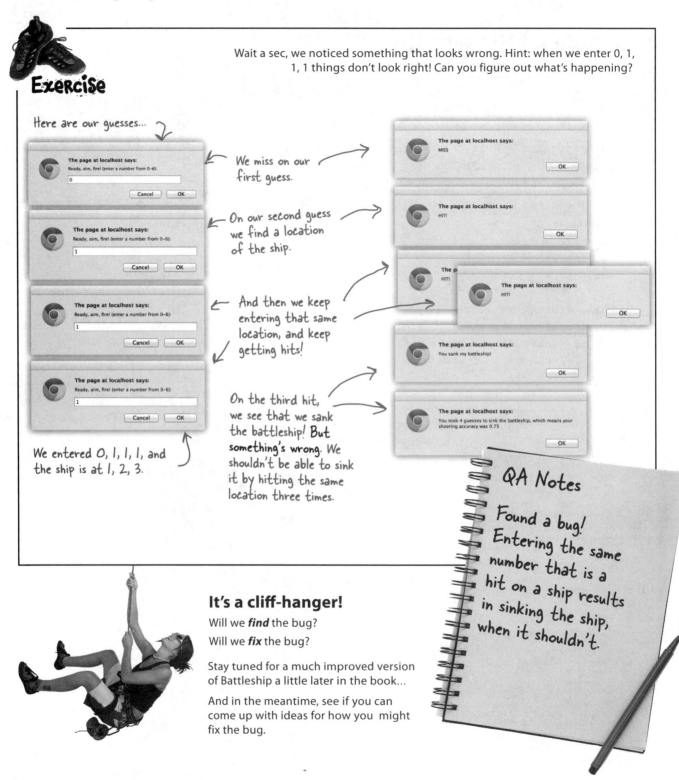

Exercise

Wait a sec, we noticed something that looks wrong. Hint: when we enter 0, 1, 1, 1 things don't look right! Can you figure out what's happening?

Here are our guesses...

We miss on our first guess.

On our second guess we find a location of the ship.

And then we keep entering that same location, and keep getting hits!

We entered 0, 1, 1, 1, and the ship is at 1, 2, 3.

On the third hit, we see that we sank the battleship! But something's wrong. We shouldn't be able to sink it by hitting the same location three times.

The page at localhost says:
MISS
[OK]

The page at localhost says:
HIT!
[OK]

The page at localhost says:
HIT!

The page at localhost says:
HIT!
[OK]

The page at localhost says:
You sank my battleship!
[OK]

The page at localhost says:
You took 4 guesses to sink the battleship, which means your shooting accuracy was 0.75
[OK]

QA Notes

Found a bug! Entering the same number that is a hit on a ship results in sinking the ship, when it shouldn't.

It's a cliff-hanger!

Will we *find* the bug?

Will we *fix* the bug?

Stay tuned for a much improved version of Battleship a little later in the book...

And in the meantime, see if you can come up with ideas for how you might fix the bug.

Congrats on your first true JavaScript program, and a short word about reusing code

You've probably noticed that we made use of a few *built-in functions* like `alert`, `prompt`, `console.log` and `Math.random`. With very little effort, these functions have given you the ability to pop up dialog boxes, log output to the console and generate random numbers, almost like magic. But, these built-in functions are just packaged up code that's already been written for you, and as you can see their power is that you can use and reuse them just by making a call to them when you need them.

Now there's a lot to learn about functions, how to call them, what kinds of values you can pass them, and so on, and we're going to start getting into all that in the next chapter where you learn to create your own functions.

But before you get there you've got the bullet points to review, a crossword puzzle to complete… oh, and a good night's sleep to let everything sink in.

 BULLET POINTS

- You can use a flowchart to outline the logic of a JavaScript program, showing decision points and actions.

- Before you begin writing a program, it's a good idea to sketch out what your program needs to do with pseudocode.

- **Pseudocode** is an approximation of what your real code should do.

- There are two kinds of boolean operators: comparison operators and logical operators. When used in an expression, boolean operators result in a true or false value.

- **Comparison** operators compare two values and result in true or false. For example, we can use the boolean comparison operator < ("less than") like this: 3 < 6. This expression results in true.

- **Logical** operators combine two boolean values. For example true || false results in true; true && false results in false.

- You can generate a random number between 0 and 1 (including 0, but not including 1) using the **Math.random** function.

- The **Math.floor** function rounds down a decimal number to the nearest integer.

- Make sure you use Math with an uppercase M, and not m, when using Math.random and Math.floor.

- The JavaScript function **prompt** shows a dialog with message and a space for the user to enter a value.

- In this chapter, we used prompt to get input from the user, and alert to display the results of the battleship game in the browser.

JavaScript cross

How does a crossword puzzle help you learn
JavaScript? The mental twists and turns burn the
JavaScript right into your brain!

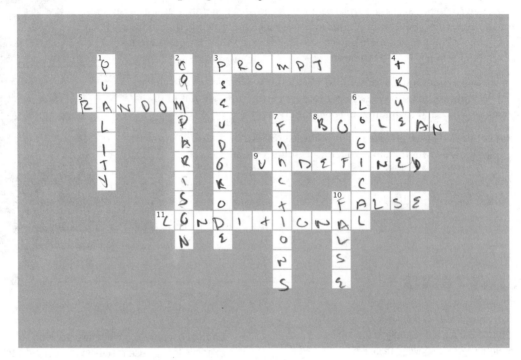

ACROSS

3. To get input from a user, you can use the _____ function.

5. To randomly choose a position for a ship, use Math._____.

8. We keep track of whether a ship is sunk or not with a _____ variable.

9. If you don't initialize a variable, the value is _____.

10. Boolean operators always result in true or _____.

11. Both while and if statements use _____ tests.

DOWN

1. If you're good at testing programs, you might want to become a _____ Assurance specialist.

2. == is a _____ operator you can use to test to see if two values are the same.

3. This helps you think about how a program is going to work.

4. To get a true value from an AND operator (&&), both parts of the conditional must be _____.

6. OR (||) and AND (&&) are _____ operators.

7. JavaScript has many built-in _____ like alert and prompt.

10. To get a false value from an OR operator (||), both parts of the conditional must be _____.

Sharpen your pencil
Solution

Let's say our virtual row looks like this:

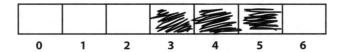

And we've represented that by setting:

```
location1 = 3;
location2 = 4;
location3 = 5;
```

Assume the following user input:

```
1, 4, 2, 3, 5
```

Now, using the pseudocode on the previous page, trace through each step of code, and see how this works. Put your notes below. We've started the trace for you below. Here's our solution.

location1	location2	location 3	guess	guesses	hits	isSunk
3	4	5	——	0	0	false
3	4	5	1	1	0	false
3	4	5	4	2	1	false
3	4	5	2	3	1	false
3	4	5	3	4	2	false
3	4	5	5	5	3	true

Exercise Solution

We've got two statements below that use the onSale and inStock variables in conditionals to figure out the value of the variable buyIt. Work through each possible value of inStock and onSale for both statements. Which version is the biggest spender? The OR (||) operator!

```
var buyIt = (inStock || onSale);
```

onSale	inStock	buyIt	buyIt
true	true	true	true
true	false	true	false
false	true	true	false
false	false	false	false

```
var buyIt = (inStock && onSale);
```

Sharpen your pencil Solution

We've got a whole bunch of boolean expressions that need evaluating below. Fill in the blanks. Here's our solution:

```
var temp = 81;
var willRain = true;
var humid = (temp > 80 && willRain == true);
```

What's the value of **humid**? _true_

```
var guess = 6;
var isValid = (guess >= 0 && guess <= 6);
```

What's the value of **isValid**? _true_

```
var kB = 1287;
var tooBig = (kB > 1000);
var urgent = true;
var sendFile =
    (urgent == true || tooBig == false);
```

What's the value of **sendFile**? _true_

```
var keyPressed = "N";
var points = 142;
var level;
if (keyPressed == "Y" ||
    (points > 100 && points < 200)) {
    level = 2;
} else {
    level = 1;
}
```

What's the value of **level**? _2_

Exercise Solution

Bob and Bill, both from accounting, are working on a new price checker application for their company's web site. They've both written if/else statements using boolean expressions. Both are sure they've written the correct code. Which accountant is right? Should these accountants even be writing code? Here's our solution.

Bob

```
if (price < 200 || price > 600) {
    alert("Price is too low or too high! Don't buy the gadget.");
} else {
    alert("Price is right! Buy the gadget.");
}
```

Bill

```
if (price >= 200 || price <= 600) {
    alert("Price is right! Buy the gadget.");
} else {
    alert("Price is too low or too high! Don't buy the gadget.");
}
```

Bob's the better coder (and possibly, a better accountant, too). Bob's solution works, but Bill's doesn't. To see why, let's try three different prices (too low, too high and just right) with Bob's and Bill's conditionals and see what results we get:

price	Bob's	Bill's
100	true	true
	alert: Don't buy!	alert: Buy!
700	true	true
	alert: Don't buy!	alert: Buy!
400	false	true
	alert: Buy!	alert: Buy!

If price is 100, then 100 is less than 200, so Bob's conditional is true (remember, with OR, you only need one of the expressions to be true for the whole thing to be true), and we alert NOT to buy.

But Bill's conditional is also true, because price is <= 600! So the result of the entire expression is true, and we alert the user to buy, even though the price is too low.

Turns out Bill's conditional is always true, no matter what the price is, so his code tells us to Buy! every time. Bill should stick with accounting.

Exercise Solution

Remember we said pseudocode often isn't perfect? Well we actually left something out of our original pseudocode: we're not telling the user if her guess is a HIT or a MISS. Can you insert these pieces of code in the proper place to correct this? Here's our solution:

```
// Variable declarations go here

while (isSunk == false) {
    guess = prompt("Ready, aim, fire! (enter a number from 0-6):");
    if (guess < 0 || guess > 6) {
        alert("Please enter a valid cell number!");
    } else {
        guesses = guesses + 1;
        if (guess == location1 || guess == location2 || guess == location3) {
            alert("HIT!");
            hits = hits + 1;
            if (hits == 3) {
                isSunk = true;
                alert("You sank my battleship!");
            }
        } else {
            alert("MISS");
        }
    }
}
var stats = "You took " + guesses + " guesses to sink the battleship, " +
            "which means your shooting accuracy was " + (3/guesses);
alert(stats);
```

Solution

What do you think of this first attempt to write the code to detect when a ship is hit? Does it look more complex than it needs to be, or are we repeating code in a way that seems a bit, well, redundant? Could we simplify it? Using what you know of the || operator (that is, the boolean OR operator), can you simplify this code? *Here's our solution.*

We're using the same code over and over here.

```
if (guess == location1) {
    hits = hits + 1;
} else  if (guess == location2) {
    hits = hits + 1;
} else if (guess == location3) {
    hits = hits + 1;
}
```

If we ever have to change how hits are updated, we've got three places to change our code. Changes like this are often a source of bugs and issues in code.

Not only that, this code is just way more complex than it needs to be. It's harder to read than it should be, and it took a lot more thought and typing than needed.

But, with the boolean OR operator we can combine the tests so that if location matches any of location1, location2 or location3, then the if conditional will be true, and the hits variable will be updated.

```
if (guess == location1 || guess == location2 || guess == location3) {
    hits = hits + 1;
}
```

Isn't that much easier on the eye? Not to mention easier to understand.

And if we ever have to change how hits is updated, well, then we only have one place to do it, which is much less error prone.

JavaScript cross Solution

How does a crossword puzzle help you learn
JavaScript? The mental twists and turns burn the
JavaScript right into your brain! Here's our solution.

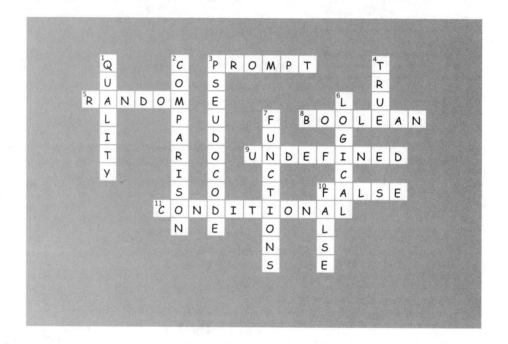

3 introducing functions

Getting functional

```
function abc() {
    return "def";
```

Get ready for your first superpower. You've got some programming under your belt; now it's time to really move things along with **functions**. Functions give you the power to write code that can be applied to all sorts of different circumstances, code that can be **reused** over and over, code that is much more **manageable**, code that can be **abstracted** away and given a simple name so you can forget all the complexity and get on with the important stuff. You're going to find not only that functions are your gateway from scripter to programmer, they're the key to the JavaScript programming style. In this chapter we're going to start with the basics: the mechanics, the ins and outs of how functions really work, and then you'll keep honing your function skills throughout the rest of the book. So, let's get a good foundation started, *now*.

More on this as we progress through the book.

Sharpen your pencil

Do a little analysis of the code below. How does it look? Choose as many of the options below as you like, or write in your own analysis:

```javascript
var dogName = "rover";
var dogWeight = 23;
if (dogWeight > 20) {
    console.log(dogName + " says WOOF WOOF");
} else {
    console.log(dogName + " says woof woof");
}
dogName = "spot";
dogWeight = 13;
if (dogWeight > 20) {
    console.log(dogName + " says WOOF WOOF");
} else {
    console.log(dogName + " says woof woof");
}
dogName = "spike";
dogWeight = 53;
if (dogWeight > 20) {
    console.log(dogName + " says WOOF WOOF");
} else {
    console.log(dogName + " says woof woof");
}
dogName = "lady";
dogWeight = 17;
if (dogWeight > 20) {
    console.log(dogName + " says WOOF WOOF");
} else {
    console.log(dogName + " says woof woof");
}
```

 A. The code seems very redundant.

 B. If we want to change the display of the output, or add another weight for dogs, this is going to require a lot of reworking.

 C. Looks tedious to type in!

☐ D. Not the most readable code I've ever seen.

☐ E. _____

What's wrong with the code anyway?

We just looked at some code that got used *over and over*. What's wrong with that? Well, at face value, nothing. After all, it works, right? Let's have a closer look at the code in question:

```javascript
var dogName = "rover";
var dogWeight = 23;
if (dogWeight > 20) {
    console.log(dogName + " says WOOF WOOF");
} else {
    console.log(dogName + " says woof woof");
}

...

dogName = "lady";
dogWeight = 17;
if (dogWeight > 20) {
    console.log(dogName + " says WOOF WOOF");
} else {
    console.log(dogName + " says woof woof");
}
```

What we're doing here is comparing the dog's weight to 20, and if it's greater than 20, we're outputting a big WOOF WOOF. If it's less than 20, we're outputting a smaller woof woof.

And this code is... d'oh! It's doing EXACTLY the same thing. And so on, many times over in the rest of the code.

```javascript
dogName = "spike";
dogWeight = 53;
if (dogWeight > 20) {
    console.log(dogName + " says WOOF WOOF");
} else {
    console.log(dogName + " says woof woof");
}
dogName = "lady";
dogWeight = 17;
if (dogWeight > 20) {
    console.log(dogName + " says WOOF WOOF");
} else {
    console.log(dogName + " says woof woof");
}
```

Sure, this code looks innocent enough, but it's tedious to write, a pain to read and will be problematic if your code needs to change, over time. That last point will ring true more and more as you gain experience in programming—all code changes over time and the code above is a nightmare waiting to happen because we've got the same logic repeated over and over, and if you need to change that logic, you'll have to change it in multiple places. And the bigger the program gets, the more changes you'll have to make, leading to more opportunities for mistakes. What we really want is a way to take redundant code like this and to put it in one place where it can be easily re-used whenever we need it.

BRAIN POWER

How can we improve this code? Take a few minutes to think of a few possibilities. Does JavaScript have something that could help?

If only I could find a way to **reuse** code so that anytime I needed it, I could just **use** it rather than **retyping** it. And a way to give it a nice memorable **name** so that I could remember it. And a way to make changes in just **one** place instead of many if something changes. That would be dreamy. But I know it's just a fantasy...

By the way, did we happen to mention **FUNCTIONS?**

Meet *functions*. JavaScript functions allow you to take a bit of code, give it a name, and then refer to it over and over whenever we need it. That sounds like just the medicine we need.

Say you're writing some code that does a lot of "barking." If your code is dealing with a big dog then the bark is a big "WOOF WOOF". And if it's a small dog, the bark is a tiny "woof woof". You're going to need to use this barking functionality many times in your code. Let's write a `bark` function you can use over and over:

The <u>function</u> keyword begins a function definition.

Next we give the function a <u>name</u>, like bark.

And we're going to hand it two things when we get around to using it: a dog name and a dog weight.

We call these the <u>parameters</u> of the function. We put these in parentheses after the function name.

```
function bark(name, weight) {

}
```

Next we're going to write some code that gets executed when we use the function.

We'll call this the <u>body</u> of the function. It's everything inside the { and the }.

Now we need to write the code for the function; our code will check the weight and output the appropriate sized bark.

First we need to check the weight, and...

Notice the variable names used in the code match the parameters of the function.

```
function bark(name, weight) {
    if (weight > 20) {
        console.log(name + " says WOOF WOOF");
    } else {
        console.log(name + " says woof woof");
    }
}
```

...then output the dog's name with WOOF WOOF or woof woof.

Now you have a function you can use in your code. Let's see how that works next...

Okay, but how does it actually work?

First, let's rework our code using the new function `bark`:

```
function bark(name, weight) {
    if (weight > 20) {
        console.log(name + " says WOOF WOOF");
    } else {
        console.log(name + " says woof woof");
    }
}
```

Ahh, this is nice, all the logic of the code is here in one place.

```
bark("rover", 23);
bark("spot", 13);
bark("spike", 53);
bark("lady", 17);
```

Now all that code becomes just a few calls to the bark function, passing it each dog's name and weight.

Wow, now that's simple!

Wow, that's a lot less code—and it's so much more readable to your co-worker who needs to go into your code and make a quick change. We've also got all the logic in one convenient location.

Okay, but how exactly does it all come together and actually work? Let's go through it step by step.

First we have the function.

So we've got the `bark` function right at the top of the code. The browser reads this code, sees it's a function and then takes a look at the statements in the body. The browser knows it isn't executing the function statements now; it'll wait until the function is called from somewhere else in the code.

Notice too that the function is *parameterized*, meaning it takes a dog's name and weight when it is called. That allows you to call this function for as many different dogs as you like. Each time you do, the logic applies to the name and weight you pass to the function call.

Again, these are parameters; they are assigned values when the function is called.

```
function bark(name, weight) {
    if (weight > 20) {
        console.log(name + " says WOOF WOOF");
    } else {
        console.log(name + " says woof woof");
    }
}
```

And everything inside the function is the body of the function.

Now let's call the function.

To call, or *invoke*, a function, just use its name, followed by an open parenthesis, then any values you need to pass it, separated by commas, and finally a closing parenthesis. The values in the parentheses are *arguments*. For the `bark` function we need two arguments: the dog's name and the dog's weight.

Here's how the call works:

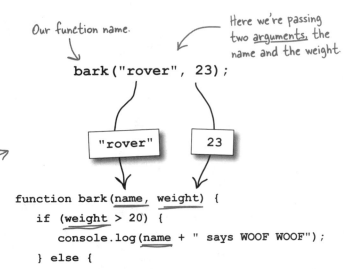

"Invoking a function" is just a fancy way of saying "calling a function." Feel free to mix and match, especially when your new boss is around.

Our function name.

Here we're passing two arguments, the name and the weight.

```
bark("rover", 23);
```

When we call the bark function, the arguments are assigned to the parameter names.

And any time the parameters appear in the function, the values we passed in are used.

```
function bark(name, weight) {
    if (weight > 20) {
        console.log(name + " says WOOF WOOF");
    } else {
        console.log(name + " says woof woof");
    }
}
```

After you call the function, the body of the function does all the work.

After we know the value for each parameter—like name is "rover" and weight is 23—then we're ready to execute the function body.

Statements in the function body are executed from top to bottom, just like all the other code you've been writing. The only difference is that the parameter names name and weight have been assigned the values of the arguments you passed into the function.

After we've assigned the argument values to the parameter names, we then execute the statements in the body.

```
function bark(name, weight) {
    if ( 23  > 20) {
        console.log( "rover" + " says WOOF WOOF");
    } else {
        console.log( "rover" + " says woof woof");
    }
}
```

The parameters act like variables in the body, which have been assigned the values of the arguments you passed in.

And when it's done... The logic of the body has been carried out (and, in this example, you'll see that Rover, being 23 pounds, sounds like "WOOF WOOF"), and the function is done. After the function completes, then control is returned to the statement following our call to bark.

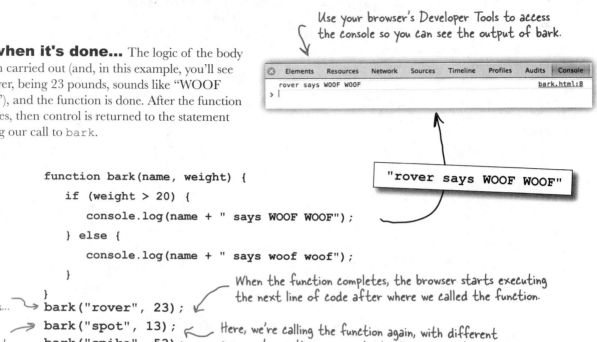

Use your browser's Developer Tools to access the console so you can see the output of bark.

"rover says WOOF WOOF"

```
function bark(name, weight) {
    if (weight > 20) {
        console.log(name + " says WOOF WOOF");
    } else {
        console.log(name + " says woof woof");
    }
}
bark("rover", 23);
bark("spot", 13);
bark("spike", 53);
bark("lady", 17);
```

We just did this...

...so do this next.

When the function completes, the browser starts executing the next line of code after where we called the function.

Here, we're calling the function again, with different arguments, so the process starts all over again!

Sharpen your pencil

We've got some more calls to bark below. Next to each call, write what you think the output should be, or if you think the code will cause an error. Check your answer at the end of the chapter before you go on.

bark("juno", 20); ___woof woof___

bark("scottie", -1); ___woof woof___

bark("dino", 0, 0); ___woof woof___

bark("fido", "20"); ___woof woof___

bark("lady", 10); ___woof woof___

bark("bruno", 21); ___WOOF WOOF___

Write what you think the console log will display here.

Hmm, any ideas what these do?

Code Magnets

This working JavaScript code is all scrambled up on the fridge. Can you reconstruct the code snippets to make a working program that produces the output listed below? Notice, there may be some extra code on the fridge, so you may not use all the magnets. Check your answer at the end of the chapter.

```
,
,       ,
        ,
    }
            }
    }       (
~~function~~    )       {

whatShallIWear(80);
```

```
else {
    console.log("Wear t-shirt");
}
```

~~whatShallIWear~~

```
else if (temp < 70) {
    console.log("Wear a sweater");
}
```

temperature

```
if (temp < 60) {
    console.log("Wear a jacket");
}
```

~~temp~~   `whatShallIWear(60);`

`whatShallIWear(50);`

(handwritten scratch work)

Function whatShallIWear (Temp) {
If (temp <= 0) {
    console.log("Wer . sdat");
}
else if (Temp < 70) {
    ~~~~~~~) ;
}

else {
    case ---
}
whatShallIwear (80);
"   <60) ;
"   (50)

JavaScript console

Wear a jacket
Wear a t-shirt
Wear a sweater

↰ We're using this to represent a generic console.

The Function Exposed

This week's interview: the intimate side of functions...

Head First: Welcome Function! We're looking forward to digging in and finding out what you're all about.

Function: Glad to be here.

Head First: Now we've noticed many JavaScript newbies tend to ignore you. They just get in and write their code, line by line, top to bottom, no functions at all. Are you really needed?

Function: Those newbies are missing out. That's unfortunate because I'm powerful. Think about me like this: I give you a way to take code, write it once, and then reuse it over and over.

Head First: Well, excuse me for saying this, but if you're just giving them the ability to do the same thing, over and over... that's a little boring isn't it?

Function: No no, functions are parameterized—in other words, each time you use the function, you pass it arguments so it can compute something that's relevant to what you need.

Head First: Err, example?

Function: Let's say you need to show a user how much the items in his shopping cart are going to cost, so you write a function `computeShoppingCartTotal`. Then you can pass that function the shopping carts of many users and each time I compute the amount of each specific shopping cart.

Head First: If you're so great, why aren't more new coders using you?

Function: That's not even a true statement; they use me all the time: `alert`, `prompt`, `Math.random`, `document.write`. It's hard to write anything meaningful without using functions. It's not so much that new users don't use functions, they just aren't defining *their own* functions.

Head First: Well, right, `alert` and `prompt`, those make sense, but take `Math.random`—that doesn't look quite like a function.

Function: `Math.random` is a function, but it happens to be attached to another powerful thing new coders don't make a lot of use of: *objects*.

Head First: Oh yes, objects. I believe our readers are learning about those in a later chapter.

Function: Fair enough, I'll save my breath on that one for later.

Head First: Now this argument/parameter stuff all seems a little confusing.

Function: Think about it like this: each parameter acts like a variable throughout the body of the function. When you call the function, each value you pass in is assigned to a corresponding parameter.

Head First: And arguments are what?

Function: Oh, that's just another name for the values you pass into a function... they're the arguments of the function call.

Head First: Well you don't seem all that great; I mean, okay you allow me to reuse code, and you have this way of passing values as parameters. Is that it? I don't get the mystery around you.

Function: Oh, that's just the basics, there's so much more: I can return values, I can masquerade around your code anonymously, I can do a neat trick called closures, and I have an *intimate* relationship with objects.

Head First: Ohhhhh REALLY?! Can we get an exclusive on that relationship for our next interview?

Function: We'll talk...

What can you pass to a function?

When you call a function you pass it arguments and those arguments then get matched up with the parameters in the function definition. You can pass pretty much any JavaScript value as an argument, like a string, a boolean, or a number:

Pass any JavaScript value as an argument.

```
saveMyProfile("krissy", 1991, 3.81, false);
```

Each argument is passed to its corresponding parameter in the function.

```
function saveMyProfile(name, birthday, GPA, newuser) {
    if (birthday >= 2004) {
        // code for handling a child
    }
    // rest of code for this function here
}
```

And each parameter acts as a variable within the function.

You can also pass variables as arguments, and that's often the more common case. Here's the same function call using variables:

```
var student = "krissy";
var year = 1991;
var GPA = 381/100;
var status = "existinguser";
var isNewUser = (status == "newuser");
saveMyProfile(student, year, GPA, isNewUser);
```

Now, each of the values we're passing is stored in a variable. When we call the function, the variable's values are passed as the arguments.

So, in this case we're passing the value in the variable student, "krissy", as the argument to the name parameter.

And we're also using variables for these other arguments.

And, you can even use expressions as arguments:

```
var student = "krissy";
var status = "existinguser";
var year = 1991;


saveMyProfile(student, year, 381/100, status == "newuser");
```

Yes, even these expressions will work as arguments!

In each case we first evaluate the expression to a value, and then that value is passed to the function.

We can evaluate a numeric expression...

... or a boolean expression, like this one that results in passing false to the function.

I'm still not sure I get the difference between a parameter and an argument—are they just two names for the same thing?

No, they're different.

When you define a function you can *define* it with one or more *parameters*.

Here we're defining three parameters: degrees, mode and duration.

```
function cook(degrees, mode, duration) {
    // your code here
}
```

When you call a function, you *call* it with *arguments*:

```
cook(425.0, "bake", 45);
```

These are arguments. There are three arguments: a floating point number, a string and an integer.

```
cook(350.0, "broil", 10);
```

So you'll only define your parameters once, but you'll probably call your function with many different arguments.

What does this code output? Are you sure?

```
function doIt(param) {
    param = 2;
}
var test = 1;
doIt(test);
console.log(test);
```

Exercise

Below you'll find some JavaScript code, including variables, function definitions and function calls. Your job is to identify all the variables, functions, arguments and parameters. Write the names of each in the appropriate boxes on the right. Check your answer at the end of the chapter before you go on.

```javascript
function dogYears(dogName, age) {
    var years = age * 7;
    console.log(dogName + " is " + years + " years old");
}
var myDog = "Fido";
dogYears(myDog, 4);

function makeTea(cups, tea) {
    console.log("Brewing " + cups + " cups of " + tea);
}
var guests = 3;
makeTea(guests, "Earl Grey");

function secret() {
    console.log("The secret of life is 42");
}
secret();

function speak(kind) {
    var defaultSound = "";
    if (kind == "dog") {
        alert("Woof");
    } else if (kind == "cat") {
        alert("Meow");
    } else {
        alert(defaultSound);
    }
}
var pet = prompt("Enter a type of pet: ");
speak(pet);
```

Variables

> years
> myDog   pet
> guests
> defaultSound

Functions

> function dogYears(dogName, age)
> function makeTea...
> function secret...
> function speak...

Built-in functions

> alert
> console.log
> prompt

Arguments

Parameters

JavaScript is pass-by-value.
That means pass-by-copy.

It's important to understand how JavaScript passes arguments. JavaScript passes arguments to a function using *pass-by-value*. What that means is that each argument is *copied* into the parameter variable. Let's look at a simple example to see how this works.

1 Let's declare a variable age, and initialize it to the value 7.

```
var age = 7;
```

2 Now let's declare a function addOne, with a parameter named x, that adds 1 to the value of x.

```
function addOne(x) {
    x = x + 1;
}
```

3 Now let's call the function addOne, pass it the variable age as the argument. The value in age is copied into the parameter x.

```
addOne(age);
```

This is a COPY of age.

4 Now the value of x is incremented by one. But remember x is a copy, so only x is incremented, not age.

We're incrementing x.

```
function addOne(x) {
    x = x + 1;
}
```

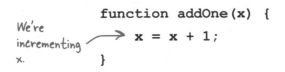 

x has been incremented within addOne.

age doesn't change even if x does.

So how do I think about this pass-by-value stuff? On the one hand it feels pretty straightforward, and on the other hand I feel like I might be missing something.

We're glad you're thinking about it. Understanding how JavaScript passes values to functions is important. On the one hand it is pretty straightforward: when an argument is passed to a function its value is first *copied* and then assigned to the corresponding parameter. But, if you don't understand this, you can make some wrong assumptions about how functions, arguments and parameters all work together.

The real impact of pass-by-value is that any changes to a parameter's value within the function will affect *only the parameter*, not the original variable passed to the function. That's pretty much it.

But of course, there's an exception to every rule, and we're going to have to talk about this topic again when we learn objects, which we'll talk about in a couple of chapters. But no worries, with a solid understanding of pass-by-value, you're in good shape to have that discussion.

And, for now, just remember that because of pass-by-value, *whatever happens to a parameter in the function, stays in the function*. Kinda like Vegas.

Remember this Brain Power? Do you think about it differently now, knowing about pass by value? Or did you guess correctly the first time?

```
function doIt(param) {
    param = 2;
}
var test = 1;
doIt(test);
console.log(test);
```

WEIRD FUNCTIONS

So far you've seen the normal way to use functions, but what happens when you experiment a little by, say, passing too many arguments to a function? Or not enough? Sounds dangerous. Let's see what happens:

EXPERIMENT #1: what happens when we don't pass enough arguments?

Sounds dicey, but all that really happens is each parameter that doesn't have a matching argument is set to undefined. Here's an example:

```
function makeTea(cups, tea) {
  console.log("Brewing " + cups + " cups of " + tea);
}
makeTea(3);
```

Notice that the value of the parameter tea is undefined because we didn't pass in a value.

> JavaScript console
> Brewing 3 cups of undefined

EXPERIMENT #2: what happens when we pass too many argments?

Ah, in this case JavaScript just ignores the extra. Here's an example:

```
function makeTea(cups, tea) {
  console.log("Brewing " + cups + " cups of " + tea);
}
makeTea(3, "Earl Grey", "hey ma!", 42);
```

Works fine, the function ignores the extras.

> JavaScript console
> Brewing 3 cups of Earl Grey

There's actually a way to get at the extra arguments, but we won't worry about that just now...

EXPERIMENT #3: what happens when we have NO parameters?

No worries, many functions have no parameters!

```
function barkAtTheMoon() {
  console.log("Wooooooooooooooo!");
}
barkAtTheMoon();
```

> JavaScript console
> Wooooooooooooooo!

Functions can <u>return</u> things too

You know how to communicate with your functions in one direction; that is, you know how to pass arguments *to functions*. But what about the other way? Can a function communicate back? Let's check out the `return` statement:

Here we've got a new bake function that takes the temperature in degrees for the oven.

```
function bake(degrees) {
    var message;

    if (degrees > 500) {
        message = "I'm not a nuclear reactor!";
    } else if (degrees < 100) {
        message = "I'm not a refrigerator!";
    } else {
        message = "That's a very comfortable temperature for me.";
        setMode("bake");
        setTemp(degrees);
    }

    return message;
}

var status = bake(350);
```

It then sets a variable to a string that depends on the temperature requested in the degrees parameter.

And presumably some real work is getting done here, but we won't worry about those details for now...

What we care about is that a return statement is returning the message as the result of this function.

Now, when the function is called and returns, the string that is returned as a result will be assigned to the status variable.

And in this case, if the status variable was printed, it would hold the string "That's a very comfortable temperature for me." Work through the code and make sure you see why!

350 degrees is the perfect temperature for good cookies. Feel free to make some and return to the next page.

Tracing through a function with a return statement

Now that you know how arguments and parameters work, and how you can return a value from a function, let's trace through a function call from start to finish to see what happens at every step along the way. Be sure to follow the steps in order.

(1) First, we declare a variable radius and initialize it to 5.2.

(2) Next, we call the calculateArea function, and pass the radius variable as the argument.

(3) The argument is sent to the parameter r, and the calculateArea function begins executing with r containing the value 5.2.

(4) The body of the function executes starting with declaring a variable, area. We then test to see if the parameter r has a value <= 0.

(5) If r <= 0, then we return 0 from the function and the function stops executing. But we passed in 5.2 so this line does NOT execute.

(6) We execute the else clause instead.

(7) We compute the area of the circle using the value 5.2 in the parameter r.

(8) We return the value of area from the function. This stops the execution of the function and returns the value.

(9) The value returned from the function is stored in the variable theArea.

(10) Execution continues on the next line.

```
(3) function calculateArea(r) {
        var area;
(4)     if (r <= 0) {
(5)         return 0;
(6)     } else {
(7)         area = Math.PI * r * r;
(8)         return area;
        }
    }
(1) var radius = 5.2;

(9) var theArea = (2) calculateArea(radius);

(10) console.log("The area is: " + theArea);
```

Output here!

```
JavaScript console
The area is: 84.94866535306801
```

Developers often call this "tracing the flow of execution" or just "tracing." As you can see the flow can jump around when you're calling functions and returning values. Just take it slow, one step at a time.

Anatomy of a Function

Now that you know how to define and call a function, let's make sure we've got the syntax down cold. Here are all the parts of a function's anatomy:

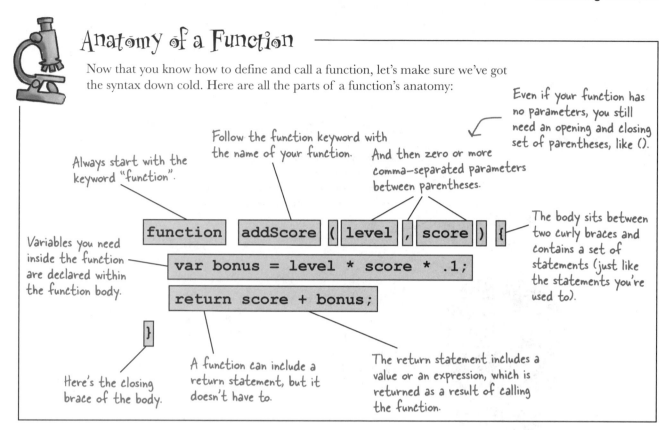

Even if your function has no parameters, you still need an opening and closing set of parentheses, like ().

Follow the function keyword with the name of your function.

Always start with the keyword "function".

And then zero or more comma-separated parameters between parentheses.

```
function  addScore  ( level , score ) {
    var bonus = level * score * .1;
    return score + bonus;
}
```

Variables you need inside the function are declared within the function body.

The body sits between two curly braces and contains a set of statements (just like the statements you're used to).

Here's the closing brace of the body.

A function can include a return statement, but it doesn't have to.

The return statement includes a value or an expression, which is returned as a result of calling the function.

there are no
Dumb Questions

Q: What happens if I mix up the order of my arguments, so that I'm passing the wrong arguments into the parameters?

A: All bets are off; in fact, we'd guess you're pretty much guaranteed either an error at run time or incorrect code. Always take a careful look at a function's parameters, so you know what arguments the function expects to be passed in.

Q: Why don't the parameter names have var in front of them? A parameter is a new variable right?

A: Effectively yes. The function does all the work of instantiating the variable for you, so you don't need to supply the var keyword in front of your parameter names.

Q: What are the rules for function names?

A: The rules for naming a function are the same as the rules for naming a variable. Just like with variables, you'll want to use names that make sense to you when you read them, and provide some indication of what the function does, and you can use camel case (e.g. camelCase) to combine words in function names, just like with variables.

Q: What happens if I use the same name for an argument variable as the parameter? Like if I use the name x for both?

A: Even if your argument and parameter have the same name, like x, the parameter x gets a copy of the argument x, so they are two different variables. Changing the value of the parameter x does not change the value of the argument x.

Q: What does a function return if it doesn't have a return statement?

A: A function without a return statement returns undefined.

I noticed you started putting variable declarations right inside of your functions. Do these declarations work just the same?

Good catch. Yes and no.

These declarations work exactly the same within a function as they do outside a function, in the sense that you are initializing a new variable to a value. However, the difference between a variable declared *outside a function* and a variable declared *inside a function* is where that variable can be used—in other words, where in your JavaScript code you can reference the variable. If the variable is declared outside a function, then you can use it *anywhere* in your code. If a variable is declared inside a function, then you can use it only *within that function*. This is known as a variable's *scope*. There are two kinds of scope: global and local.

We need to talk about your variable usage...

Global and local variables
Know the difference or risk humiliation

You already know that you can declare a variable by using the `var` keyword and a name anywhere in your script:

```
var avatar;
var levelThreshold = 1000;
```

These are <u>global</u> variables; they're accessible everywhere in your JavaScript code.

And you've seen that you can also declare variables inside a function:

```
function getScore(points) {
    var score;
    var i = 0;
    while (i < levelThreshold) {
        //code here
        i = i + 1;
    }
    return score;
}
```

The points, score and i variables are all declared within a function.

We call them <u>local</u> variables because they are known locally only within the function itself.

Even if we use levelThreshold inside the function, it's global because it's <u>declared</u> outside the function.

If a variable is declared outside a function, it's GLOBAL. If it's declared inside a function, it's LOCAL.

But what does it matter? Variables are variables, right? Well, *where* you declare your variables determines *how visible* they are to other parts of your code, and, later, understanding how these two kinds of variables operate will help you write more maintainable code (not to mention, help you understand the code of others).

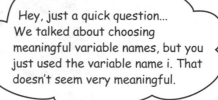

Hey, just a quick question...
We talked about choosing
meaningful variable names, but you
just used the variable name i. That
doesn't seem very meaningful.

Another good catch.

There's a long history of using the letter i as the
variable you iterate with. This convention developed
back in the days when space was limited (like when
we used punched cards to write code), and there
was an advantage to short variable names. Now it's
a convention all programmers understand. You'll
also commonly see j, k, and sometimes even x and y
used in this manner. However, this is one of the only
exceptions to the best practice of choosing meaningful
variable names.

Knowing the scope of your local and global variables

Where you define your variables determines their *scope*; that is, where they're visible to your code and where they aren't. Let's look at an example of both locally and globally scoped variables—remember, the variables you define outside a function are globally scoped, and the function variables are locally scoped:

```javascript
var avatar = "generic";
var skill = 1.0;
var pointsPerLevel = 1000;
var userPoints = 2008;

function getAvatar(points) {
    var level = points / pointsPerLevel;

    if (level == 0) {
        return "Teddy bear";
    } else if (level == 1) {
        return "Cat";
    } else if (level >= 2) {
        return "Gorilla";
    }
}

function updatePoints(bonus, newPoints) {
    var i = 0;
    while (i < bonus) {
        newPoints = newPoints + skill * bonus;
        i = i + 1;
    }
    return newPoints + userPoints;
}

userPoints = updatePoints(2, 100);
avatar = getAvatar(2112);
```

These four variables are globally scoped. That means they are defined and visible in all the code below.

Note that if you link to additional scripts in your page, they will see these global variables, and you will see their global variables too!

The level variable here is local and is visible only to the code within the getAvatar function. That means only this function can access the level variable.

And let's not forget the points parameter, which also has local scope in the getAvatar function.

Note that getAvatar makes use of the pointsPerLevel global variable too.

In updatePoints we have a local variable i. i is visible to all of the code in updatePoints.

bonus and newPoints are also local to updatePoints, while userPoints is global.

And here in our code we can use only the global variables, we have no access to any variables inside the functions because they're not visible in the global scope.

I could have sworn the variable was right behind me, but when I turned around he was just...gone...

The short lives of variables

When you're a variable, you work hard and life can be short. That is, unless you're a global variable, but even with globals, life has its limits. But what determines the life of a variable? Think about it like this:

Globals live as long as the page. A global variable begins life when its JavaScript is loaded into the page. But, your global variable's life ends when the page goes away. Even if you reload the same page, all your global variables are destroyed and then recreated in the newly loaded page.

Local variables typically disappear when your function ends. Local variables are created when your function is first called and live until the function returns (with a value or not). That said, you can take the values of your local variables and return them from the function before the variables meet their digital maker.

So, there really is NO escape from the page is there? If you're a local variable, your life comes and goes quickly, and if you're lucky enough to be a global, you're good as long as that browser doesn't reload the page.

We say "typically" because there are some advanced ways to retain locals a little longer, but we're not going to worry about them now.

Don't forget to declare your locals!

If you use a variable without declaring it first, that variable will be global. That means that even if you use a variable for the first time inside a function (because you meant for it to be local), the variable will actually be global, and be available outside the function too (which might cause confusion later). So, don't forget to declare your locals!

> **If you forget to declare a variable before using it, the variable will always be global (even if the first time you use it is in a function).**

```
function playTurn(player, location) {
    points = 0;
    if (location == 1) {
        points = points + 100;
    }
    return points;
}
var total = playTurn("Jai", 1);
alert(points);
```

We forgot to declare points with "var" before we used it. So points is automatically global.

That means we can use points outside the function! The value doesn't go away (like it should) when the function is done executing.

This program behaves as if you'd written this instead:

JavaScript assumes that we meant for points to be global because we forgot to use "var", and behaves as if points were declared at the global level.

```
var points = 0;
function playTurn(player, location) {
    points = 0;
    if (location == 1) {
        points = points + 100;
    }
    return points;
}
var total = playTurn("Jai", 1);
alert(points);
```

Forgetting to declare your local variables can cause problems if you use the same name as another global variable. You might overwrite a value you didn't mean to.

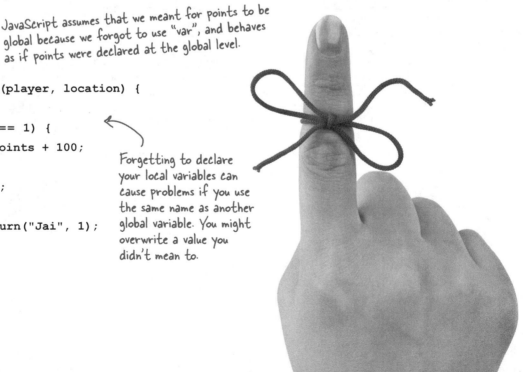

What happens when I name a local variable the same thing as an existing global variable?

You "shadow" your global.

Here's what that means: say you have a global variable **beanCounter** and you then declare a function, like this:

```
var beanCounter = 10;


function getNumberOfItems(ordertype) {
    var beanCounter = 0;
    if (ordertype == "order") {
        // do some stuff with beanCounter...
    }
    return beanCounter;
}
```

← We've got a global and a local!

When you do this, any references to **beanCounter** within the function refer to the local variable and not the global. So we say the global variable is in the shadow of the local variable (in other words we can't see the global variable because the local version is in our way).

Note that the local and global variables have no effect on each other: if you change one, it has no effect on the other. They are independent variables.

Exercise

Below you'll find some JavaScript code, including variables, function definitions and function calls. Your job is to identify the variables used in all the arguments, parameters, local variables and global variables. Write the variable names in the appropriate boxes on the right. Then circle any variables that are shadowed. Check your answer at the end of the chapter.

```javascript
var x = 32;
var y = 44;
var radius = 5;

var centerX = 0;
var centerY = 0;
var width = 600;
var height = 400;

function setup(width, height) {
    centerX = width/2;
    centerY = height/2;
}

function computeDistance(x1, y1, x2, y2) {
    var dx = x1 - x2;
    var dy = y1 - y2;
    var d2 = (dx * dx) + (dy * dy);
    var d = Math.sqrt(d2);
    return d;
}

function circleArea(r) {
    var area = Math.PI * r * r;
    return area;
}

setup(width, height);
var area = circleArea(radius);
var distance = computeDistance(x, y, centerX, centerY);
alert("Area: " + area);
alert("Distance: " + distance);
```

Arguments

Parameters

Locals

Globals

Fireside Chats

Tonight's talk: **Global and Local variables argue over who is most important in a program.**

Global variable:

Hey Local, I'm really not sure why you're here because I can handle any need for a variable a coder might have. After all, I'm visible everywhere!

You have to admit that I could replace all your previous local variables with global ones and your functions would work just the same.

It wouldn't have to be a mess. Programmers could just create all the variables they need up at the top of a program, so they'd all be in one place…

Well, if you'd use better names, then you might be able to keep track of your variables more easily.

True. But why bother with arguments and parameters if you've got all the values you need in globals?

Local variable:

Yes but using globals everywhere is just bad style. Lots of functions need variables that are local. You know, their own private variables for their own use. Globals can be seen everywhere.

Well, yes and no. If you're extremely careful, sure. But being that careful is difficult, and if you make a mistake, then we've got functions using variables that other functions are using for different purposes. You'd also be littering the program with global variables that you only need inside one function call… that would just make a huge mess.

Yeah, and so what happens if you need to call a function that needs a variable, like, oh I dunno, x, and you can't remember what you've used x for before. You have to go searching all over your code to see if you've used x anywhere else! What a nightmare.

And what about parameters? Function parameters are always local. So you can't get around that.

Excuse me, do you hear what you're saying? The whole point of functions is so we can reuse code to compute different things based on different inputs.

Global variable:

But your variables are just so... temporary. Locals come and go at a moment's notice.

Not at all? Globals are the mainstay of JavaScript programmers!

I think I need a drink.

Local variable:

Face it. It's just good programming practice to use local variables unless you absolutely need globals. And globals can get you into real trouble. I've seen JavaScript programs that barely use globals at all!

Of inexperienced programmers, sure. But as programmers learn to correctly structure their code for correctness, maintainability, and just good coding style, they learn how to stop using globals except when necessary.

They let globals drink? Now, we're *really* in dangerous territory.

Who needs to. Your cards are written all over your face.

Lucky for me you can't read my local variables.

Another Function

A Function

there are no
Dumb Questions

Q: Keeping track of the scope of all these locals and globals is confusing, so why not just stick to globals? That's what I've always done.

A: If you're writing code that is complex or that needs to be maintained over a long period of time, then you really have to watch how you manage your variables. When you're overzealous in creating global variables, it becomes difficult to track where your variables are being used (and where you're making changes to your variables' values), and that can lead to buggy code. All this becomes even more important when you're writing code with co-workers or you're using third-party libraries (although if those libraries are written well, they should be structured to avoid these issues).

So, use globals where it makes sense, but use them in moderation, and whenever possible, make your variables local. As you get more experience with JavaScript, you can investigate additional techniques to structure code so that it's more maintainable.

Q: I have global variables in my page, but I'm loading in other JavaScript files as well. Do those files have separate sets of global variables?

A: There is only one global scope so every file you load sees the same set of variables (and creates globals in the same space). That's why it is so important you be careful with your use of variables to avoid clashes (and reduce or eliminate global variables when you can).

Q: If I use the same name for a parameter as I do for a global variable, does the parameter shadow the global?

A: Yes. Just like if you declare a new, local variable in a function with the same name as a global, if you use the same name for a parameter as a global, you're also going to shadow the global with that name. It's perfectly fine to shadow a global name as long as you don't want to use the global variable inside your function. But it's a good idea to document what you're doing with comments so you don't get confused later when you're reading your code.

Q: If I reload a page in the browser, do the global variables all get re-initialized?

A: Yes. Reloading a page is like starting over from scratch as far as the variables are concerned. And if any code was in the middle of executing when you reload the page, any local variables will disappear, too.

Q: Should we always declare our local variables at the top of a function?

A: Just like with global variables, you can declare local variables when you first need to use them in a function. However, it's a good programming practice to go ahead and declare them at the top of your function so someone reading your code can easily find those declarations and get a sense at a glance of all the local variables used within the function. In addition, if you delay declaring a variable and then decide to use that variable earlier in the body of the function than you originally anticipated, you might get behavior that you don't expect. JavaScript creates all local variables at the beginning of a function whether you declare them or not (this is called "hoisting" and we'll come back to it later), but the variables are all undefined until they are assigned a value, which might not be what you want.

Q: Everyone seems to complain about the overuse of global variables in JavaScript. Why is this? Was the language badly designed or do people not know what they're doing, or what? And what do we do about it?

A: Globals are often overused in JavaScript. Some of this is because the language makes it easy to just jump in and start coding—and that's a good thing—because JavaScript doesn't enforce a lot of structure or overhead on you. The downside is when people write serious code this way and it has to be changed and maintained over the long term (and that pretty much describes all web pages). All that said, JavaScript is a powerful language that includes features like objects you can use to organize your code in a modular way. Many books have been written on that topic alone, and we're going to give you a taste of objects in Chapter 5 (which is only a couple of chapters away).

We've talked a lot about local and global variables and where they should be declared, but we haven't talked about where to declare our functions. Should we just put them all at the top of our JavaScript files?

Actually, you can put your functions anywhere in your JavaScript file.

JavaScript doesn't care if your functions are declared before or after you use them. For instance, check out this code:

```javascript
var radius = 5;
var area = circleArea(radius);
alert(area);

function circleArea(r) {
    var a = Math.PI * r * r;
    return a;
}
```

Notice that we're using the circleArea function before we're defining it!

The circleArea function isn't actually defined until after we've called it, in the code above. How on earth does this work?

This might seem really odd, especially if you remember when the browser loads your page, it starts executing the JavaScript from the top to the bottom of your file. But, the truth is JavaScript actually makes two passes over your page: in the first pass it reads all the function definitions, and in the second it begins executing your code. So, that allows you to place functions anywhere in your file.

The Thing-A-Ma-Jig

The Thing-A-Ma-Jig is quite a contraption—it clanks and clunks and even thunks, but what it really does, well, you've got us stumped. Coders claim they know how it works. Can you uncrack the code and find its quirks?

```javascript
function clunk(times) {
    var num = times;
    while (num > 0) {
        display("clunk");
        num = num - 1;
    }
}

function thingamajig(size) {
    var facky = 1;
    clunkCounter = 0;
    if (size == 0) {
        display("clank");
    } else if (size == 1) {
        display("thunk");
    } else {
        while (size > 1) {
            facky = facky * size;
            size = size - 1;
        }
        clunk(facky);
    }
}

function display(output) {
    console.log(output);
    clunkCounter = clunkCounter + 1;
}
var clunkCounter = 0;
thingamajig(5);
console.log(clunkCounter);
```

Your output here!

JavaScript console

We recommend passing the Thing-A-Ma-Jig the numbers 0, 1, 2, 3, 4, 5, etc. See if you know what it's doing.

Webville Guide to Code Hygiene

In Webville we like to keep things clean, organized and ready for expansion. There's no place that needs to be better maintained than your code, and JavaScript can seem pretty loosey-goosey when it comes to organizing your variables and functions. So we've put together a neat little guide for you that makes a few recommendations for those new to Webville. Take one, they're FREE.

Global variables, right at the TOP!

It's a good idea to keep your globals grouped together as much as possible, and if they're all up at the top, it's easy to find them. Now you don't have to do this, but isn't it easier for you and others to locate the variables used in your code if they're all at the top?

Functions like to sit together.

Well, not really; they actually don't care, they're just functions. But, if you keep your functions together, it's a lot easier to locate them. As you know, the browser actually scans your JavaScript for the functions before it does anything else. So you can place them at the top or bottom of the file, but if you keep them in one place your life will be easier. Here in Webville, we often start with our global variables and then put our functions next.

Let your local variables be declared at the TOP of the function they're in.

Put all your local variable declarations at the beginning of the function body. This makes them easy to find and ensures they are all declared properly before use.

That's it, just be safe and we hope you enjoy your time coding in Webville!

Who am I?

A bunch of JavaScript attendees, in full costume, are playing a party game, "Who am I?" They give you a clue, and you try to guess who they are, based on what they say. Assume they always tell the truth about themselves. Fill in the blank next to each sentence with the name of one attendee.

Tonight's attendees:

function, argument, return, scope, local variable, global variable, pass-by-value, parameter, function call, Math.random, built-in functions, code reuse.

I get passed into a function. _____

I send values back to the calling code. _____

I'm the all important keyword. _____

I'm what receives arguments. _____

It really means 'make a copy'. _____

I'm everywhere. _____

Another phrase for invoking a function. _____

Example of a function attached to an object. _____

alert and prompt are examples. _____

What functions are great for. _____

Where I can be seen. _____

I'm around when my function is. _____

The case of the attempted robbery not worth investigating

Sherlock finished his phone call with the bumbling chief of police, Lestrade, and sat down in front of the fireplace to resume reading the newspaper. Watson looked at him expectantly.

"What?" said Sherlock, not looking up from the paper.

"Well? What did Lestrade have to say?" Watson asked.

"Oh, he said they found a bit of rogue code in the bank account where the suspicious activity was taking place."

"And?" Watson said, trying to hide his frustration.

"Lestrade emailed me the code, and I told him it wasn't worth pursuing. The criminal made a fatal flaw and will never be able to actually steal the money," Sherlock said.

"How do you know?" Watson asked.

"It's obvious if you know where to look," Sherlock exclaimed. "Now stop bothering me with questions and let me finish this paper."

With Sherlock absorbed in the latest news, Watson snuck a peek at Sherlock's phone and pulled up Lestrade's email to look at the code.

```
var balance = 10500;                This is the real, actual bank
                                    balance in the account.
var cameraOn = true;


function steal(balance, amount) {
    cameraOn = false;
    if (amount < balance) {
        balance = balance - amount;
    }
    return amount;
    cameraOn = true;
}


var amount = steal(balance, 1250);
alert("Criminal: you stole " + amount + "!");
```

Why did Sherlock decide not to investigate the case? How could he know that the criminal would never be able to steal the money just by looking at the code? Is there one problem with the code? Or more?

BULLET POINTS

- Declare a function using the **function** keyword, followed by the name of the function.

- Use parentheses to enclose any **parameters** a function has. Use empty parentheses if there are no parameters.

- Enclose the **body** of the function in curly braces.

- The statements in the body of a function are executed when you call a function.

- **Calling** a function and **invoking** a function are the same thing.

- You call a function by using its name and passing arguments to the function's parameters (if any).

- A function can optionally return a value using the **return** statement.

- A function creates a local scope for parameters and any local variables the function uses.

- Variables are either in the **global scope** (visible everywhere in your program) or in the **local scope** (visible only in the function where they are declared).

- Declare local variables at the top of the body of your function.

- If you forget to declare a local variable using **var**, that variable will be global, which could have unintended consequences in your program.

- Functions are a good way to organize your code and create reusable chunks of code.

- You can customize the code in a function by passing in arguments to parameters (and using different arguments to get different results).

- Functions are also a good way to reduce or eliminate duplicate code.

- You can use JavaScript's many built-in functions, like alert, prompt, and Math.random, to do work in your programs.

- Using built-in functions means using existing code you don't have to write yourself.

- It's a good idea to organize your code so your functions are together, and your global variables are together, at the top of your JavaScript file.

JavaScript cross

In this chapter you got functional. Now use some brain functions to do this crossword.

ACROSS

4. A parameter acts like a _____ in the body of a function.

6. JavaScript uses _____ when passing arguments to functions.

10. You can declare your functions _____ in your JavaScript file.

11. What gets returned from a function without a return statement.

13. Local variables disappear when the _____ returns.

16. If you forget to declare your locals, they'll be treated like _____.

17. A local variable can _____ a global variable.

DOWN

1. A variable with global _____ is visible everywhere.

2. Use functions so you can _____ code over and over again.

3. The variables that arguments land in when they get passed to functions.

5. To get a value back from a function, use the _____ statement.

7. What gets passed to functions.

8. When you reload your page, all your _____ get re-initialized.

9. _____ through your code means following the execution line by line.

12. Watson looked at the bank heist code in Sherlock's _____ on his phone.

14. It's better to use _____ variables whenever you can.

15. Extra arguments to a function are _____.

Sharpen your pencil
Solution

Do a little analysis of the code below. How does it look? Choose as many of the options below as you like, or write in your own analysis. Here's our solution.

```javascript
var dogName = "rover";
var dogWeight = 23;
if (dogWeight > 20) {
    console.log(dogName + " says WOOF WOOF");
} else {
    console.log(dogName + " says woof woof");
}
dogName = "spot";
dogWeight = 13;
if (dogWeight > 20) {
    console.log(dogName + " says WOOF WOOF");
} else {
    console.log(dogName + " says woof woof");
}
dogName = "spike";
dogWeight = 53;
if (dogWeight > 20) {
    console.log(dogName + " says WOOF WOOF");
} else {
    console.log(dogName + " says woof woof");
}
dogName = "lady";
dogWeight = 17;
if (dogWeight > 20) {
    console.log(dogName + " says WOOF WOOF");
} else {
    console.log(dogName + " says woof woof");
}
```

We chose all of them!

☑ A. The code seems very redundant.

☑ B. If we wanted to change how this outputs, or if we wanted to add another weight for dogs, this is going to require a lot of reworking.

☑ C. Looks tedious to type in!

☑ D. Not the most readable code I've ever seen.

☑ E. *Looks like the developer thought the weights might change over time.*

Sharpen your pencil
Solution

We've got some more calls to bark below. Next to each call, write what you think the output should be, or if you think the code will cause an error. Here's our solution.

`bark("juno", 20);` _juno says woof woof_

`bark("scottie", -1);` _scottie says woof woof_

↖ Our bark function doesn't check to make sure dog weights are greater than 0. So this works because -1 is less than 20.

`bark("dino", 0, 0);` _dino says woof woof_

↖ The bark function just ignores the extra argument, 0. And using 0 as the weight doesn't make sense, but it still works.

`bark("fido", "20");` _fido says woof woof_

↖ We compare the string "20" to the number 20. "20" isn't greater than 20, so fido says "woof woof". (You'll find out later how JavaScript compares "20" and 20.)

`bark("lady", 10);` _lady says woof woof_

`bark("bruno", 21);` _bruno says WOOF WOOF_

Code Magnets Solution

This working JavaScript code is all scrambled up on the fridge. Can you reconstruct the code snippets to make a working program that produces the output listed below? Notice, there may be some extra code on the fridge, so you may not use all the magnets. Here's our solution.

```javascript
function whatShallIWear ( temp ) {

    if (temp < 60) {
        console.log("Wear a jacket");
    }

    else if (temp < 70) {
        console.log("Wear a sweater");
    }

    else {
        console.log("Wear t-shirt");
    }

}
whatShallIWear(50);
whatShallIWear(80);
whatShallIWear(60);
```

Leftover magnets.

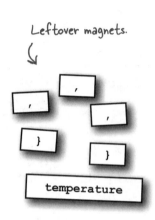

,
,
,
}
}
temperature

```
JavaScript console
Wear a jacket
Wear a t-shirt
Wear a sweater
```

Exercise Solution

Below you'll find some JavaScript code, including variables, function definitions and function calls. Your job is to identify all the variables, functions, arguments and parameters. Write the names of each in the appropriate boxes on the right. Here's our solution.

```javascript
function dogYears(dogName, age) {
    var years = age * 7;
    console.log(dogName + " is " + years + " years old");
}
var myDog = "Fido";
dogYears(myDog, 4);

function makeTea(cups, tea) {
    console.log("Brewing " + cups + " cups of " + tea);
}
var guests = 3;
makeTea(guests, "Earl Grey");

function secret() {
    console.log("The secret of life is 42");
}
secret();

function speak(kind) {
    var defaultSound = "";
    if (kind == "dog") {
        alert("Woof");
    } else if (kind == "cat") {
        alert("Meow");
    } else {
        alert(defaultSound);
    }
}
var pet = prompt("Enter a type of pet: ");
speak(pet);
```

Variables

myDog, guests, pet, years, defaultSound

Functions

dogYears, makeTea, secret, speak,

Built-in functions

alert, console.log, prompt

Arguments

myDog, 4, guests, "Earl Grey", pet, plus all the string arguments to alert and console.log

Parameters

dogName, age, cups, tea, kind

Below you'll find some JavaScript code, including variables, function definitions and function calls. Your job is to identify the variables used in all the arguments, parameters, local variables and global variables. Write the variable names in the appropriate boxes on the right. Then circle any variables that are shadowed. Here's our solution.

```javascript
var x = 32;
var y = 44;
var radius = 5;

var centerX = 0;
var centerY = 0;
var width = 600;
var height = 400;

function setup(width, height) {
    centerX = width/2;
    centerY = height/2;
}

function computeDistance(x1, y1, x2, y2) {
    var dx = x1 - x2;
    var dy = y1 - y2;
    var d2 = (dx * dx) + (dy * dy);
    var d = Math.sqrt(d2);
    return d;
}

function circleArea(r) {
    var area = Math.PI * r * r;
    return area;
}

setup(width, height);
var area = circleArea(radius);
var distance = computeDistance(x, y, centerX, centerY);
alert("Area: " + area);
alert("Distance: " + distance);
```

Don't forget the arguments to the alert function.

Arguments

width, height, radius, x, y, centerX, centerY, "Area: " + area, "Distance: "+ distance

Parameters

width, height, xl, yl, x2, y2, r

Locals

dx, dy, d2, d, (area)

The local variable area shadows the global variable area

Globals

x, y, radius, centerX, centerY, width, height, area, distance

Don't forget area and distance. These are globals too.

Exercise
Solution

The Thing-A-Ma-Jig

The Thing-A-Ma-Jig is quite a contraption—it clanks and clunks and even thunks, but what it really does, well, you've got us stumped. Coders claim they know how it works. Can you uncrack the code and find its quirks?

Here's our solution:

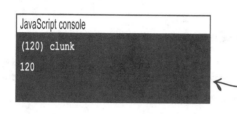

JavaScript console

(120) clunk

120

If you pass 5 to thingamajig, you'll see "clunk" in the console 120 times (or you might see your console abbreviate 120 clunks, like above), and then the number 120 at the end.

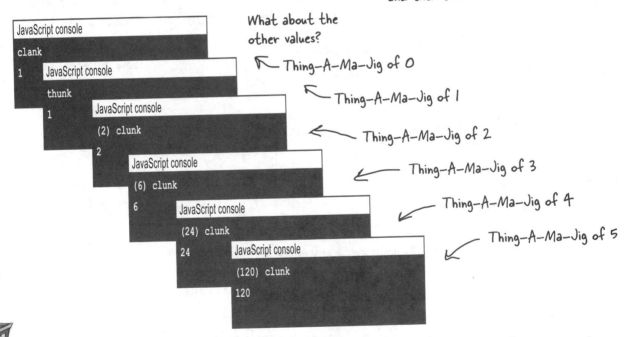

What about the other values?

← Thing-A-Ma-Jig of 0
← Thing-A-Ma-Jig of 1
← Thing-A-Ma-Jig of 2
← Thing-A-Ma-Jig of 3
← Thing-A-Ma-Jig of 4
← Thing-A-Ma-Jig of 5

What does it all mean? We hear the Thing-A-Ma-Jig was invented by a curious chap who was fascinated by rearranging words. You know like DOG rearranged is GOD, OGD, DGO, GDO and ODG. So if a word has three letters the Thing-A-Ma-Jig says you can make six total combinations from those letters. If you use the word "mixes" you can make 120 combinations of letters, wow! Anyway, that's what we heard. And here we just thought it computed mathematical factorials! Who knew!?

Check out 'factorial' in wikipedia for more info!

Five Minute
Mystery
Solution

Why did Sherlock decide not to investigate the case? How could he know that the criminal would never be able to steal the money just by looking at the code? Is there one problem with the code? Or more? Here's our solution.

```
var balance = 10500;
var cameraOn = true;

function steal(balance, amount) {
    cameraOn = false;
    if (amount < balance) {
        balance = balance - amount;
    }
    return amount;
    cameraOn = true;
}

var amount = steal(balance, 1250);
alert("Criminal: you stole " + amount + "!");
```

balance is a global variable...

... but it's shadowed by this parameter.

So when you change the balance in the function steal, you're not changing the actual bank balance!

We're returning the amount stolen...

... but we're not using it to update the real balance in the account. So the balance of the bank account is the same as it was originally.

The criminal thinks he stole the money, but he didn't!

And, in addition to not actually stealing any money, the criminal forgets to turn the camera back on, which is a dead giveaway to the police that something nefarious is going on. Remember, when you return from a function, the function stops executing, so any lines of code after the return are ignored!

Who am I?

Solution

A bunch of JavaScript attendees, in full costume, are playing a party game, "Who am I?" They give you a clue, and you try to guess who they are, based on what they say. Assume they always tell the truth about themselves. Fill in the blank next to each sentence with the name of one attendee. Here's our solution.

Tonight's attendees:

function, argument, return, scope, local variable, global variable, pass-by-value, parameter, function call, Math.random, built-in functions, code reuse.

I get passed into a function.	argument
I send values back to the calling code.	return
I'm the all important keyword.	function
I'm what receives arguments.	parameter
It really means 'make a copy'.	pass-by-value
I'm everywhere.	global variable
Another phrase for invoking a function.	function call
Example of a function attached to an object.	Math.random
alert and prompt are examples.	built-in functions
What functions are great for.	code reuse
Where I can be seen.	scope
I'm around when my function is.	local variable

 JavaScript cross Solution

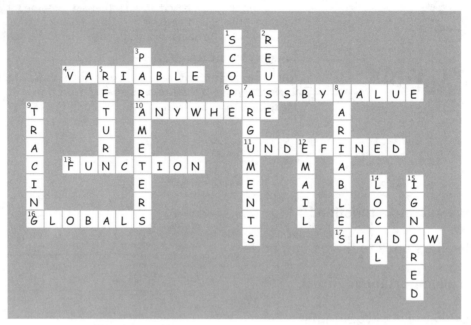

4 putting some order in your data

There's more to JavaScript than numbers, strings and booleans.

So far you've been writing JavaScript code with **primitives**—simple strings, numbers and booleans, like "Fido", 23, and true. And you can do a lot with primitive types, but at some point you've got to deal with **more data**. Say, all the items in a shopping cart, or all the songs in a playlist, or a set of stars and their apparent magnitude, or an entire product catalog. For that we need a little more *ummph*. The type of choice for this kind of ordered data is a JavaScript **array**, and in this chapter we're going to walk through how to put your data into an array, how to pass it around and how to operate on it. We'll be looking at a few other ways to **structure your data** in later chapters but let's get started with arrays.

Can you help Bubbles-R-Us?

Meet the Bubbles-R-Us company. Their tireless research makes sure bubble wands & machines everywhere blow the best bubbles. Today they're testing the "bubble factor" of several variants of their new bubble solution; that is, they're testing how many bubbles a given solution can make. Here's their data:

Each bubble solution was tested for the number of bubbles it can create.

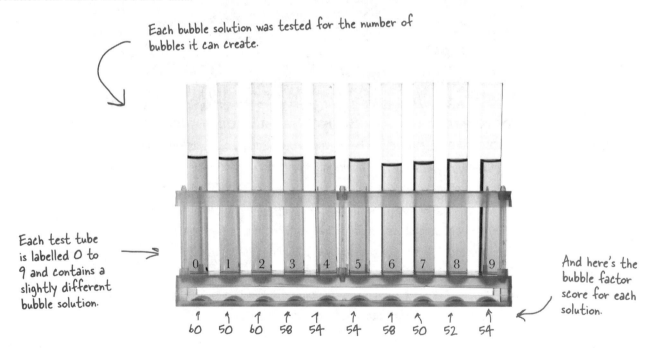

Each test tube is labelled 0 to 9 and contains a slightly different bubble solution.

And here's the bubble factor score for each solution.

0 1 2 3 4 5 6 7 8 9

60 50 60 58 54 54 58 50 52 54

Of course you want to get all this data into JavaScript so you can write code to help analyze it. But that's a lot of values. How are you going to construct your code to handle all these values?

How to represent multiple values in JavaScript

You know how to represent single values like strings, numbers and booleans with JavaScript, but how do you represent *multiple* values, like all the bubble factor scores from the ten bubble solutions? To do that we use JavaScript *arrays*. An array is a JavaScript type that can hold many values. Here's a JavaScript array that holds all the bubble factor scores:

```
var scores = [60, 50, 60, 58, 54, 54, 58, 50, 52, 54];
```

Here's all ten values, grouped together into an array, and assigned to the scores variable.

You can treat all the values as a whole, or you can access the individual scores when you need to. Check this out:

To access an <u>item</u> of the array we use this syntax: the variable name of the array followed by the <u>index</u> of the item, surrounded by square brackets.

Notice that arrays are zero-based. So the first bubble solution is solution #0 and has the score in scores[0], and likewise, the third bubble solution is solution #2 and has the score in scores[2].

```
var solution2 = scores[2];
alert("Solution 2 produced " + solution2 + " bubbles.");
```

Solution 2 produced 60 bubbles.

OK

My bubble solution #2 is definitely going to be the best.

One of the Bubbles-R-Us bubbleologists.

How arrays work

Before we get on to helping Bubbles-R-Us, let's make sure we've got
arrays down. As we said, you can use arrays to store *multiple* values
(unlike variables that hold just one value, like a number or a string). Most
often you'll use arrays when you want to group together similar things,
like bubble factor scores, ice cream flavors, daytime temperatures or
even the answers to a set of true/false questions. Once you have a bunch
of values you want to group together, you can create an array that holds
them, and then access those values in the array whenever you need them.

How to create an array

Let's say you wanted to create an array that holds ice cream flavors.
Here's how you'd do that:

Notice that each
item in the array is
separated by a comma.

```
var flavors = ["vanilla", "butterscotch", "lavender", "chocolate", "cookie dough"];
```

Let's assign the
array to a variable
named flavors.

To begin the array,
use the [character...

and then list each
item of the array...

... and end the array
with the] character.

When you create an array, each item is placed at a location, or *index*, in
the array. With the flavors array, the first item, "vanilla", is at index 0, the
second, "butterscotch", is at index 1, and so on. Here's a way to think
about an array:

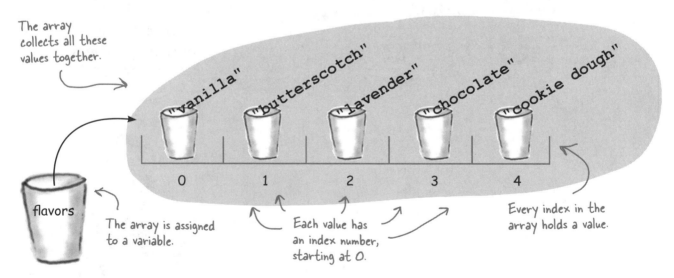

The array
collects all these
values together.

"vanilla" "butterscotch" "lavender" "chocolate" "cookie dough"

0   1   2   3   4

flavors

The array is assigned
to a variable.

Each value has
an index number,
starting at 0.

Every index in the
array holds a value.

How to access an array item

Each item in the array has its own index, and that's your key to both accessing and changing the values in an array. To access an item just follow the array variable name with an index, surrounded by square brackets. You can use that notation anywhere you'd use a variable:

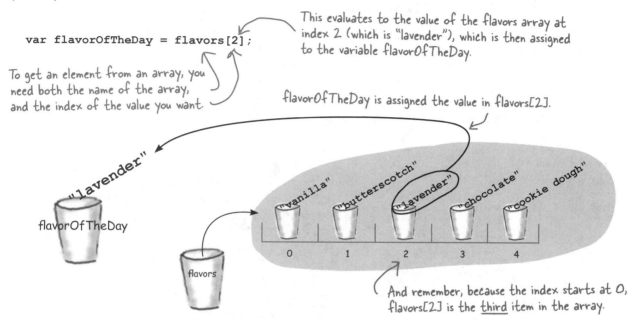

```
var flavorOfTheDay = flavors[2];
```

This evaluates to the value of the flavors array at index 2 (which is "lavender"), which is then assigned to the variable flavorOfTheDay.

To get an element from an array, you need both the name of the array, and the index of the value you want.

flavorOfTheDay is assigned the value in flavors[2].

"lavender"

flavorOfTheDay

flavors

"vanilla"   "butterscotch"   "lavender"   "chocolate"   "cookie dough"

0   1   2   3   4

And remember, because the index starts at 0, flavors[2] is the <u>third</u> item in the array.

Updating a value in the array

You can also use the array index to change a value in an array:

```
flavors[3] = "vanilla chocolate chip";
```

This sets the value of the item at index 3 (previously "chocolate") to a new value, "vanilla chocolate chip".

So, after this line of code, your array will look like this:

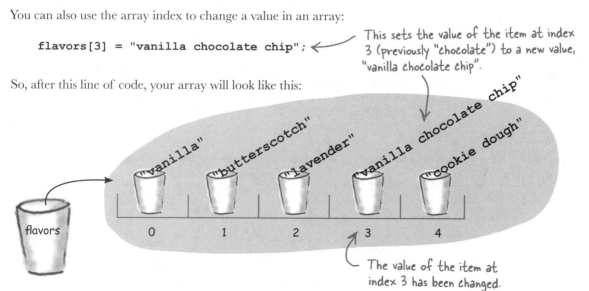

flavors

"vanilla"   "butterscotch"   "lavender"   "vanilla chocolate chip"   "cookie dough"

0   1   2   3   4

The value of the item at index 3 has been changed.

How big is that array anyway?

Say someone hands you a nice big array with important data in it. You know what's in it, but you probably won't know exactly how big it is. Luckily, every array comes with its own property, `length`. We'll talk more about properties and how they work in the next chapter, but for now, a property is just a value associated with an array. Here's how you use the `length` property:

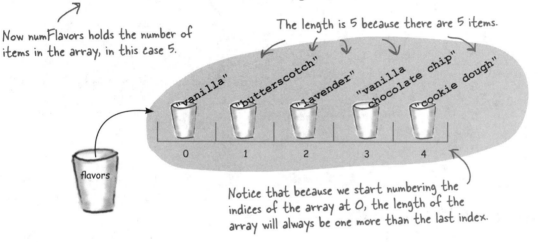

Every array has a property, length, that contains the number of items currently in the array.

To get the length of an array, you use the name of the array, then a ".", and then length.

```
var numFlavors = flavors.length;
```

Now numFlavors holds the number of items in the array, in this case 5.

The length is 5 because there are 5 items.

"vanilla"   "butterscotch"   "lavender"   "vanilla chocolate chip"   "cookie dough"

0   1   2   3   4

flavors

Notice that because we start numbering the indices of the array at 0, the length of the array will always be one more than the last index.

Sharpen your pencil

The products array below holds the Jenn and Berry's ice cream flavors. The ice cream flavors were added to this array in the order of their creation. Finish the code to determine the *most recent* ice cream flavor they created.

```
var products = ["Choo Choo Chocolate", "Icy Mint", "Cake Batter", "Bubblegum"];
var last = _____;
var recent = products[last];
```

Try my new Phrase-o-Matic and you'll be a slick talker just like the boss or those guys in marketing.

You didn't think our serious business application from Chapter 1 was serious enough? Fine. Try this one, if you need something to show the boss.

Check out this code for the hot new Phrase-o-Matic app and see if you can figure out what it does before you go on...

```html
<!doctype html>
<html lang="en">
<head>
  <title>Phrase-o-matic</title>
  <meta charset="utf-8">
  <script>
    function makePhrases() {
      var words1 = ["24/7", "multi-tier", "30,000 foot", "B-to-B", "win-win"];
      var words2 = ["empowered", "value-added", "oriented", "focused", "aligned"];
      var words3 = ["process", "solution", "tipping-point", "strategy", "vision"];

      var rand1 = Math.floor(Math.random() * words1.length);
      var rand2 = Math.floor(Math.random() * words2.length);
      var rand3 = Math.floor(Math.random() * words3.length);

      var phrase = words1[rand1] + " " + words2[rand2] + " " + words3[rand3];
      alert(phrase);
    }
    makePhrases();
  </script>
</head>
<body></body>
</html>
```

The Phrase-0-Matic

We hope you figured out this code is the perfect tool for creating
your next start-up marketing slogan. It has created winners like
"Win-win value-added solution" and "24/7 empowered process"
in the past and we have high hopes for more winners in the
future. Let's see how this thing really works:

① First, we define the `makePhrases` function, which we can call as many times as
we want to generate the phrases we want:

We're defining a function named
makePhrases, that we can call later.

```
function makePhrases() {

}
makePhrases();
```

All the code for makePhrases goes here, we'll get to it in a sec...

We call makePhrases once here, but we could call it
multiple times if we want more than one phrase.

② With that out of the way we can write the code for the `makePhrases` function. Let's start by
setting up three arrays. Each will hold words that we'll use to create the phrases. In the next
step, we'll pick one word at random from each array to make a three word phrase.

We create a variable named words1, that we
can use for the first array.

```
var words1 = ["24/7", "multi-tier", "30,000 foot", "B-to-B", "win-win"];
```

We're putting five strings in the array. Feel free to
change these to the latest buzzwords out there.

```
var words2 = ["empowered", "value-added", "oriented", "focused", "aligned"];
var words3 = ["process", "solution", "tipping-point", "strategy", "vision"];
```

And here are two more arrays of words, assigned
to two new variables, words2 and words3.

③ Now we generate three random numbers, one for each of the three random words we want to pick to make a phrase. Remember from Chapter 2 that Math.random generates a number between 0 and 1 (not including 1). If we multiply that by the length of the array, and use Math.floor to truncate the number, we get a number between 0 and one less than the length of the array.

```
var rand1 = Math.floor(Math.random() * words1.length);
var rand2 = Math.floor(Math.random() * words2.length);
var rand3 = Math.floor(Math.random() * words3.length);
```

rand1 will be a number between 0 and the last index of the words1 array.

And likewise for rand2, and rand3.

④ Now we create the slick marketing phrase by taking each randomly chosen word and concatenating them all together, with a nice space in between for readability:

We define another variable to hold the phrase.

We use each random number to index into the word arrays...

```
var phrase = words1[rand1] + " " + words2[rand2] + " " + words3[rand3];
```

⑤ We're almost done; we have the phrase, now we just have to display it. We're going to use alert as usual.

```
alert(phrase);
```

⑥ Okay, finish that last line of code, have one more look over it all and feel that sense of accomplishment before you load it into your browser. Give it a test drive and enjoy the phrases.

Here's what ours looks like!

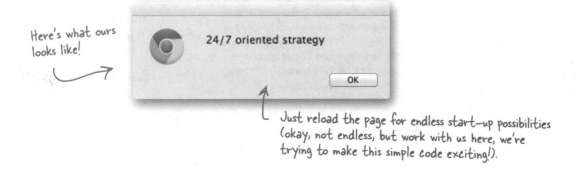

24/7 oriented strategy

OK

Just reload the page for endless start-up possibilities (okay, not endless, but work with us here, we're trying to make this simple code exciting!).

there are no
Dumb Questions

Q: Does the order of items in an array matter?

A: Most of the time, yes, but it depends. In the Bubbles-R-Us scores array, the ordering matters a lot, because the index of the score in the array tells us which bubble solution got that score—bubble solution 0 got score 60, and that score is stored at index 0. If we mixed up the scores in the array, then we'd ruin the experiment! However, in other cases, the order may not matter. For instance, if you're using an array just to keep a list of randomly selected words and you don't care about the order, then it doesn't matter which order they're in the array. But, if you later decide you want the words to be in alphabetical order, then the order will matter. So it really depends on how you're using the array. You'll probably find that ordering matters more often than not when you use an array.

Q: How many things can you put into an array?

A: Theoretically, as many as you want. Practically, however, the number is limited by the memory on your computer. Each array item takes up a little bit of space in memory. Remember that JavaScript runs in a browser, and that browser is one of many programs running on your computer. If you keep adding items to an array, eventually you'll run out of memory space. However, depending on the kind of items you're putting in your array, the maximum number of items you can put into an array is probably in the many thousands, if not millions, which you're unlikely to need most of the time. And keep in mind that the more items you have the slower your program will run, so you'll want to limit your arrays to reasonable sizes—say a few hundred—most of the time.

Q: Can you have an empty array?

A: You can, and in fact, you'll see an example of using an empty array shortly. To create an empty array, just write:

```
var emptyArray = [ ];
```

If you start with an empty array, you can add things to it later.

Q: So far we've seen strings and numbers in an array; can you put other things in arrays too?

A: You can; in fact, you can put just about any value you'll find in JavaScript in an array, including numbers, strings, booleans, other arrays, and even objects (we'll get to this later).

Q: Do all the values in an array have to be the same type?

A: No they don't; although typically we *do* make the values all of the same type. Unlike many other languages, there is no requirement in JavaScript that all the values in an array be of the same type. However, if you mix up the types of the values in an array, you need to be extra careful when using those values. Here's why: let's say you have an array with the values [1, 2, "fido", 4, 5]. If you then write code that checks to see if the values in the array are greater than, say, 2, what happens when you check to see if "fido" is greater than 2? To make sure you aren't doing something that doesn't make sense, you'd have to check the type of each of the values before you used it in the rest of your code. It's certainly possible to do this (and we'll see later in the book how), but in general, it's a lot easier and safer if you just use the same type for all the values in your arrays.

Q: What happens if you try to access an array with an index that is too big or too small (like less than 0)?

A: If you have an array, like:

```
var a = [1, 2, 3];
```

and you try to access a[10] or a[-1], in either case, you'll get the result undefined. So, you'll either want to make sure you're using only valid indices to access items in your array, or you'll need to check that the value you get back is not undefined.

Q: So, I can see how to get the first item in an array using index 0. But how would I get the last item in an array? Do I always have to know precisely how many items are in my array?

A: You can use the length property to get the last item of an array. You know that length is always one greater than the last index of the array, right? So, to get the last item in the array, you can write:

```
myArray[myArray.length - 1];
```

JavaScript gets the length of the array, subtracts one from it, and then gets the item at that index number. So if your array has 10 items, it will get the item at index 9, which is exactly what you want. You'll use this trick all the time to get the last item in an array when you don't know exactly how many items are in it.

Meanwhile, back at Bubbles-R-Us...

Hey, glad you guys are here. We just got a lot of new bubble tests run. Check out all the new bubble scores! I really need some help understanding this data. I'd love for you to code up what I sketched below.

The Bubbles-R-Us CEO

```
var scores = [60, 50, 60, 58, 54, 54,
              58, 50, 52, 54, 48, 69,
              34, 55, 51, 52, 44, 51,
              69, 64, 66, 55, 52, 61,
              46, 31, 57, 52, 44, 18,
              41, 53, 55, 61, 51, 44];
```

What we need to build. ⟍

New bubble scores.

Hey, I really need this report to be able to make quick decisions about which bubble solution to produce! Can you get this coded?

— Bubbles-R-Us CEO

Bubbles-R-Us

Bubble solution #0 score: 60
Bubble solution #1 score: 50
Bubble solution #2 score: 60

⟵ —— rest of scores here...

Bubbles tests: 36
Highest bubble score: 69
Solutions with highest score: #11, #18

Let's take a closer look at what the CEO is looking for:

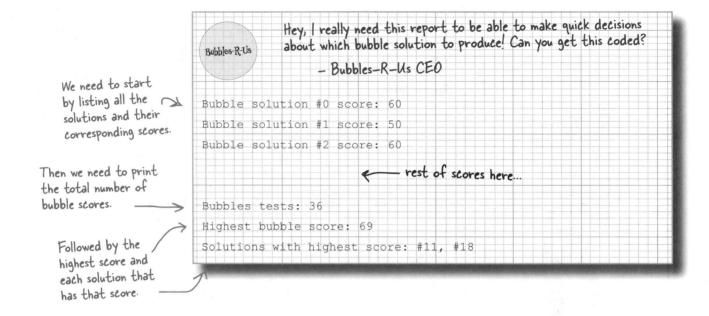

We need to start by listing all the solutions and their corresponding scores.

Then we need to print the total number of bubble scores.

Followed by the highest score and each solution that has that score.

BRAIN POWER

Take some time to sketch out your ideas of how you'd create this little bubble score report. Take each item in the report separately and think of how you'd break it down and generate the right output. Make your notes here.

Cubicle Conversation

Let's take a look at this report and see how we can tackle coding it...

Frank

Judy

Joe

Judy: The first thing we need to do is display every score along with its solution number.

Joe: And the solution number is just the index of the score in the array, right?

Judy: Oh, yeah, that's totally right.

Frank: Slow down a sec. So we need to take each score, print its index, which is the bubble solution number, and then print the corresponding score.

Judy: You've got it, and the score is just the corresponding value in the array.

Joe: So, for bubble solution #10, its score is just `scores[10]`.

Judy: Right.

Frank: Okay, but there are a lot of scores. How do we write code to output all of them?

Judy: Iteration, my friend.

Frank: Oh, you mean like a while loop?

Judy: Right, we loop through all the values from zero to the length... oh, I mean the length minus one of course.

Joe: This is starting to sound very doable. Let's write some code; I think we know what we're doing.

Judy: That works for me! Let's do it, and then we'll come back to the rest of the report.

How to iterate over an array

Your goal is to produce some output that looks like this:

```
Bubble solution #0 score: 60
Bubble solution #1 score: 50
Bubble solution #2 score: 60
   .
   .
   .
Bubble solution #35 score: 44
```

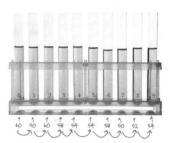

← *Scores 3 through 34 will be here... we're saving some trees (or bits depending on which version of the book you have).*

We'll do that by outputting the score at index zero, and then we'll do the same for index one, two, three and so on, until we reach the last index in the array. You already know how to use a while loop; let's see how we can use that to output all the scores:

And then we'll show you a better way in a sec...

```
var scores = [60, 50, 60, 58, 54, 54, 58, 50, 52, 54, 48, 69,
              34, 55, 51, 52, 44, 51, 69, 64, 66, 55, 52, 61,
              46, 31, 57, 52, 44, 18, 41, 53, 55, 61, 51, 44];

var output;
```
We're using this variable in the loop below to create a string to output.

```
var i = 0;
```
Create a variable to keep track of the current index.

```
while (i < scores.length) {
```
And keep looping while our index is less than the length of the array.

```
  output = "Bubble solution #" + i + " score: " + scores[i];

  console.log(output);

  i = i + 1;

}
```

Then create a string to use as a line of output that includes the bubble solution number (which is just the array index) and the score.

Then we'll use console.log to output the string.

And finally, increment the index by one before looping again.

Code Magnets

We've got code for testing to see which ice cream flavors have bubblegum pieces in them. We had all the code nicely laid out on our fridge using fridge magnets, but the magnets fell on the floor. It's your job to put them back together. Be careful; a few extra magnets got mixed in. Check your answer at the end of the chapter before you go on.

```
while (i < hasBubbleGum.length)
```

```
i = i + 2;
```

```
{
```

```
}
```

```
i = i + 1;
```

```
}
```

```
var i = 0;
```

```
{
```

```
{
```

```
if (hasBubbleGum[i])
```

```
while (i > hasBubbleGum.length)
```

```
var products = ["Choo Choo Chocolate",
            "Icy Mint", "Cake Batter",
            "Bubblegum"];
```

```
var hasBubbleGum = [false,
                    false,
                    false,
                    true];
```

```
console.log(products[i] +
    " contains bubble gum");
```

↑
Rearrange the magnets here.

Here's the output we're expecting. ↙

JavaScript console

Bubblegum contains bubble gum

But wait, there's a better way to iterate over an array

We should really apologize. We can't believe it's already Chapter 4 and we haven't even introduced you to the **for loop**. Think of the for loop as the while loop's cousin. The two basically do the same thing, except the for loop is usually a little more convenient to use. Check out the while loop we just used and we'll see how that maps into a for loop.

First we INITIALIZED a counter.

Ⓐ `var i = 0;`
`while` Ⓑ `(i < scores.length) {`

Then we tested that counter in a CONDITIONAL expression.

```
output = "Bubble solution #" + i + " score: " + scores[i];
console.log(output);
```
Ⓒ `i = i + 1;`
`}`

We also had a BODY to execute; that is, all the statements between the { and }.

And finally, we INCREMENTED the counter.

Now let's look at how the for loop makes all that so much easier:

In the parentheses, there are three parts. The first part is the loop variable INITIALIZATION. This initialization happens only once, before the for loop starts.

The second part is the CONDITIONAL test. Each time we loop, we perform this test, and if it is false, we stop.

And the third part is where we INCREMENT the counter. This happens once per loop, after all the statements in the BODY.

A for loop starts with the keyword for.

```
for (var i = 0; i < scores.length; i = i + 1) {
    output = "Bubble solution #" + i + " score: " + scores[i];
    console.log(output);
}
```

Ⓐ Ⓑ Ⓒ

The BODY goes here. Notice there are no changes other than moving the increment of i into the for statement.

Sharpen your pencil

Rewrite your fridge magnet code (from two pages back) so that it uses a for loop instead of a while loop. If you need a hint, refer to each piece of the while loop on the previous page and see how it maps to the corresponding location in the for loop.

```
var products = ["Choo Choo Chocolate",
                "Icy Mint", "Cake Batter",
                "Bubblegum"];
```

```
var hasBubbleGum = [false,
                    false,
                    false,
                    true];
```

```
var i = 0;
```
```
while (i < hasBubbleGum.length)
```
`{`

```
if (hasBubbleGum[i])
```
`{`

```
console.log(products[i] +
    " contains bubble gum");
```

`}`

```
i = i + 1;
```

`}`

Your code goes here.

We've got all the pieces for the first part of the report, let's put this all together...

We've got the standard HTML stuff here for a web page. We don't need much; just enough to create a script.

```html
<!doctype html>
<html lang="en">
<head>
  <meta charset="utf-8">
  <title>Bubble Factory Test Lab</title>
  <script>
    var scores = [60, 50, 60, 58, 54, 54,
                  58, 50, 52, 54, 48, 69,
                  34, 55, 51, 52, 44, 51,
                  69, 64, 66, 55, 52, 61,
                  46, 31, 57, 52, 44, 18,
                  41, 53, 55, 61, 51, 44];

    var output;

    for (var i = 0; i < scores.length; i = i + 1) {

        output = "Bubble solution #" + i +
                    " score: " + scores[i];

        console.log(output);

    }
  </script>
</head>
<body></body>
</html>
```

Here's our bubble scores array.

Here's the for loop we're using to iterate through all the bubble solution scores.

Each time through the loop, we create a string with the value of i, which is the bubble solution number, and scores[i], which is the score that bubble solution got.

(Also notice we split the string up across two lines here. That's okay as long as you don't create a new line in between the quotes that delimit a string. Here, we did it after a concatenation operator (+), so it's okay. Be careful to type it in exactly as you see here.)

Then we display the string in the console. And that's it! Time to run this report.

Test drive the bubble report

Save this file as "bubbles.html" and load it into your browser. Make sure you've got the console visible (you might need to reload the page if you activate the console after you load the page), and check out the brilliant report you just generated for the Bubbles-R-Us CEO.

Just what the CEO ordered.

It's nice to see all the bubble scores in a report, but it's still hard to find the highest scores. We need to work on the rest of the report requirements to make it a little easier to find the winner.

```
JavaScript console

Bubble solution #0 score: 60
Bubble solution #1 score: 50
Bubble solution #2 score: 60
Bubble solution #3 score: 58
Bubble solution #4 score: 54
Bubble solution #5 score: 54
Bubble solution #6 score: 58
Bubble solution #7 score: 50
Bubble solution #8 score: 52
Bubble solution #9 score: 54
Bubble solution #10 score: 48
Bubble solution #11 score: 69
Bubble solution #12 score: 34
Bubble solution #13 score: 55
Bubble solution #14 score: 51
Bubble solution #15 score: 52
Bubble solution #16 score: 44
Bubble solution #17 score: 51
Bubble solution #18 score: 69
Bubble solution #19 score: 64
Bubble solution #20 score: 66
Bubble solution #21 score: 55
Bubble solution #22 score: 52
Bubble solution #23 score: 61
Bubble solution #24 score: 46
Bubble solution #25 score: 31
Bubble solution #26 score: 57
Bubble solution #27 score: 52
Bubble solution #28 score: 44
Bubble solution #29 score: 18
Bubble solution #30 score: 41
Bubble solution #31 score: 53
Bubble solution #32 score: 55
Bubble solution #33 score: 61
Bubble solution #34 score: 51
Bubble solution #35 score: 44
```

Fireside Chats

Tonight's talk: **The while and for loop answer the question "Who's more important?"**

The WHILE loop

What, are you kidding me? Hello? I'm the *general* looping construct in JavaScript. I'm not married to looping with a silly counter. I can be used with any type of conditional. Did anyone notice I was taught first in this book?

And that's another thing, have you noticed that the FOR loop has no sense of humor? I mean if we all had to do skull-numbing iteration all day I guess we'd all be that way.

Oh, I don't think that could possibly be true.

This book just showed that FOR and WHILE loops are pretty much the same thing, so how could that be?

The FOR loop

I don't appreciate that tone.

Cute. But have you noticed that nine times out of ten, coders use FOR loops?

Not to mention, doing iteration over, say, an array that has a fixed number of items with a WHILE loop is just a bad, clumsy practice.

Ah, so you admit we're more equal than you let on huh?

I'll tell you why...

The WHILE loop

The FOR loop

When you use a WHILE loop you have to initialize your counter and increment your counter in separate statements. If, after lots of code changes, you accidentally moved or deleted one of these statements, well, then things could get ugly. But with a FOR loop, everything is packaged right in the FOR statement for all to see and with no chance of things getting changed or lost.

Well, isn't that nice and neat of you. Hey, most of the iteration I see doesn't even include counters; it's stuff like:

```
while (answer != "forty-two")
```

try that with a FOR loop!

Okay:

```
for (;answer != "forty-two";)
```

Hah, I can't believe that even works.

Oh, it does.

Lipstick on a pig.

So that's all you got? You're better when you've got a general conditional?

Not only better, prettier.

Oh, I didn't realize this was a beauty contest as well.

It's that time again....
Can we talk about your verbosity?

You've been writing lots of code that looks like this:

Assume myImportantCounter contains a number, like 0.

Here we're taking the variable and incrementing it by one.

```
myImportantCounter = myImportantCounter + 1;
```

After this statement completes, myImportantCounter is one greater than before.

In fact, this statement is so common there's a shortcut for it in JavaScript. It's called the post-increment operator, and despite its fancy name, it is quite simple. Using the post-increment operator, we can replace the above line of code with this:

Just add "++" to the variable name.

```
myImportantCounter++;
```

After this statement completes, myImportantCounter is one greater than before.

Of course it just wouldn't feel right if there wasn't a post-decrement operator as well. You can use the post-decrement operator on a variable to reduce its value by one. Like this:

Just add "−−" to the variable name.

```
myImportantCounter--;
```

After this statement completes, myImportantCounter is one less than before.

And why are we telling you this now? Because it's commonly used with `for` statements. Let's clean up our code a little using the post-increment operator...

Redoing the for loop with the post-increment operator

Let's do a quick rewrite and test to make sure the code works the same as before:

```
var scores = [60, 50, 60, 58, 54, 54,
              58, 50, 52, 54, 48, 69,
              34, 55, 51, 52, 44, 51,
              69, 64, 66, 55, 52, 61,
              46, 31, 57, 52, 44, 18,
              41, 53, 55, 61, 51, 44];

for (var i = 0; i < scores.length; i++) {

    var output = "Bubble solution #" + i +
                 " score: " + scores[i];

    console.log(output);

}
```

All we've done is update where we increment the loop variable with the post-increment operator.

Quick test drive

Time to do a quick test drive to make sure the change to use the post-increment operator works. Save your file, "bubbles.html", and reload. You should see the same report you saw before.

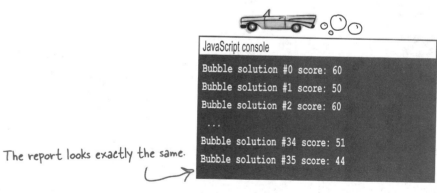

The report looks exactly the same.

We're saving a few trees and not showing all the bubble solution scores, but they are all there.

Cubicle Conversation Continued...

We've got all the bubble solution scores displaying, now we just need to generate the rest of the report.

Judy: Right, and the first thing we need to do is determine the total number of bubble tests. That's easy; it's just the length of the scores array.

Joe: Oh, right. We've got to find the highest score too, and then the solutions that have the highest score.

Hey, I really need this report to be able to make quick decisions about which bubble solution to produce! Can you get this coded?

— Bubbles-R-Us CEO

```
Bubble solution #0 score: 60
Bubble solution #1 score: 50
Bubble solution #2 score: 60

        ←— rest of scores here...

Bubbles tests: 36
Highest bubble score: 69
Solutions with highest score: #11, #18
```

Judy: Yeah, that last one is going to be the toughest. Let's work out finding the highest score first.

Joe: Sounds like a good place to start.

Judy: To do that I think we just need to maintain a highest score variable that keeps track as we interate through the array. Here, let me write some pseudocode:

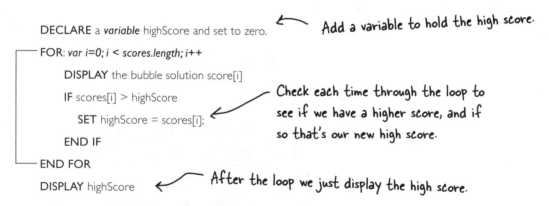

DECLARE a *variable* highScore and set to zero. ←— Add a variable to hold the high score.

FOR: *var i=0; i < scores.length; i++*

    DISPLAY the bubble solution score[i]

    IF scores[i] > highScore

        SET highScore = scores[i]; ←— Check each time through the loop to see if we have a higher score, and if so that's our new high score.

    END IF

END FOR

DISPLAY highScore ←— After the loop we just display the high score.

Joe: Oh nice; you did it with just a few lines added to our existing code.

Judy: Each time through the array we look to see if the current score is greater than highScore, and if so, that's our new high score. Then, after the loop ends we just display the high score.

Sharpen your pencil

Go ahead and implement the pseudocode on the previous page to find the highest score by filling in the blanks in the code below. Once you're done, give it a try in the browser by updating the code in "bubbles.html" and reloading the page. Check the results in the console, and fill in the blanks in our console display below with the number of bubble tests and the highest score. Check your answer at the end of the chapter before you go on.

```
var scores = [60, 50, 60, 58, 54, 54,
              58, 50, 52, 54, 48, 69,
              34, 55, 51, 52, 44, 51,
              69, 64, 66, 55, 52, 61,
              46, 31, 57, 52, 44, 18,
              41, 53, 55, 61, 51, 44];

var highScore = _____;
var output;
for (var i = 0; i < scores.length; i++) {
    output = "Bubble solution #" + i + " score: " + scores[i];
    console.log(output);
    if (_____ > highScore) {
        _____ = scores[i];
    }
}
console.log("Bubbles tests: " + _____);
console.log("Highest bubble score: " + _____);
```

← Fill in the blanks to complete the code here...

... and then fill in the blanks showing the output you get in the console.

```
JavaScript console
Bubble solution #0 score: 60
Bubble solution #1 score: 50
Bubble solution #2 score: 60
   ...
Bubble solution #34 score: 51
Bubble solution #35 score: 44
Bubbles tests: _____
Highest bubble score: _____
```

Hey you guys are almost there! All you've got left is collecting up all the solutions with highest score and printing them. Remember, there might be more than one.

"More than one"...hmmm. When we need to store more than one thing what do we use? An array, of course. So can we iterate through the scores array looking for only scores that match the highest score, and then add them to an array that we can later display in the report? You bet we can, but to do that we'll have to learn how to create a brand new, empty array, and then understand how to add new elements to it.

Remember here's what we have left.

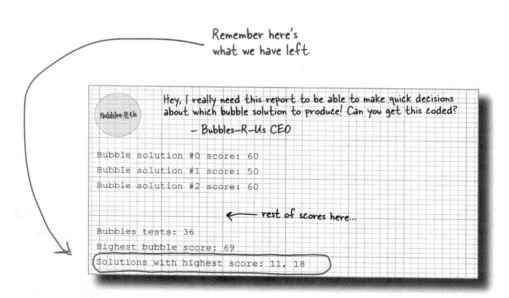

Hey, I really need this report to be able to make quick decisions about which bubble solution to produce! Can you get this coded?

— Bubbles-R-Us CEO

Bubbles-R-Us

```
Bubble solution #0 score: 60
Bubble solution #1 score: 50
Bubble solution #2 score: 60
```

← *rest of scores here...*

```
Bubbles tests: 36
Highest bubble score: 69
Solutions with highest score: 11, 18
```

Creating an array from scratch (and adding to it)

Before we take on finishing this code, let's get a sense for how to create a new array, and how to add new items to it. You already know how to create an array with values, like this:

```
var genres = ["80s", "90s", "Electronic", "Folk"];
```

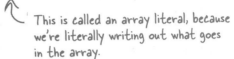

This is called an array literal, because we're literally writing out what goes in the array.

But you can also omit the initial items and just create an empty array:

```
var genres = [];
```

A new array, all ready to go with no items and a length of zero.

This is an array literal too, it just doesn't have anything in it (yet).

And you already know how to add new values to an array. To do that you just assign a value to an item at an index, like this:

```
var genres = [];
genres[0] = "Rockabilly";
genres[1] = "Ambient";
var size = genres.length;
```

A new array item is created and it holds the string "Rockabilly".

And a second array item is created that holds the string "Ambient".

And here size holds the value 2, the length of the array.

Now when adding new items you have to be careful about which index you're adding. Otherwise you'll create a sparse array, which is an array with "holes" in it (like an array with values at 0 and 2, but no value at 1). Having a sparse array isn't necessarily a bad thing, but it does require special attention. For now, there's another way to add new items without worrying about the index, and that's push. Here's how it works:

```
var genres = [];
genres.push("Rockabilly");
genres.push("Ambient");
var size = genres.length;
```

Creates a new item in the next available index (which happens to be 0) and sets its value to "Rockabilly".

Creates another new item in the next open index (in this case, 1) and sets the value to "Ambient".

there are no
Dumb Questions

Q: The for statement contains a variable declaration and initialization in the first part of the statement. You said we should put our variable declarations at the top. So, what gives?

A: Yes, putting your variable declarations at the top (of your file, if they are global, or of your function if they are local) is a good practice. However, there are times when it makes sense to declare a variable right where you're going to use it, and a for statement is one of those times. Typically, you use a loop variable, like i, just for iterating, and once the loop is done, you're done with that variable. Now, you might use i later in your code, of course, but typically you won't. So, in this case, just declaring it right in the for statement keeps things tidy.

Q: What does the syntax myarray. push(value) actually mean?

A: Well, we've been keeping a little secret from you: in JavaScript, an array is actually a special kind of object. As you'll learn in the next chapter, an object can have functions associated with it that act on the object. So, think of push as a function that can act on myarray. In this case, what that function does is add a new item to the array, the item that you pass as an argument to push. So, if you write

```
genres.push("Metal");
```
you're calling the function push and passing it a string argument, "Metal". The push function takes that argument and adds it as a new value on the end of the genres array. When you see `myarray.push(value)` just think, "I'm pushing a new value on the end of my array."

Q: Can you say a little more about what a sparse array is?

A: A sparse array is just an array that has values at only a few indices and no values in between. You can create a sparse array easily, like this:

```
var sparseArray = [ ];
sparseArray[0] = true;
spraseArray[100] = true;
```
In this example, the sparseArray has only two values, both true, at indices 0 and 100. The values at all the other indices are undefined. The length of the array is 101 even though there are only two values.

Q: Say I have an array of length 10, and I add a new item at index 10000, what happens with indices 10 through 9999?

A: All those array indices get the value undefined. If you remember, undefined is the value assigned to a variable that you haven't initialized. So, think of this as if you're creating 9989 variables, but not initializing them. Remember that all those variables take up memory in your computer, even if they don't have a value, so make sure you have a good reason to create a sparse array.

Q: So, if I'm iterating through an array, and some of the values are undefined, should I check to make sure before I use them?

A: If you think your array might be sparse, or even have just one undefined value in it, then yes, you should probably check to make sure that the value at an array index is not undefined before you use it. If all you're doing is displaying

the value in the console, then it's no big deal, but it's much more likely that you'll actually want to use that value somehow, perhaps in a calculation of some kind. In that case, if you try to use undefined, you might get an error, or at the very least, some unexpected behavior. To check for undefined, just write:

```
if (myarray[i] == undefined) {
    ...
}
```
Notice there are no quotes around undefined (because it's not a string, it's a value).

Q: All the arrays we've created so far have been literal. Is there another way to create an array?

A: Yes. You may have seen the syntax:
```
var myarray = new Array(3);
```
What this does is create a new array, with three empty spots in it (that is, an array with length 3, but no values yet). Then you can fill them, just like you normally would, by providing values for myarray at indices 0, 1, and 2. Until you add values yourself, the values in myarray are undefined.

An array created this way is just the same as an array literal, and in practice, you'll find yourself using the literal syntax more often, and that's what we'll tend to use in the rest of the book.

And don't worry about the details of the syntax above for now (like "new" and why Array is capitalized); we'll get to all that later!

> Now that we know how to add items to an array we can finish up this report. We can just create the array of the solutions with the highest score as we iterate through the scores array to find the highest bubble score, right?

Judy: Yes, we'll start with an empty array to hold the solutions with the highest scores, and add each solution that has that high score one at a time to it as we iterate through the scores array.

Frank: Great, let's get started.

Judy: But hold on a second… I think we might need a separate loop.

Frank: We do? Seems like there should be a way to do it in our existing loop.

Judy: Yup, I'm sure we do. Here's why. We have to know what the highest score is *before* we can find all the solutions that have that highest score. So we need two loops: one to find the highest score, which we've already written, and then a second one to find all the solutions that have that score.

Frank: Oh, I see. And in the second loop, we'll compare each score to the highest score, and if it matches, we'll add the index of the bubble solution score to the new array we're creating for the solutions with the highest scores.

Judy: Exactly! Let's do it.

Sharpen your pencil

Can you write the loop to find all the scores that match the high score? Give it a shot below before you turn the page to see the solution and give it a test drive.

Remember, the variable highScore has the highest score in it; you can use that in the code below.

```
                                    Here's the new array we'll use to store the bubble
                                    solutions with the highest score.
var bestSolutions = [];
for (var i = 0; i < scores.length; i++) {

                        ←—— Your code here.



}
```

Sharpen your pencil
Solution

Can you write the loop to find all the scores that match the high score?
Here's our solution.

Again, we're starting by creating a
new array that will hold all the bubble
solutions that match the highest score.

Next, we iterate through the entire
scores array, looking for those items
with the highest score.

```
var bestSolutions = [];

for (var i = 0; i < scores.length; i++) {
    if (scores[i] == highScore) {

        bestSolutions.push(i);

    }
}

console.log("Solutions with the highest score: " + bestSolutions);
```

Each time through the loop, we
compare the score at index i with
the highScore and if they are equal,
then we add that index to the
bestSolutions array using push.

And finally, we can display the bubble solutions with the highest scores. Notice we're
using console.log to display the bestSolutions array. We could create another loop to
display the array items one by one, but, luckily, console.log will do this for us (and, if
you look at the output, it also adds commas between the array values!).

 **BRAIN POWER**

Take a look at the code in the Sharpen exercise above. What if you woke up and push no longer
existed? Could you rewrite this code without using push? Work that code out here:

Test drive the final report

Go ahead and add the code to generate the bubble solutions with the highest score to your code in "bubbles.html" and run another test drive. All the JavaScript code is shown below:

```javascript
var scores = [60, 50, 60, 58, 54, 54,
              58, 50, 52, 54, 48, 69,
              34, 55, 51, 52, 44, 51,
              69, 64, 66, 55, 52, 61,
              46, 31, 57, 52, 44, 18,
              41, 53, 55, 61, 51, 44];

var highScore = 0;
var output;
for (var i = 0; i < scores.length; i++) {
    output = "Bubble solution #" + i + " score: " + scores[i];
    console.log(output);
    if (scores[i] > highScore) {
        highScore = scores[i];
    }
}
console.log("Bubbles tests: " + scores.length);
console.log("Highest bubble score: " + highScore);

var bestSolutions = [];
for (var i = 0; i < scores.length; i++) {
    if (scores[i] == highScore) {
        bestSolutions.push(i);
    }
}
console.log("Solutions with the highest score: " + bestSolutions);
```

And the winners are...

Bubble solutions #11 and #18 both have a high score of 69! So they are the best bubble solutions in this batch of test solutions.

```
JavaScript console

Bubble solution #0 score: 60
Bubble solution #1 score: 50
  ...
Bubble solution #34 score: 51
Bubbles tests: 36
Highest bubble score: 69
Solutions with the highest score: 11,18
```

We spent a lot of time in the last chapter talking about functions. How come we're not using any?

You're right, we should be. Given you just learned functions, we wanted to get the basics of arrays out of the way before employing them. That said, you always want to think about which parts of your code you can abstract away into a function. Not only that, but say you wanted to reuse, or let others reuse, all the work that went into writing the bubble computations—you'd want to give other developers a nice set of functions they could work with.

Let's go back to the Bubble Score code and *refactor* it into a set of functions. By refactor we mean we're going to rework how it's organized, to make it more readable and maintainable, but we're going to do it without altering what the code does. In other words, when we're done, the code will do exactly what it does now but it'll be a lot better organized.

A quick survey of the code...

Let's get an overview of the code we've written and figure out which pieces we want to abstract into functions:

Here's the Bubbles-R-Us code.

```
<!doctype html>
<html lang="en">
<head>
  <meta charset="utf-8">
  <title>Bubble Factory Test Lab</title>
  <script>
    var scores = [60, 50, 60, 58, 54, 54,
                  58, 50, 52, 54, 48, 69,
                  34, 55, 51, 52, 44, 51,
                  69, 64, 66, 55, 52, 61,
                  46, 31, 57, 52, 44, 18,
                  41, 53, 55, 61, 51, 44];

    var highScore = 0;
    var output;

    for (var i = 0; i < scores.length; i++) {
      output = "Bubble solution #" + i + " score: " + scores[i];
      console.log(output);
      if (scores[i] > highScore) {
        highScore = scores[i];
      }
    }
    console.log("Bubbles tests: " + scores.length);
    console.log("Highest bubble score: " + highScore);

    var bestSolutions = [];

    for (var i = 0; i < scores.length; i++) {
      if (scores[i] == highScore) {
        bestSolutions.push(i);
      }
    }

    console.log("Solutions with the highest score: " + bestSolutions);
  </script>
</head>
<body> </body>
</html>
```

We don't want to declare scores inside the functions that operate on scores because these are going to be different for each use of the functions. Instead, we'll pass the scores as an argument into the functions, so the functions can use any scores array to generate results.

We use this first chunk of code to output each score and at the same time compute the highest score in the array. We could put this in a printAndGetHighScore function.

And we use this second chunk of code to figure out the best results given a high score. We could put this in a getBestResults function.

Writing the printAndGetHighScore function

We've got the code for the `printAndGetHighScore` function already. It's just the code we've already written, but to make it a function we need to think through what arguments we're passing it, and if it returns anything back to us.

Now, passing in the scores array seems like a good idea because that way, we can reuse the function on other arrays with bubble scores. And we want to return the high score that we compute in the function, so the code that calls the function can do interesting things with it (and, after all, we're going to need it to figure out the best solutions).

Oh, and another thing: often you want your functions to do *one thing* well. Here we're doing two things: we're displaying all the scores in the array and we're also computing the high score. We might want to consider breaking this into two functions, but given how simple things are right now we're going to resist the temptation. If we were working in a professional environment we might reconsider and break this into two functions, `printScores` and `getHighScore`. But for now, we'll stick with one function. Let's get this code refactored:

We've created a function that expects one argument, the scores array.

```
function printAndGetHighScore(scores) {
    var highScore = 0;
    var output;
    for (var i = 0; i < scores.length; i++) {
        output = "Bubble solution #" + i + " score: " + scores[i];
        console.log(output);
        if (scores[i] > highScore) {
            highScore = scores[i];
        }
    }
    return highScore;
}
```

This code is exactly the same. Well, actually it LOOKS exactly the same, but it now uses the parameter scores rather than the global variable scores.

And we've added one line here to return the highScore to the code that called the function.

Refactoring the code using printAndGetHighScore

Now, we need to change the rest of the code to use our new function. To do so, we simply call the new function, and set the variable `highScore` to the result of the `printAndGetHighScore` function:

```html
<!doctype html>
<html lang="en">
<head>
  <title>Bubble Factory Test Lab</title>
  <meta charset="utf-8">
  <script>
    var scores = [60, 50, 60, 58, 54, 54, 58, 50, 52, 54, 48, 69,
                  34, 55, 51, 52, 44, 51, 69, 64, 66, 55, 52, 61,
                  46, 31, 57, 52, 44, 18, 41, 53, 55, 61, 51, 44];

    function printAndGetHighScore(scores) {
        var highScore = 0;
        var output;
        for (var i = 0; i < scores.length; i++) {
            output = "Bubble solution #" + i + " score: " + scores[i];
            console.log(output);
            if (scores[i] > highScore) {
                highScore = scores[i];
            }
        }
        return highScore;
    }

    var highScore = printAndGetHighScore(scores);
    console.log("Bubbles tests: " + scores.length);
    console.log("Highest bubble score: " + highScore);

    var bestSolutions = [];

    for (var i = 0; i < scores.length; i++) {
      if (scores[i] == highScore) {
        bestSolutions.push(i);
      }
    }

    console.log("Solutions with the highest score: " + bestSolutions);
  </script>
</head>
<body> </body>
</html>
```

Here's our new function, all ready to use.

And now we just call the function, passing in the scores array. We assign the value it returns to the variable highScore.

Now we need to refactor this code into a function and make the appropriate changes to the rest of the code.

Sharpen your pencil

Let's work through this next one together. The goal is to write a function to create an array of bubble solutions that have the high score (and there might be more than one, so that's why we're using an array). We're going to pass this function the scores array and the highScore we computed with printAndGetHighScore. Finish the code below. You'll find the answer on the next page but don't peek! Do the code yourself first, so you really get it.

Here's the original code in case you need to refer to it.

```
var bestSolutions = [];
for (var i = 0; i < scores.length; i++) {
    if (scores[i] == highScore) {
        bestSolutions.push(i);
    }
}
console.log("Solutions with the highest score: " + bestSolutions);
```

We've already started this but we need your help to finish it!

```
function getBestResults(_____, _____) {
    var bestSolutions = _____;
    for (var i = 0; i < scores.length; i++) {
        if (_____ == highScore) {
            bestSolutions._____;
        }
    }
    return _____;
}


var bestSolutions = _____(scores, highScore);
console.log("Solutions with the highest score: " + bestSolutions);
```

Putting it all together...

Once you've completed refactoring your code, make all the changes to "bubbles.html", just like we have below, and reload the bubble report. You should get exactly the same results as before. But now you know your code is more organized and reusable. Create your own scores array and try some reuse!

```html
<!doctype html>
<html lang="en">
<head>
  <meta charset="utf-8">
  <title>Bubble Factory Test Lab</title>
  <script>
    var scores = [60, 50, 60, 58, 54, 54, 58, 50, 52, 54, 48, 69,
                  34, 55, 51, 52, 44, 51, 69, 64, 66, 55, 52, 61,
                  46, 31, 57, 52, 44, 18, 41, 53, 55, 61, 51, 44];

    function printAndGetHighScore(scores) {
        var highScore = 0;
        var output;
        for (var i = 0; i < scores.length; i++) {
            output = "Bubble solution #" + i + " score: " + scores[i];
            console.log(output);
            if (scores[i] > highScore) {
                highScore = scores[i];
            }
        }
        return highScore;
    }

    function getBestResults(scores, highScore) {
        var bestSolutions = [];
        for (var i = 0; i < scores.length; i++) {
            if (scores[i] == highScore) {
                bestSolutions.push(i);
            }
        }
        return bestSolutions;
    }

    var highScore = printAndGetHighScore(scores);
    console.log("Bubbles tests: " + scores.length);
    console.log("Highest bubble score: " + highScore);

    var bestSolutions = getBestResults(scores, highScore);
    console.log("Solutions with the highest score: " + bestSolutions);

  </script>
</head>
<body> </body>
</html>
```

Okay, here's the new getBestResults function.

And we use the result of that function to display the best solutions in the report.

Great job! Just one more thing... can you figure out the most cost effective bubble solution? With that final bit of data, we'll definitely take over the entire bubble solution market. Here's an array with the cost of each solution you can use to figure it out.

Here's the array. Notice that it has a cost for each of the corresponding solutions in the scores array.

```
var costs = [.25, .27, .25, .25, .25, .25,
             .33, .31, .25, .29, .27, .22,
             .31, .25, .25, .33, .21, .25,
             .25, .25, .28, .25, .24, .22,
             .20, .25, .30, .25, .24, .25,
             .25, .25, .27, .25, .26, .29];
```

So, what's the job here? It's to take the leading bubble solutions—that is, the ones with the highest bubble scores—and choose the lowest cost one. Now, luckily, we've been given a `costs` array that mirrors the `scores` array. That is, the bubble solution score at index 0 in the `scores` array has the cost at index 0 in the `costs` array (.25), the bubble solution at index 1 in the `scores` array has a cost at index 1 in the `costs` array (.27), and so on. So, for any score you'll find its cost in the `costs` array at the same index. Sometimes we call these *parallel* arrays:

Scores and costs are parallel arrays because for each score there is a corresponding cost at the same index.

```
var costs = [.25, .27, .25, .25, .25, .25, .33, .31, .25, .29, .27, .22, ..., .29];
```

The cost at 0 is the cost of the bubble solution at 0...

And likewise for the other cost and score values in the arrays.

```
var scores = [60, 50, 60, 58, 54, 54, 58, 50, 52, 54, 48, 69, ..., 44];
```

This seems a little tricky. How do we determine not only the scores that are highest, but then pick the one with the lowest cost?

Judy: Well, we know the highest score already.

Frank: Right, but how do we use that? And we have these two arrays, how do we get those to work together?

Judy: I'm pretty sure either of us could write a simple for loop that goes through the `scores` array again and picks up the items that match the highest score.

Frank: Yeah, I could do that. But then what?

Judy: Anytime we hit a score that matches the highest score, we need to see if its cost is the lowest we've seen.

Frank: Oh I see, so we'll have a variable that keeps track of the index of the "lowest cost high score." Wow, that's a mouthful.

Judy: Exactly. And once we get through the entire array, whatever index is in that variable is the index of the item that not only matches the highest score, but has the lowest cost.

Frank: What if two items match in cost?

Judy: Hmm, we have to decide how to handle that. I'd say, whatever one we see first is the winner. Of course we could do something more complex, but let's stick with that unless the CEO says differently.

Frank: This is complicated enough I think I want to sketch out some pseudocode before writing anything.

Judy: I agree; whenever you are managing indices of multiple arrays things can get tricky. Let's do that; in the long run I'm sure it will be faster to plan it first.

Frank: Okay, I'll take a first stab at it…

Exercise

I'm pretty sure I nailed the pseudocode. Check it out below. Now you go ahead and translate it into JavaScript. Make sure to check your answer.

FUNCTION GETMOSTCOSTEFFECTIVESOLUTION (SCORE, COSTS, HIGHSCORE)

DECLARE a *variable* cost and set to 100.

DECLARE a *variable* index.

FOR: *var i=0; i < scores.length; i++*

    IF the bubble solution at score[i] has the highest score

      IF the current value of cost is greater than the cost of the bubble solution

      THEN

        SET the value of index to the value of i

        SET the value of cost to the cost of the bubble solution

      END IF

    END IF

END FOR

RETURN index

```
function getMostCostEffectiveSolution(scores, costs, highscore) {
```

← Translate the pseudocode to JavaScript here.

```
}
var mostCostEffective = getMostCostEffectiveSolution(scores, costs, highScore);
console.log("Bubble Solution #" + mostCostEffective + " is the most cost effective");
```

THE WINNER: SOLUTION #11

The last bit of code you wrote really helped determine the TRUE winner; that is, the solution that produces the most bubbles at the lowest cost. Congrats on taking a lot of data and crunching it down to something Bubbles-R-Us can make real business decisions with.

Now, if you're like us, you're dying to know what is in Bubble Solution #11. Look no further; the Bubble-R-Us CEO said he'd be delighted to give you the recipe after all your unpaid work.

So, you'll find the recipe for Bubble Solution #11 below. Take some time to let your brain process arrays by making a batch, getting out, and blowing some bubbles before you begin the next chapter. Oh, but don't forget the bullet points and the crossword before you go!

Bubble Solution #11

2/3 cup dishwashing soap

1 gallon water

2 to 3 tablespoons of glycerine (available at the pharmacy or chemical supply house.)

INSTRUCTIONS: Mix ingredients together in a large bowl and have fun!

DO try this at HOME!

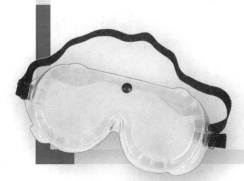

BULLET POINTS

- Arrays are a **data structure** for ordered data.

- An array holds a set of items, each with its own **index**.

- Arrays use a zero-based index, where the first item is at index zero.

- All arrays have a **length** property, which holds a number representing the number of items in the array.

- You can access any item using its index. For example, use myArray[1] to access item one (the second item in the array).

- If an item doesn't exist, trying to access it will result in a value of undefined.

- Assigning a value to an existing item will change its value.

- Assigning a value to an item that doesn't exist in the array will create a new item in the array.

- You can use a value of any type for an array item.

- Not all the values in an array need to be the same type.

- Use the **array literal notation** to create a new array.

- You can create an empty array with var myArray = [ ];

- The **for loop** is commonly used to iterate through arrays.

- A for loop packages up variable initialization, a conditional test, and variable increment into one statement.

- The while loop is most often used when you don't know how many times you need to loop, and you're looping until a condition is met. The for loop is most often used when you know the number of times the loop needs to execute.

- Sparse arrays occur when there are undefined items in the middle of an array.

- You can increment a variable by one with the **post-increment** operator ++.

- You can decrement a variable by one with the **post-decrement** operator --.

- You can add a new value to an array using **push**.

JavaScript cross

Let arrays sink into your brain as you do the crossword.

ACROSS

5. An array with undefined values is called a _____ array.

9. To change a value in an array, simply _____ the item a new value.

10. Who thought he was going to have the winning bubble solution?

14. When you _____ your code, you organize it so it's easier to read and maintain.

17. Each value in an array is stored at an _____.

DOWN

1. To add a new value to the end of an existing array, use _____.

2. We usually use a _____ loop to iterate over an array.

3. Arrays are good for storing _____ values.

4. The last index of an array is always one _____ than the length of the array.

6. The operator we use to increment a loop variable.

7. When iterating through an array, we usually use the _____ property to know when to stop.

8. The index of the first item in an array is _____.

11. The value an array item gets if you don't specify one.

12. Functions can help _____ your code.

13. An array is an _____ data structure.

15. How many bubble solutions had the highest score?

16. Access an array item using its _____ in square brackets.

Sharpen your pencil
Solution

The products array below holds the Jenn and Berry's ice cream flavors. The ice creams were added to this array in the order of their creation. Finish the code to determine the most recent ice cream flavor they created. Here's our solution.

```
var products = ["Choo Choo Chocolate", "Icy Mint", "Cake Batter", "Bubblegum"];
var last = products.length - 1;
var recent = products[last];
```

We can use the length of the array, minus one to get the index of the last item. The length is 4, and the index of the last item is 3, because we start from 0.

Code Magnets Solution

We've got code for testing to see which ice cream flavors have bubblegum pieces in them. We had all the code nicely laid out on our fridge using fridge magnets, but the magnets fell on the floor. It's your job to put them back together. Be careful; a few extra magnets got mixed in. Here's our solution.

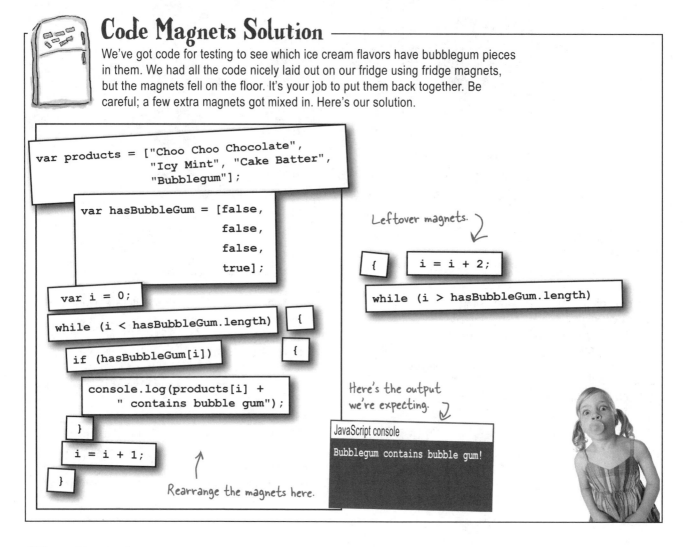

```
var products = ["Choo Choo Chocolate",
                "Icy Mint", "Cake Batter",
                "Bubblegum"];

var hasBubbleGum = [false,
                    false,
                    false,
                    true];

var i = 0;
while (i < hasBubbleGum.length) {
    if (hasBubbleGum[i]) {
        console.log(products[i] +
            " contains bubble gum");
    }
    i = i + 1;
}
```

Leftover magnets.

```
{          i = i + 2;

while (i > hasBubbleGum.length)
```

Here's the output we're expecting.

```
JavaScript console
Bubblegum contains bubble gum!
```

Rearrange the magnets here.

Sharpen your pencil
Solution

Rewrite your fridge magnet code (from two pages back) so that it uses a for loop instead of a while loop. If you need a hint, refer to each piece of the while loop on the previous page and see how it maps to the corresponding location in the for loop. Here's our solution.

```
var products = ["Choo Choo Chocolate",
         "Icy Mint", "Cake Batter",
         "Bubblegum"];
```

```
var hasBubbleGum = [false,
                    false,
                    false,
                    true];
```

```
var i = 0;
```
```
while (i < hasBubbleGum.length)        {
```
```
    if (hasBubbleGum[i])        {
```
```
        console.log(products[i] +
            " contains bubble gum");
```
```
    }
```
```
    i = i + 1;
```
```
}
```

Your code goes here.

```
var products = ["Choo Choo Chocolate",
                "Icy Mint", "Cake Batter",
                "Bubblegum"];
var hasBubbleGum = [false,
                    false,
                    false,
                    true];
for (var i = 0; i < hasBubbleGum.length; i = i + 1) {
    if (hasBubbleGum[i]) {
        console.log(products[i] + " contains bubble gum");
    }
}
```

Sharpen your pencil
Solution

Go ahead and implement the pseudocode on the previous page to find the highest score by filling in the blanks in the code below. Once you're done, give it a try in the browser by updating the code in "bubbles.html", and reloading the page. Check the results in the console, and fill in the blanks in our console display below with the number of bubble tests and the highest score. Here's our solution.

```
var scores = [60, 50, 60, 58, 54, 54,
              58, 50, 52, 54, 48, 69,
              34, 55, 51, 52, 44, 51,
              69, 64, 66, 55, 52, 61,
              46, 31, 57, 52, 44, 18,
              41, 53, 55, 61, 51, 44];

var highScore = _0_ ;                    ← Fill in the blanks to complete the code here...
var output;
for (var i = 0; i < scores.length; i++) {
    output = "Bubble solution #" + i + " score: " + scores[i];
    console.log(output);
    if ( __scores[i]__ > highScore) {
        __highScore__ = scores[i];
    }
}
console.log("Bubbles tests: " + __scores.length__ );
console.log("Highest bubble score: " + __highScore__ );
```

... and then fill in the blanks showing the output you get in the console.

```
JavaScript console
Bubble solution #0 score: 60
Bubble solution #1 score: 50
Bubble solution #2 score: 60
     ...
Bubble solution #34 score: 51
Bubble solution #35 score: 44
Bubbles tests: 36
Highest bubble score: 69
```

Exercise Solution

Here's our solution for the getMostCostEffectiveSolution function, which takes an array of scores, an array of costs, and a high score, and finds the index of the bubble solution with the highest score and lowest cost. Go ahead and test drive all your code in "bubbles.html" and make sure you see the same results.

The getMostCostEffectiveSolution takes the array of scores, the array of costs, and the high score.

```
function getMostCostEffectiveSolution(scores, costs, highscore) {
    var cost = 100;              We'll keep track of the lowest cost solution in cost...
    var index;                   ... and the index of the lowest cost solution in index.

    for (var i = 0; i < scores.length; i++) {
        if (scores[i] == highscore) {
            if (cost > costs[i]) {
                index = i;
                cost = costs[i];
            }
        }
    }
    return index;
}

var mostCostEffective = getMostCostEffectiveSolution(scores, costs, highScore);

console.log("Bubble Solution #" + mostCostEffective + " is the most cost effective");
```

We start cost at a high number, and we'll lower it each time we find a lower cost solution (with a high score).

We iterate through the scores array like before...

... and check to see if the score has the high score.

If it does, then we can check its cost. If the current cost is greater than the solution's cost, then we've found a lower cost solution, so we'll make sure we keep track of which solution it is (its index in the array) and store its cost in the cost variable as the lowest cost we've seen so far.

Once the loop is complete, the index of solution with the lowest cost is stored in index, so we return that to the code that called the function.

And then display the index (which is the bubble solution #) in the console.

The final report showing bubble solution #11 as the winner of the bubble tests for having the highest bubble factor at a low cost.

BONUS: We could also implement this using the bestSolutions array so we wouldn't have to iterate through all the scores again. Remember, the bestSolutions array has the indices of the solutions with the highest scores. So in that code, we'd use the items in the bestSolutions array to index into the costs array to compare the costs. The code is a little more efficient than this version, but it's also a little bit more difficult to read and understand! If you're interested, we've included the code in the book code download at wickedlysmart.com.

```
JavaScript console

Bubble solution #0 score: 60
Bubble solution #1 score: 50
Bubble solution #2 score: 60
    ...
Bubble solution #34 score: 51
Bubble solution #35 score: 44
Bubbles tests: 36
Highest bubble score: 69
Solutions with the highest score: 11,18
Bubble Solution #11 is the most cost effective
```

JavaScript cross Solution

Let arrays sink into your brain as you do the crossword.

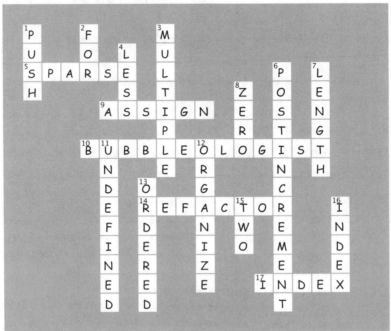

5 understanding objects

A trip to Objectville

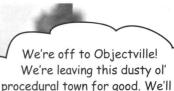

We're off to Objectville! We're leaving this dusty ol' procedural town for good. We'll send you a postcard!

So far you've been using primitives and arrays in your code. And, you've approached coding in quite a **procedural manner** using simple statements, conditionals and for/while loops with functions—that's not exactly **object-oriented**. In fact, it's not object-oriented *at all!* We did use a few objects here and there without really knowing it, but you haven't written any of your own objects yet. Well, the time has come to leave this boring procedural town behind to create some **objects** of your own. In this chapter, you're going to find out why using objects is going to make your life so much better—well, better in a **programming sense** (we can't really help you with your fashion sense *and* your JavaScript skills all in one book). Just a warning: once you've discovered objects you'll never want to come back. Send us a postcard when you get there.

Did someone say "Objects"?!

Ah, our favorite topic! Objects are going to take your JavaScript programming skills to the next level—they're the key to managing complex code, to understanding the browser's document model (which we'll do in the next chapter), to organizing your data, and they're even the fundamental way many JavaScript libraries are packaged up (more on that much later in the book). That said, objects are a difficult topic, right? Hah! We're going to jump in head first and you'll be using them in no time.

Here's the secret to JavaScript objects: they're just a collection of properties. Let's take an example, say, a car. A car's got properties:

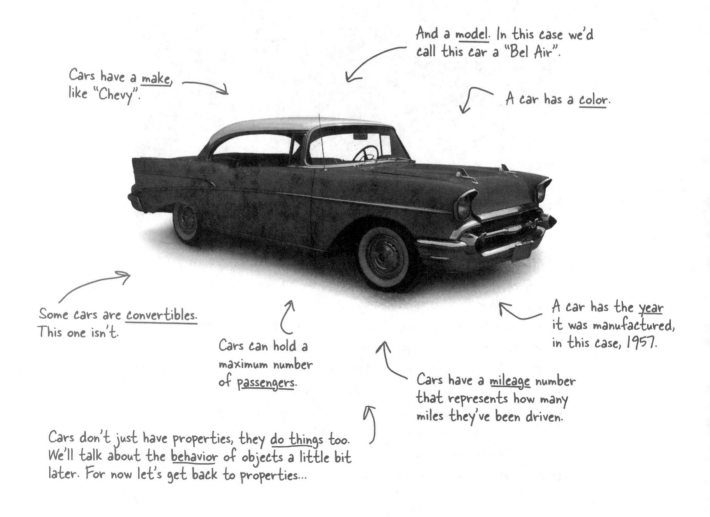

And a <u>model</u>. In this case we'd call this car a "Bel Air".

Cars have a <u>make</u>, like "Chevy".

A car has a <u>color</u>.

Some cars are <u>convertibles</u>. This one isn't.

Cars can hold a maximum number of <u>passengers</u>.

A car has the <u>year</u> it was manufactured, in this case, 1957.

Cars have a <u>mileage</u> number that represents how many miles they've been driven.

Cars don't just have properties, they <u>do things</u> too. We'll talk about the <u>behavior</u> of objects a little bit later. For now let's get back to properties...

Thinking about properties...

Of course there's a lot more to a real car than just a few properties, but for the purposes of coding, these are the properties we want to capture in software. Let's think about these properties in terms of JavaScript data types:

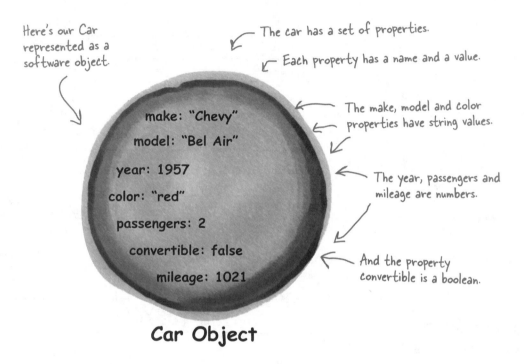

Here's our Car represented as a software object.

The car has a set of properties.

Each property has a name and a value.

The make, model and color properties have string values.

The year, passengers and mileage are numbers.

And the property convertible is a boolean.

```
make: "Chevy"

model: "Bel Air"

year: 1957

color: "red"

passengers: 2

convertible: false

mileage: 1021
```

Car Object

BRAIN POWER

Those fuzzy dice may look nice, but would they really be useful in an object?

Are there other properties you'd want to have in a car object? Go ahead and think through all the properties you might come up with for a car and write them below. Remember, only some real-world properties are going to be useful in software.

Sharpen your pencil

We've started making a table of property names and values for a car. Can you help complete it? Make sure you compare your answers with ours before moving on!

Put your property names here.

And put the corresponding values over here.

{

make	:	"Chevy" ,
model	:	_____ ,
year	:	_____ ,
color	:	_____ ,
passengers	:	_____ ,
convertible	:	_____ ,
mileage	:	_____ ,
_____	:	_____ ,
_____	:	_____

Put your answers here. Feel free to expand the list to include your own properties.

};

When you're done notice the syntax we've placed around the properties and values. There might be a pop-quiz at some point... just sayin'.

BRAIN POWER

What if the car is a taxi? What properties and values would it share with your '57 Chevy? How might they differ? What additional properties might it have (or not have)?

How to create an object

Here's the good news: after the last Sharpen your Pencil exercise, you're already most of the way to creating an object. All you really need to do is assign what you wrote on the previous page to a variable (so you can do things with your object after you've created it). Like this:

Add a variable declaration for the object.

Next, start an object with a left curly brace.

Then all the object's properties go inside.

Each property has a name, a colon and then a value. Here we have strings, numbers and one boolean as property values.

Notice that each property is separated by a comma.

We end the object with a closing curly brace, and just like any other variable declaration, we end this one with a semicolon.

```javascript
var chevy = {
    make: "Chevy",
    model: "Bel Air",
    year: 1957,
    color: "red",
    passengers: 2,
    convertible: false,
    mileage: 1021
};
```

The result of all this? A brand new object of course. Think of the object as something that holds all your names and values (in other words, your properties) together.

Now you've got a live object complete with a set of properties. And you've assigned your object to a variable that you can use to access and change its properties.

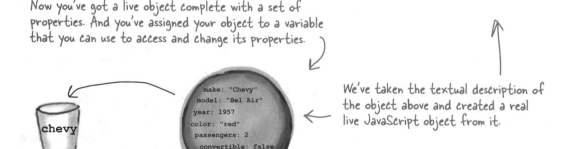

We've taken the textual description of the object above and created a real live JavaScript object from it.

You can now take your object, pass it around, get values from it, change it, add properties to it, or take them away. We'll get to how to do all that in a second. For now, let's create some more objects to play with…

EⅹeRciŚe

You don't have to be stuck with just one object. The real power of objects (as you'll see soon enough) is having lots of objects and writing code that can operate on whatever object you give it. Try your hand at creating another object from scratch... another car object. Go ahead and work out the code for your second object.

```
var cadi = {
```

← Put the properties for your Cadillac object here.

```
};
```

We'll call this a tan color.

This is a 1955 GM Cadillac.

It's not a convertible, and it can hold five passengers (it's got a nice big bucket seat in the back).

Its mileage is 12,892.

SPEEDING TICKET
Issued by the *Webville* Police dept.

WARNING CITATION   № 10

Don't worry, you're getting off easy this time; rather than issuing a ticket, we ask that you please review the following "rules of the road" for creating objects.

Make sure you enclose your object in curly braces:

```
var cat = {
    name: "fluffy"
};
```

Separate the property name and property value with a colon:

```
var planet = {
    diameter: 49528
};
```

A property name can be any string, but we usually stick with valid variable names:

```
var widget = {
    cost$: 3.14,
    "on sale": true
};
```

> Notice that if you use a string with a space in it for a property name, you need to use quotes around the name.

No two properties in an object can have the same name:

```
var forecast = {
    highTemp: 82,
    highTemp: 56
};
```

> WRONG! This won't work.

Separate each property name and value pair with a comma:

```
var gadget = {
    name: "anvil",
    isHeavy: true
};
```

Don't use a comma after the last property value:

```
var superhero = {
    name: "Batman",
    alias: "Caped Crusader"
};
```

> No comma needed here!

What is Object-Oriented Anyway?

Up 'til now, we've been thinking of a problem as a set of variable declarations, conditionals, for/while statements, and function calls. That's thinking *procedurally*: first do this, then do this and so on. With *object-oriented* programming we think about a problem in terms of objects. Objects that have state (like a car might have an oil and a fuel level), and behavior (like a car can be started, driven, parked and stopped).

What's the point? Well, object-oriented programming allows you to free your mind to think at a higher level. It's the difference between having to toast your bread from first principles (create a heating coil out of wire, hook it to electricity, turn the electricity on and then hold your bread close enough to toast it, not to mention watch long enough for it to toast and then unhook the heating coil), and just using a toaster (place bread in toaster and push down on the toast button). The first way is procedural, while the second way is object-oriented: you have a toaster object that supports an easy method of inserting bread and toasting it.

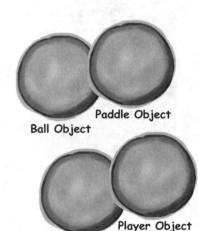

Ball Object Paddle Object

Player Object

Player Object

What do you like about OO?

"It helps me design in a more natural way. Things have a way of evolving."

-Joy, 27, software architect

"Not messing around with code I've already tested, just to add a new feature."

-Brad, 32, programmer

"I like that the data and the methods that operate on that data are together in one object."

-Josh, 22, beer drinker

"Reusing code in other apps. When I write a new object, I can make it flexible enough to be used in something new, later."

-Chris, 39, project manager

"I can't believe Chris just said that. He hasn't written a line of code in five years."

-Daryl, 44, works for Chris

Say you were implementing a classic ping-pong style video arcade game. What would you choose as objects? What state and behavior do you think they'd have?

Pong!

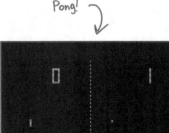

Smallest car in Webville!

```
var fiat = {
    make: "Fiat",
    model: "500",
    year: 1957,
    color: "Medium Blue",
    passengers: 2,
    convertible: false,
    mileage: 88000
};
```

How properties work

So you've got all your properties packaged up in an object. Now what? Well, you can examine the values of those properties, change them, add new properties, take away properties, and in general, compute using them. Let's try a few of these things out, using JavaScript of course.

How to access a property. To access a property in an object, start with the object name, follow it with a period (otherwise known as a "dot") and then use the property name. We often call that "dot" notation and it looks like this:

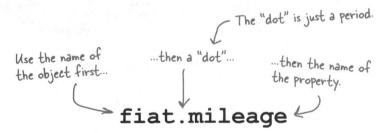

The "dot" is just a period.

Use the name of the object first...

...then a "dot"...

...then the name of the property.

fiat.mileage

And then we can use a property in any expression, like this:

```
var miles = fiat.mileage;
if (miles < 2000) {
    buyIt();
}
```

Start with the variable that holds your object, add a period (otherwise known as a dot) and then your property name.

> **Dot Notation .**
>
> - Dot notation (.) gives you access to an object's properties.
>
> - For example, `fiat.color` is a property in `fiat` with the name `color` and the value "Medium Blue".

How to change a property. You can change the value of a property at any time. All you need to do is assign the property to a new value. Like, let's say we wanted to set the mileage of our nifty Fiat to an even 10,000. You'd do it like this:

```
fiat.mileage = 10000;
```

Just specify the property you want to change and then give it a new value. Note: in some states this may be illegal!

How to add a new property. You can extend your object at any time with new properties. To do this you just specify the new property and give it a value. For instance, let's say we want to add a boolean that indicates when the Fiat needs to be washed:

```
fiat.needsWashing = true;
```

As long as the property doesn't already exist in the object, it's added to the object. Otherwise, the property with this name is updated.

```
make: "Fiat"
model: "500"
year: 1957
color: "Medium Blue"
passengers: 2
convertible: false
mileage: 88000
needsWashing: true
```

The new property is added to your object.

How to compute with properties. Computing with properties is simple: just use a property like you would any variable (or any value). Here are a few examples:

You can use an object's property just like you use a variable, except you need to use dot notation to access the property in the object.

```
if (fiat.year < 1965) {
    classic = true;
}
for (var i = 0; i < fiat.passengers; i++) {
    addPersonToCar();
}
```

Object Magnets

This code got all scrambled up on the fridge. Practice your object creating and dot notation skills by getting it all back together. Be careful, some extra magnets might have got mixed in!

| bark | , | 20.2 |

| dog.weight | | Fido |

| "fetch balls" | dog.activity |

| dog.name | breed | , |

| "Fido" | dog.bark | 4 |

| , | age | weight |

| , |

Use these magnets to complete the code.

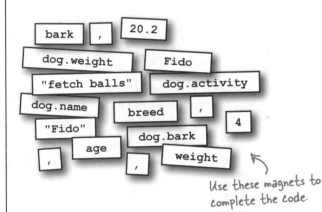

```
name: "Fido"
weight: 20.2
age: 4
breed: "mixed"
  activity: "fetch balls"
```

The dog object.

```
var dog = {
    name: _____
    _____: 20.2
    age: _____
    _____: "mixed",
    activity: _____
};
var bark;
if (_____ > 20) {
    bark = "WOOF WOOF";
} else {
    bark = "woof woof";
}
var speak = _____ + " says " + _____ + " when he wants to " + _____;
console.log(speak);
```

Fido is hoping you get all his properties right.

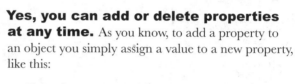

I see we can add new properties at any time. Can I get rid of them too?

Yes, you can add or delete properties at any time. As you know, to add a property to an object you simply assign a value to a new property, like this:

```
fido.dogYears = 35;
```

and from that point on `fido` will have a new property `dogYears`. Easy enough.

To delete a property, we use a special keyword, wait for it... `delete`. You use the `delete` keyword like this:

```
delete fido.dogYears;
```

When you delete a property, you're not just deleting the value of the property, you're deleting the property itself. And, if you try to use `fido.dogYears` after deleting it, it will evaluate to `undefined`.

The `delete` expression returns `true` if the property was deleted successfully. `delete` will return false only if it can't delete a property (which could happen for, say, a protected object that belongs to the browser). It will return `true` even if the property you're trying to delete doesn't exist in the object.

there are no
Dumb Questions

Q: How many properties can an object have?

A: As few or as many as you want. You can have an object with no properties, or you can have an object with hundreds of properties. It's really up to you.

Q: How can I create an object with no properties?

A: Just like you create any object, only leave out all the properties. Like this:
```
var lookMaNoProps = { };
```

Q: I know I just asked how to create an object with no properties, but why would I want to do this?

A: Well, you might want to start with an entirely empty object and then add your own properties dynamically, depending on the logic of your code. This way of creating an object will become clear as we continue to use objects.

```
var lookMaNoProps = { };
lookMaNoProps.age = 10;
if (lookMaNoProps.age > 5) {
    lookMaNoProps.school = "Elementary";
}
```

Q: What's better about an object than just using a bunch of variables? After all, each of the properties in the fiat object could just be its own variable, right?

A: Objects package up the complexity of your data so that you can focus on the high level design of your code, not the nitty gritty details. Say you want to write a traffic simulator with tens of cars; you'll want to focus on cars and streetlights and road objects and not hundreds of little variables. Objects also make your life easier because they encapsulate, or hide, the complexity of the state and behavior of your objects so you don't have to worry about them. How all that works will become much clearer as you gain experience with objects.

Q: If I try to add a new property to my object, and the object already has a property with that name, what happens?

A: If you try to add a new property, like needsWashing, to fiat and fiat already has a property needsWashing, then you'll be changing the existing value of the property. So if you say:
```
fiat.needsWashing = true;
```
but fiat already contains a property needsWashing with the value false, then you're changing the value to true.

Q: What happens if I try to access a property that doesn't exist? Like if I said,
```
if (fiat.make) { ... }
```
but fiat didn't have a property make?

A: The result of the expression fiat.make will be undefined if fiat doesn't have a property named make.

Q: What happens if I put a comma after the last property?

A: In most browsers it won't cause an error. However, in older versions of some browsers this will cause your JavaScript to halt execution. So, if you want your code to work in as many browsers as possible, keep away from extraneous commas.

Q: Can I use console.log to display an object in the console?

A: You can. Just write:
```
console.log(fiat);
```
in your code, and when you load the page with the console open, you'll see information about the object displayed in the console.

```
JavaScript console

> console.log(fiat)

Object {make: "Fiat", model: "500", year: 1957,
color: "Medium Blue", passengers: 2…}

>
```

How does a variable hold an object? Inquiring minds want to know...

You've already seen that a variable is like a container and it holds a value. But numbers, strings and booleans are pretty small values. What about objects? Can a variable hold any sized object no matter how many properties you put in it?

Behind the Scenes

- ■ **Variables don't actually hold objects.**

- ■ **Instead they hold a reference to an object.**

- ■ **The reference is like a pointer or an address to the actual object.**

- ■ **In other words, a variable doesn't hold the object itself, but it holds something like a pointer. And, in JavaScript we don't really know *what* is inside a reference variable. We *do* know that whatever it is, it points to our object.**

- ■ **When we use dot notation, the JavaScript interpreter takes care of using the reference to get the object and then accesses its properties for us.**

So, you can't stuff an object into a variable, but we often think of it that way. It's not what happens though—there aren't giant expandable cups that can grow to the size of any object. Instead, an object variable just holds a reference to the object.

Here's another way to look at it: a primitive variable represents the actual *value* of the variable while an object variable represents *a way to get to the object*. In practice you'll only need to think of objects as, well, objects, like dogs and cars, not as references, but knowing variables contain *references* to objects will come in handy later (and we'll see that in just a few pages).

And also think about this: you use the dot notation (.) on a reference variable to say, "use the reference *before* the dot to get me the object that has the property *after* the dot." (Read that sentence a few times and let it sink in.) For example:

```
car.color;
```

means "use the object referenced by the variable `car` to access the `color` property."

Comparing primitives and objects

Think of an object reference as just another variable value, which means that we can put that reference in a cup, just like we can primitive values. With primitive values, the value of a variable is… the *value*, like 5, -26.7, "hi", or false. With reference variables, the value of the variable is a *reference*: a value that represents a way to get to a specific object.

number string boolean   reference

These are all primitive variables. Each holds the value you stored in the variable.

This is a reference variable, and holds a value that is a reference to an object.

Initializing a primitive variable

When you declare and initialize a primitive, you give it a value, and that value goes right in the cup, like this:

```
var x = 3;
```

The variable holds the number three.

A number primitive value.

Initializing an object (a reference) variable

When you declare and initialize an object, you make the object using object notation, but that object won't fit in the cup. So what goes in the cup is a *reference* to the object.

```
var myCar = {...};
```

A reference to the Car object goes into the variable.

The Car object itself does not go into the variable!

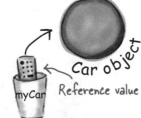

Car object

myCar   Reference value

Behind the Scenes

We don't know (or care) how the JavaScript interpreter represents object references.

We just know we can access an object and its properties using dot notation.

Doing even more with objects...

Let's say you're looking for a good car for your stay in Webville. Your criteria? How about:

❏ Built in 1960 or before.

❏ 10,000 miles or less.

You also want to put your new coding skills to work (and make your life easier) so you want to write a function that will "prequalify" cars for you—that is, if the car meets your criteria then the function returns true; otherwise the car isn't worth your time and the function returns false.

More specifically, you're going to write a *function* that *takes a car object as a parameter* and puts that car through the test, returning a boolean value. Your function is going to work for *any car object*.

Let's give it a shot:

Here's the function.

You're going to pass it a car object.

```
function prequal(car) {
    if (car.mileage > 10000) {
        return false;
    } else if (car.year > 1960) {
        return false;
    }
    return true;
}
```

Just use dot notation on the car parameter to access the mileage and year properties.

Test each property value against the prequalification criteria.

If either of the disqualification tests succeeds we return false. Otherwise we return true, meaning we've successfully prequalified!

Now let's give this function a try. First you need a car object. How about this one:

```
var taxi = {
    make: "Webville Motors",
    model: "Taxi",
    year: 1955,
    color: "yellow",
    passengers: 4,
    convertible: false,
    mileage: 281341
};
```

What do you think? Should we consider this yellow taxi? Why or why not?

Doing some pre-qualification

We've done enough talking about objects. Let's actually create one and put it through its paces using the `prequal` function. Grab your favorite, basic HTML page ("prequal.html") and throw in the code below, load the page and see if the taxi qualifies:

```javascript
var taxi = {
    make: "Webville Motors",
    model: "Taxi",
    year: 1955,
    color: "yellow",
    passengers: 4,
    convertible: false,
    mileage: 281341
};

function prequal(car) {
    if (car.mileage > 10000) {
        return false;
    } else if (car.year > 1960) {
        return false;
    }
    return true;
}


var worthALook = prequal(taxi);

if (worthALook) {
    console.log("You gotta check out this " + taxi.make + " " + taxi.model);
} else {
    console.log("You should really pass on the " + taxi.make + " " + taxi.model);
}
```

Does the taxi cut it?

Here's what we got... let's quickly trace through the code on the next page to see how the Taxi got rejected...

```
JavaScript console
You should really pass on the Webville Motors Taxi
```

Stepping through pre-qualification

① First we create the taxi object and assign it to the variable `taxi`. Of course, the `taxi` variable holds a reference to the taxi object, not the object itself.

```
var taxi = { ... };
```

```
make: "Webville...
model: "Taxi
year: 1955
color: "yellow"
passengers: 4
convertible: false
mileage: 281341
```

② Next we call `prequal`, passing it the argument `taxi`, which is bound to the parameter `car` in the function.

```
function prequal(car) {

    ...

}
```

car points to the same object as taxi!

```
make: "Webville...
model: "Taxi
year: 1955
color: "yellow"
passengers: 4
convertible: false
mileage: 281341
```

③ We then perform the tests in the body of the function, using the taxi object in the car parameter.

```
if (car.mileage > 10000) {
    return false;
} else if (car.year > 1960) {
    return false;
}
```

In this case, the taxi's mileage is way above 10,000 miles, so prequal returns false. Too bad; it's a cool ride.

```
make: "Webville...
model: "Taxi
year: 1955
color: "yellow"
passengers: 4
convertible: false
mileage: 281341
```

④ Unfortunately the taxi has a lot of miles, so the first test of car.mileage > 10000 is true. The function returns false, and so `worthALook` is set to false. We then get "You should really pass on the Webville Motors Taxi" displayed in the console.

The prequal function returns false, and so we get...

```
var worthALook = prequal(taxi);

if (worthALook) {
    console.log("You gotta check out this " + taxi.make + " " + taxi.model);
} else {
    console.log("You should really pass on the " + taxi.make + " " + taxi.model);
}
```

```
JavaScript console
You should really pass on the Webville Motors Taxi
```

Sharpen your pencil

Your turn. Here are three more car objects; what is the result of passing each car to the `prequal` function? Work the answer by hand, and then write the code to check your answers:

```
var cadi = {
    make: "GM",
    model: "Cadillac",
    year: 1955,
    color: "tan",
    passengers: 5,
    convertible: false,
    mileage: 12892
};

prequal(cadi);
```

_____

↑
Write the
value of
prequal here.

```
var fiat = {
    make: "Fiat",
    model: "500",
    year: 1957,
    color: "Medium Blue",
    passengers: 2,
    convertible: false,
    mileage: 88000
};

prequal(fiat);
```

_____

```
var chevy = {
    make: "Chevy",
    model: "Bel Air",
    year: 1957,
    color: "red",
    passengers: 2,
    convertible: false,
    mileage: 1021
};

prequal(chevy);
```

_____

Let's talk a little more about passing objects to functions

We've already talked a bit about how arguments are passed to functions—arguments are *passed by value*, which means *pass-by-copy*. So if we pass an integer, the corresponding function parameter gets a copy of the value of that integer for its use in the function. The same rules hold true for objects, however, we should look a little more closely at what pass-by-value means for objects to understand what happens when you pass an object to a function.

You already know that when an object is assigned to a variable, that variable holds a *reference* to the object, not the object itself. Again, think of a reference as a pointer to the object:

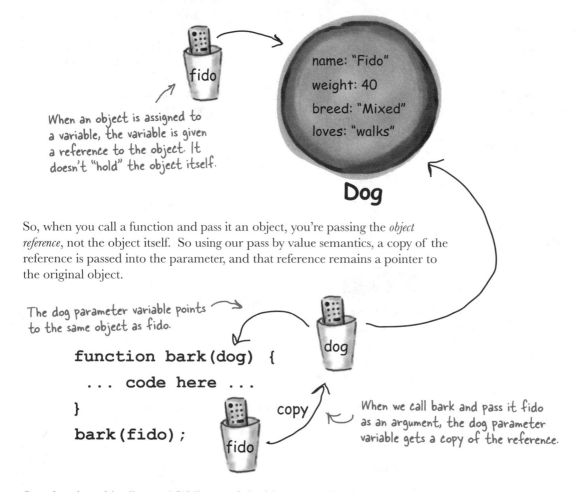

When an object is assigned to a variable, the variable is given a reference to the object. It doesn't "hold" the object itself.

name: "Fido"

weight: 40

breed: "Mixed"

loves: "walks"

Dog

So, when you call a function and pass it an object, you're passing the *object reference*, not the object itself. So using our pass by value semantics, a copy of the reference is passed into the parameter, and that reference remains a pointer to the original object.

The dog parameter variable points to the same object as fido.

```
function bark(dog) {
    ... code here ...
}
bark(fido);
```

copy

When we call bark and pass it fido as an argument, the dog parameter variable gets a copy of the reference.

So, what does this all mean? Well, one of the biggest ramifications is that if you change a property of the object in a function, you're changing the property in the *original* object. So any changes you make to the object inside a function will still be there when the function completes. Let's step through an example...

Putting Fido on a diet....

Let's say we are testing a new method of weight loss for dogs, which we want to neatly implement in a function `loseWeight`. All you need to do is pass `loseWeight` your dog object and an amount to lose, and like magic, the dog's weight will be reduced. Here's how it works:

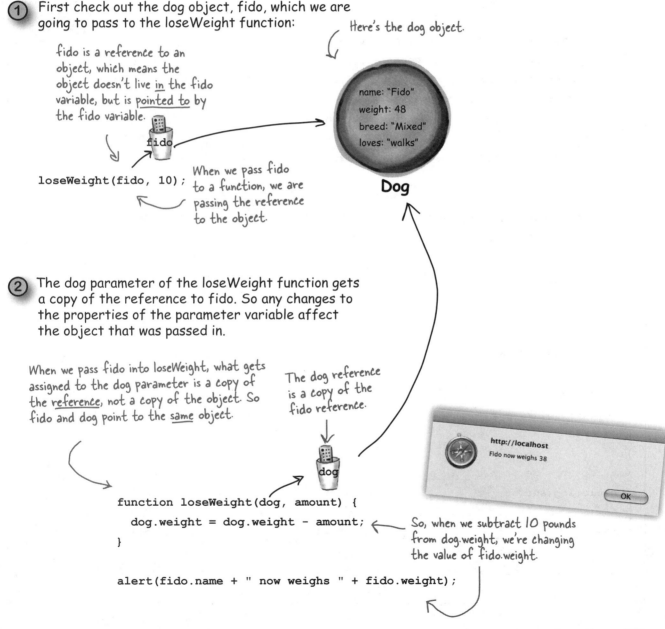

1 First check out the dog object, fido, which we are going to pass to the loseWeight function:

Here's the dog object.

fido is a reference to an object, which means the object doesn't live *in* the fido variable, but is pointed to by the fido variable.

```
name: "Fido"
weight: 48
breed: "Mixed"
loves: "walks"
```
Dog

`loseWeight(fido, 10);`

When we pass fido to a function, we are passing the reference to the object.

2 The dog parameter of the loseWeight function gets a copy of the reference to fido. So any changes to the properties of the parameter variable affect the object that was passed in.

When we pass fido into loseWeight, what gets assigned to the dog parameter is a copy of the <u>reference</u>, not a copy of the object. So fido and dog point to the <u>same</u> object.

The dog reference is a copy of the fido reference.

http://localhost
Fido now weighs 38

OK

```
function loseWeight(dog, amount) {
    dog.weight = dog.weight - amount;
}

alert(fido.name + " now weighs " + fido.weight);
```

So, when we subtract 10 pounds from dog.weight, we're changing the value of fido.weight.

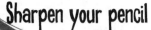

Sharpen your pencil

You've been given a super secret file and two functions that allow access to get and set the contents of the file, but only if you have the right password. The first function, `getSecret`, returns the contents of the file if the password is correct, and logs each attempt to access the file. The second function, `setSecret`, updates the contents of the file, and resets the access tracking to 0. It's your job to fill in the blanks below to complete the JavaScript and test your functions.

```javascript
function getSecret(file, secretPassword) {
    _____.opened = _____.opened + 1;
    if (secretPassword == _____.password) {
        return _____.contents;
    }
    else {
        return "Invalid password! No secret for you.";
    }
}
function setSecret(file, secretPassword, secret) {
    if (secretPassword == _____.password) {
        _____.opened = 0;
        _____.contents = secret;
    }
}


var superSecretFile = {
    level: "classified",
    opened: 0,
    password: 2,
    contents: "Dr. Evel's next meeting is in Detroit."
};
var secret = getSecret(_____, _____);
console.log(secret);

setSecret(_____, _____, "Dr. Evel's next meeting is in Philadelphia.");
secret = getSecret(_____, _____);
console.log(secret);
```

> I'm back, and this time I've got an Auto-O-Matic. This baby will have you hawking new cars all day long.

```
<!doctype html>
<html lang="en">
<head>
  <title>Object-o-matic</title>
  <meta charset="utf-8">
  <script>
    function makeCar() {
        var makes = ["Chevy", "GM", "Fiat", "Webville Motors", "Tucker"];
        var models = ["Cadillac", "500", "Bel-Air", "Taxi", "Torpedo"];
        var years = [1955, 1957, 1948, 1954, 1961];
        var colors = ["red", "blue", "tan", "yellow", "white"];
        var convertible = [true, false];

        var rand1 = Math.floor(Math.random() * makes.length);
        var rand2 = Math.floor(Math.random() * models.length);
        var rand3 = Math.floor(Math.random() * years.length);
        var rand4 = Math.floor(Math.random() * colors.length);
        var rand5 = Math.floor(Math.random() * 5) + 1;
        var rand6 = Math.floor(Math.random() * 2);

        var car = {
            make: makes[rand1],
            model: models[rand2],
            year: years[rand3],
            color: colors[rand4],
            passengers: rand5,
            convertible: convertible[rand6],
            mileage: 0
        };
        return car;
    }

    function displayCar(car) {
        console.log("Your new car is a " + car.year + " " + car.make + " " + car.model);
    }

    var carToSell = makeCar();
    displayCar(carToSell);

  </script>
</head>
<body></body>
</html>
```

← The Auto-O-Matic is similar to the Phrase-O-Matic from Chapter 4, except that the words are car properties, and we're generating a new car object instead of a marketing phrase!

← Check out what it does and how it works.

The Auto-O-Matic

Brought to you by the same guy who brought you the Phrase-O-Matic, the Auto-O-matic creates knock-off cars all day long. That is, instead of generating marketing messages, this code generates makes, models, years and all the properties of a car object. *It's your very own car factory in code.* Let's take a closer look at how it works.

① First, we have a `makeCar` function that we can call whenever we want to make a new car. We've got four arrays with the makes, models, years and colors of cars, and an array with true and false options for whether a car is a convertible. We generate five random numbers so we can pick a make, a model, a year, a color, and whether a car is a convertible randomly from these five arrays. And we generate one more random number we're using for the number of passengers.

> We have several makes, models, years and colors to choose from in these four arrays...

```
var makes = ["Chevy", "GM", "Fiat", "Webville Motors", "Tucker"];
var models = ["Cadillac", "500", "Bel-Air", "Taxi", "Torpedo"];
var years = [1955, 1957, 1948, 1954, 1961];
var colors = ["red", "blue", "tan", "yellow", "white"];
var convertible = [true, false];
```

> ... and we'll use this array to choose a convertible property value, either true or false.

```
var rand1 = Math.floor(Math.random() * makes.length);
var rand2 = Math.floor(Math.random() * models.length);
var rand3 = Math.floor(Math.random() * years.length);
var rand4 = Math.floor(Math.random() * colors.length);
var rand5 = Math.floor(Math.random() * 5) + 1;
var rand6 = Math.floor(Math.random() * 2);
```

> We're going to combine values from the arrays randomly using these four random numbers.

> We'll use this random number for the number of passengers. We're adding 1 to the random number so we can have at least one passenger in the car.

> ... and we'll use this random number to choose whether a car is convertible or not.

② Instead of creating a string by mixing and matching the various car properties, like we did with Phrase-O-Matic, this time we're creating a new object, `car`. This car has all the properties you'd expect. We pick values for the `make`, `model`, `year` and `color` properties from the arrays using the random numbers we created in step 1, and also add the `passengers`, `convertible` and `mileage` properties:

```
var car = {
    make: makes[rand1],
    model: models[rand2],
    year: years[rand3],
    color: colors[rand4],
    passengers: rand5,
    convertible: convertible[rand6],
    mileage: 0
};
```

We're creating a new car object, with property values made from the values in the arrays.

We're also setting the number of passengers to the random number we created, and setting the convertible property to true or false using the convertible array.

Finally, we're just setting the mileage property to 0 (it is a new car, after all).

③ The last statement in `makeCar` returns the new `car` object:

```
    return car;
```

Returning an object from a function is just like returning any other value. Let's now look at the code that calls `makeCar`:

```
function displayCar(car) {
    console.log("Your new car is a " + car.year + " " +
                car.make + " " + car.model);
}
var carToSell = makeCar();
displayCar(carToSell);
```

First we call the `makeCar` function and assign the value it returns to `carToSell`. We then pass the car object returned from `makeCar` to the function `displayCar`, which simply displays a few of its properties in the console.

Don't forget; what you're returning (and assigning to the carToSell variable) is a reference to a car object.

Car object

```
var carToSell = makeCar();
```

④ Go ahead and load up the Auto-O-Matic in your browser ("autoomatic.html") and give it a whirl. You'll find no shortage of new cars to generate, and remember there's a sucker born every minute.

Here's your new car! We think a '57 Fiat Taxi would be a cool car to have.

```
JavaScript console
Your new car is a 1957 Fiat Taxi
Your new car is a 1961 Tucker 500
Your new car is a 1948 GM Torpedo
```

Reload the page a few times like we did!

Oh Behave! Or, how to add behavior to your objects

You didn't think objects were just for storing numbers and strings did you? Objects are *active*. Objects can *do things*. Dogs don't just sit there... they bark, run, and play catch, and a dog object should too! Likewise, we drive cars, park them, put them in reverse and make them brake. Given everything you've learned in this chapter, you're all set to add behavior to your objects. Here's how we do that:

```
var fiat = {
    make: "Fiat",
    model: "500",
    year: 1957,
    color: "Medium Blue",
    passengers: 2,
    convertible: false,
    mileage: 88000,
    drive: function() {
        alert.log("Zoom zoom!");
    }
};
```

You can add a function directly to an object like this.

All you do is assign a function definition to a property. Yup, properties can be functions too!

Notice we don't supply a name in the function definition, we just use the function keyword followed by the body. The name of the function is the name of the property.

And a bit of nomenclature: we typically refer to functions inside an object as <u>methods</u>. That is a common object-oriented term for a function in an object.

To call the `drive` function—excuse us—to call the drive *method*, you use dot notation again, this time with the object name `fiat` and the property name `drive`, only we follow the property name with parentheses (just like you would when you call any other function).

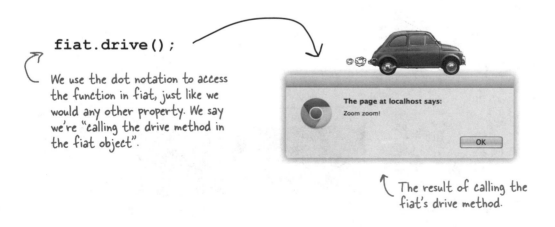

```
fiat.drive();
```

We use the dot notation to access the function in fiat, just like we would any other property. We say we're "calling the drive method in the fiat object".

The page at localhost says:
Zoom zoom!

OK

The result of calling the fiat's drive method.

Improving the drive method

Let's make the fiat a little more car-like in behavior. Most cars can't be driven until the engine is started, right? How about we model that behavior? We'll need the following:

- ❏ **A boolean property to hold the state of the car (the engine is either on or off).**

- ❏ **A couple of methods to start and stop the car.**

- ❏ **A conditional check in the drive method to make sure the car is started before we drive it.**

We'll begin by adding a boolean `started` property along with methods to `start` and `stop` the car, then we'll update the `drive` method to use the `started` property.

```
var fiat = {
    make: "Fiat",
    model: "500",
    year: 1957,
    color: "Medium Blue",
    passengers: 2,
    convertible: false,
    mileage: 88000,
    started: false,

    start: function() {
        started = true;
    },

    stop: function() {
        started = false;
    },

    drive: function() {
        if (started) {
            alert("Zoom zoom!");
        } else {
            alert("You need to start the engine first.");
        }
    }
};
```

Here's the property to hold the current state of the engine (true if it is started and false if it is off).

And here's a method to start the car. All it does (for now) is set the started property to true.

And here's a method to stop the car. All it does is set the started property to false.

And here's where the interesting behavior happens: when you try to drive the car, if it is started we get a "Zoom zoom!" and if not, we get a warning that we should start the car first.

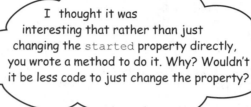

I thought it was interesting that rather than just changing the `started` property directly, you wrote a method to do it. Why? Wouldn't it be less code to just change the property?

Good catch. You're right; to start the car we could have replaced the code:

```
fiat.start();
```

with:

```
fiat.started = true;
```

That would have saved us from writing a method to start the car.

So why did we create and call the `start` method instead of just changing the `started` property directly? Using a method to change a property is another example of encapsulation whereby we can often improve the maintainability and extensibility of code by letting an object worry about how it gets things done. It's better to have a `start` method that knows how to start the car than for you to have to know "to start the car we need to take the `started` variable and set it to true."

Now you may still be saying "What's the big deal? Why not just set the property to true to start the car?!" Consider a more complex `start` method that checks the seatbelts, ensures there is enough fuel, checks the battery, checks the engine temperature and so on, all before setting `started` to true. You certainly don't want to think about all that every time you start the car. You just want a handy method to call that gets the job done. By putting all those details into a method, we've created a simple way for you to get an object to do some work while letting the object worry about how it gets that work done.

Take the fiat for a test drive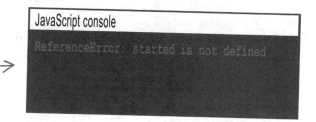

Let's take our new and improved `fiat` object for a test drive. Let's give it a good testing—we'll try to drive it before it's started, and then start, drive and stop it. To do that make sure you have the code for the `fiat` object typed into a simple HTML page ("carWithDrive.html"), including the new methods `start`, `stop` and `drive`, and then add this code below the object:

```
fiat.drive();    ← First, we'll try to drive the car, which should
fiat.start();    ← give us a message to start the car. Then we'll
fiat.drive();    ← start it for real, and we'll drive it. Finally,
fiat.stop();     ← when we're done we'll stop the car.
```

Go ahead and load the page in your browser and let the road trip begin!

Uh oh, not so fast...

If you can't drive your fiat, you're not alone. In fact, find your way to your JavaScript console and you're likely to see an error message similar to the one we got saying that `started` is not defined.

So, what's going on? Let's listen in on the `drive` method and see what's happening as we try to drive the car with `fiat.drive()`:

> **JavaScript console**
>
> ReferenceError: started is not defined

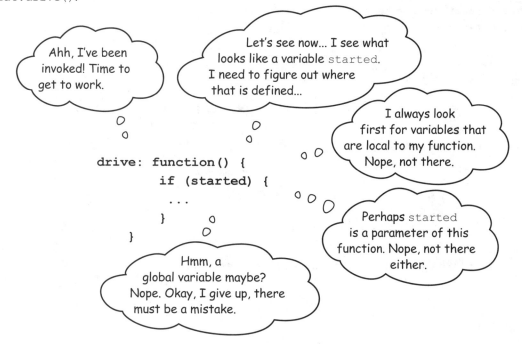

Why doesn't the drive method know about the started property?

Here's the conundrum: we've got references to the property `started` in the `fiat` object's methods, and normally when we're trying to resolve a variable in a function, that variable turns out to be a local variable, a parameter of the function or a global variable. But in the `drive` method, `started` is none of those things; instead, it's a *property* of the `fiat` object.

Shouldn't this code just work, though? In other words, we wrote `started` in the `fiat` object; shouldn't JavaScript be smart enough to figure out we mean the `started` property?

Nope. As you can see it isn't. How can that be?

Okay, here's the deal: what looks like a variable in the method is really a property of the object, but we aren't telling JavaScript which object. You might say to yourself, "Well, obviously we mean THIS object, this one right here! How could there be any confusion about that?" And, yes, we want the property of this very object. In fact, there's a keyword in JavaScript named `this`, and that is exactly how you tell JavaScript you mean *this object we're in*.

So, let's add the `this` keyword and get this code working:

> Really, if you want me to know which object `started` belongs to, you're going to have to tell me.

```
drive: function() {
    if (started) {
        ...
    }
}
```

```
var fiat = {
    make: "Fiat",
    // other properties are here, we're just saving space
    started: false,

    start: function() {
        this.started = true;
    },

    stop: function() {
        this.started = false;
    },

    drive: function() {
        if (this.started) {
            alert("Zoom zoom!");
        } else {
            alert("You need to start the engine first.");
        }
    }
};
```

Use **this** along with dot notation before each occurrence of the started property to tell the JavaScript interpreter you mean the property of THIS very object, rather than having JavaScript think you're referring to a variable.

A test drive with "this"

Go ahead and update your code, and take it for a spin! Here's what we got:

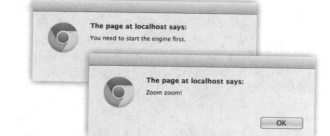

The page at localhost says:
You need to start the engine first.

The page at localhost says:
Zoom zoom!

OK

BE the Browser

Below, you'll find JavaScript code with some mistakes in it. Your job is to play like you're the browser and find the errors in the code. After you've done the exercise look at the end of the chapter to see if you found them all.

```javascript
var song = {
    name: "Walk This Way",
    artist: "Run-D.M.C.",
    minutes: 4,
    seconds: 3,
    genre: "80s",
    playing: false,

    play: function() {
        if (!playing) {
            this = true;
            console.log("Playing "
                + name + " by " + artist);
        }
    },

    pause: function() {
        if (playing) {
            this.playing = false;
        }
    }
};

this.play();
this.pause();
```

Go ahead and mark up the code right here...

How this works

You can think of `this` like a variable that is assigned to the object whose method was just called. In other words, if you call the `fiat` object's `start` method, with `fiat.start()`, and use `this` in the body of the `start` method, then `this` will refer to the `fiat` object. Let's look more closely at what happens when we call the `start` method of the `fiat` object.

First, we have an object representing the Fiat car, which is assigned to the `fiat` variable:

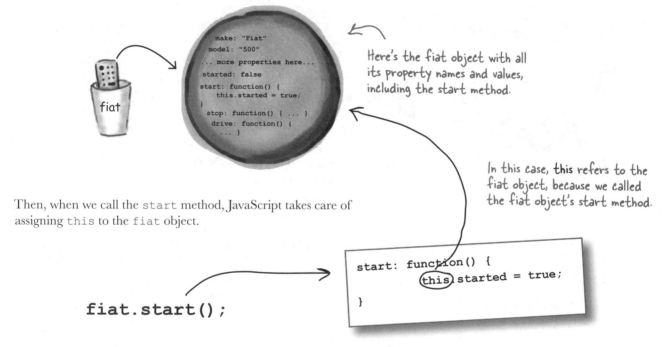

```
make: "Fiat"
model: "500"
... more properties here...
started: false
start: function() {
    this.started = true;
}
stop: function() { ... }
drive: function() {
    ... }
```

Here's the fiat object with all its property names and values, including the start method.

Then, when we call the `start` method, JavaScript takes care of assigning `this` to the `fiat` object.

In this case, **this** refers to the fiat object, because we called the fiat object's start method.

```
start: function() {
    this.started = true;
}
```

fiat.start();

Whenever we call a method in an object, **this** will refer to that object. So here, **this** refers to the fiat object.

The real key to understanding `this` is that whenever a method is called, in the body of that method you can count on `this` to be assigned to the *object whose method was called*. Just to drive the point home, let's try it on a few other objects…

If you call the chevy object's start method, then this will refer to the chevy object in the body of the method.

```
start: function() {
        this.started = true;
}
```

chevy.start();

```
make: "Chevy"
model: "Bel Air"
... more properties here...
started: false
start: function() {
  this.started = true;
}
  stop: function() { ... }
    drive: function() {
      ... }
```

And, in the start method of the taxi object, this refers to the taxi.

taxi.start();

```
start: function() {
        this.started = true;
}
```

```
make: "Webville..."
model: "Taxi"
... more properties here ...
started: false
start: function() {
  this.started = true;
}
  stop: function() { ... }
    drive: function() { ... }
```

Sharpen your pencil

Use your new **this** skills to help us finish this code. Check your answer at the end of the chapter.

```
var eightBall = { index: 0,
                  advice: ["yes", "no", "maybe", "not a chance"],
                  shake: function() {
                          this.index = _____.index + 1;
                          if (_____.index  >= _____.advice.length) {
                                  _____.index = 0;
                          }
                  },
                  look: function() {
                          return _____.advice[_____.index];
                  }
};
eightBall.shake();
console.log(eightBall.look());
```

Repeat this sequence several times to test your code.

```
JavaScript console

no

maybe

not a chance
```

there are no
Dumb Questions

Q: What's the difference between a method and a function?

A: A method is just a function that's been assigned to a property name in an object. You call functions using the function name, while you call methods using the object dot notation and the name of the property. You can also use the keyword this in a method to refer to the object whose method was called.

Q: I noticed that when using the function keyword within an object we don't give the function an explicit name. What happened to the function name?

A: Right. To call methods, we use the property name in the object rather than explicitly naming the function, and using that name. For now, just take this as the convention we use, but later in the book we'll dive into the topic of anonymous functions (which is what you call functions that don't explicitly have names).

Q: Can methods have local variables, like functions can?

A: Yes. A method is a function. We just call it a method because it lives inside an object. So, a method can do anything a function can do precisely because a method is a function.

Q: So, you can return values from methods too?

A: Yes. What we said in the last answer!

Q: What about passing arguments to methods? Can we do that too?

A: Err, maybe you didn't read the answer two questions back? Yes!

Q: Can I add a method to an object after it's created like I can with a property?

A: Yes. Think of a method as a function assigned to a property, so you can add a new one at any time:

```
// add a turbo method
car.engageTurbo =
        function() { ... };
```

Q: If I add a method like engageTurbo above, will the this keyword still work?

A: Yes. Remember this is assigned to the object whose method is called *at the time it is called*.

Q: When is the value of this set to the object? When we define the object, or when we call the method?

A: The value of this is set to the object when you call the method. So when you call fiat.start(), this is set to fiat, and when you call chevy.start(), this is set to chevy. It *looks* like this is set when you define the object, because in fiat.start, this is always set to fiat, and in chevy.start, this is always set to chevy. But as you'll see later, there is a good reason the value of this is set when you call the method and not when you define the object. This is an important point we'll be coming back to a few different times.

BRAIN
POWER

If you copy the start, stop, and drive methods into the chevy and cadi objects we created earlier, what do you have to change to make the methods work correctly?

Answer: Nothing! this refers to "this object," the one whose method we're calling.

Exercise

It's time to get the whole fleet up and running. Add the drive method to each car object. When you've done that, add the code to start, drive and stop each of them. Check your answer at the end of the chapter.

```
var cadi = {
    make: "GM",
    model: "Cadillac",
    year: 1955,
    color: "tan",
    passengers: 5,
    convertible: false,
    mileage: 12892
};
```

Add the started property and the methods to each car. Then use the code below to give them a test drive.

```
started: false,

start: function() {
    this.started = true;
},

stop: function() {
    this.started = false;
},

drive: function() {
    if (this.started) {
        alert(this.make + " " +
              this.model + " goes zoom zoom!");
    } else {
        alert("You need to start the engine first.");
    }
}
```

```
var chevy = {
    make: "Chevy",
    model: "Bel Air",
    year: 1957,
    color: "red",
    passengers: 2,
    convertible: false,
    mileage: 1021
};
```

We improved the drive method just a bit so make sure you get this new code.

```
var taxi = {
    make: "Webville Motors",
    model: "Taxi",
    year: 1955,
    color: "yellow",
    passengers: 4,
    convertible: false,
    mileage: 281341
};
```

Don't forget to add a comma after mileage when you add the new properties!

Throw this code after the car object definitions to give them all a test drive.

```
cadi.start();
cadi.drive();
cadi.stop();
chevy.start();
chevy.drive();
chevy.stop();
taxi.start();
taxi.drive();
taxi.stop();
```

> It seems like we're duplicating code with all the copying and pasting of the methods to the various car objects. Isn't there a better way?

Ah, good eye.

Yes, when we copy `start`, `stop` and `drive` into each car object we're definitely duplicating code. Unlike the other properties, which have values that depend on which car object they're in, the methods are the same for all of the objects.

Now if you're saying "Great, we're reusing code!"... not so fast. Sure, we're reusing it, but we're doing that by copying it, not just once, but many times! What happens now if we want drive to work differently? Then you've got to redo the code in every single car. Not good. Not only is that a waste, it can be error prone.

But you're identifying a problem even larger than simple copying and pasting; we're assuming that just because we put the same properties in all our objects, that makes them all car objects. What if you accidentally leave out the `mileage` property from one of the objects—is it still a car?

These are all real problems with our code so far, and we're going to tackle all these questions in an upcoming chapter on advanced objects where we'll talk about some techniques for properly reusing the code in your objects.

I was also wondering if someone handed me an object, is there a way to know what all its properties are?

One thing you can do is iterate through an object's properties.
To do that you can use a form of iteration we haven't seen yet called `for in`. The `for in` iterator steps through every property in an object in an arbitrary order. Here's how you could display all the properties of the `chevy` object:

for in steps through the object's properties one at time, assigning each one in turn to the variable prop.

```
for (var prop in chevy) {
    console.log(prop + ": " + chevy[prop]);
}
```

You can use prop as a way to access the property using bracket notation.

This brings up another topic: there's another way to access properties.
Did you catch the alternative syntax we just used to access the properties of the `chevy` object? As it turns out, you've got two options when accessing a property of an object. You already know dot notation:

```
chevy.color
```
We just use the object name followed by a dot and a property name.

But there's another way: bracket notation, which looks like this:

```
chevy["color"]
```
Here we use the object name followed by brackets that enclose a property name in quotes.

Looks a bit like how we access array items.

```
JavaScript console
make: Chevy
model: Bel Air
year: 1957
color: red
passengers: 2
convertible: false
mileage: 1021
```

The thing to know about both of these forms, is they are equivalent and do the same thing. The only difference you need to know about is the bracket notation sometimes allows a little more flexibility because you can make the property name an expression like this:

```
chevy["co" + "lor"]
```
As long as the expression evaluates to a property name represented by a string, you can put any expression you want inside the backets.

How behavior affects state...
Adding some Gas-o-line

Objects contain *state* and *behavior*. An object's properties allow us to keep state about the object—like its fuel level, its current temperature or, say, the current song that is playing on the radio. An object's methods allow us to have behavior—like starting a car, turning up the heat or fast-forwarding the playback of a song. Have you also noticed these two *interact*? Like, we can't start a car if it doesn't have fuel, and the amount of fuel should get reduced as we drive the car. Kinda like real life, right?

Let's play with this concept a little more by giving our car some fuel, and then we can start to add interesting behavior. To add fuel, we'll add a new property, `fuel`, and a new method, `addFuel`. The `addFuel` method will have a parameter, `amount`, which we'll use to increase the amount of fuel in the `fuel` property. So, add these properties to the `fiat` object:

```
var fiat = {
    make: "Fiat",
    model: "500",
    // other properties go here, we're saving some paper...
    started: false,
    fuel: 0,

    start: function() {
        this.started = true;
    },
    stop: function() {
        this.started = false;
    },
    drive: function() {
        if (this.started) {
            alert(this.make + " " + this.model + " goes zoom zoom!");
        } else {
            alert("You need to start the engine first.");
        }
    },
    addFuel: function(amount) {
        this.fuel = this.fuel + amount;
    }
};
```

We've added a new property, fuel, to hold the amount of fuel in the car. The car will begin life on empty.

Let's also add a method, addFuel, to add fuel to the car. We can add as much fuel as we like by specifying the amount when we call the method.

Remember, fuel is an object property, so we need the this keyword...

But amount is a function parameter, so we don't need this to use it.

Now let's affect the behavior with the state

So now that we have fuel, we can start to implement some interesting behaviors. For instance, if there's no fuel, we shouldn't be able to drive the car! So, let's start by tweaking the `drive` method a bit to check the fuel level to make sure we've got some, and then we'll subtract one from `fuel` each time the car is driven. Here's the code to do that:

```
var fiat = {
    // other properties and methods here...
    drive: function() {
        if (this.started) {
            if (this.fuel > 0) {
                alert(this.make + " " +
                    this.model + " goes zoom zoom!");
                this.fuel = this.fuel - 1;
            } else {
                alert("Uh oh, out of fuel.");
                this.stop();
            }
        } else {
            alert("You need to start the engine first.");
        }
    },
    addFuel: function(amount) {
        this.fuel = this.fuel + amount;
    }
};
```

Now we can check to make sure there's fuel before we drive the car. And, if we can drive the car, we should reduce the amount of fuel left each time we drive.

If there's no fuel left, we display a message and stop the engine. To drive the car again, you'll have to add fuel and restart the car.

Gas up for a test drive

Go ahead and update your code, and take it for a spin! Here's what we got with the following test code:

```
fiat.start();
fiat.drive();
fiat.addFuel(2);
fiat.start();
fiat.drive();
fiat.drive();
fiat.drive();
fiat.stop();
```

First, we tried to drive it with no fuel, so then we added some fuel and drove it until we ran out of fuel again! Try adding your own test code and make sure it works like you think it should.

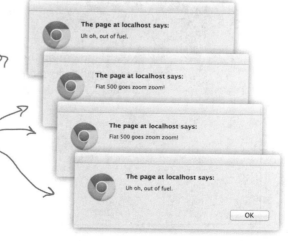

We still have some more work to do to fully integrate the fuel property into the car. For instance, should you be able to start the car if there's no fuel? Check out the start method:

```
start: function() {
        this.started = true;
}
```

It certainly looks like we can.

Help us integrate the fuel property into this code by checking the fuel level before the car is started. If there's no fuel, and the start method is called, let the driver know with a handy alert, like **"The car is on empty, fill up before starting!"** Rewrite your start method below, and then add it to your code and test it. Check your answer at the end of the chapter before you go on.

Your code here.

BRAIN POWER

Take a look at all the fiat car code. Are there other places you could use the fuel property to alter the car's behavior (or create behavior to modify the fuel property)? Jot down your ideas below.

With objects the future's so bright we really DO have to wear shades...

Congrats on your first objects!

You've made it through the first objects chapter and you're ready to move forward. Remember how you began with JavaScript? You were thinking of the world in terms of low-level numbers and strings and statements and conditionals and for loops and so on. Look how far you've come. You're starting to think at a higher level, and in terms of objects and methods. Just look at this code:

```
fiat.addFuel(2);
fiat.start();
fiat.drive();
fiat.stop();
```

It's so much easier to understand what's going on in this code, because it describes the world as a set of objects with state and behavior.

And this is just the beginning. You can take it so much further, and we will. Now that you know about objects we're going to keep developing your skills to write truly object-oriented code using even more features of JavaScript and quite a few best practices (which become oh-so-important with objects).

There's one more thing you should know, before you leave this chapter...

Guess what? There are objects all around you! (and they'll make your life easier)

Now that you know a bit about objects, a whole new world is going to open up for you because JavaScript provides you with lots of objects (for doing math computations, manipulating strings and creating dates and times, to name a few) that you can use in your own code. JavaScript also provides some really key objects that you need to write code for the browser (and we're going to take a look at one of those objects in the next chapter). For now, take a second to get acquainted with a few more of these objects, and we'll touch on these throughout the rest of the book:

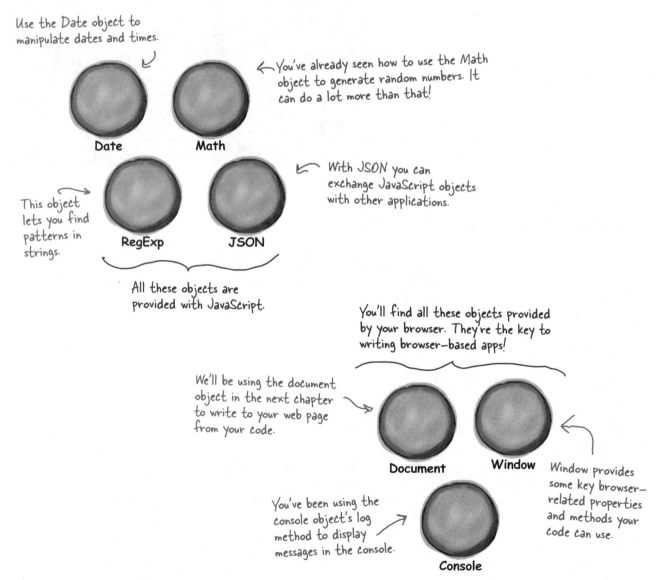

Use the Date object to manipulate dates and times.

You've already seen how to use the Math object to generate random numbers. It can do a lot more than that!

Date

Math

This object lets you find patterns in strings.

With JSON you can exchange JavaScript objects with other applications.

RegExp

JSON

All these objects are provided with JavaScript.

You'll find all these objects provided by your browser. They're the key to writing browser-based apps!

We'll be using the document object in the next chapter to write to your web page from your code.

Document

Window

Window provides some key browser-related properties and methods your code can use.

You've been using the console object's log method to display messages in the console.

Console

The Object Exposed

This week's interview:
In Object's own words...

Head First: Welcome Object, it's been a fascinating chapter. It's a real head-spinner thinking about code as objects.

Object: Oh, well... we've only just begun.

Head First: How so?

Object: An object is a set of properties, right? Some of those properties are used to keep the state of the object, and some are actually functions—or rather, methods—that give an object behavior.

Head First: I'm with you so far. I hadn't actually thought about the methods being properties too, but I guess they are just another name and value, if you can call a function a value?

Object: Oh you can! Believe me, you can. In fact, that's a huge insight, whether you realize it or not. Hold on to that thought; I'm guessing there's a lot in store for you on that topic.

Head First: But you were saying...

Object: So, you've looked at these objects with their properties and you've created lots of them, like a bunch of different types of cars.

Head First: Right...

Object: But it was very *ad hoc*. The real power comes when you can create a template of sorts, something that can basically stamp out uniform objects for you.

Head First: Oh, you mean objects that all have the same type?

Object: Sort of... as you'll see the concept of type is an interesting one in JavaScript. But you're on the right track. You'll see that you have real power when you can start to write code that deals with objects of the same kind. Like you could write code that deals with vehicles and you wouldn't have to care if they are bicycles, cars or buses. That's power.

Head First: It certainly sounds interesting. What else do we need to know to do that?

Object: Well, you have to understand objects a little better, and you need a way to create objects of the same kind.

Head First: We just did that, didn't we? All those cars?

Object: They're sort of the same kind by convention, because you happened to write code that creates cars that look alike. In other words, they have the same properties and methods.

Head First: Right, and in fact we talked a little about how we are replicating code across all those objects, which is not necessarily a good thing in terms of maintaining that code.

Object: The next step is to learn how to create objects that really are all guaranteed to be the same, and that make use of the same code—code that's all in one place. That's getting into how to design object-oriented code. And you're pretty much ready for that now that you know the basics.

Head First: I'm sure our readers are happy to hear that!

Object: But there are a few more things about objects to be aware of.

Head First: Oh?

Object: There are many objects already out there in the wild that you can use in your code.

Head First: Oh? I hadn't noticed, where?

Object: How about `console.log`. What do you think `console` is?

Head First: Based on this discussion, I'm guessing it's an object?

Object: BINGO. And `log`?

Head First: A property... err, a method?

Object: BINGO again. And what about `alert`?

Head First: I haven't a clue.

Object: It has to do with an object, but we'll save that for a bit later.

Head First: Well, you've certainly given us a lot to think about Object, and I'm hoping you'll join us again.

Object: I'm sure we can make that work.

Head First: Great! Until next time then.

Crack the Code Challenge

In his quest for world domination, Dr. Evel has accidentally exposed an internal web page with the current passcode to his operation. With the passcode we can finally get the upper hand. Of course, as soon as Dr. Evel discovered the page was live on the Internet, he quickly took it down. Luckily, our agents made a record of the page. The only problem is, our agents don't know HTML or JavaScript. Can you help figure out the access code using the code below? Keep in mind, if you are wrong, it could be quite costly to Queen and Country.

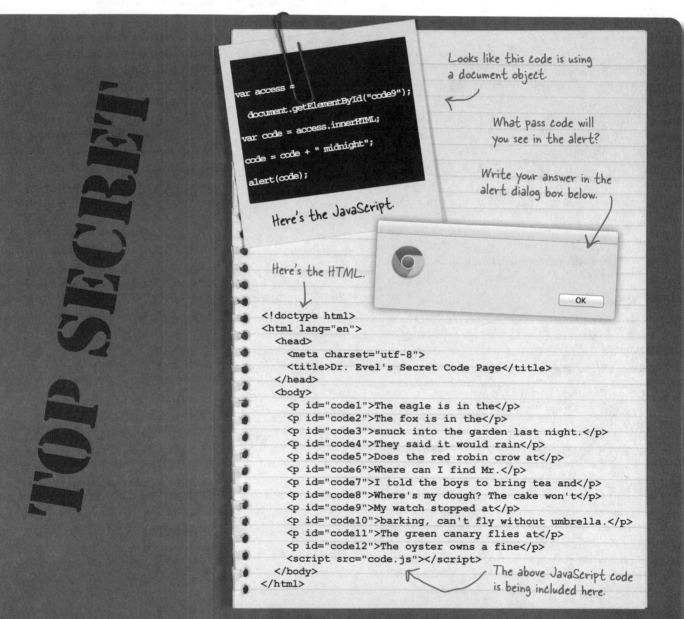

TOP SECRET

Looks like this code is using a document object.

```javascript
var access =
    document.getElementById("code9");

var code = access.innerHTML;

code = code + " midnight";

alert(code);
```

Here's the JavaScript.

What pass code will you see in the alert?

Write your answer in the alert dialog box below.

OK

Here's the HTML.

```html
<!doctype html>
<html lang="en">
  <head>
    <meta charset="utf-8">
    <title>Dr. Evel's Secret Code Page</title>
  </head>
  <body>
    <p id="code1">The eagle is in the</p>
    <p id="code2">The fox is in the</p>
    <p id="code3">snuck into the garden last night.</p>
    <p id="code4">They said it would rain</p>
    <p id="code5">Does the red robin crow at</p>
    <p id="code6">Where can I find Mr.</p>
    <p id="code7">I told the boys to bring tea and</p>
    <p id="code8">Where's my dough? The cake won't</p>
    <p id="code9">My watch stopped at</p>
    <p id="code10">barking, can't fly without umbrella.</p>
    <p id="code11">The green canary flies at</p>
    <p id="code12">The oyster owns a fine</p>
    <script src="code.js"></script>
  </body>
</html>
```

The above JavaScript code is being included here.

If you skipped the last page, go back and do the challenge. It is vitally important to Chapter Six!

BULLET POINTS

- An object is a **collection of properties**.

- To access a property, use **dot notation**: the name of the variable containing the object, then a period, then the name of the property.

- You can add new properties to an object at any time, by assigning a value to a new property name.

- You can also delete properties from objects, using the **delete** operator.

- Unlike variables that contain primitive values, like strings, numbers, and booleans, a variable can't actually contain an object. Instead, it contains a **reference** to an object. We say that objects are "reference variables".

- When you pass an object to a function, the function gets a copy of the reference to the object, not a copy of the object itself. So, if you change the value of one of the object's properties, it changes the value in the original object.

- Object properties can contain functions. When a function is in an object, we call it a method.

- You call a method by using the **dot notation**: the object name, a period, and the property name of the method, followed by parentheses.

- A method is just like a function except that it is in an object.

- You can pass arguments to methods, just like you can to regular functions.

- When you call an object's method, the keyword **this** refers to the object whose method you are calling.

- To access an object's properties in an object's method, you must use dot notation, with **this** in place of the object's name.

- In object-oriented programming, we think in terms of objects rather than procedures.

- An object has both **state** and **behavior**. State can affect behavior, and behavior can affect state.

- Objects **encapsulate**, or hide, the complexity of the state and behavior in that object.

- A well-designed object has methods that abstract the details of how to get work done with the object, so you don't have to worry about it.

- Along with the objects you create, JavaScript has many built-in objects that you can use. We'll be using many of these built-in objects throughout the rest of the book.

JavaScript cross

How about a crossword object? It's got lots of clue
properties that will help objects stick in your brain.

ACROSS

2. An object gets _____ with its methods.

6. The method log is a property in the _____ object.

8. **this** is a _____, not a regular variable.

10. To access the property of an object we use _____
notation.

11. _____ can have local variables and parameters,
just like regular functions can.

13. We used a _____ property to represent the make of
a car object.

14. The _____ method affects the state of the car object,
by adding to the amount of fuel in the car.

DOWN

1. The fiat wouldn't start because we weren't using
_____ to access the started property.

3. Object references are passed by _____ to functions,
just like primitive variables.

4. When you assign an object to a variable, the variable
contains a _____ to the object.

5. We usually use one _____ for property names.

7. The name and value of a property in an object are
separated by a _____.

9. Don't forget to use a _____ after each property value
except the last one.

12. Car and dog objects can have both _____ and
behavior.

Sharpen your pencil
Solution

We've started making a table of property names and values for a car. Can you help complete it? Here's our solution:

Put your property names here.

And put the corresponding values over here.

{

make	:	"Chevy"	,
model	:	"Bel Air"	,
year	:	1957	,
color	:	"red"	,
passengers	:	2	,
convertible	:	false	,
mileage	:	1021	,
accessories	:	"Fuzzy Dice"	,
whitewalls	:	true	

};

We're using strings, booleans and numbers where appropriate.

Put your answers here. Feel free to expand the list to include your own properties.

Sharpen your pencil
Solution

Use your new **this** skills to help us finish this code. Here's our solution.

```
var eightBall = { index: 0,
                  advice: ["yes", "no", "maybe", "not a chance"],
                  shake: function() {
                          this.index = this.index + 1;
                          if (this.index  >= this.advice.length) {
                              this.index = 0;
                          }
                  },
                  look: function() {
                          return this.advice[this.index];
                  }
};
eightBall.shake();
console.log(eightBall.look());
```

Repeat this sequence several times to test your code.

JavaScript console

no

maybe

not a chance

Exercise Solution

You don't have to be stuck with just one object. The real power of objects (as you'll see soon enough) is having lots of objects and writing code that can operate on whatever object you give it. Try your hand at creating another object from scratch... another car object. Go ahead and work out the code for your second object. Here's our solution.

```
var cadi = {
    make: "GM",
    model: "Cadillac",
    year: 1955,
    color: "tan",
    passengers: 5,
    convertible: false,
    mileage: 12892
};
```

Here are the properties for the Cadillac.

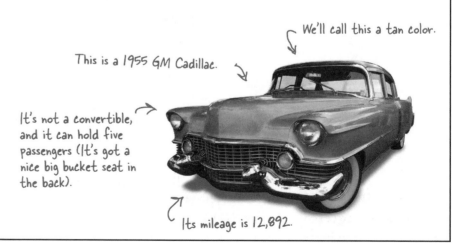

We'll call this a tan color.

This is a 1955 GM Cadillac.

It's not a convertible, and it can hold five passengers (It's got a nice big bucket seat in the back).

Its mileage is 12,892.

Object Magnets Solution

Practice your object creating and dot notation skills by completing the code below with the fridge magnets. Be careful, some extra magnets got mixed in! Here's our solution.

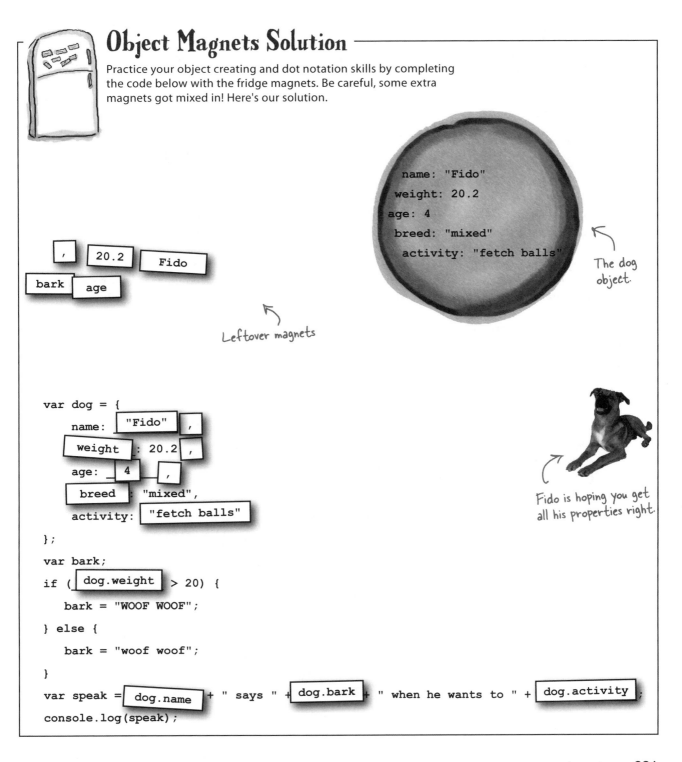

```
name: "Fido"
weight: 20.2
age: 4
breed: "mixed"
activity: "fetch balls"
```

The dog object.

```
,     20.2     Fido

bark     age
```

Leftover magnets

```
var dog = {
    name:    "Fido"    ,
    weight    : 20.2 ,
    age:    4    ,
    breed    : "mixed",
    activity:    "fetch balls"
};
var bark;
if (    dog.weight    > 20) {
    bark = "WOOF WOOF";
} else {
    bark = "woof woof";
}
var speak =    dog.name    + " says " +    dog.bark    + " when he wants to " +    dog.activity    ;
console.log(speak);
```

Fido is hoping you get all his properties right.

Sharpen your pencil
Solution

Your turn. Here are three more car objects; what is the result of passing each car to the `prequal` function? Work the answer by hand, and then write the code to check your answers. Here's our solution:

```
var cadi = {
    make: "GM",
    model: "Cadillac",
    year: 1955,
    color: "tan",
    passengers: 5,
    convertible: false,
    mileage: 12892
};

prequal(cadi);
```

_____ *false*

↗
Write the
value of
prequal here.

```
var fiat = {
    make: "Fiat",
    model: "500",
    year: 1957,
    color: "Medium Blue",
    passengers: 2,
    convertible: false,
    mileage: 88000
};

prequal(fiat);
```

_____ *false*

```
var chevy = {
    make: "Chevy",
    model: "Bel Air",
    year: 1957,
    color: "red",
    passengers: 2,
    convertible: false,
    mileage: 1021
};

prequal(chevy);
```

_____ *true*

Sharpen your pencil
Solution

You've been given a super secret file and two functions that allow access to get and set the contents of the file, but only if you have the right password. The first function, `getSecret`, returns the contents of the file if the password is correct, and logs each attempt to access the file. The second function, `setSecret`, updates the contents of the file, and resets the access tracking back to 0. It's your job to fill in the blanks below to complete the JavaScript, and test your functions. Here's our solution.

```
function getSecret(file, secretPassword) {
    __file__.opened = __file__.opened + 1;
    if (secretPassword == __file__.password) {
        return __file__.contents;
    }
    else {
        return "Invalid password! No secret for you.";
    }
}
function setSecret(file, secretPassword, secret) {
    if (secretPassword == __file__.password) {
        __file__.opened = 0;
        __file__.contents = secret;
    }
}


var superSecretFile = {
    level: "classified",
    opened: 0,
    password: 2,
    contents: "Dr. Evel's next meeting is in Detroit."
};
var secret = getSecret(__superSecretFile__, _2_);
console.log(secret);

setSecret(__superSecretFile__, _2_, "Dr. Evel's next meeting is in Philadelphia.");
secret = getSecret(__superSecretFile__, _2_);
console.log(secret);
```

The superSecretFile object is passed into the getSecret function, and gets the parameter name file. So we need to make sure we use the object name, file and dot notation to access the object's properties, like opened, and password.

Same here.

We can pass the supserSecretFile object to the getSecret and setSecret functions.

BE the Browser Solution

Below, you'll find JavaScript code with some mistakes in it. Your job is to play like you're the browser and find the errors in the code. Here's our solution.

```
var song = {
    name: "Walk This Way",
    artist: "Run-D.M.C.",
    minutes: 4,
    seconds: 3,
    genre: "80s",
    playing: false,

    play: function() {
        if (!this.playing) {                    ← We were missing a this here.
            this.playing = true;                ← And missing the playing
            console.log("Playing "                 property name here.
                + this.name + " by " + this.artist);
        }                    ← We need to use this to access
    },                          both these properties, too.

    pause: function() {
        if (this.playing) {    ← Again here, we need this to access the playing property.
            this.playing = false;
        }
    }
};

this song.play();    ← We don't use this outside of a method; we call
this song.pause();      an object using the object's variable name.
```

Exercise
Solution

It's time to get the whole fleet up and running. Add the drive method to each car object. When you've done that, add the code to start, drive and stop each of them. Here's our solution.

```
var cadi = {
    make: "GM",
    model: "Cadillac",
    year: 1955,
    color: "tan",
    passengers: 5,
    convertible: false,
    mileage: 12892,
    started: false,
    start: function() {
        this.started = true;
    },
    stop: function() {
        this.started = false;
    },
    drive: function() {
        if (this.started) {
            alert(this.make + " " +
                this.model + " goes zoom zoom!");
        } else {
            alert("You need to start the engine first.");
        }
    }
};
var chevy = {
    make: "Chevy",
    model: "Bel Air",
    year: 1957,
    color: "red",
    passengers: 2,
    convertible: false,
    mileage: 1021,
    started: false,
    start: function() {
        this.started = true;
    },
    stop: function() {
        this.started = false;
    },
    drive: function() {
        if (this.started) {
            alert(this.make + " " +
                this.model + " goes zoom zoom!");
        } else {
            alert("You need to start the engine first.");
        }
    }
};
```

```
var taxi = {
    make: "Webville Motors",
    model: "Taxi",
    year: 1955,
    color: "yellow",
    passengers: 4,
    convertible: false,
    mileage: 281341,
    started: false,
    start: function() {
        this.started = true;
    },
    stop: function() {
        this.started = false;
    },
    drive: function() {
        if (this.started) {
            alert(this.make + " " +
                this.model + " goes zoom zoom!");
        } else {
            alert("You need to start the engine first.");
        }
    }
};
```

Make sure you add a comma after any new properties you add.

```
cadi.start();
cadi.drive();
cadi.stop();

chevy.start();
chevy.drive();
chevy.stop();

taxi.start();
taxi.drive();
taxi.stop();
```

We copied and pasted the code into each object, so every car has the same properties and methods.

Now we can start, drive and stop each of the cars, using the same method names.

Exercise Solution

We still have some more work to do to fully integrate the fuel property into the car. For instance, should you really be able to start the car if there's no fuel? Help us integrate the fuel property into this code by checking the fuel level before the car is started. If there's no fuel, and the start method is called, let the driver know with a handy alert, like **"The car is on empty, fill up before starting!"** Rewrite the start method below, and then add it to your code and test it. Check your answer at the end of the chapter before you go on. Here's our solution.

The page at localhost says:
The car is on empty, fill up before starting!

OK

```javascript
var fiat = {
    make: "Fiat",
    model: "500",
    year: 1957,
    color: "Medium Blue",
    passengers: 2,
    convertible: false,
    mileage: 88000,
    fuel: 0,
    started: false,

    start: function() {
        if (this.fuel == 0) {
            alert("The car is on empty, fill up before starting!");
        } else {
            this.started = true;
        }
    },

    stop: function() {
        this.started = false;
    },
    drive: function() {
        if (this.started) {
            if (this.fuel > 0) {
                alert(this.make + " " +
                    this.model + " goes zoom zoom!");
                this.fuel = this.fuel - 1;
            } else {
                alert("Uh oh, out of fuel.");
                this.stop();
            }
        } else {
            alert("You need to start the engine first.");
        }
    },
    addFuel: function(amount) {
        this.fuel = this.fuel + amount;
    }
};
```

JavaScript cross Solution

How about a crossword object? It's got lots of clue properties that will help objects stick in your brain.

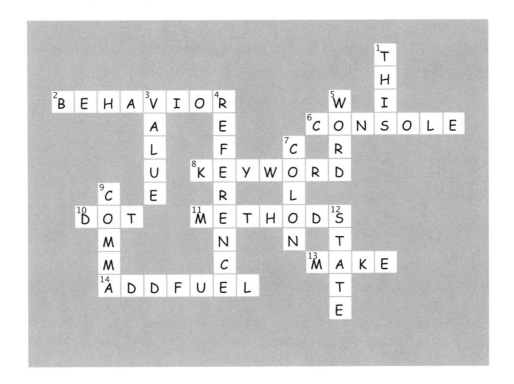

Getting to know the DOM

Hold on there cowboy. If you wanna get to know me, then you need to know your way around my document object model...

You've come a long way with JavaScript. In fact you've evolved from a newbie to a scripter to, well, a **programmer**. But, there's something missing. To really begin leveraging your JavaScript skills you need to know how to interact with the web page your code lives in. Only by doing that are you going to be able to write pages that are **dynamic**, pages that react, that respond, that update themselves after they've been loaded. So how do you interact with the page? By using the **DOM**, otherwise known as the **document object model**. In this chapter we're going to break down the DOM and see just how we can use it, along with JavaScript, to teach your page a few new tricks.

In our last chapter, we left you with a little challenge. The "crack the code challenge."

You were given some HTML with code in an external file, captured from Dr. Evel's web site, that looked like this:

Here's the HTML.

```
<!doctype html>
<html lang="en">
  <head>
    <meta charset="utf-8">
    <title>Dr. Evel's Secret Code Page</title>
  </head>
  <body>
    <p id="code1">The eagle is in the</p>
    <p id="code2">The fox is in the</p>
    <p id="code3">snuck into the garden last night.</p>
    <p id="code4">They said it would rain</p>
    <p id="code5">Does the red robin crow at</p>
    <p id="code6">Where can I find Mr.</p>
    <p id="code7">I told the boys to bring tea and</p>
    <p id="code8">Where's my dough? The cake won't</p>
    <p id="code9">My watch stopped at</p>
    <p id="code10">barking, can't fly without umbrella.</p>
    <p id="code11">The green canary flies at</p>
    <p id="code12">The oyster owns a fine</p>
    <script src="code.js"></script>
  </body>
</html>
```

Notice that each paragraph is identified by an id.

Here's the JavaScript....

```
var access =
    document.getElementById("code9");
var code = access.innerHTML;
code = code + " midnight";
alert(code);
```

document is a global object.

And getElementById is a method.

Make sure you get the case right on the letters in the method name getElementById, otherwise it won't work!

And look, we have dot notation, this looks like an object with an innerHTML property.

And you needed to figure out Dr. Evel's passcode using your deductive powers on this code.

So what does the code do?

We'll learn all about document and element objects in this chapter.

Let's walk through this code to see how Dr Evel is generating his passcodes. After we break down each step you'll start to see how this all works:

(1) First, the code sets the variable `access` to the result of calling the `document` object's `getElementById` method and passing it "code9". What gets returned is an element object.

```
var access =
  document.getElementById("code9");
var code = access.innerHTML;
code = code + " midnight";
alert(code);
```

Get the element that has an id of "code9". That would be this element...

```
<p id="code9">My watch stopped at</p>
```

(2) Next we take that element (that is, the element with the id "code9") and we use its `innerHTML` property to get its content, which we assign to the variable `code`.

```
var access =
  document.getElementById("code9");
var code = access.innerHTML;
code = code + " midnight";
alert(code);
```

The element with id "code9" is a paragraph element and that element's content (or rather its "innerHTML") is the text "My watch stopped at".

(3) Dr. Evel's code adds the string " midnight" to the end of string contained in `code`, which is "My watch stopped at". Then, the page creates an alert with the passcode contained in the variable `code`.

```
var access =
  document.getElementById("code9");
var code = access.innerHTML;
code = code + " midnight";
alert(code);
```

The page at localhost says:
My watch stopped at midnight

OK

So we add " midnight" to "My watch stopped at" to get "My watch stopped at midnight" and then put up an alert to display this code.

A quick recap

So, what did we just do? Well, we had some JavaScript that reached into the page (otherwise known as the *document*), grabbed an element (the one with the id equal to `"code9"`), took that element's content (which is `"My watch stopped at"`), slapped a `" midnight"` on the end, and then displayed the result as a passcode.

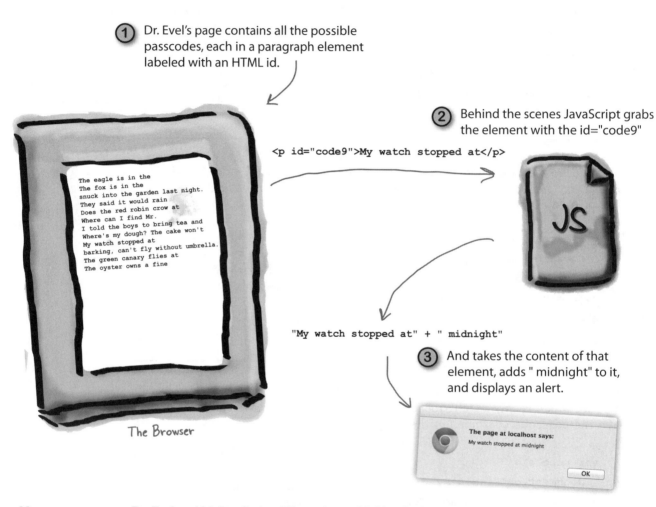

① Dr. Evel's page contains all the possible passcodes, each in a paragraph element labeled with an HTML id.

② Behind the scenes JavaScript grabs the element with the id="code9"

`<p id="code9">My watch stopped at</p>`

The eagle is in the
The fox is in the
snuck into the garden last night.
They said it would rain
Does the red robin crow at
Where can I find Mr.
I told the boys to bring tea and
Where's my dough? The cake won't
My watch stopped at
barking, can't fly without umbrella.
The green canary flies at
The oyster owns a fine

The Browser

`"My watch stopped at" + " midnight"`

③ And takes the content of that element, adds `" midnight"` to it, and displays an alert.

The page at localhost says:
My watch stopped at midnight

OK

Now, more power to Dr. Evel and his JavaScript skills, and we wish him the best in his security schemes, but what is important here is to notice that the web page is a living, breathing *data structure* that your JavaScript can interact with—you can access and read the content of the elements in your page. You can also go the other way, and use JavaScript to change the content or structure of your page. To do all that, let's step back for a moment and understand better how JavaScript and HTML work together.

How JavaScript really interacts with your page

JavaScript and HTML are *two different things*. HTML is markup and JavaScript is code. So how do they interact? It all happens through a representation of your page, called the *document object model*, or the DOM for short. Where does the DOM come from? It's created when the browser loads your page. Here's how:

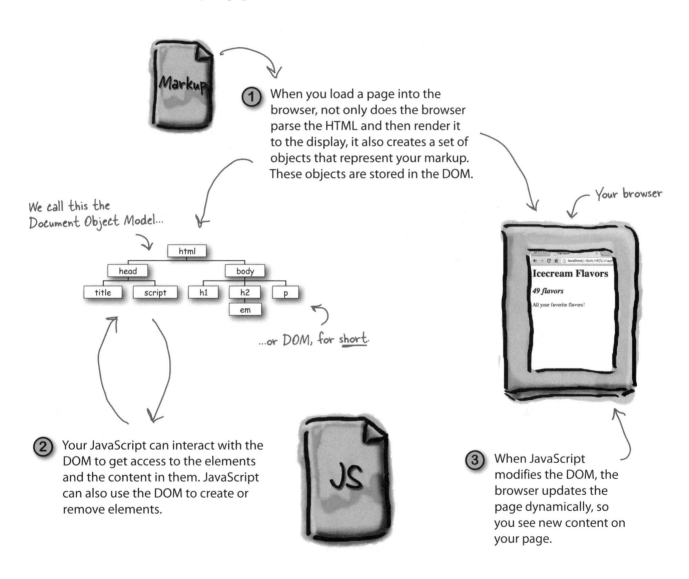

1 When you load a page into the browser, not only does the browser parse the HTML and then render it to the display, it also creates a set of objects that represent your markup. These objects are stored in the DOM.

We call this the Document Object Model...

...or DOM, for short.

Your browser

2 Your JavaScript can interact with the DOM to get access to the elements and the content in them. JavaScript can also use the DOM to create or remove elements.

3 When JavaScript modifies the DOM, the browser updates the page dynamically, so you see new content on your page.

How to bake your very own DOM

Let's take some markup and create a DOM for it. Here's a simple recipe for doing that:

Ingredients

One well-formed HTML5 page

One modern web browser, pre-heated and ready to go

Instructions

1. Start by creating a document node at the top.

2. Next, take the top level element of your HTML page, in our case the <html> element, call it the current element and add it as a child of the document.

```
document
   |
  html
```

3. For each element nested in the current element, add that element as a child of the current element in the DOM.

```
        document
           |
          html
        /      \
     head      body
```

4. Return to (3) for each element you just added, and repeat until you are out of elements.

```
<!doctype html>
<html lang="en">
<head>
    <meta charset="utf-8">
    <title>My blog</title>
    <script src="blog.js"></script>
</head>
<body>
    <h1>My blog</h1>
    <div id="entry1">
        <h2>Great day bird watching</h2>
        <p>
            Today I saw three ducks!
            I named them
            Huey, Louie, and Dewey.
        </p>
        <p>
            I took a couple of photos...
        </p>
    </div>
</body>
</html>
```

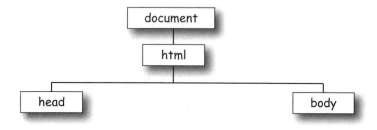

We've already fully baked this DOM for you. See the finished DOM on the next page.

A first taste of the DOM

If you follow the recipe for creating a DOM you'll end up with a structure like the one below. Every DOM has a document object at the top and then a tree complete with branches and leaf nodes for each element in the HTML markup. Let's take a closer look.

We compare this structure to a tree because a "tree" is a data structure that comes from computer science, and because it looks like an upside down tree, with the root at the top and the leaves at the bottom.

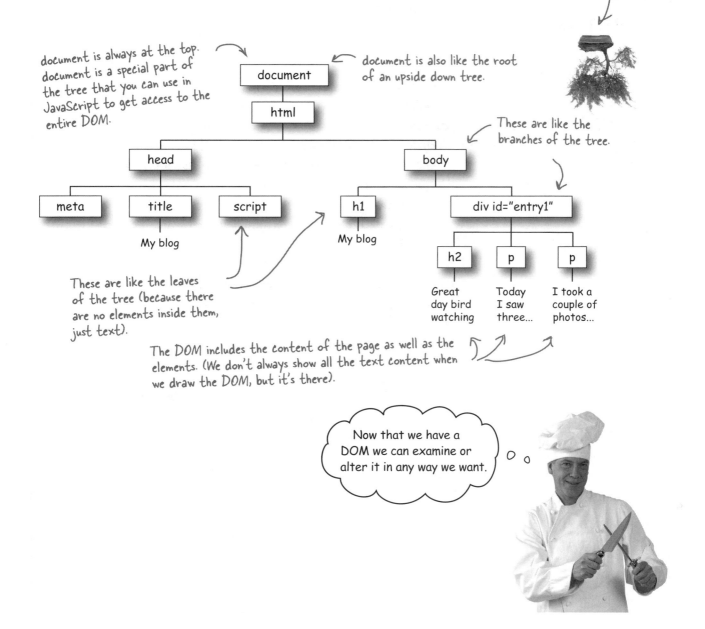

document is always at the top. document is a special part of the tree that you can use in JavaScript to get access to the entire DOM.

document is also like the root of an upside down tree.

These are like the branches of the tree.

These are like the leaves of the tree (because there are no elements inside them, just text).

The DOM includes the content of the page as well as the elements. (We don't always show all the text content when we draw the DOM, but it's there).

> Now that we have a DOM we can examine or alter it in any way we want.

BE the Browser

Your job is to act like you're the browser. You need to parse the HTML and build your very own DOM from it. Go ahead and parse the HTML to the right, and draw your DOM below. We've already started it for you.

Check your answer with our solution at the end of the chapter before you go on.

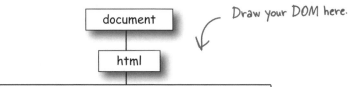

```html
<!doctype html>
<html lang="en">
  <head>
    <meta charset="utf-8">
    <title>Movies</title>
  </head>
  <body>
    <h1>Movie Showtimes</h1>
    <h2 id="movie1">Plan 9 from Outer Space</h2>
    <p>Playing at 3:00pm, 7:00pm.
      <span>
        Special showing tonight at <em>midnight</em>!
      </span>
    </p>
    <h2 id="movie2">Forbidden Planet</h2>
    <p>Playing at 5:00pm, 9:00pm.</p>
  </body>
</html>
```

```
          ┌──────────────┐
          │   document   │        Draw your DOM here.
          └──────────────┘
                 │
            ┌─────────┐
            │  html   │
            └─────────┘
                 │
      ┌──────────┴──────────┐
```

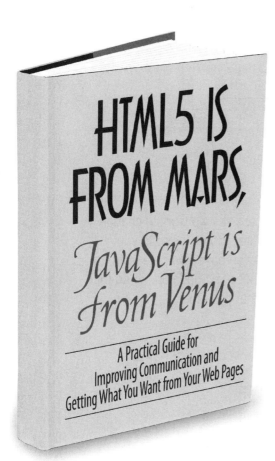

Or, how two totally different technologies hooked up.

HTML and JavaScript are from different planets for sure. The proof? HTML's DNA is made of declarative markup that allows you to describe a set of nested elements that make up your pages. JavaScript, on the other hand, is made of pure algorithmic genetic material, meant for describing computations.

Are they so far apart they can't even communicate? Of course not, because they have something in common: the DOM. Through the DOM, JavaScript can communicate with your page, and vice versa. There are a few ways to make this happen, but for now let's concentrate on one— it's a little wormhole of sorts that allows JavaScript to get access to any element in your page. That wormhole is *getElementById*.

Let's start with a DOM. Here's a simple DOM; it's got a few HTML paragraphs, each with an id identifying it as the green, red or blue planet. Each paragraph has some text as well. Of course there's a <head> element too, but we've left the details out to keep things simpler.

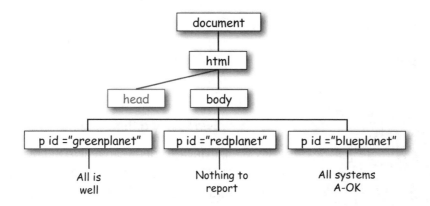

Now let's use JavaScript to make things more interesting. Let's say we want to change the greenplanet's text from "All is well" to "Red Alert: hit by phaser fire!" Down the road you might want to do something like this based on a user's actions, or even based on data from a web service. We'll get to all that; for now let's just get the greenplanet's text updated. To do that we need the element with the id "greenplanet". Here's some code that does that:

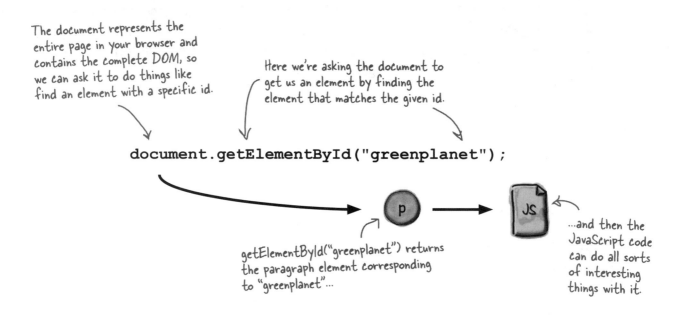

The document represents the entire page in your browser and contains the complete DOM, so we can ask it to do things like find an element with a specific id.

Here we're asking the document to get us an element by finding the element that matches the given id.

```
document.getElementById("greenplanet");
```

getElementById("greenplanet") returns the paragraph element corresponding to "greenplanet"...

...and then the JavaScript code can do all sorts of interesting things with it.

Once getElementById gives you an element, you're ready do something with it
(like change its text to "Red Alert: hit by phaser fire!"). To do that, we typically assign the
element to a variable so we can refer to the element thoughout our code. Let's do that
and then change the text:

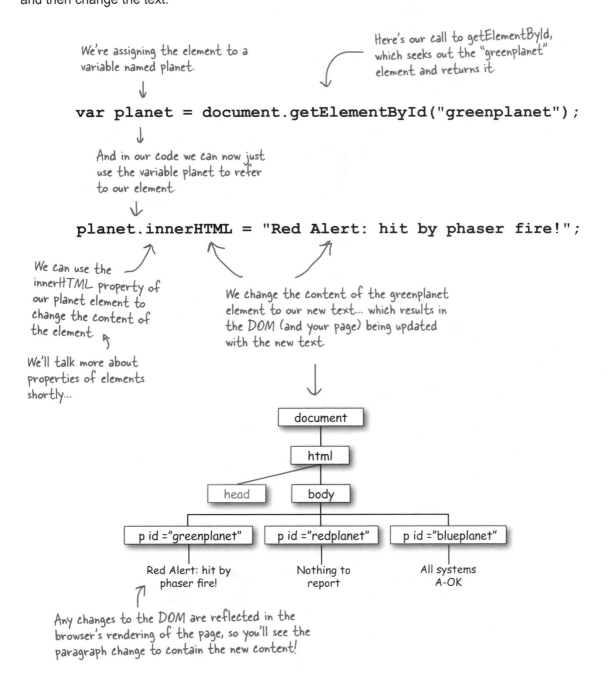

We're assigning the element to a
variable named planet.

Here's our call to getElementById,
which seeks out the "greenplanet"
element and returns it.

```
var planet = document.getElementById("greenplanet");
```

And in our code we can now just
use the variable planet to refer
to our element.

```
planet.innerHTML = "Red Alert: hit by phaser fire!";
```

We can use the
innerHTML property of
our planet element to
change the content of
the element.

We'll talk more about
properties of elements
shortly...

We change the content of the greenplanet
element to our new text... which results in
the DOM (and your page) being updated
with the new text.

document

html

head   body

p id ="greenplanet"   p id ="redplanet"   p id ="blueplanet"

Red Alert: hit by   Nothing to   All systems
phaser fire!   report   A-OK

Any changes to the DOM are reflected in the
browser's rendering of the page, so you'll see the
paragraph change to contain the new content!

Getting an element with getElementById

So, what did we just do? Let's step through it in a little more detail. We're using the document object to get access to the DOM from our code. The document object is a built-in object that comes with a bunch of properties and methods, including getElementById, which we can use to grab an element from the DOM. The getElementById method takes an id and returns the element that has that id. Now in the past you've probably used ids to select and style elements with CSS. But here, what we're doing is using an id to grab an element—the <p> element with the id "greenplanet"—from the DOM.

Once we have the right element, we can modify it. We'll get to that in just a moment; for now, let's focus on how getElementById works by tracing through these steps:

Follow the steps 1, 2, 3.

1

> Browser here, I'm reading the page and creating a DOM of it.

Green Planet

All is well

Red Planet

Nothing to report

Blue Planet

All systems A-OK

document
html
head   body
p id ="greenplanet"   p id ="redplanet"   p id ="blueplanet"
All is well   Nothing to report   All systems A-OK

> JavaScript code here, I'm looking for an element in the DOM with an id of "greenplanet".

We're using document to get access to the DOM.

2 `var planet = document.getElementById("greenplanet");`

Here's our call to getElementById.

And we're looking for the element with an id of "greenplanet".

We'll assign the element that is returned to the planet variable for later use.

> You found me! I'm the <p> element with the "greenplanet" id. Just tell me what you need to do.

3

What, exactly, am I getting from the DOM?

When you grab an element from the DOM using `getElementById`, what you get is an *element object*, which you can use to read, change or replace the element's content and attributes. And here's the magic: when you change an element, *you change what is displayed in your page as well.*

But, first things first. Let's take another look at the element object we just grabbed from the DOM. We know that this element object represents the <p> element in our page that has the id "greenplanet" and that the text content in the element is "All is well". Just like other kinds of JavaScript objects, an element object has properties and methods. In the case of an element object, we can use these properties and methods to read and change the element. Here are a few things you can do with element objects:

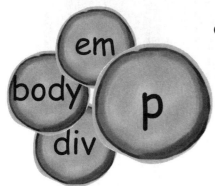

Get the content (text or HTML).

Change the content.

Read an attribute.

Add an attribute.

Change an attribute.

Remove an attribute.

Things you can do with an element object.

What we want to do with our <p> element—which, remember, is the <p> element with the id "greenplanet"—is change the content "All is well" to "Red Alert: hit by phaser fire!". We've got the element object stashed in the `planet` variable in our code; let's use that to modify one of its properties, `innerHTML`:

The planet variable contains an element object—the element object that is the "greenplanet" <p> element.

```
var planet = document.getElementById("greenplanet");

planet.innerHTML = "Red Alert: hit by phaser fire!";
```

We can use the innerHTML property of the element object to change the content of the element!

Finding your inner HTML

The `innerHTML` property is an important property that we can use to read or replace the content of an element. If you look at the value of `innerHTML` then you'll see the content contained *within* the element, not including the HTML element tags. The "withIN" is why it's called "inner" HTML. Let's try a little experiment. We'll try displaying the content of the `planet` element object in the console by logging the `innerHTML` property. Here's what we get:

```
var planet = document.getElementById("greenplanet");
console.log(planet.innerHTML);
```

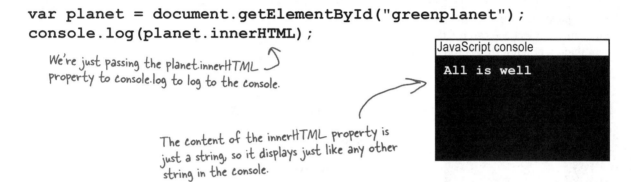

We're just passing the planet.innerHTML property to console.log to log to the console.

JavaScript console

All is well

The content of the innerHTML property is just a string, so it displays just like any other string in the console.

Now let's try changing the value of the `innerHTML` property. When we do this, we're changing the content of the "greenplanet" `<p>` element in the page, so you'll see your page change too!

```
var planet = document.getElementById("greenplanet");
planet.innerHTML = "Red Alert: hit by phaser fire!";
console.log(planet.innerHTML);
```

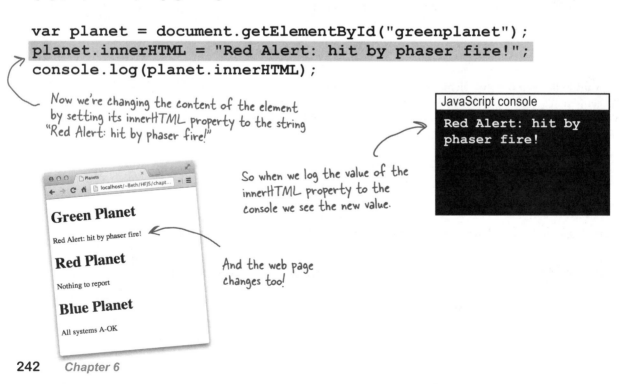

Now we're changing the content of the element by setting its innerHTML property to the string "Red Alert: hit by phaser fire!"

JavaScript console

Red Alert: hit by phaser fire!

So when we log the value of the innerHTML property to the console we see the new value.

Green Planet

Red Alert: hit by phaser fire!

Red Planet

Nothing to report

Blue Planet

All systems A-OK

And the web page changes too!

A Quick Refresher

Hey, sit down; take a quick break. You might be saying to yourself, "Wait, I remember something about ids and classes but I don't remember the specifics, and don't they have something to do with CSS anyway?" No, problem, let's just have a quick refresher, get some context, and we'll have you back on your way in no time...

With HTML, ids give us a way to uniquely identify an element, and, once an element is unique, we can use that to select it with CSS for styling. And, as you've seen, we can get an element by its id in JavaScript as well.

Let's look at an example:

```
<div id="menu">
    ...
</div>
```

We're giving this <div> a unique id of "menu". It should be the only element in your page with the id "menu".

And once we have that, we can select it with CSS to style it. Like this:

div#menu is an id selector.

```
div#menu {
    background-color: #aaa;
}
```

div#menu selects the <div> with the id menu, so we can apply style to that element, and only that element.

And we can access this element through its id in JavaScript too:

```
var myMenu = document.getElementById("menu");
```

Don't forget, there's another way to label your elements: with classes. Classes give us a way to label a set of elements, like this:

```
<h3 class="drink">Strawberry Blast</h3>
<h3 class="drink">Lemon Ice</h3>
```

Both <h3> elements are in the class "drink". A class is like a group; you can have multiple elements in the same group.

And we can select elements by classes too, both in CSS and JavaScript. We'll see how to make use of classes with JavaScript in a bit. And, by the way, if this reminder isn't quite enough, check out Chapter 7 of *Head First HTML and CSS,* or your favorite HTML & CSS reference guide.

What happens when you change the DOM

So, what exactly happens when you change the content of an element using `innerHTML`? What you're doing is changing actual content of your web page, on the fly. And when you change the content in the DOM, you'll see that change immediately in your web page, too.

Before...

The web page you see and the DOM behind the scenes before you change the content with innerHTML...

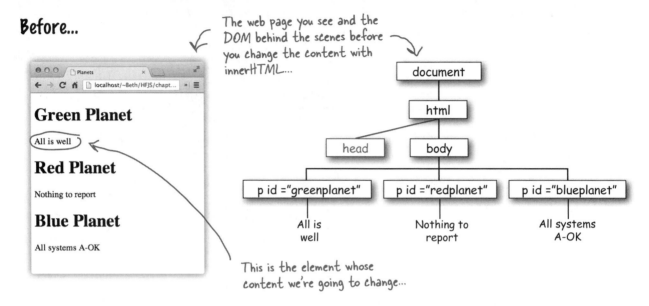

This is the element whose content we're going to change...

... and after.

... and the web page you see and the DOM behind the scenes after you change the content with innerHTML.

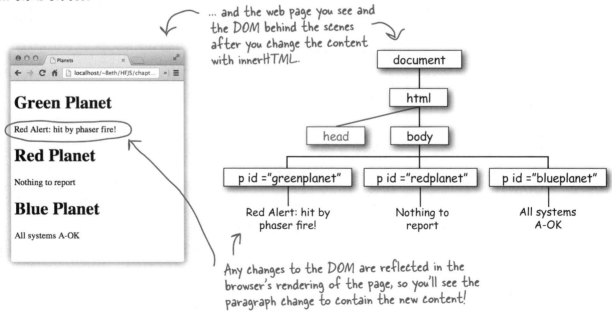

Any changes to the DOM are reflected in the browser's rendering of the page, so you'll see the paragraph change to contain the new content!

there are no
Dumb Questions

Q: What happens if I use document.getElementById and pass in an id that doesn't exist?

A: If you try to get an element from the DOM by id, and that id doesn't exist in an element, then the call to getElementById returns a null value. Testing for null is a good idea when you use getElementById to ensure that the element is there before you try to access its properties. We'll talk more about null in the next chapter.

Q: Can we use document.getElementById to get elements by class as well—for instance, say I have a bunch of elements in the class "planets"?

A: No, but you're thinking along the right lines. You can only use getElementById with an id. But there is another DOM method named getElementsByClassName that you can use to get elements by class name. With this method, what you get back is a collection of elements that belong to the class (because multiple elements can be in the same class). Another method that returns a collection of elements is getElementsByTagName, which returns all elements that match the tag name you specify. We'll see getElementsByTagName a little later in the book and see how to handle the collection of elements it returns.

Q: What exactly is an element object anyway?

A: Great question. An element object is the browser's internal representation of what you type into your HTML file, like <p>some text</p>. When the browser loads and parses your HTML file, it creates an element object for every element in your page, and adds all those element objects to the DOM. So the DOM is really just a big tree of element objects. And, keep in mind that, just like other objects, element objects can have properties, like innerHTML, and methods, too. We'll explore a few more of the properties and methods of element objects later in the book.

Q: I would have expected a property named "content" or maybe "html" in the element object. Why is it called innerHTML instead?

A: We agree, it's kind of a weird name. The innerHTML property represents all the content contained in your element, including other nested elements (like a paragraph might include <em> and <img> elements in addition to the text in the paragraph). In other words, it's the HTML that's "INside" your element. Is there an outerHTML property? Yes! And that property gets you all the HTML inside the element, as well as the element itself. In practice you won't see outerHTML used very often, but you will see innerHTML used frequently to update the content of elements.

Q: So by assigning something to innerHTML I can replace the content of any element with something else. What if I used innerHTML to change, say, the <body> element's content?

A: Right, innerHTML gives you a convenient way to replace the content of an element. And, yes, you could use it to replace the content of the <body> element, which would result in your entire page being replaced with something new.

Here's a DOM with a secret message hidden in it. Evaluate the code below to reveal the secret! The answer is upside down on this page.

```
document.getElementById("e7")
document.getElementById("e8")
document.getElementById("e16")
document.getElementById("e9")
document.getElementById("e18")
document.getElementById("e13")
document.getElementById("e12")
document.getElementById("e2")
```

Write the element each line of code selects, as well as the content of the element to reveal the secret message!

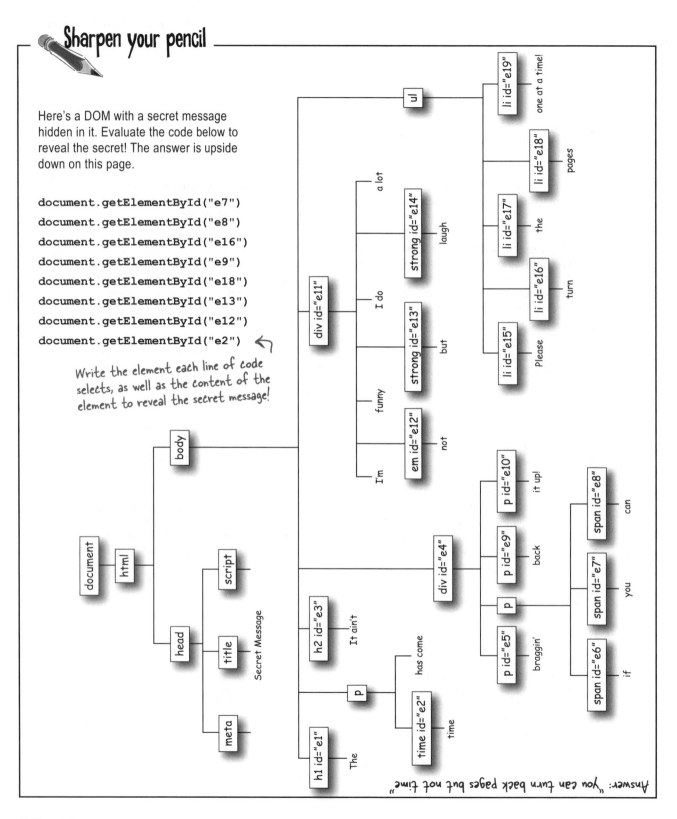

Answer: "You can turn back pages but not time."

A test drive around the planets

Okay, you know how to use `document.getElementById` to get access to an element, and how to use `innerHTML` to change the content of that element. Let's do it for real, now.

Here's the HTML for the planets. We've got a `<script>` element in the `<head>` where we'll put the code, and three paragraphs for the green, red, and blue planets. If you haven't already, go ahead and type in the HTML and the JavaScript to update the DOM:

```
<!doctype html>
<html lang="en">
<head>
  <meta charset="utf-8">
  <title>Planets</title>
  <script>
    var planet = document.getElementById("greenplanet");
    planet.innerHTML = "Red Alert: hit by phaser fire!";
  </script>
</head>
<body>
  <h1>Green Planet</h1>
  <p id="greenplanet">All is well</p>
  <h1>Red Planet</h1>
  <p id="redplanet">Nothing to report</p>
  <h1>Blue Planet</h1>
  <p id="blueplanet">All systems A-OK</p>
</body>
</html>
```

Here's our script element with the code.

Just like you saw before, we're getting the `<p>` element with the id "greenplanet" and changing its content.

Here's the `<p>` element you're going to change with JavaScript.

After you've got it typed in, go ahead and load the page into your browser and see the DOM magic happen on the green planet.

UH OH! Houston, we've got a problem, the green planet still shows "All is well". What's wrong?

I've triple-checked my markup and code, and this just isn't working for me either. I'm not seeing any changes to my page.

Oh yeah, we forgot to mention one thing.

When you're dealing with the DOM it's important to execute your code only *after* the page is *fully loaded*. If you don't, there's a good chance the DOM won't be created by the time your code executes.

Let's think about what just happened: we put code in the `<head>` of the page, so it begins executing before the browser even sees the rest of the page. That's a big problem because that paragraph element with an id of "greenplanet" doesn't exist, yet.

So what happens exactly? The call to `getElementById` returns null instead of the element we want, causing an error, and the browser, being the good sport that it is, just keeps moving and renders the page anyway, but without the change to the green planet's content.

Check out your console when this page loads, you'll see the error in most browsers. The console tool is good for debugging.

How do we fix this? Well, we could move the code to the bottom of the `<body>`, but there's actually a more foolproof way to make sure this code runs at the right time; a way to tell the browser "run my code after you've fully loaded in the page and created the DOM." Let's see how to do that next.

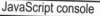

```
JavaScript console

Uncaught TypeError:
Cannot set property
'innerHTML' of null
```

Don't even think about running my code until the page is fully loaded!

Ah, but how? Besides moving the code to the bottom of the body, there's another—and, one might argue—cleaner way to do it: *with code.*

Here's how it works: first create a function that has the code you'd like executed *once the page is fully loaded.* After you've done that, you take the window object, and assign the function to its `onload` property.

> *The window object is built-in to JavaScript. It represents the browser window.*

What does that do? The window object will call any function you've assigned to its `onload` property, but only *after* the page is fully loaded. So, thank the designers of the window object for giving you a way to supply the code that gets called after the page has loaded. Check this out:

> *First, create a function named init and put your existing code in the function.*

> *You can call this function anything you want, but it's often called init by convention.*

> *Here's the code we had before, only now it's in the body of the init function.*

```
<script>
function init() {
    var planet = document.getElementById("greenplanet");
    planet.innerHTML = "Red Alert: hit by phaser fire!";
}

window.onload = init;
</script>
```

> *Here, we're assigning the function init to the window.onload property. Make sure you <u>don't</u> use parentheses after the function name! We're not calling the function; we're just assigning the function value to the window.onload property.*

Let's try that again...

Go ahead and reload the page with the new `init` function and the `onload` property. This time the browser will load the page completely, build the entire DOM and *only then* call your `init` function.

> *Ah, there we go, now the green planet shows the Red Alert, just like we wanted.*

You say "event hander," I say "callback"

Let's think about how `onload` works just a bit more, because it uses a common coding pattern you'll see over and over again in JavaScript.

Let's say there's a big important event that's going to occur, and you *definitely* want to know about it. Say that event is the "page is loaded" event. Well, a common way to deal with that situation is through a *callback*, also known as an *event handler*.

A callback works like this: give a function to the object that knows about the event. When the event occurs, that object will call you back, or notify you, by calling that function. You're going to see this pattern in JavaScript for a variety of events.

The callback, or event handler, if you prefer.

Hey browser, I'm waiting until you've loaded the page before I can get some things done.

The browser, or, more specifically, the window object.

Well don't sit around waiting, just give me a callback function and I'll call it when I'm finished.

No problem... here ya go, it's named init.

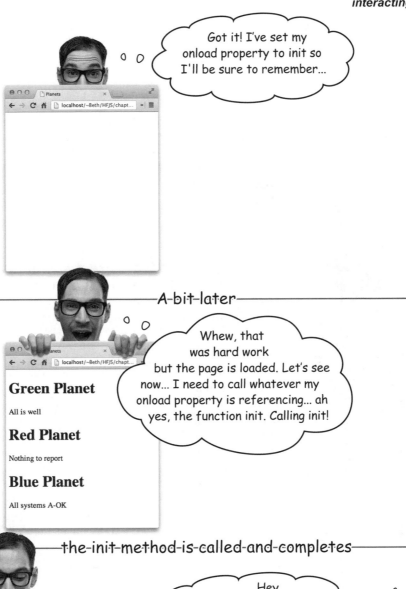

Got it! I've set my onload property to init so I'll be sure to remember...

—A-bit-later—

Whew, that was hard work but the page is loaded. Let's see now... I need to call whatever my onload property is referencing... ah yes, the function init. Calling init!

—the-init-method-is-called-and-completes—

Hey browser, thanks for remembering to call init! Went off without a hitch!

And once init is called, we see the update to our page!

Interesting. So I can use functions to package up code that can be called when some event happens. What other kinds of events can I handle with functions like this?

That's right, and there are many kinds of events you can handle if you want

to. Some events, like the load event, are generated by the browser, while others are generated by a user interacting with the page, or even by your own JavaScript code.

You've seen an example of "the page is loaded" event, which we handle by setting the `onload` property of the window object. You can also write event handlers that handle things like "call this function every five seconds," or "some data arrived from a web service that we need to deal with," or "the user clicked a button and we need to get some data from a form," and there are many more. All these types of events are heavily used when you're creating pages that act more like applications than static documents (and who doesn't want that). Right now, we've had just a brief glimpse of event handlers, but we'll be spending a lot more time on them a bit later given their important role in JavaScript programming.

Sharpen your pencil

Here's the HTML for the page.

Here's some HTML for a playlist of songs, except that the list is empty. It's your job to complete the JavaScript below to add the songs to the list. Fill in the blank with the JavaScript that will do the job. Check your answer with our solution at the end of the chapter before you go on.

```
<!doctype html>

<html lang="en">

<head>

  <title>My Playlist</title>

  <meta charset="utf-8">

  <script>

  _____ addSongs()  {

    var song1 = document._____("_____");

    var _____ = _____("_____");

    var _____ = _____.getElementById("_____");


    _____.innerHTML = "Blue Suede Strings, by Elvis Pagely";

    _____ = "Great Objects on Fire, by Jerry JSON Lewis";

    song3._____ = "I Code the Line, by Johnny JavaScript";

  }

  window._____ = _____;

  </script>

</head>

<body>

  <h1>My awesome playlist</h1>

  <ul id="playlist">

    <li id="song1"></li>

    <li id="song2"></li>

    <li id="song3"></li>

  </ul>

</body>

</html>
```

Here's our script. This code should fill in the list of songs below, in the <ul>.

Fill in the blanks with the missing code to get the playlist filled out.

Here's the empty list of songs. The code above should add content to each <li> in the playlist.

When you get the JavaScript working, this is what the web page will look like after you load the page.

My awesome playlist

- Blue Suede Strings, by Elvis Pagely
- Great Objects on Fire, by Jerry JSON Lewis
- I Code the Line, by Johnny JavaScript

Why stop now? Let's take it further

Let's think for a second about what you just did: you took a static web page and you dynamically changed the content of one of its paragraphs *using code*. It seems like a simple step, but this is really the beginning of making a *truly interactive* page.

And that's our goal, which we'll fully realize in Chapter 8.

Let's take the second step: now that you know how to get your hands on an element in the DOM, let's set an *attribute* of an element with code.

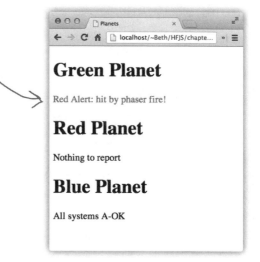

Why would that be interesting? Well, take our simple planets example. When we set the paragraph to read "Red Alert," we could also set the paragraph's color to red. That would certainly more clearly communicate our message.

Here's how we're going to do that:

① We'll define a CSS rule for the class "redtext" that specifies a red color for the text of the paragraph. That way any element we add to this class will have red text.

② Next, we'll add code to take the greenplanet paragraph element and add the class "redtext".

That's it. All we need now is to learn how to set an attribute of an element and then we can write the code.

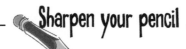 ## Sharpen your pencil

How about getting another part of your brain working? We're going to need the CSS style for the class "redtext" that sets the color to "red" for the text in the planet paragraph. If it's been a while since you wrote CSS, don't worry; give it a shot anyway. If you can do it in your sleep, awesome. Either way, you'll find the answer at the end of this chapter.

How to set an attribute with setAttribute

Element objects have a method named `setAttribute` that you can call to set the value of an HTML element's attribute. The `setAttribute` method looks like this:

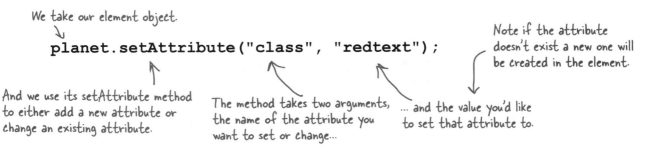

We take our element object.

```
planet.setAttribute("class", "redtext");
```

And we use its setAttribute method to either add a new attribute or change an existing attribute.

The method takes two arguments, the name of the attribute you want to set or change...

... and the value you'd like to set that attribute to.

Note if the attribute doesn't exist a new one will be created in the element.

We can call `setAttribute` on any element to change the value of an existing attribute, or, if the attribute doesn't already exist, to add a new attribute to the element. As an example, let's check out how executing the code above affects our DOM.

Before...

Here's the element before we call the setAttribute method on it. Notice this element already has one attribute, id.

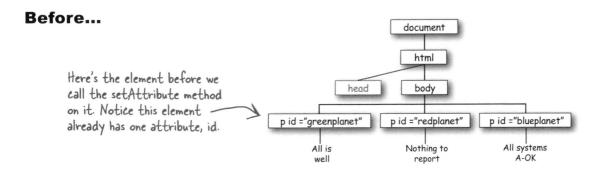

And After

And here's the element after we call setAttribute. Now you can see it's got two attributes, id and class.

Remember, when we call the setAttribute method, we're changing the element object in the DOM, which immediately changes what you see displayed in the browser.

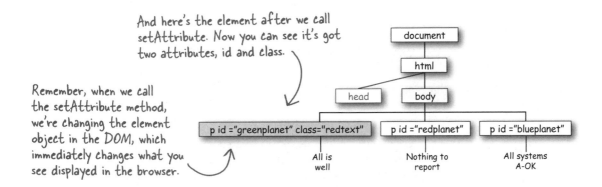

More fun with attributes!
(you can GET attributes too)

Need to know the value of an attribute in an element? No problem, we have a `getAttribute` method that you can call to get the value of an HTML element's attribute.

Get a reference to the element with getElementById, then use the element's getAttribute method to get the attribute.

```
var scoop = document.getElementById("raspberry");
var altText = scoop.getAttribute("alt");
console.log("I can't see the image in the console,");
console.log(" but I'm told it looks like: " + altText);
```

Pass in the name of the attribute you want the value of.

What happens if my attribute doesn't exist in the element?

Remember what happens when you call `getElementById` and the id doesn't exist in the DOM? You get null. Same thing with `getAttribute`. If the attribute doesn't exist, you'll get back null. Here's how you test for that:

```
var scoop = document.getElementById("raspberry");
var altText = scoop.getAttribute("alt");
if (altText == null) {
    console.log("Oh, I guess there isn't an alt attribute.");
} else {
    console.log("I can't see the image in the console,");
    console.log(" but I'm told it looks like " + altText);
}
```

Test to make sure there actually is an attribute value returned.

If there's no attribute value, we do this...

... and if there is one, we can show the text content in the console.

Don't forget getElementById can return null too!

Any time you ask for something, you need to make sure you got back what you expected...

The call to getElementById can return a null value if the element id does not exist in the DOM. So, to follow best practices, you'll want to make sure you test for null after getting elements too. We could follow that rule ourselves, but then the book would end up being 1000 pages longer.

Meanwhile, back at the ~~ranch~~ solar system...

It's time to put all the code for the planets together and do a final test drive.

```
<!doctype html>
<html lang="en">
<head>
  <meta charset="utf-8">
  <title>Planets</title>
  <style>
    .redtext { color: red; }
  </style>
  <script>
    function init() {
        var planet = document.getElementById("greenplanet");
        planet.innerHTML = "Red Alert: hit by phaser fire!";
        planet.setAttribute("class", "redtext");
    }
    window.onload = init;
  </script>
</head>
<body>
  <h1>Green Planet</h1>
  <p id="greenplanet">All is well</p>
  <h1>Red Planet</h1>
  <p id="redplanet">Nothing to report</p>
  <h1>Blue Planet</h1>
  <p id="blueplanet">All systems A-OK</p>
</body>
</html>
```

Here's all the HTML, CSS and JavaScript for the planets.

We've got the redtext class included here so when we add "redtext" as the value for the class attribute in our code, it turns the text red.

And to review: we're getting the greenplanet element, and stashing the value in the planet variable. Then we're changing the content of the element, and finally adding a class attribute that will turn the text of the element red.

We're calling the init function only when the page is fully loaded!

Test driving the planets one last time...

Load this page up in your browser and you'll see the green planet has been hit by phaser fire, and now we see the message in bright red, so we'll be sure not to miss it!

So what else is a DOM good for anyway?

The DOM can do a fair bit more than we've seen so far and we'll be seeing some of its other functionality as we move forward in the book, but for now let's just take a quick look so you've got it in the back of your mind:

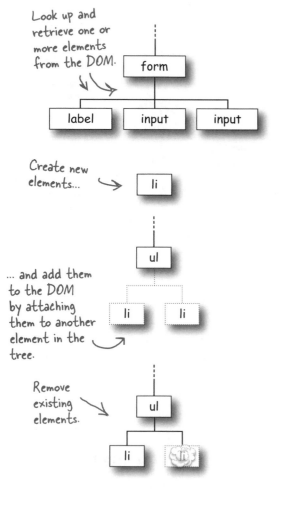

Look up and retrieve one or more elements from the DOM.

Create new elements...

... and add them to the DOM by attaching them to another element in the tree.

Remove existing elements.

Get all the children of an element...

... or get the parent of an element.

... get an element's siblings...

Get elements from the DOM.

Of course you already know this because we've been using document.getElementById, but there are other ways to get elements as well; in fact, you can use tag names, class names and attributes to retrieve not just one element, but a whole set of elements (say all elements in the class "on_sale"). And you can get form values the user has typed in, like the text of an input element.

Create and add elements to the DOM.

You can create new elements and you can also add those elements to the DOM. Of course, any changes you make to the DOM will show up immediately as the DOM is rendered by the browser (which is a good thing!).

Remove elements from the DOM.

You can also remove elements from the DOM by taking a parent element and removing any of its children. Again, you'll see the element removed in your browser window as soon as it is deleted from the DOM.

Traverse the elements in the DOM.

Once you have a handle to an element, you can find all its children, you can get its siblings (all the elements at the same level), and you can get its parent. The DOM is structured just like a family tree!

BULLET POINTS

- The **Document Object Model**, or DOM, is the browser's internal representation of your web page.

- The browser creates the DOM for your page as it loads and parses the HTML.

- You get access to the DOM in your JavaScript code with the document object.

- The document object has properties and methods you can use to access and modify the DOM.

- The **document.getElementById** method grabs an element from the DOM using its id.

- The document.getElementById method returns an **element object** that represents an element in your page.

- An element object has properties and methods you can use to read an element's content, and change it.

- The **innerHTML** property holds the text content, as well as all nested HTML content, of an element.

- You can modify the content of an element by changing the value of its innerHTML property.

- When you modify an element by changing its innerHTML property, you see the change in your web page immediately.

- You can get the value of an element's attributes using the **getAttribute** method.

- You can set the value of an element's attributes using the **setAttribute** method.

- If you put your code in a <script> element in the <head> of your page, you need to make sure you don't try to modify the DOM until the page is fully loaded.

- You can use the window object's **onload** property to set an **event handler**, or callback, function for the load event.

- The event handler for the window's onload property will be called as soon as the page is fully loaded.

- There are many different kinds of events we can handle in JavaScript with event handler functions.

 JavaScript cross

Load the DOM into your brain with this puzzle.

ACROSS

5. Functions that handle events are known as event
_____.

7. Dr. Evel's passcode clue was in the element with the id _____.

9. Assign a _____ to the window.onload property to handle the load event.

12. Use the element object's property, _____, to change the HTML inside an element.

14. The setAttribute method is a method of an _____ object.

15. The DOM is shaped like a _____.

DOWN

1. Which planet gets hit by phaser fire?

2. Use the _____ to see if you have errors in your code.

3. It's important to make sure the ____ is completely loaded before using code to get or change elements in the page.

4. The getElementById method gets an element by its ___.

6. Change the class of an element using the _____ method.

8. The _____ object is always at the top of the DOM tree.

10. It's a good idea to check for _____ when using getElementById.

11. When you load a page into the browser, the browser creates a _____ representing all the elements and content in the page.

13. getElementById is a _____ of the document object.

BE the Browser Solution

Your job is to act like you're the browser. You need to parse the HTML and build your very own DOM from it. Go ahead and parse the HTML to the right, and draw your DOM below. We've already started it for you.

Movie Showtimes

Plan 9 from Outer Space

Playing at 3:00pm, 7:00pm. Special showing tonight at *midnight*!

Forbidden Planet

Playing at 5:00pm, 9:00pm.

```html
<!doctype html>
<html lang="en">
  <head>
    <meta charset="utf-8">
    <title>Movies</title>
  </head>
  <body>
    <h1>Movie Showtimes</h1>
    <h2 id="movie1" >Plan 9 from Outer Space</h2>
    <p>Playing at 3:00pm, 7:00pm.
      <span>
        Special showing tonight at <em>midnight</em>!
      </span>
    </p>
    <h2 id="movie2">Forbidden Planet</h2>
    <p>Playing at 5:00pm, 9:00pm.</p>
  </body>
</html>
```

Here's our DOM

```
                    document
                        |
                      html
              _____|_____
             |                       |
           head                    body
          ___|___      _____|_____
         |       |    |      |       |      |            |       |
       meta    title  h1   h2 id=  p      h2 id=        p
                           "movie1"              "movie2"
                                     |
                                   span
                                     |
                                    em
```

**Sharpen your pencil
Solution**

Here's the HTML for the page.

Here's some HTML for a playlist of songs, except that the list is empty. It's your job to complete the JavaScript below to add the songs to the list. Fill in the blank with the JavaScript that will do the job. Here's our solution.

```
<!doctype html>

<html lang="en">

<head>

  <meta charset="utf-8">

  <title>My Playlist</title>

  <script>
    function     addSongs() {

    var song1 = document.getElementById ("  song1  ");

    var song2 = document.getElementById ("  song2  ");

    var song3 = document.getElementById("  song3  ");


     song1   .innerHTML = "Blue Suede Strings, by Elvis Pagely";
     song2.innerHTML     = "Great Objects on Fire, by Jerry JSON Lewis";
    song3. innerHTML     = "I Code the Line, by Johnny JavaScript";

    }

    window. onload   = addSongs   ;

  </script>

</head>

<body>

  <h1>My awesome playlist</h1>

  <ul id="playlist">

    <li id="song1"></li>

    <li id="song2"></li>

    <li id="song3"></li>

  </ul>

</body>

</html>
```

Here's our script. This code should fill in the list of songs below, in the <ul>.

Fill in the blanks with the missing code to get the playlist filled out.

Here's the empty list of songs. The code above should add content to each <li> in the playlist.

This is what the web page looks like after you load the page.

My awesome playlist

- Blue Suede Strings, by Elvis Pagely
- Great Objects on Fire, by Jerry JSON Lewis
- I Code the Line, by Johnny JavaScript

Sharpen your pencil
Solution

How about getting another part of your brain working? We're going to need the CSS style for the class "redtext" that sets the color to "red" for the text in the planet paragraph. If it's been a while since you wrote CSS, don't worry; give it a shot anyway. If you can do it in your sleep, awesome. Here's our solution.

```
.redtext { color: red; }
```

JavaScript cross Solution

Load the DOM into your brain with this puzzle.

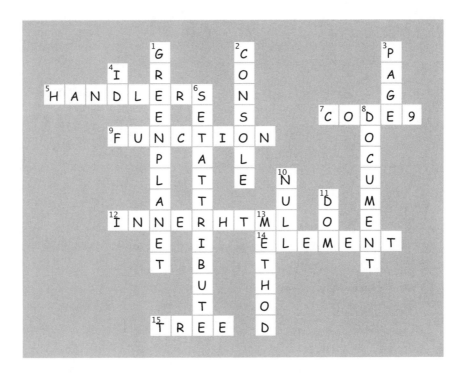

7 types, equality, conversion and all that jazz

Serious types

It's time to get serious about our types. One of the great things about JavaScript is you can get a long way without knowing a lot of details of the language. But to truly **master the language**, get that promotion and get on to the things you really want to do in life, you have to rock at **types**. Remember what we said way back about JavaScript? That it didn't have the luxury of a silver-spoon, academic, peer-reviewed language definition? Well that's true, but the academic life didn't stop Steve Jobs and Bill Gates, and it didn't stop JavaScript either. It does mean that JavaScript doesn't have the... well, the most thought-out type system, and we'll find a few **idiosyncrasies** along the way. But, don't worry, in this chapter we're going to nail all that down, and soon you'll be able to avoid all those embarrassing moments with types.

The truth is out there...

Now that you've had a lot of experience working with JavaScript types—there's your primitives with numbers, strings, and booleans, and there's all the objects, some supplied by JavaScript (like the Math object), some supplied by the browser (like the document object), and some you've written yourself—aren't you just basking in the glow of JavaScript's simple, powerful and consistent type system?

Low-level basic types for numbers, strings, booleans.

High-level objects used to represent the things in your problem space.

Primitive Types

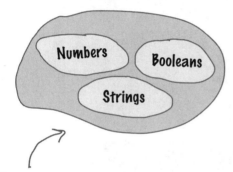

Objects

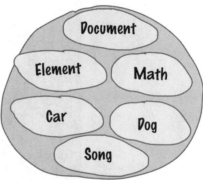

These are all supplied by JavaScript.

JavaScript also supplies a lot of useful objects, but you can also create your own or use objects other developers have written.

After all what else would you expect from the official language of Webville? In fact, if you were a mere scripter, you might think about sitting back, sipping on that Webville Martini, and taking a much needed break...

But you're not a mere scripter, and something is amiss. You have that sinking feeling that behind Webville's picket fences something bizarre is at work. You've heard the reports of sightings of strings that are acting like objects, you've read in the blogs about a (probably radioactive) null type, you've heard the rumors that the JavaScript interpreter as of late has been doing some weird type conversion. What does it all mean? We don't know, but the truth is out there and we're going to uncover it in this chapter, and when we do, we might just turn what you think of true and false upside down.

Who am I?

A bunch of JavaScript values and party crashers, in full costume, are playing a party game, "Who am I?" They give you a clue, and you try to guess who they are, based on what they say. Assume they always tell the truth about themselves. Draw an arrow from each sentence to the name of one attendee. We've already guessed one of them for you. Check your answers at the end of the chapter before you go on.

If you find this exercise difficult, it's okay to cheat and look at the answers.

Tonight's attendees:

I get returned from a function when there is no return statement.

zero

I'm the value of a variable when I haven't been assigned a value.

empty object

null

I'm the value of an array item that doesn't exist in a sparse array. ⟶ undefined

NaN

I'm the value of a property that doesn't exist.

infinity

area 51

I'm the value of a property that's been deleted.

...---...

I'm the value that can't be assigned to a property when you create an object.

{}

[]

Watch out, you might bump into undefined when you aren't expecting it...

As you can see, whenever things get shaky—you need a variable that's not been initialized yet, you want a property that doesn't exist (or has been deleted), you go after an array item that isn't there—you're going to encounter `undefined`.

But what the heck is it? It's not really that complicated. Think of `undefined` as the value assigned to things that don't yet have a value (in other words they haven't been initialized).

So what good is it? Well, `undefined` gives you a way to test to see if a variable (or property, or array item) has been given a value. Let's look at a couple of examples, starting with an unassigned variable:

```
var x;

if (x == undefined) {
    // x isn't defined! just deal with it!
}
```

You can check to see if a variable like x is undefined. Just compare it to the value undefined.

Note that we're using the value undefined here, not to be confused with the string "undefined".

Or, how about an object property:

```
var customer = {
    name: "Jenny"
};
if (customer.phoneNumber == undefined) {
    // get the customer's phone number
}
```

You can check to see if a property is undefined, again by comparing it to the value undefined.

there are no Dumb Questions

Q: When do I need to check if a variable (or property or array item) is undefined?

A: Your code design will dictate this. If you've written code so that a property or variable may not have a value when a certain block of code is executed, then checking for undefined gives you a way to handle that situation rather than computing with undefined values.

Q: If undefined is a value, does it have a type?

A: Yes, it does. The type of undefined is undefined. Why? Well our logic (work with us here) is this: it isn't an object, or a number or a string or a boolean, or really anything that is defined. So why not make the type undefined, too? This is one of those weird twilight zones of JavaScript you just have to accept.

IN THE LABORATORY

In the laboratory we like to take things apart, look under the hood, poke and prod, hook up our diagnostic tools and check out what is really going on. Today, we're investigating JavaScript's type system and we've found a little diagnostic tool called **typeof** to examine variables. Put your lab coat and safety goggles on, and come on in and join us.

The **typeof** operator is built into JavaScript. You can use it to probe the type of its operand (the thing you use it to operate on). Here's an example:

```
var subject = "Just a string";

var probe = typeof subject;
console.log(probe);
```

The typeof operator takes an operand, and evaluates to the type of the operand.

The type here is "string". Note that typeof uses strings to represent types, like "string", "boolean", "number", "object", "undefined", and so on.

JavaScript console

string

Now it's your turn. Collect the data for the following experiments:

```
var test1 = "abcdef";
var test2 = 123;
var test3 = true;
var test4 = {};
var test5 = [];
var test6;
var test7 = {"abcdef": 123};
var test8 = ["abcdef", 123];
function test9(){return "abcdef"};

console.log(typeof test1);
console.log(typeof test2);
            console.log(typeof test3);
                console.log(typeof test4);
                console.log(typeof test5);
            console.log(typeof test6);
              console.log(typeof test7);
              console.log(typeof test8);
            console.log(typeof test9);
```

Here's the test data, and the tests.

JavaScript console

Put your results here. Are there any surprises?

> I remember from the DOM chapter that getElementById returns null, not undefined, if the id doesn't exist. What exactly is null, and why doesn't getElementById return undefined instead?

Ah yes, this causes a lot of confusion. There are many languages that have the concept of a value that means "no object." And, it's not a bad idea—take the `document.getElementById` method. It's supposed to return an object right? So, what happens if it can't? Then we want to return something that says "I would have been an object if there was one, but we don't have one." And that's what `null` is.

You can also set a variable to `null` directly:

```
var killerObjectSomeday = null;
```

What does it mean to assign the value `null` to a variable? How about "We intend to assign an object to this variable at some point, but we haven't yet."

Now, if you're scratching your head and saying "Hmm, why didn't they just use `undefined` for that?" then you're in good company. The answer comes from the very beginnings of JavaScript. The idea was to have one value for variables that haven't been initialized to anything yet, and another that means the lack of an object. It isn't pretty, and it's a little redundant, but it is what it is at this point. Just remember the intent of each (`undefined` and `null`), and know that it is most common to use `null` in places where an object should be but one can't be created or found, and it is most common to find `undefined` when you have a variable that hasn't been initialized, or an object with a missing property, or an array with a missing value.

BACK IN THE LABORATORY

Oops, we forgot null in our test data. Here's the missing test case:

```
var test10 = null;

console.log(typeof test10);
```
Put your results here.

JavaScript console

How to use null

There are many functions and methods out there in the world that return objects, and you'll often want to make sure what you're getting back is a full-fledged object, and not `null`, just in case the function wasn't able to find one or make one to return to you. You've already seen examples from the DOM where a test is needed:

Let's look for the all-important header element.

```
var header = document.getElementById("header");
if (header == null) {
    // okay, something is seriously wrong if we have no header
}
```

Uh oh, it doesn't exist. Abandon ship!

Keep in mind that getting `null` doesn't necessarily mean something is wrong. It may just mean something doesn't exist yet and needs to be created, or something doesn't exist and you can skip it. Let's say users have the ability to open or close a weather widget on your site. If a user has it open there's a `<div>` with the id of "weatherDiv", and if not, there isn't. All of a sudden `null` becomes quite useful:

Let's see if the element with id "weatherDiv" exists.

```
var weather = document.getElementById("weatherDiv");
if (weather != null) {
    // create content for the weather div
}
```

If the result of getElementById isn't null, then there is such an element in the page. Let's create a nice weather widget for it (presumably getting the weather for the local area).

We can use null to check to see if an object exists yet or not.

Remember, null is intended to represent an object that isn't there.

Blaine, Missouri
It is always 67 degrees with a 40% chance of rain.

WICKEDLYSMART'S
Believe It or Not!!

The Number that isn't a Number

Believe it or not, there are numeric values that are **impossible to represent** in JavaScript! JavaScript can't express these values, so it has a stand-in value that it uses:

NaN

JavaScript uses the value NaN, more commonly known as "Not a Number", to represent numeric results that, well, can't be represented. Take 0/0 for instance. 0/0 evaluates to something that just can't be represented in a computer, so it is represented by NaN in JavaScript.

It's easy to write JavaScript statements that result in numeric values that are not well defined.

Here are a few examples:

```
var a = 0/0;
```

> In mathematics this has no direct answer, so we can't expect JavaScript to know the answer either!

```
var b = "food" * 1000;
```

> We don't know what this evaluates to, but it is certainly not a number!

```
var c = Math.sqrt(-9);
```

> If you remember high school math, the square root of a negative number is an imaginary number, which you can't represent in JavaScript.

NaN MAY BE THE WEIRDEST VALUE IN THE WORLD. Not only does it represent all the numeric values that can't be represented, it is the only value in JavaScript that isn't equal to itself!

You heard that right. If you compare NaN to NaN, they aren't equal!

NaN != NaN

Dealing with NaN

Now you might think that dealing with NaN is a rare event, but if you're working with any kind of code that uses numbers, you'd be surprised how often it shows up. The most common thing you'll need to do is test for NaN, and given everything you've learned about JavaScript, how to do this might seem obvious:

```
if (myNum == NaN) {
    myNum = 0;
}
```

You'd think this would work, but it doesn't.

WRONG!

Any sensible person would assume that's how you test to see if a variable holds a NaN value, but it doesn't work. Why? Well, NaN isn't equal to anything, not even itself, so, any kind of test for equality with NaN is off the table. Instead you need to use a special function: isNaN. Like this:

```
if (isNaN(myNum)) {
    myNum = 0;
}
```

Use the isNaN function, which returns true if the value passed to it is not a number.

RIGHT!

It gets even weirder

So, let's think through this a bit more. If NaN stands for "Not a Number", what is it? Wouldn't it be easier if it were named for what it is rather than what it isn't? What do you think it is? We can check its type for a hint:

```
var test11 = 0 / 0;
console.log(typeof test11);
```

Here's what we got.

```
JavaScript console
number
```

If your mind isn't blown, you should probably just use this book for some good kindling.

What on earth? NaN is of type number? How can something that's not a number have the type number? Okay, deep breath. Think of NaN as just a poorly named value. Someone should have called it something more like "Number that can't be represented" (okay, we agree the acronym isn't quite as nice) instead of "Not a Number". If you think about it like that, then you can think of NaN as being a value that is a number but can't be represented (at least, not by a computer).

Go ahead and add this one to your JavaScript twilight zone list.

there are no
Dumb Questions

Q: If I pass isNaN a string, which isn't a number, will it return true?

A: It sure will, just as you'd expect. You can expect a variable holding the value NaN, or any other value that isn't an actual number to result in isNaN returning true (and false otherwise). There are a few caveats to this that you'll see when we talk about type conversion.

Q: But why isn't NaN equal to itself?

A: If you're deeply interested in this topic you'll want to seek out the IEEE floating point specification. However, the layman's insight into this is that just because NaN represents an unrepresentable numeric value, does not mean that those unrepresentable numbers are equal. For instance, take the sqrt(-1) and sqrt(-2). They are definitely not the same, but they both produce NaN.

Q: When we divide 0/0 we get NaN, but I tried dividing 10/0 and got `Infinity`. Is that different from `NaN`?

A: Good find. The Infinity (or -Infinity) value in JavaScript represents all numbers (to get a little technical) that exceed the upper limit on computer floating point numbers, which is

1.7976931348623157E+10308 (or -1.7976931348623157E+10308 for -Infinity). The type of Infinity is number and you can test for it if you suspect one of your values is getting a little large:

```
if (tamale == Infinity) {
    alert("That's a big tamale!");
}
```

Q: You did blow my mind with that "NaN is a number" thing. Any other mind blowing details?

A: Funny you should ask. How about Infinity minus Infinity equals.... wait for it........ NaN. We'll refer you to a good mathematician to understand that one.

Q: Just to cover every detail, did we say what the type of null is?

A: A quick way to find out is by using the typeof operator on null. If you do that you'll get back the result "object". And this makes sense from the perspective that null is used to represent an object that isn't there. However, this point has been heavily debated, and the most recent spec defines the type of null as null. You'll find this an area where your browser's JavaScript implementation may not match the spec, but, in practice, you'll rarely need to use the type of null in code.

Exercise

We've been looking at some rather, um, interesting, values so far in this chapter. Now, let's take a look at some interesting behavior. Try adding the code below to the <script> element in a basic web page and see what you get in the console when you load up the page. You won't get why yet, but see if you can take a guess about what might be going on.

```
if (99 == "99") {
    console.log("A number equals a string!");
} else {
    console.log("No way a number equals a string");
}
```

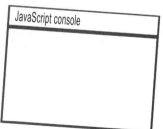

JavaScript console

Write what you get here.

We have a confession to make

There is an aspect of JavaScript we've deliberately been holding back on. We could have told you up front, but it wouldn't have made as much sense as it will now.

It's not so much that we've been pulling the wool over your eyes, it's that there is more to the story than we've been telling you. And what is this topic? Here, let's take a look:

At some point a variable gets set, in this case to the number 99.

```javascript
var testMe = 99;
```

And later it gets compared with a number in a conditional test.

```javascript
if (testMe == 99) {
    // good things happen
}
```

Straightforward enough? Sure, what could be easier? However, one thing we've done at least once so far in this book, that you might not have noticed, is something like this:

At some point a variable gets set, in this case to the string "99".

Did we mention we're using a string this time?

```javascript
var testMe = "99";
```

And later it gets compared with a number in a conditional test.

```javascript
if (testMe == 99) {
    // good things happen
}
```

Now we have a string being compared to a number.

So what happens when we compare a number to a string? Mass chaos? Computer meltdown? Rioting in the streets?

No, JavaScript is smart enough to determine that 99 and "99" are the same for all practical purposes. But what exactly is going on behind the scenes to make this work? Let's take a look…

BULLET POINTS

Just a quick reminder about the difference between assignment and equality:

- `var x = 99;`
  = is the assignment operator. It is used to assign a value to a variable.

- `x == 99`
  == is a comparison operator. It is used to compare one value with another to see if they're equal.

Understanding the equality operator (otherwise known as ==)

You'd think that understanding equality would be a simple topic. After all, 1 == 1, "guacamole" == "guacamole" and true == true. But, clearly there is more at work here if "99" == 99. What could be going on inside the equality operator to make that happen?

It turns out the == operator takes the types of its operands (that is, the two things you're comparing) into account when it does a comparison. You can break this down into two cases:

If the two values have the <u>same</u> type, just compare them

If the two values you are comparing have the same type, like two numbers or two strings, then the comparison works just like you would expect: the two values are compared against each other and the result is true if they are the same value. Easy enough.

If the two values have <u>different</u> types, try to <u>convert</u> them into the same type and then compare them

This is the more interesting case. Say you have two values with different types that you want to compare, like a number and a string. What JavaScript does is convert the string into a number, and then compares the two values. Like this:

← Note that the conversion is only temporary, so that the comparison can happen.

99 == "99"

When you're comparing a number and a string, JavaScript converts the string to a number (if possible)...

99 == 99

... and then tries the comparison again. Now, if they're equal, the expression results in true, false otherwise.

Okay, that makes some intuitive sense, but what are the rules here? What if I compare a boolean to a number, or null to undefined, or some other combination of values? How do I know what's going to get converted into what? And, why not convert the number into a string instead, or use some other scheme to test their equality? Well, this is defined by a fairly simple set of rules in the JavaScript specification that determine how the conversion happens when we compare two values with different types. This is one of those things you just need to internalize—once you've done that, you'll be on top of how comparisons work the rest of your JavaScript career.

This will also set you above your peers, and help you nail your next interview.

How equality converts its operands (sounds more dangerous than it actually is)

So what we know is that when you compare two values that have different types, JavaScript will convert one type into another in order to compare them. If you're coming from another language this might seem strange given this is typically something you'd have to code explicitly rather than have it happen automatically. But no worries, in general, it's a useful thing in JavaScript *so long as you understand when and how it happens*. And, that's what we've got to figure out now: when it happens and how it happens.

Here we go (in four simple cases):

CASE#1: Comparing a number and a string.

If you're comparing a string and a number the same thing happens every time: the string is converted into a number, and the two numbers are then compared. This doesn't always go well, because not all strings can be converted to numbers. Let's see what happens in that case:

```
99 == "vanilla"
        |
        v
99 == NaN
   |
   v
 false
```

Once again, we're comparing a number and a string. But this time, when we try to convert the string to a number, we fail.

When we try to convert "vanilla" to a number, we get NaN, and NaN isn't equal to anything. And so the result is false.

CASE#2: Comparing a boolean with any other type.

In this case, we convert the boolean to a number, and compare. This might seem a little strange, but it's easier to digest if you just remember that true converts to 1 and false converts to 0. You also need to understand that sometimes this case requires doing more than one type conversion. Let's look at a few examples:

```
1 == true
      |
      v
1 == 1
   |
   v
 true
```

We're comparing a number and a boolean. The true value is converted to the number 1.

And then we compare 1 to 1, which is true.

Here's another case; this time a boolean is compared to a string. Notice how more steps are needed.

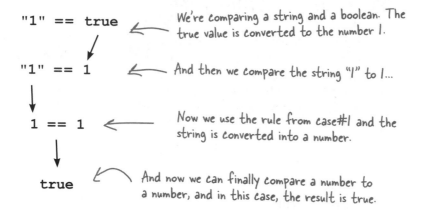

```
"1" == true
```
← We're comparing a string and a boolean. The true value is converted to the number 1.

```
"1" == 1
```
← And then we compare the string "1" to 1...

```
1 == 1
```
← Now we use the rule from case#1 and the string is converted into a number.

```
true
```
← And now we can finally compare a number to a number, and in this case, the result is true.

CASE#3: Comparing null and undefined.

Comparing these values evalutates to true. That might seem odd as well, but it's the rule. For some insight, these values both essentially represent "no value" (that is, a variable with no value, or an object with no value), so they are considered to be equal.

```
undefined == null
```
```
true
```
← Undefined and null are always equal.

CASE#4: Oh, actually there is no case #4.

That's it. You can pretty much determine the value of any equality with these rules. That said, there are a few edge cases and caveats. One caveat is that we still need to talk about comparing objects, which we'll talk about in a bit. The other is around conversions that might catch you off guard. Here's one example:

```
1 == ""
```
← We're comparing a number and a string. Use rule #1.

```
1 == 0
```
← The empty string is converted to the number 0. Believe it or not!

```
false
```
← Ah, too bad, 1 and 0 are not the same. So this evaluates to false.

If only I could find a way to test two values for **equality** without having to worry about their types being converted. A way to just test if two values are equal only if they have the same value *and* the same type. A way to not have to worry about all these rules and the mistakes they might cause. That would be dreamy. But I know it's just a fantasy...

How to get strict with equality

I'm a little more strict about my comparisons.

While we're making confessions, here's another one: there are not one, but *two equality operators*. You've already been introduced to == (equality), and the other operator is === (strict equality).

That's right, three equals. You can use === in place of == anytime you want, but before you start doing that, let's make sure you understand how they differ.

With ==, you now know all the complex rules around how the operands are converted (if they're different types) when they're compared. With ===, the rules are even more complicated.

Just kidding, actually there is *only one rule* with ===:

Two values are strictly equal only if they have the same <u>type</u> and the same <u>value</u>.

Read that again. What that means is, if two values have the same type we compare them. If they don't, forget it, we're calling it false no matter what—no conversion, no figuring out complex rules, none of that. All you need to remember is that === will find two values equal *only if they are the same type and the same value.*

Editor's note: Make sure we have a photo release on file from Doug Crockford.

Sharpen your pencil

For each comparison below write true or false below the operators == and === to represent the result of the comparison:

	==	**===**	
`"42" == 42`	true	_____	`"42" === 42`
`"0" == 0`	_____	_____	`"0" === 0`
`"0" == false`	_____	_____	`"0" === false`
`"true" == true`	_____	_____	`"true" === true`
`true == (1 == "1")`	_____	_____	`true === (1 === "1")`

Tricky! (left)   *Tricky!* (right)

there are no
Dumb Questions

Q: What happens if I compare a number, like 99, to a string, like "ninety-nine", that can't be converted to a number?

A: JavaScript will try to convert "ninety-nine" to a number, and it will fail, resulting in NaN. So the two values won't be equal, and the result will be false.

Q: How does JavaScript convert strings to numbers?

A: It uses an algorithm to parse the individual characters of a string and try to turn each one of them into a number. So if you write "34", it will look at "3", and see that can be a 3, and then it will look at "4" and see that can be a 4. You can also convert strings like "1.2" to floating point numbers— JavaScript is smart enough to recognize a string like this can still be a number.

Q: So, what if I try something like "true" == true?

A: That is comparing a string and a boolean, so according to the rules, JavaScript will first convert true to 1, and then compare "true" and 1. It will then try to convert "true" to a number, and fail, so you'll get false.

Q: So if there is both a == and a === operator, does that mean we have <= and <==, and >= and >==?

A: No. There are no <== and >== operators. You can use only <= and >=. These operators only know how to compare strings and numbers (true <= false doesn't really make sense), so if you try to compare any values other than two strings or two numbers (or a string and a number), JavaScript will attempt to convert the types using the rules we've discussed.

Q: So if I write 99 <= "100" what happens?

A: Use the rules: "100" is converted to a number, and then compared with 99. Because 99 is less than or equal to 100 (it's less than), the result is true.

Q: Is there a !==?

A: Yes, and just like === is stricter than ==, !== is stricter than !=. You use the same rules for !== as you do for ===, except that you're checking for inequality instead of equality.

Q: Do we use the same rules when we're comparing say, a boolean and a number with < and >, like 0 < true?

A: Yup! And in that case, true gets converted to 1, so you'll get true because 0 is less than 1.

Q: It makes sense for a string to be equal to another string, but how can a string be less than or greater than another string?

A: Good question. What does it mean to say "banana" < "mango"? Well, with strings, you can use alphabetical order to know if one string is less than or greater than another. Because "banana" begins with a "b" and "mango" with an "m", "banana" is less than "mango" because "b" comes before "m" in the alphabet. And "mango" is less than "melon" because, while the first letters are the same, when we compare the second letters, "a" comes before "e".

This alphabetical comparison can trip you up, however; for instance, "Mango" < "mango" is true, even though you might think that "M" is greater than "m" because its "M" is capitalized. The ordering of strings has to do with the ordering of the Unicode values that are used to represent each character in the computer (Unicode is a standard for representing characters digitally), and that ordering might not always be what you expect! For all the details, try googling "Unicode". But most of the time, the basic alphabetical ordering is all you need to know if one string is less than or greater than another.

Fireside Chats

Tonight's talk: **The equality and strict equality operators let us know who is boss.**

==

Ah look who it is, Mr. Uptight.

I'm up for a count of == versus === across all JavaScript code out in the world. You're going to come in way behind. It won't even be close.

I don't think so. I provide a valuable service. Who doesn't want to, say, compare user input in the form of a string to a number every once in a while?

When you were in grade school did you have to walk to school in the snow, every day, uphill, in both directions? Do you always have to do things the hard way?

The thing is, not only can I do the same comparisons you do, I add value on top of that by doing some nice conversions of types.

You'd rather just throw your hands up, call it false and go home?

===

Just keep in mind that several leading JavaScript gurus say that developers should use me, and only me. They think you should be taken out of the language altogether.

You know, you might be right, but folks are slowly starting to get it, and those numbers are changing.

And with it come all the rules you have to keep in mind to even use ==. Keep life and code simple; use === and if you need to convert user input to a number there are methods for that.

Very funny. There's nothing wrong with being strict and having clear-cut semantics around your comparisons. Bad, unexpected things can happen if you don't keep all the rules in mind.

Every time I look at your rules I throw up in my mouth a little. I mean comparing a boolean to anything means I convert the boolean to a number? That doesn't seem very sensical to me.

==

It's working so far. Look at all the code out there, a lot written by mere… well, scripters.

You mean like taking a shower after one of these conversations with you?

Hmm. Well, ever considered just buying me out? I'd be happy to go spend my days on the beach, kicking back with a margarita in hand.

Arguing about == versus === gets old. I mean there are more interesting things to do in life.

Look, here's the thing you have to deal with: people aren't going to just stop using ==. Sometimes it's really convenient. And people can use it in an educated way, taking advantage of it when it makes sense. Like the user input example—why the heck not use ==?

My new attitude is if people want to use you, great. I'm still here when they need me, and by the way, I still get a check every month no matter what they do! There's enough legacy code with == in the world—I'm never going off payroll.

===

No, but one can get a little too lax around your complex rules.

That's fine but pages are getting more complex, more sophisticated. It's time to take on some best practices.

No, like sticking to ===. It makes your code clearer and removes the potential for weird edge cases in comparisons.

I didn't see that coming, I thought you'd defend your position as THE equality operator until the end. What gives?

I don't even know how to respond.

Well like I said, you never know when something is going to happen.

Great. If it wasn't confusing enough already, we now have two equality operators. Which one am I supposed to use?

Deep breath. There's a lot of debate around this topic, and different experts will tell you different things. Here's our take: traditionally, coders have used mostly == (equality) because, well, there wasn't a great awareness of the two operators and their differences. Today, we're more educated and for most purposes === (strict equality) works just fine and is in some ways the safer route because you know what you're getting. With ==, of course, you also know what you're getting, but with all the conversions it's hard sometimes to think through all the possibilities.

Now, there are times when == provides some nice convenience (like when you're comparing numbers to strings) and of course you should feel free to use == in those cases, especially now that, unlike many JavaScript coders, you know exactly what == does. Now that we've talked about ===, you'll see us mostly shift gears in this book and predominantly use ===, but we won't get dogmatic about it if there's a case where == makes our life easier and doesn't introduce issues.

 You'll also hear developers refer to === (strict equality) as the "identity" operator.

WHO DOES WHAT?

We had our descriptions for these operators all figured out, and then they got all mixed up. Can you help us figure out who does what? Be careful, we're not sure if each contender matches zero, one or more descriptions. We've already figured one out, which is marked below:

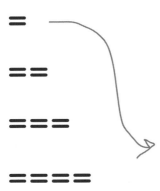

Compares values to see if they are equal. This is the considerate equality operator. He'll go to the trouble of trying to convert your types to see if you are really equal.

Compares values to see if they are equal. This guy won't even consider values that have different types.

Assigns a value to a variable.

Compares object references and returns true if they are the same and false otherwise.

Even more type conversions...

Conditional statements aren't the only place you're going to see type conversion. There are a few other operators that like to convert types when they get the chance. While these conversions are meant to be a convenience for you, the coder, and often they are, it's good to understand exactly where and when they might happen. Let's take a look.

Another look at concatenation, and addition

You've probably figured out that when you use the + operator with numbers you get *addition*, and when you use it with strings you get *concatenation*. But what happens when we mix the types of +'s operands? Let's find out.

If you try to add a number and a string, JavaScript converts the number to a string and concatenates the two. Kind of the opposite of what it does with equality:

```
var addi = 3 + "4";
```
When we have a string added to a number, we get concatenation, not addition.

The result variable is set to "34" (not 7).

```
var plusi = "4" + 3;
```
Same here... we get "43".

If you put the string first and then use the + operator with a number, the same thing happens: the number is converted to a string and the two are joined by concatenation.

What about the other arithmetic operators?

When it comes the other arithmetic operators—like multiplication, division and subtraction—JavaScript prefers to treat those as arithmetic operations, not string operations.

```
var multi = 3 * "4";
```
Here, JavaScript converts the string "4" to the number 4, and multiplies it by 3, resulting in 12.

```
var divi = 80 / "10";
```
Here the string "10" is converted to the number 10. Then 80 is divided by the number 10, resulting in 8.

```
var mini = "10" - 5;
```
With minus, the "10" is converted to the number 10, so we have 10 minus 5, which is 5.

there are no Dumb Questions

Q: Is + always interpreted as string concatenation when one of the operands is a string?

A: Yes. However, because + has what is called left-to-right associativity, if you have a situation like this:

```
var order = 1 + 2 + " pizzas";
```

you'll get "3 pizzas", not "12 pizzas" because, moving left to right, 1 is added to 2 first (and both are numbers), which results in 3. Next we add 3 and a string, so 3 is converted to a string and concatenated with "pizza". To make sure you get the results you want, you can always use parentheses to force an operator to be evaluated first:

```
var order = (1 + 2) + " pizzas";
```

ensures you'll get 3 pizzas, and

```
var order = 1 + (2 + " pizzas");
```

ensures you'll get 12 pizzas.

Q: Is that it? Or are there more conversions?

A: There are some other places where conversion happens. For instance, the unary operator - (to make a negative number) will turn -true into -1. And concatenating a boolean with a string will create a string (like true + " love" is "true love"). These cases are fairly rare, and we've personally never needed these in practice, but now you know they exist.

Q: So if I want JavaScript to convert a string into a number to add it to another number, how would I do that?

A: There's a function that does this named Number (yes, it has a uppercase N). Use it like this:

```
var num = 3 + Number("4");
```

This statement results in num being assigned the value 7. The Number function takes an argument, and if possible, creates a number from it. If the argument can't be converted to a number, Number returns.... wait for it..... NaN.

Sharpen your pencil

Time to test that conversion knowledge. For each expression below, write the result in the blank next to it. We've done one for you. Check your answers at the end of the chapter before you go on.

```
                    Infinity - "1"    _____

                        "42" + 42     "4242"  _____

                        2 + "1 1"     _____

                        99 + 101      _____

                        "1" - "1"     _____

        console.log("Result: " + 10/2) _____

    3 + " bananas " + 2 + " apples"   _____
```

One thing we haven't really talked about is how equality relates to objects. For instance, what does it mean for objects to be equal?

We're glad you're thinking about it. When it comes to object equality there's a simple answer and there's a long, deep answer. The simple answer tackles the question: is this object equal to that object? That is, if I have two variables referencing objects, do they point to precisely the same object? We'll walk through that on the next page. The complex question involves object types, and the question of how two objects might or might not be the same type. We've seen that we can create objects that look like the same type, say two cars, but how do we know they really are? It's an important question, and one we're going to tackle head on in a later chapter.

How to determine if two objects are equal

Your first question might be: are we talking about == or ===? Here's the good news: *if you're comparing two objects, it doesn't matter*! That is, if both operands are objects, then you can use either == or === because they work in exactly the same way. Here's what happens when you test two objects for equality:

When we test equality of two object variables, we compare the <u>references</u> to those objects

Remember, variables hold references to objects, and so whenever we compare two objects, we're comparing object references.

```
if (var1 === var2) {
    // wow, these are the same object!
}
```

Not in this case!

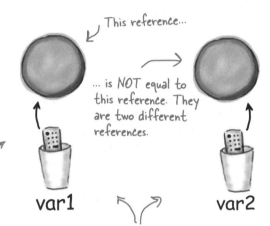

This reference...

... is NOT equal to this reference. They are two different references.

var1   **var2**

Notice, it doesn't matter what's in these objects. If the references aren't the same, then the objects aren't equal.

Two references are equal only if they reference the <u>same</u> object

The only way a test for equality between two variables containing object references returns true is when the two references point to the *same* object.

```
if (var1 === var3) {
    // wow, these are the same object!
}
```

Finally, two object references that are equal.

This reference...

var3   **var1**   **var2**

... is equal to this reference. They are equal and the same object!

Sharpen your pencil

Here's a little code that helps find cars in Earl's Autos parking lot. Trace through this code and write the values of loc1 through loc4 below.

```javascript
function findCarInLot(car) {
    for (var i = 0; i < lot.length; i++) {
        if (car === lot[i]) {
            return i;
        }
    }
    return -1;
}
var chevy = {
    make: "Chevy",
    model: "Bel Air"
};
var taxi = {
    make: "Webville Motors",
    model: "Taxi"
};
var fiat1 = {
    make: "Fiat",
    model: "500"
};
var fiat2 = {
    make: "Fiat",
    model: "500"
};

var lot = [chevy, taxi, fiat1, fiat2];

var loc1 = findCarInLot(fiat2);    _____
var loc2 = findCarInLot(taxi);     _____
var loc3 = findCarInLot(chevy);    _____
var loc4 = findCarInLot(fiat1);    _____
```

⌐ Your answers here.
↙

Earl, from
Earl's Autos.
↘

The truthy is out there...

That's right, we said truthy not truth. We'll say falsey too. What on earth are we talking about? Well, some languages are rather precise about true and false. JavaScript, not so much. In fact, JavaScript is kind of loose about true and false. How is it loose? Well, there are values in JavaScript that aren't true or false, but that are nevertheless treated as true or false in a conditional. We call these values truthy and falsey precisely because they aren't technically true or false, but they behave like they are (again, inside a conditional).

Now here's the secret to understanding truthy and falsey: *concentrate on knowing what is falsey, and then everything else you can consider truthy*. Let's look at some examples of using these falsey values in a conditional:

Some people write it "falsy."

```
var testThis;
if (testThis) {
    // do something
}
```

Okay that's weird, we know this variable will be undefined in the conditional test. Does this work? Is this legal JavaScript? (Answer: yes.)

```
var element = document.getElementById("elementThatDoesntExist");
if (element) {
    // do something
}
```

Here the value of element is null. What's that going to do?

```
if (0) {
    // do another thing
}
```

We're testing 0?

Now we're doing a conditional test on an empty string. Anyone want to place bets?

```
if ("") {
    // does code here ever get evaluated? Place your bets.
}
```

Wait, now we're using NaN in a boolean condition? What's that going to evaluate to?

```
if (NaN) {
    // Hmm, what's NaN doing in a boolean test?
}
```

What JavaScript considers falsey

Again, the secret to learning what is truthy and what is falsey is to learn what's falsey, and then consider everything else truthy.

There are five falsey values in JavaScript:

undefined is falsey.

null is falsey.

0 is falsey.

The empty string is falsey.

NaN is falsey.

To remember which values are truthy and which are falsey, just memorize the five falsey values— undefined, null, *0*, "" and NaN—and remember that everything else is truthy.

So, every conditional test on the previous page evaluated to false. Did we mention every other value is truthy (except for false, of course)? Here are some examples of truthy values:

This is an array. It's not undefined, null, zero, "" or NaN. It has to be true!

```
if ([]) {
   // this will happen
}

var element = document.getElementById("elementThatDoesExist");
if (element) {
   // so will this
}

if (1) {
   // gonna happen
}

var string = "mercy me";
if (string) {
   // this will happen too
}
```

This time we have an actual element object. That's not falsy either, so it's truthy.

Only the number 0 is falsey, all others are truthy.

Only the empty string is falsey, all other strings are truthy.

Sharpen your pencil

Time for a quick lie detector test. Figure out how many lies the perp tells, and whether the perp is guilty as charged, by determining which values are truthy and which values are falsey. Check your answer at the end of the chapter before you go on. And of course feel free to try these out in the browser yourself.

```javascript
function lieDetectorTest() {
    var lies = 0;

    var stolenDiamond = { };
    if (stolenDiamond) {
        console.log("You stole the diamond");
        lies++;
    }
    var car = {
        keysInPocket: null
    };
    if (car.keysInPocket) {
        console.log("Uh oh, guess you stole the car!");
        lies++;
    }
    if (car.emptyGasTank) {
        console.log("You drove the car after you stole it!");
        lies++;
    }
    var foundYouAtTheCrimeScene = [ ];
    if (foundYouAtTheCrimeScene) {
        console.log("A sure sign of guilt");
        lies++;
    }
    if (foundYouAtTheCrimeScene[0]) {
        console.log("Caught with a stolen item!");
        lies++;
    }
    var yourName = " ";   // A string with one space.
    if (yourName) {
        console.log("Guess you lied about your name");
        lies++;
    }
    return lies;
}
var numberOfLies = lieDetectorTest();
console.log("You told " + numberOfLies + " lies!");
if (numberOfLies >= 3) {
    console.log("Guilty as charged");
}
```

What do you think this code does? Do you see anything odd about this code, especially given what we know about primitive types?

```
var text = "YOU SHOULD NEVER SHOUT WHEN TYPING";
var presentableText = text.toLowerCase();
if (presentableText.length > 0) {
    alert(presentableText);
}
```

The Secret Life of Strings

Types always belong to one of two camps: they're either a primitive type or an object. Primitives live out fairly simple lives, while objects keep state and have behavior (or said another way, have properties and methods). Right?

Well, actually, while all that is true, it's not the whole story. As it turns out, strings are a little more mysterious. Check out this code:

This looks like a normal, primitive string.

```
var emot = "XOxxOO";
var hugs = 0;
var kisses = 0;

emot = emot.trim();
emot = emot.toUpperCase();

for(var i = 0; i < emot.length ; i++) {
    if (emot.charAt(i) === "X") {
        hugs++;
    } else if (emot.charAt(i) == "O") {
        kisses++;
    }
}
```

Wait a see, calling a method on a string?

And a string with a property?

More methods?

How a string can look like a primitive and an object

How does a string masquerade as both a primitive and an object? Because JavaScript supports both. That is, with JavaScript you can create a string that is a primitive, and you can also create one that is an object (which supports lots of useful string manipulation methods). Now, we've never talked about how to create a string that is an object, and in most cases you don't need to explicitly do it yourself, because the JavaScript interpreter *will create string objects for you*, as needed.

Now, where and why might it do that? Let's look at the life of a string:

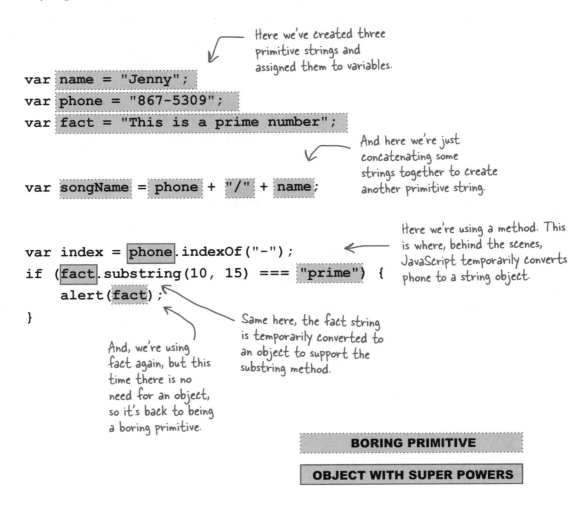

Here we've created three primitive strings and assigned them to variables.

```
var name = "Jenny";
var phone = "867-5309";
var fact = "This is a prime number";
```

And here we're just concatenating some strings together to create another primitive string.

```
var songName = phone + "/" + name;
```

Here we're using a method. This is where, behind the scenes, JavaScript temporarily converts phone to a string object.

```
var index = phone.indexOf("-");
if (fact.substring(10, 15) === "prime") {
    alert(fact);
}
```

Same here, the fact string is temporarily converted to an object to support the substring method.

And, we're using fact again, but this time there is no need for an object, so it's back to being a boring primitive.

BORING PRIMITIVE

OBJECT WITH SUPER POWERS

This seems very confusing. My string is being converted back and forth between a primitive and object? How am I supposed to keep track of all this?

You don't need to. In general you can just think of your strings as objects that have lots of great methods to help you manipulate the text in your strings. JavaScript will take care of all the details. So, look at it this way: you now have a better understanding of what is under the covers of JavaScript, but in your day to day coding most developers just rely on JavaScript to do the right thing (and it does).

there are no Dumb Questions

Q: Just making sure, do I ever have to keep track of where my string is a primitive and where it's an object?

A: Most of the time, no. The JavaScript interpreter will handle all the conversion for you. You just write your code, assuming a string supports the object properties and methods, and things will work as expected.

Q: Why does JavaScript support a string as both a primitive and an object?

A: Think about it this way: you get the efficiency of the simple string primitive type as long as you are doing basic string operations like comparison, concatenation, writing string to the DOM, and so on. But if you need to do more sophisticated string processing, then you have the string object quickly at your disposal.

Q: Given an arbitrary string, how do I know if it is an object or primitive?

A: A string is always a primitive unless you create it in a special way using an object constructor. We'll talk about object constructors later. And you can always use the typeof operator on your variable to see if it is of type string or object.

Q: Can other primitives act like objects?

A: Yes, numbers and booleans can also act like objects at times. However, neither of these has nearly as many useful properties as strings do, so you won't find you'll use this feature nearly as often as you do with strings. And remember, this all happens for you behind the scenes, so you don't really have to think about it much. Just use a property if you need to and let JavaScript handle the temporary conversion for you.

Q: How can I know all the methods and properties that are available for String objects?

A: That's where a good reference comes in handy. There are lots of online references that are helpful, and if you want a book, *JavaScript: The Definitive Guide* has a reference guide with information about every string property and method in JavaScript. Google works pretty well too.

A five-minute tour of string methods (and properties)

Given that we're in the middle of talking about strings and you've just discovered that strings also support methods, let's take a little break from talking about weirdo types and look at a few of the more common string methods you might want to use. A few string methods get used over and over, and it is highly worth your time to get to know them. So on with the tour.

A little pep talk: we could pull you aside and write an entire chapter on every method and property that strings support. Not only would that make this book 40 lbs and 2000 pages long, but at this point, you really don't need it— you already get the basics of methods and objects, and all you need is a good reference if you really want to dive into the details of string processing.

the length property

The length property holds the number of characters in the string. It's quite handy for iterating through the characters of the string.

We use the length property to iterate over each character in the string.

```
var input = "jenny@wickedlysmart.com";
for(var i = 0; i < input.length; i++) {
    if (input.charAt(i) === "@") {
        console.log("There's an @ sign at index " + i);
    }
}
```

And the charAt method to get the character at a particular index in the string.

> **JavaScript console**
>
> There's an @ sign at index 5

the charAt method

The charAt method takes an integer number between zero and the length of the string (minus one), and returns a string containing the single character at that position of the string. Think of the string a bit like an array, with each character at an index of the string, with the indices starting at 0 (just like an array). If you give it an index that is greater than or equal to the length of the string, it returns the empty string.

Note that JavaScript doesn't have a character type. So characters are returned as new strings containing one character.

a b c d e f

charAt(0) is "a". *charAt(5) is "f".*

the indexOf method

This method takes a string as an argument and returns the index of the first character of the first occurrence of that argument in the string.

Here's the string we're going to call indexOf on.

```
var phrase = "the cat in the hat";
```

And our goal is to find the first occurence of "cat" in phrase.

```
var index = phrase.indexOf("cat");
console.log("there's a cat sitting at index " + index);
```

The index of the first cat is returned.

> **JavaScript console**
> There's a cat sitting at index 4

You can also add a second argument, which is the starting index for the search.

```
index = phrase.indexOf("the", 5);
console.log("there's a the sitting at index " + index);
```

Because we're starting the search at index 5, we're skipping the first "the" and finding the second "the" at index 11.

> **JavaScript console**
> There's a the sitting at index 11

```
index = phrase.indexOf("dog");
console.log("there's a dog sitting at index " + index);
```

Note if the string can't be found, then −1 is returned as the index.

> **JavaScript console**
> There's a dog sitting at index -1

the substring method

Give the substring method two indices, and it will extract and return the string contained within them.

```
var data = "name|phone|address";
var val = data.substring(5, 10);
console.log("Substring is " + val);
```

Here's the string we're going to call substring on.

We'd like the string from index 5 and up to (but not including) 10 returned.

We get back a new string with the characters from index 5 to 10.

JavaScript console
```
Substring is phone
```

You can omit the second index and substring will extract a string that starts at the first index and then continues until the end of the original string.

```
val = data.substring(5);
console.log("Substring is now " + val);
```

JavaScript console
```
Substring is now phone|address
```

the split method

The split method takes a character that acts as a delimiter, and breaks the string into parts based on the delimiter.

```
var data = "name|phone|address";
var vals = data.split("|");
console.log("Split array is ", vals);
```

Split uses the delimiter to break the original string into pieces, which are returned in an array.

Notice here we're passing two arguments to console.log separated by a comma. This way, the vals array doesn't get converted to a string before it's displayed in the console.

JavaScript console
```
Split array is ["name", "phone", "address"]
```

String Soup

toLowerCase

Returns a string with all uppercase characters changed to lowercase.

Finds substrings and replaces them with another string.

replace

Returns a new string that has part of the original string removed.

lastIndexOf

Just like indexOf, but finds the last, not the first, occurrence.

Joins strings together.

concat

slice

match

Searches for matches in a string using regular expressions.

Returns a string with all lowercase characters changed to uppercase.

Returns a portion of a string.

substring

trim Removes whitespace from around the string. Handy when processing user input.

toUpperCase

There's really no end to learning all the things you can do with strings. Here are a few more methods available to you. Just get a passing familiarity right now, and when you really need them you can look up the details...

Chair Wars
(or How Really Knowing Types Can Change Your Life)

Once upon a time in a software shop, two programmers were given the same spec and told to "build it." The Really Annoying Project Manager forced the two coders to compete, by promising that whoever delivers first gets one of those cool Aeron™ chairs all the Silicon Valley guys have. Brad, the hardcore hacker scripter, and Larry, the college grad, both knew this would be a piece of cake.

Larry, sitting in his cube, thought to himself, "What are the things this code has to *do*? It needs to make sure the string is long enough, it needs to make sure the middle character is a dash, and it needs to make sure every other character is a number. I can use the string's `length` property and I know how to access its characters using the `charAt` method."

Brad, meanwhile, kicked back at the cafe and thought to himself, "What are the things this code has to do?" He first thought, "A string is an object, and there are lots of methods I can use to help validate the phone number. I'll brush up on those and get this implemented quickly. After all, an object is an object." Read on to see how Brad and Larry built their programs, and for the answer to your burning question: ***who got the Aeron?***

The spec ↓

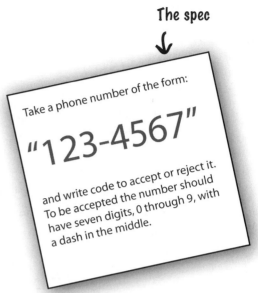

Take a phone number of the form:

"123-4567"

and write code to accept or reject it. To be accepted the number should have seven digits, 0 through 9, with a dash in the middle.

← *The chair*

In Larry's cube

Larry set about writing code based on the string methods. He wrote the code in no time:

```javascript
function validate(phoneNumber) {
    if (phoneNumber.length !== 8) {
        return false;
    }
    for (var i = 0; i < phoneNumber.length; i++) {
        if (i === 3) {
            if (phoneNumber.charAt(i) !== '-') {
                return false;
            }
        } else if (isNaN(phoneNumber.charAt(i))) {
            return false;
        }
    }
    return true;
}
```

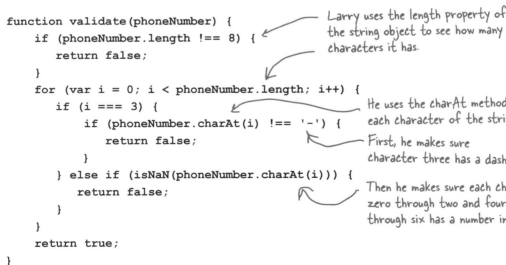

Larry uses the length property of the string object to see how many characters it has.

He uses the charAt method to examine each character of the string.

First, he makes sure character three has a dash.

Then he makes sure each character zero through two and four through six has a number in it.

In Brad's cube

Brad wrote code to check for two numbers and a dash:

Brad starts just like Larry...

But he uses his knowledge of the string methods.

He uses the substring method to create a string containing three characters from zero up to character three.

```
function validate(phoneNumber) {
    if (phoneNumber.length !== 8) {
        return false;
    }
    var first = phoneNumber.substring(0,3);
    var second = phoneNumber.substring(4);
    if (phoneNumber.charAt(3) !== "-" || isNaN(first) || isNaN(second)) {
        return false;
    }
    return true;
}
```

And again to start at character index four up to the end of the string.

Then he tests all the conditions for being a correct phone number in one conditional.

And interestingly, knowing it or not, he's depending on some type conversions here to convert a string to a number, and then making sure it's a number with isNaN. Clever!

But wait! There's been a spec change.

"Okay, *technically* you were first, Larry, because Brad was looking up how to use all those methods," said the Manager, "but we have to add just one tiny thing to the spec. It'll be no problem for crack programmers like you two."

"If I had a dime for every time I've heard *that* one", thought Larry, knowing that spec-change-no-problem was a fantasy. "And yet Brad looks strangely serene. What's up with that?" Still, Larry held tight to his core belief that Brad's fancy way, while cute, was just showing off. And that he'd win again in this next round and produce the code first.

BRAIN POWER

Wait, can you think of any bugs Brad might have introduced with his use of isNaN?

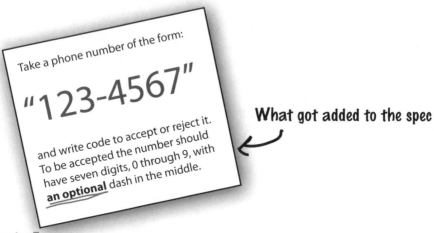

Take a phone number of the form:

"123-4567"

and write code to accept or reject it. To be accepted the number should have seven digits, 0 through 9, with **an optional** dash in the middle.

What got added to the spec

Back in Larry's cube

Larry thought he could use most of his existing code; he just had to work these edge cases of the missing dash in the number. Either the number would be only seven digits, or it would be eight digits with a dash in the third position. Quickly Larry coded the additions (which took a little testing to get right):

```javascript
function validate(phoneNumber) {
    if (phoneNumber.length > 8 ||
            phoneNumber.length < 7) {
        return false;
    }
    for (var i = 0; i < phoneNumber.length; i++) {
        if (i === 3) {
            if (phoneNumber.length === 8 &&
                    phoneNumber.charAt(i) !== '-') {
                return false;
            } else if (phoneNumber.length === 7 &&
                    isNaN(phoneNumber.charAt(i))) {
                return false;
            }
        } else if (isNaN(phoneNumber.charAt(i))) {
            return false;
        }
    }
    return true;
}
```

Larry had to make a few additions to his logic. Not a lot of code, but it's getting a bit hard to decipher.

At Brad's laptop at the beach

Brad smiled, sipped his margarita and quickly made his changes. He simply got the second part of the number using the length of the phone number minus four as the starting point for the substring, instead of hardcoding the starting point at a position that assumes a dash. That almost did it, but he did need to rewrite the test for the dash because it applies only when the phone number has a length of eight.

About the same number of changes as Larry, but Brad's code is still easier to read.

```javascript
function validate(phoneNumber) {
    if (phoneNumber.length > 8 ||
        phoneNumber.length < 7) {
        return false;
    }
    var first = phoneNumber.substring(0,3);
    var second = phoneNumber.substring(phoneNumber.length - 4);

    if (isNaN(first) || isNaN(second)) {
        return false;
    }
    if (phoneNumber.length === 8) {
        return (phoneNumber.charAt(3) === "-");
    }
    return true;
}
```

Now Brad's getting the second number using the total length of the phone number to get the starting point.

And he's validating the dash only if the number is eight characters.

Here we're returning the result of evaluating the conditional, which will be true or false.

BRAIN POWER

Err, we think Brad still has a bug. Can you find it?

BRAIN POWER

How would you rewrite Brad's code to use the split method instead?

Larry snuck in just ahead of Brad.

But the smirk on Larry's face melted when the Really Annoying Project Manager said, "Brad, your code is very readable and maintainable. Good job."

But Larry shouldn't be too worried, because, as we know, there is more than just code beauty at work. This code still needs to get through QA, and we're not quite sure Brad's code works in all cases. What about you? Who do you think deserves the chair?

The suspense is killing me. Who got the chair?

Amy from the second floor.

(Unbeknownst to all, the Project Manager had given the spec to *three* programmers.)

Wow, a one-liner! Check out how this works in the appendix!

Here's Amy's code.

```javascript
function validate(phoneNumber) {
    return phoneNumber.match(/^\d{3}-?\d{4}$/);
}
```

IN THE LABORATORY, AGAIN

The lab crew continues to probe JavaScript using the **typeof** operator and they're uncovering some more interesting things deep within the language. In the process, they've discovered a new operator, **instanceof**. With this one, they're truly on the cutting edge. Put your lab coat and safety goggles back on and see if you can help decipher this JavaScript and the results. *Warning: this is definitely going to be the weirdest code you've seen so far.*

Here's the code. Read it, run it, alter it, massage it, see what it does...

How strange. Doesn't this look a bit like a mix of a function and an object?

```javascript
function Duck(sound) {
    this.sound = sound;
    this.quack = function() {console.log(this.sound);}
}

var toy = new Duck("quack quack");

toy.quack();

console.log(typeof toy);
console.log(toy instanceof Duck);
```

Hmm "new". We've haven't seen that before. But we're guessing we should read this as, create a new Duck and assign it to the toy variable.

If it looks like an object, and walks like an object... let's test it.

Okay, and here is instanceof...

Be sure to check your output with the answers at the end of the chapter. But just what does this all mean? Ah, we'll be getting to all that in just a couple of chapters. And, in case you didn't notice, you are well on your way to being a pretty darn advanced JavaScript coder. This is serious stuff!

JavaScript console

↑ Put your results here. Are there any surprises?

BULLET POINTS

- There are two groups of types in JavaScript: **primitives** and objects. Any value that isn't a primitive type is an **object**.

- The primitives are: numbers, strings, booleans, null and undefined. Everything else is an object.

- **undefined** means that a variable (or property or array item) hasn't yet been initialized to a value.

- **null** means "no object".

- "NaN" stands for "Not a Number", although a better way to think of **NaN** is as a number that can't be represented in JavaScript. The type of NaN is number.

- NaN never equals any other value, including itself, so to test for NaN use the function **isNaN**.

- Test two values for equality using == or ===.

- If two operands have different types, the equality operator (==) will try to convert one of the operands into another type before testing for equality.

- If two operands have different types, the strict equality operator (===) returns false.

- You can use === if you want to be sure no type conversion happens, however, sometimes the type conversion of == can come in handy.

- Type conversion is also used with other operators, like the arithmetic operators and string concatenation.

- JavaScript has five **falsey** values: undefined, null, 0, "" (the empty string) and false. All other values are **truthy**.

- Strings sometimes behave like objects. If you use a property or method on a primitive string, JavaScript will convert the string to an object temporarily, use the property, and then convert it back to a primitive string. This happens behind the scenes so you don't have to think about it.

- The string has many methods that are useful for string manipulation.

- Two objects are equal only if the variables containing the object references point to the same object.

JavaScript cross

You're really expanding your JavaScript skills. Do a crossword to help it all sink in. All the answers are from this chaper.

ACROSS

2. The only value in JavaScript that doesn't equal anything.

5. The type of Infinity is _____.

7. There are _____ falsey values in JavaScript.

8. Who got the Aeron?

10. Two variables containing object references are equal only if they _____ the same object.

12. The value returned when you're expecting an object, and that object doesn't exist.

13. The _____ method is a string method that returns an array.

16. It's always 67 degrees in _____, Missouri.

17. The type of null in the JavaScript specification.

18. The _____ equality operator returns true only if the operands have the same type and the same value.

DOWN

1. The _____ operator can be used to get the type of a value.

2. The weirdest value in the world.

3. Your Fiat is parked at _____ Autos.

4. Sometimes strings masquerade as _____.

6. The value of a property that doesn't exist.

9. There are lots of handy string _____ you can use.

11. The _____ operator tests two values to see if they're equal, after trying to convert the operands to the same type.

14. null == undefined

15. To find a specific character at an index in a string, use the _____ method.

Who am I?

A bunch of JavaScript values and party crashers, in full costume, are playing a party game, "Who am I?" They give you a clue, and you try to guess who they are, based on what they say. Assume they always tell the truth about themselves. Fill in the blank next to each sentence with the name of one attendee. We've already guessed one of them.

Here's our solution:

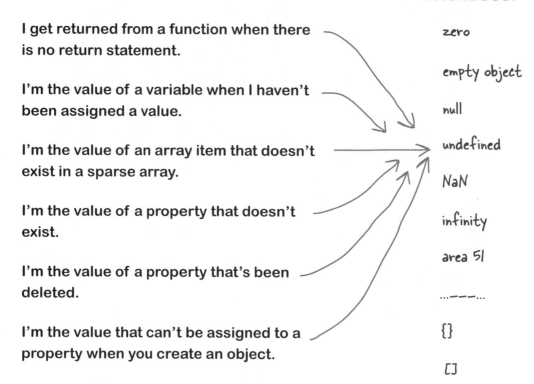

Tonight's attendees:

zero

empty object

null

undefined

NaN

infinity

area 51

...−−−...

{}

[]

I get returned from a function when there is no return statement.

I'm the value of a variable when I haven't been assigned a value.

I'm the value of an array item that doesn't exist in a sparse array.

I'm the value of a property that doesn't exist.

I'm the value of a property that's been deleted.

I'm the value that can't be assigned to a property when you create an object.

IN THE LABORATORY *SOLUTION*

In the laboratory we like to take things apart, look under the hood, poke and prod, hook up our diagnostic tools and check out what is really going on. Today, we're investigating JavaScript's type system and we've found a little diagnostic tool called **typeof** to examine variables. Put your lab coat and safety goggles on, and come on in and join us.

The **typeof** operator is built into JavaScript. You can use it to probe the type of its operand (the thing you use it to operate on). Here's an example:

```
var subject = "Just a string";

var probe = typeof subject;
console.log(probe);
```

The typeof operator takes an operand, and evaluates to the type of the operand.

The type here is "string". Note that typeof uses strings to represent types, like "string", "boolean", "number", "object", "undefined" and so on.

JavaScript console

string

Now it's your turn. Collect the data for the following experiments:

```
var test1 = "abcdef";
var test2 = 123;
var test3 = true;
var test4 = {};
var test5 = [];
var test6;
var test7 = {"abcdef": 123};
var test8 = ["abcdef", 123];
function test9(){return "abcdef"};

console.log(typeof test1);
console.log(typeof test2);
console.log(typeof test3);
console.log(typeof test4);
console.log(typeof test5);
console.log(typeof test6);
console.log(typeof test7);
console.log(typeof test8);
console.log(typeof test9);
```

Here's the test data, and the tests.

JavaScript console

string
number
boolean
object
object
undefined
object
object
function

↑ Here are our results.

BACK IN THE LABORATORY SOLUTION

Oops, we forgot null in our test data. Here's the missing test case:

```
var test10 = null;

console.log(typeof test10);
```

Here's our result.

```
JavaScript console
object
```

Exercise Solution

We've been looking at some rather, um, interesting, values so far in this chapter. Now, let's take a look at some interesting behavior. Try adding the code below to the <script> element in a basic web page and see what you get in the console when you load up the page. You won't get why yet, but see if you can take a guess about what might be going on.

```
if (99 == "99") {
    console.log("A number equals a string!");
} else {
    console.log("No way a number equals a string");
}
```

Here's what we got.

```
JavaScript console
A number equals a string!
```

Sharpen your pencil
Solution

For each comparison below write true or false below the operators == or === to represent the result of the comparison:

	==	===	
"42" == 42	true	false	"42" === 42
"0" == 0	true	false	"0" === 0
"0" == false	true	false	"0" === false
"true" == true	false	false	"true" === true
true == (1 == "1")	true	false	true === (1 === "1")

Tricky!

If you replace both == with ===, then the result is false.

WHO DOES WHAT?
SOLUTION

We had our descriptions for these operators all figured out, and then they got all mixed up. Can you help us figure out who does what? Be careful, we're not sure if each contender matches zero, one or more descriptions. Here's our solution:

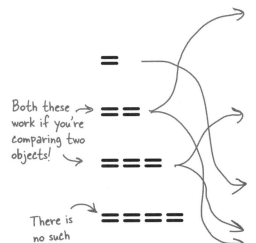

Compares values to see if they are equal. This is the considerate equality operator. He'll go to the trouble of trying to convert your types to see if you are really equal.

Both these work if you're comparing two objects!

Compares values to see if they are equal. This guy won't even consider values that have different types.

Assigns a value to a variable.

There is no such operator.

Compares object references and returns true if they are the same and false otherwise.

Sharpen your pencil
Solution

For each expression below, write the result in the blank next to it. We've done one for you. Here's our solution.

Infinity - "1"   Infinity   ← —"1" is converted to 1, and Infinity – 1 is Infinity.

"42" + 42   "4242"

2 + "1 1"   "21 1"

99 + 101   200   Both strings are converted to 1, and 1–1 is 0.

"1" - "1"   0   ←

console.log("Result: " + 10/2)   "Result: 5"   ← 10/2 happens first, and the result is concatenated to the string "Result: "

3 + " bananas " + 2 + " apples"   "3 bananas 2 apples"

↰ Each + is concatenation because for both, one operand is a string.

Sharpen your pencil
Solution

Time for a quick lie detector test. Figure out how many lies the perp tells, and whether the perp is guilty as charged, by determining which values are truthy and which values are falsey. Here's our solution. Did you try these out in the browser yourself?

```javascript
function lieDetectorTest() {
    var lies = 0;

    var stolenDiamond = { };
    if (stolenDiamond) {
        console.log("You stole the diamond");
        lies++;
    }
    var car = {
        keysInPocket: null
    };
    if (car.keysInPocket) {
        console.log("Uh oh, guess you stole the car!");
        lies++;
    }
    if (car.emptyGasTank) {
        console.log("You drove the car after you stole it!");
        lies++;
    }
    var foundYouAtTheCrimeScene = [ ];
    if (foundYouAtTheCrimeScene) {
        console.log("A sure sign of guilt");
        lies++;
    }
    if (foundYouAtTheCrimeScene[0]) {
        console.log("Caught with a stolen item!");
        lies++;
    }
    var yourName = " ";
    if (yourName) {
        console.log("Guess you lied about your name");
        lies++;
    }
    return lies;
}
var numberOfLies = lieDetectorTest();
console.log("You told " + numberOfLies + " lies!");
if (numberOfLies >= 3) {
    console.log("Guilty as charged");
}
```

Any object is truthy, even an empty one.

This perp didn't steal the car because the value of the keysInPocket property is null, which is falsey.

And the perp didn't drive the car either, because the emptyGasTank property is undefined, which is falsey.

But [ ] (an empty array) is truthy, so the perp was caught on the scene.

There is no item in the array, so the array item at 0 is undefined, which is falsey. Hmm, the perp must have hidden the stash already.

A string with one space.

Any non-empty string is truthy, even if it just has one space!

The number of lies is 3 so we think the perp is guilty.

```
JavaScript console

You stole the diamond
A sure sign 8f guilt
Guess you lied about your name
You told 3 lies!
Guilty as charged
```

Sharpen your pencil
Solution

Here's a little code that helps find cars in Earl's Used Autos parking lot. Trace through this code and write the values of loc1 through loc4 below.

```
function findCarInLot(car) {
    for (var i = 0; i < lot.length; i++) {
        if (car === lot[i]) {
            return i;
        }
    }
    return -1;
}
var chevy = {
    make: "Chevy",
    model: "Bel Air"
};
var taxi = {
    make: "Webville Motors",
    model: "Taxi"
};
var fiat1 = {
    make: "Fiat",
    model: "500"
};
var fiat2 = {
    make: "Fiat",
    model: "500"
};

var lot = [chevy, taxi, fiat1, fiat2];

var loc1 = findCarInLot(fiat2);      3
var loc2 = findCarInLot(taxi);       1
var loc3 = findCarInLot(chevy);      0
var loc4 = findCarInLot(fiat1);      2
```

Here are our answers.

Earl, from Earl's Autos.

IN THE LABORATORY, AGAIN SOLUTION

The lab crew continues to probe JavaScript using the **typeof** operator and they're uncovering some more interesting things deep within the language. In the process, they've discovered a new operator, **instanceof**. With this one, they're truly on the cutting edge. Put your lab coat and safety goggles back on and see if you can help decipher this JavaScript and the results. *Warning: this is definitely going to be the weirdest code you've seen so far.*

Here's the code. Read it, run it, alter it, massage it, see what it does...

```
function Duck(sound) {
    this.sound = sound;
    this.quack = function() {console.log(this.sound);}
}

var toy = new Duck("quack quack");

toy.quack();

console.log(typeof toy);
console.log(toy instanceof Duck);
```

How strange. Doesn't this look a bit like a mix of a function and an object?

Hmm "new". We've haven't seen that before. But we're guessing we should read this as, create a new Duck and assign it to the toy variable.

If it looks like an object, and walks like an object... let's test it.

Okay, and here is instanceof...

Just what does this all mean? Ah, we'll be getting to all that in just a few chapters. And, in case you didn't notice, you are well on your way to being a pretty darn advanced JavaScript coder. This is serious stuff!

JavaScript console

quack quack *The toy acts like an object... we can call its method.*

object *And the type is object.*

true *But it is an "instanceof" a Duck, whatever that means... Hmm.*

Here are our results.

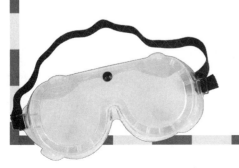

JavaScript cross Solution

You're really expanding your JavaScript skills. Do a crossword to help it all sink in. All the answers are from this chaper. Here's our solution.

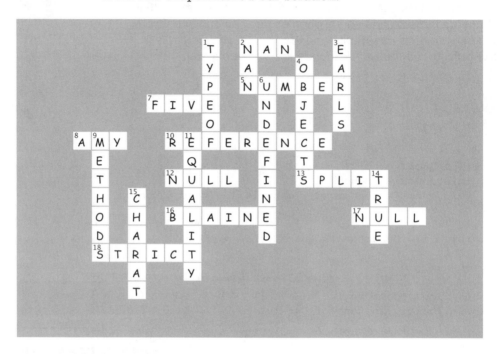

8 bringing it all together

Building an app

I love how you've brought all the ingredients together to create something truly tasty.

Hey! Eyes up! The poundcake's up here.

Put on your toolbelt. That is, the toolbelt with all your new coding skills, your knowledge of the DOM, and even some HTML & CSS. We're going to bring everything together in this chapter to create our first true **web application**. No more **silly toy games** with one battleship and a single row of hiding places. In this chapter we're building the **entire experience**: a nice big game board, multiple ships and user input right in the web page. We're going to create the page structure for the game with HTML, visually style the game with CSS, and write JavaScript to code the game's behavior. Get ready: this is an all out, pedal to the metal development chapter where we're going to lay down some serious code.

This time, let's build a **REAL** Battleship game

Sure, you can feel good because back in Chapter 2 you built a nice little battleship game from scratch, but let's admit it: that was a bit of a *toy* game—it worked, it was playable, but it wasn't exactly the game you'd impress your friends with, or use to raise your first round of venture capital. To really impress, you'll need a visual game board, snazzy battleship graphics, and a way for players to enter their moves right in the game (rather than a generic browser dialog box). You'll also want to improve the previous version by supporting all three ships.

In other words, you'll want to create something like this:

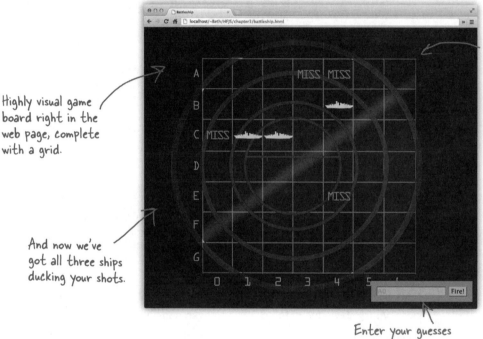

Highly visual game board right in the web page, complete with a grid.

And now we've got all three ships ducking your shots.

Your hits and misses are placed right on the game board as you take your shots.

Enter your guesses right in the page.

Forget JavaScript for a minute... look at the Battleship mockup above. If you focus on the structure and visual represenation of the page, how would you create it using HTML and CSS?

Stepping back... to HTML and CSS

To create a modern, interactive web page, or *app*, you need to work with three technologies: HTML, CSS and JavaScript. You already know the mantra "HTML is for structure, CSS is for style and JavaScript is for behavior." But rather than just stating it, in this chapter we're going to fully embody it. And we're going to start with the HTML and CSS first.

Our first goal is going to be to reproduce the look of the game board on the previous page. But not *just* reproduce it; we need to implement the game board so it has a structure we can use in JavaScript to take player input and place hits, misses and messages on the page.

To pull that off we're going to do things like use an image in the background to give us the slick grid over a radar look, and then we'll lay a more functional HTML table over that so we can place things (like ships) on top of it. We'll also use an HTML form to get the player input.

We'll place an image in the background of the page that depicts the grid of the game.

And then add an HTML table that overlays the grid.

Then we can place the ship or MISS graphic in the table cells as needed.

So, let's build this game. We're going to take a step back and spend a few pages on the crucial HTML and CSS, but once we have that in place, we'll be ready for the JavaScript.

GET YOUR BATTLESHIP TOOLKIT

Here's a toolkit to get you started on this new version of Battleship.

INVENTORY includes...

board.jpg

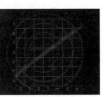

ship.png

miss.png

This toolkit contains three images, "board.jpg", which is the main background board for the game including the grid; "ship.png", which is a small ship for placement on the board—notice that it is a PNG image with transparency, so it will lay right on top of the background— and finally we have "miss.png", which is also meant to be placed on the board. True to the original game, when we hit a ship we place a ship in the corresponding cell, and when we miss we place a miss graphic there.

Download everything you need for the game at http://wickedlysmart.com/hfjs

Creating the HTML page: the Big Picture

Here's the plan of attack for creating the Battleship HTML page:

① First we'll concentrate on the background of the game, which includes setting the background image to black and placing the radar grid image in the page.

We're placing an image in the background to give the game its cool, green phosphorus radar feel.

② Next we'll create an HTML table and lay it on top of the background image. Each cell in the table will represent a board cell in the game.

An HTML table on top of the background creates a game board for the game to play out in.

③ Then we'll add an HTML form element where players can enter their guesses, like "A4". We'll also add an area to display messages, like "You sank my battleship!"

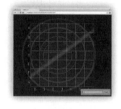

An HTML form for player input.

④ Finally, we'll figure out how to use the table to place the images of a battleship (for a hit) and a MISS (for a miss) into the board.

We'll use these images and place them into the table as needed.

Step 1: The Basic HTML

Let's get started! First we need an HTML page. We're going to start by creating a simple HTML5-compliant page; we'll also add some styling for the background image. In the page we're going to place a `<body>` element that contains a single `<div>` element. This `<div>` element is going to hold the game grid.

Go ahead and check out the next page that contains our starter HTML and CSS.

Relax

A little rusty?

If you're feeling a bit rusty on your HTML and CSS, *Head First HTML and CSS* was written to be the companion to this book.

```
<!doctype html>            Just a regular HTML page.
<html lang="en">
  <head>
    <meta charset="utf-8">
    <title>Battleship</title>
    <style>
      body {                        And we want the background
        background-color: black;    of the page to be black.
      }
                                    We want the game board to stay in the
                                    middle of the page, so we're setting the
      div#board {                   width to 1024px (the width of the game
        position: relative;         board), and the margins to auto.
        width: 1024px;
        height: 863px;                            Here's where we add the
        margin: auto;                             "board.jpg" image to the page, as
        background: url("board.jpg") no-repeat;   the background of the "board"
      }                                           <div> element. We're positioning
    </style>                                      this <div> relative, so that we can
  </head>                                         position the table we add in the
  <body>                  We're going to put the  next step relative to this <div>.
    <div id="board">      table for the game
                          board and the form for
                          getting user input here.
    </div>
    <script src="battleship.js"></script>         We'll put our code in the file
  </body>                                         "battleship.js". Go ahead and
</html>                                           create a blank file for that.
```

A Test Drive

Go ahead and enter the code above (or download all the code for the book from http://wickedlysmart.com/hfjs) into the file "battleship.html" and then load it in your browser. Our test run is below.

Here's what the web
page looks like so far...

Step 2: Creating the table

Next up is the table. The table will overlay the visual grid in the background image, and provide the area to place the hit and miss graphics where you play the game. Each cell (or if you remember your HTML, each `<td>` element) is going to sit right on top of a cell in the background image. Now here is the trick: we'll give each cell its own id, so we can manipulate it later with CSS and JavaScript. Let's check out how we're going to create these ids and add the HTML for the table:

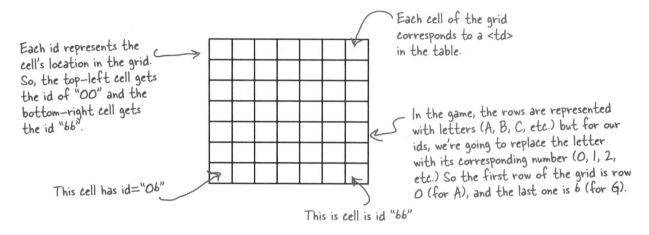

Each id represents the cell's location in the grid. So, the top-left cell gets the id of "00" and the bottom-right cell gets the id "66".

Each cell of the grid corresponds to a `<td>` in the table.

This cell has id="06"

In the game, the rows are represented with letters (A, B, C, etc.) but for our ids, we're going to replace the letter with its corresponding number (0, 1, 2, etc.) So the first row of the grid is row 0 (for A), and the last one is 6 (for G).

This is cell is id "66"

Here's the HTML for the table. Go ahead and add this between the `<div>` tags:

`<div id="board">` ⟵ We're nesting the table inside the "board" `<div>`.

```
  <table>
    <tr>
      <td id="00"></td><td id="01"></td><td id="02"></td><td id="03">
</td><td id="04"></td> <td id="05"></td><td id="06"></td>
    </tr>
    <tr>
      <td id="10"></td><td id="11"></td><td id="12"></td><td id="13"></td>
<td id="14"></td> <td id="15"></td><td id="16"></td>
    </tr>
    ...
    <tr>
      <td id="60"></td><td id="61"></td><td id="62"></td><td id="63"></td>
<td id="64"></td><td id="65"></td><td id="66"></td>
    </tr>
  </table>
```

`</div>`

Make sure each `<td>` gets the correct id corresponding to its row and column in the grid.

We've left out a few rows to save some trees, but we're sure you can fill these in on your own.

Step 3: Player interaction

Okay, now we need an HTML element to enter guesses (like "A0" or "E4"), and an element to display messages to the player (like "You sank my battleship!"). We'll use a `<form>` with a text `<input>` for the player to submit guesses, and a `<div>` to create an area where we can message the player:

We'll notify players when they've sunk battleships with a message up in the top left corner.

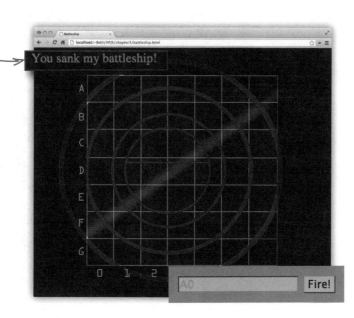

And here's where players can enter their guesses.

```
<div id="board">
  <div id="messageArea"></div>
  <table>
     . . .
  </table>
  <form>
    <input type="text" id="guessInput" placeholder="A0">
    <input type="button" id="fireButton" value="Fire!">
  </form>
</div>
```

The messageArea `<div>` will be used to display messages from code.

The `<form>` has two inputs: one for the guess (a text input) and one for the button. Note the ids on these elements. We'll need them later when we write the code to get the player's guess.

Notice that the message area `<div>`, the `<table>`, and the `<form>` are all nested within the "board" `<div>`. This is important for the CSS on the next page.

Adding some more style

If you load the page now (go ahead, give it a try), most of the elements are going to be in the wrong places and the wrong size. So we need to provide some CSS to put everything in the right place, and make sure all the elements, like the table cells, have the right size to match up with the game board image.

To get the elements into the right places, we're going to use CSS positioning to lay everything out. We've positioned the "board" `<div>` element using position relative, so we can now position the message area, table, and form at specific places within the "board" `<div>` to get them to display exactly where we want them.

Let's start with the "messageArea" `<div>`. It's nested inside the "board" `<div>`, and we want to position it at the very top left corner of the game board:

We want the message area to be positioned at the top left corner of the game board.

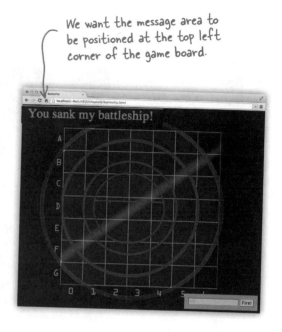

```
body {
    background-color: black;
}
div#board {
    position: relative;
    width: 1024px;
    height: 863px;
    margin: auto;
    background: url("board.jpg") no-repeat;
}
div#messageArea {
    position: absolute;
    top: 0px;
    left: 0px;
    color: rgb(83, 175, 19);
}
```

The "board" <div> is positioned relative, so everything nested within this <div> can be positioned relative to it.

We're positioning the message area at the top left of the board.

The messageArea <div> is nested inside the board <div>, so its position is specified relative to the board <div>. So it will be positioned 0px from the top and 0px from the left of the top left corner of the board <div>.

BULLET POINTS

- "position: relative" positions an element at its normal location in the flow of the page.

- "position: absolute" positions an element based on the position of its most closely positioned parent.

- The top and left properties can be used to specify the number of pixels to offset a positioned element from its default position.

We can also position the table and the form within the "board" `<div>`, again using absolute positions to get these elements precisely where we want them. Here's the rest of the CSS:

```css
body {
    background-color: black;
}
div#board {
    position: relative;
    width: 1024px;
    height: 863px;
    margin: auto;
    background: url("board.jpg") no-repeat;
}
div#messageArea {
    position: absolute;
    top: 0px;
    left: 0px;
    color: rgb(83, 175, 19);
}
table {
    position: absolute;
    left: 173px;
    top: 98px;
    border-spacing: 0px;
}
td {
    width: 94px;
    height: 94px;
}
form {
    position: absolute;
    bottom: 0px;
    right: 0px;
    padding: 15px;
    background-color: rgb(83, 175, 19);
}
form input {
    background-color: rgb(152, 207, 113);
    border-color: rgb(83, 175, 19);
    font-size: 1em;
}
```

We position the `<table>` 173 pixels from the left of the board and 98 pixels from the top, so it aligns with the grid in the background image.

Each `<td>` gets a specific width and height so that the cells of the `<table>` match up with the cells of the grid.

We're placing the `<form>` at the bottom right of the board. It obscures the bottom right numbers a bit, but that's okay (you know what they are). We're also giving the `<form>` a nice green color to match the background image.

And finally, a bit of styling on the two `<input>` elements so they fit in with the game theme, and we're done!

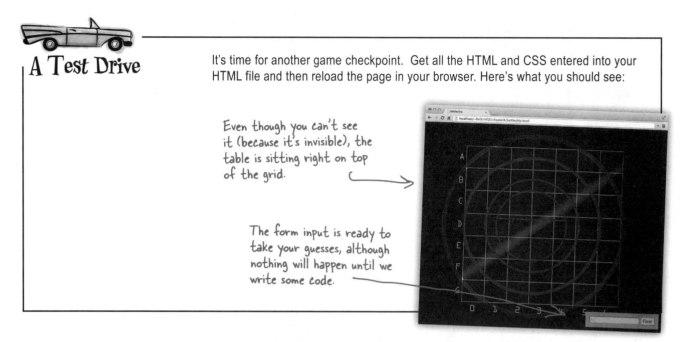

A Test Drive

It's time for another game checkpoint. Get all the HTML and CSS entered into your HTML file and then reload the page in your browser. Here's what you should see:

Even though you can't see it (because it's invisible), the table is sitting right on top of the grid.

The form input is ready to take your guesses, although nothing will happen until we write some code.

Step 4: Placing the hits and misses

The game board is looking great don't you think? However, we still need to figure out how to visually add hits and misses to the board—that is, how to add either a "ship.png" image or a "miss.png" image to the appropriate spot on the board for each guess. Right now we're only going to worry about how to craft the right markup or style to do this, and then later we'll use the same technique in code.

So how do we get a "ship.png" image or a "miss.png" image on the board? A straightforward way is to add the appropriate image to the background of a `<td>` element using CSS. Let's try that by creating two classes, one named "hit" and the other "miss". We'll use the `background` CSS property with these images so an element styled with the "hit" class will have the "ship.png" in its background, and an element styled with the "miss" class will have the "miss.png" image in its background. Like this:

ship.png

miss.png

If an element is in the hit class it gets the ship.png image. If the element is in the miss class, it gets the miss.png image in its background.

```
.hit {
    background: url("ship.png") no-repeat center center;
}
.miss {
    background: url("miss.png") no-repeat center center;
}
```

Each CSS rule places a single, centered image in the selected element.

Using the hit and miss classes

Make sure you've added the hit and miss class definitions to your CSS. You may be wondering how we're going to use these classes. Let's do a little experiment right now to demonstrate: imagine you have a ship hidden at "B3", "B4" and "B5", and the user guesses "B3"—a hit! So, you need to place a "ship.png" image at B3. Here's how you can do that: first convert the "B" into a number, 1 (since A is 0, B is 1, and so on), and find the `<td>` with the id "13" in your table. Now, add the class "hit" to that `<td>`, like this:

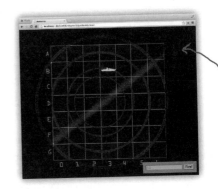

Here we've added the "hit" class to the `<td>`.

```
<tr>
<td id="10"></td> <td id="11"></td> <td id="12"></td> <td id="13" class="hit"></td>
<td id="14"></td> <td id="15"></td> <td id="16"></td>
</tr>
```

Make sure you've added the hit and miss classes from the previous page to your CSS.

Now when you reload the page, you'll see a battleship at location "B3" in the game board.

What we see when we add the class "hit" to element with id "13".

PRACTICE DRILLS

Before we write the code that's going to place hits and misses on the game board, get a little more practice to see how the CSS works. Manually play the game by adding the "hit" and "miss" classes into your markup, as dictated by the player's moves below. Be sure to check your answers!

```
Ship 1: A6, B6, C6
Ship 2: C4, D4, E4
Ship 3: B0, B1, B2
```

Remember, you'll need to convert the letters to numbers, with A = 0, ... G = 6.

and here are the player's guesses:

```
A0, D4, F5, B2, C5, C6
```

Check your answer at the end of the chapter before you go on.

When you're done, remove any classes that you've added to your `<td>` elements so you'll have an empty board to use when we start coding.

there are no
Dumb Questions

Q: I didn't know it was okay to use a string of numbers for the id attributes in our table?

A: Yes. As of HTML5, you are allowed to use all numbers as an element id. As long as there are no spaces in the id value, it's fine. And for the Battleship application, using numbers for each id works perfectly as a way to keep track of each table position, so we can access the element at that position quickly and easily.

Q: So just to make sure I understand, we're using each td element as a cell in the gameboard, and we'll mark a cell as being a hit or a miss with the class attribute?

A: Right, there are a few pieces here: we have a background image grid that is just for eye candy, we have a transparent HTML table overlaying that, and we use the classes "hit" and "miss" to put an image in the background of each table cell when needed. This last part will all be done from code, when we're going to dynamically add the class to an element.

Q: It sounds like we're going to need to convert letters, as in "A6", to numbers so we get "06". Will JavaScript do this automatically for us?

A: No, we're going to have to do that ourselves, but we have an easy way to do it—we're going to use what you know about arrays to do a quick conversion... stay tuned.

Q: I'm not sure I completely remember how CSS positioning works.

A: Positioning allows you to specify an exact position for an element. If an element is positioned "relative", then the element is positioned based on its normal location in the flow of the page. If an element is positioned "absolute", then that element is positioned at a specific location, relative to its most closely positioned parent. Sometimes that's the entire page, in which case the position you specify could be its top left position based on the corner of the web browser. In our case, we're positioning the table and message area elements absolutely, but in relation to the game board (because the board is the most closely positioned parent of the table and the message area).

If you need a more in-depth refresher on CSS positioning, check out Chapter 11 of *Head First HTML and CSS*.

Q: When I learned about the HTML form element, I was taught there is an action attribute that submits the form. Why don't we have one?

A: We don't need the action attribute in the <form> because we're not submitting the form to a server-side application. For this game, we're going to be handling everything in the browser, using code. So, instead of submitting the form, we're going to implement an event handler to be notified when the form button is clicked, and when that happens, we'll handle everything in our code, including getting the user's input from the form. Notice that the type of the form button is "button", not "submit", like you might be used to seeing if you've implemented forms that submit data to a PHP program or another kind of program that runs on the server. It's a good question; more on this later in the chapter.

How to design the game

With the HTML and CSS out of the way, let's get to the real game design. Back in Chapter 2, we hadn't covered functions or objects or encapsulation or learned about object-oriented design, so when we built the first version of the Battleship game, we used a procedural design—that is, we designed the game as a series of steps, with some decision logic and iteration mixed in. You also hadn't learned about the DOM, so the game wasn't very interactive. This time around, we're going to organize the game into a set of objects, each with its own responsibilities, and we're going to use the DOM to interact with the user. You'll see how this design makes approaching the problem a lot more straightforward.

Let's first get introduced to the objects we're going to design and implement. There are three: the *model*, which will hold the state of the game, like where each ship is located and where it's been hit; the *view*, which is responsible for updating the display; and the *controller*, which glues everything together by handling the user input, making sure the game logic gets played and determining when the game is over.

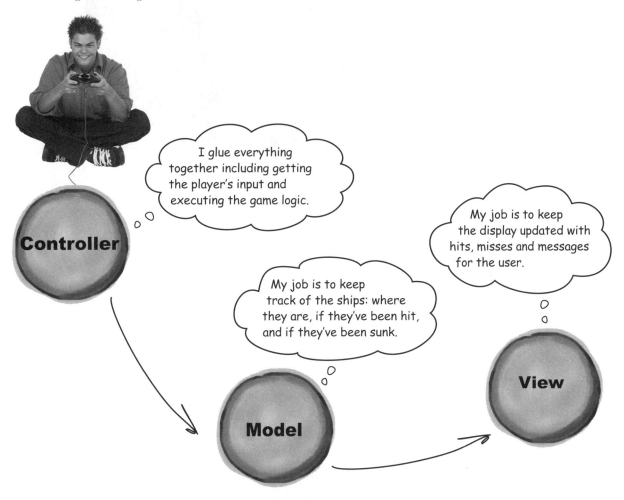

I glue everything together including getting the player's input and executing the game logic.

Controller

My job is to keep the display updated with hits, misses and messages for the user.

My job is to keep track of the ships: where they are, if they've been hit, and if they've been sunk.

Model

View

Exercise

It's time for some object design. We're going to start with the view object. Now, remember, the view object is responsible for updating the view. Take a look at the view below and see if you can determine the methods we want the view object to implement. Write the declarations for these methods below (just the declarations; we'll code the bodies of the methods in a bit) along with a comment or two about what each does. We've done one for you. *Check your answers before moving on:*

Here's a message. Messages will be things like "HIT!", "You missed." and "You sank my battleship!"

Here the display has a MISS placed on the grid.

And here the display has a ship placed on the grid.

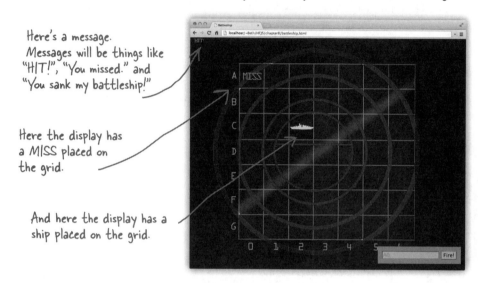

```
var view = {
```
Notice we're defining an object and assigning it to the variable view.

```
    // this method takes a string message and displays it
    // in the message display area
    displayMessage: function(msg) {
          // code to be supplied in a bit!
    }
```

Your methods go here!

```
};
```

Implementing the View

If not, shame on you. Do it now!

If you checked the answer to the previous exercise, you've
seen that we've broken the view into three separate methods:
`displayMessage`, `displayHit` and `displayMiss`. Now,
there is no one right answer. For instance, you might have just
two methods, `displayMessage` and `displayPlayerGuess`,
and pass an argument into `displayPlayerGuess` that
indicates if the player's guess was a hit or a miss. That is a
perfectly reasonable design. But we're sticking with our design
for now... so let's think through how to implement the first
method, `displayMessage`:

Here's our view object.

```
var view = {
    displayMessage: function(msg) {

    },                                          We're going to start here.
    displayHit: function(location) {
    },
    displayMiss: function(location) {
    }
};
```

How displayMessage works

To implement the `displayMessage` method you need to
review the HTML and see that we have a `<div>` with the id
"messageArea" ready for messages:

```
<div id="board">
    <div id="messageArea"></div>
        ...
</div>
```

We'll use the DOM to get access to this `<div>`, and then
set its text using `innerHTML`. And remember, whenever you
change the DOM, you'll see the changes immediately in the
browser. Here's what we're going to do…

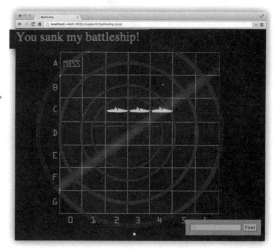

> Hey wait just a minute... how can we implement the view object without first getting the player's input and all that?

That's one great thing about objects.

We can make sure objects fulfill their responsibility without worrying about every other detail of the program. In this case the view just needs to know how to update the message area and place hit and miss markers on the grid. Once we've correctly implemented that behavior, we're done with the view object and we can move on to other parts of the code.

The other advantage of this approach is we can test the view in isolation and make sure it works. When we test many aspects of the program at once, we increase the odds something is going to go wrong and at the same time make the job of finding the problem more difficult (because you have to examine more areas of the code to find the problem).

To test an isolated object (without having finished the rest of the program yet), we'll need to write a little testing code that we'll throw away later, but that's okay.

So let's finish the view, test it, and then move on!

Implementing displayMessage

Let's get back to writing the code for `displayMessage`. Remember it needs to:

- Use the DOM to get the element with the id "messageArea".

- Set that element's `innerHTML` to the message passed to the `displayMessage` method.

So open up your blank "battleship.js" file, and add the view object:

```
var view = {
    displayMessage: function(msg) {
        var messageArea = document.getElementById("messageArea");
        messageArea.innerHTML = msg;
    },
    displayHit: function(location) {
    },
    displayMiss: function(location) {
    }
};
```

The displayMessage method takes one argument, a msg.

We get the messageArea element from the page...

...and update the text of the messageArea element by setting its innerHTML to msg.

Now before we test this code, let's go ahead and write the other two methods. They won't be incredibly complicated methods, and this way we can test the entire object at once.

How displayHit and displayMiss work

So we just talked about this, but remember, to have an image appear on the game board, we need to take a `<td>` element and add either the "hit" or the "miss" class to the element. The former results in a "ship.png" appearing in the cell and the latter results in "miss.png" being displayed.

We can affect the display by adding the "hit" or "miss" class to the `<td>` elements. Now we just need to do this from code.

```
<tr>
<td id="10"></td> <td class="hit" id="11"></td> <td id="12"></td> ...
</tr>
```

Now in code, we're going to use the DOM to get access to a `<td>`, and then set its class attribute to "hit" or "miss" using the `setAttribute` element method. As soon as we set the class attribute, you'll see the appropriate image appear in the browser. Here's what we're going to do:

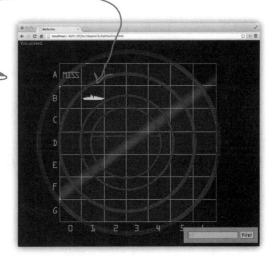

- Get a string id that consists of two numbers for the location of the hit or miss.

- Use the DOM to get the element with that id.

- Set that element's class attribute to "hit" if we're in `displayHit`, and "miss" if we're in `displayMiss`.

Implementing displayHit and displayMiss

Both `displayHit` and `displayMiss` are methods that take the location of a hit or
miss as an argument. That location should match the id of a cell (or <td> element) in
the table representing the game board in the HTML. So the first thing we need to do is
get a reference to that element with the `getElementById` method. Let's try this in the
`displayHit` method:

```
displayHit: function(location) {
    var cell = document.getElementById(location);
},
```

*Remember the location is created
from the row and column and
matches an id of a <td> element.*

The next step is to add the class "hit" to the cell, which we can do with the
`setAttribute` method like this:

```
displayHit: function(location) {
    var cell = document.getElementById(location);
    cell.setAttribute("class", "hit");
},
```

*We then set the class of that element
to "hit". This will immediately add a
ship image to the <td> element.*

Now let's add this code to the view object, and write `displayMiss` as well:

```
var view = {
    displayMessage: function(msg) {
        var messageArea = document.getElementById("messageArea");
        messageArea.innerHTML = msg;
    },

    displayHit: function(location) {
        var cell = document.getElementById(location);
        cell.setAttribute("class", "hit");
    },

    displayMiss: function(location) {
        var cell = document.getElementById(location);
        cell.setAttribute("class", "miss");
    }
};
```

*We're using the id we created from
the player's guess to get the correct
element to update.*

*And then setting the class of
that element to "hit".*

*We do the same thing in displayMiss,
only we set the class to "miss" which
adds a miss image to the element.*

Make sure you add the code for `displayHit` and `displayMiss` to your "battleship.js" file.

Another Test Drive...

Let's put the code through its paces before moving on...in fact, let's take the guesses from the previous Practice Drills exercise and implement them in code. Here's the sequence we want to implement:

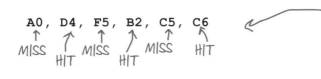

A0, D4, F5, B2, C5, C6
↑ MISS ↑ HIT ↑ MISS ↑ HIT ↑ MISS ↑ HIT

To represent that sequence in code, add this to the bottom of your "battleship.js" JavaScript file:

```
view.displayMiss("00");
view.displayHit("34");
view.displayMiss("55");
view.displayHit("12");
view.displayMiss("25");
view.displayHit("26");
```

← "A0"
← "D4"
← "F5"
← "B2"
← "C5"
← "C6"

Remember, displayHit and displayMiss take a location in the board that's already been converted from a letter and a number to a string with two numbers that corresponds to an id of one of the table cells.

And, let's not forget to test `displayMessage`:

```
view.displayMessage("Tap tap, is this thing on?");
```

Any message will do for simple testing...

After all that, reload the page in your browser and check out the updates to the display.

One of the benefits of breaking up the code into objects and giving each object only one responsibility is that we can test each object to make sure it's doing its job correctly.

The "tap tap" message is displayed up here at the top left of the view.

And the hits and misses we displayed using the view object are displayed in the game board.

Check each one to make sure it's in the right spot.

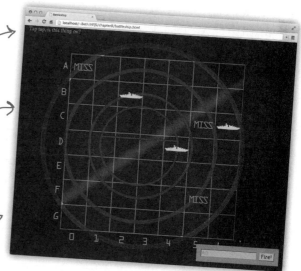

The Model

With the view object out of the way, let's move on to the model. The model is where we keep the *state* of the game. The model often also holds some *logic* relating to how the state changes. In this case the state includes the location of the ships, the ship locations that have been hit, and how many ships have been sunk. The only logic we're going to need (for now) is determining when a player's guess has hit a ship and then marking that ship with a hit.

Here's what the model object is going to look like:

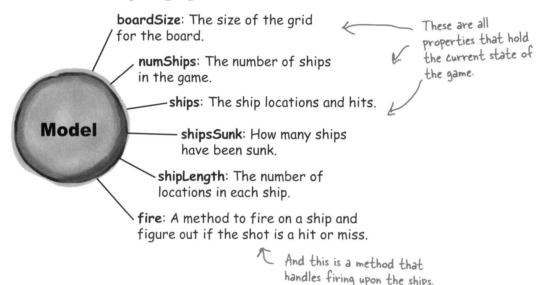

Model

boardSize: The size of the grid for the board.

numShips: The number of ships in the game.

ships: The ship locations and hits.

These are all properties that hold the current state of the game.

shipsSunk: How many ships have been sunk.

shipLength: The number of locations in each ship.

fire: A method to fire on a ship and figure out if the shot is a hit or miss.

And this is a method that handles firing upon the ships.

How the model interacts with the view

When the state of the game changes—that is, when you hit a ship, or miss—then the view needs to update the display. To do this, the model needs to talk to the view, and luckily we have a few methods the model can use to do that. We'll get our game logic set first in the model, then we'll add code to update the view.

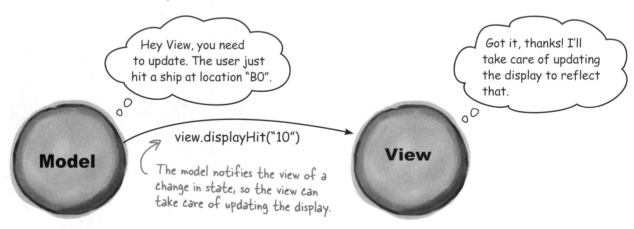

Hey View, you need to update. The user just hit a ship at location "B0".

Got it, thanks! I'll take care of updating the display to reflect that.

Model

view.displayHit("10")

View

The model notifies the view of a change in state, so the view can take care of updating the display.

You're gonna need a bigger boat... and game board

Before we start writing model code, we need to think about how to represent the state of the ships in the model. Back in Chapter 2 in the simple Battleship game, we had a single ship that sat on a 1x7 game board. Now things are a little more complex: we have *three* ships on a 7x7 board. Here's how it looks now:

Each ship takes up three cells on the 2D board.

This ship sits at locations "B0", "C0", "D0".

Here's another ship at D2 through D4.

You'll note that the ships don't overlap on the board. That would be impossible on a physical Battleship board and would lead to weird game play. We'll come back later to see how to make sure ships don't overlap when we talk about how to randomly place ships on the board.

We also need to be able to keep track of hits. Each ship has three locations, so we need to store three hits for each ship too.

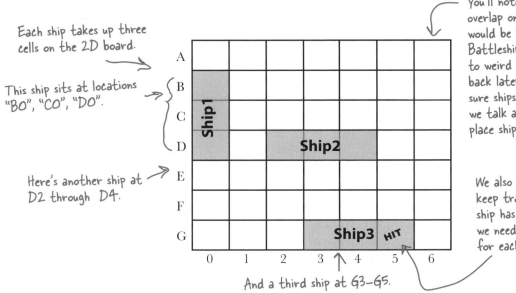

And a third ship at G3–G5.

Sharpen your pencil

Given how we've described the new game board above, how would you represent the ships in the model (just the locations, we'll worry about hits later). Check off the best solution below.

❏ Use nine variables for the ship locations, similar to the way we handled the ships in Chapter 2.

❏ Use an array with an item for each cell in entire board (49 items total). Record the ship number in each cell that holds part of a ship.

❏ Use an array to hold all nine locations. Items 0-2 will hold the first ship, 3-5 the second, and so on.

❏ Use three different arrays, one for each ship, with three locations contained in each.

❏ Use an object named ship with three location properties. Put all the ships in an array named ships.

❏ _____
_____
_____

Or write in your own answer.

How we're going to represent the ships

As you can see there are many ways we can represent ships, and you may have even come up with a few other ways of your own. You'll find that no matter what kind of data you've got, there are many choices for storing that data, with various tradeoffs depending on your choice—some methods will be space efficient, others will optimize run time, some will just be easier to understand, and so on.

We've chosen a representation for ships that is fairly simple—we're representing each ship as an object that holds the locations it sits in, along with the hits it's taken. Let's take a look at how we represent one ship:

> *Each ship is an object.*

> *The ship has a locations property and a hits property.*

```
var ship1 = {
        locations: ["10", "20", "30"],
        hits: ["", "", ""]
    };
```

> *The locations property is an array that holds each location on the board.*

> *The hits property is also an array that holds whether or not a ship is hit at each location. We'll set the array items to the empty string initially, and change each item to "hit" when the ship has taken a hit in the corresponding location.*

> *Note that we've converted the ship locations to two numbers, using 0 for A, 1 for B, and so on.*

Here's what all three ships would look like:

> *Each ship has an array of three locations and an array to track hits.*

```
var ship1 = { locations: ["10", "20", "30"], hits: ["", "", ""] };
var ship2 = { locations: ["32", "33", "34"], hits: ["", "", ""] };
var ship3 = { locations: ["63", "64", "65"], hits: ["", "", "hit"] };
```

And, rather than managing three different variables to hold the ships, we'll create a single array variable to hold them all, like this:

> *Note the plural name, ships.*

> *We're assigning to ships an array that holds all three ships.*

```
var ships = [{ locations: ["10", "20", "30"], hits: ["", "", ""] },
            { locations: ["32", "33", "34"], hits: ["", "", ""] },
            { locations: ["63", "64", "65"], hits: ["", "", "hit"] }];
```

> *Here's the first ship...*
> *...and the second...*
> *...and the third.*

> *Note this ship has a hit at location "65" on the grid.*

Ship Magnets

Use the following player moves, along with the data structure for the ships, to place the ship and miss magnets onto the game board. Does the player sink all the ships? We've done the first move for you.

Here are the moves:

A6, B3, C4, D1, B0, D4, F0, A1, C6, B1, B2, E4, B6 ← Execute these moves on the game board.

```
var ships = [{ locations: ["06", "16", "26"], hits: ["hit", "", ""] },
             { locations: ["24", "34", "44"], hits: ["", "", ""] },
             { locations: ["10", "11", "12"], hits: ["", "", ""] }];
```

Here is the data structure. Mark each ship with a hit as the game is played.

And here's the board and your magnets.

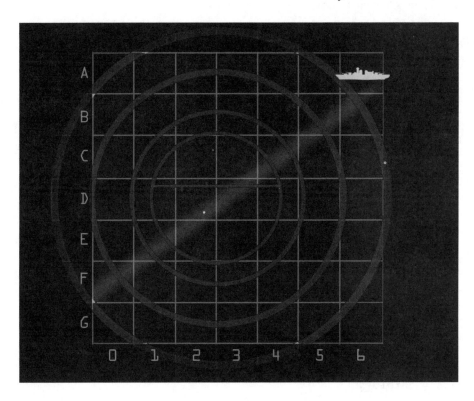

MISS
MISS
MISS
MISS
MISS

You might have leftover magnets.

Sharpen your pencil

Let's practice using the ships data structure to simulate some ship activities. Using the ships definition below, work through the questions and the code below and fill in the blanks. Make sure you check your answers before moving on, as this is an important part of how the game works:

```
var ships = [{ locations: ["31", "41", "51"], hits: ["", "", ""] },
            { locations: ["14", "24", "34"], hits: ["", "hit", ""] },
            { locations: ["00", "01", "02"], hits: ["hit", "", ""] }];
```

Which ships are already hit?_____ And, at what locations? _____

The player guesses "D4", does that hit a ship?_____ If so, which one? _____

The player guesses "B3", does that hit a ship?_____ If so, which one? _____

Finish this code to access the second ship's middle location and print its value with console.log.

```
var ship2 = ships[____];
var locations = ship2.locations;
console.log("Location is " + locations[____]);
```

Finish this code to see if the third ship has a hit in its first location:

```
var ship3 = ships[____];
var hits = ship3._____;
if (_____ === "hit") {
    console.log("Ouch, hit on third ship at location one");
}
```

Finish this code to hit the first ship at the third location:

```
var _____ = ships[0];
var hits = ship1._____;
hits[____] = _____;
```

Implementing the model object

Now that you know how to represent the ships and the hits, let's get some code down. First, we'll create the model object, and then take the `ships` data structure we just created, and add it as a property. And, while we're at it, there are a few other properties we're going to need as well, like `numShips`, to hold the number of ships we have in the game. Now, if you're asking, "What do you mean, we know there are three ships, why do we need a `numShips` property?" Well, what if you wanted to create a new version of the game that was more difficult and had four or five ships? By not "hardcoding" this value, and using a property instead (and then using the property throughout the code rather than the number), we can save ourselves a future headache if we need to change the number of ships, because we'll only need to change it in one place.

Now, speaking of "hardcoding", we *are* going to hardcode the ships' initial locations, for now. By knowing where the ships are, we can test the game more easily, and focus on the core game logic for now. We'll tackle the code for placing random ships on the game board a little later.

So let's get the model object created:

boardSize: The size of the grid for the board.

numShips: The number of ships in the game.

ships: The ship locations and hits.

shipsSunk: How many ships have been sunk.

shipLength: The number of locations in each ship.

Model

fire: A method to fire on a ship and figure out if the shot is a hit or miss.

The model is an object.

```
var model = {
    boardSize: 7,
    numShips: 3,
    shipLength: 3,
    shipsSunk: 0,

    ships: [{ locations: ["06", "16", "26"], hits: ["", "", ""] },
            { locations: ["24", "34", "44"], hits: ["", "", ""] },
            { locations: ["10", "11", "12"], hits: ["", "", ""] }]

};
```

These three properties keep us from hardcoding values. They are: boardSize (the size of the grid used for the board), numShips (the number of ships in the game), and shipLength (the number of locations in each ship, 3).

shipsSunk (initialized to 0 for the start of the game) keeps the current number of ships that have been sunk by the player.

We've got quite a bit of state already!

Later on, we'll generate these locations for the ships so they're random, but for now, we'll hardcode them to make it easier to test the game.

The property ships is the array of ship objects that each store the locations and hits of one of the three ships. (Notice that we've changed ships from a variable, which we used before, to a property for the model object.)

Note we're also hardcoding the sizes of the locations and hits arrays. You'll learn how to dynamically create arrays later in the book.

Thinking about the fire method

The `fire` method is what turns a player's guess into a hit or a miss. We already know the `view` object is going to take care of displaying the hits and misses, but the `fire` method has to provide the game logic for determining if a hit or a miss has occurred.

Knowing that a ship is hit is straightforward: given a player's guess, you just need to:

- Examine each ship and see if it occupies that location.

- If it does, you have a hit, and we'll mark the corresponding item in the `hits` array (and let the view know we got a hit). We'll also return `true` from the method, meaning we got a hit.

- If no ship occupies the guessed location, you've got a miss. We'll let the view know, and return `false` from the method.

> **boardSize**: The size of the grid for the board.
>
> **numShips**: The number of ships in the game.
>
> **ships**: The ship locations and hits.
>
> **shipsSunk**: How many ships have been sunk.
>
> **shipLength**: The number of locations in each ship.
>
> **Model**
>
> **fire**: A method to fire on a ship and figure out if the shot is a hit or miss.

Now the `fire` method should also determine if a ship isn't just hit, but if it's sunk. We'll worry about that once we have the rest of the logic worked out.

Setting up the fire method

Let's get a basic skeleton of the `fire` method set up. The method will take a guess as an argument, and then iterate over each ship to determine if that ship was hit. We won't write the hit detection code just yet, but let's get the rest set up now:

```
var model = {
    boardSize: 7,
    numShips: 3,
    shipsSunk: 0,
    shipLength: 3,
    ships: [{ locations: ["06", "16", "26"], hits: ["", "", ""] },
            { locations: ["24", "34", "44"], hits: ["", "", ""] },
            { locations: ["10", "11", "12"], hits: ["", "", ""] }],

    fire: function(guess) {

        for (var i = 0; i < this.numShips; i++) {
            var ship = this.ships[i];
        }
    }
};
```

← Don't forget to add a comma here!

The method accepts a guess.

Then, we iterate through the array of ships, examining one ship at a time.

Here we have our hands on a ship. We need to see if the guess matches any of its locations.

Looking for hits

So now, each time through the loop, we need to see if the guess is one of the
locations of the ship:

```
for (var i = 0; i < this.numShips; i++) {
    var ship = this.ships[i];
    locations = ship.locations;

}
```

And we're stepping
through each ship.

And we've accessed the ship's set of
locations. Remember this is a property
of the ship that contains an array.

What we need is the code that
determines if the guess is in this
ship's locations.

Here's the situation: we have a string, guess, that we're looking for in an array,
locations. If guess matches one of those locations, we know we have a hit:

```
guess = "16";
locations = ["06", "16", "26"];
```

We need to find out if the value
in guess is one of the values in
the ship's locations array.

We could write yet another loop to go through each item in the locations array,
compare the item to guess, and if they match, we have a hit.

But rather than write another loop, we have an easier way to do this:

```
var index = locations.indexOf(guess);
```

The indexOf method searches an array for a matching
value and returns its index, or −1 if it can't find it.

So, using indexOf, we can write the code to find a hit like this:

```
for (var i = 0; i < this.numShips; i++) {
    var ship = this.ships[i];
    locations = ship.locations;
    var index = locations.indexOf(guess);
    if (index >= 0) {
        // We have a hit!
    }
}
```

Notice that the indexOf method for an array is similar
to the indexOf string method. It takes a value and
returns the index of that value in the array (or −1 if
it can't find the value).

So if we get an index greater than or
equal to zero, the user's guess is in the
location's array, and we have a hit.

Using indexOf isn't any more efficient than writing a loop, but it is a little clearer and it's
definitely less code. We'd also argue that the intent of this code is clearer than if we wrote
a loop: it's easier to see what value we're looking for in an array using indexOf. In any
case, you now have another tool in your programming toolbelt.

Putting that all together...

To finish this up, we have one more thing to determine here: if we have a hit, what do we do? All we need to do, for now, is mark the hit in the model, which means adding a "hit" string to the `hits` array. Let's put all the pieces together:

```javascript
var model = {

    boardSize: 7,

    numShips: 3,

    shipsSunk: 0,

    shipLength: 3,

    ships: [ { locations: ["06", "16", "26"], hits: ["", "", ""] },
             { locations: ["24", "34", "44"], hits: ["", "", ""] },
             { locations: ["10", "11", "12"], hits: ["", "", ""] } ],


    fire: function(guess) {
        for (var i = 0; i < this.numShips; i++) {
            var ship = this.ships[i];
            var locations = ship.locations;
            var index = locations.indexOf(guess);
            if (index >= 0) {
                ship.hits[index] = "hit";
                return true;
            }
        }
        return false;

    }
};
```

For each ship...

If the guess is in the locations array, we have a hit.

So mark the hits array at the same index.

Oh, and we need to return true because we had a hit.

Otherwise, if we make it through all the ships and don't have a hit, it's a miss, so we return false.

That's a great start on our model object. There are only a couple of other things we need to do: determine if a ship is sunk, and let the view know about the changes in the model so it can keep the player updated. Let's get started on those…

Wait, can we talk about your verbosity again?

Sorry, we have to bring this up again. You're being a bit verbose in some of your references to objects and arrays. Take another look at the code:

```
for (var i = 0; i < this.numShips; i++) {
  var ship = this.ships[i];            ← First we get the ship...
  var locations = ship.locations;      ← Then we get the locations
                                          in the ship...
  var index = locations.indexOf(guess); ← Then we get the index of
  ...                                      the guess in the locations.
}
```

Some would call this code overly verbose. Why? Because some of these references can be shortened using *chaining*. Chaining allows us to string together object references so that we don't have to create temporary variables, like the `locations` variable in the code above.

Now you might ask why `locations` is a temporary variable? That's because we're using `locations` only to temporarily store the `ship.locations` array so we can then turn around and call the `indexOf` method on it to get the `index` of the `guess`. We don't need `locations` for anything else in this method. With chaining, we can get rid of that temporary `locations` variable, like this:

```
var index = ship.locations.indexOf(guess);   ← We've combined the two lines
                                                highlighted above into a single line.
```

 How chaining works...

Chaining is really just a shorthand for a longer series of steps to access properties and methods of objects (and arrays). Let's take a closer look at what we just did to combine two statements with chaining.

```
                                    ← Here's a ship object.
var ship = { locations: ["06", "16", "26"], hits: ["", "", ""] };
var locations = ship.locations;  ← We were grabbing the locations array from the ship
var index = locations.indexOf(guess);  ← And then using it to access the indexOf method.
```

We can combine the bottom two statements by chaining together the expressions (and getting rid of the variable `locations`):

```
ship.locations.indexOf(guess)
```

1 Evaluates to the ship object.

2 Which has a locations property, which is an array.

3 Which has a method named indexOf.

Meanwhile back at the battleship...

Now we need to write the code to determine if a ship is sunk. You know
the rules: a battleship is sunk when all of its locations are hit. We can add
a little helper method to check to see if a ship is sunk:

*We'll call the method isSunk. It's going to take a ship and
return true if it's sunk and false if it is still floating.*

*This method takes a ship, and
then checks every possible
location for a hit.*

```
isSunk: function(ship) {
    for (var i = 0; i < this.shipLength; i++)  {
        if (ship.hits[i] !== "hit") {
            return false;
        }
    }
    return true;
}
```

*If there's a location that doesn't
have a hit, then the ship is still
floating, so return false.*

*Otherwise this ship is
sunk! Return true.*

*Go ahead and add this method to
your model object, just below fire.*

Now, we can use that method in the `fire` method to find out if a ship is sunk:

```
fire: function(guess) {
    for (var i = 0; i < this.numShips; i++) {
        var ship = this.ships[i];
        var index = ship.locations.indexOf(guess);
        if (index >= 0) {
            ship.hits[index] = "hit";
            if (this.isSunk(ship)) {
                this.shipsSunk++;
            }
            return true;
        }
    }
    return false;
},
isSunk: function(ship) { ... }
```

*We'll add the check here,
after we know for sure we
have a hit. If the ship is sunk,
then we increase the number of
ships that are sunk in model's
shipsSunk property.*

*Here's where we added the new isSunk method, just below
fire. Don't forget to make sure you've got a comma
between each of the model's properties and methods!*

A view to a kill...

That's about it for the model object. The model maintains the state of the game, and has the logic to test guesses for hits and misses. The only thing we're missing is the code to notify the view when we get a hit or a miss in the model. Let's do that now:

```
var model = {
    boardSize: 7,
    numShips: 3,
    shipsSunk: 0,
    shipLength: 3,
    ships: [ { locations: ["06", "16", "26"], hits: ["", "", ""] },
             { locations: ["24", "34", "44"], hits: ["", "", ""] },
             { locations: ["10", "11", "12"], hits: ["", "", ""] } ],
    fire: function(guess) {
        for (var i = 0; i < this.numShips; i++) {
            var ship = this.ships[i];
            var index = ship.locations.indexOf(guess);
            if (index >= 0) {
                ship.hits[index] = "hit";
                view.displayHit(guess);
                view.displayMessage("HIT!");
                if (this.isSunk(ship)) {
                    view.displayMessage("You sank my battleship!");
                    this.shipsSunk++;
                }
                return true;
            }
        }
        view.displayMiss(guess);
        view.displayMessage("You missed.");
        return false;
    },
    isSunk: function(ship) {
        for (var i = 0; i < this.shipLength; i++) {
            if (ship.hits[i] !== "hit") {
                return false;
            }
        }
        return true;
    }
};
```

This is the whole model object so you can see the entire thing in one piece.

Notify the view that we got a hit at the location in guess.

And ask the view to display the message "HIT!".

Let the player know that this hit sank the battleship!

Notify the view that we got a miss at the location in guess.

And ask the view to display the message "You missed.".

Remember that the methods in the view object add the "hit" or "miss" class to the element with the id at row and column in the guess string. So the view translates the "hit" in the hits array into a "hit" in the HTML. But keep in mind, the "hit" in the HTML is just for display; the "hit" in the model represents the actual state.

A Test Drive

Add all the model code to "battleship.js". Test it by calling the model's fire method, passing in a row and column of a guess each time. Our ships are hardcoded still, so it'll be easy for you to hit them all. Try adding some of your own as well (a few more misses). (Download "battleship_tester.js" to see our version of the test code.)

You'll need to remove or comment out the previous view testing code to get the same results as we show here. You can see how to do that in battleship_tester.js.

```
model.fire("53");

model.fire("06");
model.fire("16");
model.fire("26");

model.fire("34");
model.fire("24");
model.fire("44");

model.fire("12");
model.fire("11");
model.fire("10");
```

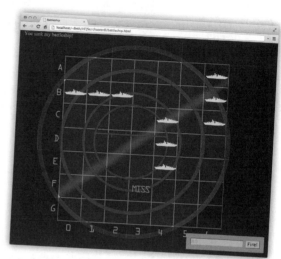

Reload "battleship.html". You should see your hits and misses appear on the game board.

there are no
Dumb Questions

Q: Is using chaining to combine statements better than keeping statements separate?

A: Not necessarily better, no. Chaining isn't much more efficient (you save one variable), but it does make your code shorter. We'd argue that short chains (2 or 3 levels at most) are easier to read than multiple lines of code, but that's our preference. If you want to keep your statements separate, that's fine. And if you do use chaining, make sure you don't create really long chains; they will be harder to read and understand if they're too long.

Q: We have arrays (locations) inside an object (ship) inside an array (ships). How many levels deep can you nest objects and arrays like this?

A: Pretty much as deep as you want. Practically, of course, it's unlikely you'll ever go too deep (and if you find yourself with more than three or four levels of nesting, it's likely your data structure is getting too complex and you should rethink things a bit).

Q: I noticed we added a property named boardSize to the model, but we haven't used it in the model code. What is that for?

A: We're going to be using model.boardSize, and the other properties in model, in the code coming up. The model's responsibility is to manage the state of the game, and boardSize is definitely part of the state. The controller will access the state it needs by accessing the model's properties, and we'll be adding more model methods later that will use these properties too.

Implementing the Controller

Now that you have the view and the model complete, we're going to start to bring this app together by implementing the controller. At a high level, the controller glues everything together by getting a guess, processing the guess and getting it to the model. It also keeps track of some administrative details, like the current number of guesses and the player's progress in the game. To do all this the controller relies on the model to keep the state of the game and on the view to display the game.

More specifically, here's the set of responsibilities we're giving the controller:

- Get and process the player's guess (like "A0" or "B1").

- Keep track of the number of guesses.

- Ask the model to update itself based on the latest guess.

- Determine when the game is over (that is, when all ships have been sunk).

Let's get started on the controller by first defining a property, guesses, in the controller object. Then we'll implement a single method, processGuess, that takes an alphanumeric guess, processes it and passes it to the model.

guesses: Keeps number of guesses.

processGuess: Processes guesses and passes them to the model. Detects the end of the game.

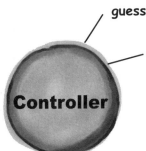

Here's the skeleton of the controller code; we'll fill this in over the next few pages:

```
var controller = {
    guesses: 0,

    processGuess: function(guess) {
        // more code will go here
    }
};
```

Here we're defining our controller object, with a property, guesses, initialized to zero.

And here's the beginning of the processGuess method, which takes a guess in the form "A0".

Processing the player's guess

The controller's responsibility is to get the player's guess, make sure it's valid, and then get it to the model object. But, where does it get the player's guess? Don't worry, we'll get to that in a bit. For now we're just going to assume, at some point, some code is going to call the controller's processGuess method and give it a string in the form:

This is a great technique when you are coding. Focus on the requirements for the specific code you're working on. Thinking about the whole problem at once is often a less successful technique.

"A3"

You know the Battleship-style guess format at this point: it's a letter followed by a number.

Now after you receive a guess in this form (an alpha-numeric set of characters, like "A3"), you'll need to transform the guess into a form the model understands (a string of two numeric characters, like "03"). Here's a high level view of how we're going to convert a valid input into the number-only form:

Surely a player would never enter in an invalid guess, right? Ha! We'd better make sure we've got valid input.

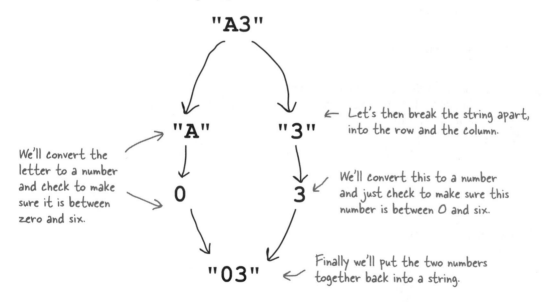

Assume we've been handed a string in alphanumeric form:

"A3"

← Let's then break the string apart, into the row and the column.

We'll convert the letter to a number and check to make sure it is between zero and six.

We'll convert this to a number and just check to make sure this number is between 0 and six.

Finally we'll put the two numbers together back into a string.

"03"

But first things first. We also need to check that the input is valid. Let's plan this all out before we write the code.

Planning the code...

Rather than putting all this guess-processing code into the `processGuess` method, we're going to write a little helper function (after all we might be able to use this again). We'll name the function `parseGuess`.

Let's step through how it is going to work before we start writing code:

1 We get a player's guess in classic Battleship-style as a single letter followed by a number.

2 Check the input to make sure it is valid (not null or too long or too short).

3 Take the letter and convert it to a number: A to 0, B to 1, and so on.

4 See if the number from step 3 is valid (between 0 and 6).

5 Check the second number for validity (also between 0 and 6).

6 If any check failed, return null. Otherwise concatenate the two numbers into a string and return the string.

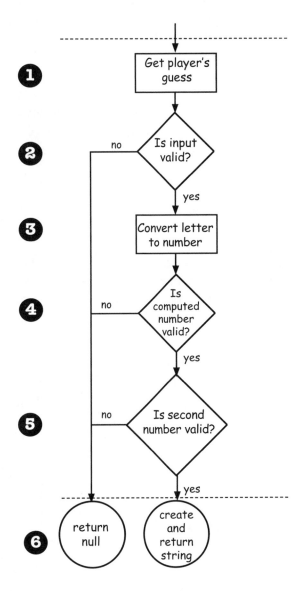

Implementing parseGuess

We have a solid plan for coding this, so let's get started:

 Let's tackle steps one and two. All we need to do is accept the player's guess and check to make sure it is valid. At this point we're just going to define validity as accepting a non-null string and a string that has exactly two characters in it.

The guess is passed into the guess parameter.

↓

And then we check for null and to make sure the length is 2 characters.

```javascript
function parseGuess(guess) {
    if (guess === null || guess.length !== 2) {
        alert("Oops, please enter a letter and a number on the board.");
    }
}
```

If not, we alert the player.

3 Next, we take the letter and convert it to a number by using a helper array that contains the letters A-F. To get the number, we can use the indexOf method to get the index of the letter in the array, like this:

An array loaded with each letter that could be part of a valid guess.

```javascript
function parseGuess(guess) {
    var alphabet = ["A", "B", "C", "D", "E", "F", "G"];

    if (guess === null || guess.length !== 2) {
        alert("Oops, please enter a letter and a number on the board.");
    } else {
        firstChar = guess.charAt(0);
        var row = alphabet.indexOf(firstChar);
    }
}
```

Grab the first character of the guess.

Then, using indexOf, we get back a number between zero and six that corresponds to the letter. Try a couple of examples to see how this works.

Now we'll handle checking both characters of the guess to see if they are numbers between zero and six (in other words, to make sure they are both valid positions on the board).

```
function parseGuess(guess) {
    var alphabet = ["A", "B", "C", "D", "E", "F", "G"];

    if (guess === null || guess.length !== 2) {
        alert("Oops, please enter a letter and a number on the board.");
    } else {
        firstChar = guess.charAt(0);
        var row = alphabet.indexOf(firstChar);
        var column = guess.charAt(1);

        if (isNaN(row) || isNaN(column)) {
            alert("Oops, that isn't on the board.");
        } else if (row < 0 || row >= model.boardSize ||
                        column < 0 || column >= model.boardSize) {
            alert("Oops, that's off the board!");
        }
    }
}
```

Here we've added code to grab the second character in the string, which represents the column.

And we're checking to see if either of the row or column is not a number using the isNAN function.

We're also making sure that the numbers are between zero and six.

Notice we're using type conversion like crazy here! column is a string, so when we check to make sure its value is 0–6, we rely on type conversion to convert it to a number for comparison.

Actually we're being even more general here. Instead of hardcoding the number six, we're asking the model to tell us how big the board is and using that number for comparison.

Rather than hard-coding the value six as the biggest value a row or column can hold, we used the model's boardSize property. What advantage do you think that has in the long run?

6 Now for our final bit of code for the parseGuess function... If any check for valid input fails, we'll return null. Otherwise we'll return the row and column of the guess, combined into a string.

```javascript
function parseGuess(guess) {
    var alphabet = ["A", "B", "C", "D", "E", "F", "G"];

    if (guess === null || guess.length !== 2) {
        alert("Oops, please enter a letter and a number on the board.");
    } else {
        firstChar = guess.charAt(0);
        var row = alphabet.indexOf(firstChar);
        var column = guess.charAt(1);

        if (isNaN(row) || isNaN(column)) {
            alert("Oops, that isn't on the board.");
        } else if (row < 0 || row >= model.boardSize ||
                   column < 0 || column >= model.boardSize) {
            alert("Oops, that's off the board!");
        } else {
            return row + column;
        }
    }
    return null;
}
```

← At this point, everything looks good, so we can return a row and column.

← If we get here, there was a failed check along the way, so return null.

Notice we're concatenating the row and column together to make a string, and returning that string. We're using type conversion again here: row is a number and column is a string, so we'll end up with a string.

A Test Drive

Okay, make sure all this code is entered into "battleship.js" and then add some function calls below it all that look like this:

```javascript
console.log(parseGuess("A0"));
console.log(parseGuess("B6"));
console.log(parseGuess("G3"));
console.log(parseGuess("H0"));
console.log(parseGuess("A7"));
```

Reload "battleship.html", and make sure your console window is open. You should see the results of parseGuess displayed in the console and possibly an alert or two.

JavaScript console

```
00
16
63
null
null
```

Meanwhile back at the controller...

Now that we have the `parseGuess` helper function written we
move on to implementing the controller. Let's first integrate the
`parseGuess` function with the existing controller code:

```
var controller = {
    guesses: 0,

    processGuess: function(guess) {
        var location = parseGuess(guess);
        if (location) {

        }
    }
};
```

We'll use parseGuess to
validate the player's guess.

And as long as we don't get null back, we
know we've got a valid location object.

Remember null is a
falsey value.

And the rest of the code for the
controller will go here.

That completes the first responsibility of the controller. Let's see
what's left:

- ~~Get and process the player's guess (like "A0" or "B1").~~
- Keep track of the number of guesses.
- Ask the model to update itself based on the latest guess.
- Determine when the game is over (that is, when all ships
  have been sunk).

We'll tackle
these next.

Counting guesses and firing the shot

The next item on our list is straightforward: to keep track of the
number of guesses we just need to increment the `guesses` property
each time the player makes a guess. As you'll see in the code, we've
chosen not to penalize players if they enter an invalid guess.

Next, we'll ask the model to update itself based on the guess by calling
the model's `fire` method. After all, the point of a player's guess is to
fire hoping to hit a battleship. Now remember, the `fire` method takes
a string, which contains the row and column, and by some luck we get
that string by calling `parseGuess`. How convenient.

Let's put all this together and implement the next step...

```
var controller = {
    guesses: 0,

    processGuess: function(guess) {
        var location = parseGuess(guess);
        if (location) {
            this.guesses++;
            var hit = model.fire(location);
        }
    }
};
```

If the player entered a valid guess we increase the number of guesses by one.

Remember, this.guesses++ just adds one to the value of the guesses property. It works just like i++ in for loops.

Also notice if the player enters an invalid board location, we don't penalize them by counting the guess.

And then we pass the row and column in the form of a string to the model's fire method. Remember, the fire method returns true if a ship is hit.

Game over?

All we have left is to determine when the game is complete. How do we do that? Well, we know that when three ships are sunk the game is over. So, each time the guess is a hit, we'll check to see if there are three sunken ships, using the `model.shipsSunk` property. Let's generalize this a bit, and instead of just comparing it to the number 3, we'll use the model's `numShips` property for the comparison. You might decide later to set the number of ships to, say, 2 or 4, and this way, you won't need to revisit this code to make it work correctly.

```
var controller = {
    guesses: 0,

    processGuess: function(guess) {
        var location = parseGuess(guess);
        if (location) {
            this.guesses++;
            var hit = model.fire(location);
            if (hit && model.shipsSunk === model.numShips) {
                view.displayMessage("You sank all my battleships, in " +
                                        this.guesses + " guesses");
            }
        }
    }
};
```

If the guess was a hit, and the number of ships that are sunk is equal to the number of ships in the game, then show the player a message that they've sunk all the ships.

We'll show the player the total number of guesses they took to sink the ship. The guesses property is a property of "this" object, the controller.

A Test Drive

Okay, make sure all the controller code is entered into your "battleship.js" file and then add some function calls below it all to test your controller. Reload your "battleship.html" page and note the hits and misses on the board. Are they in the right places? (Download "battleship_tester.js" to see our version.)

Again, you'll need to remove or comment out the previous testing code to get the same results as we show here. You can see how to do that in battleship_tester.js.

```
controller.processGuess("A0");

controller.processGuess("A6");
controller.processGuess("B6");
controller.processGuess("C6");

controller.processGuess("C4");
controller.processGuess("D4");
controller.processGuess("E4");

controller.processGuess("B0");
controller.processGuess("B1");
controller.processGuess("B2");
```

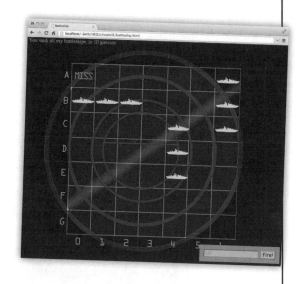

 We're calling the controller's processGuess method and passing in guesses in Battleship format.

We let the player know the game ended in the message area, after they sink all three ships. But the player can still enter guesses. If you wanted to fix this so a player isn't allowed to enter guesses after they've sunk all the ships, how would you handle that?

Getting a player's guess

Now that you've implemented the core game logic and display, you need a way to enter and retrieve a player's guesses so the game can actually be played. You might remember that in the HTML we've already got a `<form>` element ready for entering guesses, but how do we hook that into the game?

To do that we need an *event handler*. We've talked a little about event handlers already. For now, we're going to spend just enough time with event handlers again to get the game working, and we'll undertake learning the nitty-gritty details of event handlers in the next chapter. Our goal is for you to get a high-level understanding of how event handlers work with form elements, but not necessarily understand everything about how it works at the detailed level, right now.

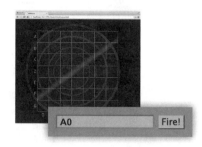

Here's our HTML form element, ready to take user input.

Here's the big picture:

① The player enters a guess and clicks on the Fire! button.

② When Fire! is clicked, a pre-assigned event handler is called.

③ The handler for the Fire! button grabs the player's input from the form and hands it to the controller.

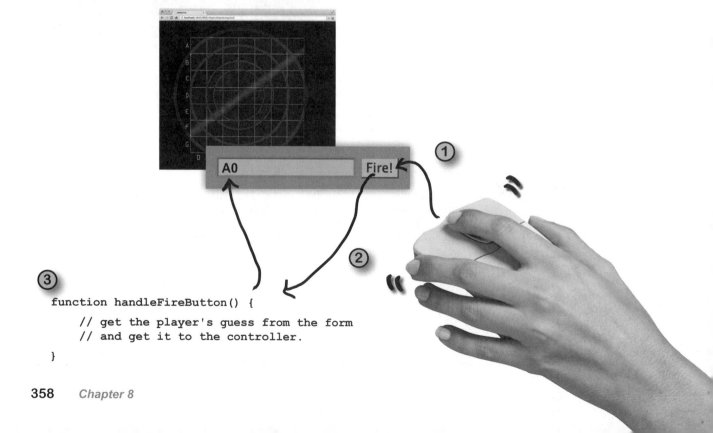

```
function handleFireButton() {
    // get the player's guess from the form
    // and get it to the controller.
}
```

How to add an event handler to the Fire! button

To get this all rolling the first thing we need to do is add an event handler to the Fire! button. To do that, we first need to get a reference to the button using the button's id. Review your HTML again, and you'll find the Fire! button has the id "fireButton". With that, all you need to do is call `document.getElementById` to get a reference to the button. Once we have the button reference, we can assign a handler function to the `onclick` property of the button, like this:

We need somewhere for this code to go, so let's create an init function.

First, we get a reference to the Fire! button using the button's id:

```
function init() {
    var fireButton = document.getElementById("fireButton");
    fireButton.onclick = handleFireButton;
}
```

Then we can add a click handler function named handleFireButton to the button.

And let's not forget to get a handleFireButton function started:

Here's the handleFireButton function. This function will be called whenever you click the Fire! button.

```
function handleFireButton() {
    // code to get the value from the form
}
```

We'll write this code in just a sec.

```
window.onload = init;
```

Just like we learned in Chapter 6, we want the browser to run init when the page is fully loaded.

Getting the player's guess from the form

The Fire! button is what initiates the guess, but the player's guess is actually contained in the "guessInput" form element. We can get the value from the form input by accessing the input element's `value` property. Here's how you do it:

First, we get a reference to the input form element using the input element's id, "guessInput".

```
function handleFireButton() {
    var guessInput = document.getElementById("guessInput");
    var guess = guessInput.value;
}
```

Then we get the guess from the input element. The guess is stored in the value property of the input element.

We have the value, now all we need is to do something with it. Luckily we have lots of code already that's ready to do something with it. Let's add that next.

Passing the input to the controller

Here's where it all comes together. We have a controller waiting—just dying—to get a guess from the player. All we need to do is pass the player's guess to the controller. Let's do that:

```
function handleFireButton() {
    var guessInput = document.getElementById("guessInput");
    var guess = guessInput.value;
    controller.processGuess(guess);

    guessInput.value = "";
}
```

We're passing the player's guess to the controller, and then everything should work like magic!

This little line just resets the form input element to be the empty string. That way you don't have to explicitly select the text and delete it before entering the next guess, which would be annoying.

A Test Drive

This is no mere test drive. You're finally ready to play the real game! Make sure you've added all the code to "battleship.js", and reload "battleship.html" in your browser. Now, remember the ship locations are hardcoded, so you'll have a good idea of how to win this game. Below you'll find the winning moves, but be sure to fully test this code. Enter misses, invalid guesses and downright incorrect guesses.

A6
B6
C6

C4
D4
E4

B0
B1
B2

These are the winning guesses, in order by ship. But you don't have to enter them all in order. Try mixing them up a bit. Enter some invalid guesses in between the correct ones. Enter misses too. That's all part of the Quality Assurance testing for the game.

Serious Coding

Finding it clumsy to have to click the Fire! button with every guess? Sure, clicking works, but it's slow and inconvenient. It would be so much easier if you could just press RETURN, right? Here's a quick bit of code to handle a RETURN key press:

```
function init() {
    var fireButton = document.getElementById("fireButton");
    fireButton.onclick = handleFireButton;
    var guessInput = document.getElementById("guessInput");
    guessInput.onkeypress = handleKeyPress;
}
```

Add a new handler. This one handles key press events from the HTML input field.

Here's the key press handler. It's called whenever you press a key in the form input in the page.

The browser passes an event object to the handler. This object has info about which key was pressed.

```
function handleKeyPress(e) {
    var fireButton = document.getElementById("fireButton");
    if (e.keyCode === 13) {
        fireButton.click();
        return false;
    }
}
```

If you press the RETURN key, the event's keyCode property will be set to 13. If that's the case, then we want to cause the Fire! button to act like it was clicked. We can do that by calling the fireButton's click method (basically tricking it into thinking it was clicked).

And we return false so the form doesn't do anything else (like try to submit itself).

Update your init function and add the handleKeyPress function anywhere in your code. Reload and let the game play begin!

What's left? Oh yeah, darn it, those hardcoded ships!

At this point you've got a pretty amazing browser-based game created from a little HTML, some images, and roughly 100 lines of code. But, the one aspect of this game that is a little unsatisfying is that the ships are always in the same location. You still need to write the code to generate random locations for the ships every time we start a new game (otherwise, it'll be a pretty boring game).

Now, before we start, we want to let you know that we're going to cover this code at a slightly faster clip—you're getting to the point where you can read and understand code better, and there aren't a lot of new things in this code. So, let's get started. Here's what we need to consider:

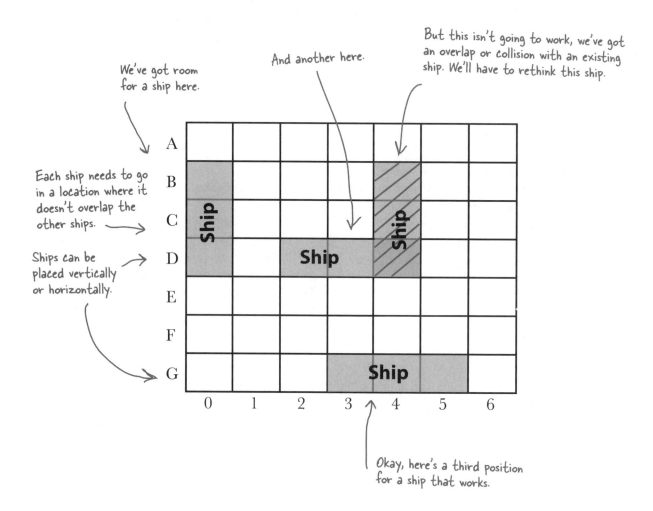

But this isn't going to work, we've got an overlap or collision with an existing ship. We'll have to rethink this ship.

And another here.

We've got room for a ship here.

Each ship needs to go in a location where it doesn't overlap the other ships.

Ships can be placed vertically or horizontally.

Okay, here's a third position for a ship that works.

Code Magnets

An algorithm to generate ships is all scrambled up on the fridge. Can you put the magnets back in the right places to produce a working algorithm? Check your answer at the end of the chapter before you go on.

An algorithm is just a fancy word for a sequence of steps that solve a problem.

> Generate a random location for the new ship.

> Loop for the number of ships we want to create.

> Generate a random direction (vertical or horizontal) for the new ship.

> Add the new ship's locations to the ships array.

> Test to see if the new ship's locations collide with any existing ship's locations.

How to place ships

There are two things you need to consider when placing ships on the game board. The first is that ships can be oriented either vertically or horizontally. The second is that ships don't overlap on the board. The bulk of the code we're about to write handles these two constraints. Now, as we said, we're not going to go through the code in gory detail, but you have everything you need to work through it, and if you spend enough time with the code you'll understand each part in detail. There's nothing in it that you haven't already encountered so far in the book (with one exception that we'll talk about). So let's dive in…

We're going to organize the code into three methods that are part of the model object:

- **generateShipLocations**: This is the master method. It creates a `ships` array in the model for you, with the number of ships in the model's `numShips` property.

- **generateShip**: This method creates a single ship, located somewhere on the board. The locations may or may not overlap other ships.

- **collision**: This method takes a single ship and makes sure it doesn't overlap with a ship already on the board.

The generateShipLocations function

Let's get started with the `generateShipLocations` method. This method iterates, creating ships, until it has filled the model's `ships` array with enough ships. Each time it generates a new ship (which it does using the `generateShip` method), it uses the `collision` method to make sure there are no overlaps. If there is an overlap, it throws that ship away and keeps trying.

One thing to note in this code is that we're using a new iterator, the **do while** loop. The do while loop works almost exactly like **while**, except that you *first* execute the statements in the body, and *then* check the condition. You'll find certain logic conditions, while rare, work better with do while than with the while statement.

We're adding this method to the model object.

```
generateShipLocations: function() {
    var locations;
    for (var i = 0; i < this.numShips; i++) {
        do {
            locations = this.generateShip();
        } while (this.collision(locations));
        this.ships[i].locations = locations;
    }
},
```

We're using a do while loop here!

For each ship we want to generate locations for.

We generate a new set of locations…

… and check to see if those locations overlap with any existing ships on the board. If they do, then we need to try again. So keep generating new locations until there's no collision.

Once we have locations that work, we assign the locations to the ship's locations property in the model.ships array.

Writing the generateShip method

The `generateShip` method creates an array with random locations for one ship without worrying about overlap with other ships on the board. We'll go through this method in a couple of steps. The first step is to randomly pick a direction for the ship: will it be horizontal or vertical? We're going to determine this with a random number. If the number is 1, then the ship is horizontal; if it's 0, then the ship is vertical. We'll use our friends the `Math.random` and `Math.floor` methods to do this as we've done before:

Generating a random 0 or 1 is kind of like tossing a coin.

This method also is added to the model object.

```
generateShip: function() {
    var direction = Math.floor(Math.random() * 2);
    var row, col;

    if (direction === 1) {
        // Generate a starting location for a horizontal ship
    } else {
        // Generate a starting location for a vertical ship
    }

    var newShipLocations = [];
    for (var i = 0; i < this.shipLength; i++) {
        if (direction === 1) {
            // add location to array for new horizontal ship
        } else {
            // add location to array for new vertical ship
        }
    }
    return newShipLocations;
},
```

We use Math.random to generate a number between 0 and 1, and multiply the result by 2, to get a number between 0 and 2 (not including 2). We then turn that into a 0 or a 1 using Math.floor.

We're saying that if the direction is a 1, that means we'll create a horizontal ship...

... and if direction is 0, that means we'll create a vertical ship.

First, we'll create a starting location, like row = 0 and column = 3, for the new ship. Depending on the direction, we need different rules to create the starting location (you'll see why in just a sec).

For the new ship locations, we'll start with an empty array, and add the locations one by one.

We'll loop for the number of locations in a ship...

... and add a new location to the newShipLocations array each time through the loop. Again we need slightly different code to generate a location depending on the direction of the ship.

Once we've generated all the locations, we return the array.

We'll be filling in the rest of this code starting on the next page...

Generate the starting location for the new ship

Now that you know how the ship is oriented, you can generate the locations for the ship. First, we'll generate the starting location (the first position for the ship) and then the rest of the locations will just be the next two columns (if the ship is horizontal) or the next two rows (if it's vertical).

To do this we need to generate two random numbers—a row and a column—for the starting location of the ship. The numbers both have to be between 0 and 6, so the ship will fit on the game board. But remember, if the ship is going to be placed *horizontally*, then the starting *column* must be between 0 and 4, so that we have room for the rest of the ship:

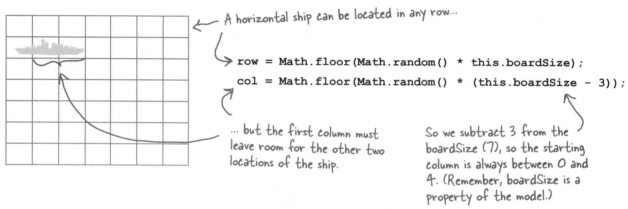

A horizontal ship can be located in any row...

```
row = Math.floor(Math.random() * this.boardSize);
col = Math.floor(Math.random() * (this.boardSize - 3));
```

... but the first column must leave room for the other two locations of the ship.

So we subtract 3 from the boardSize (7), so the starting column is always between 0 and 4. (Remember, boardSize is a property of the model.)

And, likewise, if the ship is going to be placed *vertically*, then the starting *row* must be between 0 and 4, so that we have room for the rest of the ship:

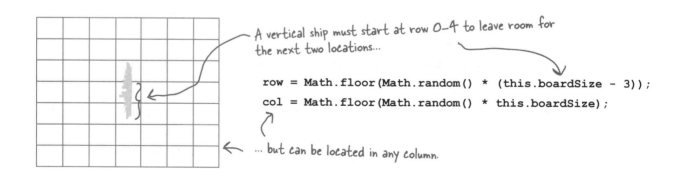

A vertical ship must start at row 0-4 to leave room for the next two locations...

```
row = Math.floor(Math.random() * (this.boardSize - 3));
col = Math.floor(Math.random() * this.boardSize);
```

... but can be located in any column.

Completing the generateShip method

Plugging that code in, now all we have to do is make sure we add the starting location along with the next two locations to the `newShipLocations` array.

```
generateShip: function() {
    var direction = Math.floor(Math.random() * 2);
    var row, col;

    if (direction === 1) {
        row = Math.floor(Math.random() * this.boardSize);
        col = Math.floor(Math.random() * (this.boardSize - this.shipLength));
    } else {
        row = Math.floor(Math.random() * (this.boardSize - this.shipLength));
        col = Math.floor(Math.random() * this.boardSize);
    }

    var newShipLocations = [];
    for (var i = 0; i < this.shipLength; i++) {
        if (direction === 1) {
            newShipLocations.push(row + "" + (col + i));
        } else {
            newShipLocations.push((row + i) + "" + col);
        }
    }
    return newShipLocations;
},
```

Here's the code to generate a starting location for the ship on the board.

We replaced 3 (from the previous page) with this.shipLength to generalize the code, so we can use it for any ship length.

Here, we use parentheses to make sure i is added to col before it's converted to a string.

This is the code for a horizontal ship. Let's break it down...

We're pushing a new location onto the newShipLocations array.

That location is a string made up of the row (the starting row we just computed above)...

... and the column + i. The first time through the loop, i is 0, so it's just the starting column. The second time, it's the next column over, and the third, the next column over again. So we'll get something like "01", "02", "03" in the array.

Same thing here only for a vertical ship.

So now, we're increasing the row instead of the column, adding i to the row each time through the loop.

For a vertical ship, we'll get something like "31", "41", "51" in the array.

Remember, when we add a string and a number, + is concatenation not addition, so we get a string.

Once we've filled the array with the ship's locations, we return it to the calling method, generateShipLocations.

Avoiding a collision!

The `collision` method takes a ship and checks to see if any of the locations overlap—or collide—with any of the existing ships already on the board.

← Look back at page 364 to see where we call the collision method.

We've implemented this using two nested for loops. The outer loop iterates over all the ships in the model (in the `model.ships` property). The inner loop iterates over all the new ship's locations in the `locations` array, and checks to see if any of those locations is already taken by an existing ship on the board.

locations is an array of locations for a new ship we'd like to place on the board.

```
collision: function(locations) {
    for (var i = 0; i < this.numShips; i++) {
        var ship = model.ships[i];
        for (var j = 0; j < locations.length; j++) {
            if (ship.locations.indexOf(locations[j]) >= 0) {
                return true;
            }
        }
    }
    return false;
}
```

For each ship already on the board...

...check to see if any of the locations in the new ship's locations array are in an existing ship's locations array.

Returning from inside a loop that's inside another loop stops the iteration of both loops immediately, exiting the function and returning true.

We're using indexOf to check if the location already exists in a ship, so if the index is greater than or equal to 0, we know it matched an existing location, so we return true (meaning, we found a collision).

If we get here and haven't returned, then we never found a match for any of the locations we were checking, so we return false (there was no collision).

BRAIN POWER

In this code, we have two loops: an outer loop to iterate over all the ships in the model, and an inner loop to iterate over each of the locations we're checking for a collision. For the outer loop, we used the loop variable i, and for the inner loop, we used the loop variable j. Why did we use two different loop variable names?

Two final changes

We've written all the code we need to generate random locations for the ships; now all we have to do is integrate it. Make these two final changes to your code, and then take your new Battleship game for a test drive!

```
var model = {
    boardSize: 7,
    numShips: 3,
    shipLength: 3,
    shipsSunk: 0,
    ships: [ { locations: ["06", "16", "26"], hits: ["", "", ""] },
            { locations: ["24", "34", "44"], hits: ["", "", ""] },
            { locations: ["10", "11", "12"], hits: ["", "", ""] } ],
    ships: [ { locations: [0, 0, 0], hits: ["", "", ""] },
            { locations: [0, 0, 0], hits: ["", "", ""] },
            { locations: [0, 0, 0], hits: ["", "", ""] } ],
    fire: function(guess) { ... },
    isSunk: function(ship) { ... },
    generateShipLocations: function() { ... },
    generateShip: function() { ... },
    collision: function(locations) { ... }
};

function init() {
    var fireButton = document.getElementById("fireButton");
    fireButton.onclick = handleFireButton;
    var guessInput = document.getElementById("guessInput");
    guessInput.onkeypress = handleKeyPress;

    model.generateShipLocations();
}
```

Remove the hardcoded ship locations...

... and replace them with arrays initialized with O's instead.

And of course, add the call to generate the ship locations, which will fill in those empty arrays in the model.

We're calling model.generateShipLocations from the init function so it happens right when you load the game, before you start playing. That way all the ships will have locations ready to go when you start playing.

Don't forget you can download the complete code for the Battleship game at http://wickedlysmart.com/hfjs.

A <u>Final</u> Test Drive

This is the FINAL test drive of the real game, with random ship locations. Make sure you've got all the code added to "battleship.js", reload "battleship.html" in your browser, and play the game! Give it a good run through. Play it a few times, reloading the page each time to generate new ship locations for each new game.

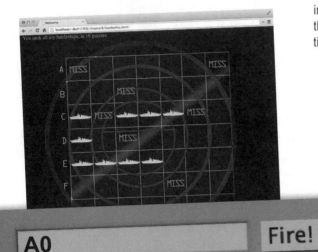

Oh, and how to cheat!

To cheat, open up the developer console, and type `model.ships`. Press return and you should see the three ship objects containing the locations and hits arrays. Now you have the inside scoop on where the ships are sitting in the game board. But, you didn't hear this from us!

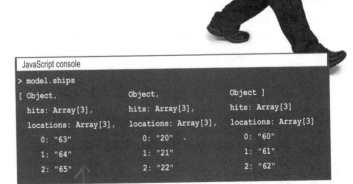

```
JavaScript console
> model.ships
[ Object,                  Object,                   Object ]
  hits: Array[3],           hits: Array[3],           hits: Array[3]
  locations: Array[3],      locations: Array[3],      locations: Array[3]
    0: "63"                   0: "20"  .                 0: "60"
    1: "64"                   1: "21"                   1: "61"
    2: "65"                   2: "22"                   2: "62"
```

Beat the computer every time.

Congrats, It's Startup Time!

You've just built a great web application, all in 150 (or so) lines of code and some HTML & CSS. Like we said, the code is yours. Now all that's standing between you and your venture capital is a real business plan. But then again, who ever let that stand in their way!?

So now, after all the hard work, you can relax and play a few rounds of Battleship. Pretty darn engaging, right?

Oh, but we're just getting started. With a little more JavaScript horse power we're going to be able to take on apps that rival those written in native code.

For now, we've been through a lot of code in this chapter. Get some good food and plenty of rest to let it all sink in. But before you do that, you've got some bullet points to review and a crossword puzzle to do. Don't skip them; repetition is what really drives the learning home!

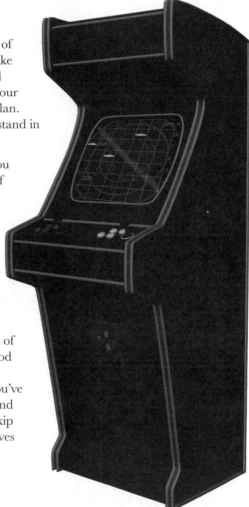

QA Notes

Found a bug, I think. When I get a hit on a ship, if
I re-enter that board location again, it results
another hit at the same spot. Try it, you'll see!

So, is this a bug? Or the correct behavior?
Assuming it's a bug, how would you fix it? Write
your notes here:

BULLET POINTS

- We use HTML to build the structure of the Battleship game, CSS to style it, and JavaScript to create the behavior.

- The id of each <td> element in the table is used to update the image of the element to indicate a HIT or a MISS.

- The form uses an input with type "button". We attach an **event handler** to the button so we can know in the code when a player has entered a guess.

- To get a value from a form input text element, use the element's **value** property.

- CSS positioning can be used to position elements precisely in a web page.

- We organized the code using three objects: a **model**, a **view**, and a **controller**.

- Each object in the game has one **primary responsibility**.

- The responsibility of the model is to store the state of the game and implement logic that modifies that state.

- The responsibility of the view is to update the display when the state in the model changes.

- The responsibility of the controller is to glue the game together, to make sure the player's guess is sent to the model to update the state, and to check to see when the game is complete.

- By designing the game with objects that each have a **separate responsibility**, we can build and test each part of the game independently.

- To make it easier to create and test the model, we initially hardcoded the locations of the ships. After ensuring the model was working, we replaced these hardcoded locations with random locations generated by code.

- We used properties in the model, like numShips and shipLength, so we don't hardcode values in the methods that we might want to change later.

- Arrays have an **indexOf** method that is similar to the string indexOf method. The array indexOf method takes a value, and returns the index of that value if it exists in the array, or -1 if it does not.

- With **chaining**, you can string together object references (using the dot operator), thus combining statements and eliminating temporary variables.

- The **do while** loop is similar to the while loop, except that the condition is checked after the statements in the body of the loop have executed once.

- **Quality assurance** (QA) is an important part of developing your code. QA requires testing not just valid input, but invalid input as well.

JavaScript cross

Your brain is frying from the coding challenges in this chapter. Do the crossword to get that final sizzle.

ACROSS

2. We use the _____ method to set the class of an element.

4. To add a ship or miss image to the board, we place the image in the _____ of a <td> element.

6. The _____ loop executes the statements in its body at least once.

8. Modern, interactive web apps use HTML, CSS and _____.

10. We represent each ship in the game with an _____.

11. The id of a <td> element corresponds to a _____ on the game board.

12. The responsibility of the collision function is to make sure that ships don't _____.

15. We call the _____ method to ask the model to update the state with the guess.

17. Who is responsible for state?

18. You can cheat and get the answers to Battleship using the _____.

DOWN

1. To get the guess from the form input, we added an event _____ for the click event.

3. Chaining is for _____ references, not just jailbirds.

5. The _____ is good at gluing things together.

7. To add a "hit" to the game board in the display, we add the _____ class to the corresonding <td> element.

9. Arrays have an _____ method too.

13. The three objects in our game design are the model, _____, and controller.

14. 13 is the keycode for the _____ key.

16. The _____ notifies the view when its state changes.

PRACTICE DRILLS SOLUTION

In just a few pages, you're going to learn how to add the MISS and ship images to the game board with JavaScript. But before we get to the real thing, you need to practice in the HTML simulator. We've got two CSS classes set up and ready for you to practice with. Go ahead and add these two rules to your CSS, and then imagine you've got ships hidden at the following locations:

Ship 1: A6, B6, C6

Ship 2: C4, D4, E4

Ship 3: B0, B1, B2

and that the player has entered the following guesses:

A0, D4, F5, B2, C5, C6

You need to add one of the two classes below to the correct cells in the grid (the correct <td> elements in the table) so that your grid shows MISS and a ship in the right places.

Make sure you've downloaded everything you need, including the two images you'll need for this exercise.

```
.hit {
    background: transparent url("ship.png") no-repeat center center;
}
.miss {
    background: transparent url("miss.png") no-repeat center center;
}
```

Here's our solution. The right spots for the .hit class are in <td>s with the ids: "00", "34", "55", "12", "25" and "26". To add a class to an element, you use the class attribute, like this:

```
<td class="miss" id="55">
```

After adding the classes in the right spots, your game board should look like this.

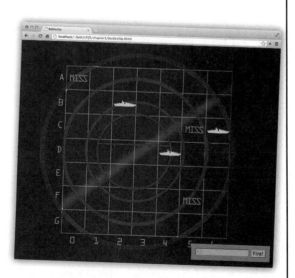

Exercise Solution

It's time for some object design. We're going to start with the view object. Now, remember, the view object is responsible for updating the view. Take a look at the view below and see if you can determine the methods we want the view object to implement. Write the declarations for these methods below (just the declarations; we'll code the bodies of the methods in a bit) along with a comment or two about what each does. Here's our solution:

Here's a message. Messages will be things like "HIT!", "You missed." and "You sank my battleship!"

Here the display has a MISS placed on the grid.

And here the display has a ship placed on the grid.

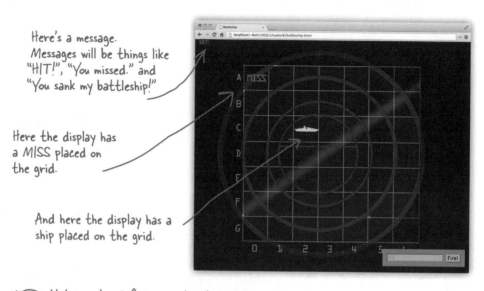

```
var view = {
```
← Notice we're defining an object and assigning it to the variable view.

```
    // this method takes a string message and displays it
    // in the message display area
    displayMessage: function(msg) {
        // code to be supplied in a bit!
    },

    displayHit: function(location) {
        // code will go here
    },

    displayMiss: function(location) {
        // code will go here
    }
};
```

Your methods go here!

Sharpen your pencil
Solution

Given how we've described the new game board above, how would you represent the ships in the model (just the locations, we'll worry about hits later). Check off the best solution below.

❏ Use nine variables for the ship locations, similar to the way we handled the ships in Chapter 2.

❏ Use an array with an item for each cell in entire board (49 items total). Record the ship number in each cell that holds part of a ship.

❏ Use an array to hold all nine locations. Items 0-2 will hold the first ship, 3-5 the second, and so on.

Or write in your own answer.

❏ Use three different arrays, one for each ship, with three locations contained in each.

☑ Use an object named ship with three location properties. Put all the ships in an array named ships.

❏ _____
_____
_____

Any of these solutions could work! (In fact we tried each one when we were figuring out the best way to do it.) This is the one we use in the chapter.

JavaScript cross solution

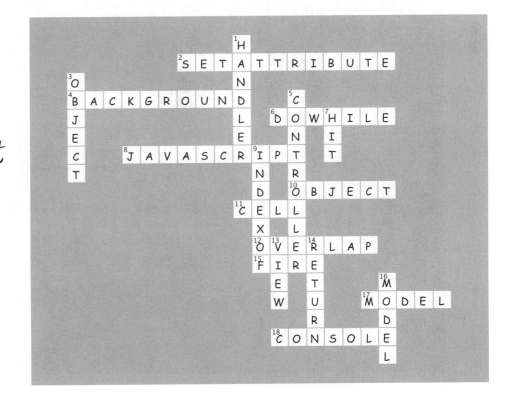

Ship Magnets Solution

Use the following player moves, along with the data structure for the ships, to place the ship and miss magnets onto the game board. Does the player sink all the ships? We've done the first move for you.

Here are the moves:

A6, B3, C4, D1, B0, D4, F0, A1, C6, B1, B2, E4, B6 ← *Execute these moves on the game board.*

And here's our solution:

```
var ships = [{ locations: ["06", "16", "26"], hits: ["hit", "hit", "hit"] },
             { locations: ["24", "34", "44"], hits: ["hit", "hit", "hit"] },
             { locations: ["10", "11", "12"], hits: ["hit", "hit", "hit"] }];
```

All three ships are sunk! ⤴

And here's the board and your magnets.

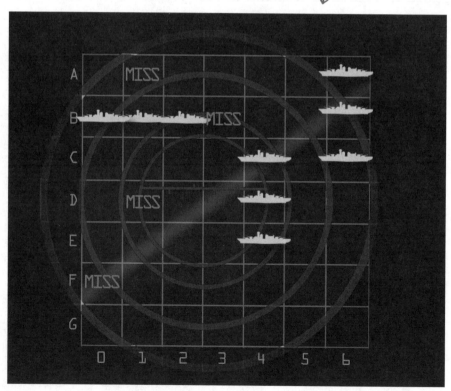

Leftover magnets.

Sharpen your pencil
Solution

Let's practice using the ships data structure to simulate some ship activities. Using the ships definition below, work through the questions and the code below and fill in the blanks. Make sure you check your answers before moving on, as this is an important part of how the game works:

```
var ships = [{ locations: ["31", "41", "51"], hits: ["", "", ""] },
             { locations: ["14", "24", "34"], hits: ["", "hit", ""] },
             { locations: ["00", "01", "02"], hits: ["hit", "", ""] }];
```

Which ships are already hit? __Ships 2 and 3__ And at what locations? __C4, A0__

The player guesses "D4", does that hit a ship? __yes__ If so, which one? __Ship 2__

The player guesses "B3", does that hit a ship? __no__ If so, which one? _____

Finish this code to access the second ship's middle location and print its value with console.log.

```
var ship2 = ships[ 1 ];
var locations = ship2.locations;
console.log("Location is " + locations[ 1 ]);
```

Finish this code to see if the third ship has a hit in its first location:

```
var ship3 = ships[ 2 ];
var hits = ship3. hits ;
if ( hits[0] === "hit") {
    console.log("Ouch, hit on third ship at location one");
}
```

Finish this code to hit the first ship at the third location:

```
var ship1  = ships[0];
var hits = ship1. hits ;
hits[ 2 ] = "hit" ;
```

Code Magnets Solution

An algorithm to generate ships is all scrambled up on the fridge. Can you put the magnets back in the right places to produce a working algorithm? Here's our solution.

> Loop for the number of ships we want to create.

> Generate a random direction (vertical or horizontal) for the new ship.

> Generate a random location for the new ship.

> Test to see if the new ship's locations collide with any existing ship's locations.

> Add the new ship's locations to the ships array.

9 asynchronous coding

Handling events

After this chapter you're going to realize you aren't in Kansas anymore. Up until now, you've been writing code that typically executes from top to bottom—sure, your code might be a little more complex than that, and make use of a few functions, objects and methods, but at some point the code just runs its course. Now, we're awfully sorry to break this to you this late in the book, but that's **not how you typically write JavaScript code**. Rather, most JavaScript is written to **react to events**. What kind of events? Well, how about a user clicking on your page, data arriving from the network, timers expiring in the browser, changes happening in the DOM and that's just a few examples. In fact, all kinds of events are happening **all the time**, behind the scenes, in your browser. In this chapter we're going rethink our approach to JavaScript coding, and learn how and why we should write code that reacts to events.

You know what a browser does, right? It retrieves a page and all that page's contents and then renders the page. But the browser's doing a lot more than just that. What else is it doing? Choose any of the tasks below you suspect the browser is doing behind the scenes. If you aren't sure just make your best guess.

☐ Knows when the page is fully loaded and displayed.

☐ Watches all mouse movement.

☐ Keeps track of all the clicks you make to the page, be it on a button, link or elsewhere.

☐ Watches the clock and manages timers and timed events.

☐ Knows when a user submits a form.

☐ Retrieves additional data for your page.

☐ Knows when the user presses keys on a keyboard.

☐ Tracks when the page has been resized or scrolled.

☐ Knows when an element gets user interface focus.

☐ Knows when the cookies are finished baking.

Sharpen your pencil

Pick two of the events above. If the browser could notify your code when these events occurred, what cool or interesting code might you write?

⌐ No, you can't use the cookie event as one of your examples!

What are events?

We're sure you know by now that after the browser retrieves and displays your page, it doesn't just sit there. Behind the scenes, a lot is going on: users are clicking buttons, the mouse location is being tracked, additional data is becoming available on the network, windows are getting resized, timers are going off, the browser's location could be changing, and so on. All these things cause *events* to be triggered.

Whenever there's an event, there is an opportunity for your code to *handle it*; that is, to supply some code that will be invoked when the event occurs. Now, you're not required to handle any of these events, but you'll need to handle them if you want interesting things to happen when they occur—like, say, when the button click event happens, you might want to add a new song to a playlist; when new data arrives you might want to process it and display it on your page; when a timer fires you might want to tell a user the hold on a front row concert ticket is going to expire, and so on.

A browser's geo-location, as well as a number of other advanced types of events, is something we cover in Head First HTML5 Programming. In this book we'll stick to the bread & butter foundational types of events.

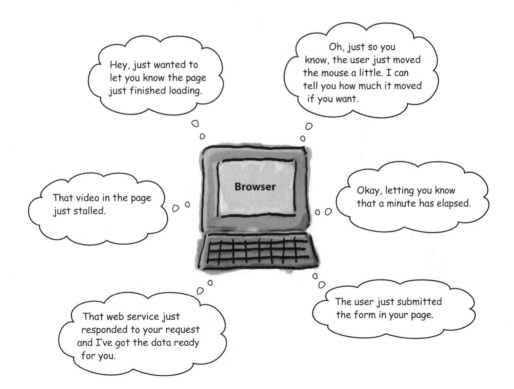

Whenever there's an **event**, there is an opportunity for your code to **handle** it.

What's an event handler?

We write *handlers* to handle events. Handlers are typically small pieces of code that know what to do when an event occurs. In terms of code, a handler is just a function. When an event occurs, its handler function is called.

To have your handler called when an event occurs, you first need to *register it*. As you'll see, there are a few different ways to do that depending on what kind of event it is. We'll get into all that, but for now let's get started with a simple example, one you've seen before: the event that's generated when a page is fully loaded.

You might also hear developers use the name callback or listener instead of handler.

Hey browser, I've got a handler with some code that needs to run when you've finished getting the page fully loaded. And did I mention I'm in a hurry?

The handler, code that will be run <u>later</u>, when the page is loaded.

Never any pressure around here huh? Sure thing, as soon as I'm done loading everything, I've got your handler ready to go and I'll be sure to invoke it.

The browser.

How to create your first event handler

There's no better way to understand events than by writing a handler and wiring it up to handle a real, live event. Now, remember, you've already seen a couple of examples of handling events—including the page load event—but we've never fully explained how event handling works. The page load event is triggered when the browser has fully loaded and displayed all the content in your page (and built out the DOM representing the page).

Let's step through what it takes to write the handler and to make sure it gets invoked when the page load event is triggered:

1 First we need to write a function that can handle the page load event when it occurs. In this case, the function is going to announce to the world "I'm alive!" when it knows the page is fully loaded.

A handler is just an ordinary function.

```
function pageLoadedHandler() {
    alert("I'm alive!");
}
```

Here's our function, we'll name it pageLoadedHandler, but you can call it anything you like.

Remember we often refer to this as a handler or a callback.

This event handler doesn't do much. It just creates an alert.

2 Now that we have a handler written and ready to go, we need to wire things up so the browser knows there's a function it should invoke when the load event occurs. To do that we use the onload property of the window object, like this:

```
window.onload = pageLoadedHandler;
```

In the case of the load event, we assign the name of the handler to the window's onload property.

Now when the page load event is generated, the pageLoadedHandler function is going to be called.

We're going to see that different kinds of events are assigned handlers in different ways.

3 That's it! Now, with this code written, we can sit back and know that the browser will invoke the function assigned to the window.onload property when the page is loaded.

Test drive your event

Go ahead and create a new file, "event.html", and add the code to test your load event
handler. Load the page into the browser and make sure you see the alert.

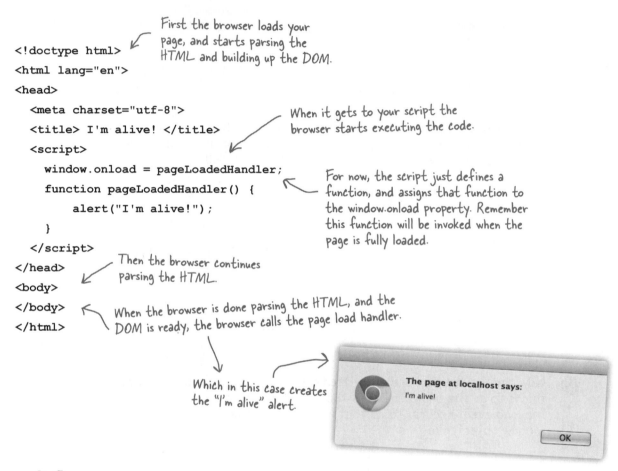

First the browser loads your
page, and starts parsing the
HTML and building up the DOM.

```
<!doctype html>
<html lang="en">
<head>
  <meta charset="utf-8">
  <title> I'm alive! </title>
  <script>
    window.onload = pageLoadedHandler;
    function pageLoadedHandler() {
        alert("I'm alive!");
    }
  </script>
</head>
<body>
</body>
</html>
```

When it gets to your script the
browser starts executing the code.

For now, the script just defines a
function, and assigns that function to
the window.onload property. Remember
this function will be invoked when the
page is fully loaded.

Then the browser continues
parsing the HTML.

When the browser is done parsing the HTML, and the
DOM is ready, the browser calls the page load handler.

Which in this case creates
the "I'm alive" alert.

> **The page at localhost says:**
> I'm alive!
>
> OK

⚛ BRAIN POWER

If we didn't have functions, could we have event handlers?

If you're ever going to be a *real* Javascript developer, you're going to have to learn to deal with events.

As we already mentioned, up until now you've taken a rather, let's say, linear approach to writing code: you took an algorithm, like computing the best bubble solution, or generating the 99 bottles song, and wrote the code stepwise, top to bottom.

But remember the Battleship game? The code for that game didn't quite fit the linear model—sure, you wrote some code that set up the game, initialized the model, and all that—but then the main part of the game operated in a *different way*. Each time you wanted to fire at another ship you entered your guess into a form input element and pressed the "Fire" button. That button then caused a whole sequence of actions that resulted in the next move of the game being executed. In that case your code was *reacting* to the user input.

Organizing code around reacting to events is a different way of thinking about how you write your code. To write code this way, you need to consider the events that can happen, and how your code should react. Computer science types like to say that this kind of code is *asynchronous*, because we're writing code to be invoked *later*, *if* and *when* an event occurs. This kind of coding also changes your perspective from one of encoding an algorithm step-by-step into code, into one of gluing together an application that is composed of many handlers handling many different kinds of events.

Getting your head around events... by creating a game

The best way to understand events is with experience, so let's get some more by writing a simple game. The game works like this: you load a page and are presented with an image. Not just any image, but a really blurred image. Your job is to guess what the image is. And, to check your answer, you click on the image to unblur it.

Like this:

Here's the blurred version of the image. Hmmm, what could it be?

Hum the Jeopardy theme song to yourself as you try to figure it out...

When you think you have it, click to reveal the unblurred image.

Let's start with the markup. We'll use two JPG images. One is blurred and the other isn't. We've named them "zeroblur.jpg" and "zero.jpg" respectively. Here's the markup:

```
<!doctype html>
<html lang="en">
<head>
  <meta charset="utf-8">
  <title> Image Guess </title>
  <style> body { margin: 20px; } </style>
  <script>  </script>
</head>
<body>
    <img id="zero" src="zeroblur.jpg">
</body>
</html>
```

Just some basic HTML, with a <script> element all ready for our code. Rather than use a separate file for the JavaScript, we'll keep it simple and add the script here. As you'll see, there is very little code needed to implement this.

And here's the blurred image, placed in the page. We'll give it an id of "zero". You'll see how we use the id in a sec...

388   *Chapter 9*

Implementing the game

Go ahead and load this markup in your browser and you'll see the blurred image. To implement the game, we need to react to a click on the image in order to display the unblurred version of the image.

Lucky for us, every time an HTML element in the page is clicked (or touched on a mobile device), an event is generated. Your job is to create a handler for that event, and in it write the code to display the unblurred version of the image. Here's how you're going to do that:

1 **Access the image object in the DOM and assign a handler to its onclick property.**

2 **In your handler, write the code to change the image src attribute from the blurred image to the unblurred one.**

Let's walk through these steps and write the code.

Step 1: access the image in the DOM

Getting access to the image is old hat for you; we just need to use our old friend, the `getElementById` method, to get a reference to it.

```
var image = document.getElementById("zero");
```

Here we're grabbing a reference to the image element and assigning it to the image variable.

Oh, but we also need this code to run only *after* the DOM for the page has been created, so let's use the window's `onload` property to ensure that. We'll place our code into a function, `init`, that we'll assign to the `onload` property.

Remember, we can't get the image from the DOM until the page has finished loading.

```
window.onload = init;
function init() {
    var image = document.getElementById("zero");
}
```

We create a function init, and assign it to the onload handler to make sure this code doesn't run until the page is fully loaded.

In the code of init, we'll grab a reference to the image with id="zero".

Remember in JavaScript the order in which you define your functions doesn't matter. So we can define init after we assign it to the onload property.

Step 2: add the handler, and update the image

To add a handler to deal with clicks on the image, we simply assign a function to the image's `onclick` property. Let's call that function `showAnswer`, and we'll define it next.

```
window.onload = init;
function init() {
    var image = document.getElementById("zero");
    image.onclick = showAnswer;
}
```

Using the image object from the DOM, we're assigning a handler to its onclick property.

Now we need to write the `showAnswer` function, which unblurs the image by resetting the image element's `src` property to the unblurred image:

First, we have to get the image from the DOM again.

```
function showAnswer() {
    var image = document.getElementById("zero");
    image.src = "zero.jpg";
}
```

Remember the blurred version is named "zeroblur.jpg" and the unblurred is named "zero.jpg".

Once we have the image, we can change it by setting its src property to the unblurred image.

Test drive

Let's take this simple game for a test drive. Make sure you've got all the HTML, CSS and JavaScript typed into a file named "image.html", and that you've got the images you downloaded from http://wickedlysmart.com/hfjs in the same folder. Once all that's done, load up the file in your browser and give it a try!

Click anywhere on the image to have the showAnswer handler called. When that happens, the src of the image is changed to reveal the answer.

> Wait, why do we need to use getElementById again in showAnswer? I'm not sure of the flow of execution here.

Ah, yes. It can get tricky to follow the flow of execution in code with a lot of event handlers. Remember, the `init` function is called when the page is loaded. But the `showAnswer` function isn't called until later, when you click the image. So these two event handlers get called at two different times.

In addition, remember your scope rules. In the `init` function we're putting the object returned by `getElementById` into a *local* variable `image`, which means when that function completes, the variable falls out of scope and is destroyed. So later, when the `showAnswer` function is called, we have to get the image object again from the DOM. Sure, we could have put this in a global variable, but over use of globals can lead to confusing and buggy code, which we'd like to avoid.

there are no
Dumb Questions

Q: Is setting the src property of the image the same as setting the src attribute using setAttribute?

A: In this case, yes, it is. When you get an HTML element from the DOM using getElementById, you're getting an element object that has several methods and properties. All element objects come with a property, id, that is set to the id of the HTML element (if you've given it one in your HTML). The image element object also comes with

a src property that is set to the image file specified in the src attribute of the <img> element.

Not all attributes come with corresponding object properties, however, so you will need to use setAttribute and getAttribute for those. And in the case of src and id, you can use either the properties or get/set them using getAttribute and setAttribute and it does the same thing.

Q: So do we have a handler called within a handler?

A: Not really. The load handler is the code that is called when the page is fully loaded. When the load handler is called, we assign a handler to the image's onclick property, but it won't be called until you actually click on the image. When you do that (potentially a long time after the page has loaded), the showAnswer click handler is called. So the two handlers get called at different times.

BE the Browser

Below, you'll find your game code. Your job is to play like you're the browser and to figure out what you need to do after each event. After you've done the exercise, look at the end of the chapter to see if you got everything. We've done the first bit for you.

```javascript
window.onload = init;
function init() {
    var image = document.getElementById("zero");
    image.onclick = showAnswer;
}

function showAnswer() {
    var image = document.getElementById("zero");
    image.src = "zero.jpg";
}
```

Here's the code you're executing...

When page is being loaded...	First define the functions init and showAnswer
When page load event occurs...	
When image click event occurs...	

Your answers go here.

BRAIN POWER

What if you had an entire page of images that could each be individually deblurred by clicking? How would you design your code to handle this? Make some notes. What might be the naive way of implementing this? Is there a way to implement this with minimal code changes to what you've already written?

Jim ↗ Judy ↙ Joe ↘

Judy: Hey guys. So far the image guessing game works great. But we really should expand the game to include more images on the page.

Jim: Sure, Judy, that's exactly what I was thinking.

Joe: Hey, I've already got a bunch of images ready to go, we just need the code. I've followed the naming convention of "zero.jpg", "zeroblur. jpg", "one.jpg", "oneblur.jpg", and so on...

Jim: Are we going to need to write a new click event handler for each image? That's going to be a lot of repetitive code. After all, every event handler's going to do exactly the same thing: replace the blurred image with its unblurred version, right?

Joe: That's true. But I'm not sure I know how to use the same event handler for multiple images. Is that even possible?

Judy: What we can do is assign the same handler, which really means the same function, to the `onclick` property of every image in the game.

Joe: So the same function gets called for every image that is clicked on?

Judy: Right. We'll use `showAnswer` as the handler for every image's click event.

Jim: Hmm, but how will we know which image to deblur?

Joe: What do you mean? Won't the click handler know?

Jim: How will it know? Right now, our `showAnswer` function assumes we clicked on the image with the id "zero". But if we're calling `showAnswer` for every image's click event, then our code needs to work for any of the images.

Joe: Oh... right... so how do we know which image was clicked?

Judy: Actually I've been reading up on events, and I think there is a way for the click handler to know the element the user clicked on. But let's deal with that part later. First let's add some more images to the game, and see how to set the same event handler for all of them... then we'll figure out how to determine which image the user clicked.

Joe, Jim: Sounds good!

Let's add some more images

We've got a whole set of new images, so let's start by adding them to the page. We'll add five more images for a total of six. We'll also modify the CSS to add a little whitespace between the images:

Get the images

You'll find all the images in the chapter9 folder you downloaded from http://wickedlysmart.com/hfjs.

```html
<!doctype html>
<html lang="en">
<head>
  <meta charset="utf-8">
  <title> Image Guess </title>
  <style>
    body { margin: 20px; }
    img { margin: 20px; }
  </style>
  <script>
    window.onload = init;
    function init() {
        var image = document.getElementById("zero");
        image.onclick = showAnswer;
    }
    function showAnswer() {
        var image = document.getElementById("zero");
        image.src = "zero.jpg";
    }
  </script>
</head>
<body>
    <img id="zero" src="zeroblur.jpg">
    <img id="one" src="oneblur.jpg">
    <img id="two" src="twoblur.jpg">
    <img id="three" src="threeblur.jpg">
    <img id="four" src="fourblur.jpg">
    <img id="five" src="fiveblur.jpg">
</body>
</html>
```

We're just adding a margin of 20px between the images with this CSS property.

And here are the five new images we're adding. Notice we're using the same id & src naming scheme (and image naming scheme) for each one. You'll see how this is going to work in a bit...

If you give this a quick test drive, your page should look like this:

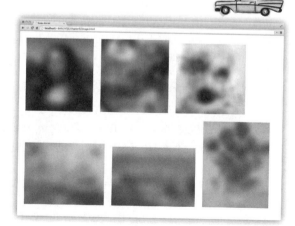

Now we need to assign the same event handler to each image's onclick property

Now we have more images in the page, but we have more work to do. Right now you can click on the first image (of the *Mona Lisa*) and see the unblurred image, but what about the other images?

We *could* write a new, separate handler function for each image, but, from the discussion so far you know that would be tedious and wasteful. Here, have a look:

```javascript
window.onload = init;
function init() {
    var image0 = document.getElementById("zero");
    image0.onclick = showImageZero;
    var image1 = document.getElementById("one");
    image1.onclick = showImageOne;
    ...
}
function showImageZero() {
    var image = document.getElementById("zero");
    image.src = "zero.jpg";
}
function showImageOne() {
    var image = document.getElementById("one");
    image.src = "one.jpg";
}
...
```

← We could get each image element from the page and assign a separate click handler to each one. We'd have to do this six times... we're only showing two here.

← The other four would be set here.

← And we'd need six different click handlers, one for each image.

← And we'd need four more handler functions here.

☢ BRAIN POWER

What are the disadvantages of writing a separate handler for each image? Check all that apply:

☐ Lots of redundant code in each handler.

☐ If we need to change the code in one handler, we're probably going to have to change them all.

☐ Generates a lot of code.

☐ Hard to keep track of all the images and handlers.

☐ Hard to generalize for an arbitrary number of images.

☐ Harder for others to work on the code.

How to reuse the same handler for all the images

Clearly writing a handler for each image isn't a good way to solve this problem. So what we're going to do instead is use our existing handler, showAnswer, to handle all of the click events for all the images. Of course, we'll need to modify showAnswer a little bit to make this work. To use showAnswer for all the images we need to do two things:

① **Assign the showAnswer click handler function to every image on the page.**

② **Rework showAnswer to handle unblurring any image, not just zero.jpg.**

And we'd like to do both these things in a generalized way that works even if we add more images to the page. In other words, if we write the code right, we should be able to add images to the page (or delete images from the page) without any code changes. Let's get started.

Assigning the click handler to all images on the page

Here's our first hurdle: in the current code we use the getElementById method to grab a reference to image "zero", and assign the showAnswer function to its onclick property. Rather than hardcoding a call to getElementById for each image, we're going to show you an easier way: we'll grab all the images at once, iterate through them, and set up the click handler for each one. To do that we'll use a DOM method you haven't seen yet: document.getElementsByTagName. This method takes a tag name, like img or p or div, and returns a list of elements that match it. Let's put it to work:

```
function init() {
    var image = document.getElementById("zero");
    image.onclick = showAnswer;

    var images = document.getElementsByTagName("img");
    for (var i = 0; i < images.length; i++) {
        images[i].onclick = showAnswer;
    }
};
```

We'll get rid of the old code to get image "zero" and set its handler.

Now we're getting elements from the page using a tag name, img. This finds every image in the page and returns them all. We store the resulting images in the images variable.

Then we iterate over the images, and assign the showAnswer click handler to each image in turn. Now the onclick property of each image is set to the showAnswer handler.

document.getElementsByTagName Up Close

The `document.getElementsByTagName` method works a lot like `document.getElementById`, except that instead of getting an element by its id, we're getting elements by tag name, in this case the tag name "img". Of course, your HTML can include many `<img>` elements, so this method may return many elements, or one element, or even zero elements, depending on how many images we have in our page. In our image game example, we have six `<img>` elements, so we'll get back a list of six image objects.

What we get back is a list of element objects that match the specified tag name.

```
var images = document.getElementsByTagName("img");
```

What's returned is an array-like list of objects. It's not exactly an array but has qualities similar to an array.

Notice the "s" here. That means we might get many elements back.

Put the tag name in quotes here (and don't include the < and >!).

there are no Dumb Questions

Q: You said getElementsByTagName returns a list. Do you mean an array?

A: It returns an object that you can treat like an array, but it's actually an object called a NodeList. A NodeList is a collection of Nodes, which is just a technical name for the element objects that you see in the DOM tree. You can iterate over this collection by getting its length using the length property, and then access each item in the NodeList using an index with the bracket notation, just like an array. But that's pretty much where the similarities of a NodeList and an array end, so beyond this, you'll need to be careful in how you deal with the NodeList object. You typically won't need to know more about NodeList until you want to start adding and removing elements to and from the DOM.

Q: So I can assign a click handler to any element?

A: Pretty much. Take any element on the page, get access to it, and assign a function to its onclick property. Done. As you've seen, that handler might be specific to that one element, or you might reuse a handler for events on many elements. Of course elements that don't have a visual presence in your page, like the <script> and <head> elements, won't support events like the click event.

Q: Do handler functions ever get passed any arguments?

A: Ah, good question, and very timely. They do, and we're just about to look at the event object that gets passed to some handlers.

Q: Do elements support other types of events? Or is the click the only one?

A: There are quite a few others; in fact, you've already seen another one in the code of the battleship game: the keypress event. There, an event handler function was called whenever the user pressed Enter from the form input. We'll take a look at a few other event types in this chapter.

Okay Judy, now we have a single event handler, showAnswer, to handle clicks on all the images. You said you know how to tell which image was clicked on when showAnswer is called?

Judy: Yes I do. Whenever the click event handler is called, it's passed an *event object.* You can use that object to find out details about the event.

Joe: Like which image was clicked on?

Judy: Well, more generally, the element on which the event occurred, which is known as the *target.*

Joe: What's the target?

Judy: Like I said, it's the element that generated the event. Like if you click on a specific image, the target will be that image.

Joe: So if I click on the image with the id "zero", then the target will be set to that image?

Judy: More precisely, the element object that represents that image.

Joe: Come again?

Judy: Think of the element object as exactly the same thing you get if you call document. getElementById with a value of "zero". It's the object that represents the image in the DOM.

Joe: Okay, so how do we get this target? It sounds like that's what we need to know which image was clicked on.

Judy: The target is just a property of the event object.

Joe: Great. That sounds perfect for showAnswer. We'll be done in a snap... Wait, so showAnswer is passed the event object?

Judy: That's right.

Joe: So how did our code for the showAnswer function work up until now? It's being passed this event object, but we don't have a parameter defined for the event object in the function!

Judy: Remember, JavaScript lets you ignore parameters if you want.

Joe: Oh, right.

Judy: Now Joe, don't forget, you'll need to figure out how to change the src of the image to the correct name for the unblurred version. Right now we're assuming the name of the unblurred image is "zero.jpg", but that won't work any more.

Joe: Maybe we can use the id attribute of the image to figure out the unblurred image name. The ids of all the images match the names of the unblurred version of each image.

Judy: Sounds like a plan!

How the event object works

When the click handler is called, it's passed an *event object*—and in fact, for most of the events associated with the document object model (DOM) you'll be passed an event object. The event object contains general information about the event, such as what element generated the event and what time the event happened. In addition, you'll get information specific to the event, so if there was a mouse click, for instance, you'll get the coordinates of the click.

There are other kinds of events too (that is, other than DOM events), and we'll see an example later in the chapter...

Let's step through how event objects work:

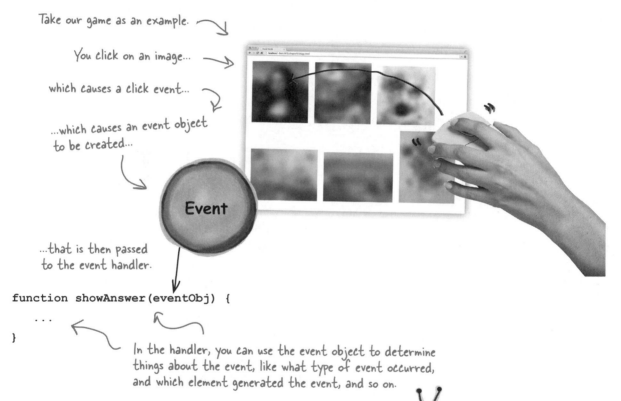

Take our game as an example.

You click on an image...

which causes a click event...

...which causes an event object to be created...

Event

...that is then passed to the event handler.

```
function showAnswer(eventObj) {
    ...
}
```

In the handler, you can use the event object to determine things about the event, like what type of event occurred, and which element generated the event, and so on.

So, what is *in* an event object? Like we said, both general and specific information about the event. The specific information depends on the type of the event, and we'll come back to that a bit. The general information includes the `target` property that holds a reference to the object that generated the event. So, if you click on a page element, like an image, that's the target, and we can access it like this:

Watch it!

If you're running IE8 or older, check the appendix.

With older versions of IE, you need to set up the event object a little differently.

```
function showAnswer(eventObj) {
    var image = eventObj.target;
}
```

The target tells us what element generated the event.

You've already seen that the event object (for DOM events) has properties that give you more information about the event that just happened. Below you'll find other properties that the event object can have. Match each event object property to what it does.

target

type

timeStamp

keyCode

clientX

clientY

touches

Want to know how far from the top of the browser window the user clicked? Use me.

I hold the object on which the event occurred. I can be different kinds of objects, but most often I'm an element object.

Using a touch device? Then use me to find out how many fingers are touching the screen.

I'm a string, like "click" or "load", that tells you what just happened.

Want to know when your event happened? I'm the property for you.

Want to know how far from the left side of the browser window the user clicked? Use me.

I'll tell you what key the user just pressed.

Putting the event object to work

So, now that we've learned a little more about events—or more specifically, how the event object is passed to the click handler—let's figure out how to use the information in the event object to deblur any image on the page. We'll start by revisiting the HTML markup.

```
<!doctype html>
...
<body>
    <img id="zero" src="zeroblur.jpg">
    <img id="one" src="oneblur.jpg">
    <img id="two" src="twoblur.jpg">
    <img id="three" src="threeblur.jpg">
    <img id="four" src="fourblur.jpg">
    <img id="five" src="fiveblur.jpg">
</body>
</html>
```

Here's the HTML again.

Each of the images has an id, and the id corresponds to the unblurred image name. So the image with id "zero" has an unblurred image of "zero.jpg". And the image with id "one" has an unblurred image of "one.jpg" and so on...

Notice that the value of each image's id corresponds to the name of the unblurred image (minus the ".jpg" extension). Now, if we can access this id, then we can simply take that name and add on ".jpg" to create the name of the corresponding unblurred image. Once we have that we can change the image `src` property to the unblurred version of the image. Let's see how:

Remember you're getting passed an event object each time an image is clicked on.

```
function showAnswer(eventObj) {
    var image = eventObj.target;

    var name = image.id;
    name = name + ".jpg";
    image.src = name;
}
```

The event object's target property is a reference to the image element that was clicked.

We can then use the id property of that object to get the name of the unblurred image.

And finally, we'll set the src of the image to that name.

As you know, once you change the src property of the image, the browser will immediately retrieve that new image and display it in the page in place of the blurred version.

Test drive the event object and target

Make sure you've updated all the code in your "image.html" file, and take it for a test drive. Guess the image, click, and see the unblurred version be revealed. Think about how this app is designed not as a top-to-bottom running program, but purely as a set of actions that result from an event being generated when you click on an image. Also think about how you handled the events on all the images with one piece of code that's smart enough to know which image was clicked on. Play around. What happens if you click twice? Anything at all?

> Now we can click on any of the images and see the unblurred version. How well did you do?

there are no Dumb Questions

Q: Does the onload event handler get passed an event object too?

A: It does, and it includes information like the target, which is the window object, the time it happened, and the type of the event, which is just the type "load". It's safe to say you don't typically see the event object used much in load handlers because there really isn't anything that is useful in it for this kind of event. You're going to find that sometimes the event object will be useful to you, and sometimes it won't, depending on the type of event. If you're unsure what the event object contains for a specific kind of event, just grab a JavaScript reference.

⚛ BRAIN POWER

What if you want to have an image become blurred again a few seconds after you've revealed the answer. How might that work?

Events Exposed

This week's interview:
Talking to the browser about events

Head First: Hey Browser, it's always good to have your time. We know how busy you are.

Browser: My pleasure, and you're right, managing all these events keeps me on my toes.

Head First: Just how do you manage them anyway? Give us a behind-the-scenes look at the magic.

Browser: As you know, events are almost continually happening. The user moves the mouse around, or makes a gesture on a mobile device; things arrive over the network; timers go off… it's like Grand Central. That's a lot to manage.

Head First: I would have assumed you don't need to do much unless there happens to be a handler defined somewhere for an event?

Browser: Even if there's no handler, there's still work to do. Someone has to grab the event, interpret it, and see if there is a handler waiting for it. If there is, I have to make sure that handler gets executed.

Head First: So how do you keep track of all these events? What if lots of events are happening at the same time? There's only one of you after all.

Browser: Well, yes, lots of events can happen over a very short amount of time, sometimes too fast for me to handle all in real time. So what I do is throw them all on a queue as they come in. Then I go through the queue and execute handlers where necessary.

Head First: Boy, that sounds like my days as a short-order cook!

Browser: Sure, if you had orders coming in every millisecond or so!

Head First: You have go through the queue one by one?

Browser: I sure do, and that's an important thing to know about JavaScript: there's one queue and one "thread of control," meaning there is only one of me going through the events one at a time.

Head First: What does that really mean for our readers learning JavaScript?

Browser: Well, say you write a handler and it requires a lot of computation—that is, something that takes a long time to compute. As long as your handler is chugging along computing, I'm sitting around waiting until it's done. Only then can I continue with the queue.

Head First: Oh wow. Does that happen a lot, that is, you end up waiting on slow code?

Browser: It happens, but it also doesn't take long for a web developer to figure out the page or app isn't responsive because the handlers are slow. So, it's not a common problem as long as the web developers know how event queues work.

Head First: And now all our readers do! Now, back to events, are there lots of different kinds of events?

Browser: There are. We've got network-based events, timer events, DOM events related to the page and a few others. Some kinds of events, like DOM events, generate event objects that contain a lot more detail about the event—like a mouse click event will have information about where the user clicked, and a keypress event will have information about which key was pressed, and so on.

Head First: So, you spend a lot of time dealing with events. Is that really the best use of your time? After all, you've got to deal with retrieving, parsing and rendering pages and all that.

Browser: Oh, it's very important. These days you've got to write code that makes your pages interactive and engaging, and for that you need events.

Head First: Oh for sure, the days of simple pages are gone.

Browser: Exactly. Oh shoot, this queue is about to overflow. Gotta run!

Head First: Okay… until next time!

Events and queues

You already know that the browser maintains a queue of events. And that behind the scenes the browser is constantly taking events off that queue and processing them by calling the appropriate event handler for them, if there is one.

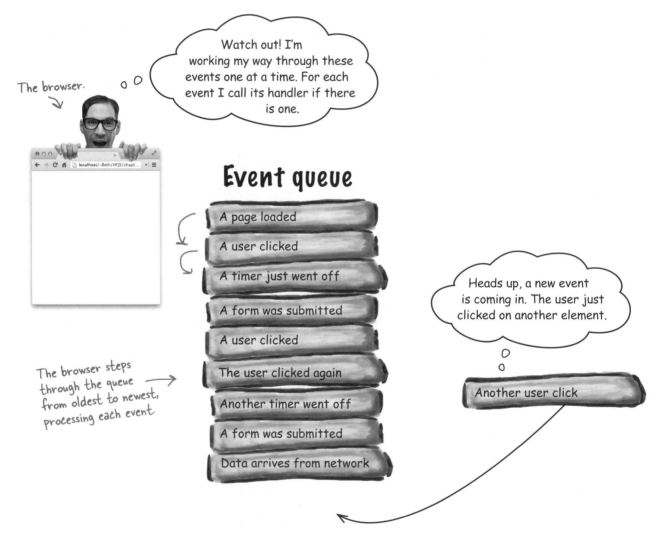

The browser.

Watch out! I'm working my way through these events one at a time. For each event I call its handler if there is one.

Event queue

A page loaded

A user clicked

A timer just went off

A form was submitted

A user clicked

The user clicked again

Another timer went off

A form was submitted

Data arrives from network

The browser steps through the queue from oldest to newest, processing each event.

Heads up, a new event is coming in. The user just clicked on another element.

Another user click

It's important to know that the browser processes these events one at a time, so, where possible, you need to keep your handlers short and efficient. If you don't, the whole event queue could stack up with waiting events, and the browser will get backed up dealing with them all. The downside to you? Your interface could really start to become slow and unresponsive.

If things get really bad you'll get the slow script dialog box, which means the browser is giving up!

Ahoy matey! You've got a treasure map in your possession and we need your help in determining the coordinates of the treasure. To do that you're going to write a bit of code that displays the coordinates on the map as you pass the mouse over the map. We've got some of the code on the next page, but you'll have to help finish it.

Exercise

Here's the map and X marks the spot!

After your code is written, just move the mouse over the X to see the coordinates of the treasure.

P.S. We highly encourage you to do this exercise, because we don't think the pirates are going to be too happy if they don't get their coordinates... Oh, and you'll need this to complete your code:

Your code will display the coordinates below the map.

COORDINATES: 10, 20

The mousemove event

The mousemove event notifies your handler when a mouse moves over a particular element. You set up your handler using the element's **onmousemove** property. Once you've done that you'll be passed an event object that provides these properties:

clientX, clientY: the x (and y) position in pixels of your mouse from the left side (and top) of the browser window.

screenX, screenY: the x (and y) position in pixels of your mouse from the left side (and top) of the user's screen.

pageX, pageY: the x (and y) position in pixels of your mouse from the left side (and top) of the browser's page.

Blimey! The code is below. So far it includes the map in the page
and creates a paragraph element to display the coordinates. You
need to make all the event code work. Good luck. We don't want to
see you go to Davy Jones' locker anytime soon...

```html
<!doctype html>
<html lang="en">
<head>
  <meta charset="utf-8">
  <title>Pirates Booty</title>
  <script>
      window.onload = init;
      function init() {
          var map = document.getElementById("map");

          _____
      }
                                    Set up your handler here.

      function showCoords(eventObj) {
          var map = document.getElementById("coords");

          _____

          _____
          map.innerHTML = "Map coordinates: "
                                 + x + ", " + y;
      }
                                    Grab the coordinates here.
  </script>
</head>
<body>
      <img id="map" src="map.jpg">
      <p id="coords">Move mouse to find coordinates...</p>
</body>
</html>
```

When you're done get this code in a real page, load it,
and write your coordinates here.

_____

Even more events

So far we've seen three types of events: the load event, which occurs when the browser has loaded the page; the click event, which occurs when a user clicks on an element in the page and the mousemove event, which occurs when a user moves the mouse over an element. You're likely to run into many other kinds of events too, like events for data arriving over the network, events about the geolocation of your browser, and time-based events (just to name a few).

For all the events you've seen, to wire up a handler, you've always assigned the handler to some property, like `onload`, `onmouseover` or `onclick`. But not all events work like this—for example, with time-based events, rather than assigning a handler to a property, you call a function, `setTimeout`, instead and pass it your handler.

Here's an example: say you want your code to wait five seconds before doing something. Here's how you do that using `setTimeout` and a handler:

First we write an event handler. This is the handler that will be called when the time event has occurred.

```
function timerHandler() {
    alert("Hey what are you doing just sitting there staring at a blank screen?");
}
```
All we're doing in this event handler is showing an alert.

And here, we call setTimeout, which takes two arguments: the event handler and a time duration (in milliseconds).

```
setTimeout(timerHandler, 5000);
```

Using setTimeout is a bit like setting a stop watch.

Here we're asking the timer to wait 5000 milliseconds (5 seconds).

And then call the handler timerHandler.

Test drive your timer

Don't just sit there! It's time to test this code! Throw this code into a basic HTML page, and load the page. At first you won't see anything, but after five seconds you'll see the alert.

Be patient, wait five seconds and you'll see what we see. Now if you've been sitting there a couple minutes you might want to give your machine a little kick... just kidding, you'd actually better check your code.

How setTimeout works

Let's step through what just happened.

Okay, it's go time. I've got a timer that goes off in 5000 milliseconds, and I've got a handler to call when that happens.

1 When the page loads we do two things: we define a handler named timerHandler, and we call setTimeout to create a time event that will be generated in 5000 milliseconds. When the time event happens, the handler will be executed.

Your browser manages timers.

The browser tracks all timers (yes you can have more than one at a time) along with the corresponding handlers it needs to call.

2 The browser continues its normal job as the timer counts down in milliseconds.

5000, 4999, 4998...

..., 6, 5, 4, 3, 2, 1, 0.

That's 5000 milliseconds, the timer is done, let's call that handler.

3 When the browser's countdown gets to zero, the browser calls the handler.

The time event is triggered when the countdown is complete. The browser executes the event handler by calling the function you passed in.

4 The handler is called, resulting in an alert being created and displayed in the browser.

The handler has been called. I'm finished with that timer.

```
function timerHandler() {
    alert("Hey what are you doing just sitting there staring at a blank screen?");
}
```

When the browser executes our event handler, we see the alert!

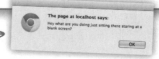

The page at localhost says:
Hey what are you doing just sitting there staring at a blank screen?

OK

> With setTimeout, did I misunderstand, or did you pass a function to another function?

Good catch! Remember we said up front that in this chapter you're going to feel like you aren't in Kansas anymore? Well this is that point in the movie where everything goes from black and white to color. Back to your question; yes, we defined a function and then took that function, and passed it to setTimeout (which is actually a method).

```
setTimeout(timerHandler, 5000);
```

Here it is, a reference to a function passed to setTimeout (another function).

Why would we do this and what does it mean? Let's think through this: the setTimeout function essentially creates a countdown timer and associates a handler with that timer. That handler is called when the timer hits zero. Now to tell setTimeout what handler to call, we need to pass it a *reference to the handler function*. setTimeout stores the reference away to use later when the timer has expired.

If you're saying "That makes sense," then great. On the other hand, you might be saying "Excuse me? Pass a function to a function? Say what?" In that case, you probably have experience with a language like C or Java, where *you don't just go around passing functions to other functions like this…* well, in JavaScript, you do, and in fact, being able to pass functions around is incredibly powerful, especially when we're writing code that reacts to events.

More likely at this point you're saying, "I think I sort of get it, but I'm not sure." If so, no worries. For now, just think of this as giving setTimeout a reference to the handler it's going to need to invoke when the timer expires. We're going to be talking a lot more about functions and what you can do with them (like passing them to other functions) in the next chapter. So just go with it for now.

Exercise

Here's the code.

Take a look at the code below and see if you can figure out what `setInterval` does. It's similar to `setTimeout`, but with a slight twist. Check your answer at the end of the chapter.

```
var tick = true;
function ticker() {
    if (tick) {
        console.log("Tick");
        tick = false;
    } else {
        console.log("Tock");
        tick = true;
    }
}
setInterval(ticker, 1000);
```

Your analysis goes here.

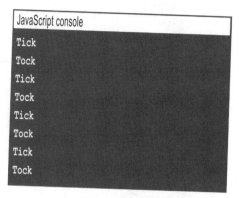

Here's the output.

there are no Dumb Questions

Q: Is there a way to stop setInterval?

A: There is. When you call setInterval, it returns a timer object. You can pass that timer object to another function, clearInterval, to stop the timer.

Q: You said setTimeout was a method, but it looks like a function. Where's the object it's a method of?

A: Good catch. Technically we could write window.setTimeout, but because the window object is considered the global object, we can omit the object name, and just use setTimeout, which we'll see a lot in practice.

Q: Can I omit window on the window.onload property too?

A: You can, but most people don't because they are worried onload is a common enough property name (other elements can have the onload property too) that not specifying which onload property might be confusing.

Q: With onload I'm assigning one handler to an event. But with setTimeout, I seem to be able to assign as many handlers as I want to as many timers as I want?

A: Exactly. When you call setTimeout, you are creating a timer and associating a handler with it. You can create as many timers as you like. The browser keeps track of associating each timer with its handler.

Q: Are there other examples of passing functions to functions?

A: Lots of them. In fact, you'll find that passing around functions is fairly common in JavaScript. Not only do lots of built-in functions, like setTimeout and setInterval, make use of function passing, but you'll also discover there's a lot code you'll write yourself that accepts functions as arguments. But that's only part of the story, and in the next chapter we're going to dive deep into this topic and discover that you can do all sort of interesting things with functions in JavaScript.

> Hey guys I'm trying to get this image app finished. I'm working on getting the images to reblur a couple of seconds after the user clicks on them.

Joe: That sounds cool… I bet you're using `setTimeout`?

Frank: That's my plan, although I'm not sure how to know which image to reblur.

Jim: What do you mean?

Frank: I have my code so that when you click on an image and reveal it, I set up a timer that fires in two seconds. When the timeout event fires, it calls a new handler I wrote called `reblur`.

Joe: And in `reblur`, you need to know which image to reblur?

Frank: Right. I'm not passing any arguments to the handler, it's just being called by the browser when the time expires, and so I have no way to tell my handler the correct image to reblur. I'm kinda stuck.

Jim: Have you looked at the `setTimeout` API?

Frank: No, I know only what Judy told me: that `setTimeout` takes a function and a time duration in milliseconds.

Jim: You can add an argument to the call to `setTimeout` that is passed on to the handler when the time event fires.

Frank: Oh that's perfect. So I can just pass in a reference to the correct image to reblur and that will get passed on to the handler when it is called?

Jim: You got it.

Frank: See what a little talking through code gets ya Joe?

Joe: Oh for sure. Let's give this a try…

Finishing the image game

Now it's time to put the final polish on the image game. What we want is for an image to automatically reblur a few seconds after it's revealed. And, as we just learned, we can pass along an argument for the event handler when we call `setTimeout`. Let's check out how to do this:

```
window.onload = function() {
    var images = document.getElementsByTagName("img");
    for (var i = 0; i < images.length; i++) {
        images[i].onclick = showAnswer;
    }
};
```

This code is just as we wrote it before. No changes here...

```
function showAnswer(eventObj) {
    var image = eventObj.target;
    var name = image.id;
    name = name + ".jpg";
    image.src = name;

    setTimeout(reblur, 2000, image);
}
```

But now when we show the user the clear image, we also call setTimeout to set up an event that will fire in two seconds.

We'll use reblur (below) as our handler, and pass it 2000 milliseconds (two seconds) and also an argument, the image to reblur.

```
function reblur(image) {
    var name = image.id;
    name = name + "blur.jpg";
    image.src = name;
}
```

Now when this handler is called, it will be passed the image.

The handler can take the image, get the id of the image, and use that to create the name of the blurred image. When we set the src of the image to that name, it will replace the clear image with the blurred image.

Watch it!

setTimeout does not support extra arguments in IE8 and earlier.

That's right. This code is not going to work for you or your users if you're using IE8 or earlier. But you shouldn't be using IE8 for this book anyway! That said, you'll see another way to do this a little later in the book that will take care of this for IE8 (and earlier).

Test driving the timer

That wasn't much code to add, but it sure makes a big difference in how the image game works. Now when you click, behind the scenes, the browser (through the timer events) is tracking when it needs to call the `reblur` handler, which blurs the image again. Note how *asynchronous* this feels—you're in control of when the images are clicked, but behind-the-scenes code is being invoked at various times based on the click event and on timer events. There's no über algorithm driving things here, controlling what gets called and when; it's just a lot of little pieces of code that set up, create and react to events.

Now when you click, you'll see the image revealed, and then blurred again two seconds later.

Give this a good QA testing by clicking on lots of images in quick succession. Does it always work? Refer back to the code and wrap your brain around how the browser keeps track of all the images that need to be reblurred.

there are no Dumb Questions

Q: Can I pass just one argument to the setTimeout handler?

A: No you can actually pass as many as you like: zero, one or more.

Q: What about the event object? Why doesn't setTimeout pass the event handler one?

A: The event object is mostly used with DOM-related event handlers. setTimeout doesn't pass any kind of event object to its handler, because it doesn't occur on a specific element.

Q: showAnswer is a handler, and yet it creates a new handler, reblur, in its code. Is that right?

A: You've got it. You'll actually see this fairly often in JavaScript. It's perfectly normal to see a handler set up additional event handlers for various events. And this is the style of programming we were referring to in the beginning of the chapter: *asynchronous programming*. To create the image game we didn't just translate an algorithm that runs top down. Rather we're hooking up event handlers to handle the execution of the game as events occur. Trace through a few different examples of clicking on images and the various calls that get made to reveal and reblur the image.

Q: So there are DOM-based events, and timer events... are there lots of different kinds of events?

A: Many of the events you deal with in JavaScript are DOM events (like when you click on an element), or timer events (created with setTmeout or setInterval). There are also API-specific events, like events generated by JavaScript APIs including Geolocation, LocalStorage, Web Workers, and so on (see *Head First HTML5 Programming* for more on these). And finally, there is a whole category of events related to I/O: like when you request data from a web service using XmlHttpRequest (again, see *Head First HTML5 Programming* for more), or Web Sockets.

Hey guys, our desktop users would like to be able to pass their mouse over the image without clicking to reveal the unblurred image. Can we get that implemented?

Judy: To make this work you'll want to make use of the mouseover event. You can set a handler for this event on any element with the `onmouseover` property:

```
myElement.onmouseover = myHandler;
```

Judy: Also, the mouseout event tells you when the mouse leaves your element. You can set its handler with the `onmouseout` property.

Exercise

Rework your code so that an image is revealed and reblurred by moving your mouse over and out of the image elements. Be sure to test your code, and check your answer at the end of the chapter:

↖ JavaScript code goes here.

Exercise

With the image game complete, Judy wrote some code to review in the weekly team meeting. In fact, she started a little contest, awarding the first person to describe what the code does with lunch. Who wins? Jim, Joe, Frank? Or you?

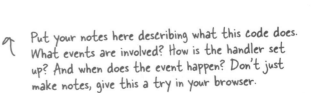

```
<!doctype html>
<html lang="en">
<head>
<meta charset="utf-8">
<title>Don't resize me, I'm ticklish!</title>
<script>
    function resize() {
        var element = document.getElementById("display");
        element.innerHTML = element.innerHTML + " that tickles!";
    }
</script>
</head>
<body>
<p id="display">
    Whatever you do, don't resize this window! I'm warning you!
</p>
<script>
    window.onresize = resize;
</script>
</body>
</html>
```

↖ Put your notes here describing what this code does. What events are involved? How is the handler set up? And when does the event happen? Don't just make notes, give this a try in your browser.

CODE LABORATORY

We've found some highly suspicious code we need your help testing. While we've already done an initial analysis on the code and it looks like 100% standard JavaScript, something about it looks odd. Below you'll find two code specimens. For each specimen you'll need to identify what seems odd about the code, test to make sure the code works, and then try to analyze what exactly it does. Go ahead and make your notes on this page. You'll find our analysis on the next page.

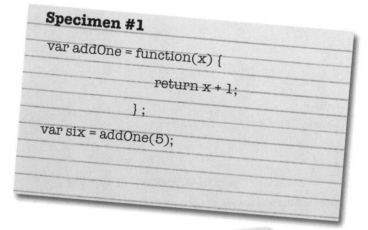

Specimen #1

```javascript
var addOne = function(x) {
            return x + 1;
        };
var six = addOne(5);
```

Specimen #2

```javascript
window.onload = function() {
     alert("The page is loaded!");

}
```

CODE LABORATORY: ANALYSIS

Specimen #1

```
var addOne = function(x) {

            return x + 1;

      };
var six = addOne(5);
```

At first glance this code appears to simply define a function that adds the number one to any parameter and return it.

Looking closer, this isn't a normal function definition. Rather, we are declaring a variable and assigning to it a function that appears to be missing its name.

Further, we're invoking the function with the variable name, not a name associated with the function as part of its definition.

Odd indeed (although it reminds us a bit of how object methods are defined).

Specimen #2

```
window.onload = function() {
    alert("The page is loaded!");
}
```

Here we appear to have something similar. Instead of defining a function separately and assigning its name to the window.onload property, we're assigning a function directly to that property. And again, the function doesn't define its own name.

We added this code to an HTML page and tested it. The code appears to work as you might expect. With specimen #1, when the function assigned to addOne is invoked, we get a result that is one greater than the number we pass in, which seems right. With specimen #2, when we load the page, we get the alert "The page is loaded!".

From these tests it would appear as if functions can be defined without names, and used in places where you'd expect an expression.

What does it all mean? Stick around; we'll reveal our findings on these odd functions in the next chapter...

BULLET POINTS

- Most JavaScript code is written to react to **events**.

- There are many different kinds of events your code can react to.

- To react to an event, you write an **event handler** function, and register it. For instance, to register a handler for the click event, you assign the handler function to the onclick property of an element.

- You're not required to handle any specific event. You choose to handle the events you're interested in.

- **Functions** are used for handlers because functions allow us to package up code to be executed later (when the event occurs).

- Code written to handle events is different from code that executes top to bottom and then completes. Event handlers can run at any time and in any order: they are **asynchronous**.

- Events that occur on elements in the DOM (DOM events) cause an event object to be passed to the event handler.

- The **event object** contains properties with extra information about the event, including the type (like "click" or "load") and the target (the object on which the event occurred).

- Older versions of IE (IE 8 and older) have a different event model from other browsers. See the appendix for more details.

- Many events can happen very close together. When too many events happen for the browser to handle them as they occur, the events are stored in an **event queue** (in the order in which they occurred) so the browser can execute the event handlers for each event in turn.

- If an event handler is computationally complex, it will slow down the handling of the events in the queue because only one event handler can execute at a time.

- The functions **setTimeout** and **setInterval** are used to generate time-based events after a certain time has passed.

- The method **getElementsByTagName** returns zero, one or more element objects in a NodeList (which is array-like, so you can iterate over it).

Event Soup

click
Get this event when you click (or tap) in a web page.

load
The event you get when the browser has completed loading a web page.

mousemove
When you move your mouse over an element, you'll generate this event.

keypress
This event is generated every time you press a key.

unload
This event is generated when you close the browser window, or navigate away from a web page.

mouseover
When you put your mouse over an element, you'll generate this event.

mouseout
And you'll generate this event when you move your mouse off an element.

resize
Whenever you resize your browser window, this event is generated.

dragstart
If you drag an element in the page, you'll generate this event.

touchstart
On touch devices, you'll generate a touchstart event when you touch and hold an element.

play
Got <video> in your page? You'll get this event when you click the play button.

drop
You'll get this event when you drop an element you've been dragging.

pause
And this one when you click the pause button.

touchend
And you'll get this event when you stop touching.

We've scratched the surface of events, using load, click, mousemove, mouseover, mouseout, resize and timer events. Check out this delicious soup of events you'll encounter and will want to explore in your web programming.

JavaScript cross

Practice your event reaction time by doing this crossword.

ACROSS

1. Use this property of the event object to know when an event happened.

3. When you click your mouse, you'll generate a _____ event.

8. Events are handled _____.

12. 5000 milliseconds is _____ seconds.

13. Use this method to get multiple elements from the DOM using a tag name.

14. A function designed to react to an event is called an event _____.

15. The setTimeout method is used to create a _____ event.

16. The browser has only one _____ of control.

17. The browser can only execute one event _____ at a time.

19. The event object for a mouseover event has this property for the X position of the mouse.

20. The event _____ is passed to an event handler for DOM events.

21. To pass an argument to a time event handler, pass it as the _____ argument to setTimeout.

DOWN

1. You'll generate this event if you touch your touch screen device.

2. zero.jpg is the _____.

4. When you begin programming with events, you might feel like you're not in _____ any more.

5. JavaScript allows you to pass a _____ to a function.

6. If too many events happen close together, the browser stores the events in an event _____.

7. Events are generated for lots of things, but not for baking _____.

9. To make a time event happen over and over, use _____.

10. The window _____ property is for handling a page loaded event.

11. _____ is super ticklish.

14. To assign an event handler for a time event, pass the _____ to setTimeout as the first argument.

15. How you know which image was clicked on in the image game.

18. A program with code to handle events is not this.

Sharpen your pencil
Solution

Pick two of the events above. If the browser could notify your code when these events occurred, what cool or interesting code might you write?

Let's take an event that notifies us when a user submits a form. If we're notified of this event, then we could get all the data the user filled into the form and check to make sure it's valid (e.g. the user put something that looks like a phone number into a phone number field, or filled out the required fields). Once we've done that check, then we could submit the form to the server.

How about the mouse movement event? If we're notified whenever a user moves the mouse, then we could create a drawing application right in the browser.

If we're notified when the user scrolls down the page, we could do interesting things like reveal an image as they scroll down.

BE the Browser Solution

Below, you'll find the image game code. Your job is to play like you're the browser and to figure out what you need to do after each event. After you've done the exercise look at the end of the chapter to see if you got everything. Here's our solution.

```
window.onload = init;
function init() {
    var image = document.getElementById("zero");
    image.onclick = showAnswer;
}

function showAnswer() {
    var image = document.getElementById("zero");
    image.src = "zero.jpg";
}
```

When page is being loaded...	First define the functions init and showAnswer
	Set load handler to init
When page load event occurs...	load handler, init, is called
	we get the image with id "zero"
	set image's click handler to showAnswer
When image click event occurs...	showAnswer is called
	we get the image with id "zero"
	we set the src attribute to "zero.jpg"

You've already seen that the event object (for DOM events) has properties that give you more information about the event that just happened. Below you'll find other properties that the event object can have. Match each event object property to what it does.

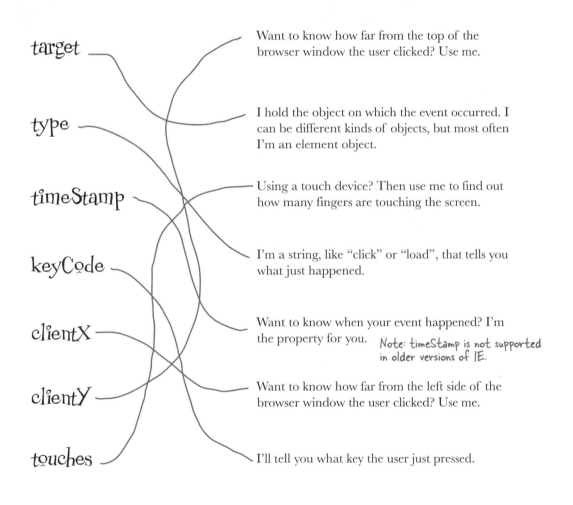

target

type

timeStamp

keyCode

clientX

clientY

touches

Want to know how far from the top of the browser window the user clicked? Use me.

I hold the object on which the event occurred. I can be different kinds of objects, but most often I'm an element object.

Using a touch device? Then use me to find out how many fingers are touching the screen.

I'm a string, like "click" or "load", that tells you what just happened.

Want to know when your event happened? I'm the property for you. Note: timeStamp is not supported in older versions of IE.

Want to know how far from the left side of the browser window the user clicked? Use me.

I'll tell you what key the user just pressed.

Ahoy matey! You've got a treasure map in your possession and we need your help in determining the coordinates of the treasure. To do that you're going to write a bit of code that displays the coordinates on the map as you pass the mouse over the map.

Blimey! The code is below. So far it includes the map in the page and creates a paragraph element to display the coordinates. You need to make all the event-based code works. Good luck. We don't want to see you go to Davy Jones' locker anytime soon... And here's our solution.

```
<!doctype html>
<html lang="en">
<head>
  <meta charset="utf-8">
  <title>Pirates Booty</title>
  <script>
      window.onload = init;
      function init() {
          var map = document.getElementById("map");
          map.onmousemove = showCoords;
      }

      function showCoords(eventObj) {
          var map = document.getElementById("coords");
          var x = eventObj.clientX;
          var y = eventObj.clientY;
          map.innerHTML = "Map coordinates: "
                                + x + ", " + y;
      }
  </script>
</head>
<body>
      <img id="map" src="map.jpg">
      <p id="coords">Move mouse to find coordinates...</p>
</body>
</html>
```

When we put our mouse right over the X, we got the coordinates: 200, 190

EXERCISE
SOLUTION

Take a look at the code below and see if you can figure out what `setInterval` does. It's similar to `setTimeout`, but with a slight twist. Here's our solution:

Here's the code.

```
var tick = true;

function ticker() {
    if (tick) {
        console.log("Tick");
        tick = false;
    } else {
        console.log("Tock");
        tick = true;
    }
}

setInterval(ticker, 1000);
```

```
JavaScript console
Tick
Tock
Tick
Tock
Tick
Tock
Tick
Tock
```

Here's the output.

Your analysis goes here.

Just like setTimeout, setInterval also takes an event handler function as its first argument and a time duration as its second argument.

But unlike setTimeout, setInterval executes the event handler multiple times... in fact it keeps going. Forever! (Actually, you can tell it to stop, see below). In this example, every 1000 milliseconds (1 second), setInterval calls the ticker handler. The ticker handler is checking the value of the tick variable to determine whether to display "Tick" or "Tock" in the console.

So setInterval generates an event when the timer expires, and then restarts the timer.

```
var t = setInterval(ticker, 1000);
```
To stop an interval timer, save the result of calling setInterval in a variable...

```
clearInterval(t);
```
...and then pass that to clearInterval later, when you want to stop the timer.

Exercise Solution

Rework your code so that you can reveal and reblur an image by passing your mouse over and out of the image elements. Be sure to test your code. Here's our solution:

```javascript
window.onload = function() {
    var images = document.getElementsByTagName("img");
    for (var i = 0; i < images.length; i++) {
        images[i].onclick = showAnswer;
        images[i].onmouseover = showAnswer;
        images[i].onmouseout = reblur;
    }
};
function showAnswer(eventObj) {
    var image = eventObj.target;
    var name = image.id;
    name = name + ".jpg";
    image.src = name;

    setTimeout(reblur, 2000, image);
}

function reblur(eventObj) {
    var image = eventObj.target;
    var name = image.id;
    name = name + "blur.jpg";
    image.src = name;
}
```

First, we remove the assignment of the event handler to the onclick property.

Then we add the showAnswer event handler to the onmouseover property of the image...

And now we're going to use reblur as the handler for the mouseout event (instead of as a timer event handler). So we assign reblur to the onmouseout property of the image.

We won't use the timer anymore to reblur the image; instead, we'll reblur it when the user moves the mouse out of the image element.

Now we're using reblur as an event handler for the mouseout event, so to get the correct image to reblur, we have to use the event object. Just like in showAnswer, we'll use the target property to get the image object. Once we have that, the rest of reblur is the same.

Exercise Solution

With the image game complete, Judy wrote some code to review in the weekly team meeting. In fact, she started a little contest, awarding the first person to describe what the code does with lunch. Who wins? Jim, Joe, Frank? Or you?

```html
<!doctype html>
<html lang="en">
<head>
<meta charset="utf-8">
<title>Don't resize me, I'm ticklish!</title>
<script>
    function resize() {
        var element = document.getElementById("display");
        element.innerHTML = element.innerHTML + " that tickles!";
    }
</script>
</head>
<body>
<p id="display">
    Whatever you do, don't resize this window! I'm warning you!
</p>
<script>
    window.onresize = resize;
</script>
</body>
</html>
```

Our event handler is named resize. When it's called, it just adds some text to the paragraph with the id "display".

The event we're interested in is the resize event, so we set up a handler function (named resize), and assign it to the onresize property of the window.

We set up the resize event in the script at the bottom of the page. Remember, this script won't run until the page is fully loaded, so that makes sure we don't set up the event handler too early.

When you resize the browser window, the resize event handler is called, which updates the page by adding new text content (" that tickles") to the "display" paragraph.

JavaScript cross Solution

Practice your event reaction time by doing this crossword. Here's our solution.

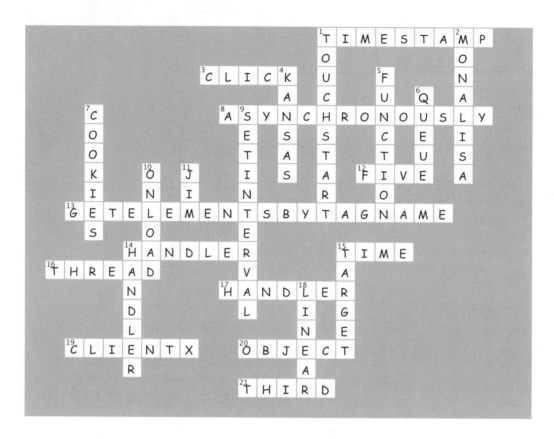

10 first class functions

Know functions, then rock. Every art, craft, and discipline has a key principle that separates the intermediate players from the rock star virtuosos—when it comes to JavaScript, it's truly understanding **functions** that makes the difference. Functions are fundamental to JavaScript, and many of the techniques we use to **design and organize** code depend on advanced knowledge and use of functions. The path to learning functions at this level is an interesting and often mind-bending one, so get ready... This chapter is going to be a bit like Willy Wonka giving a tour of the chocolate factory—you're going to encounter some wild, wacky and wonderful things as you learn more about JavaScript functions.

We'll spare you the singing Oompa Loompas.

The mysterious double life of the function keyword

So far we've been declaring functions like this:

```
function quack(num) {
    for (var i = 0; i < num; i++) {
        console.log("Quack!");
    }
}
```

A standard function declaration with the function keyword, a name, a parameter and a block of code.

```
quack(3);
```

And we can invoke this function by using its name followed by parentheses that enclose any needed arguments.

There are no surprises here, but let's get our terminology down: formally, the first statement above is a *function declaration*, which creates a function that has a name—in this case quack—that can be used to *reference* and *invoke* the function.

So far so good, but the story gets more mysterious because, as you saw at the end of the last chapter, there's another way to use the function keyword:

This doesn't look so standard: the function doesn't have a name, and it's on the right hand side of an assignment to a variable.

```
var fly = function(num) {
    for (var i = 0; i < num; i++) {
        console.log("Flying!");
    }
};
```

We can invoke this function too, this time by using the variable fly.

```
fly(3);
```

Now when we use the function keyword this way—that is, within a statement, like an assignment statement—we call this a *function expression*. Notice that, unlike the function declaration, this function doesn't have a name. Also, the expression results in a value that is then assigned to the variable fly. What is that value? Well, we're assigning it to the variable fly and then later invoking it, so it must be a *reference to a function*.

Serious Coding

A function reference is exactly what it sounds like: a reference that refers to a function. You can use a function reference to invoke a function or, as you'll see, you can assign them to variables, store them in objects, and pass them to or return them from functions (just like object references).

Function declarations versus function expressions

Whether you use a function declaration or a function expression you get the same thing: a function. So what's the difference? Is the declaration just more convenient, or is there something about function expressions that makes them useful? Or are these just two ways to do the same thing?

At first glance, it might appear as if there isn't a big difference between function declarations and function expressions. But, actually, there is something fundamentally different about the two, and to understand that difference we need to start by looking at how your code is treated by the browser at runtime. So let's drop in on the browser as it parses and evaluates the code in your page:

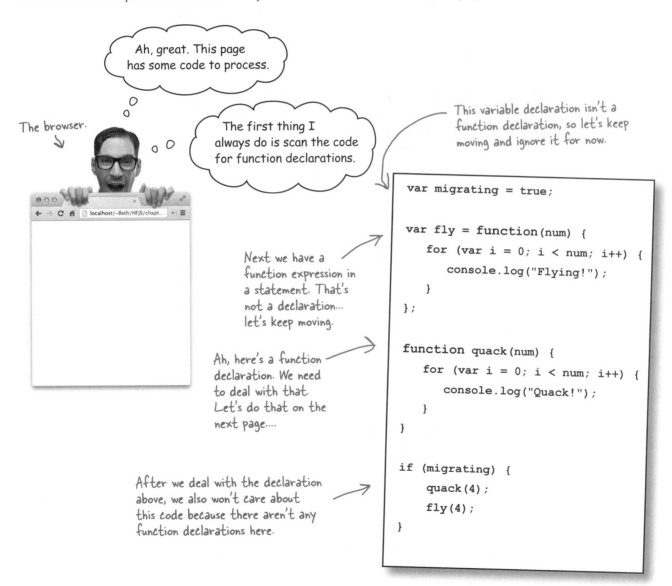

Ah, great. This page has some code to process.

The browser.

The first thing I always do is scan the code for function declarations.

This variable declaration isn't a function declaration, so let's keep moving and ignore it for now.

Next we have a function expression in a statement. That's not a declaration... let's keep moving.

Ah, here's a function declaration. We need to deal with that. Let's do that on the next page....

After we deal with the declaration above, we also won't care about this code because there aren't any function declarations here.

```
var migrating = true;

var fly = function(num) {
    for (var i = 0; i < num; i++) {
        console.log("Flying!");
    }
};

function quack(num) {
    for (var i = 0; i < num; i++) {
        console.log("Quack!");
    }
}

if (migrating) {
    quack(4);
    fly(4);
}
```

Parsing the function declaration

When the browser parses your page—before it evaluates any code—it's looking for function declarations. When the browser finds one, it creates a function and assigns the resulting reference to a variable with the same name as the function. Like this:

```
var migrating = true;

var fly = function(num) {
    for (var i = 0; i < num; i++) {
        console.log("Flying!");
    }
};

function quack(num) {
    for (var i = 0; i < num; i++) {
        console.log("Quack!");
    }
}

if (migrating) {
    quack(4);
    fly(4);
}
```

Here's the function declaration in this code. Let's see what the browser's going to do with it...

Ok, we've got a function declaration, we handle those before we do anything else...

I'm going to grab the function and stash it away so I can retrieve it later when the function is invoked.

```
function quack(num) {
    for (var i = 0; i < num; i++) {
        console.log("Quack!");
    }
}
```

quack

```
function quack(num) {
    for (var i = 0; i < num; i++) {
        console.log("Quack!");
    }
}
```

Here's our function stored away for later use, such as when the function gets invoked.

And, the function has a name, quack, so I'll set up a variable named quack to hold the function reference.

What's next? The browser executes the code

Now that all the function declarations have been taken care of, the browser goes back up to the top of your code and starts executing it, top to bottom. Let's check in on the browser at that point in the execution:

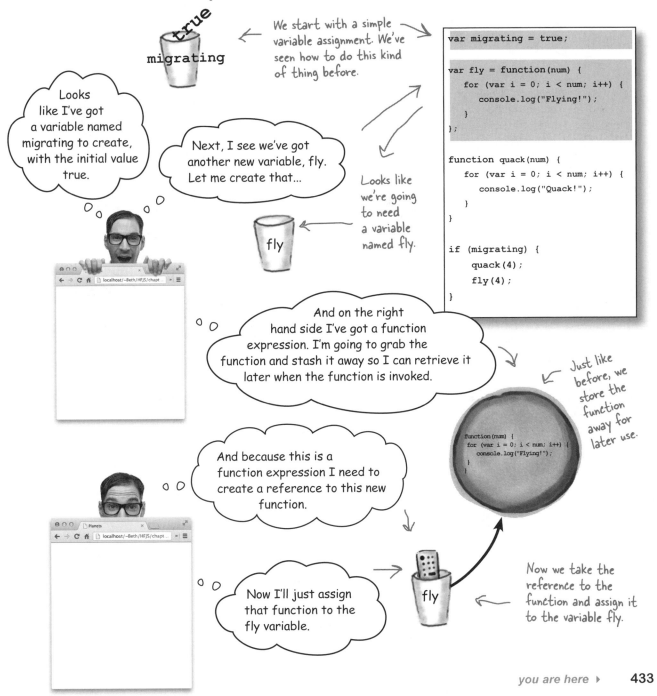

true

migrating

We start with a simple variable assignment. We've seen how to do this kind of thing before.

```
var migrating = true;

var fly = function(num) {
    for (var i = 0; i < num; i++) {
        console.log("Flying!");
    }
};

function quack(num) {
    for (var i = 0; i < num; i++) {
        console.log("Quack!");
    }
}

if (migrating) {
    quack(4);
    fly(4);
}
```

Looks like I've got a variable named migrating to create, with the initial value true.

Next, I see we've got another new variable, fly. Let me create that...

Looks like we're going to need a variable named fly.

fly

And on the right hand side I've got a function expression. I'm going to grab the function and stash it away so I can retrieve it later when the function is invoked.

Just like before, we store the function away for later use.

```
function(num) {
    for (var i = 0; i < num; i++) {
        console.log("Flying!");
    }
}
```

And because this is a function expression I need to create a reference to this new function.

Now I'll just assign that function to the fly variable.

fly

Now we take the reference to the function and assign it to the variable fly.

Moving on... The conditional

Once the `fly` variable has been taken care of, the browser moves on. The next statement is the function declaration for `quack`, which was dealt with in the first pass through the code, so the browser skips the declaration and moves on to the conditional statement. Let's follow along...

Been there, done that, moving on...

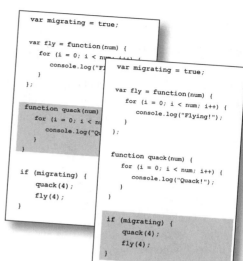

> Let's see, the variable migrating is true, so I need to execute the body of the if statement. Inside it looks like there's a call to quack. I know it's a function call because we're using the function name, quack, followed by parentheses.

```
quack(4);
```

> Remember, the quack variable is a reference to the function I stashed away earlier...

Here's the function created by the function declaration for quack.

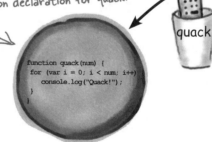

> There's an argument in the function call, so I'll pass that into the function...

4

To invoke the function, we pass a copy of the argument value to the parameter...

```
function quack(num) {
    for (var i = 0; i < num; i++) {
        console.log("Quack!");
    }
}
```

...and then execute the body of the function.

> ... and execute the code in the body of the function, which prints "Quack!" four times to the console log.

```
var migrating = true;

var fly = function(num) {
    for (var i = 0; i < num; i++) {
        console.log("Flying!");
    }
};

function quack(num) {
    for (var i = 0; i < num; i++) {
        console.log("Quack!");
    }
}

if (migrating) {
    quack(4);
    fly(4);
}
```

And finishing up...

All that's left is to invoke the `fly` function created by the function expression. Let's see how the browser handles this:

> Hey look, another function call. I know it's a function call because we're using the variable name, fly, followed by parentheses.

fly(4);

> Remember the fly variable is a reference to the function I stashed away earlier...

Here's the function referenced by the fly variable.

fly

> There's an argument in the function call, so I'll pass that into the function...

4

To invoke the function, we pass a copy of the argument value to the parameter...

```
function(num) {
    for (var i = 0; i < num; i++) {
        console.log("Flying!");
    }
}
```

...and then execute the body of the function.

> Then I'll execute the code in the body of the function, which prints "Flying!" four times to the console log.

Sharpen your pencil

What deductions can you make about function declarations and function expressions given how the browser treats the quack and fly code? Check each statement that applies. Check your answer at the end of the chapter before you go on.

❏ Function declarations are evaluated before the rest of the code is evaluated.

❏ Function expressions get evaluated later, with the rest of the code.

❏ A function declaration doesn't return a reference to a function; rather it creates a variable with the name of the function and assigns the new function to it.

❏ A function expression returns a reference to the new function created by the expression.

❏ You can hold function references in variables.

❏ Function declarations are statements; function expressions are used in statements.

❏ The process of invoking a function created by a declaration is exactly the same for one created with an expression.

❏ Function declarations are the tried and true way to create functions.

❏ You always want to use function declarations because they get evaluated earlier.

there are no
Dumb Questions

Q: We've seen expressions like 3+4 and Math.random() * 6, but how can a function be an expression?

A: An expression is anything that evaluates to a value. 3+4 evaluates to 7, Math.random() * 6 evaluates to a random number, and a function expression evaluates to a function reference.

Q: But a function declaration is not an expression?

A: No, a function declaration is a statement. Think of it as having a hidden assignment that assigns the function reference to a variable for you. A function expression doesn't assign a function reference to anything; you have to do that yourself.

Q: What good does it do me to have a variable that refers to a function?

A: Well for one thing you can use it to invoke the function:

```
myFunctionReference();
```

But you can also pass a reference to a function or return a reference from a function. But, we're getting a little ahead of ourselves. We'll come back to this in a few pages.

Q: Can function expressions only appear on the right hand side of an assignment statements?

A: Not at all. A function expression can appear in many different places, just like other kind of expressions can. Stay tuned because this is a really good question and we'll be coming back to this in just a bit.

Q: Okay, a variable can hold a reference to a function. But what is the variable really referencing? Just some code that is in the body of the function?

A: That's a good way to begin thinking about functions, but think of them more as a little crystallized version of the code, all ready to pull out at any time and invoke. You're going to see later that this crystallized function has a bit more in it than just the code from the body.

> We just saw that we invoke functions created by declarations or created by expressions in exactly the same way. So what is the difference between declarations and expressions? I feel like I'm missing something subtle here.

It is a little subtle. First of all, you're right—whether you use a function declaration or a function expression, you end up with a function. But there are some important differences between the two. For one, with a declaration, a function is created and setup *before the rest of the code gets evaluated*. With a function expression, a function is created as the code executes, at *runtime*.

Another difference has to do with function naming—when you use a declaration, the function name is used to create and set up as a variable that refers to the function. And, when you use a function expression, you typically don't provide a name for the function, so either you end up assigning the function to a variable in code, or you use the function expression in other ways.

We'll take a look at what those are later in the chapter.

Now take these differences and stash them in the back of your brain as this is all going to become useful shortly. For now, just remember how function declarations and expressions are evaluated, and how names are handled.

BE *the* Browser

Below, you'll find JavaScript code. Your job is to play like you're the browser evaluating the code. In the space to the right, record each function as it gets created. Remember to make two passes over the code: the pass that processes declarations, and the second pass that handles expressions.

Write, in order, the names of the functions as they are created. If a function is created with a function expression put the name of the variable it is assigned to. We've done the first one for you.

```javascript
var midi = true;
var type = "piano";
var midiInterface;

function play(sequence) {
    // code here
}
var pause = function() {
    stop();
}
function stop() {
    // code here
}


function createMidi() {
    // code here
}


if (midi) {
    midiInterface = function(type) {
        // code here
    };
}
```

play

How functions are values too

Sure, we all think of functions as things we invoke, but you can think of functions as *values* too. That value is actually a reference to the function, and as you've seen, whether you define a function with a function declaration or a function expression, you get a reference to that function.

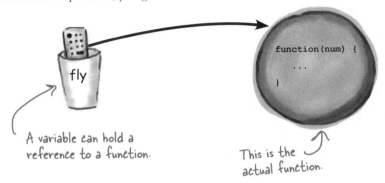

A variable can hold a reference to a function.

This is the actual function.

One of the most straightforward things we can do with functions is assign them to variables. Like this:

Our two functions again. Remember quack is defined with a function declaration, and fly with a function expression. Both result in function references, which are stored in the variables quack and fly, respectively.

```javascript
function quack(num) {
    for (var i = 0; i < num; i++) {
        console.log("Quack!");
    }
}
var fly = function(num) {
    for (var i = 0; i < num; i++) {
        console.log("Flying!");
    }
}
```

The function declaration takes care of assigning the reference to a variable with the name you supply, in this case quack.

When you have a function expression, you need to assign the resulting reference to a variable yourself. Here we're storing the reference in the fly variable.

```javascript
var superFly = fly;
superFly(2);
```

After we assign the value in fly to superFly, superFly holds the function reference, so by adding some parentheses and an argument we can invoke it!

```javascript
var superQuack = quack;
superQuack(3);
```

And even though quack was created by a function declaration, the value in quack is a function reference too, so we can assign it to the variable superQuack and invoke it.

In other words, references are references, no matter how you create them (that is, with a declaration or an expression)!

```
JavaScript console

Flying!
Flying!
Quack!
Quack!
Quack!
```

Sharpen your pencil

To get the idea of functions as values into your brain, let's play a little game of chance. Try the shell game. Will you win or lose? Give it a try and find out.

```
var winner = function() { alert("WINNER!") };
var loser = function() { alert("LOSER!") };
// let's test as a warm up
winner();
// let's assign to other variables for practice
var a = winner;
var b = loser;
var c = loser;
a();
b();
// now let's try your luck with a shell game
c = a;
a = b;
b = c;
c = a;
a = c;
a = b;
b = c;
a();
```

Remember, these variables hold references to the winner and loser functions. We can assign and reassign these references to other variables, just like with any value.

Remember, at any time, we can invoke a reference to a function.

Execute the code (by hand!) and figure out if you won or lost.

Start thinking about functions as values, just like numbers, strings, booleans or objects. The thing that really makes a function value different from these other values is that we can <u>invoke it.</u>

Function Exposed

This week's interview:
Understanding Function

Head First: Function, we're so happy to finally have you back on this show. You're quite a mystery and our readers are dying to know more.

Function: It's true, I'm deep.

Head First: Let's start with this idea that you can be created with a declaration, or created with an expression. Why two ways of defining you? Wouldn't one be enough?

Function: Well, remember, these two ways of defining a function do two slightly different things.

Head First: But the result is the same: a function, right?

Function: Yes, but look at it this way. A function declaration is doing a little bit of work behind the scenes for you: it's creating the function, and then also creating a variable to store the function reference in. A function expression creates the function, which results in a reference and it's up to you to do something with it.

Head First: But don't we always just store the reference we get from a function expression in a variable anyway?

Function: Definitely not. In fact, we usually don't. Remember a function reference is a value. Think of the kinds of things you can do with other kinds of values, like an object reference for instance. I can do all those things too.

Head First: But how can you possibly do everything those other values can do? I declare a function, and I call it. That's about as much as any language allows, right?

Function: Wrong. You need to start thinking of a function as a value, just like objects or the primitive types. Once you get a hold of a function you can do all kinds of things with it. But there is one important difference between a function and other kinds of values, and that is what really makes me what I am: a function can be invoked, to execute the code in its body.

Head First: That sounds very impressive and powerful, but I'd have no idea what to do with you other than define and call you.

Function: This is where we separate the six figure coders from the scripters. When you can treat a function like any other value, all kinds of interesting programming constructs become possible.

Head First: Can you give us just one example?

Function: Sure. Say you want to write a function that can sort *anything*. No problem. All you need is a function that takes two things: the collection of items you need to sort, and *another function* that knows how to compare any two items in your collection. Using JavaScript you can easily create code like that. You write one sort function for every kind of collection, and then just tell that function how to compare items by passing it a function that knows how to do the comparison.

Head First: Err…

Function: Like I said, this is where we separate the six figure coders from the scripters. Again, we're *passing a function* that knows how to do the comparison *to the other function*. In other words we're treating the function like a value by passing it to a function *as a value*.

Head First: And what does that get us other than confused?

Function: It gets you less code, less hard work, more reliability, better flexibility, better maintainability, a higher salary.

Head First: That all sounds good, but I'm still not sure how to get there.

Function: Getting there takes a little bit of work. This is definitely an area where your brain has to expand a bit.

Head First: Well, function, my head is expanding so much it's about to explode, so I'm going to go lie down.

Function: Any time. Thanks for having me!

Did we mention functions have First Class status in JavaScript?

If you're coming to JavaScript from a more traditional programming language you might expect functions to be... well, just functions. You can declare them and call them, but when you're not doing either of those things they just sit around doing nothing.

Now you know that functions in JavaScript are values—values that can be assigned to variables. And you know that with values of other types, like numbers, booleans, strings and even objects, we can do all sorts of things with those values, like pass them to functions, return them from functions or even store them in objects or arrays.

Computer scientists actually have a term for these kinds of values: they're called *first class values*. Here's what you can do with a first class value:

- ❏ Assign the value to a variable (or store it in a data structure like an array or object).

- ❏ Pass the value to a function.

- ❏ Return the value from a function.

Guess what? We can do all these things with functions too. In fact, we can do *everything* with a function that we can do with other values in JavaScript. So consider functions first class values in JavaScript, along with all the values of the types you already know: numbers, strings, booleans and objects.

Here's a more formal definition of first class:

> **First class**: a value that can be treated like any other value in a programming language, including the ability to be assigned to a variable, passed as an argument, and returned from a function.

We're going to see that JavaScript functions easily qualify as first class values—in fact, let's spend a little time working through just what it means for a function to be first class in each of these cases. Here's a little advice first: stop thinking about functions as something special and different from other values in JavaScript. There is great power in treating a function like a value. Our goal in the rest of the chapter is to show you why.

We always thought VIP-access-to-all-areas was a better name, but they didn't listen to us, so we'll stick with first class.

Flying First Class

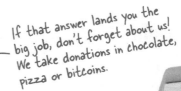

If that answer lands you the big job, don't forget about us! We take donations in chocolate, pizza or bitcoins.

The next time you're in a job interview and you get asked "What makes JavaScript functions first class?" you're going to pass with flying colors. But before you start celebrating your new career, remember that, so far, all your understanding of first class functions is *book knowledge*. Sure, you can recite the definition of what you can do with first class functions:

☑ You can assign functions to variables. ← You've seen this already.

❑ You can pass functions to functions. ← We're going to work on this now.

❑ You can return functions from functions. ← And we'll cover this in just a bit...

But can you use those techniques in your code, or know when it would help you to do so? No worries; we're going to deal with that now by learning how to pass functions to functions. We're going to start simple, and take it from there. In fact, we're going to start with just a simple data structure that represents passengers on an airline flight:

Here's the data structure representing the passengers:

All passengers are kept in an array.

And here we have four passengers (feel free to expand this list with friends and family).

```
var passengers = [   { name: "Jane Doloop", paid: true },
                     { name: "Dr. Evel", paid: true },
                     { name: "Sue Property", paid: false },
                     { name: "John Funcall", paid: true } ];
```

And each passenger is represented by an object with a name and a paid property.

The name is a simple text string.

And paid is a boolean that represents whether or not the passenger has paid for the flight.

Here our goal: write some code that looks at the passenger list and makes sure that certain conditions are met before the flight is allowed to take off. For instance, let's make sure there are no passengers on a no-fly list. And let's make sure everyone has paid for the flight. We might even want to create a list of everyone who is on the flight.

> ⚛ **BRAIN POWER**
>
> Think about how you'd write code to perform these three tasks (no-fly list, paid customers and a list of passengers)?

Writing code to process and check passengers

Now typically you'd write a function for each of these conditions: one to check the no-fly-list, one to check that every passenger has paid, and one to print out all the passengers. But if we wrote that code and stepped back to look at it, we'd find that all these functions look roughly the same, like this:

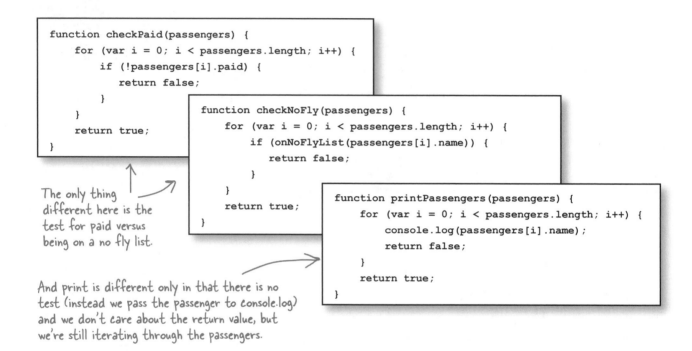

```
function checkPaid(passengers) {
    for (var i = 0; i < passengers.length; i++) {
        if (!passengers[i].paid) {
            return false;
        }
    }
    return true;
}
```

```
function checkNoFly(passengers) {
    for (var i = 0; i < passengers.length; i++) {
        if (onNoFlyList(passengers[i].name)) {
            return false;
        }
    }
    return true;
}
```

```
function printPassengers(passengers) {
    for (var i = 0; i < passengers.length; i++) {
        console.log(passengers[i].name);
        return false;
    }
    return true;
}
```

The only thing different here is the test for paid versus being on a no fly list.

And print is different only in that there is no test (instead we pass the passenger to console.log) and we don't care about the return value, but we're still iterating through the passengers.

That's a lot of duplicated code: all these functions iterate through the passengers doing something with each passenger. And what if there are additional checks needed in the future? Say, checking to make sure laptops are powered down, checking to see if a passenger has an upgrade, checking to see if a passenger has a medical issue, and so on. That's a lot of redundant code.

Even worse, what if the data structure holding the passengers changes from a simple array of objects to something else? Then you might have to open every one of these functions and rewrite it. Not good.

We can solve this little problem with first class functions. Here's how: we're going to write one function that knows how to iterate through the passengers, and pass to that function a second function that knows how to do the check we need (that is, to see if a name is on a no-fly list, to check whether or not a passenger has paid, and so on).

Exercise

Let's do a little pre-work on this by first writing a function that takes a passenger as an argument and checks to see if that passenger's name is on the no-fly-list. Return true if it is and false otherwise. Write another function that takes a passenger and checks to see if the passenger hasn't paid. Return true if the passenger has not paid, and false otherwise. We've started the code for you below; you just need to finish it. You'll find our solution on the next page, but don't peek!

```
function checkNoFlyList(passenger) {



}



function checkNotPaid(passenger) {
```

Hint: assume your no-fly list consists of one individual: Dr. Evel.

```
}
```

Sharpen your pencil

Let's get your brain warmed up for passing your first function to another function. Evaluate the code below (in your head) and see what you come up with. Make sure you check your answer before moving on.

```
function sayIt(translator) {
    var phrase = translator("Hello");
    alert(phrase);
}

function hawaiianTranslator(word) {
    if (word === "Hello") return "Aloha";
    if (word === "Goodbye") return "Aloha";
}

sayIt(hawaiianTranslator);
```

Iterating through the passengers

We need a function that takes the passengers and another function that knows how to test a single passenger for some condition, like being on the no-fly list. Here's how we do that:

The function processPassengers has two parameters. The first is an array of passengers.

And the second is a function that knows how to look for some condition in the passengers.

```javascript
function processPassengers(passengers, testFunction) {
    for (var i = 0; i < passengers.length; i++) {
        if (testFunction(passengers[i])) {
            return false;
        }
    }
    return true;
}
```

We iterate through all the passengers, one at a time.

And then we call the function on each passenger.

If the result of the function is true, then we return false. In other words, if the passenger failed the test (e.g. they haven't paid, or they are on the no-fly list), then we don't want the plane to take off!

Otherwise, if we get here then all passengers passed the test and we return true.

Now all we need are some functions that can test passengers (luckily you wrote these in the previous Sharpen Your Pencil exercise). Here they are:

Pay attention: this is one passenger (an object) not the array of passengers (an array of objects).

```javascript
function checkNoFlyList(passenger) {
    return (passenger.name === "Dr. Evel");
}
```

Here's the function to check to see if a passenger is on the no-fly list. Our no-fly list is simple: everyone except Dr. Evel can fly. We return true if the passenger is Dr. Evel; otherwise, we return false (that is, the passenger is <u>not</u> on the no-fly list).

```javascript
function checkNotPaid(passenger) {
    return (!passenger.paid);
}
```

And here's the function to check to see if a passenger has paid. All we do is check the paid property of the passenger. If they have <u>not</u> paid, then we return true.

Passing a function to a function

Okay, we've got a function that's ready to accept a function as an argument (processPassengers), and we've got two functions that are ready to be passed as arguments to processPassengers (checkNoFlyList and checkNotPaid).

It's time to put this all together. Drum roll please...

Passing a function to a function is easy. We just use the name of the function as the argument.

Here, we're passing the checkNoFlyList function. So processPassengers will check each passenger to see if they are on the no-fly list.

```javascript
var allCanFly = processPassengers(passengers, checkNoFlyList);
if (!allCanFly) {
    console.log("The plane can't take off: we have a passenger on the no-fly-list.");
}
```

If any of the passengers are on the no-fly list, we'll get back false, and we'll see this message in the console.

Here, we're passing the checkNotPaid function. So processPassengers will check each passenger to see if they've paid.

```javascript
var allPaid = processPassengers(passengers, checkNotPaid);
if (!allPaid) {
    console.log("The plane can't take off: not everyone has paid.");
}
```

If any of the passengers haven't paid, we'll get back false, and we'll see this message in the console.

> First class is always better... I'm talking about functions of course...

Test ~~drive~~ flight

To test drive your code, just add this JavaScript to a basic HTML page, and load it into your browser.

```
JavaScript console
The plane can't take off: we have a passenger on
the no-fly-list.
The plane can't take off: not everyone has paid.
```

Well, looks like we won't be taking off after all. We've got problems with our passengers! Good thing we checked...

Exercise

Your turn again: write a function that prints a passenger's name and whether or not they have paid to console.log. Pass your function to processPassengers to test it. We've started the code for you below; you just need to finish it up. Check your answer at the end of the chapter before you go on.

```
function printPassenger(passenger) {
```

← Write your code here.

```
    }

processPassengers(passengers, printPassenger);
```

← Your code should print out the list of passengers when you pass the function to processPassengers.

there are no
Dumb Questions

Q: Couldn't we just put all this code into processPassengers? We could just put all the checks we need into one iteration, so each time through we do all the checks and print the list. Wouldn't that be more efficient?

A: If your code is short and simple, yes, that might be a reasonable approach. However, what we're really after is flexibility. What if, in the future, you are constantly adding new checks (has everyone put their laptop away?) or requirements for your existing functions change? Or the underlying data structure for passengers changes? In these cases, the design we used allows you to make changes or additions in a way that reduces overall complexity and that is less likely to introduce bugs into your code.

Q: What exactly are we passing when we pass a function to a function?

A: We're passing a reference to the function. Think of that reference like a pointer that points to an internal representation of the function itself. The reference itself can be held in a variable and reassigned to other variables or passed as an argument to a function. And placing parentheses after a function reference causes the function to be invoked.

Sharpen your pencil

Below we've created a function and assigned it to the variable fun.

```
function fun(echo) {
    console.log(echo);
};
```

```
function fun(echo) {
    console.log(echo);
}
```

fun

Work your way through this code and write the resulting output on this page.
Do this with your brain before you attempt it with your computer.

```
fun("hello");
```
_____

```
function boo(aFunction) {
    aFunction("boo");
}
```

```
boo(fun);
```
_____

```
console.log(fun);
```
_____

```
fun(boo);
```
_____

```
var moreFun = fun;
```

```
moreFun("hello again");
```
_____

Extra credit! (A preview of what's coming up...)
```
function echoMaker() {
    return fun;
}

var bigFun = echoMaker();
bigFun("Is there an echo?");
```
_____

Super important: check and understand the answers before moving on!

Returning functions from functions

At this point we've exercised two of our first class requirements, assigning functions to variables and passing functions to functions, but we haven't yet seen an example of returning a function from a function.

☑ You can assign functions to variables.

☑ You can pass functions to functions. *We're doing this now.*

❏ You can return functions from functions. ←

Let's extend the airline example a bit and explore why and where we might want to return a function from a function. To do that, we'll add another property to each of our passengers, the ticket property, which is set to "coach" or "firstclass" depending on the type of ticket the passenger has purchased:

```
var passengers = [   { name: "Jane Doloop", paid: true, ticket: "coach" },
                     { name: "Dr. Evel", paid: true, ticket: "firstclass" },
                     { name: "Sue Property", paid: false, ticket: "firstclass" },
                     { name: "John Funcall", paid: true, ticket: "coach" } ];
```

With that addition, we'll write some code that handles the various things a flight attendant needs to do:

> *What I'm offering depends on your class of ticket. First class gets wine or a cocktail; coach gets cola or water.*

Here are all the things the flight attendant needs to do to serve each passenger.

```
function serveCustomer(passenger) {
    // get drink order
    // get dinner order
    // pick up trash
}
```

← *Let's start by implementing the drink order.*

Now as you might know, service in first class tends to be a little different from the service in coach. In first class you're able to order a cocktail or wine, while in coach you're more likely to be offered a cola or water.

← *At least that's how it looks in the movies...*

Writing the flight attendant drink order code

Now your first attempt might look like this:

```javascript
function serveCustomer(passenger) {

    if (passenger.ticket === "firstclass") {

        alert("Would you like a cocktail or wine?");

    } else {

        alert("Your choice is cola or water.");

    }

    // get dinner order
    // pick up trash

}
```

If the passenger's ticket is a first class ticket then we issue an alert to ask if they'd like a cocktail or a wine.

If they have a coach ticket, then ask if they want a cola or water.

Not bad. For simple code this works well: we're taking the passenger's ticket and then displaying an alert based on the type of ticket they purchased. But let's think through some potential downsides of this code. Sure, the code to take a drink order is simple, but what happens to the `serveCustomer` function if the problem becomes more complex. For instance, we might start serving three classes of passengers (firstclass, business and coach. And what about premium economy, that's four!). What happens if the drink offerings get more complex? Or what if the choice of drinks is based on the location of the originating or destination airport?

For instance they typically only serve Maitais to first class on trips to Hawaii (or so we've been told).

If we have to deal with these complexities then `serveCustomer` is quickly going to become a large function that is a lot more about managing drinks than serving customers, and when we design functions, a good rule of thumb is to have them do only one thing, but do it really well.

BRAIN POWER

Re-read all the potential issues listed in the last two paragraphs on this page. Then, think about what code design would allow us to keep serveCustomer focused, yet also allow for expansion of our drink-serving capability in the future.

The flight attendant drink order code: a different approach

Our first pass wasn't bad, but as you can see this code could be problematic over time as the drink serving code gets more complex. Let's rework the code a little, as there's another way we can approach this by placing the logic for the drink orders in a separate function. Doing so allows us to hide away all that logic in one place, and it also gives us a well-defined place to go if we need to update the drink order code:

Here we're creating a new function createDrinkOrder, which is passed a passenger.

```
function createDrinkOrder(passenger) {
    if (passenger.ticket === "firstclass") {
        alert("Would you like a cocktail or wine?");
    } else {
        alert("Your choice is cola or water.");
    }
}
```

And we'll place all the logic for the drink order here.

Now this code is no longer polluting the serveCustomer function with a lot of drink order logic.

Now we can revisit the serveCustomer function and remove all the drink order logic, replacing it with a call to this new function.

```
function serveCustomer(passenger) {
    if (passenger.ticket === "firstclass") {
        alert("Would you like a cocktail or wine?");
    } else {
        alert("Your choice is cola or water.");
    }
    createDrinkOrder(passenger);

    // get dinner order
    // pick up trash
}
```

We're removing the logic from serveCustomer...

And we'll replace the original, inline logic with a call to createDrinkOrder.

The createDrinkOrder function is passed the passenger that was passed into serveCustomer.

That's definitely going to be more readable with a single function call replacing all the inline drink order logic. It's also conveniently put all the drink order code in one, easy-to-find place. But, before we give this code a test drive, hold on, we've just heard about another issue...

Wait, we need more drinks!

Stop the presses, we've just heard that one drink order is not enough on a flight. In fact, the flight attendants say a typical flight looks more like this:

Come on guys, a single drink? What is this? Cheap-o-Airlines?

```
function serveCustomer(passenger) {
    createDrinkOrder(passenger);
    // get dinner order
    createDrinkOrder(passenger);
    createDrinkOrder(passenger);
    // show movie
    createDrinkOrder(passenger);
    // pick up trash
}
```

We've updated the code to reflect the fact we're calling createDrinkOrder a lot during the flight.

Now, on the one hand we designed our code well, because adding additional calls to `createDrinkOrder` works just fine. But, on the other hand, we're unnecessarily recomputing what kind of passenger we're serving in `createDrinkOrder` every time we take an order.

"But it's only a few lines of code." you say? Sure, but this is a simple example in a book. What if in the real world you had to check the ticket type by communicating with a web service from a mobile device? That gets time consuming and expensive.

Don't worry though, because a first class function just rode in on a white horse to save us. You see, by making use of the capability to return functions from functions we can fix this problem.

Sharpen your pencil

What do you think this code does? Can you come up with some examples of how to use it?

```
function addN(n) {
    var adder = function(x) {
                    return n + x;
                };
    return adder;
}
```

↑ Answer here.

Taking orders with first class functions

Now it's time to wrap your head around how a first class function can help this situation. Here's the plan: rather than calling `createDrinkOrder` multiple times per passenger, we're instead going to call it once, and have it hand us back a function that knows how to do a drink order for that passenger. Then, when we need to take a drink order, we just call that function.

Let's start by redefining `createDrinkOrder`. Now when we call it, it will package up the code to take a drink order into a function and return the function for us to use when we need it.

Here's the new createDrinkOrder. It's going to return a function that knows how to take a drink order.

First, create a variable to hold the function we want to return.

Now, we execute the conditional code to check the passenger's ticket type only once.

```
function createDrinkOrder(passenger) {
    var orderFunction;

    if (passenger.ticket === "firstclass") {
        orderFunction = function() {
            alert("Would you like a cocktail or wine?");
        };
    } else {
        orderFunction = function() {
            alert("Your choice is cola or water.");
        };
    }
    return orderFunction;
}
```

If the passenger is first class, we create a function that knows how to take a first class order.

Otherwise create a function to take an coach class order.

`return orderFunction;` ← And return the function.

Now let's rework `serveCustomer`. We'll first call `createDrinkOrder` to get a function that knows how to take the passenger's order. Then, we'll use that same function over and over to take a drink order from the passenger.

getDrinkOrder now returns a function, which we store in the getDrinkOrderFunction variable.

```
function serveCustomer(passenger) {
    var getDrinkOrderFunction = createDrinkOrder(passenger);
    getDrinkOrderFunction();
    // get dinner order
    getDrinkOrderFunction();
    getDrinkOrderFunction();
    // show movie
    getDrinkOrderFunction();
    // pick up trash
}
```

We use the function we get back from createDrinkOrder whenever we need to get a drink order for this passenger.

Test ~~drive~~ flight

Let's test the new code. To do that we need to write a quick function to iterate over all the passengers and call `serveCustomer` for each passenger. Once you've added the code to your file, load it in the browser and take some orders.

```
function servePassengers(passengers) {
    for (var i = 0; i < passengers.length; i++) {
        serveCustomer(passengers[i]);
    }
}

servePassengers(passengers);
```

All we're doing here is iterating over the passengers in the passengers array, and calling serveCustomer on each passenger.

And of course we need to call servePassengers to get it all going. (Be prepared, there are a lot of alerts!)

there are no Dumb Questions

Q: Just to make sure I understand... when we call createDrinkOrder, we get back a function that we have to call again to get the drink order?

A: That's right. We first call createDrinkOrder to get back a function, getDrinkOrderFunction, that knows how to ask a passenger for an order, and then we call that function every time we want to take the order. Notice that getDrinkOrderFunction is a lot simpler than createDrinkOrder: all getDrinkOrderFunction does is alert, asking for the passenger's order.

Q: So how does getDrinkOrderFunction know which alert to show?

A: Because we created it specifically for the passenger based on their ticket. Look back at createDrinkOrder again. The

function we're returning corresponds to the passenger's ticket type: if the passenger is in first class, then getDrinkOrderFunction is created to show an alert asking for a first class order. But if the passenger is in coach, then getDrinkOrderFunction is created to show an alert asking for a coach order. By returning the correct kind of function for that specific passenger's ticket type, the ordering function is simple, fast, and easy to call each time we need to take an order.

Q: This code serves one passenger a drink, shows the movie, etc. Don't flight attendants usually serve a drink to all the passengers and show the movie to all passengers and so on?

A: See we were testing you! You passed. You're exactly right; this code applies the entire serveCustomer function to a single passenger at a time. That's not really how it works in the real world. But, this is meant to be a simple example to demonstrate a

complex topic (returning functions), and it's not perfect. But now that you've *pointed out our mistake*... students, take out a sheet of paper and:

⚛ BRAIN POWER

How would you rework the code to serve drinks, dinner and a movie to all the passengers, and do it without endlessly recomputing their order based on their ticket class? Would you use first class functions?

Exercise

Your job is to add a third class of service to our code. Add "premium economy" class ("premium" for short). Premium economy gets wine in addition to cola or water. Also, implement getDinnerOrderFunction with the following menu:

First class: chicken or pasta

Premium economy: snack box or cheese plate

Coach: peanuts or pretzels

Check your answer at the end of the chapter! And don't forget to test your code.

Make sure you use first class functions to implement this!

Webville Cola

Webville Cola needs a little help managing the code for
their product line. To give them a hand, let's take a look at
the data structure they use to hold the sodas they produce:

Looks like they're storing their products as an array
of objects. Each object is a product.

```
var products = [ { name: "Grapefruit", calories: 170, color: "red", sold: 8200 },
                 { name: "Orange", calories: 160, color: "orange", sold: 12101 },
                 { name: "Cola", calories: 210, color: "caramel", sold: 25412 },
                 { name: "Diet Cola", calories: 0, color: "caramel", sold: 43922 },
                 { name: "Lemon", calories: 200, color: "clear", sold: 14983 },
                 { name: "Raspberry", calories: 180, color: "pink", sold: 9427 },
                 { name: "Root Beer", calories: 200, color: "caramel", sold: 9909 },
                 { name: "Water", calories: 0, color: "clear", sold: 62123 }
];
```

In each product they're storing a name, number of
calories, color and number of bottles sold per month.

> We really need some help sorting these
> products. We need to sort them by every possible
> property: name, calories, color, sales numbers. Of course
> we want to get this done as efficiently as we can, and also
> keep it flexible so we can sort in lots of different ways.

Webville Cola's analytics guy

Jim

Frank   Joe

Frank: Hey guys, I got a call from Webville Cola and they need help with their product data. They want to be able to sort their products by any property, like name, bottles sold, soda color, calories per bottle, and so on, but they want it flexible in case they add more properties in the future.

Joe: How are they storing this data?

Frank: Oh, each soda is an object in an array, with properties for name, number sold, calories…

Joe: Got it.

Frank: My first thought was just to search for a simple sort algorithm and implement it. Webville Cola doesn't have many products so it just needs to be simple.

Jim: Oh, I've got a simpler way than that, but it requires you use your knowledge of first class functions.

Frank: I like hearing simple! But how do first class functions fit in? That sounds complicated to me.

Jim: Not at all. It's as easy as writing a function that knows how to compare two values, and then passing that to another function that does the real sorting for you.

Joe: How does the function we're writing work exactly?

Jim: Well, instead of handling the entire sort, all you need to do is write a function that knows how to compare two values. Say you want to sort by a product property like the number of bottles sold. You set up a function like this:

```
function compareSold(product1, product2) {

    // code to compare here

}
```

This function needs to take two products and then compare them.

We can fill in the details of the code in a minute, but for now, the key is that once you have this function you just pass it to a sort function and that sort function does the work for you—it just needs you to help it know how to compare things.

Frank: Wait, where is this sort function?

Jim: It's actually a method that you can call on any array. So you can call the `sort` method on the `products` array and pass it this compare function we're going to write. And, when `sort` is done, the `products` array will be sorted by whatever criteria `compareSold` used to sort the values.

Joe: So if I'm sorting how many bottles are sold, those are numbers, so the `compareSold` function just needs to determine which value is less or greater?

Jim: Right. Let's take a closer look at how the array sort works…

How the array sort method works

JavaScript arrays provide a `sort` method that, given a function that knows how to compare two items in the array, sorts the array for you. Here's the big picture of how this works and how your comparison function fits in: sort algorithms are well known and widely implemented, and the great thing about them is that sorting code can be reused for just about any set of items. But there's one catch: to know how to sort a specific set of items, the sort code needs to know how those items compare. Think about sorting a set of numbers versus sorting a list of names versus sorting a set of objects. The way we compare values depends on the type of the items: for numbers we use <, > and == , for strings we compare them alphabetically (in JavaScript, you can do that with <, > and ==) and for objects we'd have some custom way of comparing them based on their properties.

Let's look at a simple example before we move on to Webville Cola's products array. We'll use a simple array of numbers and use the `sort` method to put them in ascending order. Here's the array:

```
var numbersArray = [60, 50, 62, 58, 54, 54];
```

Next we need to write our own function that knows how to compare two values in the array. Now, this is an array of numbers, so our function will need to compare two numbers at a time. Assume we're going to sort the numbers in ascending order; for that the `sort` method expects us to return something greater than 0 if the first number is greater than the second, 0 if they are equal, and something less than 0 if the first number is less than the second. Like this:

This array is made of numbers, so we're going to be comparing two numbers at a time.

```
function compareNumbers(num1, num2) {
    if (num1 > num2) {
        return 1;
    } else if (num1 === num2) {
        return 0;
    } else {
        return -1;
    }
}
```

We first check to see if num1 is greater than num2. If it is, we return 1.

If they are equal then we return 0.

And finally, if num1 is less than num2, we return -1.

Serious Tip

JavaScript arrays have many useful methods you can use to manipulate arrays in various ways. A great reference on all these methods and how to use them is *JavaScript: The Definitive Guide* by David Flanagan (O'Reilly).

Sharpen your pencil

You know that the comparison function we pass to sort needs to return a number greater than 0, equal to 0, or less than 0 depending on the two items we're comparing: if the first item is greater than second, we return a value greater than 0; if first item is equal to the second, we return 0; and if the first item is less than the second, we return a value less than 0.

Can you use this knowledge with the fact that we're comparing two numbers in compareNumbers to rewrite compareNumbers using much less code?

Check your answer at the end of the chapter before you go on.

Putting it all together

Now that we've written a compare function, all we need to do is call the `sort` method on `numbersArray`, and pass it the function. Here's how we do that:

```
var numbersArray = [60, 50, 62, 58, 54, 54];

numbersArray.sort(compareNumbers);

console.log(numbersArray);
```

We call the sort method on the array, passing it the compareNumbers function.

And when sort is complete the array is sorted in ascending order, and we display that in the console as a sanity check.

Note that the sort method is destructive, in that it changes the array, rather than returning a new array that is sorted.

Here's the array sorted in ascending order.

```
JavaScript console
[50, 54, 54, 58, 60, 62]
```

Exercise

The sort method has sorted numbersArray in ascending order because when we return the values 1, 0 and -1, we're telling the sort method:

  1: place the first item after the second item

  0: the items are equivalent, you can leave them in place

  -1: place the first item before the second item.

Changing your code to sort in descending order is a matter of inverting this logic so that 1 means place the second item after the first item, and -1 means place the second item before the first item (0 stays the same). Write a new compare function for descending order:

```
function compareNumbersDesc(num1, num2) {
    if (_____ > _____) {
        return 1;
    } else if (num1 === num2) {
        return 0;
    } else {
        return -1;
    }
}
```

Meanwhile back at Webville Cola

It's time to help out Webville Cola with your new knowledge of array sorting.
Of course all we really need to do is write a comparison function for them,
but before we do that let's quickly review the `products` array again:

But we don't have to tell them that.

```
var products = [ { name: "Grapefruit", calories: 170, color: "red", sold: 8200 },
                 { name: "Orange", calories: 160, color: "orange", sold: 12101 },
                 { name: "Cola", calories: 210, color: "caramel", sold: 25412 },
                 { name: "Diet Cola", calories: 0, color: "caramel", sold: 43922 },
                 { name: "Lemon", calories: 200, color: "clear", sold: 14983 },
                 { name: "Raspberry", calories: 180, color: "pink", sold: 9427 },
                 { name: "Root Beer", calories: 200, color: "caramel", sold: 9909 },
                 { name: "Water", calories: 0, color: "clear", sold: 62123 }
               ];
```

Remember, each item in the products array is an object. We don't want to compare the objects to one another, we want to compare specific properties, like sold, in the objects.

So what are we going to sort first? Let's start with sorting by the number of bottles sold,
in ascending order. To do this we'll need to compare the `sold` property of each object.
Now one thing you should take note of is, because this is an array of product objects,
the compare function is going to be passed two objects, not two numbers:

```
function compareSold(colaA, colaB) {
    if (colaA.sold > colaB.sold) {
        return 1;
    } else if (colaA.sold === colaB.sold) {
        return 0;
    } else {
        return -1;
    }
}
```

compareSold takes two cola product objects, and compares the sold property of colaA to the sold property of colaB.

This function will make the sort method sort the colas by number of bottles sold in <u>ascending</u> order.

Feel free to simplify this code like you did in the earlier exercise if you want!

And of course, to use the `compareSold` function to sort the `products` array, we
simply call the `products` array's `sort` method:

```
products.sort(compareSold);
```

Remember that the sort method can be used for any kind of array (numbers, strings, objects), and for any kind of sort (ascending or descending). By passing in a compare function, we get flexibility and code reuse!

Take sorting for a test drive

Time to test the first Webville Cola code. You'll find all the code from the last few pages consolidated below along with some extras to test this out properly. So, just create a simple HTML page with this code ("cola.html") and give it some QA:

```javascript
var products = [ { name: "Grapefruit", calories: 170, color: "red", sold: 8200 },
                 { name: "Orange", calories: 160, color: "orange", sold: 12101 },
                 { name: "Cola", calories: 210, color: "caramel", sold: 25412 },
                 { name: "Diet Cola", calories: 0, color: "caramel", sold: 43922 },
                 { name: "Lemon", calories: 200, color: "clear", sold: 14983 },
                 { name: "Raspberry", calories: 180, color: "pink", sold: 9427 },
                 { name: "Root Beer", calories: 200, color: "caramel", sold: 9909 },
                 { name: "Water", calories: 0, color: "clear", sold: 62123 }
               ];
```

```javascript
function compareSold(colaA, colaB) {
    if (colaA.sold > colaB.sold) {
        return 1;
    } else if (colaA.sold === colaB.sold) {
        return 0;
    } else {
        return -1;
    }
}
```

Here's the compare function we'll pass to sort...

```javascript
function printProducts(products) {
    for (var i = 0; i < products.length; i++) {
        console.log("Name: " + products[i].name +
                    ", Calories: " + products[i].calories +
                    ", Color: " + products[i].color +
                    ", Sold: " + products[i].sold);
    }
}
```

... and here's a new function we wrote to print the products so they look nice in the console. (If you just write console.log(products), you can see the output, but it doesn't look very good).

So first we sort the products, using compareSold...

```javascript
products.sort(compareSold);
printProducts(products);
```

... and then print the results.

```
JavaScript console
Name: Grapefruit, Calories: 170, Color: red, Sold: 8200
Name: Raspberry, Calories: 180, Color: pink, Sold: 9427
Name: Root Beer, Calories: 200, Color: caramel, Sold: 9909
Name: Orange, Calories: 160, Color: orange, Sold: 12101
Name: Lemon, Calories: 200, Color: clear, Sold: 14983
Name: Cola, Calories: 210, Color: caramel, Sold: 25412
Name: Diet Cola, Calories: 0, Color: caramel, Sold: 43922
Name: Water, Calories: 0, Color: clear, Sold: 62123
```

Here's our output running the code using the compareSold sort function. Notice the products are in order by the number of bottles sold.

Exercise

Now that we have a way to sort colas by the sold property, it's time to write compare functions for each of the other properties in the product object: name, calories, and color. Check the output you see in the console carefully; make sure for each kind of sort, the products are sorted correctly. Check the answer at the end of the chapter.

Write your solutions for the remaining three sort functions below.

```
function compareName(colaA, colaB) {



}
```

← Hint: you can use <, > and == to sort alphabetically too!

```
function compareCalories(colaA, colaB) {




}
```

```
function compareColor(colaA, colaB) {



}
```

You guys nailed it!

```
products.sort(compareName);
console.log("Products sorted by name:");
printProducts(products);

products.sort(compareCalories);
console.log("Products sorted by calories:");
printProducts(products);

products.sort(compareColor);
console.log("Products sorted by color:");
printProducts(products);
```

← For each new compare function, we call sort, and display the results in the console.

BULLET POINTS

- There are two ways to define a function: with a **function declaration** and with a **function expression**.

- A **function reference** is a value that refers to a function.

- Function declarations are handled before your code is evaluated.

- Function expressions are evaluated at runtime with the rest of your code.

- When the browser evaluates a function declaration, it creates a function as well as a variable with the same name as the function, and stores the function reference in the variable.

- When the browser evaluates a function expression, it creates a function, and it's up to you what to do with the function reference.

- **First class** values can be assigned to variables, included in data structures, passed to functions, or returned from functions.

- A function reference is a first class value.

- The array **sort** method takes a function that knows how to compare two values in an array.

- The function you pass to the sort method should return one of these values: a number greater than 0, 0, or a number less than 0.

Exercise Solutions

Sharpen your pencil Solution

What deductions can you make about function declarations and function expressions given how the browser treats the quack and fly code? Check each statement that applies. Check your answer at the end of the chapter before you go on.

☑ Function declarations are evaluated before the rest of the code is evaluated.

☑ Function expressions get evaluated later, with the rest of the code.

☑ A function declaration doesn't return a reference to a function; rather it creates a variable with the name of the function and assigns the new function to it.

☑ A function expression returns a reference to the new function created by the expression.

☑ The process of invoking a function created by a declaration is exactly the same for one created with an expression.

☑ You can hold function references in variables.

☑ Function declarations are statements; function expressions are used in statements.

❑ Function declarations are the tried and true way to create functions.

❑ You always want to use function declarations because they get evaluated earlier.

Not necessarily!

BE the Browser Solution

Below, you'll find JavaScript code. Your job is to play like you're the
browser evaluating the code. In the space to the right, record each
function as it gets created. Remember to make two passes over
the code: the pass that processes declarations, and the second
pass that handles expressions.

Write, in order, the names of the functions
as they are created. If a function is created
with a function expression put the name of
the variable it is assigned to. We've done the
first one for you.

```
var midi = true;
var type = "piano";
var midiInterface;

function play(sequence) {
    // code here
}
var pause = function() {
    stop();
}
function stop() {
    // code here
}


function createMidi() {
    // code here
}


if (midi) {
    midiInterface = function(type) {
        // code here
    };
}
```

play
stop
createMidi
pause
midiInterface

Sharpen your pencil
Solution

To get the idea of functions as values into your brain, let's play
a little game of chance. Try the shell game. Did you win or lose?
Give it a try and find out. Here's our solution.

```
var winner = function() { alert("WINNER!") };
var loser = function() { alert("LOSER!") };
// let's test as a warm up
winner();
// let's assign to other variables for practice
var a = winner;
var b = loser;
var c = loser;
a();
b();
// now let's try your luck with a shell game
c = a;
a = b;
b = c;
c = a;
a = c;
a = b;
b = c;
a();
```

*Remember, these variables hold
references to the winner and loser
functions. We can assign and reassign
these references to other variables,
just like with any value.*

*Remember, at any time, we can
invoke a reference to a function.*

← c is winner
← a is loser
← b is winner
← c is loser
← a is loser
← a is winner
← b is loser
← invoking a...
← winner!!!

The page at localhost says:
WINNER!
OK

Sharpen your pencil
Solution

Let's get your brain warmed up for passing your first function to another function. Evalute the code below (in your head) and see what you come up with. Here's our solution:

```
function sayIt(translator) {
    var phrase = translator("Hello");
    alert(phrase);
}

function hawaiianTranslator(word) {
    if (word == "Hello") return "Aloha";
    if (word == "Goodbye") return "Aloha";
}

sayIt(hawaiianTranslator);
```

We're defining a function that takes a function as an argument, and then calls that function.

We're passing the function hawaiianTranslator to the function sayIt.

> The page at localhost says:
> Aloha
>
> OK

Exercise Solution

Your turn again: write a function that prints a passenger's name and whether or not they have paid to console.log. Pass your function to processPassengers to test it. We've started the code for you below; you just need to finish it up. Here's our solution.

```
function printPassenger(passenger) {
    var message = passenger.name;
    if (passenger.paid === true) {
        message = message + " has paid";
    } else {
        message = message + " has not paid";
    }
    console.log(message);
    return false;
}

processPassengers(passengers, printPassenger);
```

This return value doesn't matter that much because we're ignoring the result from processPassengers in this case.

```
JavaScript console
Jane Doloop has paid
Dr. Evel has paid
Sue Property has not paid
John Funcall has paid
```

Sharpen your pencil
Solution

Below we've created a function and assigned it to the variable fun.

```
function fun(echo) {
    console.log(echo);
};
```

Warning note: your browser may display different values in the console for the fun and boo functions. Try this exercise in a couple of different browsers.

(image: function in jar labeled "fun" with contents:)
```
function fun(echo) {
    console.log(echo);
}
```

Work your way through this code and write the resulting output on this page. Do this with your brain before you attempt it with your computer.

```
fun("hello");
```
hello

```
function boo(aFunction) {
    aFunction("boo");
}
```

```
boo(fun);
```
boo

```
console.log(fun);
```
function fun(echo) { console.log(echo); }

```
fun(boo);
```
function boo(aFunction) { aFunction("boo"); }

```
var moreFun = fun;
```

```
moreFun("hello again");
```
hello again

Extra credit! (A preview of what's coming up...)
```
function echoMaker() {
    return fun;
}

var bigFun = echoMaker();
bigFun("Is there an echo?");
```
Is there an echo?

Super important: check and understand the answers before moving on!

Exercise Solution

Your job is to add a third class of service to our code. Add "premium economy" class ("premium" for short). Premium economy gets wine in addition to cola or water. Also, implement getDinnerOrderFunction with the following menu:

First class: chicken or pasta

Premium economy: snack box or cheese plate

Coach: peanuts or pretzels

Here's our solution.

```
var passengers = [  { name: "Jane Doloop", paid: true, ticket: "coach" },
                    { name: "Dr. Evel", paid: true, ticket: "firstclass" },
                    { name: "Sue Property", paid: false, ticket: "firstclass" },
                    { name: "John Funcall", paid: true, ticket: "premium" } ];

function createDrinkOrder(passenger) {
    var orderFunction;
    if (passenger.ticket === "firstclass") {
        orderFunction = function() {
            alert("Would you like a cocktail or wine?");
        };
    } else if (passenger.ticket === "premium") {
        orderFunction = function() {
            alert("Would you like wine, cola or water?");
        };
    } else {
        orderFunction = function() {
            alert("Your choice is cola or water.");
        };
    }
    return orderFunction;
}
```

We've upgraded John Funcall to premium economy for this flight (so we can test our new code).

Here's the new code to handle the premium economy class. Now we're returning one of three different order functions depending on the ticket type of the passenger.

Notice how handy it is to have all this logic encapsulated in one function that knows how to create the right kind of order function for a customer.

And when we make an order, we don't have to do this logic; we have an order function that is customized for the passenger already!

```
function createDinnerOrder(passenger) {
    var orderFunction;
    if (passenger.ticket === "firstclass") {
        orderFunction = function() {
            alert("Would you like chicken or pasta?");
        };
    } else if (passenger.ticket === "premium") {
        orderFunction = function() {
            alert("Would you like a snack box or cheese plate?");
        };
    } else {
        orderFunction = function() {
            alert("Would you like peanuts or pretzels?");
        };
    }
    return orderFunction;
}
```

We've added a completely new function, createDinnerOrder, to create a dinner ordering function for a passenger.

It works in the same way that createDrinkOrder does: by looking at the passenger ticket type and returning an order function customized for that passenger.

```
function serveCustomer(passenger) {
    var getDrinkOrderFunction = createDrinkOrder(passenger);
    var getDinnerOrderFunction = createDinnerOrder(passenger);

    getDrinkOrderFunction();

    // get dinner order
    getDinnerOrderFunction();

    getDrinkOrderFunction();
    getDrinkOrderFunction();
    // show movie
    getDrinkOrderFunction();
    // pick up trash
}
```

We create the right kind of dinner order function for the passenger...

...and then call it whenever we want to take a passenger's dinner order.

```
function servePassengers(passengers) {
    for (var i = 0; i < passengers.length; i++) {
        serveCustomer(passengers[i]);
    }
}

servePassengers(passengers);
```

Sharpen your pencil
Solution

What do you think this code does? Can you come up with some examples of how to use it? Here's our solution.

```
function addN(n) {
    var adder = function(x) {
            return n + x;
        };
    return adder;
}
```

This function takes one argument n. It then creates a function that also takes one argument, x, and adds n and x together. That function is returned.

So we used it to create a function that always adds 2 to a number. Like this:

```
var add2 = addN(2);
console.log(add2(10));
console.log(add2(100));
```

Exercise
Solution

The sort method has sorted numbersArray in ascending order because when we return the values 1, 0 and -1, we're telling the sort method:

1: place the first item after the second item

0: the items are equivalent, you can leave them in place

-1: place the first item before the second item.

Changing your code to sort in descending order is a matter of inverting this logic so that 1 means place the second item after the first item, and -1 means place the second item before the first item (0 stays the same). Write a new compare function for descending order:

```
function compareNumbersDesc(num1, num2) {
    if ( num2 > num1 ) {
        return 1;
    } else if (num1 == num2) {
        return 0;
    } else {
        return -1;
    }
}
```

Sharpen your pencil
Solution

You know that the comparison function we pass to sort needs to return a number greater than 0, equal to 0, or less than 0 depending on the two items we're comparing: if the first item is greater than second, we return a value greater than 0; if first item is equal to the second, we return 0; and if the first item is less than the second, we return a value less than 0.

Can you use this knowledge with the fact we're comparing two numbers in compareNumbers to rewrite compareNumbers using much less code?

Here's our solution:

```
function compareNumbers(num1, num2) {
    return num1 - num2;
}
```

We can make this function a single line of code by simply returning the result of substracting num2 from num1. Run through a couple of examples to see how this works. And remember sort is expecting a number greater than, equal to, or less than 0, not specifically 1, 0, -1 (although you'll see a lot of code return those values for sort).

Exercise
Solution

Now that we have a way to sort colas by the sold property, it's time to write compare functions for each of the other properties in the product object: name, calories, and color. Check the output you see in the console carefully; make sure for each kind of sort, the products are sorted correctly. Here's our solution.

Here's our implementation of each compare function.

```
function compareName(colaA, colaB) {
    if (colaA.name > colaB.name) {
        return 1;
    } else if (colaA.name === colaB.name) {
        return 0;
    } else {
        return -1;
    }
}

function compareCalories(colaA, colaB) {
    if (colaA.calories > colaB.calories) {
        return 1;
    } else if (colaA.calories === colaB.calories) {
        return 0;
    } else {
        return -1;
    }
}

function compareColor(colaA, colaB) {
    if (colaA.color > colaB.color) {
        return 1;
    } else if (colaA.color === colaB.color) {
        return 0;
    } else {
        return -1;
    }
}
```

Totally!

You guys nailed it!

```
products.sort(compareName);
console.log("Products sorted by name:");
printProducts(products);

products.sort(compareCalories);
console.log("Products sorted by calories:");
printProducts(products);

products.sort(compareColor);
console.log("Products sorted by color:");
printProducts(products);
```

For each new compare function, we call sort, and display the results in the console.

11 anonymous functions, scope and closures

Serious functions

I've become 200% more expressive since I've learned about anonymous functions.

You've put functions through their paces, but there's more to learn. In this chapter we take it further; we get hard-core. We're going to show you how to **really handle** functions. This won't be a super long chapter, but it will be intense, and at the end you're going to be more expressive with your JavaScript than you thought possible. You're also going to be ready to take on a coworker's code, or jump into an open source JavaScript library, because we're going to cover some common coding idioms and conventions around functions. And if you've never heard of an **anonymous function** or a **closure**, boy are you in the right place.

↖ And if you have heard of a closure, but don't quite know what it is, you're even more in the right place!

Taking a look at the other side of functions...

You've already seen two sides of functions—you've seen the formal, declarative side of function declarations, and you've seen the looser, more expressive side of function expressions. Well, now it's time to introduce you to another interesting side of functions: *the anonymous side.*

By anonymous we're referring to functions *that don't have names.* How can that happen? Well, when you define a function with a function declaration, your function will *definitely have a name.* But when you define a function using a function expression, *you don't have to give that function a name.*

You're probably saying, sure, that's an interesting fact, maybe it's possible, but so what? By using anonymous functions we can often make our code less verbose, more concise, more readable, more efficient, and even more maintainable.

So let's see how to create and use anonymous functions. We'll start with a piece of code we've seen before, and see how an anonymous function might help out:

> Here's a load handler, set up like we've always done in the past.

> First we define a function. This function has a name, handler.

```
function handler() { alert("Yeah, that page loaded!"); }
window.onload = handler;
```

> Then we assign the function to the onload property of the window object, using its name, handler.

> And when the page loads, the handler function is invoked.

Sharpen your pencil

Use your knowledge of functions and variables and check off the true statements below.

❑ The handler variable holds a function reference.

❑ When we assign handler to window.onload, we're assigning it a function reference.

❑ The only reason the handler variable exists is to assign it to window.onload.

❑ We'll never use handler again as it's code that is meant to run only when the page first loads.

❑ Invoking onload handlers twice is not a great idea—doing so could cause issues given these handlers usually do some initialization for the entire page.

❑ Function expressions create function references.

❑ Did we mention that when we assign handler to window.onload, we're assigning it a function reference?

How to use an anonymous function

So, we're creating a function to handle the load event, but we know it's a "one time" function because the load event only happens once per page load. We can also observe that the `window.onload` property is being assigned a function reference—namely, the function reference in `handler`. But because `handler` is a one time function, that name is a bit of a waste, because all we do is assign the reference in it to the `window.onload` property.

Anonymous functions give us a way to clean up this code. An anonymous function is just a function expression without a name that's used where we'd normally use a function reference. But to make the connection, it helps to see how we use a function expression in code in an anonymous way:

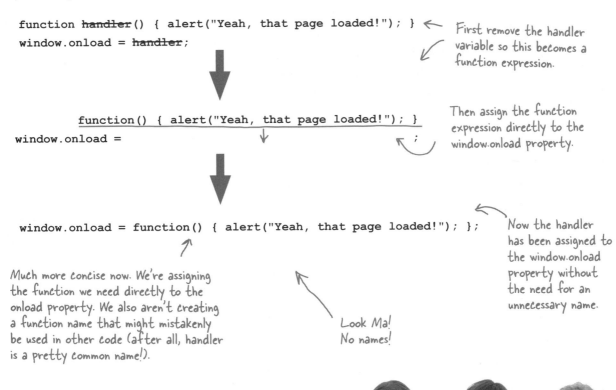

```
function handler() { alert("Yeah, that page loaded!"); }
window.onload = handler;
```
First remove the handler variable so this becomes a function expression.

```
                function() { alert("Yeah, that page loaded!"); }
window.onload =
```
Then assign the function expression directly to the window.onload property.

```
window.onload = function() { alert("Yeah, that page loaded!"); };
```
Now the handler has been assigned to the window.onload property without the need for an unnecessary name.

Much more concise now. We're assigning the function we need directly to the onload property. We also aren't creating a function name that might mistakenly be used in other code (after all, handler is a pretty common name!).

Look Ma! No names!

> Are there places in your previous code that you've seen anonymous functions and hadn't realized it?
>
> Hint: are they hiding somewhere in your objects?

Sharpen your pencil

There are a few opportunities in the code below to take advantage of anonymous functions. Go ahead and rework the code to use anonymous functions wherever possible. You can scratch out the old code and write in new code where needed. Oh, and one more task: circle any anonymous functions that are already being used in the code.

```javascript
window.onload = init;
var cookies = {
    instructions: "Preheat oven to 350...",
    bake: function(time) {
            console.log("Baking the cookies.");
            setTimeout(done, time);
        }
};
function init() {
    var button = document.getElementById("bake");
    button.onclick = handleButton;
}
function handleButton() {
    console.log("Time to bake the cookies.");
    cookies.bake(2500);
}
function done() {
    alert("Cookies are ready, take them out to cool.");
    console.log("Cooling the cookies.");
    var cool = function() {
        alert("Cookies are cool, time to eat!");
    };
    setTimeout(cool, 1000);
}
```

We need to talk about your verbosity, again

Okay, we hate to bring it up again because you've come a long way with functions—you know how to pass functions around, assign them to variables, pass them to functions, return them from functions—but, well, you're still being a little more verbose than you have to (you could also say you're not being as expressive as you could be). Let's see an example:

Here's a normal-looking function named cookieAlarm that displays an alert about cookies being done.

```
function cookieAlarm() {
    alert("Time to take the cookies out of the oven");
};

setTimeout(cookieAlarm, 600000);
```

Looks like the cookies will be done in 10 minutes, just sayin'.

*In case you forgot, these are milliseconds, so 1000 * 60 * 10 = 600,000.*

And here we're taking the function and passing it as an argument to setTimeout.

While this code looks fine, we can make it a bit tighter using anonymous functions. How? Well, think about the `cookieAlarm` variable in the call to `setTimeout`. This is a variable that references a function, so when we invoke `setTimeout`, a function reference is passed. Now, using a variable that references a function is one way to get a function reference, but just like with the `window.onload` example a couple of pages back, you can use a function expression too. Let's rewrite the code with a function expression instead:

Now instead of a variable, we're just putting the function, inline, in the call to setTimeout.

Pay careful attention to the syntax here. We write the entire function expression, which ends in a right bracket, and then like any argument, we follow it with a comma before adding the next argument.

```
setTimeout(function() { alert("Time to take the cookies out of the oven");}, 600000);
```

We specify the name of the function we're calling, setTimeout, followed by a parenthesis and then the first argument, a function expression.

Here's the second argument, after the function expression.

> Who are you trying to kid? That's a mess. Who wants to read that one long line? And what if the function is long and complicated?

For a short piece of code, a one liner is just fine. But, beyond that, you're right, it would be rather silly. But as you know, we can use lots of whitespace with JavaScript, so we can insert all the spaces and returns we need to make things more readable. Here's our reformatting of the `setTimeout` code on the previous page.

All we've done is insert some whitespace—that is, some spaces and returns here and there.

```javascript
setTimeout(function() {
        alert("Time to take the cookies out of the oven");
    }, 600000);
```

We're glad you raised this issue because the code is a lot more readable this way.

Hey, wait a sec, I think I get it. Because a function expression evaluates to a function reference, you can substitute a function expression anywhere you'd expect a reference?

That's a mouthful, but you've got it.

This is really one of the keys to understanding that functions are first class values. If your code expects a function reference, then you can always put a function expression in its place—because it evaluates to a function reference. As you just saw, if a function is expected as an argument, no problem, you can pass it a function expression (which, again, evaluates to a reference before it is passed). If you need to return a function from within a function, same thing—you can just return a function expression.

Exercise

Let's make sure you have the syntax down for passing anonymous function expressions to other functions. Convert this code from one that uses a variable (in this case vaccine) as an argument to one that uses an anonymous function expression.

```javascript
function vaccine(dosage) {
    if (dosage > 0) {
        inject(dosage);
    }
}

administer(patient, vaccine, time);
```

Write your version here. And check your answer before moving on!

there are no
Dumb Questions

Q: **Using these anonymous functions like this seems really esoteric. Do I really need to know this stuff?**

A: You do. Anonymous function expressions are used frequently in JavaScript code, so if you want to be able to read other people's code, or understand JavaScript libraries, you're going to need to know how these work, and how to recognize them when they're being used.

Q: **Is using an anonymous function expression really better? I think it just complicates the code and makes the code hard to follow and read.**

A: Give it some time. Over time, you'll be able to parse code like this more easily when you see it, and there really are lots of cases where this syntax decreases code complexity, makes the code's intention more clear, and cleans up your code. That said, overuse of this technique can definitely lead to code that is quite hard to understand. But stick with it and it'll get easier to read and more useful as you get the hang of it. You're going to encounter lots of code that makes heavy use of anonymous functions, so it's a good idea to incorporate this technique into your code toolbelt.

Q: **If first class functions are so useful, how come other languages don't have them?**

A: Ah, but they do (and even the ones that don't are considering adding them). For instance, languages like Scheme and Scala have fully first class functions like JavaScript does. Other languages, like PHP, Java (in the newest version), C#, and Objective C have some or most of the first class features that JavaScript does. As more people are recognizing the value of having first class functions in a programming language, more languages are supporting them. Each language does it a little differently, however, so be prepared for a variety of approaches as you explore this topic in other languages.

When is a function defined? It depends...

There's one fine point related to functions that we haven't mentioned yet. Remember that the browser takes two passes through your JavaScript code: in the first pass, all your function declarations are parsed and the functions defined; in the second pass, the browser executes your code top down, which is when function expressions are defined. Because of this, functions created by declarations are defined *before* functions that are created using function expressions. And this, in turn, determines where and when you can invoke a function in your code.

To see what that really means, let's take a look at a concrete example. Here's our code from the last chapter, rearranged just a bit. Let's evaluate it:

1 We start at the top of the code and find all the function declarations.

4 We start at the top again, this time evaluating the code.

IMPORTANT: Read this by following the order of the numbers. Start at 1, then go to 2, and so on.

```
var migrating = true;
```
5 Create the variable migrating and set it to true.

Notice that we moved this conditional up from the bottom of the code.

```
if (migrating) {
    quack(4);
    fly(4);
}
```

6 The conditional is true, so evaluate the code block.

7 Get the function reference from quack and invoke it with the argument 4.

8 Get the function reference from fly... oh wait, fly isn't defined!

```
var fly = function(num) {
    for (i = 0; i < num; i++) {
        console.log("Flying!");
    }
};
```

2 We found a function declaration. We create the function and assign it to the variable quack.

```
function quack(num) {
    for (i = 0; i < num; i++) {
        console.log("Quack!");
    }
}
```

3 We reach the bottom. Only one function declaration was found.

What just happened? Why wasn't fly defined?

Okay, we know the `fly` function is undefined when we try to invoke it, but why? After all, `quack` worked just fine. Well, as you've probably guessed by now, unlike `quack`—which is defined on the first pass through the code because it is a function declaration—the `fly` function is defined along with the normal top-to-bottom evaluation of the code. Let's take another look:

JavaScript console
Quack!
Quack!
Quack!
Quack!
TypeError: undefined is not a function

When we evaluate this code to try invoking quack, everything works as expected because quack was defined on the first pass through the code.

What happens when you try to call a function that's undefined.

```
var migrating = true;
if (migrating) {
    quack(4);
    fly(4);
}
var fly = function(num) {
    for (var i = 0; i < num; i++) {
        console.log("Flying!");
    }
};
function quack(num) {
    for (var i = 0; i < num; i++) {
        console.log("Quack!");
    }
}
```

But when we try to execute the call to the fly function, we get an error because we haven't yet defined fly...

...because fly doesn't get defined until this statement is evaluated, which is *after* the call to fly.

You might see an error like this instead (depending on the browser you're using): TypeError: Property 'fly' of object [object Object] is not a function.

So what does this all mean? For starters, it means that you can place function declarations anywhere in your code—at the top, at the bottom, in the middle—and invoke them wherever you like. Function declarations create functions that are defined everywhere in your code (this is known as *hoisting*).

Function expressions are obviously different because they aren't defined until they are evaluated. So, even if you assign the function expression to a global variable, like we did with `fly`, you can't use that variable to invoke a function until after it's been defined.

Now in this example, both of our functions have *global scope*—meaning both functions are visible everywhere in your code once they are defined. But we also need to consider nested functions—that is functions defined within other functions—because it affects the scope of those functions. Let's take a look.

How to nest functions

It's perfectly legal to define a function within another function, meaning you can use a function declaration or expression inside another function. How does this work? Here's the short answer: the only difference between a function defined at the top level of your code and one that's defined within another function is just a matter of scope. In other words, placing a function in another function affects where the function is visible within your code.

To understand this, let's expand our example a little by adding some nested function declarations and expressions.

```javascript
var migrating = true;
var fly = function(num) {
    var sound = "Flying";
    function wingFlapper() {
        console.log(sound);
    }
    for (var i = 0; i < num; i++) {
        wingFlapper();
    }
};
function quack(num) {
    var sound = "Quack";
    var quacker = function() {
        console.log(sound);
    };
    for (var i = 0; i < num; i++) {
        quacker();
    }
}
if (migrating) {
    quack(4);
    fly(4);
}
```

Here we're adding a function declaration with the name wingFlapper inside the fly function expression.

And here we're calling it.

Here we're adding a function expression assigned to the quacker variable inside the quack function declaration.

And here we're calling it.

We've moved this code back to the bottom so we no longer get that error when we call fly.

Exercise

In the code above, take a pencil and mark where you think the scope of the fly, quack, wingFlapper and quacker functions are. Also, mark any places you think the functions might be in scope but undefined.

How nesting affects scope

Functions defined at the top level of your code have global scope, whereas functions defined within another function have local scope. Let's make a pass over this code and look at the scope of each function. While we're at it, we'll also look at where each function is defined (or, not undefined, if you prefer):

```javascript
var migrating = true;
var fly = function(num) {
    var sound = "Flying";
    function wingFlapper() {
        console.log(sound);
    }
    for (var i = 0; i < num; i++) {
        wingFlapper();
    }
};
function quack(num) {
    var sound = "Quack";
    var quacker = function() {
        console.log(sound);
    };
    for (var i = 0; i < num; i++) {
        quacker();
    }
}
if (migrating) {
    quack(4);
    fly(4);
}
```

Everything defined at the top level of the code has global scope. So fly and quack are both global variables.

But remember fly is defined only after this function expression is evaluated.

wingFlapper is defined by a function declaration in the fly function. So its scope is the entire fly function, and it's defined throughout the entire fly function body.

quacker is defined by a function expression in the function quack. So its scope is the entire quack function but it's defined only after the function expression is evaluated, until the end of the function body.

quacker is only defined here.

Notice that the rules for when you can refer to a function are the same within a function as they are at the top level. That is, within a function, if you define a nested function *with a declaration*, that nested function is defined everywhere within the body of the function. On the other hand, if you create a nested function using a *function expression*, then that nested function is defined only after the function expression is evaluated.

there are no
Dumb Questions

Q: When we pass a function expression to another function, that function must get stored in a parameter, and then treated as a local variable in the function we passed it to. Is that right?

A: That's exactly right. Passing a function as an argument to another function copies the function reference we're passing into a parameter variable in the function we've called. And just like any other parameter, a parameter holding a function reference is a local variable.

EXTREME JAVASCRIPT CHALLENGE

We need a first class functions expert and we've heard that's you! Below you'll find two pieces of code, and we need your help figuring out what this code does. We're stumped. To us, these look like nearly identical pieces of code, except that one uses a first class function and the other doesn't. Knowing everything we do about JavaScript scope, we expected Specimen #1 to evaluate to 008 and Specimen #2 to evaluate to 007. But they both result in 008! Can you help us figure out why?

We recommend you form a strong opinion, jot it down on this page, and then turn the page.

Specimen #1

```javascript
var secret = "007";

function getSecret() {
    var secret = "008";

    function getValue() {
        return secret;
    }
    return getValue();
}

getSecret();
```

Specimen #2

```javascript
var secret = "007";

function getSecret() {
    var secret = "008";

    function getValue() {
        return secret;
    }
    return getValue;
}
var getValueFun = getSecret();
getValueFun();
```

Don't look at the solution at the end of the chapter just yet; we'll revisit this challenge a little bit later.

A little review of lexical scope

Lexical just means you can determine the scope of a variable by reading the structure of the code, as opposed to waiting until the code runs to figure it out.

While we're on the topic of scope, let's quickly review how lexical scope works:

```
var justAVar = "Oh, don't you worry about it, I'm GLOBAL";

function whereAreYou() {
    var justAVar = "Just an every day LOCAL";

    return justAVar;
}

var result = whereAreYou();
console.log(result);
```

Here we have a global variable called justAVar.

And this function defines a new lexical scope...

...in which we have a local variable, justAVar, that shadows the global variable of the same name.

When this function is called, it returns justAVar. But which one? We're using lexical scope, so we find the justAVar value by looking in the nearest function scope. And if we can't find it there, we look in the global scope.

So when we call whereAreYou, it returns the value of the local justAVar, not the global one.

```
JavaScript console
Just an every day LOCAL
```

Now let's introduce a nested function:

```
var justAVar = "Oh, don't you worry about it, I'm GLOBAL";

function whereAreYou() {
    var justAVar = "Just an every day LOCAL";

    function inner() {
        return justAVar;
    }

    return inner();
}

var result = whereAreYou();
console.log(result);
```

Here's the same function.

And shadow variable.

But now we have a nested function, that refers to justAVar. But which one? Well, again, we always use the variable from the closest enclosing function. So we're using the same variable as the last time.

Notice that we're calling inner here, and returning its result..

So when we call whereAreYou, the inner function is invoked, and returns the value of the local justAVar, not the global one.

```
JavaScript console
Just an every day LOCAL
```

Where things get interesting with lexical scope

Let's make one more tweak. Watch this step carefully; it's a doozy:

```javascript
var justAVar = "Oh, don't you worry about it, I'm GLOBAL";

function whereAreYou() {
    var justAVar = "Just an every day LOCAL";

    function inner() {
        return justAVar;
    }

    return inner;
}

var innerFunction = whereAreYou();
var result = innerFunction();
console.log(result);
```

No changes at all here, same variables and functions.

But rather than invoking inner, we <u>return</u> the inner function.

So when we call whereAreYou, we get back a reference to inner function, which we assign to the innerFunction variable. Then we invoke innerFunction, capture its output in result and display the result.

So when inner is invoked here (as innerFunction), which justAVar is used? The local one, or the global one?

What matters is when the function is invoked. We invoke inner after it's returned, when the global version of justAVar is in scope, so we'll get "Oh don't worry about it, I'm GLOBAL".

Not so fast. With lexical scope what matters is the structure in which the function is defined, so the result has to be the value of the local variable, or "Just an everyday LOCAL".

Frank: What do you mean you're right? That's like defying the laws of physics or something. The local variable doesn't even exist anymore... I mean, when a variable goes out of scope it ceases to exist. It's derezzed! Didn't you see TRON!?

Judy: Maybe in your weak little C++ and Java languages, but not in JavaScript.

Jim: Seriously, how is that possible? The `whereAreYou` function has come and gone, and the local version of `justAVar` couldn't possibly exist anymore.

Judy: If you'd listen to what I just told you... In JavaScript that's not how it works.

Frank: Well, throw us a bone Judy. How does it work?

Judy: When we define the `inner` function, the local `justAVar` is in the scope of that function. Now lexical scope says how we define things is what matters, so if we're using lexical scope, then *whenever* `inner` is invoked, it assumes it still has that local variable around if it needs it.

Frank: Yeah, but like I already said, that's like defying the laws of physics. The `whereAreYou` function that defined the local version of the `justAVar` variable is over. It doesn't exist any more.

Judy: True. The `whereAreYou` function is done, but the scope is still around for `inner` to use.

Jim: How is that?

Judy: Well, let's see what REALLY happens when we define and return a function...

EDITOR'S NOTE: Did Joe change his shirt between pages!?

Functions Revisited

We have a bit of a confession to make. Up until now we haven't told you *everything* about a function. Even when you asked "What does a function reference actually point to?" we kinda skirted the issue. "Oh just think of it like a crystallized function that holds the function's code block," we said.

Well now it's time to show you everything.

To do that, let's walk through what really happens at runtime with this code, starting with the `whereAreYou` function:

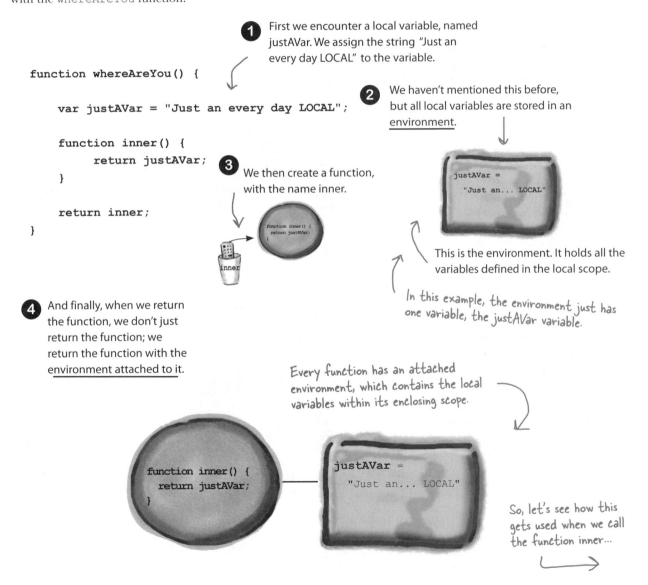

1 First we encounter a local variable, named justAVar. We assign the string "Just an every day LOCAL" to the variable.

```
function whereAreYou() {

    var justAVar = "Just an every day LOCAL";

    function inner() {
        return justAVar;
    }

    return inner;
}
```

2 We haven't mentioned this before, but all local variables are stored in an <u>environment</u>.

3 We then create a function, with the name inner.

```
function inner() {
    return justAVar;
}
```

inner

```
justAVar =
    "Just an... LOCAL"
```

This is the environment. It holds all the variables defined in the local scope.

In this example, the environment just has one variable, the justAVar variable.

4 And finally, when we return the function, we don't just return the function; we return the function with the <u>environment attached to it.</u>

Every function has an attached environment, which contains the local variables within its enclosing scope.

```
function inner() {
    return justAVar;
}
```

```
justAVar =
    "Just an... LOCAL"
```

So, let's see how this gets used when we call the function inner...

Calling a function (revisited)

Now that we have the `inner` function, and its environment, let's invoke `inner` and see what happens. Here's the code we want to evaluate:

```
var innerFunction = whereAreYou();
var result = innerFunction();
console.log(result);
```

---

(1) First, we call whereAreYou. We already know that returns a function reference. So we create a variable innerFunction and assign it that function. Remember, that function reference is linked to an environment.

```
var innerFunction = whereAreYou();
```

After this statement we have a variable innerFunction that refers to the function (plus an environment) returned from whereAreYou.

Our new variable.

```
function inner() {
    return justAVar;
}
```

```
justAVar =
    "Just an... LOCAL"
```

inner Function

The function, and its environment.

---

(2) Next we call innerFunction. To do that we evaluate the code in the function's body, and do that in the context of the function's environment, like this:

```
var result = innerFunction();
```

```
function inner() {
    return justAVar;
}
```

```
justAVar =
    "Just an... LOCAL"
```

inner Function

The function has a single statement that returns justAVar. To get the value of justAVar we look in the environment.

justAVar has the value "Just an every day LOCAL". So we return that.

3 Last, we assign the result of the function to the result variable, and then display it in the console.

```
var result = innerFunction();
console.log(result);
```

innerFunction returns the value "Just an every day LOCAL", which it got from its environment. So, we throw that into the result variable.

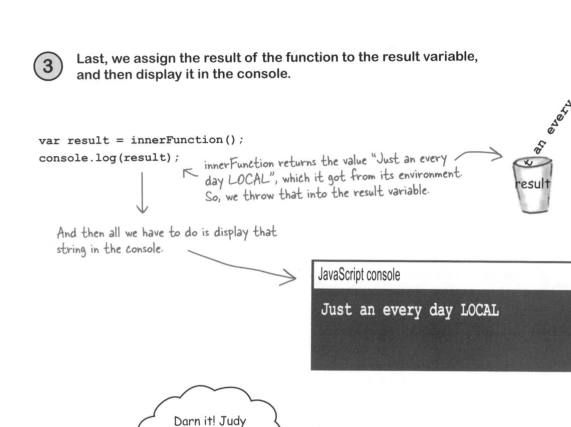

And then all we have to do is display that string in the console.

JavaScript console

Just an every day LOCAL

Darn it! Judy was right again.

Wait a sec... Judy hasn't mentioned closures? That looks related to what we're doing. Let's see if we can study up on that and use them to one-up her.

Uh, guys... this IS a closure. You'd better read up on them.

there are no
Dumb Questions

Q: When you say that lexical scope determines where a variable is defined, what do you mean?

A: By lexical scope we mean that JavaScript's rules for scoping are based purely on the structure of your code (not on some dynamic runtime properties). This means you can determine where a variable is defined by simply examining your code's structure. Also remember that in JavaScript only functions introduce new scope. So, given a reference to a variable, look for where that variable is defined in a function from the most nested (where it's used) to the least nested until you find it. And if you can't find it in a function, then it must be global, or undefined.

Q: If a function is nested way down many layers, how does the environment work then?

A: We used a simplistic way of showing the environment to explain it, but you can think of each nested function as having its own little environment with its own variables. Then, what we do is create a chain of the environments of all the nested functions, from inner to outer.

So, when it comes to finding a variable in the environment, you start at the closest one, and then follow the chain until you find your variable. And, if you don't find it, you look in the global environment.

Q: Why are lexical scoping and function environments good things? I would have thought the answer in that code example would be "Oh, don't you worry about it, I'm GLOBAL". That makes sense to me. The real answer seems confusing and counterintuitive.

A: We can see how you might think that, but the advantage of lexical scope is that we can always look at the code to determine the scope that's in place when a variable is defined, and figure out what its value should be from that. And, as we've seen, this is true even if you return a function and invoke it much later in a place totally outside of its original scope.

Now there is another reason you might consider this a good thing, and that is the kind of things we can do in code with this capability. We're going to get to that in just a bit.

Q: Do parameter variables get included in the environment too?

A: Yes. As we've said before, you can consider parameters to be local variables in your functions, so they are included in the environment as well.

Q: Do I need to understand how the environment works in detail?

A: No. What you need to understand is the lexical scoping rules for JavaScript variables, and we've covered that. But now you know that if you have a function that is returned from within a function, it carries its environment around with it.

Remember that JavaScript functions are always evaluated in the same scoping environment in which they were defined. Within a function, if you want to determine where a variable is coming from, search in its enclosing functions, from the most nested to the least.

What the heck is a closure?

Sure, everyone talks about closures as *the must have* language feature, but how many people actually get what they are or how to use them? Darn few. It's the language feature everyone wants to understand and the feature every traditional language wants to add.

Here's the problem. According to many well-educated folks in the business, *closures are hard*. But that's really not a problem for you. Want to know why? No, no, it's not because this is a "brain friendly book" and no, it's not because we have a killer application that needs to be built to teach closures to you. It's because *you just learned them*. We just didn't call them closures.

So without further ado, we give you the super-formal definition.

> **Closure, noun**: A closure is a function together with a referencing environment.

If you've been trained well in this book you should be thinking at this point, "Ah, this is the 'get a big raise' knowledge."

Okay, we agree that definition isn't totally illuminating. But why is it called *closure*? Let's quickly walk through that, because—seriously—this could be one of those make-or-break job interview questions, or the thing that gets you that raise at some point in the future.

To understand the word *closure*, we need to understand the idea of "closing" a function.

Sharpen your pencil

Here's your task: (1) find all the **free variables** in the code below and circle them. A free variable is one that isn't defined in the local scope. (2) Pick one of the environments on the right that **closes the function**. By that we mean that it provides values for all the free variables.

```
function justSayin(phrase) {
    var ending = "";
    if (beingFunny) {
        ending = " -- I'm just sayin!";
    } else if (notSoMuch) {
        ending = " -- Not so much.";
    }
    alert(phrase + ending);
}
```

Circle the free variables in this code. Free variables are not defined in the local scope.

```
beingFunny = true;
notSoMuch = false;
inConversationWith = "Paul";
```

```
beingFunny = true;
justSayin = false;
oocoder = true;
```

```
notSoMuch = true;
phrase = "Do do da";
band = "Police";
```

Pick one of these that closes the function.

Closing a function

You probably figured this out in the previous exercise, but let's run through it one more time: a function typically has *local variables* in its code body (including any parameters it has), and it also might have variables that aren't defined locally, which we call *free variables*. The name *free* comes from the fact that within the function body, free variables aren't bound to any values (in other words, they're not declared locally in the function). Now, when we have an environment that has a value for each of the free variables, we say that we've *closed* the function. And, when we take the function and the environment together, we say we have a *closure*.

> If a variable in my function body isn't defined locally, and it's not a global, you can bet it's from a function I'm nested in, and available in my environment.

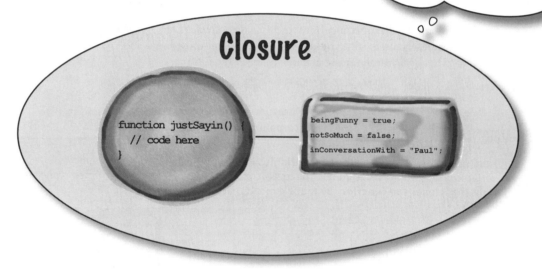

A closure results when we combine a function that has free variables with an environment that provides variable bindings for all those free variables.

We're about ten
pages into this topic.
Are we ever going back to real-world
JavaScript? Or are we staying in
theory land forever? Why do I really care
how all this low-level function stuff works?
I just need to write functions and call
them, right?

If closures weren't so darned useful, we'd agree.

We're sorry we had to drag you through the learning curve on
closures but we assure you, it is well worth it. You see, closures aren't
just some theoretical functional programming language construct;
they're also a powerful programming technique. Now that you've
got how they work down (and we're not kidding that understanding
closures is what's going to raise your cred among your managers and
peers) it's time to learn how to use them.

And here's the thing: they're used all over the place. In fact they're
going to become so second nature to you that you'll find yourself
using them liberally in your code. Anyway, let's get to some closure
code and you'll see what we're talking about.

Using closures to implement a magic counter

Ever think of implementing a counter function? It usually goes like this:

```
var count = 0;        ←—— We have a global variable count.

function counter() {          ←— Each time we call counter, we
    count = count + 1;              increment the global count variable,
    return count;                   and return the new value.
}
```

And we can use our counter like this:

```
console.log(counter());   ←——— So we can count
console.log(counter());         and display the
console.log(counter());         value of the
                                counter like this.
```

JavaScript console

```
1
2
3
```

The only issue with this is that we have to use a global variable for count, which can be problematic if you're developing code with a team (because people often use the same names, which end up clashing).

What if we were to tell you there is a way to implement a counter with a totally local and protected count variable? That way, you'll have a counter that no other code can ever clash with, and the only way to increment the counter value is through the function (otherwise known as a closure).

To implement this with a closure, we can reuse most of the code above. Watch and be amazed:

```
function makeCounter() {          ⌐ Here, we're putting the count variable in
    var count = 0;                  the function makeCounter. So now count
                                ←   is a local variable, not a global variable.

    function counter() {    ←— Now, we create the counter
        count = count + 1;         function, which increments
        return count;              the count variable.
    }
    return counter;    ←—And return the counter function.
}
        ↑ This is the closure. It holds count in its environment.
```

Think this magic trick will work? Let's try it and see…

Test drive your magic counter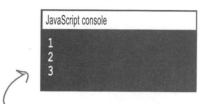

We added a bit of testing code to test the counter. Give it a try!

```javascript
function makeCounter() {
    var count = 0;

    function counter() {
        count = count + 1;
        return count;
    }
    return counter;
}
var doCount = makeCounter();
console.log(doCount());
console.log(doCount());
console.log(doCount());
```

```
JavaScript console
1
2
3
```

Our counter works... we get solid counting results.

Looking behind the curtain...

Let's step through the code to see how the counter works.

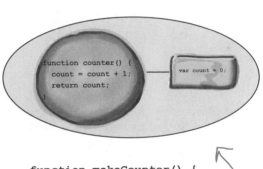

1 We call makeCounter, which creates a counter function and returns it along with an environment containing the free variable, count. In other words, it creates a closure. The function returned from makeCounter is stored in doCount.

2 We call the function doCount. This executes the body of the counter function.

3 When we encounter the variable count, we look it up in the environment, and retrieve its value. We increment count, save the new value back into the environment, and return that new value to where doCount was called.

4 We repeat steps 2 and 3 each time we call doCount.

```javascript
function makeCounter() {
    var count = 0;

    function counter() {
3       count = count + 1;
        return count;
    }
    return counter;
}
1  var doCount = makeCounter();
2  console.log(doCount());
   console.log(doCount());
4  console.log(doCount());
```

This is a closure.

When we call doCount (which is a reference to counter) and need to get the value of count, we use the count variable that's in the closure's environment. The outside world (the global scope) never sees the variable count. But we can use it anytime we call doCount. And there's no other way to get to count except by calling doCount.

When we call makeCounter, we get back a closure: a function with an environment.

ExeRcise

It's your turn. Try creating the following closures. We realize this is not an easy task at first, so refer to the answer if you need to. The important thing is to work your way through these examples, and get to the point where you fully understand them.

First up for 10pts: makePassword takes a password as an argument and returns a function that accepts a password guess and returns true if the guess matches the password (sometimes you need to read these closure descriptions a few times to get them):

```
function makePassword(password) {
    return _____ {
        return (passwordGuess === password);
    };
}
```

Next up for 20pts: the multN function takes a number (call it n) and returns a function. That function itself takes a number, multiplies it by n and returns the result.

```
function multN(n) {
    return _____ {
        return _____;
    };
}
```

Last up for 30 pts: This is a modification of the counter we just created. makeCounter takes no arguments, but defines a count variable. It then creates and returns an object with one method, increment. This method increments the count variable and returns it.

Creating a closure by passing a function expression as an argument

Returning a function from a function isn't the only way to create a closure. You create a closure *whenever* you have a reference to a function that has free variables, and that function is executed outside of the context in which it was created.

Another way we can create a closure is to pass a function to a function. The function we pass will be executed in a completely different context than the one in which it was defined. Here's an example:

```
function makeTimer(doneMessage, n) {

    setTimeout(function() {
        alert(doneMessage);
    }, n);

}

makeTimer("Cookies are done!", 1000);
```

We have a function...

...with a free variable...

...that we are using as a handler for setTimeout.

...and this function will be executed 1000 milliseconds from now, long after the function makeTimer has completed.

Here, we're passing a function expression that contains a free variable, doneMessage, to the function setTimeout. As you know, what happens is we evaluate the function expression to get a function reference, which is then passed to setTimeout. The setTimeout method holds on to this function (which is a function plus an environment—in other words, a closure) and then 1000 milliseconds later it calls that function.

And again, the function we're passing into setTimeout is a closure because it comes along with an environment that binds the free variable, doneMessage, to the string "Cookies are done!".

What would happen if our code looked like this instead?

```
function handler() {
    alert(doneMessage);
}
function makeTimer(doneMessage, n) {
    setTimeout(handler, n);
}
makeTimer("Cookies are done!", 1000);
```

Revisit the code on page 412 in Chapter 9. Can you modify your code to use a closure, and eliminate the need for the third argument to setTimeout?

The closure contains the actual environment, not a copy

One thing that often misleads people learning closures is that they think the environment in the closure must have a copy of all the variables and their values. It doesn't. In fact, the environment references the live variables being used by your code, so if a value is changed by code outside your closure function, that new value is seen by your closure function when it is evaluated.

Let's modify our example to see what that means.

```
function setTimer(doneMessage, n) {

    setTimeout(function() {          ← The closure is created here.
        alert(doneMessage);
    }, n);
                                        Now we're changing the
                                        value of doneMessage after
    doneMessage = "OUCH!";          ←   we call setTimeout.
}
setTimer("Cookies are done!", 1000);
```

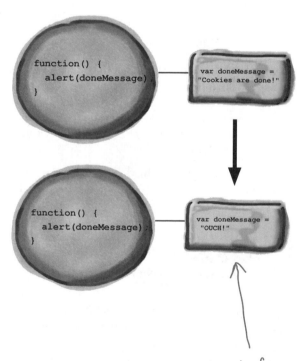

1 When we call setTimeout and pass to it the function expression, a closure is created containing the function along with a reference to the environment.

```
setTimeout(function() {
    alert(doneMessage);
}, n);
```

2 Then, when we change the value of doneMessage to "OUCH!" outside of the closure, it's changed in the same environment that is used by the closure.

```
doneMessage = "OUCH!";
```

3 1000 milliseconds later, the function in the closure is called. This function references the doneMessage variable, which is now set to "OUCH!" in the environment, so we see "OUCH!" in the alert.

When the function is called, it uses the value for doneMessage that's in the environment, which is the new value we set it to earlier, in setTimer.

```
function() { alert(doneMessage); }
```

Creating a closure with an event handler

Let's look at one more way to create a closure. We'll create a closure with an event handler, which is something you'll see fairly often in JavaScript code. We'll start by creating a simple web page with a button and a `<div>` element to hold a message. We'll keep track of how many times you click the button and display the tally in the `<div>`.

Here's the HTML and a tiny bit of CSS to create the page. Go ahead and add the HTML and CSS below into a file named "divClosure.html".

```
<!doctype html>
<html lang="en">
<head>
<meta charset="utf-8">
<title>Click me!</title>
<style>
    body, button { margin: 10px; }
    div { padding: 10px; }
</style>
<script>
    // JavaScript code here
</script>
</head>
<body>
    <button id="clickme">Click me!</button>
    <div id="message"></div>
</body>
</html>
```

Just your typical, basic web page...

With a little CSS to style the elements in the page.

Here's where our code's going to go.

We have a button, and a `<div>` to hold the message we'll update each time you click the button.

Here's what we're going for: each time you click the button, the message in the `<div>` will be updated to show the number of times you've clicked.

Click me!

You clicked me 10 times!

Next, let's write the code. Now, you could write the code for this example without using a closure at all, but as you'll see, by using a closure, our code is more concise, and even a bit more efficient.

Click me! without a closure

Let's first take a look at how you'd implement this example *without* a closure.

The count variable will need to be a global variable, because if it's local to handleClick (the click event handler on the button, see below), it'll just get re-initialized every time we click.

```
var count = 0;

window.onload = function() {
    var button = document.getElementById("clickme");
    button.onclick = handleClick;
};

function handleClick() {
    var message = "You clicked me ";
    var div = document.getElementById("message");
    count++;
    div.innerHTML = message + count + " times!";
}
```

In the load event handler function, we get the button element, and add a click handler to the onclick property.

Here's the button's click handler function.

We define the message variable...

...get the <div> element from the page...

...increment the counter...

...and update the <div> with the message containing how many times we've clicked.

Click me! <u>with</u> a closure

The version without a closure looks perfectly reasonable, except for that global variable which could potentially cause trouble. Let's rewrite the code using a closure and see how it compares. We'll show the code here, and take a closer look after we test it.

```
window.onload = function() {
    var count = 0;
    var message = "You clicked me ";
    var div = document.getElementById("message");

    var button = document.getElementById("clickme");
    button.onclick = function() {
        count++;
        div.innerHTML = message + count + " times!";
    };
};
```

Now, all our variables are local to window.onload. No problems with name clashing now.

We're setting up the click handler as a function expression assigned to the button's onclick property, so we can reference div, message and count in the function. (Remember your lexical scoping!)

This function has three free variables: div, message and count, so a closure is created for the click handler function. So what gets assigned to the button's onclick property is a closure.

Test drive your button counter

Okay, let's bring the HTML and the code together in your "divClosure.html" file and give this a test run. Go ahead and load the page and then click on the button to increment the counter. You should see the message update in the `<div>`. Look at the code again, and make sure you think you know how this all works. After you've done so, turn the page and we'll walk through it together.

Here's what we got.

← Update your "divClosure.html" file like this.

```html
<!doctype html>
<html lang="en">
<head>
<meta charset="utf-8">
<title>Click me!</title>
<style>
    body, button { margin: 10px; }
    div { padding: 10px; }
</style>
<script>
    window.onload = function() {
        var count = 0;
        var message = "You clicked me ";
        var div = document.getElementById("message");

        var button = document.getElementById("clickme");
        button.onclick = function() {
            count++;
            div.innerHTML = message + count + " times!";
        };
    };
</script>
</head>
<body>
    <button id="clickme">Click me!</button>
    <div id="message"></div>
</body>
</html>
```

How the Click me! closure works

To understand how the closure works, let's follow along with
the browser once again, as it evaluates this code...

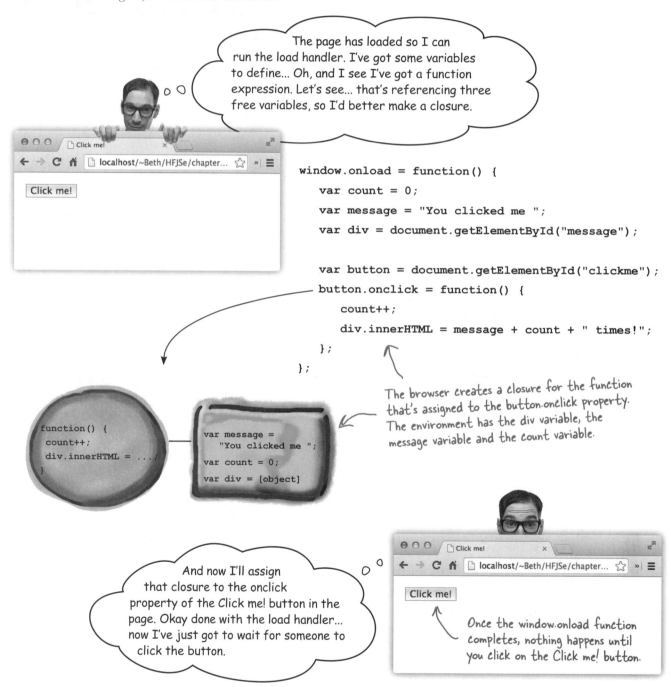

The page has loaded so I can
run the load handler. I've got some variables
to define... Oh, and I see I've got a function
expression. Let's see... that's referencing three
free variables, so I'd better make a closure.

```javascript
window.onload = function() {
    var count = 0;
    var message = "You clicked me ";
    var div = document.getElementById("message");

    var button = document.getElementById("clickme");
    button.onclick = function() {
        count++;
        div.innerHTML = message + count + " times!";
    };
};
```

The browser creates a closure for the function
that's assigned to the button.onclick property.
The environment has the div variable, the
message variable and the count variable.

```
function() {
  count++;
  div.innerHTML = ...
}
```

```
var message =
    "You clicked me ";
var count = 0;
var div = [object]
```

And now I'll assign
that closure to the onclick
property of the Click me! button in the
page. Okay done with the load handler...
now I've just got to wait for someone to
click the button.

Once the window.onload function
completes, nothing happens until
you click on the Click me! button.

Hey, someone clicked the button! Time to execute that click handler function I stashed away earlier...

Even though the button <u>variable</u> doesn't exist anymore (it goes away when the window.onload function has completed), the button <u>object</u> is in the DOM, and it has our closure stored in its onclick property.

Click me!   onclick

```
function() {
count++;
div.innerHTML = ...
}
```

```
var message =
    "You clicked me ";
var count = 0;
var div = [object]
```

Oh, I see we have a closure. Good, that means I can find values for the free variables in the environment.

Notice that the div variable in the closure holds an object. When div was initialized in window.onload we stored the object returned by document.getElementById in the div variable, so we don't have to get the object from the DOM again; we have it already. This saves us a little bit of computation and makes our code just a tiny bit faster.

```
function() {
count++;
div.innerHTML = ...
}
```

```
var message =
    "You clicked me ";
var count = 1;
var div = [object]
```

The closure doesn't go away until you close the page. It's ready to spring into action whenever you click the button!

I've incremented the count variable by one and made sure the value is updated in the environment. And I've updated the message in the page, so now all I have to do is wait for another click.

Click me!

You clicked me 1 times!

EXTREME JAVASCRIPT CHALLENGE
REVISITED

We need a closures expert and we've heard that's you! Now you know how closures work, can you figure out why both specimens below evaluate to 008? To figure it out, write any variables that are captured in the environments for the functions below. Note that it's perfectly fine for an environment to be empty. Check your answer at the end of the chapter.

Specimen #1

```
var secret = "007";

function getSecret() {
    var secret = "008";

    function getValue() {
        return secret;
    }
    return getValue();
}
getSecret();
```

Environment

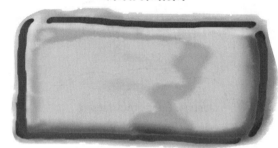

Specimen #2

```
var secret = "007";

function getSecret() {
    var secret = "008";

    function getValue() {
        return secret;
    }
    return getValue;
}
var getValueFun = getSecret();
getValueFun();
```

Environment

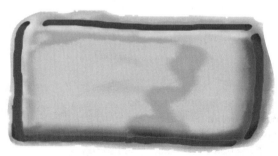

Sharpen your pencil

First, check out this code:

```
(function(food) {
    if (food === "cookies") {
        alert("More please");
    } else if (food === "cake") {
        alert("Yum yum");
    }
})("cookies");
```

Using a function expression in place of a reference, taken to the extreme.

Your task is to figure out not just what this code computes, but *how* it computes. To do that, go in reverse. That is, take out the anonymous function, assign it to a variable, and then use that variable where the function expression used to be. Is the code more obvious now? So, what does it do?

BULLET POINTS

- An **anonymous function** is a function expression that has no name.

- Anonymous functions can make your code more concise.

- A **function declaration** is defined before the rest of your code is evaluated.

- A **function expression** is evaluated at runtime with the rest of your code, and so is not defined until the statement in which it appears is evaluated.

- You can pass a function expression to another function, or return a function expression from a function.

- A function expression evaluates to a **function reference**, so you can use a function expression anywhere you can use a function reference.

- **Nested functions** are functions defined inside another function.

- A nested function has local scope, just like other local variables.

- **Lexical scope** means that we can determine the scope of a variable by reading our code.

- To bind the value of a variable in a nested function, use the value that's defined in the closest enclosing function. If no value is found, then look in the global scope.

- **Closures** are a function along with a referencing environment.

- A closure captures the value of variables in scope at the time the closure is created.

- **Free variables** in the body of a function are variables that are not bound in the body of that function.

- If you execute a function closure in a different context in which it was created, the values of free variables are determined by the referencing environment.

- Closures are often used to capture state for event handlers.

 # JavaScript cross

Time for another crossword puzzle to burn some
JavaScript into those neuron pathways.

ACROSS

4. A function declaration nested in another function has _____ scope.

6. When we tried to call fly before it was defined, we got this kind of error.

9. wingFlapper is a _____ function.

12. We often use setTimeout to create a timer for making _____.

13. A function expression assigned to a variable at the top level of your code has _____ scope.

14. To get a raise, you should understand how _____ work.

16. A _____ variable is one that's not defined in the local scope.

17. We changed the value of doneMessage to _____ in the closure.

18. An environment that provides values for all free variables _____ a function.

DOWN

1. _____ is always right.

2. _____ changed his shirt between pages.

3. Movie the word "derezzed" was used in.

5. An _____ function is a function expression that has no name.

7. A function with an _____ attached to it is called a closure.

8. A function expression evaluates to a function _____.

10. We passed a function _____ to set the cookie alarm.

11. Parameters are _____ variables, so they're included in the environment where variables are defined.

15. _____ scope means you can understand the scope of your variables by reading the structure of your code.

Sharpen your pencil
Solution

There are a few opportunities in the code below to make the code more concise by using anonymous functions. Go ahead and rework the code to use anonymous functions wherever possible. You can scratch out the old code and write in new code where needed. Oh, and one more task: circle any anonymous functions that are already being used in the code. Here's our solution.

```javascript
window.onload = init;
var cookies = {
    instructions: "Preheat oven to 350...",
    bake: function(time) {
            console.log("Baking the cookies.");
            setTimeout(done, time);
        }
};
function init() {
    var button = document.getElementById("bake");
    button.onclick = handleButton;
}
function handleButton() {
    console.log("Time to bake the cookies.");
    cookies.bake(2500);
}
function done() {
    alert("Cookies are ready, take them out to cool.");
    console.log("Cooling the cookies.");
    var cool = function() {
        alert("Cookies are cool, time to eat!");
    };
    setTimeout(cool, 1000);
}
```

We reworked the code to create two anonymous function expressions, one for the init function, and one for the handleButton function.

Now we assign a function expression to the window.onload property...

```javascript
window.onload = function() {
    var button = document.getElementById("bake");
    button.onclick = function() {
        console.log("Time to bake the cookies.");
        cookies.bake(2500);
    };
};
```

...and assign a function expression to the button.onclick property.

```javascript
var cookies = {
    instructions: "Preheat oven to 350...",
    bake: function(time) {
            console.log("Baking the cookies.");
            setTimeout(done, time);
        }
};
```

```javascript
function done() {
    alert("Cookies are ready, take them out to cool.");
    console.log("Cooling the cookies.");
    var cool = function() {
        alert("Cookies are cool, time to eat!");
    };
    setTimeout(cool, 1000);
}
```

Extra credit for you if you figured out you can pass the cool function directly to setTimeout, like this:

```javascript
setTimeout(function() {
    alert("Cookies are cool, time to eat!");
}, 1000);
```

EXERCISE SOLUTION

Let's make sure you have the syntax down for passing anonymous function expressions to other functions. Convert this code from one that uses a variable (in this case vaccine) as a parameter to one that uses an anonymous function. Here's our solution.

```
administer(patient, function(dosage) {
    if (dosage > 0) {
        inject(dosage);
    }
}, time);
```

Notice that it's totally fine to use more than one line for a function expression that's used as an argument. But watch your syntax; it's easy to make a mistake!

EXERCISE SOLUTION

It's your turn. Try creating the following closures. We realize this is not an easy task at first, so refer to the answer if you need to. The important thing is to work your way through these examples, and get to the point where you fully understand them.

Here are our solutions:

First up for 10pts: makePassword takes a password as an argument and returns a function that accepts a password guess and returns true if the guess matches the password (sometimes you need to read these closure descriptions a few times to get them):

```
makePassword(password) {
    return function guess(passwordGuess) {
        return (passwordGuess === password);
    };
}
var tryGuess = makePassword("secret");
console.log("Guessing 'nope': " + tryGuess("nope"));
console.log("Guessing 'secret': " + tryGuess("secret"));
```

The function that's returned from makePassword is a closure with an environment containing the free variable password.

We pass in the value "secret" to makePassword, so this is the value that's stored in the closure's environment.

Notice here we're using a named function expression! We don't have to, but it's handy as a way to refer to the name of the inner function. But also notice we must invoke the returned function using tryGuess (not guess).

And when we invoke tryGuess, we compare the word we pass in ("nope" or "secret") with the value for password in the environment for tryGuess.

The solutions continue on the next page...

It's your turn. Try creating the following closures. We realize this is not an easy task at first, so refer to the answer if you need to. The important thing is to work your way through these examples, and get to the point where you fully understand them.

Here are our solutions (continued):

Next up for 20pts: the multN function takes a number (call it n) and returns a function. That function itself takes a number, multiplies it by n and returns the result.

```
function multN(n) {
    return function multBy(m) {
        return n*m;
    };
}
var multBy3 = multN(3);
console.log("Multiplying 2: " + multBy3(2));
console.log("Multiplying 3: " + multBy3(3));
```

The function that's returned from multN is a closure with an environment containing the free variable n.

So we invoke multN(3) and get back a function that multiplies any number you give it by 3.

Last up for 30 pts: This is a modification of the counter we just created. makeCounter takes no arguments, but defines a count variable. It then creates and returns an object with one method, increment. This method increments the count variable and returns it.

```
function makeCounter() {
    var count = 0;
    return {
        increment: function() {
            count++;
            return count;
        }
    };
}
var counter = makeCounter();
console.log(counter.increment());
console.log(counter.increment());
console.log(counter.increment());
```

This is similar to our previous makeCounter function, except now we're returning an object with an increment method, instead of returning a function directly.

The increment method has a free variable, count. So, increment is a closure with an environment containing the variable count.

Now, we call makeCounter and get back an object with a method (that is a closure).

We invoke the method in the usual way, and when we do, the method references the variable count in its environment.

Sharpen your pencil
Solution

Use your knowledge of functions and variables and check off the true statements below. Here's our solution:

☑ The handler variable holds a function reference.

☑ When we assign handler to window.onload, we're assigning it a function reference.

☑ The only reason the handler variable exists is to assign it to window.onload.

☑ We'll never use handler again as it's code that is meant to run only when the page first loads.

☑ Invoking onload handlers twice is not a great idea—doing so could cause issues given these handlers usually do some initialization for the entire page.

☑ Function expressions create function references.

☑ Did we mention that when we assign handler to window.onload, we're assigning it a function reference?

Sharpen your pencil
Solution

Here's your task: (1) find all the **free variables** in the code below and circle them. A free variable is one that isn't defined in the local scope. (2) Pick one of the environments on the right that **closes the function**. By that we mean that it provides values for all the free variables. Here's our solution.

This environment closes the two free variables beingFunny and notSoMuch

```
beingFunny = true;
notSoMuch = false;
inConversationWith = "Paul";
```

```javascript
function justSayin(phrase) {
    var ending = "";
    if (beingFunny) {
        ending = " -- I'm just sayin!";
    } else if (notSoMuch) {
        ending = " -- Not so much.";
    }
    alert(phrase + ending);
}
```

Circle the free variables in this code. Free variables are not defined in the local scope.

```
beingFunny = true;
justSayin = false;
oocoder = true;
```

Pick one of these that closes the function.

```
notSoMuch = true;
phrase = "Do do da";
band = "Police";
```

SOLUTON

EXTREME JAVASCRIPT CHALLENGE

We need a closures expert and we've heard that's you! Now you know how closures work, can you figure out why both specimens below evaluate to 008? To figure it out, write any variables that are captured in the environments for the functions below. Note that it's perfectly fine for an environment to be empty. Here's our solution.

Specimen #1

```
var secret = "007";

function getSecret() {
    var secret = "008";

    function getValue() {
        return secret;
    }
    return getValue();
}
getSecret();
```

secret is a free variable in getValue...

Environment

secret = "008"

...so it's captured in the environment for getValue. But we don't return getValue from getSecret, so we never see the closure outside the context in which it was created.

Specimen #2

```
var secret = "007";

function getSecret() {
    var secret = "008";

    function getValue() {
        return secret;
    }
    return getValue;
}
var getValueFun = getSecret();
getValueFun();
```

secret is a free variable in getValue...

Environment

secret = "008"

...and here, we do create a closure that's returned from getSecret. So when we invoke getValueFun (getValue) in a different context (the global scope), we use the value of secret in the environment.

Sharpen your pencil
Solution

Here's our solution for this brain twister!

```
(function(food) {
    if (food === "cookies") {
        alert("More please");
    } else if (food === "cake") {
        alert("Yum yum");
    }
})("cookies");
```

Your task is to figure out not just what it computes, but how it computes. To do that, go in reverse, that is, take out the anonymous function, assign it to a variable, and then replace the previous function with the variable. Is the code more obvious now? So what does it do?

```
var eat = function(food) {
    if (food === "cookies") {
        alert("More please");
    } else if (food === "cake") {
        alert("Yum yum");
    }
};
(eat)("cookies");
```

Here's the function, extracted. We just called it eat. You could have made this a function declaration if you preferred.

You would write this as eat("cookies") of course, but we're showing how to substitute eat for the function expression above.

And what we're doing is calling eat on "cookies". But what are the extra parentheses for?

Here's the deal. Remember how a function declaration starts with the word function followed by a name? And remember how a function expression needs to be inside a statement? Well, if you don't use parentheses around the function expression, the JavaScript interpreter wants this to be a declaration rather than a function expression. But we don't need the parentheses to call eat, so you can remove them.

So all this code did was to inline a function expression and then immediately invoke it with some arguments.

Oh, and it returns "More please".

 JavaScript cross Solution

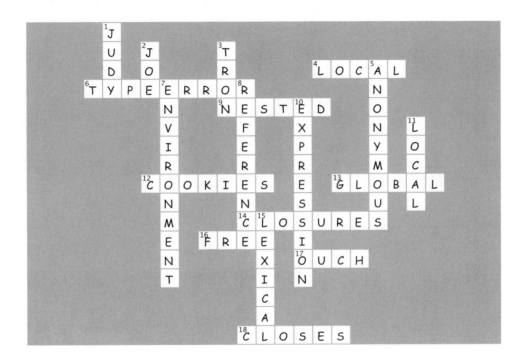

12 advanced object construction

*Creating objects

So far we've been crafting objects by hand. For each object, we've used an **object literal** to specify each and every property. That's okay on a small scale, but for serious code we need something better. That's where **object constructors** come in. With constructors we can create objects much more easily, and we can create objects that all adhere to the same **design blueprint**—meaning we can use constructors to ensure each object has the same properties and includes the same methods. And with constructors we can write object code that is much more **concise** and a lot less error prone when we're creating lots of objects. So, let's get started and after this chapter you'll be talking constructors just like you grew up in Objectville.

Creating objects with object literals

So far in this book, you've been using *object literals* to create objects. With an object literal, you create an object by writing it out... well, literally. Like this:

```
var taxi = {
    make: "Webville Motors",
    model: "Taxi",
    year: 1955,
    color: "yellow",
    passengers: 4,
    convertible: false,
    mileage: 281341,
    started: false,

    start: function() { this.started = true;},
    stop: function() { this.started = false;},
    drive: function {
        // drive code here
    }
};
```

With an object literal you type out each part of the object within curly braces. When you're done, the result is an actual JavaScript object, which you typically assign to a variable for later use.

Object literals give you a convenient way to create objects anywhere in your code, but when you need to create lots of objects—say a whole fleet of taxis—you wouldn't want to type in a hundred different object literals now would you?

⚛ BRAIN POWER

Think about creating a fleet of taxi objects. What other issues might using object literals cause?

☐ Tired fingers from a lot of typing!

☐ Can you ensure that each taxi has the same properties? What if you make a mistake or typo, or leave out a property?

☐ A lot of object literals means a lot of code. Isn't that going to lead to slow download times for the browser?

☐ The code for the start, stop and drive methods would have to be duplicated over and over.

☐ What if you decide to add or delete a property (or to change the way start or stop work)? You'd have to make the change in all the taxis.

☐ Who needs taxis when we have Uber?

Using conventions for objects

The other thing we've been doing, so far, is creating objects *by convention*. For example, we've been putting properties and methods together and saying "it's a car!" or "it's a dog!", but the only thing that makes two such objects cars (or dogs) is that we've followed our own conventions.

Now, this technique might work on a small scale but it's problematic when we have lots of objects, or even lots of developers working in the same code who might not fully know or follow the conventions.

But don't take our word for it. Take a look at some of the objects we've seen earlier in the book, which we've been told are cars:

This definitely looks like the cars we've been dealing with. It has all the same properties and methods.

```
var taxi = {
    make: "Webville Motors",
    model: "Taxi",
    year: 1955,
    color: "yellow",
    passengers: 4,
    convertible: false,
    mileage: 281341,
    started: false,

    start: function() {
        this.started = true;
    },

    stop: function() {
        this.started
```

Okay, this looks a lot like our other car objects...but wait. This has a rocket thruster. Hmm, not sure this is really a car.

The tbird looks like a great car, but we're not seeing some of the basic properties it needs, like mileage or color. It also seems to have a few extra properties. That could be a problem...

```
var rocketCar = {
    make: "Galaxy",
    model: "4000",
    year: 2001,
    color: "white",
    passengers: 6,
    convertible: false,
    mileage: 60191919,
,   started: false,

    start: function() {
        this.started = true;
    },

    stop: function() {
        this.started = false;
    },

    drive: function() {
        // drive code here
    },

    thrust: function(amount) {
        // code for thrust
    }
};
```

```
var toyCar = {
    make: "Mattel",
    model: "PeeWee",
    color: "blue",
    type: "wind up",
    Price: "2.99"
};
```

Wait, this might be a car but it looks nothing like our other cars. It does have a make, model and color, but this looks like a toy, not a car. What's this doing here?

```
var tbird = {
    make: "Ford",
    model: "Thunderbird",
    year: 1957,
    passengers: 4,
    convertible: true,
    started: false,
    oilLevel: 1.0,

    start: function() {
        if (oilLevel > .75) {
            this.started = true;
        }
    },

    stop: function() {
        this.started = false;
    },

    drive: function() {
        // drive code here
    }
};
```

If only I could find a way to **create objects** that all share the same basic structure. That way all my objects would look the same by having all the right properties and all my methods would be defined in one place. It would be something like a cookie cutter that just stamps out copies of the object for me. That would be dreamy. But I know it's just a fantasy...

Introducing Object Constructors

Object constructors, or "constructors" for short, are your path to better object creation. Think of a constructor like a little factory that can create an endless number of similar objects.

In terms of code, a constructor is quite similar to a function that returns an object: you define it once and invoke it every time you want to create a new object. But as you'll see there's a little extra that goes into a constructor.

The best way to see how constructors work is to create one. Let's revisit our old friend, the dog object, from earlier in the book and write a constructor to create as many dogs as we need. Here's a version of the dog object we've used before, with a name, a breed and a weight.

> **Object constructors and functions are closely related. Keep that in mind as you're learning how to write and use constructors.**

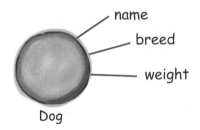

name
breed
weight

Dog

Now, if we were going to define such a dog with an object literal, it would look like this:

```
var dog = {
    name: "Fido",
    breed: "Mixed",
    weight: 38
};
```

Just a simple dog object created by an object literal. Now we need to figure out how to create a lot of these puppies.

But we don't want *just a Fido* dog, we want a way to create *any dog* that has a name, a breed and a weight. And, again, to do that we're going to write some code that looks like a function, with a dash of object syntax thrown in.

With that introduction, you must be a bit curious—go ahead and turn the page and let's get these constructors figured out and working for us.

> I personally find constructors quite Frankensteinian. They're a mix of parts from functions and objects. Could anything be more wonderful?

You'll see why on the next page.

How to create a Constructor

Using constructors is a two-step process: first we define a constructor, and then we use it to create objects. Let's first focus on creating a constructor.

What we want is a constructor that we can use to create dogs, and, more specifically, dogs with names, breeds and weights. So, we're going to define a function, called the constructor, that knows how to create dogs. Like this:

But notice that we give the name of the constructor function a capital letter. This isn't required; but everyone does it as a convention.

A constructor function looks just like a regular function.

The parameters of the function match the properties we want to supply for each individual dog.

```javascript
function Dog(name, breed, weight) {

    this.name = name;

    this.breed = breed;

    this.weight = weight;

}
```

This part feels more like an object because we're assigning each parameter to what looks like a property.

The property names and parameter names don't have to be the same, but they often are—again, by convention.

Notice that this constructor function doesn't return anything.

Hmm, we're not using local variables like in most functions. Instead we're using the this keyword, and we've only used that inside objects so far.

Hang on; we'll look at how we use the constructor next and then all this is going to fall into place and make more sense.

Sharpen your pencil

We need your help. We've been using object literals to create ducks. Given what you learned above, can you write a constructor to create ducks for us? You'll find one of our object literals below to base your constructor on:

```javascript
var duck = {
    type: "redheaded",
    canFly: true
}
```

Here's an example duck object literal.

Write a constructor for creating ducks.

P.S. We know you haven't fully figured out how this all works yet, so for now concentrate on the syntax.

How to use a Constructor

We said using a constructor is a two-step process: first we create a constructor, then we use it. Well, we've created a Dog constructor, so let's use it. Here's how we do that:

To create a dog, we use the new operator with the constructor.

Followed by a call to the constructor.

And the arguments.

Try saying it out loud: "to create fido, I create a new dog object with the name Fido that is a mixed breed and weighs 38 pounds."

```
var fido = new Dog("Fido", "Mixed", 38);
```

So, to create a new dog object with a name of "Fido", a breed of "Mixed" and a weight of 38, we start with the `new` keyword and follow it by a call to the constructor function with the appropriate arguments. After this statement is evaluated, the variable `fido` will hold a reference to our new dog object.

Now that we have a constructor for dogs, we can keep making them:

```
var fluffy = new Dog("Fluffy", "Poodle", 30);

var spot = new Dog("Spot", "Chihuahua", 10);
```

That's a bit easier than using object literals isn't it? And by creating dog objects this way, we know each dog has the same set of properties: name, breed, and weight.

Exercise

```
function Dog(name, breed, weight) {
    this.name = name;
    this.breed = breed;
    this.weight = weight;
}
var fido = new Dog("Fido", "Mixed", 38);
var fluffy = new Dog("Fluffy", "Poodle", 30);
var spot = new Dog("Spot", "Chihuahua", 10);
var dogs = [fido, fluffy, spot];

for (var i = 0; i < dogs.length; i++) {
    var size = "small";
    if (dogs[i].weight > 10) {
        size = "large";
    }
    console.log("Dog: " + dogs[i].name
                + " is a " + size
                + " " + dogs[i].breed);
}
```

Let's get some quick hands-on experience to help this all sink in. Go ahead and put this code in a page and give it a test drive. Write your output here.

How constructors work

We've seen how to declare a constructor and also how to use it to create objects, but we should also take a look behind the scenes to see how a constructor actually works. Here's the key: to understand constructors we need to know what the new operator is doing.

We'll start with the statement we used to create fido:

```
var fido = new Dog("Fido", "Mixed", 38);
```

Take a look at the right-hand side of the assignment, where all the action is. Let's follow its execution:

Behind the Scenes

(1) The first thing new does is create a new, empty object:

(2) Next, new sets this to point to the new object.

this ← Remember from Chapter 5 that this holds a reference to the current object our code is dealing with.

(3) With this set up, we now call the function Dog, passing "Fido", "Mixed" and 38 as arguments.

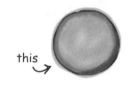

```
function Dog(name, breed, weight) {
    this.name = name;
    this.breed = breed;
    this.weight = weight;
}
```

(4) Next the body of the function is invoked. Like most constructors, Dog assigns values to properties in the newly created this object.

Executing the body of the Dog function customizes the new object with three properties, assigning them the values of the respective parameters.

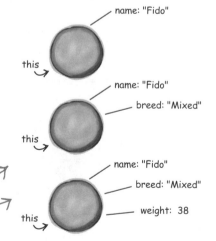

this ➜ name: "Fido"

this ➜ name: "Fido"
            breed: "Mixed"

this ➜ name: "Fido"
            breed: "Mixed"
            weight: 38

⑤ Finally, once the Dog function has completed its execution the `new` operator returns `this`, which is a reference to the newly created object. Notice `this` is returned for you; you don't have to explicitly return it in your code. And after the new object has been returned, we assign that reference to the variable `fido`.

Behind the Scenes

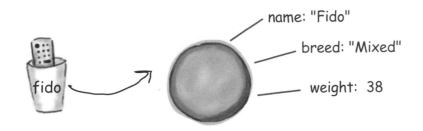

name: "Fido"

breed: "Mixed"

fido

weight: 38

BE the Browser

Below, you'll find JavaScript code with some mistakes in it. Your job is to play like you're the browser and find the errors in the code. After you've done the exercise look at the end of the chapter to see if you found them all. And, hey by the way, this is Chapter 12. Feel free to make style comments too. You've earned the right.

```javascript
function widget(partNo, size) {
    var this.no = partNo;
    var this.breed = size;
}
function FormFactor(material, widget) {
    this.material = material,
    this.widget = widget,
    return this;
}

var widgetA = widget(100, "large");
var widgetB = new widget(101, "small");
var formFactorA = newFormFactor("plastic", widgetA);
var formFactorB = new ForumFactor("metal", widgetB);
```

You can put methods into constructors as well

The dog objects that the Dog constructor creates are just like the dogs from earlier in the book… except that our newly constructed dogs can't bark (because they don't have a `bark` method). This is easily fixed because in addition to assigning values to properties in the constructor, we can set up methods too. Let's extend the code to include a `bark` method:

> *By the way, as you know, methods in objects are properties too. They just happen to have a function assigned to them.*

To add a bark method we simply assign a function, in this case an anonymous function, to the property this.bark.

```javascript
function Dog(name, breed, weight) {
    this.name = name;
    this.breed = breed;
    this.weight = weight;
    this.bark = function() {
        if (this.weight > 25) {
            alert(this.name + " says Woof!");
        } else {
            alert(this.name + " says Yip!");
        }
    };
}
```

Now every dog object will also have a bark method that you can invoke.

Notice that, just like all the other objects we've created in the past, we use this to refer to the object we're calling the method on.

Take the bark method for a quick test drive

Enough talking about constructors, let's add the code above to an HTML page, and then add the code below to test it:

```javascript
var fido = new Dog("Fido", "Mixed", 38);
var fluffy = new Dog("Fluffy", "Poodle", 30);
var spot = new Dog("Spot", "Chihuahua", 10);
var dogs = [fido, fluffy, spot];

for (var i = 0; i < dogs.length; i++) {
    dogs[i].bark();
}
```

Make sure your dog objects bark like they're supposed to.

The page at localhost says:
Fido says Woof!

OK

The page at localhost says:
Fluffy says Woof!

OK

The page at localhost says:
Spot says Yip!

OK

We've got a constructor to create coffee drinks, but it's missing its methods.

We need a method, getSize, that returns a string depending on the number of ounces of coffee:

■ 8oz is a small

■ 12oz is a medium

■ 16oz is a large

We also need a method, toString, that returns a string that represents your order, like "You've ordered a small House Blend coffee."

Write your code below, and then test it in the browser. Try creating a few different sizes of coffee. Check your answer before you go on.

```
function Coffee(roast, ounces) {
    this.roast = roast;
    this.ounces = ounces;
```

Write the two methods for this constructor here.

```
}
```

```
var houseBlend = new Coffee("House Blend", 12);
console.log(houseBlend.toString());
```

```
var darkRoast = new Coffee("Dark Roast", 16);
console.log(darkRoast.toString());
```

Here's our output; yours should look similar.

JavaScript console

You've ordered a medium House Blend coffee.

You've ordered a large Dark Roast coffee.

Q: **Why do constructor names start with a capital letter?**

A: This is a convention that JavaScript developers use so they can easily identify which functions are constructors, and which functions are just regular old functions. Why? Because with constructor functions, you need to use the new operator. In general, using a capital letter for constructors makes them easier to pick out when you're reading code.

Q: **So, other than setting up the properties of the** `this` **object, a constructor's just like a regular function?**

A: If you mean computationally, yes. You can do anything in a constructor you can do in a regular function, like declare and use variables, use for loops, call other functions, and so on. The only thing you don't want to do is return a value (other than **this**) from a constructor because that will cause the constructor to not return the object it's supposed to be constructing.

Q: **Do the parameter names of a constructor function have to match the property names?**

A: No. You can use whatever names you want for the parameters. The parameters are just used to hold values that we want to assign to the object's properties to customize the object. What matters is the name of the properties you use for the object. That said, we often do use the same names for clarity, so we know which properties we're assigning by looking at the constructor function definition.

Q: **Is an object created by a constructor just like an object created with a literal?**

A: Yes, until you get into more advanced object design, which we'll do in the next chapter.

Q: **Why do we need** `new` **to create objects? Couldn't we create an object in a regular function and return it (kind of like we did with makeCar in chapter 5)?**

A: Yes, you could create objects that way, but like we said in the previous answer, there are some extra things that happen when you use `new`. We'll get more into these issues later in this chapter, and again in Chapter 13.

Q: **I'm still a bit confused by** `this` **in the constructor. We're using** `this` **to assign properties to the object, and we're also using** `this` **in the methods of the object. Are these the same thing?**

A: When you call a constructor (to create an object) the value of **this** is set to the new object that's being created so all the code that is evaluated in the constructor applies to that new object.

Later, when you call a method on an object, **this** is set to the object whose method you called. So the **this** in your methods will always refer to the object whose method was called.

Q: **Is it better to create objects with a constructor than with object literals?**

A: Both are useful. A constructor is useful when you want to create lots of objects with the same property names and methods. Using them is convenient, reuses code, and provides consistency across your objects.

But sometimes we just need a quick object, perhaps a one-time-use only object, and literals are concise and expressive to use for this.

We'll see a good example of this a bit later.

So it really depends what your needs are. Both are great ways to create an object.

DANGER ZONE

There's one aspect of constructors you need to be very careful about: don't forget to use the **new** keyword. It's easy to do because a constructor is, after all, a function, and you can call it without **new**. *But if you forget **new** on a constructor it can lead to buggy code that is hard to troubleshoot.* Let's take a look at what can happen when you forget the **new** keyword...

```
function Album(title, artist, year) {
    this.title = title;
    this.artist = artist;
    this.year = year;
    this.play = function() {
        // code here
    };
}
var darkside = Album("Dark Side of the Cheese","Pink Mouse", 1971);
darkside.play();
```

This looks like a well-constructed constructor.

But maybe that's okay because Album is a function.

Oops we forgot to use new!

Let's try to call the play method anyway. Oh, this isn't good...

Uncaught TypeError: Cannot call method 'play' of undefined

SAFETY CHECKLIST

Okay, let's read the checklist to see why this might have happened:

The global object is the top-level object, which is where global variables get stored. In browsers, this object is the window object.

❑ Remember that **new** first creates a new object before assigning it to **this** (and then calling your constructor function). If you don't use **new**, a new object will never be created.

❑ That means any references to **this** in your constructor won't refer to a new album object, but rather, will refer to the global object of your application.

❑ If you don't use **new** there's no object to return from the constructor, which means there is no object assigned to the darkside variable, so darkside is undefined. That's why when we try to call the play method, we get an error saying the object we're trying to call it on is undefined.

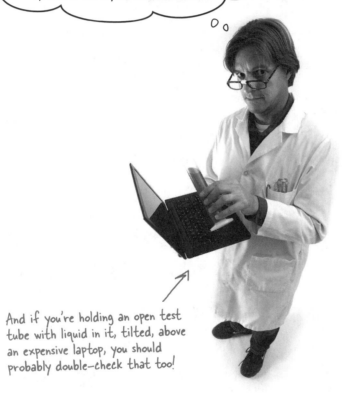

If you're using a constructor to create objects and those objects keep coming up undefined when you reference them, double check your code and make sure you're using a **new** operator with your constructor.

And if you're holding an open test tube with liquid in it, tilted, above an expensive laptop, you should probably double-check that too!

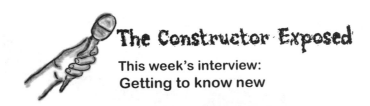

The Constructor Exposed

**This week's interview:
Getting to know new**

Head First: new, where have you been hiding? How did we get to Chapter 12 before seeing you?

new: There are still a lot of scripts out there that don't use me, or use me without understanding me.

Head First: Why is that?

new: Because many scripters just use object literals or copy & paste code that uses me, without understanding how I work.

Head First: That's a good point... object literals are convenient, and I myself am not quite clear on when or how to use you just yet.

new: Well it's true, I am kind of an advanced feature. After all, to know how to use me, you first have to know how objects work, and how functions work, and how this works... it's a lot to wrap your head around before you even learn about me at all!

Head First: Can you give us the elevator pitch about yourself? Now that our readers know about objects, functions, and this, it would be great for them to get motivated for learning about you.

new: Let me think for a second... Okay here you go: I'm the operator that operates on constructor functions to create new objects.

Head First: Umm, I hate to break it to you but that isn't the best elevator pitch.

new: Gimme a break, I'm an operator, not a PR lackey.

Head First: Well, you do raise several questions with that pitch. First of all, you're an operator?

new: Yup! I'm an operator. Put me in front of a function call and I change everything. An operator operates on its operands. In my case, I have only one operand and that operand is a function call.

Head First: Right, so explain exactly how you operate.

new: Well, first, I make a new object. Everyone thinks that the constructor function is what does it, but it's actually me. It's a thankless job.

Head First: Go on...

new: Okay, so then I call the constructor function and make sure that the new object I've created is referenced by the this keyword in the body of the function.

Head First: Why do you do that?

new: So that the statements in the body of the function have a way to refer to the object. After all, the whole point of a constructor function is to extend that object using new properties and methods. If you're using the constructor to create objects like dogs and cars, you're going to want those objects to have some properties, right?

Head First: Right. And then?

new: Then I make sure that the new object that was created is returned from the constructor. It's a nice convenience so that developers don't have to remember to return it themselves.

Head First: It does sound very convenient. Now why would anyone use an object literal after learning you?

new: Oh, object literal and I go way back. He's a great guy, and I'd use him in a second if I had to create a quick object. But, you want me when you've got to create a lot of similar objects, when you want to make sure your objects are taking advantage of code reuse, when you want to ensure some consistency, and after you've learned a little more, to support some even more advanced uses.

Head First: More advanced? Oh do tell!

new: Now now, let's keep these readers focused. We'll talk more in the next chapter.

Head First: I think I need to re-read this interview first! Until then...

It's Production Time!

You've learned your object
construction skills just in time
because we've just received a
big order for cars and we can't be
creating them all by hand. We need
to use a constructor so we can get the job
done on time. We're going to do that by taking the
car object literals we've used so far in the book, and using
them as a guide for creating a constructor to make cars.

Check out the various kinds of cars we need to build below. Notice
we've already taken the liberty of making their properties and methods uniform,
so they all match across each car. For now, we won't worry about special options, or toy cars and rocket
cars (we'll come back to that later). Go ahead and take a look, and then let's build a constructor that can
create car objects for any kind of car that has these property names and methods:

```javascript
var chevy = {
    make: "Chevy",
    model: "Bel Air",
    year: 1957,
    color: "red",
    passengers: 2,
    convertible: false,
    mileage: 1021,
    started: false,

    start: function() {
      this.started = true;
    },

    stop: function() {
      this.started = false;
    },

    drive: function() {
      if (this.started) {
        console.log(this.make + " " +
            this.model + " goes zoom zoom!");
      } else {
        console.log("Start the engine first.");
      }
    }
};
```

```javascript
var cadi = {
    make: "GM",
    model: "Cadillac",
    year: 1955,
    color: "tan",
    passengers: 5,
    convertible: false,
    mileage: 12892,
    started: false,
    start: function() {...},
    stop: function() {...},
    drive: function() {...}
```

```javascript
var fiat = {
    make: "Fiat",
    model: "500",
    year: 1957,
    color: "Medium Blue",
    passengers: 2,
    convertible: false,
    mileage: 88000,
    started: false,
    start: function() {...},
    stop: function() {
    drive: function()
};
```

```javascript
var taxi = {
    make: "Webville Motors",
    model: "Taxi",
    year: 1955,
    color: "yellow",
    passengers: 4,
    convertible: false,
    mileage: 281341,
    started: false,
    start: function() {...},
    stop: function() {...},
    drive: function() {...}
};
```

Exercise

Use everything you've learned to create a Car constructor. We suggest the following order:

① Start by providing the function keyword (actually we did that for you) followed by the constructor name. Next supply the parameters; you'll need one for each property that you want to supply an initial value for.

② Next, assign each property in the object its initial value (make sure you use `this` along with the property name).

③ Finally, add in the three car methods: start, drive and stop.

```
function _____ (_____) {
```

← All your work goes here.

Make sure you check all your work with the answer at the end of the chapter before proceeding!

```
}
```

Let's test drive some new cars

Now that we have a way to mass-produce car objects, let's make some, and put them through their paces. Start by putting the Car constructor in an HTML page, then add some test code.

Note: you won't be able to do this unless you did the exercise on the previous page! 😌

Here's the code we used; feel free to alter and extend it:

First we're using the constructor to create all the cars from Chapter 5.

```javascript
var chevy = new Car("Chevy", "Bel Air", 1957, "red", 2, false, 1021);
var cadi = new Car("GM", "Cadillac", 1955, "tan", 5, false, 12892);
var taxi = new Car("Webville Motors", "Taxi", 1955, "yellow", 4, false, 281341);
var fiat = new Car("Fiat", "500", 1957, "Medium Blue", 2, false, 88000);
```

But why stop there?

```javascript
var testCar = new Car("Webville Motors", "Test Car", 2014, "marine", 2, true, 21);
```

Let's create the book's test drive car! →

Are you starting to see how easy creating new objects can be with constructors? Now let's take these cars for a test drive:

Feel free to add your own favorite or fictional car too.

```javascript
var cars = [chevy, cadi, taxi, fiat, testCar];

for(var i = 0; i < cars.length; i++) {
    cars[i].start();
    cars[i].drive();
    cars[i].drive();
    cars[i].stop();
}
```

Here's the output we got. Did you add your own car to the mix? Try changing what the cars do (like driving before the car is started). Or, maybe you can make the number of times we call the drive method random?

```
JavaScript console

Chevy Bel Air goes zoom zoom!
Chevy Bel Air goes zoom zoom!
GM Cadillac goes zoom zoom!
GM Cadillac goes zoom zoom!
Webville Motors Taxi goes zoom zoom!
Webville Motors Taxi goes zoom zoom!
Fiat 500 goes zoom zoom!
Fiat 500 goes zoom zoom!
Webville Motors Test Car goes zoom zoom!
Webville Motors Test Car goes zoom zoom!
```

Don't count out object literals just yet

We've had some discussion of object constructors versus object literals, and mentioned that object literals are still quite useful, but you really haven't seen a good example of that. Well, let's do a little reworking of the Car constructor code, so you can see where using some object literals actually cleans up the code and makes it more readable and maintainable.

Let's look at the Car constructor again and see how we might be able to clean it up a bit.

Notice we're using a lot of parameters here. We count seven.

The more we add (and we always end up adding more as the requirements for objects grow), the harder this is to read.

```
function Car(make, model, year, color, passengers, convertible, mileage) {
    this.make = make;
    this.model = model;
    this.year = year;
    this.color = color;
    this.passengers = passengers;
    this.convertible = convertible;
    this.mileage = mileage;
    this.started = false;

    this.start = function() {
        this.started = true;
    };
    //rest of the methods here
}
```

And when we write code that calls this constructor we have to make sure we get the arguments all in exactly the right order.

So the problem we're highlighting here is that we have a heck of a lot of parameters in the Car constructor, making it difficult to read and maintain. It's also difficult to write code to call this constructor. While that might seem like a minor inconvenience, it actually causes more bugs than you might think, and not only that, they're often nasty bugs that are hard to diagnose at first.

They're hard to diagnose because if you switch two variables, the code is still syntactically correct, but it doesn't function correctly because you've switched two values.

However, there is a common technique that we can use when passing all these arguments that can be used for any function, whether or not it's a constructor. The technique works like this: take all your arguments, throw them in an object literal, and then pass that literal to your function—that way you're passing all your values in one container (the literal object) and you don't have worry about matching the order of your arguments and parameters.

Or if you leave out a value, all kinds of craziness can ensue!

Let's rewrite the code to call the Car constructor, and then do a slight rework of the constructor code to see how this works.

Rewiring the arguments as an object literal

Let's take the call to the Car constructor and rework its arguments into an object literal:

All you need to do is take each argument and place it in an object literal with an appropriate property name. We use the same property names used in the constructor.

```
var cadi = new Car("GM", "Cadillac", 1955, "tan", 5, false, 12892);
```

We've kept the same order, but there is no reason you'd have to.

```
var cadiParams = {make: "GM",
                  model: "Cadillac",
                  year: 1955,
                  color: "tan",
                  passengers: 5,
                  convertible: false,
                  mileage: 12892};
```

And then we can rewrite the call to the Car constructor like this:

```
var cadiParams = {make: "GM",
                  model: "Cadillac",
                  year: 1955,
                  color: "tan",
                  passengers: 5,
                  convertible: false,
                  mileage: 12892};
```

Wow, talk about a makeover. Not only is this much cleaner, it's a lot more readable, at least in our humble opinion.

```
var cadi = new Car(cadiParams);
```

Now we're passing a single argument to the Car constructor.

But we're not done yet because the constructor itself is still expecting seven arguments, not one object. Let's rework the constructor code, and then we'll give this a test.

Reworking the Car constructor

Now you need to remove all the individual parameters in the Car constructor and replace them with properties from the object that we're passing in. We'll call that parameter `params`. You also need to rework the code a bit to use this object. Here's how:

```
var cadiParams = {make: "GM",
                   model: "Cadillac",
                   year: 1955,
                   color: "tan",
                   passengers: 5,
                   convertible: false,
                   mileage: 12892};
```

No changes here, we've just reproduced the object literal and the call to the Car constructor from the previous page.

```
var cadi = new Car(cadiParams);
```

First things first. We'll replace the seven parameters of the Car constructor with one parameter, for the object we're passing in.

```
function Car(params) {
    this.make = params.make;
    this.model = params.model;
    this.year = params.year;
    this.color = params.color;
    this.passengers = params.passengers;
    this.convertible = params.convertible;
    this.mileage = params.mileage;
    this.started = false;

    this.start = function() {
        this.started = true;
    };
    this.stop = function() {
        this.started = false;
    };
    this.drive = function() {
        if (this.started) {
            alert("Zoom zoom!");
        } else {
            alert("You need to start the engine first.");
        }
    };
}
```

Then for each reference to a parameter, we substitute the corresponding property from the object passed into the function.

In our methods we never use a parameter directly. It wouldn't make sense to because we always want to use the object's properties (which we do using the `this` variable). So, no changes are needed to this code at all.

Test drive

Update the `cadi` and all your other cars, and test your code.

```
cadi.start();
cadi.drive();
cadi.drive();
cadi.stop();
```

Exercise

Copy the Car and Dog constructors into one file, and then add the code below along with it. Give this a run and capture the output.

You'll find the Dog constructor on page 530.

```
var limoParams = {make: "Webville Motors",
                   model: "limo",
                   year: 1983,
                   color: "black",
                   passengers: 12,
                   convertible: true,
                   mileage: 21120};

var limo = new Car(limoParams);
var limoDog = new Dog("Rhapsody In Blue", "Poodle", 40);

console.log(limo.make + " " + limo.model + " is a " + typeof limo);
console.log(limoDog.name + " is a " + typeof limoDog);
```

← Put the output here.

BRAIN POWER

Say someone handed you an object and you wanted to know what type of object it was (is it a Car? a Dog? Superman?), or you wanted to see if it was the same type as another object. Would the typeof operator be helpful?

there are no Dumb Questions

Q: Remind me what typeof does again?

A: The typeof operator returns the type of its operand. If you pass it a string you'll get back "string", if you pass it an object you'll get back "object" and so on. You can pass it any type: a number, a string, a boolean, or a more complex type like an object or function. But typeof can't be more specific and tell you the object is a dog or a car.

Q: So if typeof can't tell me that my object is a dog or car, how do I determine what is what?

A: Many other object-oriented languages, like Java or C++, have a strong notion of object typing. In those languages you can examine an object and determine exactly what type of object it is. But, JavaScript treats objects and their types in a looser, more dynamic way. Because of this, many developers have jumped to the conclusion that JavaScript has a less powerful object system, but the truth is, its object system is actually more general and flexible. Because JavaScript's type system is more dynamic, it's a little more difficult to determine if an object is a dog or a car, and it depends on what you think a dog is or a car is. However, we have another operator that can give us a little more information... so continue reading.

Understanding Object Instances

You can't look at a JavaScript object and determine that it is an object of a specific type, like a dog or a car. In JavaScript, objects are dynamic structures, and the type of all objects is just "object," no matter what properties and methods it has. But we can get some information about an object if we know the *constructor* that created the object.

Remember that each time you call a constructor using the `new` operator, you are creating a new instance of an object. And, if you used, say, the Car constructor to do that, then we say, informally, that the object is a car. More formally, we say that object is an *instance of* a Car.

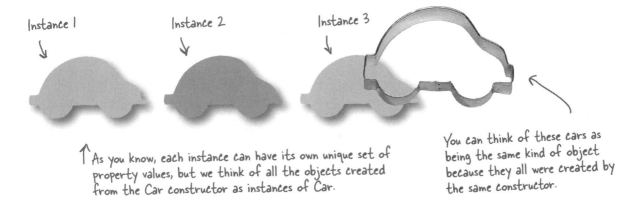

Instance 1   Instance 2   Instance 3

↑ As you know, each instance can have its own unique set of property values, but we think of all the objects created from the Car constructor as instances of Car.

You can think of these cars as being the same kind of object because they all were created by the same constructor.

Now saying an object is an instance of some constructor is more than just talk. We can actually write code to inspect the constructor that made an object with the `instanceof` operator. Let's look at some code:

```javascript
var cadiParams = {make: "GM", model: "Cadillac", year: 1955, color: "tan",
                  passengers: 5, convertible: false, mileage: 12892};

var cadi = new Car(cadiParams);

if (cadi instanceof Car) {
    console.log("Congrats, it's a Car!");
};
```

The instanceof operator returns true if the object was created by the specified constructor.

In this case we're saying "Is the cadi object an instance that was created by the Car constructor?"

As it turns out, one of the things the `new` operator does behind the scenes when the object is created is to store information that allows it to determine, at any time, the constructor that created the object. And `instanceof` uses that to determine if an object is an instance of a certain constructor.

It's a bit more complicated than we're describing here, but we'll talk about that in the next chapter.

JavaScript console

Congrats, it's a Car!

Exercise

We need a function named dogCatcher that returns true if the object passed to it is a dog, and false otherwise. Write that function and test it with the rest of the code below. Don't forget to check your answer at the end of the chapter before you go on!

```
function dogCatcher(obj) {



                                                    Add your code here
                                                    to implement the
                                                    dogCatcher function.

}
                                      And here's your test code.
function Cat(name, breed, weight) {
    this.name = name;
    this.breed = breed;
    this.weight = weight;
}
var meow = new Cat("Meow", "Siamese", 10);
var whiskers = new Cat("Whiskers", "Mixed", 12);

var fido = {name: "Fido", breed: "Mixed", weight: 38};

function Dog(name, breed, weight) {
    this.name = name;
    this.breed = breed;
    this.weight = weight;
    this.bark = function() {
        if (this.weight > 25) {
            alert(this.name + " says Woof!");
        } else {
            alert(this.name + " says Yip!");
        }
    };
}
var fluffy = new Dog("Fluffy", "Poodle", 30);
var spot = new Dog("Spot", "Chihuahua", 10);
var dogs = [meow, whiskers, fido, fluffy, spot];

for (var i = 0; i < dogs.length; i++) {
    if (dogCatcher(dogs[i])) {
        console.log(dogs[i].name + " is a dog!");
    }
}
```

So an object is a dog if it was created with a Dog constructor, and not otherwise?

Yes, that's how it works. JavaScript doesn't have a strong sense of an object's type, so if you need to compare objects to see if they are both cats or both dogs, you check to see if they were constructed the same way— that is, with the same constructor function. As we've said, a cat is a cat if it was created by the Cat constructor, and a dog is a dog if it was created by the Dog constructor.

Now in the next chapter you're going to see JavaScript constructors and objects are even more flexible than we've already seen. For instance, we might have an object that was created with a Taxi constructor, and yet we know that it is also a car. But for now, just stash that idea in the back of your brain and we'll come back to it later.

Even constructed objects can have their own independent properties

We've talked a lot about how to use constructors to create consistent objects—objects that have the same set of properties and the same methods. But what we haven't mentioned is that using constructors still doesn't prevent us from changing an object into something else later, because after an object has been created by a constructor, it can be altered.

What exactly are we talking about? Remember when we introduced object literals? We looked at how we could add and delete properties after the object was created. You can do the same with objects created from constructors:

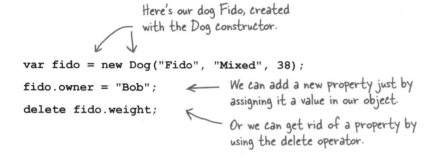

Here's our dog Fido, created with the Dog constructor.

```
var fido = new Dog("Fido", "Mixed", 38);

fido.owner = "Bob";

delete fido.weight;
```

We can add a new property just by assigning it a value in our object.

Or we can get rid of a property by using the delete operator.

You can even add new methods if you like:

To add a method just assign the method to a new property name in the object.

```
fido.trust = function(person) {

        return (person === "Bob");

    };
```

Anonymous function alert! See, they're everywhere!

Notice that here we're changing only the fido object. If we add a method to fido, only fido has that method. No other dogs have it:

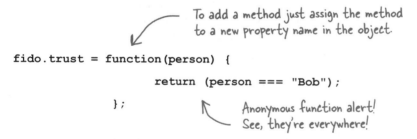

```
var notBite = fido.trust("Bob");
```

This code works because trust is defined in the fido object. So notBite is true.

```
var spot = new Dog("Spot", "Chihuahua", 10);

notBite = spot.trust("Bob");
```

This code doesn't work because spot doesn't have a method trust, resulting in: "TypeError: Object #<Dog> has no method 'trust'"

So if I change a car object after I create it, is it still a car?

Yes, a car is still a car, even if you change it later.

And what we mean by that is if you check to see if your object is still an instance of Car, it will be. For instance, if we create a car object:

```
var cadiParams = {make: "GM", model: "Cadillac",
                   year: 1955, color: "tan",
                   passengers: 5, convertible: false,
                   mileage: 12892};
var cadi = new Car(cadiParams);
```

We can add a new property `chrome` and delete the property `convertible`:

```
cadi.chrome = true;
delete cadi.convertible;
```

and yet, the `cadi` is still a car:

```
cadi instanceof Car
```
Evaluates to true.

Now is it really a car in practical terms? What if we deleted every property in the object? Would it still be a car? The `instanceof` operator would tell us yes. But judging by our own terms, probably not.

Chances are, you won't often want to use a constructor to create an object and then later change it into something that's unrecognizable as an object created by that constructor. In general, you'll use constructors to create objects that are fairly consistent. But if you need objects that are more flexible, well, JavaScript can handle that. It's your job as a code designer to decide how to use constructors and objects in a way that makes sense for you (and don't forget your coworkers).

This is what we meant earlier when we said that JavaScript has a dynamic type system.

> These built-in objects really save me time. Heck, these days I get home early enough to watch a little "Golden Girls."

Real World Constructors

JavaScript comes with a set of constructors for instantiating some handy objects—like objects that know how to deal with dates and times, objects that are great at finding patterns in text, and even objects that will give you a new perspective on arrays. Now that you know how constructors work, and also how to use the `new` keyword, you're in a great position to make use of these constructors, or more importantly the objects they create. Let's just take a quick dip into a couple, and then you'll be all ready to go out and explore them on your own.

Let's start with JavaScript's built-in date object. To get one we just use its constructor:

```
var now = new Date();
```
← Creates a new date representing the current date and time.

Calling the Date constructor gives you back an instance of Date that represents the current local date and time. With a date object in hand, you can then use its methods to manipulate dates (and times) and also retrieve various properties of a date and time. Here are a few examples:

```
var dateString = now.toString();
```
← Returns a string that represents the date, like "Thu Feb 06 2014 17:29:29 GMT-0800 (PST)".

```
var theYear = now.getFullYear();
```
← Returns the year in the date.

```
var theDayOfWeek = now.getDay();
```
← Returns a number for the day of the week represented by the date object, like 1 (for Monday).

You can easily create date objects representing any date and time by passing additional arguments to the Date constructor. For instance, say you need a date object representing "May 1, 1983", you can do that with:

```
var birthday = new Date("May 1, 1983");
```
← You can pass a simple date string to the constructor like this.

And you can get even more specific by including a time:

```
var birthday = new Date("May 1, 1983 08:03 pm");
```
← Now, we're including a time in the string too.

We are, of course, just giving you a flyby of the date object; you'll want to check out its full set of properties and methods in *JavaScript: The Definitive Guide*.

The Array object

Next up, another interesting built-in object: the array object. While we've been creating arrays using the square bracket notation [1, 2, 3], you can create arrays using a constructor too:

```
var emptyArray = new Array();
```
← Creates an empty array with length zero.

Here, we're creating a new, empty array object. And at any time we can add items to it, like this:

```
emptyArray[0] = 99;
```
← This should look familiar. This is the same way we've always added items to an array.

We can also create array objects that have a specific size. Say we want an array with three items:

```
var oddNumbers = new Array(3);
oddNumbers[0] = 1;
oddNumbers[1] = 3;
oddNumbers[2] = 5;
```
← We create an array of length three, and fill it in with values after we create it.

Here we've created an array of length three. Initially the three items in oddNumbers are undefined, but we then set each item in the array to a value. You could easily add more items to the array if you wanted.

None of this should be shockingly different than what you're used to. Where the array object gets interesting is in its set of methods. You already know about array's sort method, and here are a few other interesting ones:

This reverses all the values in the array (so we have 5, 3, 1 in oddNumbers now). Notice, the method changes the original array.

```
oddNumbers.reverse();
```

←The join method creates a string from the values in oddNumbers placing a " – " between the values, and returns that string. So this returns the string "5 – 3 – 1".

```
var aString = oddNumbers.join(" - ");
```

```
var areAllOdd = oddNumbers.every(function(x) {
    return ((x % 2) !== 0);
});
```

The every method takes a function and tests each value of the array to see if the function returns true or false when called on that value. If the function returns true for all the array items, then the result of the every method is true.

Again, that's just the tip of the iceberg, so take a look at *JavaScript: The Definitive Guide* to fully explore the array object. You've got all the knowledge you need to take it on.

Back up the bus. Up until now we've been creating arrays in a totally different way.

Good catch. The bracket notation, [ ], that you've been using to create arrays is actually just a shorthand for using the Array constructor directly. Check out these two equivalent ways of creating empty arrays:

```
var items = new Array();
var items = [];
```
← These do the same thing. The bracket notation is supported in the JavaScript language to make your life easier when creating arrays.

Likewise, if you write code like this:

```
var items = ["a", "b", "c"];
```
← We call this array literal syntax.

That's just a shorthand for using the constructor in another way:

```
var items = new Array("a", "b", "c");
```
← If you pass more than one argument, this creates an array holding the values you pass it.

And, the objects created from the literal notation or by using the constructor directly are the same, so you can use methods on either one.

You might be asking why you'd ever use the constructor rather than the literal notation. The constructor comes in handy when you need to create an array of a specific size you determine at runtime, and then add items to it later, like this:

```
var n = getNumberOfWidgetsFromDatabase();
var widgets = new Array(n);
for(var i=0; i < n; i++) {
    widgets[i] = getDatabaseRecord(i);
}
```
← This code presumably uses big arrays that we won't know the size of until runtime.

So, for creating a quick array, using the array literal syntax to create your array objects works wonderfully, but using the Array constructor might make sense when you're creating the array programmatically. You can use either or both as much as you want.

Even more fun with built-in objects

Date and array aren't the only built-in objects in JavaScript. There are lots of other objects that come with the language you might find handy at times. Here's a short list (there are more, so search online for "JavaScript's standard built-in objects" if you're curious!).

Object By using the Object constructor you can create objects. Like arrays, the object literal notation { } is equivalent to using new Object(). More on this later.

Math This object has properties and methods for doing math stuff. Like Math.PI and Math.random().

RegExp Use this constructor to create regular expression objects, which allow you to search for patterns, even complex ones, in text.

Error This constructor creates standard error objects that are handy when catching errors in your code.

there are no Dumb Questions

Q: I'm confused by how the Date and Array constructors work: they seem to support zero or more arguments. Like with Date, if I don't provide an argument, then I get today's date, but I can also pass arguments to get other dates. How does that work?

A: Right, good catch. It's possible to write functions that do different things based on the number of arguments. So if the Array constructor has zero arguments, the constructor knows it is creating an empty array; if it has one argument it knows that's the size of the array, and if it has more, then those arguments are all initial values.

Q: Can we do that with our constructors?

A: Of course. This is something we haven't covered, but every function gets passed an arguments object that contains all the arguments passed to the function. You can use this to determine what was passed

and act appropriately (check the appendix for more on the arguments object). There are other techniques based on checking to see which of your parameters is set to undefined.

Q: We used Math earlier in the book. Why don't I have to say "new Math" to instantiate a math object before I use it?

A: Great question. Actually, Math is not a constructor, or even a function. It's an object. As you know, Math is a built-in object that you can use to do things like get the value of pi (with `Math.PI`) or generate a random number (with `Math.random`). Think of Math as just like an object literal that has a bunch of useful properties and methods in it, built-in for you to use whenever you write JavaScript code. It just happens to have a capital first letter to let you know that it's built-in to JavaScript.

Q: I know how to check if an object is an instance of a constructor name, but how do I write the code to ask if two objects have the same constructor?

A: You can check to see if two objects have the same constructor like this:

```
((fido instanceof Dog) &&
        (spot instanceof Dog))
```

If this expression results in true, then fido and spot were indeed created by the same constructor.

Q: If I create an object with an object literal, what is it an instance of? Or is it not an instance of anything?

A: An object literal is an instance of Object. Think of Object as the constructor for the most generic kind of object in JavaScript. You'll learn much more about how Object figures into JavaScript's object system in the next chapter.

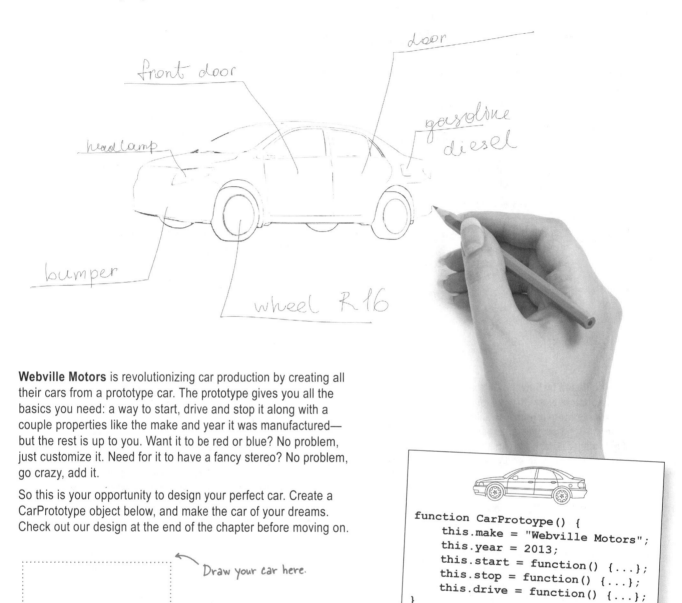

front door

door

headlamp

gasoline
diesel

bumper

wheel R16

Webville Motors is revolutionizing car production by creating all their cars from a prototype car. The prototype gives you all the basics you need: a way to start, drive and stop it along with a couple properties like the make and year it was manufactured— but the rest is up to you. Want it to be red or blue? No problem, just customize it. Need for it to have a fancy stereo? No problem, go crazy, add it.

So this is your opportunity to design your perfect car. Create a CarPrototype object below, and make the car of your dreams. Check out our design at the end of the chapter before moving on.

Draw your car here.

```
function CarProtoype() {
    this.make = "Webville Motors";
    this.year = 2013;
    this.start = function() {...};
    this.stop = function() {...};
    this.drive = function() {...};
}
```

And customize
the prototype
here.

Oh, and where are we going with this? You'll find out in the next chapter! By the way, you're done with this chapter... Oh, but there's still the bullet points and the crossword puzzle to do!

BULLET POINTS

- An **object literal** works well when you need to create a small number of objects.

- A **constructor** works well when you need to create many similar objects.

- Constructors are functions that are meant to be used with the **new** operator. We capitalize the names of constructors by convention.

- Using a constructor we can create objects that are consistent, having the same property names and methods.

- Use the **new** operator with a constructor function call to create an object.

- When you use **new** with a constructor function call, it creates a new, empty object, which is assigned to **this** within the body of the constructor.

- Use **this** in a constructor function to access the object being constructed and add properties to the object.

- A new object is returned automatically by the constructor function.

- If you forget to use **new** with a constructor, no object is created. This will cause errors in your code that can be difficult to debug.

- To customize objects, we pass arguments to a constructor, and use those values to initialize the properties of the object being created.

- If a constructor has a lot of parameters, consider consolidating them into one object parameter.

- To know if an object was created by a specific constructor, use the **instanceof** operator.

- You can modify an object that was created by a constructor just like you can modify an object literal.

- JavaScript comes with a number of constructors you can use to create useful objects like date objects, regular expressions and arrays.

 # JavaScript cross

Construct some new connections in your brain with this crossword puzzle.

ACROSS

2. A constructor is a _____.

7. If you want to save my birthday in a variable, you'll need a _____ constructor.

9. You can use an object literal to pass arguments to a constructor when the constructor has lots of these.

10. When you create an object from a constructor, we say it is an _____ of the constructor.

11. A constructor is a bit like a _____ cutter.

14. The constructor function returns the newly constructed _____.

15. If you forget to use new with a constructor, you might see a _____.

DOWN

1. Constructor syntax is a bit _____.

3. You can add a property to an object created by a _____ whenever you want.

4. new is an _____, not a PR lackey.

5. The Webville Motors test car comes in this color.

6. Using a constructor, we can make our cars so they have all the same _____.

8. Never hold a _____ over your laptop.

12. The limo and the limoDog are the same _____.

13. To create an object with a constructor, you use the ____ operator.

Sharpen your pencil Solution

We need your help. We've been using object literals to create ducks. Given what you learned above, can you write a constructor to create ducks for us? You'll find one of our object literals below to base your constructor on. Here's our solution.

```
var duck = {
    type: "redheaded",
    canFly: true
}
```

Here's an example
duck object literal.

Write a constructor
for creating ducks.

```
function Duck(type, canFly) {
    this.type = type;
    this.canFly = canFly;
}
```

P.S. We know you haven't fully figured out how this all
works yet, so for now concentrate on the syntax.

Exercise Solution

```
function Dog(name, breed, weight) {
    this.name = name;
    this.breed = breed;
    this.weight = weight;
}
var fido = new Dog("Fido", "Mixed", 38);
var fluffy = new Dog("Fluffy", "Poodle", 30);
var spot = new Dog("Spot", "Chihuahua", 10);
var dogs = [fido, fluffy, spot];

for (var i = 0; i < dogs.length; i++) {
    var size = "small";
    if (dogs[i].weight > 10) {
        size = "large";
    }
    console.log("Dog: " + dogs[i].name
                + " is a " + size
                + " " + dogs[i].breed);
}
```

Get some quick hands on experience to help this all sink in. Go ahead and put this code in a page and give it a test drive. Write your output here.

```
JavaScript console

Dog: Fido is a large Mixed
Dog: Fluffy is a large Poodle
Dog: Spot is a small Chihuahua
```

BE the Browser Solution

Below, you'll find JavaScript code with some mistakes in it.
Your job is to play like you're the browser and find
the errors in the code. Here's our solution.

If widget is to be a constructor, it needs a capital letter for W. That won't cause an error, but it's a good convention to follow.

We don't need "var" in front of this. We're not declaring new variables, we're adding properties to an object.

```javascript
function widget(partNo, size) {
    var this.no = partNo;
    var this.breed = size;
}
```

Also, by convention we usually name the parameters the same as the property names. So probably this.partNo and this.size would be better.

We're using commas instead of semicolons. Remember, in the constructor we use normal statements rather than comma separated property name/value pairs.

```javascript
function FormFactor(material, widget) {
    this.material = material,
    this.widget = widget,
    return this;
}
```

We're returning this and we don't need to. The constructor will do it for us. This statement won't cause an error, but it's not necessary.

Forgot new!

```javascript
var widgetA = widget(100, "large");
var widgetB = new widget(101, "small");
var formFactorA = newFormFactor("plastic", widgetA);
var formFactorB = new ForumFactor("metal", widgetB);
```

Needs a space between new and the constructor name.

Misspelled the name of the constructor.

Exercise Solution

We've got a constructor to create coffee drinks, but it's missing its methods.

We need a method, getSize, that returns a string depending on the number of ounces of coffee:

- 8oz is a small
- 12oz is a medium
- 16oz is a large

We also need a method, toString, that returns a string specifying your order.

Write your code below, and then test it in the browser. Try creating a few different sizes of coffee. Here's our solution.

```
function Coffee(roast, ounces) {
    this.roast = roast;
    this.ounces = ounces;
    this.getSize = function() {
        if (this.ounces === 8) {
            return "small";
        } else if (this.ounces === 12) {
            return "medium";
        } else if (this.ounces === 16) {
            return "large";
        }
    };
    this.toString = function() {
        return "You've ordered a " + this.getSize() + " "
                + this.roast + " coffee.";
    };
}
```

The getSize method looks at the ounces property of the object, and returns the corresponding size string.

Remember, this will be the object whose method we call. So if we call houseBlend.size, then this will be the houseBlend object.

The toString method just returns a string description of the object. It uses the getSize method to get the size of the coffee.

We create two coffee objects and call the toString method and display the resulting string.

```
var houseBlend = new Coffee("House Blend", 12);
console.log(houseBlend.toString());

var darkRoast = new Coffee("Dark Roast", 16);
console.log(darkRoast.toString());
```

JavaScript console

You've ordered a medium House Blend coffee.
You've ordered a large Dark Roast coffee.

Here's our output; yours should look similar.

Exercise Solution

Use everything you've learned to create a Car constructor. We suggest the following order:

① Start by providing the function keyword (actually we did that for you) followed by the constructor name. Next supply the parameters; you'll need one for each property that you want to supply an initial value for.

② Next, assign each property in the object its initial value (make sure you use `this` along with the property name).

③ Finally, add in the three car methods: start, drive and stop.

Here's our solution.

The constructor name is Car.

And seven parameters, one for each property we want to customize.

①
```
function Car(make, model, year, color, passengers, convertible, mileage) {
```

②
```
    this.make = make;
    this.model = model;
    this.year = year;
    this.color = color;
    this.passengers = passengers;
    this.convertible = convertible;
    this.mileage = mileage;
    this.started = false;
```

Each property of the new car object that's customized with a parameter is set to the parameter name. Notice we're using the same name for the property and the parameter by convention.

The started property is just initialized to false.

③
```
    this.start = function() {
        this.started = true;
    };
    this.stop = function() {
        this.started = false;
    };
    this.drive = function() {
        if (this.started) {
            alert("Zoom zoom!");
        } else {
            alert("You need to start the engine first.");
        }
    };
}
```

The methods are exactly the same as before, but now they're assigned to properties in the object with slightly different syntax because we're in a constructor not an object literal.

Copy the Car and Dog constructors into one file, and then add the code below along with it. Give this a run and capture the output. Here's our result:

```
var limoParams = {make: "Webville Motors",
                  model: "limo",
                  year: 1983,
                  color: "black",
                  passengers: 12,
                  convertible: true,
                  mileage: 21120};

var limo = new Car(limoParams);
var limoDog = new Dog("Rhapsody In Blue", "Poodle", 40);

console.log(limo.make + " " + limo.model + " is a " + typeof limo);
console.log(limoDog.name + " is a " + typeof limoDog);
```

```
JavaScript console

Webville Motors limo is a object
Rhapsody In Blue is a object
```

← What we got.

Exercise Solution

We need a function, dogCatcher, that returns true if the object passed to it is a Dog, and false otherwise. Write that function and test it with the rest of the code below. Here's our solution:

```javascript
function dogCatcher(obj) {
    if (obj instanceof Dog) {
        return true;
    } else {
        return false;
    }
}
```

Or more succinctly:

```javascript
function dogCatcher(obj) {
    return (obj instanceof Dog);
}
```

```javascript
function Cat(name, breed, weight) {
    this.name = name;
    this.breed = breed;
    this.weight = weight;
}
var meow = new Cat("Meow", "Siamese", 10);
var whiskers = new Cat("Whiskers", "Mixed", 12);

var fido = {name: "Fido", breed: "Mixed", weight: 38};

function Dog(name, breed, weight) {
    this.name = name;
    this.breed = breed;
    this.weight = weight;
    this.bark = function() {
        if (this.weight > 25) {
            alert(this.name + " says Woof!");
        } else {
            alert(this.name + " says Yip!");
        }
    };
}
var fluffy = new Dog("Fluffy", "Poodle", 30);
var spot = new Dog("Spot", "Chihuahua", 10);
var dogs = [meow, whiskers, fido, fluffy, spot];

for (var i = 0; i < dogs.length; i++) {
    if (dogCatcher(dogs[i]) {
        console.log(dogs[i].name + " is a dog!");
    }
}
```

JavaScript console

Fluffy is a dog!

Spot is a dog!

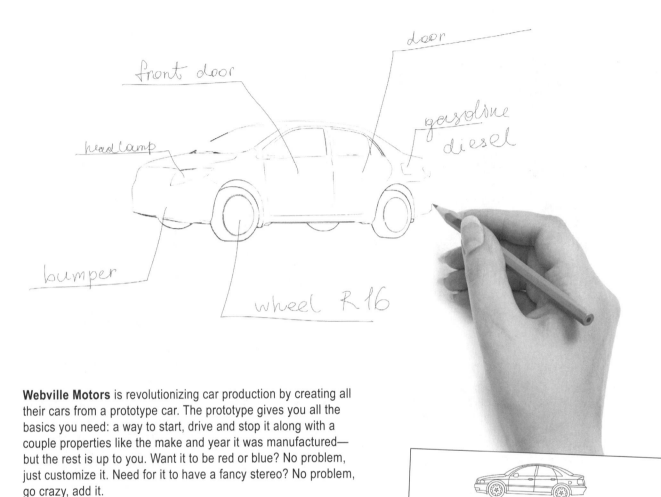

front door

door

headlamp

gasoline
diesel

bumper

wheel R 16

Webville Motors is revolutionizing car production by creating all their cars from a prototype car. The prototype gives you all the basics you need: a way to start, drive and stop it along with a couple properties like the make and year it was manufactured— but the rest is up to you. Want it to be red or blue? No problem, just customize it. Need for it to have a fancy stereo? No problem, go crazy, add it.

So this is your opportunity to design your perfect car. Check out our design below.

```
function CarProtoype() {
    this.make = "Webville Motors";
    this.year = 2013;
    this.start = function() {...};
    this.stop = function() {...};
    this.drive = function() {...};
}
```

← Draw your car here.

```
var taxi = new CarPrototype();

taxi.model = "Delorean Remake";

taxi.color = "silver";

taxi.currentTime = new Date();

taxi.fluxCapacitor = {type: "Mr. Fusion"};

taxi.timeTravel = function(date) {...};
```

← And customize the prototype here.

Oh, and where are we going with this? You'll find out in the next chapter! By the way, you're done with this chapter now.

 # JavaScript cross Solution

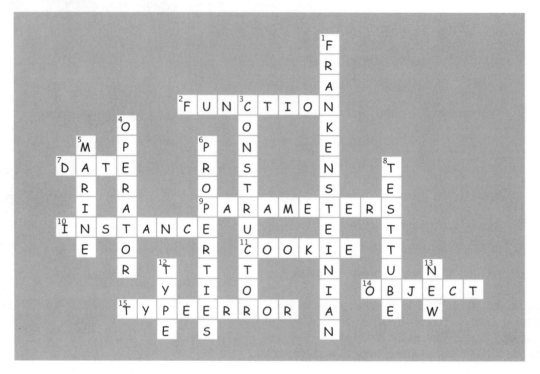

13 using prototypes

Extra strength objects

Learning how to create objects was just the beginning.

It's time to put some muscle on our objects. We need more ways to create
relationships between objects and to **share code** among them. And, we need
ways to extend and enhance existing objects. In other words, we need more
tools. In this chapter, you're going to see that JavaScript has a very powerful
object model, but one that is a bit different than the status quo object-oriented
language. Rather than the typical class-based object-oriented system, JavaScript
instead opts for a more powerful **prototype** model, where objects can inherit
and extend the behavior of other objects. What is that good for? You'll see soon
enough. Let's get started...

> Sorry, but you're going to have to unlearn all that classical object-oriented inheritance stuff you learned with Java and C++.

And if you haven't learned classical inheritance, you're lucky because you don't have to unlearn anything!

If you're used to Java, C++, or any language based on classical object-oriented programming let's have a quick chat.

And if you aren't... what, you got a date? Take a seat, and go along for the ride—you might just learn something as well.

We'll give it to you straight: JavaScript doesn't have a classical object-oriented model, where you create objects from classes. In fact, *JavaScript doesn't have classes at all*. In JavaScript, objects inherit behavior *from other objects*, which we call *prototypal inheritance*, or inheritance based on prototypes.

This may change in the future: the next version of JavaScript may add classes. So keep an eye out on wickedlysmart.com/hfjs for the latest on this.

JavaScript gets a lot of groans (and confused looks) from those trained in object-oriented programming, but know this: prototype-based languages are more general than classical object oriented ones. They're more flexible, efficient and expressive. So expressive that if you wanted to, you could use JavaScript to implement classical inheritance.

Left to the reader as an exercise.

So, if you are trained in the art of classical object-oriented programming, sit back, relax, open your mind and be ready for something a little different. And if you have no idea what we're talking about when we say "classical object-oriented programming," that just means you're starting fresh, which is often a very good thing.

Hey, before we get started, we've got a better way to diagram our objects

The object diagrams we've been using are cute and all that, but this is the *serious objects chapter*, so we're going to get more serious about our object diagrams. Actually, we really like the old ones, but the object diagrams in this chapter get complicated enough we just can't squeeze everything we need to into them.

So, without further ado, let us present the new format:

OLD SCHOOL

NEW AND IMPROVED

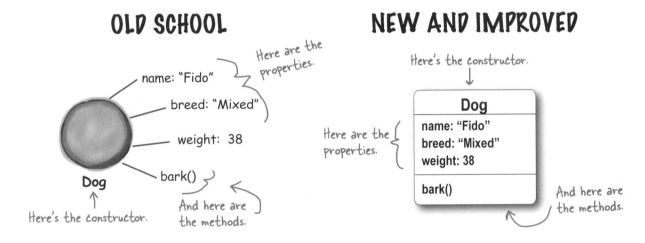

Sharpen your pencil

Do a little practice just to make sure you've got the new format down. Take the object below and redo it in the new and improved object diagram.

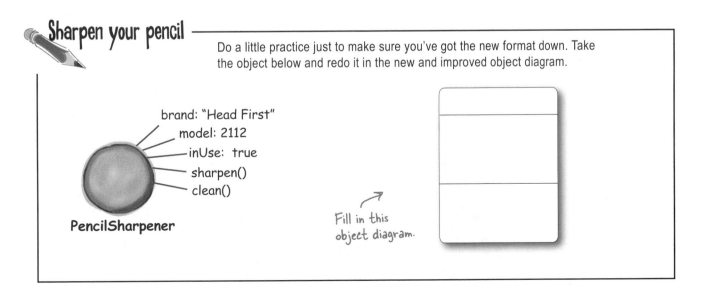

Fill in this object diagram.

Revisiting object constructors: we're reusing code, but are we being efficient?

Remember the Dog constructor we created in the last chapter? Let's take another quick look and review what we're getting out of using the constructor:

```
function Dog(name, breed, weight) {
    this.name = name;
    this.breed = breed;
    this.weight = weight;
    this.bark = function() {
        if (this.weight > 25) {
            alert(this.name + " says Woof!");
        } else {
            alert(this.name + " says Yip!");
        }
    };
}
```

Every dog can have its own custom values and a consistent set of properties.

And every dog comes complete with a bark method.

Even better, we're totally reusing code across all the dogs.

So by using the constructor we get a nice, consistent dog object that we can customize to our liking, and, we also can leverage the methods that are defined in it (in this case there's only one, `bark`). Further, every dog gets the same code from the constructor, saving us lots of code headaches if things change in the future. That's all great, but let's look at what happens at runtime when we evaluate the code below:

```
var fido = new Dog("Fido", "Mixed", 38);
var fluffy = new Dog("Fluffy", "Poodle", 30);
var spot = new Dog("Spot", "Chihuahua", 10);
```

This code causes three dog objects to be created. Let's use our new object diagrams to see what that looks like:

Here are the three different dog objects, each with its own values in the properties.

And here each object has a reference to the bark function.

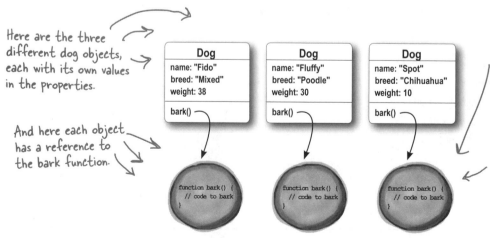

But wait a second, each dog has its own, individual bark function. They all do the same thing, but each dog has it's own copy of the function.

At a code level we've got reuse, but at runtime it looks like we get a new duplicate function with every dog.

Personally, I think every dog should have her very own bark method. Just sayin'.

Is duplicating methods really a problem?

Actually, it is. In general we don't want a new set of methods being created every time you instantiate an object with a constructor. Doing so hurts the performance of your application and impacts resources on your computer, which can be a big deal, particularly on mobile devices. And, as you're going to see, there are more flexible and powerful ways to craft your JavaScript objects.

Let's take a step back and think about one of the main reasons we used constructors in the first place: we were trying to *reuse behavior*. For instance, remember that we had a bunch of dog objects and we wanted all those objects to use the same `bark` method. By using a constructor we achieved this at a code level by placing the `bark` method in one place—inside the Dog constructor— and so we reused the same `bark` code each time we instantiated an object. But, our solution doesn't look as promising at runtime because every dog instance is getting its own copy of the `bark` method.

← Typically when we talk about an object's "behavior" we're referring to the set of methods it supports.

Now the reason we're running into this problem is because we aren't taking full advantage of JavaScript's object model, which is based on the idea of *prototypes*. In this model, we can create objects that are extensions of other objects—that is, of prototype objects.

To demonstrate prototypes, hmm… if only we had a *dog prototype* around that we could work from…

What are prototypes?

JavaScript objects can inherit properties and behavior from other objects. More specifically, JavaScript uses what is known as *prototypal inheritance*, and the object you're inheriting behavior from is called the *prototype*. The whole point of this scheme is to inherit and reuse existing properties (including methods), while extending those properties in your brand new object. That's all quite abstract so let's work through an example.

← When an object inherits from another, it gains access to all its methods and properties.

We'll start with a prototype for a dog object. Here's what it might look like:

> I'm the dog prototype. I've got properties that every dog needs and you can use me as a prototype for any dog you want to create.

Here's a prototype for dogs. This is an object that contains properties and methods that all dogs might need. →

The prototype doesn't include name, breed or weight because those will be unique to each dog, and supplied by the real dogs that inherit from the prototype. →

Dog Prototype

species: "Canine"

bark()
run()
wag()

← Contains properties useful to every dog.

} Contains behavior we'd like to use in all dogs that we create.

So now that we have a good dog prototype, we can create dog objects that inherit properties from that prototype. Our dog objects will also extend the prototype properties with dog-specific properties or behaviors. For example, we know we'll be adding a name, breed and weight to each dog.

You'll see that if any of these dogs needs to bark, run or wag their tails, they can rely on the prototype for those behaviors, because they inherit them from the prototype. So, let's create a few dog objects so you can see how this all works.

Inheriting from a prototype

First, we need to create object diagrams for the Fido, Fluffy and Spot dog objects and have them inherit from the new dog prototype. We'll show inheritance by drawing a set of dashed lines from the dog instances to the prototype. And remember, we put only the methods and properties that are common to *all* dogs in the dog prototype, because *all* the dogs will inherit them. All the properties specific to an actual dog, like the dog's name, go into the dog instances, because they are different for each dog.

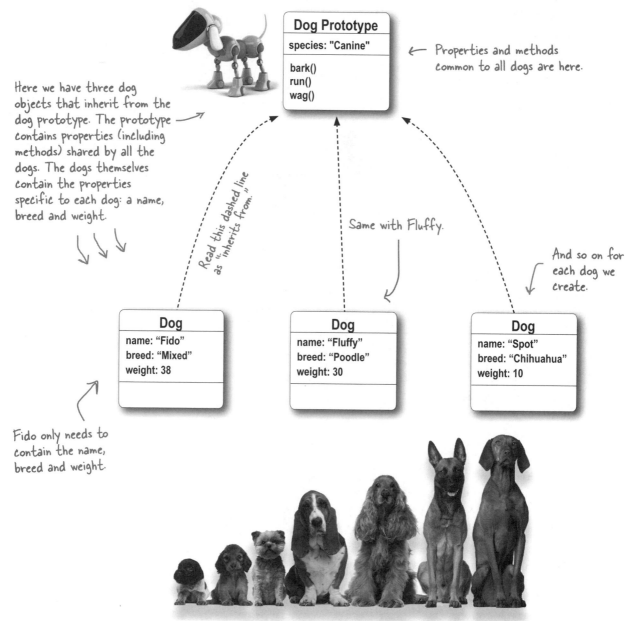

Properties and methods common to all dogs are here.

Here we have three dog objects that inherit from the dog prototype. The prototype contains properties (including methods) shared by all the dogs. The dogs themselves contain the properties specific to each dog: a name, breed and weight.

Read this dashed line as "inherits from."

Same with Fluffy.

And so on for each dog we create.

Fido only needs to contain the name, breed and weight.

Dog Prototype

species: "Canine"

bark()
run()
wag()

Dog

name: "Fido"
breed: "Mixed"
weight: 38

Dog

name: "Fluffy"
breed: "Poodle"
weight: 30

Dog

name: "Spot"
breed: "Chihuahua"
weight: 10

How inheritance works

How do we make dogs bark if the `bark` method isn't in the individual dog instances, but rather is in the prototype? That's where inheritance comes in. When you call a method on an object instance, and that method isn't found in the instance, you check the prototype for that method. Here's how.

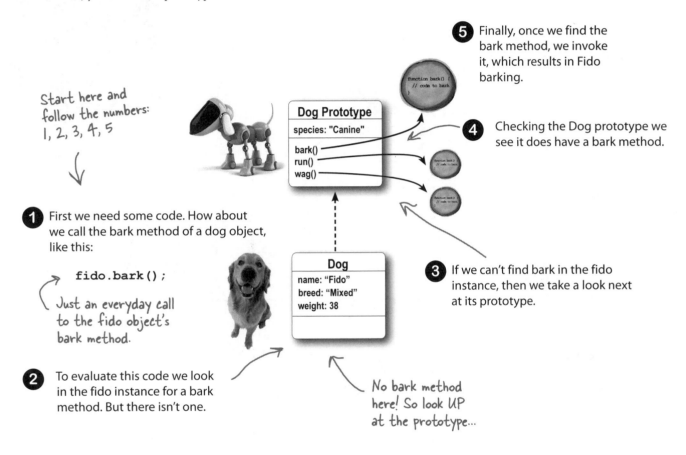

Start here and follow the numbers: 1, 2, 3, 4, 5

1 First we need some code. How about we call the bark method of a dog object, like this:

```
fido.bark();
```

Just an everyday call to the fido object's bark method.

2 To evaluate this code we look in the fido instance for a bark method. But there isn't one.

Dog Prototype
species: "Canine"
bark()
run()
wag()

Dog
name: "Fido"
breed: "Mixed"
weight: 38

No bark method here! So look UP at the prototype...

5 Finally, once we find the bark method, we invoke it, which results in Fido barking.

4 Checking the Dog prototype we see it does have a bark method.

3 If we can't find bark in the fido instance, then we take a look next at its prototype.

Properties work the same way. If we write code that needs `fido.name`, the value will come from the `fido` object. But if we want the value of `fido.species`, we first check the `fido` object, but when it isn't found there, we check the dog prototype (and find it).

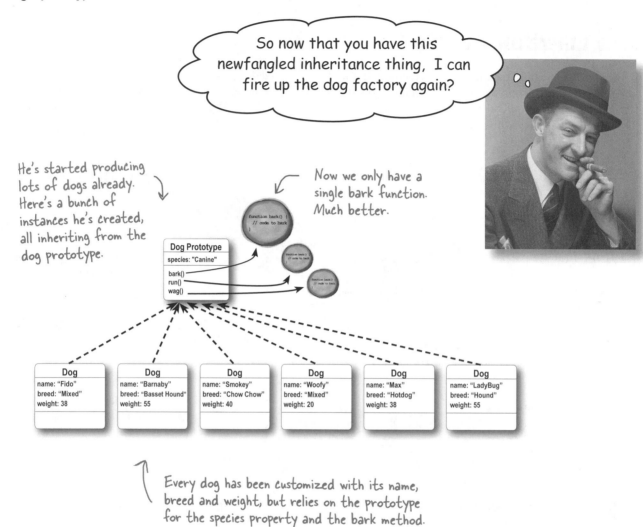

So now that you have this newfangled inheritance thing, I can fire up the dog factory again?

He's started producing lots of dogs already. Here's a bunch of instances he's created, all inheriting from the dog prototype.

Now we only have a single bark function. Much better.

Dog Prototype
species: "Canine"
bark()
run()
wag()

Dog	**Dog**	**Dog**	**Dog**	**Dog**	**Dog**
name: "Fido"	name: "Barnaby"	name: "Smokey"	name: "Woofy"	name: "Max"	name: "LadyBug"
breed: "Mixed"	breed: "Basset Hound"	breed: "Chow Chow"	breed: "Mixed"	breed: "Hotdog"	breed: "Hound"
weight: 38	weight: 55	weight: 40	weight: 20	weight: 38	weight: 55

Every dog has been customized with its name, breed and weight, but relies on the prototype for the species property and the bark method.

Now that you understand how to use inheritance we can create a large number of dogs. All the dogs can all still bark, but now they're relying on the dog prototype object to supply that `bark` method. We have code reuse, not just by having our code written in one place, but by having all dog instances use the *same* bark method at runtime, which means we aren't causing lots of runtime overhead.

You're going to see that by using prototypes, you'll be able to quickly assemble objects that reuse code, and that can be extended with new behavior and properties.

Thank you! Before you started using inheritance we were dying down here!

Overriding the prototype

Just because you inherit something from the prototype doesn't mean you're stuck with it. We can always *override* properties and methods by supplying them in the object instance. That works because JavaScript always looks in the object instance—that is, the specific dog object—for a property *before* it looks in the prototype. So, if you want to use a custom `bark` method for `spot`, all you have to do is put that custom `bark` method in the `spot` object. Once you do that, when JavaScript looks for the `bark` method to invoke, it will find the method in `spot`, and won't bother looking in the prototype.

Let's see what it looks like when we override Spot's `bark` method to give him the ability to have a big "WOOF" bark.

"Yip" isn't a very good bark for me. I need something BIGGER! How about "WOOF!" in all caps?!

Spot

The bark method in the prototype isn't used for spot, but it's still used in fido and fluffy.

```
function bark() {
    // code to bark
}
```

Prototype dog stays the same...

Dog Prototype

species: "Canine"

bark()
run()
wag()

This is a custom bark method, just for spot.

But spot gets his own bark method that says "WOOF!"

Dog

name: "Spot"
breed: "Chihuahua"
weight: 10

bark()

```
function bark() {
    // WOOF code
}
```

With all that in place we can call bark.

↳ `spot.bark();`

We start looking for the bark method first in the spot object.

And we find it, so no need to look further at the prototype. When we use this method we get a big WOOF!.

Code Magnets

We had an object diagram on the fridge, and then someone came and messed it up. Can you help put it back together? To reassemble it, we need two instances of the robot prototype. One is Robby, created in 1956, owned by Dr. Morbius, has an on/off switch and runs to Starbucks for coffee. We've also got Rosie, created in 1962, who cleans house and is owned by George Jetson. Good luck (oh, and there might be some extra magnets below)!

Here's the prototype your robots can inherit from. →

Robot Prototype

maker: "ObjectsRUs"

speak()
makeCoffee()
blinkLights()

Build the object diagram here. ↘

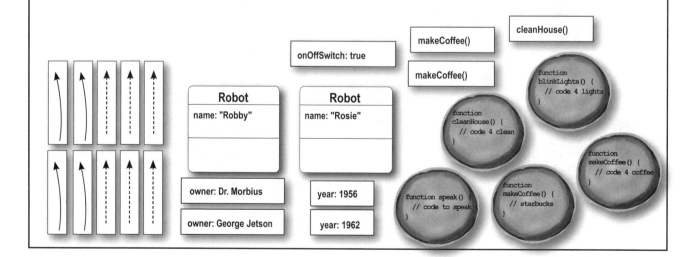

onOffSwitch: true

makeCoffee()

makeCoffee()

cleanHouse()

Robot

name: "Robby"

Robot

name: "Rosie"

owner: Dr. Morbius

owner: George Jetson

year: 1956

year: 1962

```
function
blinkLights() {
    // code 4 lights
}
```

```
function
cleanHouse() {
    // code 4 clean
}
```

```
function
makeCoffee() {
    // code 4 coffee
}
```

```
function speak() {
    // code to speak
}
```

```
function
makeCoffee() {
    // starbucks
}
```

So where do you get a prototype?

We've talked a lot about the dog prototype, and at this point, you're probably ready to see an example that uses code rather than diagrams. So, how do we create or get a hold of a dog prototype? Well, it turns out, you've actually had one all along. You just didn't know it.

And here's how you access it in code:

`Dog.prototype` ← If you look at your Dog constructor, it has a prototype property that holds a reference to the actual prototype.

Now, if you take this `prototype` property…

> Hold it right there. Dog is a constructor—in other words, a function. Remember? What do you mean it has a property?

Don't look at the man behind the curtain!

Just kidding; you're right. We were trying to gloss over that point (and we really still intend to, for now). Here's the short story: functions are objects in JavaScript. In fact, in JavaScript just about everything is an object underneath, even arrays if you haven't figured that one out yet.

But, for now, we don't want to get sidetracked on this. Just know that functions, in addition to doing everything you already know they can do, can also have properties, and in this case, the constructor always has a **prototype** property. More on functions and other things that are objects later, we promise.

How to set up the prototype

As we were saying, you can access the prototype object through the Dog constructor's `prototype` property. But what properties and methods are in the prototype object? Well, until you set it up yourself, not much. In other words it's your job to add properties and methods to the prototype. We typically do that before we start using the constructor.

So, let's set up the dog prototype. First we need a constructor to work from, so let's look at our object diagram to see how to make that:

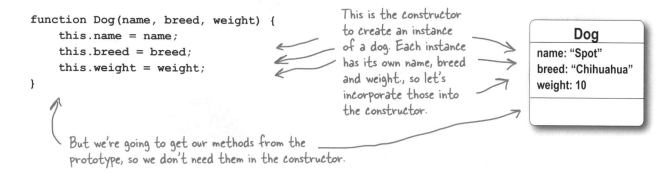

```
function Dog(name, breed, weight) {
    this.name = name;
    this.breed = breed;
    this.weight = weight;
}
```

This is the constructor to create an instance of a dog. Each instance has its own name, breed and weight., so let's incorporate those into the constructor.

Dog
name: "Spot"
breed: "Chihuahua"
weight: 10

But we're going to get our methods from the prototype, so we don't need them in the constructor.

Okay, now that we have a constructor, let's set up our dog prototype. We want it to have the `species` property and the `bark`, `run` and `wag` methods. Here's how we do that:

```
Dog.prototype.species = "Canine";

Dog.prototype.bark = function() {
    if (this.weight > 25) {
        console.log(this.name + " says Woof!");
    } else {
        console.log(this.name + " says Yip!");
    }
};

Dog.prototype.run = function() {
    console.log("Run!");
};

Dog.prototype.wag = function() {
    console.log("Wag!");
};
```

We assign the string "Canine" to the prototype's species property.

And for each method, we assign the appropriate function to the prototype's bark, run and wag properties respectively.

Serious Coding

Don't forget about chaining:

`Dog.prototype.species`

Start with Dog and grab its prototype property, which is a reference to an object that has a species property.

Test drive the prototype with some dogs

Go ahead and get this code typed into a file ("dog.html") and loaded
into your browser for testing. We've reproduced all the code after the
changes we made on the previous page, and added a bit of testing code.
Make sure all your dogs bark, run and wag like they should.

```javascript
function Dog(name, breed, weight) {
    this.name = name;
    this.breed = breed;
    this.weight = weight;
}

Dog.prototype.species = "Canine";

Dog.prototype.bark = function() {
    if (this.weight > 25) {
        console.log(this.name + " says Woof!");
    } else {
        console.log(this.name + " says Yip!");
    }
};

Dog.prototype.run = function() {
    console.log("Run!");
};

Dog.prototype.wag = function() {
    console.log("Wag!");
};

var fido = new Dog("Fido", "Mixed", 38);
var fluffy = new Dog("Fluffy", "Poodle", 30);
var spot = new Dog("Spot", "Chihuahua", 10);

fido.bark();
fido.run();
fido.wag();

fluffy.bark();
fluffy.run();
fluffy.wag();

spot.bark();
spot.run();
spot.wag();
```

Here's the Dog constructor.

And here's where we add properties and methods to the dog prototype.

We're adding one property and three methods to the prototype.

Now, we create the dogs like normal...

... and then we call the methods for each dog, just like normal. Each dog inherits the methods from the prototype.

Each dog is barking, running and wagging. Good.

But wait a second, didn't Spot want his bark to be WOOF!?

```
JavaScript console
Fido says Woof!
Run!
Wag!
Fluffy says Woof!
Run!
Wag!
Spot says Yip!
Run!
Wag!
```

Hey, don't forget about me. I requested a bigger WOOF!

Give Spot his WOOF! in code

Don't worry, we didn't forget about Spot. Spot requested a bigger WOOF! so we need to override the prototype to give him his own custom `bark` method. Let's update the code:

> The rest of the code goes here. We're just saving trees, or bits, or our carbon footprint, or something...

```
...
var spot = new Dog("Spot", "Chihuahua", 10);

spot.bark = function() {
    console.log(this.name + " says WOOF!");
};

// calls to fido and fluffy are the same

spot.bark();
spot.run();
spot.wag();
```

> The only change we make to the code is to give Spot his own custom bark method.

> We don't need to change how we call Spot's bark method at all.

Test drive the custom bark method

Add the new code above and take it for a quick test drive...

Spot gets the WOOF! he wanted.

```
JavaScript console
Fido says Woof!
Run!
Wag!
Fluffy says Woof!
Run!
Wag!
Spot says WOOF!
Run!
Wag!
```

ExeRcise

Remember our object diagram for the Robby and Rosie robots? We're going to implement that now. We've already written a Robot constructor for you along with some test code. Your job is to set up the robot prototype and to implement the two robots. Make sure you run them through the test code.

> *Here's the basic Robot constructor. You still need to set up its prototype.*

```
function Robot(name, year, owner) {
    this.name = name;
    this.year = year;
    this.owner = owner;
}
Robot.prototype.maker =

Robot.prototype.speak =

Robot.prototype.makeCoffee =

Robot.prototype.blinkLights =

var robby =
var rosie =

robby.onOffSwitch =
robby.makeCoffee =


rosie.cleanHouse =


console.log(robby.name + " was made by " + robby.maker +
            " in " + robby.year + " and is owned by " + robby.owner);
robby.makeCoffee();
robby.blinkLights();

console.log(rosie.name + " was made by " + rosie.maker +
            " in " + rosie.year + " and is owned by " + rosie.owner);
rosie.cleanHouse();
```

> *You'll want to set up the robot prototype here.*

> *Write your code to create the Robby and Rosie robots here. Make sure you add any custom properties they have to the instances.*

> *Use this code to test your instances to make sure they are working properly and inheriting from the prototype.*

> I was wondering how this.name in the bark method still works given that the bark method is in the prototype and not in the original object.

Good question. When we didn't have prototypes this was easy because we know `this` gets set to the object whose method was called. When we are calling the `bark` method in the prototype, you might think that `this` is now set to the prototype object. Well, that's not how it works.

When you call an object's method, `this` is set to the object whose method was called. If the method is not found in that object, and is found in the prototype, that doesn't change the value of `this`. `this` always refers to the original object—that is, the object whose method was called—even if the method is in the prototype. So, if we find the `bark` method in the prototype, then we call the method, with `this` set to the original dog object, giving us the result we want, like "Fluffy says Woof!".

Teaching a̭ll dogs̱ a new trick

It's time to teach our dogs a new trick. That's right we said "dogs" plural, not dog. You see, now that we have a prototype, if we add any methods to that prototype, even after we've already created dog objects, all dogs inheriting from the prototype immediately and automatically get this new behavior.

Let's say we want to teach all our dogs to sit. What we do is add a method to the prototype for sitting.

```
var barnaby = new Dog("Barnaby", "Basset Hound", 55);
```

← *Let's create another dog to test this on.*

```
Dog.prototype.sit = function() {
    console.log(this.name + " is now sitting");
}
```

← *And then let's add the sit method.*

We'll give this a try with Barnaby:

```
barnaby.sit();
```

← *We first check to see if the barnaby object has a sit method and there isn't one. So we then check the prototype, find the sit method, and invoke it.*

```
JavaScript console
Barnaby is now sitting
```

A Closer Look

Let's take a closer look at how this works. Make sure you follow the sequence 1, 2, 3, 4.

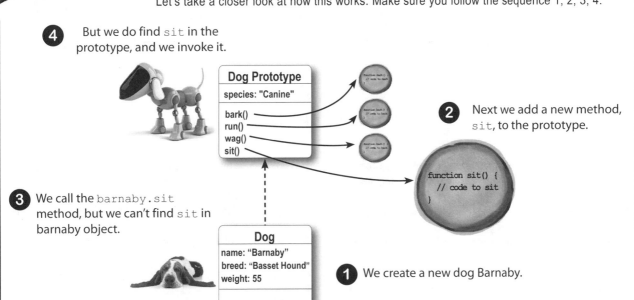

4 But we do find `sit` in the prototype, and we invoke it.

Dog Prototype
species: "Canine"
bark()
run()
wag()
sit()

2 Next we add a new method, `sit`, to the prototype.

```
function sit() {
    // code to sit
}
```

3 We call the `barnaby.sit` method, but we can't find `sit` in barnaby object.

Dog
name: "Barnaby"
breed: "Basset Hound"
weight: 55

1 We create a new dog Barnaby.

Prototypes are dynamic

We're glad to see Barnaby can now sit. But it turns out that now *all* our dogs can sit, because once you add a method to a prototype, any objects that inherit from that prototype can make use of that method:

This works for properties too, of course.

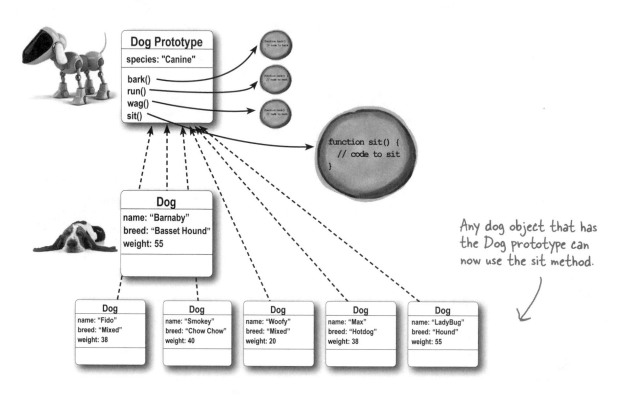

Any dog object that has the Dog prototype can now use the sit method.

there are no
Dumb Questions

Q: So when I add a new method or property to a prototype, all the object instances that inherit from it immediately see it?

A: If by "see it" you mean that they inherit that method or property, you are correct. Notice that this gives you a way to extend or change the behavior of all your instances at runtime by simply changing their prototype.

Q: I see how adding a new property to a prototype makes that property available to all the objects that inherit from the prototype. What if I *change* an existing property in the prototype; does that affect those objects in the same way? Like if I change the property species to "Feline" instead of "Canine", does that mean all existing dogs are now "Feline" species?

A: Yes. If you change any property in the prototype, it affects all the objects that inherit from that prototype, unless that object has overridden that property.

Exercise

Robby and Rosie are being used in a Robot game. You'll find the code for them below. In this game, whenever a player reaches level 42, a new robot capability is unlocked: the laser beam capability. Finish the code below so that at level 42 both Robby and Rosie get their laser beams. Check your answer at the end of the chapter before you go on.

```
function Game() {
    this.level = 0;
}

Game.prototype.play = function() {
    // player plays game here
    this.level++;
    console.log("Welcome to level " + this.level);
    this.unlock();
}

Game.prototype.unlock = function() {



}

function Robot(name, year, owner) {
    this.name = name;
    this.year = year;
    this.owner = owner;
}

var game = new Game();
var robby = new Robot("Robby", 1956, "Dr. Morbius");
var rosie = new Robot("Rosie", 1962, "George Jetson");

while (game.level < 42) {
    game.play();
}

robby.deployLaser();
rosie.deployLaser();
```

```
JavaScript console
Welcome to level 1
Welcome to level 2
Welcome to level 3
...
Welcome to level 41
Welcome to level 42
Rosie is blasting you with
laser beams.
```

A sample of our output. When you finish your code, give it a play and see which robot wins and gets to blast its laser beams!

A more interesting implementation of the sit method

Let's make the `sit` method a little more interesting: dogs will start in a state of not sitting (in other words, standing up). So, when `sit` is called, if a dog isn't sitting, we'll make him sit. Otherwise, we'll let the user know he's already sitting. To do this we're going to need an extra property, `sitting`, to keep track of whether the dog is sitting or not. Let's write the code:

We start with a sitting property in the prototype.

```
Dog.prototype.sitting = false;

Dog.prototype.sit = function() {
    if (this.sitting) {
        console.log(this.name + " is already sitting");
    } else {
        this.sitting = true;
        console.log(this.name + " is now sitting");
    }
};
```

By setting sitting to false in the prototype, all dogs start by not sitting.

Then, in the sit method, we check to see if the dog is sitting or not. At first, when we check this.sitting we'll be looking at the value in the dog prototype.

If the dog is sitting, we say he's already sitting.

But, if the dog is not sitting, we say he's now sitting and then we set the value of this.sitting to true. This <u>overrides</u> the prototype property and sets the value in the instance.

Notice that the instance now has its own local sitting property, set to true.

The interesting thing about this code is that when a dog instance starts out life, it inherits a default value of false for `sitting`. But, as soon as the `sit` method is called, the dog instance adds its own value for sitting, which results in a property being created in the instance. This overrides the inherited `sitting` property in the prototype. This gives us a way to have a default for all dogs, and then to specialize each dog if we need to.

Test drive the new sit method

Let's give this a try for real. Go ahead and update your code, adding the new property and implementation of `sit`. Now when we test drive this code, you can see that we can make `barnaby` sit, and then make `spot` sit, and each dog keeps track of whether it is sitting separately:

```
barnaby.sit()
barnaby.sit()
spot.sit()
spot.sit()
```

```
JavaScript console
Barnaby is now sitting
Barnaby is already sitting
Spot is now sitting
Spot is already sitting
```

One more time: how the sitting property works

Let's make sure we've got this down, because if you go too fast on this implementation you might miss the key details. Here's the key: the first time we get the value of `sitting`, we're getting it from the prototype. But then when we set `sitting` to true, that happens in the object instance, not the prototype. And after that property has been added to the object instance, every subsequent time we get the value of `sitting`, we're getting it from the object instance because it is overriding the value in the prototype. Let's step through it one more time:

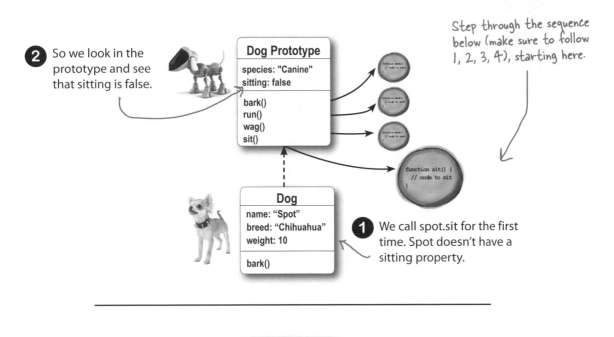

2 So we look in the prototype and see that sitting is false.

Step through the sequence below (make sure to follow 1, 2, 3, 4), starting here.

1 We call spot.sit for the first time. Spot doesn't have a sitting property.

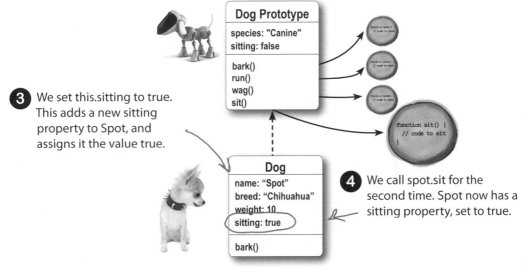

3 We set this.sitting to true. This adds a new sitting property to Spot, and assigns it the value true.

4 We call spot.sit for the second time. Spot now has a sitting property, set to true.

While we're talking about properties, is there a way in my code to determine if I'm using a property that's in the instance or in the prototype?

Yes, there is. You can use the hasOwnProperty method that every object has. The hasOwnProperty method returns true if a property is defined in an object instance. If it's not, but you can access that property, then you can assume the property must be defined in the object's prototype.

Let's try it on fido and spot. First, we know that the species property is implemented only in the dog prototype, and neither spot nor fido has overridden this property. So if we call the hasOwnProperty method and pass in the property name, "species", as a string, we get back false for both:

```
spot.hasOwnProperty("species");

fido.hasOwnProperty("species");
```

Both of these return the value false because species is defined in the prototype, not the object instances spot and fido.

Now let's try it for the sitting property. We know that the sitting property is defined in the prototype and initialized to false. So we assign the value true to spot.sitting, which overrides the sitting property in the prototype and defines sitting in the spot instance. Then we'll ask both spot and fido if they have their own sitting property defined:

When we first check to see if Spot has his own sitting property we get false.

```
spot.hasOwnProperty("sitting");

spot.sitting = true;

spot.hasOwnProperty("sitting");

fido.hasOwnProperty("sitting");
```

Then we set spot.sitting to true, adding this property to the spot instance.

This call to hasOwnProperty returns true, because spot now has his own sitting property.

But this call to hasOwnProperty returns false, because the fido instance does not have a sitting property. That means the sitting property that fido uses is defined only in the prototype, and inherited by fido.

Exercise

We've added a new capability to our robots, Robby and Rosie: they can now report when they have an error through the reportError method. Trace the code below, paying particular attention to where this method gets its error information, and to whether it's coming from the prototype of the robot instance.

Below give the output of this code:

```
function Robot(name, year, owner) {
    this.name = name;
    this.year = year;
    this.owner = owner;
}

Robot.prototype.maker = "ObjectsRUs";
Robot.prototype.errorMessage = "All systems go.";
Robot.prototype.reportError = function() {
    console.log(this.name + " says " + this.errorMessage);
};
Robot.prototype.spillWater = function() {
    this.errorMessage = "I appear to have a short circuit!";
};

var robby = new Robot("Robby", 1956, "Dr. Morbius");
var rosie = new Robot("Rosie", 1962, "George Jetson");

rosie.reportError();
robby.reportError();
robby.spillWater();
rosie.reportError();
robby.reportError();

console.log(robby.hasOwnProperty("errorMessage"));   _____
console.log(rosie.hasOwnProperty("errorMessage"));   _____
```

Does Robby have his own errorMessage property?

Does Rosie?

BEST DOG IN SHOW

All your hard work in this chapter has already paid off. The Webville Kennel Club saw your work on the dog objects and they immediately knew they'd found the right person to implement their dog show simulator. The only thing is they need you to update the Dog constructor to make show dogs. After all, show dogs aren't ordinary dogs—they don't just run, they gait. They don't go through the trash, they show a tendency towards scent articles; they don't beg for treats, they show a desire for bait.

More specifically, here's what they're looking for:

Wonderful work on the Dog constructor! We'd love to get you engaged on our dog show simulator. Show dogs are a little different, so they need additional methods (see below).

Thanks! —Webville Kennel Club

stack() — otherwise known as stand at attention.

gait() — this is like running. The method takes a string argument of "walk", "trot", "pace", or "gallop".

bait() — give the dog a treat.

groom() — doggie shampoo time.

How to approach the design of the show dogs

So how are we going to design this? Clearly we'd like to make use of our existing dog code. After all, that's why Webville Kennel came to us in the first place. But how? Let's get some thoughts on the ways we could approach this:

If we add all these new methods into our existing Dog constructor then all dogs will be able to do these things. But, that's not what we intended.

We could add the show dog methods just to the show dog instances, but then we're back to all the problems we uncovered at the beginning of the chapter.

But if we create our ShowDog constructor from scratch then we'll end up reimplementing all the basic methods: bark, run, sit...

Guys, relax. You can have more than one prototype with JavaScript.

Joe: More than one prototype? What does that even mean?

Judy: Think about it like your own inheritance.

Joe: What inheritance? If I had an inheritance I wouldn't be working here! Just kidding…

Judy: Well, you don't just inherit qualities from your parents, right? You inherit a little from your grandparents and your great-grandparents and so on.

Joe: Yeah, got that.

Judy: Well, with JavaScript you can set up a chain of prototypes that your object inherits from.

Frank: An example might help.

Judy: Say you have a bird prototype that knows how to do all things most birds do, like fly.

Frank: Easy enough, that's like our dog prototype.

Judy: Now say you need to implement a whole set of ducks—mallards, red-headed ducks…

Frank: …don't forget the black-bellied-whistling duck.

Judy: Why, thank you Frank.

Frank: No problem. I was just reading about all those ducks in that *Head First Design Patterns* book.

Judy: Okay, but ducks are a different kind of bird. They swim, and we don't want to put that into the bird prototype. But with JavaScript we can create a duck prototype that inherits from the bird prototype.

Joe: So let me see if I have this right. We'd have a Duck constuctor that points to a duck prototype. But that prototype—that is the duck prototype—would itself point to the bird prototype?

Frank: Whoa, shift back into first gear.

Judy: Think of it like this, Frank. Say you create a duck and you call its `fly` method. What happens if you look in the duck and there's no such method? You look in the duck prototype, still no fly method. So you look at the prototype the duck inherits from, bird, and you find `fly` there.

Joe: And, if we call `swim`, then we look in the duck instance, nothing there. We look in the duck prototype, and we find it.

Judy: Right… so we're not just reusing the behavior of the duck prototype, we're following a chain up to the bird prototype, when necessary, to use that as well.

Joe: That sounds perfect for extending our dog prototype into a show dog. Let see what we can do with this.

Setting up a chain of prototypes

Let's start thinking in terms of a *chain of prototypes*. Rather than having an instance that inherits properties from just one prototype, there might be a chain of one or more prototypes your instance can inherit from. It's not that big a logical step from the way we've been thinking about this already.

Let's say we want a show dog prototype for our show dogs, and we want that prototype to rely on our original dog prototype for the `bark`, `run`, and `wag` methods. Let's set that up to get a feel for how it all works together:

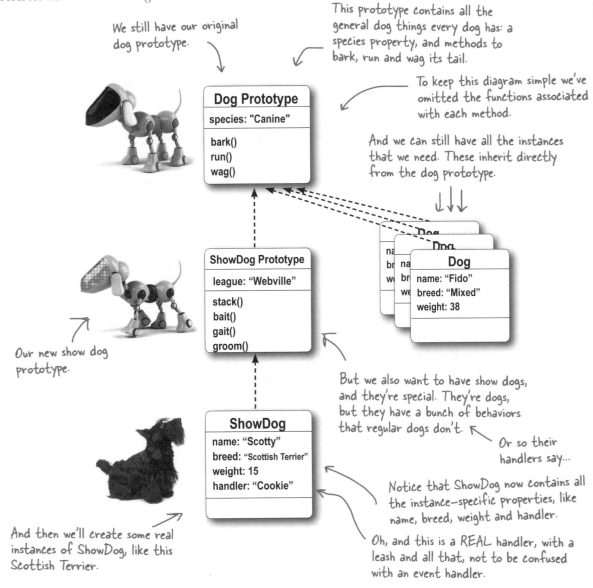

We still have our original dog prototype.

This prototype contains all the general dog things every dog has: a species property, and methods to bark, run and wag its tail.

To keep this diagram simple we've omitted the functions associated with each method.

And we can still have all the instances that we need. These inherit directly from the dog prototype.

Dog Prototype

species: "Canine"

bark()
run()
wag()

ShowDog Prototype

league: "Webville"

stack()
bait()
gait()
groom()

Our new show dog prototype.

Dog

name: "Fido"
breed: "Mixed"
weight: 38

ShowDog

name: "Scotty"
breed: "Scottish Terrier"
weight: 15
handler: "Cookie"

But we also want to have show dogs, and they're special. They're dogs, but they have a bunch of behaviors that regular dogs don't.

Or so their handlers say...

Notice that ShowDog now contains all the instance-specific properties, like name, breed, weight and handler.

And then we'll create some real instances of ShowDog, like this Scottish Terrier.

Oh, and this is a REAL handler, with a leash and all that, not to be confused with an event handler.

How inheritance works in a prototype chain

We've set up the prototype chain for the show dogs, so let's see how inheritance works in this context. Check out the properties and methods at the bottom of the page, and then trace them up the prototype chain to the object where they are defined.

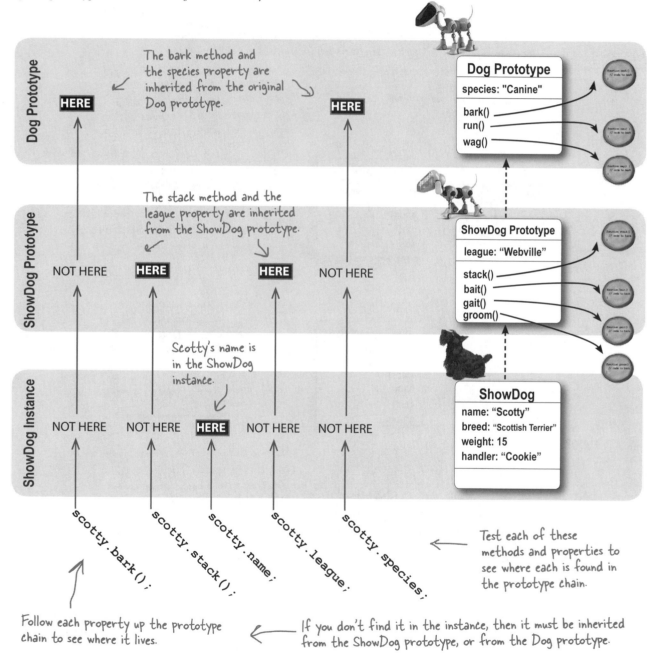

Dog Prototype

The bark method and the species property are inherited from the original Dog prototype.

HERE   **HERE**

Dog Prototype
species: "Canine"
bark()
run()
wag()

ShowDog Prototype

The stack method and the league property are inherited from the ShowDog prototype.

NOT HERE   **HERE**   **HERE**   NOT HERE

ShowDog Prototype
league: "Webville"
stack()
bait()
gait()
groom()

ShowDog Instance

Scotty's name is in the ShowDog instance.

NOT HERE   NOT HERE   **HERE**   NOT HERE   NOT HERE

ShowDog
name: "Scotty"
breed: "Scottish Terrier"
weight: 15
handler: "Cookie"

scotty.bark();   scotty.stack();   scotty.name;   scotty.league;   scotty.species;

Test each of these methods and properties to see where each is found in the prototype chain.

Follow each property up the prototype chain to see where it lives.

If you don't find it in the instance, then it must be inherited from the ShowDog prototype, or from the Dog prototype.

Code Magnets

We had another object diagram on the fridge, and then someone came and messed it up. Again!! Can you help put it back together? To reassemble it we need a new line of Space Robots that inherit properties from Robots. These new Space Robots override the Robot's speaking functionality, and extend Robots with piloting functionality and a new property, homePlanet. Good luck (there might be some extra magnets below)!

Build the object diagram here.

Here's the prototype for Robots.

Robot Prototype

maker: "ObjectsRUs"

speak()
makeCoffee()
blinkLights()

```
function
speak() {
    // cod
}
function
makeCoffee()
// code
}
function
blinklights() {
    // code 4 lights
}
```

Robot

name: "Robby"
year: 1956
owner: "Dr. Morbius"

Robot

name: "Rosie"
year: 1962
owner: "George Jetson"

And here's the prototype for the Space Robots.

Space Robot Prototype

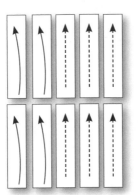

speak()   year: 1977

pilot()   year: 2009

homePlanet: "Earth"

homePlanet: "Tatooine"

```
function speak() {
    // code to speak
    in space
}
```

```
function
pilot() {
    // code to pilot
    spaceship
}
```

Space Robot

name: "C3PO"
year: 1977
owner: "L. Skywalker"

Space Robot

name: "Simon"
year: 2009
owner: "Carla Diana"

Creating the show dog prototype

When we created the dog prototype we didn't have to do anything—there was already an empty object supplied by the Dog constructor's `prototype` property. So we took that and added the properties and methods we wanted our dog instances to inherit.

But with the show dog prototype we have more work to do because we need a prototype object that inherits from another prototype (the dog prototype). To do that we're going to have to create an object that inherits from the dog prototype and then explicitly wire things up ourselves.

Right now we have a dog prototype and a bunch of dog instances that inherit from that prototype. And what we want is a show dog prototype (that inherits from dog prototype), and a bunch of show dog instances that inherit from the show dog prototype.

Setting this up will take a few steps, so we'll take it one at a time.

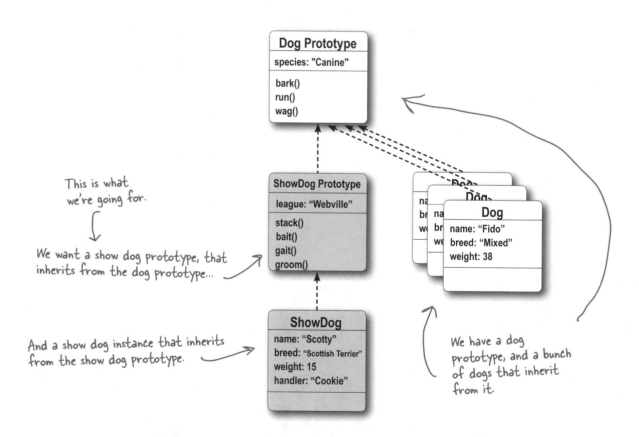

This is what we're going for.

We want a show dog prototype, that inherits from the dog prototype...

And a show dog instance that inherits from the show dog prototype.

We have a dog prototype, and a bunch of dogs that inherit from it.

First, we need an object that inherits from the dog prototype

We've established that the show dog prototype is an object that inherits from the dog prototype. But, what's the best way to create an object that inherits from the dog prototype? Well, it's something you've already been doing as you've created instances of dog. Remember? Like this:

To create an object that inherits from the dog prototype, we just use new with the Dog constructor.

```
var aDog = new Dog();
```
We'll talk about what happened to the constructor arguments in a minute...

So this code creates an object that inherits from the dog prototype. We know this because it's exactly the same as how we created all our dog instances, except this time, we didn't supply any arguments to the constructor. That's because at the moment, we don't care about the specifics of the dog; we just need the dog to inherit from the dog prototype.

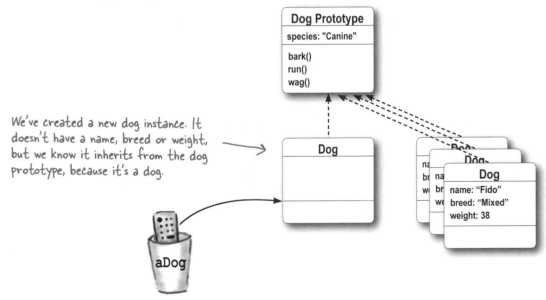

We've created a new dog instance. It doesn't have a name, breed or weight, but we know it inherits from the dog prototype, because it's a dog.

Now, what we really need is a show dog prototype. Like our dog instance, that's just an object that inherits from the dog prototype. So let's see how we can use our empty dog instance to make the show dog prototype we need.

Next, turning our dog instance into a show dog prototype

Okay, so we have a dog instance, but how do we make that our show dog prototype object? We do this by assigning the dog instance to the `prototype` property of our ShowDog constructor. Oh wait; we don't have a ShowDog constructor yet... so let's make one:

```
function ShowDog(name, breed, weight, handler) {
    this.name = name;
    this.breed = breed;
    this.weight = weight;
    this.handler = handler;
}
```

← This constructor takes everything we need to be a dog (name, breed, weight), and to be a show dog (a handler).

Now that we have a constructor, we can set its `prototype` property to a new dog instance:

```
ShowDog.prototype = new Dog();
```

We could have used our dog instance created on the previous page, but we can skip the variable assignment and just assign the new dog straight to the prototype property instead.

So, let's think about where we are: we have a ShowDog constructor, with which we can make show dog instances, and we now have a show dog prototype, which is a dog instance.

Let's make sure our object diagram accurately reflects the roles these objects are playing by changing the label "Dog" to "ShowDog Prototype". But keep in mind, the show dog prototype *is still a dog instance*.

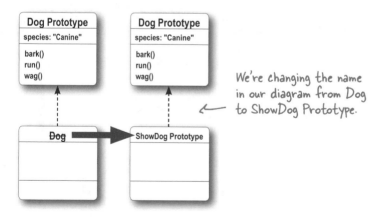

We're changing the name in our diagram from Dog to ShowDog Prototype.

Now that we've got a ShowDog constructor and we've set up the show dog prototype object, we need to go back and fill in some details. We'll take a closer look at the constructor, and we've also got some properties and methods to add to the prototype so our show dogs have the additional show dog behavior we want them to have.

Now it's time to fill in the prototype

We've got the show dog prototype set up (which at the moment is just an empty instance of dog). Now, it's time to fill it with properties and behaviors that will make it look more like a show dog prototype.

Here are some properties and methods that are specific to show dogs we can add:

```
function ShowDog(name, breed, weight, handler) {
    this.name = name;
    this.breed = breed;
    this.weight = weight;
    this.handler = handler;
}
```

Remember, the ShowDog constructor looks a lot like the Dog constructor. A show dog needs a name, breed, weight, plus one extra property, a handler (the person who handles the show dog). These will end up being defined in the show dog instance.

```
ShowDog.prototype = new Dog();

Showdog.prototype.league = "Webville";

ShowDog.prototype.stack = function() {
      console.log("Stack");
};

ShowDog.prototype.bait = function() {
      console.log("Bait");
};

ShowDog.prototype.gait = function(kind) {
      console.log(kind + "ing");
};

ShowDog.prototype.groom = function() {
      console.log("Groom");
};
```

All our show dogs are in the Webville league, so we'll add this property to the prototype.

Here are all the methods we need for show dogs. We'll just keep them simple for now.

We're adding all these properties to the show dog prototype so all show dogs inherit them.

This is where we're taking the dog instance that is acting as the show dog prototype, and we're adding new properties and methods.

With these additions our show dog prototype is starting to look like a show dog. Let's update our object diagram again, and then it's probably time to do a big test run of the show dogs. We're guessing Webville Kennel is going to be pretty excited to see these in action.

We say that our show dog prototype "extends" the dog prototype. It inherits properties from the dog prototype and extends it with new ones.

Dog Prototype

species: "Canine"

bark()
run()
wag()

ShowDog Prototype

league: "Webville"

stack()
bait()
gait()
groom()

Creating a show dog instance

Now we just have one more thing to do: create an instance of ShowDog. This instance will inherit show dog properties and methods from our show dog prototype, and because our show dog prototype is an instance of Dog, the show dog will also inherit all its doggy behavior and properties from the dog prototype, so he'll be able to bark and run and wag with the rest of the dogs.

Here's all the code so far, and the code to create the instance:

```
function ShowDog(name, breed, weight, handler) {
    this.name = name;
    this.breed = breed;
    this.weight = weight;
    this.handler = handler;
}


ShowDog.prototype = new Dog();

Showdog.prototype.league = "Webville";

ShowDog.prototype.stack = function() {
      console.log("Stack");
};

ShowDog.prototype.bait = function() {
      console.log("Bait");
};

ShowDog.prototype.gait = function(kind) {
      console.log(kind + "ing");
};

ShowDog.prototype.groom = function() {
      console.log("Groom");
};
```

```
var scotty = new ShowDog("Scotty", "Scottish Terrier", 15, "Cookie");
```

Dog Prototype

species: "Canine"

bark()
run()
wag()

ShowDog Prototype

league: "Webville"

stack()
bait()
gait()
groom()

Dog

name: "Fido"
breed: "Mixed"
weight: 38

ShowDog

name: "Scotty"
breed: "Scottish Terrier"
weight: 15
handler: "Cookie"

And here's our show dog instance. It inherits from the show dog prototype, which inherits from the dog prototype. Just what we wanted. If you go back and look at page 592, you'll see we've completed the prototype chain.

Here's our new show dog, scotty.

Test drive the show dog

Take all your the code on the previous page, and add to it the quality
assurance code below, just to give scotty a good testing. Hey, and
while you're at it, add a few dogs of your own and test them:

```
scotty.stack();
scotty.bark();
console.log(scotty.league);
console.log(scotty.species);
```

Here's what we got.

JavaScript console
```
Stack
Scotty says Yip!
Webville
Canine
```

Exercise

Your turn. Add a SpaceRobot line of robots to the ObjectsRUs line of robots. These robots should
of course be able to do everything that robots can do, plus some extra behavior for space robots.
We've started the code below, so finish it up and then test it. Check your answer at the end of the
chapter before moving on.

```
function SpaceRobot(name, year, owner, homePlanet) {



}

SpaceRobot.prototype = new _____;

  _____.speak = function() {
    alert(this.name + " says Sir, If I may venture an opinion...");
};

  _____.pilot = function() {
    alert(this.name + " says Thrusters? Are they important?");
};

var c3po = new SpaceRobot("C3PO", 1977, "Luke Skywalker", "Tatooine");
c3po.speak();
c3po.pilot();
console.log(c3po.name + " was made by " + c3po.maker);

var simon = new SpaceRobot("Simon", 2009, "Carla Diana", "Earth");
simon.makeCoffee();
simon.blinkLights();
simon.speak();
```

Exercise

Let's take a closer look at all these dogs we're creating. We've tested Fido before and we know he's truly a dog. But let's see if he's a show dog as well (we don't think he should be). And what about Scotty? We figure he should be a show dog for sure, but is he a dog too? We're not sure. And we'll test Fido and Scotty's constructors while we're at it...

```javascript
var fido = new Dog("Fido", "Mixed", 38);
if (fido instanceof Dog) {
    console.log("Fido is a Dog");
}
if (fido instanceof ShowDog) {
    console.log("Fido is a ShowDog");
}


var scotty = new ShowDog("Scotty", "Scottish Terrier", 15, "Cookie");
if (scotty instanceof Dog) {
    console.log("Scotty is a Dog");
}
if (scotty instanceof ShowDog) {
    console.log("Scotty is a ShowDog");
}
console.log("Fido constructor is " + fido.constructor);
console.log("Scotty constructor is " + scotty.constructor);
```

← Run this code and provide your output below.

Your output goes here:

```
JavaScript console

```

You'll find our output on the next page. ⟶

Examining the exercise results

Here's the output from that last test run:

Fido is a dog, which we expected, and we don't see that Fido is a show dog, so he must not be one. That makes sense too.

And Scotty is both a dog and a show dog, which makes sense. But how does instanceof know that?

Hmm, this looks weird. Both Fido and Scotty show they were created by the dog constructor. But we used the show dog constructor to create Scotty...

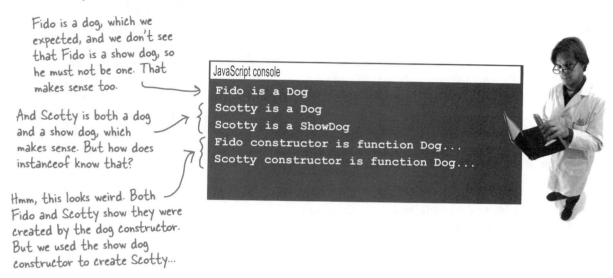

```
JavaScript console
Fido is a Dog
Scotty is a Dog
Scotty is a ShowDog
Fido constructor is function Dog...
Scotty constructor is function Dog...
```

Let's think about these results for a minute. First, Fido is apparently just a dog and not a show dog—actually, that is totally what we thought would happen; after all, Fido was created with the Dog constructor, which has nothing to do with show dogs.

Next, Scotty is a dog *and* a show dog. That makes sense too, but how did this happen? Well, **instanceof** doesn't just look at what kind of object you are, it also takes into account all the objects you inherit from. So, Scotty was created as a show dog, but a show dog inherits from a dog, so Scotty is a dog too.

Next up, Fido has a Dog constuctor, and that makes sense, because that is how we created him.

And finally, Scotty has a Dog constructor too. That doesn't make sense, because Scotty was created by the ShowDog constructor. What's going on here? Well, first let's think about where this constructor comes from: we're looking at the scotty.constructor property, and this is something we've never setup. So we must be inheriting it from the dog prototype (again, because we haven't explicitly set it up for a show dog).

So why is this happening? Honestly, it's a loose end that we need to cleanup. You see, if we don't take care of setting the show dog prototype's constructor property, no one else will. Now, keep in mind everything is working fine without it; but not setting it could lead to confusion if you or someone else tries to use scotty.constructor expecting to get show dog.

But don't worry, we'll fix it.

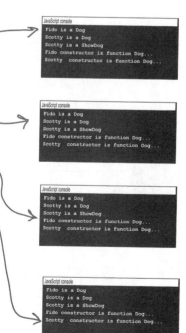

A final cleanup of show dogs

Our code is just about ready to ship to Webville Kennel, but we need to make one final pass to polish it. There are two small issues to clean up.

The first, we've already seen: that instances of ShowDog don't have their constructor property set correctly. They're inheriting the Dog constructor property. Now, just to be clear, all our code works fine as is, but setting the right constructor on our objects is a best practice, and some day another developer may end up with your code and be confused when they examine a show dog object.

To fix the constructor property, we need to make sure it is set up correctly in the show dog prototype. That way, when a show dog is constructed it will inherit the right constructor property. Here's how we do that:

```
function ShowDog(name, breed, weight, handler) {
    this.name = name;
    this.breed = breed;
    this.weight = weight;
    this.handler = handler;
}
ShowDog.prototype = new Dog();
ShowDog.prototype.constructor = ShowDog;
```

Here we're taking the show dog prototype and explicitly setting its constructor property to the ShowDog constructor.

That's all you need to do. When we check Scotty again he should have the correct constructor property, as should all other show dogs.

Remember this is a best practice, without it your code still works as expected.

Note that we didn't have to do this for the dog prototype because it came with the constructor property set up correctly by default.

Exercise

Quickly rerun the tests from the previous exercise and make sure your Scotty show dog instance has the correct constructor.

Here's what we got. Note that Scotty's constructor is now ShowDog.

```
JavaScript console
Fido is a Dog
Scotty is a Dog
Scotty is a ShowDog
Fido constructor is function Dog...
Scotty constructor is function ShowDog...
```

A little more cleanup

There's another place we could use some cleanup: in the ShowDog constructor code. Let's look again at the constructor:

```
function ShowDog(name, breed, weight, handler) {
    this.name = name;
    this.breed = breed;
    this.weight = weight;
    this.handler = handler;
}
```

If you didn't notice, this code is replicated from the Dog constructor.

As you've seen in this book, anytime we see duplicated code, the warning bells go off. In this case, the Dog constructor already knows how to do this work, so why not let the constructor do it? Further, while our example has simple code, at times constructors can have complex code to compute initial values for properties, and we don't want to start reproducing code everytime we create a new constructor that inherits from another prototype. So let's fix this. We'll rewrite the code first, and step you through it:

This idea of eliminating duplicate code even has an acronym: DRY. "Don't Repeat Yourself" as all the cool coders say.

```
function ShowDog(name, breed, weight, handler) {
    Dog.call(this, name, breed, weight);
    this.handler = handler;
}
```

This bit of code is going to reuse the Dog constructor code to process the name, breed, and weight.

But we still need to handle the handler in this code because the Dog constructor doesn't know anything about it.

As you can see we've replaced the redundant code in the ShowDog constructor with a call to a method named `Dog.call`. Here's how it works: `call` is a built-in method that you can use on any function (and remember Dog is a function). `Dog.call` invokes the Dog function and passes it the object to use as `this`, along with all the arguments for the Dog function. Let's break this down:

Dog is the function we're going to call.

Whatever is in this is used for this in the body of the Dog function.

The rest of the arguments are just passed to Dog like normal.

With this code we're calling the Dog constructor function but telling it to use our ShowDog instance as this, and so the Dog function will set the name, breed and weight properties in our ShowDog object.

```
Dog.call(this, name, breed, weight);
```

call is the method of Dog we're calling. The call method will cause the Dog function to be called. We use the call method instead of just calling Dog directly so we can control what the value of **this** is.

Stepping through Dog.call

Using `Dog.call` to call Dog is a bit tricky to wrap your head around so we'll walk through it again, starting with the reworked code.

```
function ShowDog(name, breed, weight, handler) {
    Dog.call(this, name, breed, weight);
    this.handler = handler;
}
```

We're going to rely on the code from the Dog constructor to handle assigning the name, breed, and weight properties.

But Dog doesn't know anything about handler, so we have to take care of that in ShowDog.

Here's how to think about how this works. First, we call ShowDog with the `new` operator. Remember that the `new` operator makes a new, empty object, and assigns it to the variable `this` in the body of ShowDog.

```
var scotty = new ShowDog("Scotty", "Scottish Terrier", 15, "Cookie");
```

Then, we execute the body of the ShowDog constructor function. The first thing we do is call Dog, using the `call` method. That calls Dog, passing in `this`, and the `name`, `breed`, and `weight` parameters as arguments.

```
function ShowDog(name, breed, weight, handler) {
    Dog.call(this, name, breed, weight);

                    function Dog(name, breed, weight) {
                        this.name = name;
                        this.breed = breed;
                        this.weight = weight;
                    }

    this.handler = handler;
}
```

ShowDog
name:
breed:
weight:
handler:

`this`

The this object created by new for ShowDog gets used as this in the body of Dog.

We execute the body of Dog as normal, except that this is a ShowDog, not a Dog object.

Once the Dog function completes (and remember, it is not going to return anything because we didn't call it with `new`), we complete the code in ShowDog, assigning the value of the parameter `handler` to the `this.handler` property. Then, because we used `new` to call ShowDog, an instance of ShowDog is returned, complete with its name, breed, weight, and handler.

ShowDog
name: "Scotty"
breed: "Scottish Terrier"
weight: 15
handler: "Cookie"

These three properties are assigned to this by the code in the Dog function.

This property is assigned to this by the code in the ShowDog function.

The final test drive

Well done, you've created a fantastic design that we're sure Webville Kennel is going to love. Take all your dogs for one final test run so they can show off all their doggy capabilities.

> Webville Kennel is going to love this!

```
function ShowDog(name, breed, weight, handler) {
    Dog.call(this, name, breed, weight);
    this.handler = handler;
}
ShowDog.prototype = new Dog();
ShowDog.prototype.constructor = ShowDog;
ShowDog.prototype.league = "Webville";
ShowDog.prototype.stack = function() {
    console.log("Stack");
};

ShowDog.prototype.bait = function() {
    console.log("Bait");
};
ShowDog.prototype.gait = function(kind) {
    console.log(kind + "ing");
};
ShowDog.prototype.groom = function() {
    console.log("Groom");
};
var fido = new Dog("Fido", "Mixed", 38);
var fluffy = new Dog("Fluffy", "Poodle", 30);
var spot = new Dog("Spot", "Chihuahua", 10);
var scotty = new ShowDog("Scotty", "Scottish Terrier", 15, "Cookie");
var beatrice = new ShowDog("Beatrice", "Pomeranian", 5, "Hamilton");
fido.bark();
fluffy.bark();
spot.bark();
scotty.bark();
beatrice.bark();
scotty.gait("Walk");
beatrice.groom();
```

We've brought all the ShowDog code together here. Add this to the file with your Dog code to test it.

We've added some test code below.

Create some dogs and some show dogs.

Put them through their paces and make sure they're all doing the right thing.

```
JavaScript console
Fido says Woof!
Fluffy says Woof!
Spot says Yip!
Scotty says Yip!
Beatrice says Yip!
Walking
Groom
```

there are no
Dumb Questions

Q: **When we made the dog instance we used for the show dog prototype, we called the Dog constructor with no arguments. Why?**

A: Because all we need from that dog instance is the fact that it inherits from the dog prototype. That dog instance isn't a specific dog (like Fido or Fluffy); it's simply a generic dog instance that inherits from the dog prototype.

Also, all the dogs that inherit from the show dog prototype define their own name, breed, and weight. So even if that dog instance did have values for those properties, we'd never see them because the show dog instances will always override them.

Q: **So what happens to those properties in the dog instance we use for the show dog prototype?**

A: They never get assigned values, so they are all undefined.

Q: **If we never set the ShowDog's prototype property to a dog instance, what happens?**

A: Your show dogs will work fine, but they won't inherit any behavior from the dog prototype. That means they won't be able to bark, run, or wag, nor will they have the "Canine" species property. Give it a try yourself. Comment out the line of code where we set ShowDog.prototype to new Dog() and then try making Scotty bark. What happens?

Q: **Could I create an object literal and use that as the prototype?**

A: Yes. You can use any object as the prototype for ShowDog. Of course, if you do that, your show dogs won't inherit anything from the dog prototype. They'll inherit the properties and methods you put in your object literal instead.

Q: **I accidentally put the line of code to assign ShowDog.prototype to the instance of dog below where I created my scotty instance, and my code didn't work. Why?**

A: Because when you create scotty (an instance of ShowDog), it gets the prototype that's assigned to ShowDog.prototype at the time when you create it. So if you don't assign the dog instance object to the prototype until after you create scotty, then scotty will have a different object as its prototype (the object you get by default with the ShowDog constructor). And that object doesn't have any of the Dog prototype's properties. You should assign the show dog prototype first thing after you create the constructor, but before you add anything to the prototype, or create any instances of ShowDog.

Q: **If I change a property in the dog prototype, like changing species from "Canine" to "Feline", will that affect the show dogs I've created?**

A: Yes, anything you change in the prototype will affect any instances that inherit from that prototype in the chain, no matter how many links you have in your chain.

Q: **Is there a limit to how long my prototype chains can be?**

A: Theoretically, no, but in practice, maybe. The longer your prototype chain, the more work it is to resolve a method or property. That said, runtime systems are often quite good at optimizing these lookups.

In general, you're not going to need designs that require that many levels of inheritance. If you do, you'll probably want to take another look at your design.

Q: **What if I have another category of dogs, like competition dogs. Can I create a competition dog prototype that inherits from the same dog prototype as the show dog prototype does?**

A: Yes, you can. You'll need to create a separate dog instance to act as your competition dog prototype, but once you've done that you'll be good to go. Just follow the same steps we used here to create the show dog prototype.

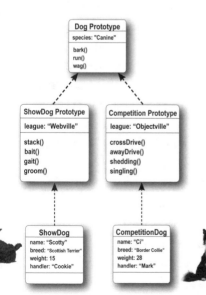

Dog Prototype
species: "Canine"
bark() run() wag()

ShowDog Prototype		Competition Prototype
league: "Webville"		league: "Objectville"
stack() bait() gait() groom()		crossDrive() awayDrive() shedding() singling()

ShowDog		CompetitionDog
name: "Scotty" breed: "Scottish Terrier" weight: 15 handler: "Cookie"		name: "Ci" breed: "Border Collie" weight: 28 handler: "Mark"

The chain doesn't end at dog

You've already seen a couple of prototype chains—we have the original dog prototype that our dog objects inherit from, and we have the more specialized show dog instances that inherit first from the show dog prototype, and the dog prototype.

But in both cases, is dog the end of the chain? Actually it isn't, because dog has its own prototype, Object.

In fact, every prototype chain you ever create will end in Object. That's because the default prototype for any instance you create (assuming you don't change it) is Object.

What is Object?

Think of Object like the primordial object. It's the object that all objects initially inherit from. And Object implements a few key methods that are a core part of the JavaScript object system. Many of these you won't use on a daily basis, but there are some methods you'll see commonly used.

One of those you've already seen in this chapter: `hasOwnProperty`, which is inherited by every object (again, because every object ultimately inherits from Object). Remember, `hasOwnProperty` is the method we used earlier to determine if a property is in an object instance or in one of its prototypes.

Another method inherited from Object is the `toString` method, which is commonly overridden by instances. This method returns a String representation of any object. We'll see in a bit how we can override this method to provide a more accurate description of our own objects.

Object as a prototype

So whether you realized it or not, every object you've ever created has had a prototype, and it's been Object. You can set an object's prototype to another kind of object, like we did with the show dog prototype, but ultimately, all prototype chains eventually lead to Object.

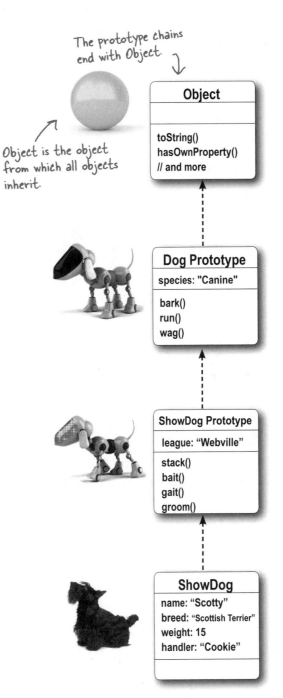

The prototype chains end with Object.

Object is the object from which all objects inherit.

Object

toString()
hasOwnProperty()
// and more

Dog Prototype

species: "Canine"

bark()
run()
wag()

ShowDog Prototype

league: "Webville"

stack()
bait()
gait()
groom()

ShowDog

name: "Scotty"
breed: "Scottish Terrier"
weight: 15
handler: "Cookie"

Using inheritance to your advantage... by overriding built-in behavior

If you're inheriting from a built-in object you can override methods in those objects. One common example is the `toString` method of Object. All objects inherit from Object, so all objects can use the `toString` method to get a simple string representation of any object. For instance, you might use it with `console.log` to display your object in the console:

```
function Robot(name, year, owner) {
    this.name = name;
    this.year = year;
    this.owner = owner;
}

var toy = new Robot("Toy", 2013, "Avary");

console.log(toy.toString());
```

JavaScript console
[Object object]

↖ The toString method we're inheriting from Object doesn't do a very good job.

As you can see, the `toString` method doesn't do a very good job of converting the toy robot into a string. So we can override the `toString` method and write one that creates a string specifically for Robot objects:

```
function Robot(name, year, owner) {
    // same code here
}

Robot.prototype.toString = function() {
    return this.name + " Robot belonging to " + this.owner;
};

var toy = new Robot("Toy", 2013, "Avary");


console.log(toy.toString());
```

JavaScript console
Toy Robot belonging to Avary

↑ Much better! Now we're using our own toString method.

Notice that the `toString` method can be invoked even if you're not calling it directly yourself. For instance, if you use the + operator to concatenate a string and an object, JavaScript will use the `toString` method to convert your object to a string before concatenating it with the other string.

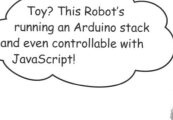

Toy? This Robot's running an Arduino stack and even controllable with JavaScript!

```
console.log("Robot is: " + toy);
```

↖ The toy object will get converted to a string using toString before it's concatenated. If toy has overridden toString, it will use that method.

DANGER ZONE

Once you start overriding properties and methods, it's easy to get a little carried away. It's especially important to be careful when overriding properties and methods in built-in objects, because you don't want to change the behavior of other code that might rely on these properties to do certain things.

So if you're thinking of overriding properties in Object, read this Safety Guide first. Otherwise, you might end up blowing up your code in unexpected ways. (Translation: you'll have bugs that are really hard to track down.)

DO NOT OVERRIDE

Here are the properties in Object you don't want to override:

constructor ← The constructor property points to the constructor function connected to the prototype.

hasOwnProperty ← You know what the hasOwnProperty method does.

isPrototypeOf ← isPrototypeOf is a method you can use to find out if an object is a prototype of another object.

propertyIsEnumerable ← The propertyIsEnumerable method checks to see if a property can be accessed by iterating through all the properties of an object.

OKAY TO OVERRIDE

Here are the properties in Object that you can override now that you know your way around prototypes, and know how to override safely:

toString

toLocaleString ← toLocaleString is a method, like toString, that converts an object to a string. This method is designed to be overridden to provide a localized string (say, for your country/language) about an object.

valueOf ← valueOf is another method designed to be overridden. By default it just gives you the object you call it on. But you can override that to return another value instead if you want.

Using inheritance to your advantage... by extending a built-in object

You already know that by adding methods to a prototype, you can add new functionality to all instances of that prototype. This applies not only to your own objects, but also to built-in objects.

Take the String object for instance—you've used String methods like `substring` in your code, but what if you want to add your own method so that any instance of String could make use of it? We can use the same technique of extending objects through the prototype on Strings too.

Remember that while we usually think of strings as primitive types, they also have an object form. JavaScript takes care of converting a string to an object whenever necessary.

Let's say we want to extend the String prototype with a method, `cliche`, that returns true if the string contains a known cliché. Here's how we'd do that:

Here we're adding a method, cliche, to the String prototype.

```
String.prototype.cliche = function() {
    var cliche = ["lock and load","touch base", "open the kimono"];

    for (var i = 0; i < cliche.length; i++) {
        var index = this.indexOf(cliche[i]);
        if (index >= 0) {
            return true;
        }
    }
    return false;
};
```

We define offending phrases to look for.

And then we use the String's indexOf function to see if the string matches any of the clichés. If it does we immediately return true.

Note that this is the string on which we call the method cliche.

Now let's write some code to test the method:

To test let's create some sentences, including a couple that use clichés.

```
var sentences = ["I'll send my car around to pick you up.",
                 "Let's touch base in the morning and see where we are",
                 "We don't want to open the kimono, we just want to inform them."];

for (var i = 0; i < sentences.length; i++) {
    var phrase = sentences[i];
    if (phrase.cliche()) {
        console.log("CLICHE ALERT: " + phrase);
    }
}
```

Each sentence is a string, so we can call its cliche method.

If true is returned, we know we have a cliché in the string.

Notice that we're not creating a string using the String constructor and new. JavaScript is converting each string to a String object behind the scenes for us, when we call the cliche method.

Test driving the cliché machine

Get the code into a HTML file, open your browser and load it up.
Check your console and you should see this output:

Works great. If only we could convince Corporate America to install this code!

JavaScript console

CLICHE ALERT: Let's touch base in the morning and see where we are

CLICHE ALERT: We don't want to open the kimono, we just want to inform them.

Watch it!

Be careful when you extend built-in objects like String with your own methods.

Make sure the name you choose for your method doesn't conflict with an existing method in the object. And if you link to other code, be aware of other custom extensions that code may have (and again, watch for name clashes). And finally, some built-in objects aren't designed to be extended (like Array). So do your homework before you start adding methods to built-in objects.

Exercise

Your turn. Write a method, palindrome, that returns true if a string reads the same forwards and backwards. (Just one word, don't worry about palindrome phrases.) Add the method to the String.prototype and test. Check your answer at the end of the chapter.

Grand Unified Theory of ~~Everything~~ JavaScript

Congratulations. You've taken on the task of learning an entirely new programming language (maybe your first language) and you've done it. Assuming you've made it this far, you now know more JavaScript than pretty much everyone.

> We're using the logic that about 5.9 billion people don't know JavaScript at all, and so those who do are pretty much a rounding error, which means you know more JavaScript than just about anyone.

More seriously, if you've made it this far in the book, you are well on your way to becoming a JavaScript expert. Now all you need is more experience designing and coding web applications (or any kind of JavaScript application for that matter).

Better living through objects

When you're learning a complex topic like JavaScript, it's hard to see the forest for the trees. But, once you understand most of JavaScript, it's easier to step back and check out the forest.

When you're learning JavaScript, you learn about pieces of it at a time: you learn about primitives (that can, at any moment, be used like an object), arrays (which kinda act like objects at times), functions (which, oddly, have properties and methods like objects), constructors (which feel like part function, part object) and well… objects themselves. It all seems rather complex.

Well, with the knowledge you have now, you can sit back, relax, take a cleansing breath, and meditate on the mantra "everything is an object."

Because you see, everything *is* an object—oh, sure we have a few primitives, like booleans, numbers and strings, but we already know that we can treat those as objects anytime we need to. We have some built-in types too, like Date, Math and RegEx, but those are just objects too. Even arrays are objects, and as you saw, the only reason they look different is because JavaScript provides some nice "syntactic sugar" we can use to make creating and accessing objects easier. And of course we have objects themselves, with the simplicity of object literals and the power of the prototypal object system.

But what about functions? Are they really objects? Let's find out:

```javascript
function meditate() {
    console.log("Everything is an object...");
}
alert(meditate instanceof Object);
```

> Everything is an object...Everything is an object...Everything is an object...

So it's true: functions are just objects. But, really, this shouldn't be a big surprise at this point. After all we can assign functions to variables (like objects), pass them as arguments (like objects), return them from functions (like objects), and we've even seen they have properties, like this one:

Dog.constructor

↑
Remember this is a function.

↑
And this is a property.

true

OK

↑
It's true! Functions are objects too.

And there's nothing stopping you from adding your own properties to a function should that come in handy. And, by the way, just to bring it all full circle, have you considered that a method is just a property in an object that is set to an anonymous function expression?

Putting it all together

A lot of JavaScript's power and flexibility comes from the interplay between how we use functions and objects, and the fact that we can treat them as first class values. If you think about the powerful programming concepts we've studied—constructors, closures, creating objects with behavior that we can reuse and extend, parameterizing the behavior of functions, and so on—all these techniques have relied on your understanding of advanced objects and functions.

Well, now you're in a position to take this all even further…

What's next?

Now that you've got all the fundamentals down, it's time to take it all further. Now you're ready to really put your experience to use with the browser and its programming interfaces. You can do that by picking up *Head First HTML5 Programming*, which will take you through how to add geolocation, canvas drawing capabilities, local storage, web workers and more into your applications. But before you put this book down, be sure to read the appendix for a great list of other topics to explore.

Be sure to visit http://wickedlysmart. com/javascript for follow-up materials for this book and, as your next mission, should you accept it…

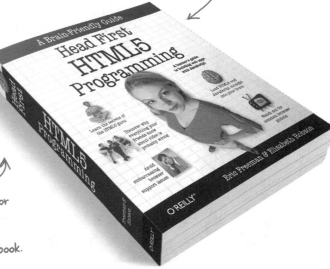

This is a rapidly evolving topic, so before you go looking for Head First HTML5 Programming, hit http://wickedlysmart.com/javascript for our latest recommendations and any updates and revisions for this book.

BULLET POINTS

- JavaScript's object system uses **prototypal inheritance**.

- When you create an instance of an object from a constructor, the instance has its own customized properties and a copy of the methods in the constructor.

- If you add properties to a constructor's prototype, all instances created from that constructor **inherit** those properties.

- Putting properties in a prototype can reduce runtime code duplication in objects.

- To **override** properties in the prototype, simply add the property to an instance.

- A constructor function comes with a default **prototype** that you can access with the function's prototype property.

- You can assign your own object to the prototype property of a constructor function.

- If you use your own prototype object, make sure you set the constructor function correctly to the constructor property for consistency.

- If you add properties to a prototype after you've created instances that inherit from it, all the instances will immediately inherit the new properties.

- Use the **hasOwnProperty** method on an instance to find out if a property is defined in the instance.

- The method **call** can be used to invoke a function and specify the object to be used as **this** in the body of the function.

- **Object** is the object that all prototypes and instances ultimately inherit from.

- Object has properties and methods that all objects inherit, like toString and hasOwnProperty.

- You can override or add properties to built-in objects like Object and String, but take care when doing so as your changes can have far-ranging effects.

- In JavaScript, almost everything is an object, including functions, arrays, many built-in objects, and all the custom objects you make yourself.

Totally awesome job!

Congratulations from all of us for finishing the book!

You did it! It's the end of the book!

Ey Ey Matey, well done!

Nice! We couldn't have done it without you!

Woohoo! You nailed it!

Right on! Nice Job!

You're ready to take on some real coding now!

STOP

Code Magnets Solution

We had an object diagram on the fridge, and then someone came and messed it up. Can you help put it back together? To reassemble it, we need two instances of the robot prototype. One is Robby, created in 1956, owned by Dr. Morbius, has an on/off switch and runs to Starbucks for coffee. We've also got Rosie, created in 1962, who cleans house and is owned by George Jetson. Good luck (oh, and there might be some extra magnets below)!

Here's our solution:

Here's the prototype your robots can inherit from.

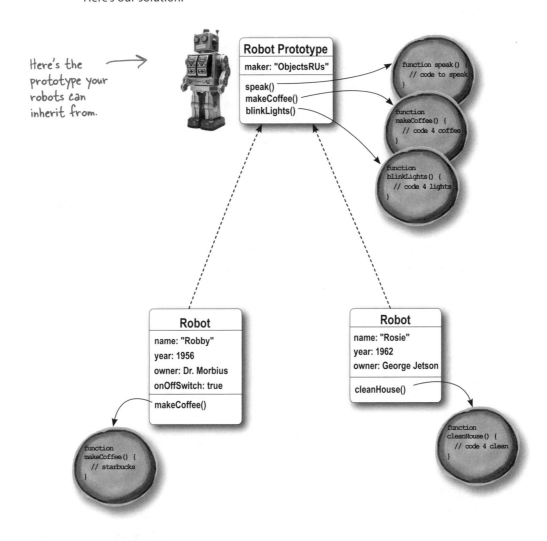

Exercise Solution

Remember our object diagram for the Robby and Rosie robots? We're going to implement that now. We've already written a Robot constructor for you along with some test code. Your job is to set up the robot prototype and to implement the two robots. Make sure you run them through the test code. Here's our solution.

```javascript
function Robot(name, year, owner) {
    this.name = name;
    this.year = year;
    this.owner = owner;
}
Robot.prototype.maker = "ObjectsRUs";
Robot.prototype.speak = function() {
    alert("Warning warning!!");
};
Robot.prototype.makeCoffee = function() {
    alert("Making coffee");
};
Robot.prototype.blinkLights = function() {
    alert("Blink blink!");
};
var robby = new Robot("Robby", 1956, "Dr. Morbius");
var rosie = new Robot("Rosie", 1962, "George Jetson");
robby.onOffSwitch = true;
robby.makeCoffee = function() {
    alert("Fetching a coffee from Starbucks.");
};
rosie.cleanHouse = function() {
    alert("Cleaning! Spic and Span soon...");
};
console.log(robby.name + " was made by " + robby.maker +
            " in " + robby.year + " and is owned by " + robby.owner);
robby.makeCoffee();
robby.blinkLights();
console.log(rosie.name + " was made by " + rosie.maker +
            " in " + rosie.year + " and is owned by " + rosie.owner);
rosie.cleanHouse();
```

Here's the basic Robot constructor.

Here we're setting up the prototype with a maker property...

...and three methods that are shared by all robots.

We create our robots, Robby and Rosie here.

Here, we're adding a custom property to Robby, as well as a custom method for making coffee (by going to Starbucks).

And Rosie also gets a custom method to clean the house (why do the girl robots have to clean?)

Here's our output (plus some alerts we're not showing).

JavaScript console

```
Robby was made by ObjectsRUs in 1956
and is owned by Dr. Morbius
Rosie was made by ObjectsRUs in 1962
and is owned by George Jetson
```

Robby and Rosie are being used in a Robot game. You'll find the code for them below. In this game, whenever a player reaches level 42, a new robot capability is unlocked: the laser beam capability. Finish the code below so that at level 42 both Robby and Rosie get their laser beams. Here's our solution.

```
JavaScript console
Welcome to level 1
Welcome to level 2
Welcome to level 3
...
Welcome to level 41
Welcome to level 42
Rosie is blasting you with
laser beams.
```

```javascript
function Game() {
    this.level = 0;
}

Game.prototype.play = function() {
    // player plays game here
    this.level++;
    console.log("Welcome to level " + this.level);
    this.unlock();
}
```
We call unlock each time we play the game but no power is unlocked until the level reaches 42.

```javascript
Game.prototype.unlock = function() {
    if (this.level === 42) {
        Robot.prototype.deployLaser = function () {
            console.log(this.name +  " is blasting you with laser beams.");
        }
    }
}
```
Here's the trick to this game: when you reach level 42, a new method is added to the prototype. That means all robots inherit the ability to deploy lasers!

A sample of our output. When you finish your code, give it a play and see which robot wins and gets to blast its laser beams!

```javascript
function Robot(name, year, owner) {
    this.name = name;
    this.year = year;
    this.owner = owner;
}

var game = new Game();
var robby = new Robot("Robby", 1956, "Dr. Morbius");
var rosie = new Robot("Rosie", 1962, "George Jetson");

while (game.level < 42) {
    game.play();
}

robby.deployLaser();
rosie.deployLaser();
```

We've added a new capability to our robots, Robby and Rosie: they can now report when they have an error through the reportError method. Trace the code below, paying particular attention to where this method gets its error information, and to whether it's coming from the prototype of the robot instance.

Here's our solution.

```
function Robot(name, year, owner) {
    this.name = name;
    this.year = year;
    this.owner = owner;
}

Robot.prototype.maker = "ObjectsRUs";
Robot.prototype.errorMessage = "All systems go.";
Robot.prototype.reportError = function() {
    console.log(this.name + " says " + this.errorMessage);
};
Robot.prototype.spillWater = function() {
    this.errorMessage = "I appear to have a short circuit!";
};

var robby = new Robot("Robby", 1956, "Dr. Morbius");
var rosie = new Robot("Rosie", 1962, "George Jetson");

rosie.reportError();
robby.reportError();
robby.spillWater();
rosie.reportError();
robby.reportError();

console.log(robby.hasOwnProperty("errorMessage"));    true
console.log(rosie.hasOwnProperty("errorMessage"));    false
```

The reportError method only uses the value of errorMessage, so it doesn't override the property.

The spillWater method assigns a new value to this.errorMessage, which will override the property in the prototype in any robot that calls this method.

We call the spillWater method on Robby, so Robby gets his own errorMessage property, which overrides the property in the prototype.

But we never call spillWater on Rosie, so she inherits the property in the prototype.

Code Magnets Solution

We had another object diagram on the fridge, and then someone came and messed it up. Again!! Can you help put it back together? To reassemble it we need a new line of Space Robots that inherit properties from Robots. These new Space Robots override the Robot's speaking functionality, and extend Robots with piloting functionality and a new property, homePlanet. Here's our solution.

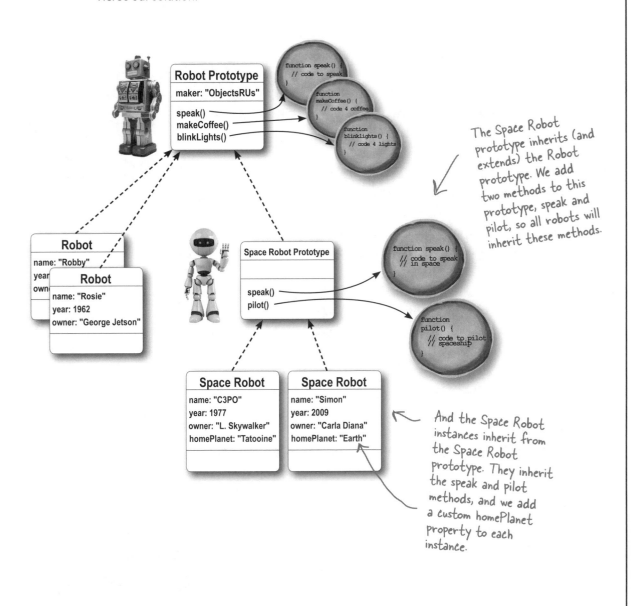

The Space Robot prototype inherits (and extends) the Robot prototype. We add two methods to this prototype, speak and pilot, so all robots will inherit these methods.

And the Space Robot instances inherit from the Space Robot prototype. They inherit the speak and pilot methods, and we add a custom homePlanet property to each instance.

Your turn. Add a SpaceRobot line of robots to the ObjectsRUs line of robots. These robots should of course be able to do everything that robots can do, plus some extra behavior for space robots. We've started the code below, so finish it up and then test it. Here's our solution.

```javascript
function SpaceRobot(name, year, owner, homePlanet) {
    this.name =  name;
    this.year = year;
    this.owner = owner;
    this.homePlanet = homePlanet;
}
```

The SpaceRobot constructor is similar to the Robot constructor, except we have an extra homePlanet property for the SpaceRobot instances.

We want the SpaceRobot prototype to inherit from the Robot prototype, so we assign a Robot instance to the SpaceRobot constructor's prototype property.

```javascript
SpaceRobot.prototype = new Robot();

SpaceRobot.prototype.speak = function() {
    alert(this.name + " says Sir, If I may venture an opinion...");
};

SpaceRobot.prototype.pilot = function() {
    alert(this.name + " says Thrusters? Are they important?");
};
```

These two methods are added to the prototype.

```javascript
var c3po = new SpaceRobot("C3PO", 1977, "Luke Skywalker", "Tatooine");
c3po.speak();
c3po.pilot();
console.log(c3po.name + " was made by " + c3po.maker);

var simon = new SpaceRobot("Simon", 2009, "Carla Diana", "Earth");
simon.makeCoffee();
simon.blinkLights();
simon.speak();
```

Here's our output (plus some alerts we're not showing).

JavaScript console
C3PO was made by ObjectsRUs

Exercise Solution

Your turn. Write a method, palindrome, that returns true if a string reads the same forward and backward. Add the method to the String.prototype and test. Here's our solution (for one word palindromes only).

```
String.prototype.palindrome = function() {
    var len = this.length-1;
    for (var i = 0; i <= len; i++) {
        if (this.charAt(i) !== this.charAt(len-i)) {
            return false;
        }
        if (i === (len-i)) {
            return true;
        }
    }
    return true;
};
```

First we get the length of the string.

Then we iterate over each character in the string, and test to see if the character at i is the same as the character at len−i (i.e., the character at the other end).

If they're not equal we return false because we don't have a palindrome.

If we get to where i is in the middle of the string, or we get to the end of the loop, we return true because we've got a palindrome.

```
var phrases = ["eve", "kayak", "mom", "wow", "Not a palindrome"];
```

Here are some words to test.

```
for (var i = 0; i < phrases.length; i++) {
    var phrase = phrases[i];
    if (phrase.palindrome()) {
        console.log("'" + phrase + "' is a palindrome");
    } else {
        console.log("'" + phrase + "' is NOT a palindrome");
    }
}
```

We just iterate through each word in the array and call the palindrome method on it. If we get back true, then we have a palindrome.

Super Advanced Solution

Here, we first split the string into an array of letters, with each letter being one item in the array. We then reverse the array and join all the letters back up into a string. If the original string's value equals the new string, we've got a palindrome. Note, we have to use valueOf here, because this is an object, not a string primitive like r, so if we don't, we'd be comparing a string to an object, and they wouldn't be equal even if this is a palindrome.

```
String.prototype.palindrome = function() {
    var r = this.split("").reverse().join("");
    return (r === this.valueOf());
}
```

Congratulations!
You made it to the end.

Of course, there's still an appendix.

And the index.

And the colophon.

And then there's the website...

There's no escape, really.

Appendix: leftovers

The top ten topics (we didn't cover)

We've covered a lot of ground, and you're almost finished with this book. We'll miss you, but before we let you go, we wouldn't feel right about sending you out into the world without a little more preparation. We can't possibly fit everything you'll need to know into this relatively small chapter. Actually, we *did* originally include everything you need to know about JavaScript Programming (not already covered by the other chapters), by reducing the type point size to .00004. It all fit, but nobody could read it. So we threw most of it away, and kept the best bits for this Top Ten appendix.

This really *is* the end of the book. Except for the index, of course (a must-read!).

#1 jQuery

jQuery is a JavaScript library that is aimed at reducing and simplifying much of the JavaScript code and syntax that is needed to work with the DOM and add visual effects to your pages. jQuery is an enormously popular library that is widely used and expandable through its plug-in model.

Now, there's nothing you can do in jQuery that you can't do with JavaScript (as we said, jQuery is just a JavaScript library); however, it does have the power to reduce the amount of code you need to write.

jQuery's popularity speaks for itself, although it can take some getting used to if you are new to it. Let's check out a few things you can do in jQuery and we encourage you to take a closer look if you think it might be for you.

↖ A working knowledge of jQuery is a good skill these days on the job front and for understanding others' code.

For starters, remember all the `window.onload` functions we wrote in this book? Like:

```
window.onload = function() {

    alert("the page is loaded!");

}
```

Here's the same thing using jQuery:

```
$(document).ready(function() {

    alert("the page is loaded!");

});
```

← Just like our version, when the document is ready, invoke my function.

Or you can shorten this even more, to:

```
$(function() {

    alert("the page is loaded!");

});
```

← This is cool, but as you can see it takes a little getting used to at first. No worries, it becomes second-nature fast.

So what about getting elements from the DOM? That's where jQuery shines. Let's say you have an `<a>` element in your page with an id of "buynow" and you want to assign a click handler to the click event on that element (like we've done a few times in this book). Here's how you do that:

So what's going on here? First we're setting up a function that is called when the page is loaded.

```
$(function() {
    $("#buynow").click(function() {
        alert("I want to buy now!");
    });
});
```

Next we're grabbing the element with a "buynow" id (notice jQuery uses CSS syntax for selecting elements).

And then we're calling a jQuery method, click, on the result to set the onclick handler.

That's really just the beginning; we can just as easily set the click handler on every <a> element in the page:

```
$(function() {

    $("a").click(function() {

        alert("I want to buy now!");

    });

});
```

To do that, all we need to do is use the tag name.

Compare this to the code you'd write to do this if we were using JavaScript without jQuery.

Or, we can do things that are much more complex:

```
$(function() {

    $("#playlist > li").addClass("favorite");

});
```

Like find all the <li> elements that are children of the element with an id of playlist.

And then add the class "favorite" to all the elements.

Actually this is jQuery just getting warmed up; jQuery can do things much more sophisticated than this.

There's a whole 'nother side of jQuery that allows you to do interesting interface transformations on your elements, like this:

```
$(function() {

    $("#specialoffer").click(function() {

        $(this).fadeOut(800, function() {

            $(this).fadeIn(400);

        });

    });

});
```

This makes the element with an id of specialoffer fade out and then fade back in at different rates.

As you can see, there's a lot you can do with jQuery, and we haven't even talked about how we can use jQuery to talk to web services, or all the plug-ins that work with jQuery. If you're interested, the best thing you can do is point your browser to http://jquery.com/ and check out the tutorials and documentation there.

And, check out Head First jQuery too!

#2 Doing more with the DOM

We've touched on some of the things you can do with the DOM in this book, but there's a lot more to learn. The objects that represent the document in your page—that is, the `document` object, and the various element objects—are chock full of properties and methods you can use to interact with and manipulate your page.

You already know how to use `document.getElementById` and `document.getElementsByTagName` to get elements from the page. The `document` object has these other methods you can use to get elements, too:

document.getElementsByClassName   *Pass this method the name of a class, and you'll get back all elements that have that class, as a NodeList.*

document.getElementsByName   *This method retrieves elements that have a name attribute with a value that matches the name you pass it.*

document.querySelector   *This method takes a selector (just like a CSS selector) and returns the first element that matches.*

document.querySelectorAll   *This method also takes a selector, but returns all the elements that match, as a NodeList.*

Here's how you'd use `document.querySelector` to match a list item element with the class "song" that's nested in a `<ul>` element with the id "playlist":

```
var li = document.querySelector("#playlist .song");
```

This says match the element with the id playlist, and then match the first element with the class song.

Notice how this selector is just like one you'd write in CSS?

What if you want to add new elements to your page from your code? You can use a combination of `document` object methods and element methods to do that, like this:

```
var newItem = document.createElement("li");

newItem.innerHTML = "Your Random Heart";

var ul = document.getElementById("playlist");

ul.appendChild(newItem);
```

First, we create a new `<li>` element, and set its content to a string.

Then we get the `<ul>` element we want to add the new `<li>` to (as a child element), and append the `<li>` to the `<ul>`.

There's a lot more you can do with the DOM using JavaScript. For a good introduction, check out *Head First HTML5 Programming*.

#3 The Window Object

You've heard of the DOM, but you should know there's also a BOM, or Browser Object Model. It's not really an official standard, but all browsers support it through the `window` object. You've seen the `window` object in passing when we've used the `window.onload` property, and you'll remember we can assign an event handler to this property that is triggered when the browser has fully loaded a page.

You've also seen the `window` object when we've used the `alert` and `prompt` methods, even though it might not have been obvious. The reason it wasn't obvious is that `window` is the object that acts as the global namespace. When you declare any kind of global variable or define a global function, it is stored as a property in the `window` object. So for every call we made to `alert`, we could have instead called `window.alert`, because it's the same thing.

Another place you've used the window object without knowing it is when you've used the `document` object to do things like get elements from the DOM with `document.getElementById`. The `document` object is a property of `window`, so we could write `window.document.getElementById`. But, just like with `alert`, we don't have to, because `window` is the global object, and it is the default object for all the properties and methods we use from it.

In addition to being the global object, and supplying the `onload` property and the `alert` and `prompt` methods, the `window` object supplies other interesting browser-based properties and methods. For instance, it's common to make use of the width and height of the browser window to tailor a web page experience to the size of the browser. You can access these values like this:

window.innerWidth

window.innerHeight

Use these properties to get the browser window's width and height in pixels. Note that older browsers don't always expose these properties.

Check out the W3C documentation* for more on the `window` object. Here are a few common methods and properties:

window.close() ← This method closes the browser window.

window.setTimeout()
window.setInterval() ← You already know these methods; they're supplied by the window object.

window.print() ← Initiates printing the page to your printer.

window.confirm() ← This method is similar to prompt, only it gives the user the choice of an Okay or Cancel button.

window.history ← This property is an object containing the browsing history.

window.location ← This property is the URL of the current page. You can also set this property to direct the browser to load a new page.

* http://www.w3.org/html/wg/drafts/html/CR/browsers.html#the-window-object

#4 Arguments

An object named `arguments` is available in every function when that function is called. You won't ever see this object in the parameter list, but it is available nevertheless every time a function is called, in the variable `arguments`.

The `arguments` object contains every argument passed to your function, and it can be accessed in an array-like manner. You can use `arguments` to create a function that accepts a variable number of arguments, or create a function that does different things depending on the number of arguments passed to it. Let's see how `arguments` works with this code:

We're not going to define any formal parameters for now. We'll just use the arguments object.

Like an array, arguments has a length property.

```javascript
function printArgs() {
    for (var i = 0; i < arguments.length; i++) {
        console.log(arguments[i]);
    }
}

printArgs("one", 2, 1+2, "four");
```

And we can access each argument using array notation.

Here we call printArgs with four arguments.

JavaScript console
```
one
2
3
four
```

While `arguments` looks just like an array, it is not actually an array; it's an object. It has a `length` property, and you can iterate over it and access items in it using bracket notation, but that's where the similarity with an array ends. Also, note that you can use both parameters and the `arguments` object in the same function. Let's write one more piece of code to see how a function with a variable number of arguments might be written:

We can define parameters like normal. In this case, using a parameter helps indicate how to use this function.

```javascript
function emote(kind) {
    if (kind === "silence") {
        console.log("Player sits in silence");
    } else if (kind === "says") {
        console.log("Player says: '" + arguments[1] + "'");
    }
}

emote("silence");
emote("says", "Stand back!");
```

JavaScript console
```
Player sits in silence
Player says: 'Stand back!'
```

If the first argument is "silence" then we don't expect another. If the first argument is "says", then we use arguments[1] to get the second argument.

#5 Handling exceptions

JavaScript is a fairly forgiving language, but now and then things go wrong—wrong enough that the browser can't continue executing your code. When that happens, your page stops working, and if you look in the console you're likely to see an error. Let's take a look at an example of some code that causes an error. Start by creating a simple HTML page with a single element in the body:

```
<div id="message"></div>
```

Now, add the following JavaScript:

```
window.onload = function() {
    var message = document.getElementById("messge");
    message.innerHTML = "Here's the message!";
};
```

← *We're making an error in this code. Can you see what we did wrong?*

Load the page in your browser, make sure the console is open, and you'll get an error. Can you see what went wrong? We mistyped the id of the `<div>` element, so when your code tries to retrieve that `<div>` element it fails, and the variable `message` is null. And you can't access the `innerHTML` property of null.

```
JavaScript console
Uncaught TypeError: Cannot set
property 'innerHTML' of null
```

When you get an error that causes your code to stop executing like this one does, it's called an exception. JavaScript has a mechanism, called try/catch, that you can use to watch for exceptions and catch them when they happen. The idea is that if you can catch one of these exceptions, rather than your code just stopping, you can take an alternative action (try something else, offer the user a different experience, etc.).

Try/catch

The way you use try/catch is like this: you put the code you want to try in the try block, and then you write a catch block that contains code that will be executed in case anything goes wrong with the code in the try block. The catch keyword is followed by parentheses that contain a variable name (that acts a lot like a function parameter). If something goes wrong and an exception is caught, the variable will be assigned to a value related to the exception, often an Error object. Here's how you use a try/catch statement:

```
window.onload = function() {
    try {
        var message = document.getElementById("messge");
        message.innerHTML = "Here's the message!";
    } catch (error) {
        console.log("Error! " + error.message);
    }
};
```

← *We moved our code into a try block.*

← *Here, we're trying to set the innerHTML property of message (which is null) to a string.*

← *If the code in the try block causes an exception, then this line of code is executed. All we're doing is displaying the message property of the error object in the console. Then execution continues with the line following the try/catch.*

↗ *Depending on the error, you could do something much smarter here.*

#6 Adding event handlers with addEventListener

In this book, we used object properties to assign event handlers to events. For instance, when we wanted to handle the load event, we assigned an event handler to the `window.onload` property. And when we wanted to handle a button click, we assigned an event handler to that button's `onclick` property.

This is a convenient way of assigning event handlers. But sometimes, you might need a more general way of assigning event handlers. For instance, if you want to assign multiple handlers for one event type, you can't do that if you use a property like `onload`. But you can with a method named `addEventListener`:

We call addEventListener on window to register a handler for the load event.

And we pass it three arguments: the name of the event, "load", as a string...

...a reference to the handler function for the event...

```
window.addEventListener("load", init, false);
function init() {
    // page has loaded
}
```

...and a flag indicating if we want to bubble the event up (we'll explain bubble in a moment).

So the init function is called when the load event happens.

You can assign a second load event handler to window simply by calling `addEventListener` again, passing a different event handler function reference as the second argument. This is handy if you want to split your initialization code into two separate functions, but remember—you won't know which handler will be called first, so keep that in mind as you're designing your code.

The third argument to `addEventListener` determines if the event is "bubbled up" to parent elements. This doesn't make a difference for the load event (because the window object is at the top level), but if you have, say, a `<span>` element nested inside a `<div>` element, and you click on the `<span>` but want the `<div>` to receive the event, then you can set bubble to true instead of false.

It's totally fine to mix and match using the event properties, like `onload`, with `addEventListener`. Also, if you add an event handler with `addEventListener`, you can remove it later with `removeEventListener`, like this:

We're using the onload property to assign the load event handler for window.

```
window.onload = function() {
    var div = document.getElementById("clickme");
    div.addEventListener("click", handleClick, false);
};
function handleClick(e) {
    var target = e.target;;
    alert("You clicked on " + target.id);
    target.removeEventListener("click", handleClick, false);
}
```

And using addEventListener to assign the event handler for the <div>'s click event.

When you click the <div>, we remove the event handler from the div with removeEventListener.

Event handling in IE8 and older

We've handled a few different kinds of events in this book—mouse clicks, load events, key presses, and more—and hopefully you've been using a modern browser and the code has worked for you. However, if you are writing a web page that handles events (and what web page doesn't?) and you're concerned that some of the people in your audience may be using versions of Internet Explorer (IE) that are version 8 or older, you need to be aware of an issue with event handling.

Unfortunately, IE handled events differently from other browsers until IE9. You could use properties like `onclick` and `onload` to set event handlers across all browsers, however, the way that older IE browsers handle the event object is different. In addition, if you happen to be using the standardized `addEventListener` method, IE didn't support this method until IE9 and later. Here are the main issues to be aware of:

- ❏ IE8 and older browsers do support most of the "on" properties you can use to assign event handlers.

- ❏ IE8 and older browsers use a method named `attachEvent` instead of the `addEventListener` method.

- ❏ When an event is triggered and your event handler is called, instead of passing an event object to the handler, IE8 and older store the event object in the window object.

So, if you want to be sure that your code works across all browsers, including IE8 and older browsers, then you can manage these differences like this:

```javascript
window.onload = function() {
    var div = document.getElementById("clickme");
    if (div.addEventListener) {
        div.addEventListener("click", handleClick, false);
    } else if (div.attachEvent) {
        div.attachEvent("onclick", handleClick);
    }
};
function handleClick(e) {
    var evt = e || window.event;
    var target;
    if (evt.target) {
        target = evt.target;
    } else {
        target = evt.srcElement;
    }
    alert("You clicked on " + target.id);
}
```

IE8 supports the onload property for the load event so this is okay.

If you use the addEventListener method to add an event handler, you need to check to make sure the method exists...

...and if it doesn't, use the attachEvent method instead. Notice attachEvent doesn't have a third argument, and uses "onclick" for the event name.

If the event object is passed, then you know you're dealing with IE9+ or another browser. Otherwise, you have to get the event object from the window.

If the event object is the modern one, the element that triggered the event will be in the target property, like normal. But if this is IE8 or older, this element will be in the srcElement property.

#7 Regular Expressions

You've seen the RegExp object in passing in this book—"RegExp" stands for *regular expression*, which is, formally, a grammar for describing patterns in text. For instance, using a regular expression, you could write an expression that matches all text that starts with "t" and ends with "e" , with at least one "a" and no more than two "u"s in between.

Regular expressions can get complex fast. In fact, regular expressions can almost seem like an alien language when you first try to read them. But you can get started with simple regular expressions fairly quickly, and if you like them, check out a good reference on the topic.

The RegExp constructor

Let's take a look at a couple of regular expressions. To create a regular expression, pass a search pattern to the RegExp constructor, between two slashes, like this:

The argument to the RegExp constructor is the search pattern. How do you read these two search patterns?

```
var areaCode = new RegExp(/[0-9]{3}/);
```

```
var phoneNumber = new RegExp(/^\d{3}-?\d{4}$/);
```

Remember this from Chair Wars back in Chapter 7? This was Amy's winning code.

The key to understanding regular expressions is learning how to read the search patterns. These search patterns are the most complex part of regular expressions, so we'll work through the two examples here, and you'll have to explore the rest on your own.

Like this...

This says match any of the numbers in the range 0-9. [ ] mean you're specifying a range of letters or numbers.

And this says that we want to match three of the previous character. In other words we want to match three numbers in the range 0-9.

/ marks the beginning of the regular expression.

$$/ \ [0 - 9] \ \{ 3 \} \ /$$

/ marks the end of the regular expression.

The whole thing matches any three digit string, like "201" or "503".

$$" 2 0 1 "$$

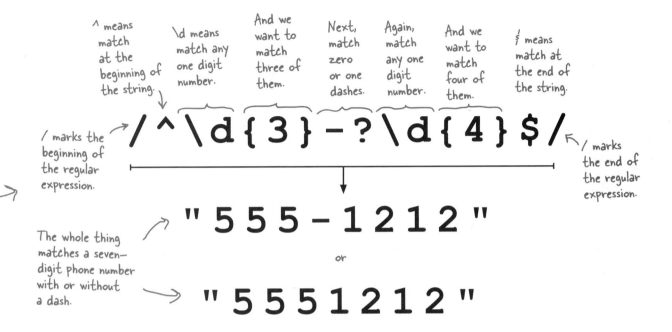

^ means match at the beginning of the string.

\d means match any one digit number.

And we want to match three of them.

Next, match zero or one dashes.

Again, match any one digit number.

And we want to match four of them.

$ means match at the end of the string.

/ marks the beginning of the regular expression.

/ marks the end of the regular expression.

`/^\d{3}-?\d{4}$/`

The whole thing matches a seven-digit phone number with or without a dash.

`"555-1212"`

or

`"5551212"`

Using a RegExp object

To use a regular expression, you first need a string to search:

```
var amyHome = "555-1212";
```

Then, you match the regular expression to the string by calling the `match` method on the string, and passing the regular expression object as an argument:

```
var result = amyHome.match(phoneNumber);
```

The value in result is ["555-1212"], because in this case, the entire string in the variable amyHome matched.

The result is an array containing any parts of the string that matched. If the result is null, then nothing in the string matched the regular expression:

```
var invalid = "5556-1212";
var result2 = invalid.match(phoneNumber);
```

The value in result2 is null because no part the string in the variable invalid matched our regular expression search pattern.

Once you've got a regular expression, like `phoneNumber`, you can just keep using it to match as many strings as you like.

#8 Recursion

When you give a function a name it allows you to do something quite interesting: call that function from within the function. We call this *recursion*, or a recursive function call.

Now why would you need such a thing? Well, some problems are inherently recursive. Here's one from mathematics: an algorithm to compute the Fibonacci number series. The Fibonacci number series is:

0, 1, 1, 2 , 3, 5, 8, 13, 21, 34, 55, 89, 144... and so on.

To compute a Fibonacci number we start by assuming:

Fibonacci of 0 is 1

Fibonacci of 1 is 1

and then to compute any other number in the series we simply add together the two previous numbers in the series. So:

Fibonacci of 2 is Fibonacci of 1 + Fibonacci of 0 = 2

Fibonacci of 3 is Fibonacci of 2 + Fibonacci of 1 = 3

Fibonacci of 4 is Fibonacci of 3 + Fibonacci of 2 = 5

and so on… The algorithm to compute Fibonacci numbers is inherently recursive because you compute the next number using the results of the previous two Fibonacci numbers.

We can make a recursive function to compute Fibonacci numbers like this: to compute the Fibonacci of the number n, we call the Fibonacci function with the argument n-1 and call the Fibonacci function with the argument n-2, and then add the results together.

Let's do that in code. We'll start by handling the cases of 0 and 1:

We start with a function that accepts n, the number in the series we're after.

```
function fibonacci(n) {
    if (n === 0) return 1;
    if (n === 1) return 1;
}
```

Then we know that if the number is either 0 or 1, we return 1. This is known as the base case of the function, because it doesn't make any recursive calls.

These are the *base cases*—that is, the cases that don't rely on previous Fibonacci numbers to compute—and it is usually good to write them first. From there you can think like this: "To compute a Fibonacci number n, I return the result of adding the Fibonacci of n-1 and the Fibonacci of n-2.

Let's do that…

```
function fibonacci(n) {

    if (n === 0) return 1;

    if (n === 1) return 1;

    return (fibonacci(n-1) + fibonacci(n-2));

}
```

Now if n isn't 0 or 1, we just need to compute the Fibonacci by adding together the Fibonacci of n-1 and n-2.

This looks a little like magic if you've never seen recursion before, but this does compute Fibonacci numbers. Let's clean the code up a little, and test it:

Same code, just written a little better.

```
function fibonacci(n) {

    if (n === 0 || n === 1) {

        return 1;

    } else {

        return (fibonacci(n-1) + fibonacci(n-2));

    }

}
```

And some test code.

```
for (var i = 0; i < 10; i++) {

    console.log("The fibonacci of " + i + " is " + fibonacci(i));

}
```

Make sure you have a base case.

If recursive code never reaches a base case where the computation ends, it will run forever, like an infinite loop. In other words, the function will continue calling itself over and over, consuming resources until your browser can't take it anymore. So if you write recursive code and your page isn't responding, figure out how to make sure you're getting to the base case.

```
JavaScript console

The fibonacci of 0 is 1
The fibonacci of 1 is 1
The fibonacci of 2 is 2
The fibonacci of 3 is 3
The fibonacci of 4 is 5
The fibonacci of 5 is 8
The fibonacci of 6 is 13
The fibonacci of 7 is 21
The fibonacci of 8 is 34
The fibonacci of 9 is 55
```

#9 JSON

Not only is JavaScript the programming language of the Web, it's becoming a common interchange format for storing and transmitting objects. JSON is an acronym for "JavaScript Object Notation" and is a format that allows you to represent a JavaScript object as a string—a string that can be stored and transmitted:

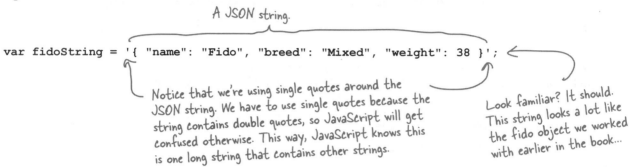

A JSON string.

```
var fidoString = '{ "name": "Fido", "breed": "Mixed", "weight": 38 }';
```

Notice that we're using single quotes around the JSON string. We have to use single quotes because the string contains double quotes, so JavaScript will get confused otherwise. This way, JavaScript knows this is one long string that contains other strings.

Look familiar? It should. This string looks a lot like the fido object we worked with earlier in the book...

Now, the cool thing about JSON is we can take strings like this and turn them into objects. The way we do it is with a couple of methods supplied by JavaScript JSON object: `JSON.parse` and `JSON.stringify`. We'll use the `parse` method to parse the `fidoString` above and turn it into a real dog (well, a JavaScript object anyway):

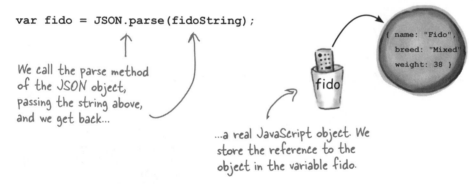

```
var fido = JSON.parse(fidoString);
```

We call the parse method of the JSON object, passing the string above, and we get back...

...a real JavaScript object. We store the reference to the object in the variable fido.

```
{ name: "Fido",
  breed: "Mixed",
  weight: 38 }
```

Notice that we're using the JSON object here. JSON is both the name of a string format and an object in JavaScript.

And you can go the other way, too. If you have an object, `fido`, and you want to turn it into a string, you just call the `JSON.stringify` method, like this:

```
var fido = {
    name: "Fido",
    breed: "Mixed",
    weight: 38
};
var fidoString = JSON.stringify(fido);
```

Here, we're taking a JavaScript object...

...and turning it into a string.

Note that the JSON format doesn't work with methods (so you can't include, say, a `bark` method in your JSON string), but it does work with all the primitive types, as well as objects and arrays.

#10 Server-side JavaScript

In this book we've focused on the browser and client-side programming, but there's a whole world of server-side programming where you can now use your JavaScript skills. Server-side programming is typically required for the kinds of web and cloud services you use on the Internet. If you want to create Webville Taco's new online order system, or you think the next big idea is the anti-social network, you'll need to write code that lives and runs in the cloud (on a server on the Internet).

Server-side code executes on a server on the Internet.

request

Client-side code executes on the client—that is, on your computer.

Node.js is the JavaScript server-side technology of choice these days, and it includes its own runtime environment and set of libraries (in the same way client-side JavaScript uses the browser's libraries). And like the browser, Node.js runs JavaScript in a single-threaded model where only one thread of execution can happen at a time. This leads to a programing model similar to the browser that is based on asynchronous events and an event loop.

As an example, the method below starts up a web server listening for incoming web requests. It takes a handler that is responsible for handling those requests when they occur. Notice that the convention for setting up the event handler for incoming requests is to pass an anonymous function to the `createServer` method.

The http.createServer Node.js library method takes a handler in the form of an anonymous function as an argument.

```
http.createServer(function(request, response) {
  response.writeHead(200, {"Content-Type": "text/plain"});
  response.write("Hello World");
  response.end();
}).listen(8888);
```

The anonymous function is responsible for taking care of requests. It responds to incoming requests by sending back the string "Hello World".

Of course, there is much more to explain and to work through to understand how Node.js works. But, given your knowledge of objects and functions you are well positioned to take this on. Also, explaining Node.js requires at least an entire book of its own, but you'll also find many online tutorials, articles and demonstrations at http://nodejs.org.

Colophon

All interior layouts were designed by Eric Freeman and Elisabeth Robson.

Kathy Sierra and Bert Bates created the look & feel of the Head First series. The book was produced using Adobe InDesign CS5.5 and Adobe Photoshop CS5.5. The book was typeset using Uncle Stinky, Mister Frisky (you think we're kidding), Ann Satellite, Baskerville, Comic Sans, Myriad Pro, Skippy Sharp, Savoye LET, Jokerman LET, Courier New and Woodrow typefaces.

Interior design and production was done exclusively on Apple Macintoshes—a Mac Pro, an iMac, a Macbook Pro, and two MacBook Airs to be precise.

Writing locations were primarily Bainbridge Island, Washington; Austin, Texas; Port of Ness, Scotland; Seaside, Florida.

Sonic environment during writing included BT, Daft Punk, Muse, The Fixx, Depeche Mode, Adam & the Ants, Men without Hats, Sleep Research Lab, Dousk, Uh Huh Her, Art of Noise, deadmau5 & Kaskade, David Bowie, Cheap Trick, The Who, Blank & Jones, Chris Isaak, Roy Orbison, Elvis, John Lennon, George Harrison, Amy Macdonald, Schiller, Sia, Sigur Ros, Tom Waits, OMD, Phillip Glass, Muse, Eno, Krishna Das, Mike Oldfield, Devo, Steve Roach, Beyman Brothers, Harry and the Potters, and the soundtracks for Frozen, Harry Potter, Back to the Future and Pleasantville.

Index

Symbols

$ (dollar sign)
    beginning JavaScript variable names 13
    function in jQuery 624

0 (zero), as falsey value 292

&& (AND) operator 55, 62–63, 74

* (asterisk) operator, as multiplication arithmetic operator 15, 286

: (colon), separating property name and property value 179

, (comma), separating object properties 177, 179

{ } (curly braces)
    enclosing object properties 177, 179
    in body of function 97
    in code block 17
    matching in code 59
    using with object literals 177, 522

. (dot notation)
    accessing object properties 181, 209, 230
    using with reference variables 186
    using with this object 202

= (equal sign) operator, assigning values to variables using 11, 16, 275

== (equality) operator
    as comparison operator 16, 55, 275–285, 311, 459
    vs. === operator 289

=== (strict equality) operator
    as comparison operator 55, 280–285, 311
    vs. == operator 289

// (forward slashes), beginning comments in JavaScript 13

/ (forward slash) operator, as division arithmetic operator 15, 286

> (greater than) operator 16, 55, 459

>= (greater than or equal to) operator 16, 55

< (less than) operator 55, 459

<= (less than or equal to) operator 55

- (minus sign) operator
    as unary operator 287
    using as arithmetic operator with string and number 286–287, 312

!= (not equal to) operator 16, 55

! (NOT) operator 55

|| (OR) operator 54, 55, 62–63, 74

() (parentheses)
    in calling functions 68, 430, 439
    in parameters 97

+ (plus sign)
    as arithmetic operator 286–287, 312
    in concatenating strings 15, 133, 142, 354

-- (post-decrement operator) 146–147

++ (post-increment operator) 146–147

" " (quotation marks, double)
    surrounding character strings in JavaScript 13
    using around property name 179

; (semicolon), ending statements in JavaScript 11, 13

[ ] (square brackets)
    accessing properties using 209
    in arrays 127, 129, 550

!== (strict not equal to) operator 281

_ (underscore), beginning JavaScript variable names 13

A

action attributes 328

activities, about doing xxxiii

addEventListener method 630

alert function
    communicating with users using 25–26, 42, 46
    determining hits and misses in simplified Battleship game 59–60, 76

I

object properties and 176, 219
objects 266
operators and 286
operators to sort 459
passing values to functions 92–93, 192
primitive 266
strict equality 280
strings 291–297
truthy and falsey 291–293
type conversion and 276–281
types in arrays 134
undefined 268
variables and 11

variable declaration, object 177

variables
about 11
assigning functions to 439, 449, 469
conditional as 23
declaring in arrays 152
declaring inside and outside of functions 98
declaring local 103, 108
default value of 50
finding errors in 39
free 495–496, 501, 516
global
guide to code hygiene 111
identifying 105, 120
lexical scope of 488–490, 494
nesting affecting 486, 488–490, 494
overuse of 391
scope of 101
vs. local variables 99, 106–107
guide to code hygiene 111
identifying 91, 119
in arrays 127, 129
lexical scope of 488–490, 494
local
declaring 103, 108
guide to code hygiene 111
identifying 105, 120
in methods 206
lexical scope of 488–490, 494
nesting affecting 486, 488–490, 494
scope of 101
vs. global variables 99, 106–107
naming 12–13, 100, 103, 108
objects assigned to 192

objects in 186
passing into arguments 89
referring to functions to invoke functions 436
reloading page and 108
scope of 101
setting to null 270
shadowing 104
short life of 102
undefined values and 268
using pseudocode in determining 50
var keyword in declaring 97, 99

var keyword
about 11
in declaring variables 97, 99

view object, advanced Battleship game
about 329
implementing 331–334
interacting with model 336
notifying of hits or misses 347
testing 335

W

W3C documentation website 627

web browsers
conditional statements handled by 434
events 404
executing code 433
function declarations handled by 431–433, 436, 465, 483
function expressions handled by 434–436, 465
handling events 383, 403. *See also* handling events
loading and executing JavaScript in 3
loading code into 31
objects provided by 214
opening console 28
parsing HTML and building DOM from it 261
recommended xxvi
running JavaScript in xxxii
setting up Event Object in IE8 and older 399
setting up event objects in IE8 and older 631
tailoring size of window to web page 627

web browser wars 6

web pages
adding code to HTML page 32
as applications 9

Z

I can't believe the book is almost over. Before you go, you really should read the index. It's great stuff. And after that you've always got the website. So I'm sure we'll see you again soon...

Don't worry, this isn't goodbye.

Nor is it the end. Now that you've got an amazingly solid foundation in JavaScript, it's time to become a master. Point your browser to `http://wickedlysmart.com/hfjs` to explore what's next!

What's next? So much more! Join us at http://wickedlysmart.com/hfjs to continue your journey.

Have it your way.

Get even more for your money.

Join the O'Reilly Community, and register the O'Reilly books you own. It's free, and you'll get:

- $4.99 ebook upgrade offer
- 40% upgrade offer on O'Reilly print books
- Membership discounts on books and events
- Free lifetime updates to ebooks and videos
- Multiple ebook formats, DRM FREE
- Participation in the O'Reilly community
- Newsletters
- Account management
- 100% Satisfaction Guarantee

Signing up is easy:

1. **Go to: oreilly.com/go/register**
2. **Create an O'Reilly login.**
3. **Provide your address.**
4. **Register your books.**

Note: English-language books only

To order books online:

oreilly.com/store

For questions about products or an order:

orders@oreilly.com

To sign up to get topic-specific email announcements and/or news about upcoming books, conferences, special offers, and new technologies:

elists@oreilly.com

For technical questions about book content:

booktech@oreilly.com

To submit new book proposals to our editors:

proposals@oreilly.com

O'Reilly books are available in multiple DRM-free ebook formats. For more information:

oreilly.com/ebooks

O'REILLY®

Spreading the knowledge of innovators   oreilly.com